W9-BQI-463

RELIGIOUS TRENDS IN ENGLISH POETRY

RELIGIOUS TRENDS IN ENGLISH POETRY

By HOXIE NEALE FAIRCHILD
PROFESSOR OF ENGLISH
HUNTER COLLEGE OF THE CITY OF NEW YORK

VOLUME IV: 1830–1880
CHRISTIANITY AND ROMANTICISM IN THE VICTORIAN ERA

NEW YORK AND LONDON
COLUMBIA UNIVERSITY PRESS

First printing 1957
Second printing 1964

Library of Congress Catalog Card Number: 39-12839
Manufactured in the United States of America

FOR ANNE AND PHILIP STEVENS

MY DAUGHTER AND HER HUSBAND

ACKNOWLEDGMENTS

THE author gratefully acknowledges the kindness of the following publishers for permission to quote from copyright material:

George Bell and Sons, Ltd., for permission to quote from Basil Champneys's *Memoirs and Correspondence of Coventry Patmore*; Constable and Company, Ltd., for permission to quote from Derek Patmore's *The Life and Times of Coventry Patmore*; Faber and Faber, Ltd., for permission to quote from T. E. Welby's *A Study of Swinburne*; Harcourt, Brace, and Company, for permission to quote from I. A. Richards's *Practical Criticism*; Houghton Mifflin Company, for permission to quote from J. H. Randall's *The Making of the Modern Mind*; The Macmillan Company (New York), for permission to quote from Graham Hough's *The Last Romantics*, from J. M. Murry's *Things to Come*, and from Charles Tennyson's *Alfred Tennyson*; Macmillan and Company, Ltd. (London), for permission to quote from A. C. Bradley's *A Commentary on Tennyson's "In Memoriam,"* from John Morley's *On Compromise*, and from Christina Rossetti's *Poetical Works*; William Morrow and Company, for permission to quote from Georges Lafourcade's *Swinburne: A Literary Biography*; Oxford University Press (New York), for permission to quote from C. B. Tinker and H. F. Lowry's *The Poetry of Matthew Arnold*; Simon and Shuster, Inc., for permission to quote from Bertrand Russell's *History of Western Philosophy*.

Thanks are also due the editors of *College English* and of *Review of Religion* for permission to quote from articles contributed to these journals by the author.

H. N. F.

PREFACE

THIS FOURTH VOLUME of *Religious Trends in English Poetry*[1] carries the subject onward from about 1830 to about 1880—from the close of the Romantic Period to what, despite the date of the Queen's death, may be regarded as the close of the Victorian Period proper. The chosen terminus entails awkward truncation of such continuing tendencies as the Catholic Revival and the Aesthetic Movement, but to press on to the end of the century would deprive the study of the relative unity which it now possesses. The careers of such representative Victorians as Tennyson and Browning have not, of course, been chopped off at 1880; conversely, poets who began to publish before 1880 but who produced most of their work after that date have been omitted. With a good deal of hesitation this principle has been applied even to Meredith and Hopkins; they will feel more at home in Volume V. Similarly I have paid little or no attention to survivors of the Romantic Period who did some writing after 1830; but it would be absurd to ignore Keble merely because *The Christian Year* was published in 1827.

I have greatly enjoyed my rash invasion of a period in which I have not hitherto been a specialist. The adventure has been good for my personal education; others must decide whether it has been good for anything else. The prospect of appearing before a largely new bench of judges is formidable but not altogether unwelcome. Since the twentieth century has no reason to feel itself superior to any earlier period in recorded history, the Stracheyan manner of sneering at the Victorians has deservedly become unfashionable, and I have no wish to revive it. Probably, however, no contemporary student of the Victorians worships Arnold, Browning, or Rossetti with the quasi-religious fervor which some eminent specialists in the Romantic Period feel toward Wordsworth, Shelley, or Keats. In the court of Victorian scholarship there will probably be no outcry of horror if I confess to some lack of admiration for the religious thought of Swinburne, who rightly regarded himself as the spiritual heir of Blake and Shelley.

[1] The three volumes of *Religious Trends in English Poetry* which have already appeared are: Vol. I: 1700–1740, *Protestantism and the Cult of Sentiment* (Columbia University Press, 1939); Vol. II: 1740–1780, *Religious Sentimentalism in the Age of Johnson* (Columbia University Press, 1942); Vol. III: 1780–1830, *Romantic Faith* (Columbia University Press, 1949).

My footnotes and bibliographical appendixes furnish clear though incomplete evidence of my heavy obligations to past and present workers in the Victorian field. I have not, however, attempted to study the innumerable scholarly books and articles as extensively as I did for Volume III. On the other hand, if I have not digested the entire mass of secondary exegesis I have read with some care the great Victorian prosemen who did so much to shape the intellectual environment of the poets.

The methodological inconsistency of this series of studies may distress readers who cherish absolutistic views on such matters. To be frank, I write these books in different ways largely to avoid being bored by concentration on a single subject throughout many years. Since I do not believe that there is any one ideal method for such a task my capriciousness does not trouble my conscience. To some extent, however, the changes in scope and treatment are also conditioned by the characteristics of the material to be discussed in a given volume.

Victorian poetry of religious pertinence is so torrentially abundant that the problem of selection, scale, and organization was especially urgent for the present book. Obviously a few major figures deserved particular attention. It seemed unwise, however, to devote this volume, like its immediate predecessor, entirely to the familiar mountain-peaks, for the minor poetry is both interesting in itself and useful for an understanding of the greater men. My solution has been to intersperse separate chapters on the major poets among "omnibus" chapters drawing on groups of minor writers whose work illustrates some general trend of religious thought. But of course no approach to exhaustiveness has been attempted, and doctoral candidates should not reproach me for ignoring the heroes of their dissertations.

Even when screened very selectively, the material remained so plentiful that I foresaw the danger of writing a longer book than my patient and quixotic publishers could be expected to print. Hence I have tried to avoid telling the reader too much of what he already knows. In this respect the ideal balance is difficult to achieve if one is writing, as I have wished to write, not only for the Victorian expert but for the mature student of literature who is not necessarily a specialist in this field. If there is too much run-of-the-mill information for some readers there is probably too little for others. A more mechanical space-saving device has been the reduction of documentation to a common-sense minimum except in acknowledging indebtedness to secondary sources. In the chapters on well-known individual poets whose work is easily accessible in several trustworthy editions, footnote references to passages quoted from their poems have been omitted. It seemed desirable, however, to document quotations from the obscurer figures who provide material for the omnibus chapters.

Partly for economy of space but chiefly for interpretative focus and impact, I have organized my materials in accordance with a perhaps excessively tight and shipshape theme which is set forth in the introductory chapter. That chapter also reminds the reader of certain governing ideas which unite the first three volumes of this series and which seem equally applicable to Victorian poetry. I may add, however, that this fourth volume is more than a performance of the same old tune on a new piano, for this period has interesting and perplexing characteristics of its own and raises problems which I have not hitherto confronted. Although it is part of a series, the book stands on its own legs and may be read as a separate study of its particular subject.

It is symptomatic of changing academic fashions that two able reviewers of Volume III should have deplored my indifference to the aesthetic implications of my subject, as if it were culpable to study literature for any other purpose than that of "pure" criticism. Trained in a tradition of scholarship which did not insist that the student of literature must be exclusively literary, I am studying the history of religious sensibility as it stands revealed in English poetry from about 1700 to the present. I use poetry because the interweaving of sense-experience, emotion, ratiocination, symbol-making, and ceremonial pattern gives religion a closer kinship with poetry than with more abstract, discursive, and rhetorical modes of expression.

Mr. I. A. Richards observes that between the realm of everyday convention and the realm of the scientifically verifiable lies "the vast *corpus* of problems, assumptions, adumbrations, fictions, prejudices, tenets; the sphere of random beliefs and hopeful guesses; the whole world, in brief, of abstract opinion and disputation about matters of feeling. To this world belongs everything about which civilized man cares most. . . . As a subject-matter for discussion, poetry is a central and typical denizen of this world. It is so both by its own nature and by the type of discussion with which it is traditionally associated. It serves, therefore, as an eminently suitable *bait* for anyone who wishes to trap the current opinions and responses in this middle field for the purpose of examining and comparing them with a view to advancing our knowledge of what may be called the natural history of human opinions and feelings."[2] This pioneer of the new criticism here refers primarily to analysis of the reader's responses, but he would doubtless grant that the

[2] *Practical Criticism*, p. 6.

study of opinions *in* poetry is a no less respectable enterprise than the study of opinions *about* poetry. From the beginning of my long task, on the other hand, I have recognized that my subject holds implications for the critic, and from time to time I have glanced at them. Although I am too old a dog to learn all the new tricks I am not willfully unresponsive to changing trends in our profession: indeed I believe that both historical scholarship and aesthetic criticism would benefit from a closer alliance. In this volume, therefore, I have gone somewhat further than before in suggesting relationships between the religious thought of the poets and their intrinsic literary qualities; and I have been so generous as to provide two concluding chapters—one for the historian and one for the critic.

Preparation of this volume has not entailed any very esoteric research or compelled me to seek the expert assistance of others. I am indebted, however, to the librarians of Hunter College, Columbia University, Cornell University, the New York Public Library, and the British Museum for the opportunity of using the collections in their charge. As always, it is a pleasure to record my gratitude to the Columbia University Press for its efficient, generous, and enlightened dealings with me and my writings from the publication of *The Noble Savage* in 1928 to the present. I also wish to thank Mr. Edwin N. Iino of the Press's staff for his valuable editorial service in connection with the present volume and Miss Lucie Wallace for her skillful compilation of the indexes.

In 1939, describing my entire project in the Preface of Volume I, I said that it would consist of five books. Quite absurdly I forgot that time would not stand still while I was reading and writing. Not five, but six books will be needed to overtake the calendar. Volume V would run from 1880 to 1920; Volume VI, from 1920 to about a year before the date of publication. At present I am sixty. Granting the continuance of good health and the survival of civilization, I feel reasonably confident of completing Volume V. The sixth and last book is more problematical. I shall write it if permitted to do so.

H. N. F.

Hunter College of the City of New York
January, 1955

CONTENTS

RELIGIOUS TRENDS IN ENGLISH POETRY

Chapter One

CHRISTIANITY AND ROMANTICISM

To a greater extent than I had anticipated at the outset, this series of books has become a study, in and through poetry, of the complex and uneasy relationships between supernaturalistic religion and romanticism. If any readers of the present volume have also read its predecessors—it is unlikely, but conceivable—they will recall that I define romanticism as an expression of "faith in the natural goodness, strength, and creativity of all human energies. The taproot of romanticism . . . is an eternal and universal fact of consciousness: man's desire for self-trust, self-expression, self-expansion." In all human beings the romantic impulse works in varying degree, mingled in varying proportions with feelings of limitation and dependence; but complete satisfaction of the impulse could be found only in complete intellectual and spiritual autonomy. That the romanticist should so frequently aspire toward "a pantheistic interfusion of real and ideal, natural and supernatural, finite and infinite, man and God" implies no desire to lose his little selfhood in a great suprapersonal wholeness. On the contrary, this emotional experience is precious to him as the culminating exploit of his creative power. "By effacing all distinctions and boundaries it permits unlimited outward projection of personal energy."[1]

This conception of romanticism still strikes me as valid. But as I grow more and more convinced that it is best to think nominalistically of all man-made abstractions in order to prevent them from tyrannizing over our thought, I grow less and less sure that I know what romanticism "is." For me the term has become a way of expressing the basic psychological motive which unites the variegated cultural manifestations of human pride. The desire to feel independently good, creative, and boundless has been one of the dominant factors in modern history. I call the expression of this impulse "romanticism" because I see it as the driving force behind those ideas and activities which are customarily labeled "romantic." The reader may prefer

[1] *Religious Trends in English Poetry*, III, 3. Those who wish to consider the grounds of this theory and its implications for the history of religious thought without detailed study of the evidence already provided might read the concluding chapters of the first three volumes and the introductory chapter of Volume III.

a different verbal symbol for the thrust toward boundlessness, using "romanticism" as a means of pointing at something else; no harm will be done so long as he understands my terminology. Of course it is intellectual malpractice to employ a familiar term in a sense so wantonly eccentric and crotchety that communication is frustrated, but so many reputable scholars conceive of romanticism more or less as I do that I believe myself guiltless of this offense. If I had substituted "humanism," as I have often been tempted to do, my readers would have demanded, "Which of the dozen or so kinds of humanism do you mean?" I should have replied, "I mean *romantic* humanism." " And what do you mean by 'romantic '?" "Pertaining to man's desire for limitless expression of self-sufficiency." "Naturalism" would incur the same circularity, and "pride" would be too pugnaciously theological for the uses of history.

The term "religion" has become no less ambiguous than "romanticism." For me, the indispensable religious ideas are the insufficiency of man and the transcendence of God. Any individual possesses a religion if he affirms the existence of a Divine Being whose status in reality is completely independent of human thought and feeling and if he acknowledges that he cannot rise above his present weakness without that Being's aid. I may think that such a man's notions of how God's aid is given and received and used are inadequate, but I regard him as a religious person. I stand with him on the same side of the chasm which divides those who believe that man makes God from those who believe that God makes man. The peculiarity which some of my critics have found difficult to understand is that in my opinion this distinction is no less crucial for the history of culture than the distinction between all those who say that they believe in God and all those who say that they do not.

For any student of our subject, these fundamental differences are complicated and sometimes obscured by the necessity of examining the way in which they have been related, in the history of culture, to organized institutional religions and preeminently of course to Christianity. Among the various formulations of creed, cult, and practice which at one time or another have been associated with the term "Christianity," some appear to have been more favorable than others to the basic religious concepts. To recognize this fact has seemed to me an essential part of my business as a historian. This empirical standard by no means provides the sole ground for my belief in traditional Christianity, but it does provide the sole ground for my using that faith as a criterion in a work of historical criticism. For the purposes of this study, one belief can be thought of as "better" than another only to the extent that it has proved itself a more effective instrument for furthering a type of religious experience in which man and God are related without being confused. Whatever absolute verities may exist beyond this psychological pragmatism are the province of theology, not of history. In these books I neither conceal my own suprahistorical commitments nor attempt to argue in their behalf. My objection to the romantic faith is not that it is heterodox in relation to any refinements of theology but that it denies the insufficiency of man and the transcendent objectivity of God.[2] The thought of Roden Noel, as we shall see later, is predominantly romantic, but in one of his critical essays he seems to recognize the distinction which I am trying to explain. He qualifies his admiration for Walt Whitman by granting that "it does make a difference whether we are to look *into ourselves, and ourselves only*, for spiritual elevation above the ordinary, or whether we are to look *out of ourselves* to a possible Source of higher manhood, which yet at present is by no means manifest in us."[3] The difference is real, obvious, and essential.

I consider romanticism non-Christian solely because it fails to recognize the two fundamental principles of supernaturalistic religion. I had no other reason for stating in Volume III:

> It is at all events a little confusing, for history no less than for theology, to apply the same title to a religion of human insufficiency, which offers redemption at the cost of humility and self-surrender, and to a religion of human sufficiency, which denies the necessity of redemption and offers man limitless self-expansion at no greater cost than the will to affirm his own goodness as part of a good universe; to a religion in which grace descends to man from a great outward Reality completely independent of his desires and imaginings, and to a religion in which grace is the echo of man's pride; to a religion which says, "Be it unto me according to thy word," and to a religion which says, with Emerson, "No law can be sacred to me but that of my own nature."[4]

Although my personal preferences are undisguised, I do not pretend to *know* which of these views comes closer to the truth. I merely insist that if the former is Christian the latter should be called something else.

[2] The terms "objective" and "subjective" are not naïve or obsolete when used by those who posit a real *not-me* world which is "external" to us in the sense that we play no part in shaping its truth. Human *experience* of that world is inevitably subjective, but there is an immense philosophical and psychological difference between a subjectivity which affirms and a subjectivity which denies the existence of objective reality.

[3] *Essays on Poetry and Poets*, p. 336. All italics in quotations are those of the author quoted unless I indicate the contrary.

[4] *Religious Trends*, III, 11. In the window of an occultist bookshop I recently saw two books by Charles Brunton: *The Inner Reality* and *The Quest of the Overself*. In the romantic faith the two subjects are identical, and "the Overself" expresses what Emerson means by "the Oversoul"—deified selfhood.

In short, I see no possibility of reconciling Christian belief in God and romantic belief in man[5] except upon the supposition that all supernatural religion is a stratagem for validating the romantic impulse without appearing to be romantic. This is the theory of Feuerbach, whose *Wesen des Christentums* became an influential Victorian book in Marian Evans's translation. He proclaims that "religion itself, not indeed on the surface, but fundamentally . . . believes in nothing else than the truth and divinity of human nature. . . . Religion is the dream of the human mind"—the human mind dreaming about its own divinity.

> Religion, expressed generally, is consciousness of the infinite; thus it is and can be nothing else than the consciousness which man has of his own—not finite and limited, but infinite nature. . . . The consciousness of the infinite is nothing else than the consciousness of the infinity of the consciousness. . . . The *absolute* to man is his own nature. . . Consciousness is self-verification, self-affirmation, self-love, joy in one's own perfection.[6]

According to Feuerbach there is no difference between religious and nonreligious feelings, for all feeling is essentially religious.

> How couldst thou perceive the divine by feeling, if feeling were not itself divine in its nature? . . . The divine nature which is discovered by feeling, is in truth nothing else than feeling enraptured, in ecstasy with itself. . . . God is pure, unlimited, free Feeling. . . . Feeling is atheistic in the sense of the orthodox belief, which attaches religion to an external God; it denies an objective God—is itself God. In this point of view, only the negation of feeling is the negation of God. . . . I doubt God only when I predicate concerning him anything which is not true of my own nature,

for "God is the nature of man regarded as absolute truth, the truth of man." Hence Feuerbach feels entitled to declare: "We have reduced the supermundane, supernatural, and superhuman nature of God to the elements of human nature as its fundamental elements. . . . The beginning, middle, and end of Religion is MAN."[7]

Although Feuerbach believes that these truths have been more grievously perverted by Catholicism than by Protestantism, he asserts that all Christianity, Protestant as well as Catholic, has been false to the spirit of love in insisting upon faith in a particular revelation of a particular God. Love would not be thus limited and constrained if we learned to say "Love is God" instead of "God is Love." Human love is not sanctified by Christ: Christ is

[5] There is of course a *Christian* belief in man, but it depends upon Christian belief in God.

[6] *The Essence of Christianity*, tr. by Marian Evans, pp. 7, 10, 21, 23, 24, 25.

[7] *Ibid.*, pp. 29, 30, 41, 42, 239.

sanctified by human love. "He therefore who loves man for the sake of man, who rises to the love of the species . . . he is a Christian, is Christ himself. He does what Christ did, what made Christ Christ." To this extent Christianity may be justified as an exoteric version of esoteric truth, but we should try to rise above it to the realization that we are *all* God-Men.[8]

But if religion is nothing but human self-deification, why should man thwart his own egotism by inventing a superhuman God before whom to prostrate himself? Feuerbach's answer is disquieting. "To enrich God," he explains, "man must become poor; that God may be all, man must be nothing. But he desires to be nothing in himself, because what he takes from himself is not lost to him, since it is preserved in God. . . . What man withdraws from himself, what he renounces in himself, he only enjoys in incomparably fuller measure in God." Both Pelagianism and Augustinianism "vindicate the goodness of man; but Pelagianism does it directly, in a rationalistic and moral form, Augustinianism indirectly, in a mystical, that is, a religious form. . . . So long as man adores a good being as his God, so long does he contemplate in God the goodness of his own nature," for "God is the mirror of man." Through the Incarnation, the purely human goodness and power which the Christian deposits in the God-idea are repaid with compound interest: "In the Incarnation religion only confesses . . . that God is an altogether human being. . . . God as God is feeling as yet shut up, hidden; only Christ is the unclosed, open feeling or heart. In Christ feeling is first perfectly certain of itself, and assured beyond doubt of the truth and divinity of its own nature." Not only the Incarnation but all other Christian doctrines " are realized wishes of the heart."[9]

If this psychological analysis is correct, Christianity is merely a peculiarly subtle way of satisfying the romantic impulse, which is identical with the religious impulse. That would leave me in a most uncomfortable position. I must admit that I do not know of any objectively conclusive evidence with which Feuerbach's theory can be refuted. The Christian's feelings rise up against it, but how is he to prove that Feuerbach's interpretation of those feelings is false? It is not impossible that Christians are self-deluded in believing that they are surrendering their wills to the will of a real transcendent Deity. If they permitted themselves to realize that they had imagined God in order to inflate their own egos the whole plan would be spoiled: their motives for subconsciously suppressing the ironic truth are strong.

[8] *Ibid.*, pp. 186, 332–336 *passim*, 339, 340.

[9] *Ibid.*, pp. 48, 51–52, 84, 93, 187, 191. See also pp. 77, 106, 107, 165, 166, 167, 172, 173, 182, 227.

Many professed Christians use their religion for romantic purposes, and it s conceivable that all of them do so. On the other hand, Christianity and romanticism produce such different effects in history and in individual personality that it is difficult to regard the former as no more than a mask for the latter. Can we suppose that C. S. Lewis has merely found a more ingenious device for obtaining precisely what John Middleton Murry wants? In my personal experience—I have tried both ways of life—the freedom and power derived from religious self-surrender are of utterly different quality from the freedom and power derived from romantic self-assertion. But would I loathe and dread human pride as strongly as I do if I myself were not eaten up with pride? There is no demonstrative proof either way; the reader must choose for himself. If he feels sure that he is right and knows that he may be wrong he will be in exactly my position.

Even if, in defiance of Feuerbach, we continue to insist on the vital difference between Christian God-worship and romantic man-worship, we must recognize that absolutely pure Christianity and absolutely pure romanticism are rare phenomena. Granting and temporarily disregarding exceptional cases, what we usually observe in others and in ourselves is a variable mingling of the impulse toward self-surrender and the impulse toward self-assertion. For historical purposes men are classifiable as Christian or romantic, not when only one of the two factors is present, but when either is strongly dominant over the other. Many minds are so close to the borderline that they cannot be classified at all. Unless he is going to be a great saint, the individual Christian is much more romantic than his creed. In a nominally Christian civilization, conversely, the romantic most easily satisfies his desires not by defying Christianity but by reinterpreting it in a romantic sense until it becomes what Mallock calls "a new firm trading under the old name, and trying to purchase the goodwill of the establish ment."[10]

The fact that this romantic reinterpretation of Christianity has been a salient feature of English literature from the sixteenth century to the present raises a prickly question. Has one type of Christianity proved to be more easily romanticized than another type? The first three volumes of this series have presented a large mass of evidence pointing toward the conclusion that the quasi-religious beliefs and feelings associated with romanticism are much more closely related to the Protestant than to the Catholic tradition. The facts seem to indicate "that seventeenth-century Protestantism, especially of the Puritan type, is the father of that eighteenth-century sentimentalism

[10] W. H. Mallock, *The New Republic*, p. 123.

which becomes romanticism on attaining maturity."[11] In the opening chapter of Volume III I observe that this historical thesis has been independently arrived at by a good many other scholars—and not merely by Roman or Anglican Catholics but by proromantic as well as antiromantic Protestants, Jews, and secularists.

To the antiromantic secularists may now be added Bertrand Russell, whose *History of Western Philosophy* shows that a completely nonreligious thinker can interpret the course of modern thought almost precisely as I do. According to this eminent agnostic

> The concept of "truth" as something dependent upon facts largely outside human control has been one of the ways in which philosophy hitherto has inculcated the necessary element of humility. When this check upon pride is removed, a farther step is taken on the road toward a certain kind of madness—the intoxication of power which invaded philosophy with Fichte, and to which modern men, whether philosophers or not, are prone. I am persuaded that this intoxication is the greatest danger of our time, and that any philosophy which, however unintentionally, contributes to it is increasing the danger of vast social disaster.

Lord Russell associates this "cosmic impiety" with romanticism, and romanticism with Protestant subjectivity. "In morals," he says, "the Protestant emphasis on the individual conscience was essentially anarchic." Thanks to habit and custom, the "intoxication of power" was held in balance for some time.

> But this was a precarious equilibrium. The eighteenth-century cult of "sensibility" began to break it down: an act was admired, not for its good consequences, or for its conformity to a moral code, but for the emotion which inspired it. Out of this attitude developed the cult of the hero as it is expressed by Carlyle and Nietzsche, and the Byronic cult of violent passion of no matter what kind.[12]

My agreement with Russell on these matters certainly does not prove that I am right, but it makes against the easy assumption that my historical interpretation is the puppet of my doctrinal commitments.[13]

I have never felt sure as to whether Protestantism is inherently romantic or whether its deliquescence into romanticism is the result of external pressure exerted upon it by historical forces which its loose organization and

[11] *Religious Trends*, III, 12; but for the whole argument see pp. 10–18. Of course I do not mean that Protestantism gives birth to the romantic impulse, which is older than Christianity itself. I mean that the religious aspects of the Romantic Movement in modern history are by-products of the deliquescence of Protestantism.

[12] Bertrand Russell, *History of Western Philosophy*, pp. 18–19, 777, 856. See also pp. 705, 718, 730, 787.

[13] Confirmation from an antithetical source is provided by Monsignor R. A. Knox's interesting study of *Enthusiasm* which appeared in the year following the publication of my third volume. Although Father Knox does not use romanticism as a historical concept his book abounds in illustrations of the impact of the romantic spirit upon Christianity.

lack of authority made it incapable of withstanding. In the past I have leaned rather heavily toward the former view, but in my present nominalistic state of mind I think the question unanswerable and perhaps even unaskable. There can be no hope of framing a logically respectable definition of the term "Protestantism." Protestantism can be *described*, but only by specifying the direction in which, at any given time, the most intelligent and influential non-Catholic Christians appear to be moving. From the seventeenth century to a quite recent date, the dominant trend in Protestantism (reversed only partially and temporarily by the Evangelical Movement) was from a God-centered to a man-centered religion. The force of that trend is by no means spent, but there are clear signs of a reaction. At present the most notable Protestant theologians and denominational leaders seem to be turning from romantic man-worship towards historically Christian supernaturalism. They are reaffirming doctrines which the sentimental humanitarians of the preceding generation condemned as disheartening and bigoted. They are emphasizing the otherness and objectivity of God, and they are beginning to balance His transcendence and His immanence through a revival (still very gingerly) of the sacramental principle and of liturgical worship. In the ecumenical movement they are reaching out toward the ideal of the Universal Church. While we await the issue of these developments we had better be content to observe the historical phenomena of our chosen period without attempting to define the undefinable. I assert only that in the seventeenth, eighteenth, and nineteenth centuries the religion of Protestants moves in a chiefly romantic direction and that the religion of Catholics does not.

As regards the present volume my thesis conflicts with the opinion, once almost universal and still widely held, that the nineteenth-century Catholic Revival was an expression of the romantic spirit. Here in the first place we should observe a distinction between the terms "Catholicism" and "Catholic Revival." The latter was not completely a renewal of the former. It would be absurd to deny that some features of the Catholic Revival were strongly influenced by some features of the Romantic Movement. But it would be equally absurd to deny that the fundamental motive of the Catholic Revival was the desire to believe and practice Catholic Christianity, a resolutely theocentric religion. Hence anyone who recognizes that human self-sufficiency is basic in romanticism must conclude that despite a good deal of superficial overlapping the Catholic Revival and the Romantic Movement point in opposite directions.[14]

[14] A more elaborate treatment of this question may be found in my "Romanticism and the Religious Revival in England," *Journal of the History of Ideas*, II, 330–338. I now feel that the article

Let us look beyond our period to John Middleton Murry, who brackets classicism with Catholicism and romanticism with Protestantism. He much prefers the latter pair. For him the statement, "The Christianity which is native to me is a Protestant Christianity. . . . I am the heir of a long succession of rebels against spiritual authority" is equivalent to "I, as my readers should know by this time, am a Romantic. . . . The words 'Conceived in sin' in the service of baptism stick in my gizzard." In rebuttal of Tolstoy he avers that "not Christianity (Church or Tolstoyan) but post-Renaissance art itself contains the highest life-conception of which Western humanity has so far proved itself capable." Jesus and Shakespeare—"I know of no two spirits more profoundly alike than theirs." But not far below these outstanding Protestants he would place the English romantic poets—Blake, Shelley, and of course Keats. The Abbé Brémond is wrong in saying that poetry " 'aspires to the condition of prayer.' It would be truer . . . to say that prayer aspires to the condition of poetry. . . . The poetic experience is the perfection of the religious experience."[15]

One day Mr. Murry made a spiritual discovery. That Feuerbach had made it a century earlier does not detract from the modern critic's originality: such revelations occur independently to people of the same general sort at different times and places. When it suddenly dawned upon him he recognized it as "essentially, my creed. . . . It is a red-letter day for me that I have said something so clearly to myself as this: What I do, God does; what I am God is. Perhaps it will give others something of the simple satisfaction it gives me."[16]

Doubtless it will. At all events, no one will question that Mr. Murry is as romantic as he proclaims himself to be. That he is the heir of Protestantism is less obvious: an actual confrontation of John Calvin (or even Martin Luther) with John Middleton Murry would be worth seeing. Nevertheless he is a clear though extreme example of what *happened to* the religion of large numbers of intelligent and high-minded Protestants. For the sake of

---

underestimates the extent to which the Catholic Revival was influenced by external manifestations of the romantic spirit, but that my main thesis, the essential antiromanticism of Catholic Christianity, will hold water. For corroboration see C. F. Harrold, *John Henry Newman*, pp. 28ff. and 246ff., and the same scholar's "The Oxford Movement: A Reconsideration," *The Reinterpretation of Victorian Literature*, pp. 34ff.

[15] John Middleton Murry, *Things to Come*, pp. 54, 122, 153, 211, 215, 263. See T. S. Eliot's discussion of Murry's views in *Selected Essays*, pp. 15–18. Eliot accepts Murry's groupings but dislikes Protestantism and romanticism as heartily as Murry dislikes Catholicism and classicism. I see no inevitable connection between Catholic belief and classical style, and I repudiate Eliot's association of Catholicism with monarchism.

[16] *Ibid.*, p. 123.

contrast, let us hear a voice from the other side of the chasm. In Newman's *Loss and Gain*, a Roman Catholic priest says to Charles Reding that Englishmen "will not be blessed, they will effect nothing in religious matters, till they begin by an act of unreserved faith in the will of God, whatever it be; till they go out of themselves, till they cease to make something within them their standard."[17]

What Emerson would have told young Reding may be gathered from the *Divinity School Address*: "That is always best which gives me to myself. The sublime is excited in me by the great stoical doctrine, Obey thyself. That which shows God in me, fortifies me. That which shows God out of me, makes me a wart and a wen." For this romantic child of Puritanism, "The true Christianity—a faith like Christ's in the infinitude of man—is lost. None believeth in the soul of man, but only in some man or person old and departed."[18] This is not far from Kingsley's declaration that "The very essential ideal of Protestantism is the dignity and divinity of man as God made him!" The last clause must be interpreted in the light of this Broad Churchman's desire to further "a lofty and enlightened Christianity, which shall be thoroughly human, and therefore thoroughly divine." The more human, the more Godlike. "Kingsley," writes Professor Baker, "is of the school of Rousseau. Indeed, the whole Reactionary Revolution—the Oxford Movement—New-Toryism—Neo-Catholicism—had for its avowed object of warfare just that extreme Rousseauistic faith in the goodness of the natural man. . . . Protestantism in Kingsley usually means reliance on natural instinct . . . on the natural man's understanding of the Bible . . . and on the natural conclusions of the human intellect."[19] Which was the truer romantic, Kingsley or Newman?

According to Hugh Walker, Carlyle was fundamentally on the same side as Newman, since "Both Carlyle and the Puseyites were in revolt against the reign of the logical understanding."[20] But Carlyle's revolt, as Professor Willey has observed, proclaimed the romantic interfusion: "God and man, supernatural and natural, spirit and matter, sacred and profane:—it was primarily by fusing these distinctions in his visionary furnace that he cast a spell over his hearers and gave them a sense of deepened insight."[21] For better or worse, no such insight was offered by Newman.

For Carlyle, Christianity is basically hero-worship. "The greatest of all

[17] *Loss and Gain*, p.386. [18] *Selected Prose and Poetry*, pp. 76, 84.
[19] J. E. Baker, *The Novel and the Oxford Movement*, pp. 88–89.
[20] *The Literature of the Victorian Era*, p. 20.
[21] Basil Willey, *Nineteenth Century Studies*, p. 105.

heroes is One—whom we do not name here!"[22] Similarly Mr. Murry describes himself as "simply a believer in humanity in its finest manifestations. In other words, I am a great believer in heroes, and the greatest of my heroes is Jesus"—whose words "have the same mystery and the same message as Shakespeare's. . . . The extreme of human love was manifested once for all, as it must be manifested, in man. Him I worship. A man can worship a man."[23] The position of the Catholic poet Aubrey de Vere is antipodal:

> The Christian creed confesses that God made man in His image. . . . That subjective philosophy, which separates ideas from external realities, replies with its counter creed, "No, it is the human Mind which creates to itself a God in its own image!" . . . May English transcendentalism long resist what is said to have deeply infected that of Germany! . . . This form of error comes from a diseased individualism. The Church, which is historical and universal, would seem to be our protection against it.[24]

But English transcendentalism, as the example of Carlyle shows, did *not* resist the infection. Drawing heavily upon the Germans, it "preserved" Christianity by romanticizing it. Professor Baker, in support of his contention that Carlyle was a pure humanist despite all his supernaturalistic thunderings, quotes from *Latter Day Pamphlets:* "Not because Heaven existed, did men know Good from Evil. . . . It was because men . . . knew, through all their being, the difference between Good and Evil, that Heaven and Hell first came to exist."[25] Christianity, in other words, is a product of human imagination. Not only Feuerbach but Carlyle has anticipated Murry's "What I am, God is."

It follows that Carlyle regards all religions as man-made symbols. Jesus, the human hero, is born of our heroism—"Higher has the human Thought not yet reached." Not yet, for as our ideals rise still higher Jesus may be rejected, as Carlyle soon rejected Him, in favor of superior imaginative fabrications. The test of the adequacy of any myth is "Feel it in thy heart, and then say whether it is of God! This is Belief; all else is Opinion."[26] Oliver Elton says of a similar passage in *Characteristics:* "This is the old doctrine of the 'inner light,' minus the theology."[27] In the preceding volumes of this series the history of the Inner Light has been traced from the seventeenth-century sectarian enthusiasts through the eighteenth-century sentimentalists

[22] *On Heroes, Hero-Worship, and the Heroic in History*, p. 105. See also pp. 354–355, where Carlyle interprets Protestantism in terms of the hero-cult.

[23] *Things to Come*, pp. 5, 32, 119.

[24] Aubrey de Vere, *Recollections*, pp. 207–208.

[25] J. E. Baker, "Our New Hellenic Renaissance," *The Reinterpretation of Victorian Literature*, p. 227.

[26] *Sartor Resartus*, pp. 146, 168.

[27] *A Survey of English Literature 1830–1880*, I, 14.

and the great romantic poets to the threshhold of the Victorian period. The beliefs which chasten Newman's strong romantic feelings stand completely apart from this development. Both in his Anglican and Romanist phases the essence of his criticism of Protestants is that they "make something within them their standard." Mr. Murry is quite correct in refusing to associate "A man can worship a man" with the Catholic tradition. The differences between Carlyle and Newman are more significant than their common opposition to positivism and logic-chopping.

The foregoing remarks call the reader's attention to facts which exist regardless of our approval or disapproval of them. Those facts forbid us to describe the Catholic Revival as a manifestation of the romantic spirit. They suggest, on the contrary, that the religious aspects of modern romanticism are end products of the disintegration of Protestantism. This of course does not mean that all Victorians who called themselves Catholics kept firm hold on the Christian essentials, or that all who called themselves Protestants forsook those essentials.[28]

The Catholic Revival is not the only factor which complicates the Victorian phase of our investigation. We must take into account the steady rise of materialism, mechanism, secularism. In many ways, to be sure, this aspect of the period offered rich satisfactions to man's pride. Science and invention, industrial development and money-making, the diffusion of knowledge, secularistic social reform, nationalism and imperialism—in a word, "progress"—gave ample scope for romantic expansiveness. There seemed to be no limit to what man—especially the Englishman—could do. But on the other hand, could man really *do* anything at all as a free creative agent? Was he not, body and mind, a bit of machinery within the great machine of the universe? If progress was an inevitable law, it was futile to talk of furthering or of resisting it. What imaginative autonomy, what boundlessness, what triumphs of personal Titanism could be enjoyed in a necessitated world?

Except to the philosophically shallow and the aesthetically insensitive, such questions were disquieting, and they were especially so to poets. In some ways the rapid changefulness of the age was inspiring, but it was too largely a mechanical changefulness that filled the poet's mind with drab and vulgar novelties with which he had formed no emotional associations. Well might Bunthorne exclaim, "Oh, Hollow! Hollow! Hollow!"

[28] Those who find my distinctions uncharitably precise may derive some ironic satisfaction from the fact that millions of Christians will think me a heretic. In Chapter IX I shall make a brief attempt to justify my inclusion of Roman and Anglican Catholicism under a single head.

What time the poet hath hymned
The writhing maid, lithe-limbed,
    Quivering on amaranthine asphodel,
How can he paint her woes,
Knowing, as well he knows,
    That all can be set right with calomel?

A later stanza suggests a solution:

Is it, and can it be,
Nature hath this decree,
    Nothing poetic in the world shall dwell?
Or that in all her works
Something poetic lurks,
    Even in colocynth and calomel?
        I cannot tell.

Even science, then, could be romanticized after a fashion, but the result was seldom very scientific or very romantic. At best one must say, "I cannot tell." It was difficult to think of the imagination as creating the cosmic machine which had created the imagination.

There was nothing radically new in all this. We merely observe the malaise of modern man growing more acute as the century advances. Carlyle's outcry against the Juggernaut of the machine in *Signs of the Times* and *Characteristics* continues Blake's outcry against the "dark Satanic mills" of Newton and Locke and Shelley's warning that "man, having enslaved the elements, remains himself a slave." In this respect the romantic Toryism of old Wordsworth and old Southey makes another bridge between the two periods. But such disquietude, indeed, goes back at least as far as Fulke Greville and John Donne. In the eighteenth century the sentimental poets had tried to derive romantic satisfaction from Newtonianism, the Whiggish glorification of commercial progress, and something very like the Victorian cult of social service. Gradually, however, they came to the realization that man's romantic brain has fabricated a universe which thwarts the outrush of man's romantic passion. The path of escape led from sentimental naturalism to sentimental subjectivism—"Consultons la lumière intérieure."

Deeply saturated in eighteenth-century thought, the young poets of the 1780–1830 period similarly attempted to achieve boundlessness through a sentimental interpretation of the religion of nature, suffered disillusionment, and turned to a more or less Rousseauistic reliance upon inward feeling. But mere indulgence in reverie could not surmount the obstacles which an increasingly mechanistic world presented to their expansive impulses; a more systematic and formidable rationalization was required. Finally, therefore, they exploited some form of transcendental metaphysics as a means of validating the romantic experience. Plato, Plotinus, Bruno, Boehme, Spinoza (carefully screened), and Berkeley could be made to serve this purpose; but Coleridge showed his brethren and their Victorian successors that the deep romantic Germans provided even more satisfying arguments for the mind's esemplastic power.

Significantly, the dominant trend in Protestant apologetics followed the same course as the apologetics of the romantic faith in human self-sufficiency —from external to internal evidence and thence to a Teutonically inspired transcendental idealism as a means of authenticating inwardness. "The main tendency of nineteenth-century religious development" has accurately been summarized by Professor Hough:

> The breakdown of the argument from design, the mainstay of eighteenth-century orthodoxy, under pressure of evolutionary ideas (an unnecessary breakdown, but still, it occurred); the similar breakdown of the traditional cosmology; the historical disintegration of the scriptures, had all, since the early years of the century, tended to drive religious thought back to subjectivism. . . . Coleridge had prophetically foreseen the necessity of something like this, and had pointed the way for this kind of apologetic: mainly through the influence of F. D. Maurice, it had found its way into current opinion among the young men both at Oxford and Cambridge, and it found its poetical expression in *In Memoriam*.[29]

One need only add that the Catholic Revival followed a different course, and that the development here described is at work even before "the early years of the century," not only in Methodism but in such works of Anglican apologetics as Soame Jenyns's *View of the Internal Evidences of the Christian Religion* (1776).[30]

The great poets studied in Volume III are so intensely romantic that they clearly illustrate the contrast between romanticism and Christianity. Precisely for that reason, however, they are likely to mislead the historian of nineteenth-century religious thought. They were highly exceptional in their day; their influence worked more strongly upon the Victorians than upon their own contemporaries. That influence, to be sure, was partly diluted and partly driven under ground by the Victorian compromise. But in this respect the difference between the 1780–1830 and 1830–1880 periods is less marked than is realized by those who forget that the so-called Romantic Period as a whole was considerably less romantic than its small cluster of distinguished poets. Throughout the entire century, overtly romantic

[29] Graham Hough, *The Last Romantics*, p. 135.

[30] See *Religious Trends*, II, 10–13.

revolt against Christianity was much rarer than the gradual, mainly unconscious, and of course never quite complete romanticizing of Christianity from within by its own declared adherents. The major romantic poets themselves do not stand wholly apart from this trend. Blake and Coleridge always thought themselves good Christians. So did Wordsworth throughout all but a few significant years of his long career, and most Victorians were able to revere him as a great Christian poet by reading his earlier poems in the light of his later Anglicanism. Shelley had openly attacked Christianity, but perhaps only because he was so "Christlike." The author of *Cain* was harder to forgive, but one could apply "Greater love hath no man" to the final gesture at Missolonghi.

If Christianity and romanticism are as different as I assert them to be, why then did they lie down together so peaceably in the minds of so many Victorian poets? For several reasons. In the first place, as I have already said, almost all Christians, Catholic or Protestant, are more romantic than their religion. Also the first three volumes of this series have shown that by 1830 Protestantism (exclusive of undiluted Evangelicalism) had already become so deeply romanticized that only a very pugnaciously romantic poet had any reasonable motive for refusing to think of himself as a Christian. After the French Revolution, furthermore, Christianity had become politically and socially respectable. At a time when progress was usually associated with avoidance of fundamental change, the traditional religion—its yoke now grown so easy—was not likely to be flouted even by those who no longer seriously believed in it. More importantly, Christianity and romanticism wove themselves together in self-defense against their common enemies—utilitarianism, positivism, scientific materialism. Confronted by opponents who seemed to believe nothing at all,[31] those who refused, on *any* grounds, to subject their minds to their senses were inclined to claim kinship with one another.

But the mutually debilitating alliance of Christianity and romanticism was by no means universal. We shall find not a few poets who are overtly anti-Christian romantics or overtly antiromantic Christians. For them the difference between "Man makes God" and "God makes man" is no less vital than the difference between materialism and immaterialism. Our principal theme, in short, is the ferment of attraction and repulsion between Christianity and romanticism in an increasingly secularistic age.

[31] "Seemed" should be emphasized: most Victorian unbelievers believed a great deal.

Chapter Two

EVANGELICAL CHRISTIANITY

EVEN THE MOST un-Evangelical poetry of our period often bears marks of the Evangelical impact upon Victorian culture, but the indirect influence of the moral temper of Evangelicalism was stronger and more enduring than the direct influence of its theology. As early as 1830 Evangelicalism was already becoming more a code than a creed, and by 1880 its spiritual force had greatly diminished with the broadening and loosening of its original doctrines. Throughout the entire period, nevertheless, there were "serious" Anglicans and Dissenters[1] whose loyalty to Reformation principles was, if anything, intensified rather than weakened by the perils of Darwinism, Broad Churchmanship, Puseyism, and Popery. Thanks to this fact, the student of religious thought in Victorian poetry is enabled to run the entire gamut from a theology which would be acceptable to a seventeenth-century Puritan down to a rejection of all Christian beliefs. But for art, as for other aspects of Victorian life, Evangelicalism was more fertile in sickness than in health. The dwindling band of the uncorrupted did not produce much poetry, and very little of what they did produce is fit to read. I am not alluding to the fact that Evangelical Christianity was the religion of large numbers of shabby, ignorant, and vulgar people. Christians had better not sneer at the power of the Evangelical Movement to carry the Gospel tidings down into subliterary levels of society. In a study of this kind we should concern ourselves with men and women who might reasonably be expected to enjoy poetry and, if sufficiently gifted, to write it.

It is not from the chaotic lodgings of Mrs. Jellyby but from the luxurious country seat of Lady Inglis, and as late as 1864, that Miss Wedgwood writes to Robert Browning: "This is a home where I should not venture to open a newspaper on Sunday to save something much more precious than my life. I always feel muzzled here."[2] In these pious circles nothing could be read on

[1] For our purposes, the basic religious differences between Anglican Evangelicals and rigorous Dissenters (including Methodists) are too slight to justify sacrificing the advantages of calling them all "Evangelicals" and treating them in a single chapter.

[2] *Robert Browning and Julia Wedgwood: A Broken Friendship as Revealed by Their Letters*, p. 28. Lady Inglis was Julia Wedgwood's aunt. Lord Neaves's poem, *Let Us All Be Unhappy on Sunday*, is of about the same date as this letter. (Charles, Lord Neaves, *Songs and Verses Social and Scientific*, pp. 120–122.)

the Sabbath except the Bible, a commentary upon it, a sermon or tract, or, if one was a trifle worldly, some non-devotional but definitely edifying work in prose. If people like Julia Wedgwood felt muzzled in such an atmosphere, what must have been the feelings of children?[3] Here is *Sunday Morning* as seen by a little boy named Charles Kingsley:

> Now the bells are ringing loud.
> People rising very early—
> Boys and girls are dressing now,
> And now they go to Sunday School
> To Church—and then come back again.
> Everybody does not work,
> But idle people do not read their Bible
> And God punishes them.
> Now Sunday evening thus comes.
> Everybody goes to bed,
> Boys and girls still remain reading their Bibles
> Till the time they go to Bed.
> Then Monday morning
> Men and women return to work.[4]

Young Charles may have found it hard to join wholeheartedly in the hymn,

> O what their joy and their glory must be,
> Those endless Sabbaths the blessed ones see!

No wonder he turned to Muscular Christianity when he grew up.[5] And yet seven-year-old Frances Havergal, who never became at all muscular, avers that "Sunday is a pleasant day":

> On Sunday hear the village bells;
> It seems as if they said,
> Go to the church where the pastor tells
> How Christ for man has bled.
>
> And if we love to pray and read
> While we are in our youth,
> The Lord will help us in our need
> And keep us in His truth.[6]

[3] Miss Wedgwood, *ibid.*, p. 64, tells Browning that she "always went to bed as a child elaborately expecting the Judgment Day, remembering that passage about its coming as a thief in the night."

[4] Margaret F. Thorp, *Charles Kingsley*, p. 6.

[5] "The happy Christian homes," said James Hinton with too much justification, "are the dark places of the world." (Quoted by A. W. Brown, *The Metaphysical Society*, p. 120.) Compare W. S. Gilbert's devastating line, "The truly happy never look quite well."

[6] E. Davies, *Frances Ridley Havergal*, p. 14. One is entitled to doubt her biographer's assertion that these lines, just as they stand, were written at the age of seven without adult aid.

On weekdays, except in unrepresentatively rigid families, saints of all ages might travel a little more freely in the realms of gold. But not very much. There was a deep suspicion against any reading, and a fortiori against any writing, which did not directly promote knowledge of saving truth. The Evangelical bard Robert Pollok died before he was able to write a great prose work which he had projected. According to his brother it was to have been a "review in which the literature of all ages would be brought to the test and standard of Christianity." The strong heathen influence on almost all the poetry of the Christian era would be exposed and deplored. "Milton was to be the first poet who would stand the test. From the moralists, he had selected Addison and Johnson, and their morality was to be carefully examined. Novels of all sorts he was prepared to condemn entirely; and he meant to give the novels of Sir Walter Scott a thorough scrutiny." He also planned to show that many sermons, past and present, were "tinctured, more or less, with heathen philosophy."[7]

The delightfulness of merely secular literature was a snare, like the one cigar which Leslie Stephen's father smoked in an unguarded moment "and found it so delicious that he never smoked again."[8] In the Evangelical attitude toward the arts, ascetic Hebraism went hand in hand with utilitarian Philistinism: beauty was both morally dangerous and commercially useless. Arnold gleefully cites a newspaper report "of the suicide of a Mr. Smith, secretary to some insurance company, who, it was said, 'labored under the apprehension that he would come to poverty, and that he was eternally lost.' " The pleasures of poetry would have fostered neither of those "two grand objects of concern," which, says Arnold, poor Mr. Smith shared with "the strongest, most respectable, and most representative part of our nation."[9]

The Evangelicals sundered themselves from the Hellenic tradition in English poetry not merely because the Greeks worshipped false gods but because they delighted in the joys of sense. (In this respect Arnold was rather closer to the puritans whom he derided than to the ancients whom he glorified.) When Charles Tennyson returned to his manse after the long victorious struggle against opium, he brought with him "A memory stored with forms of ancient art" and looked at village life through an aura of classical reminiscence. With a sense of guilt he prays that he may not

[7] Robert Pollok, *The Course of Time*, pp. 393–394. It is my not wholly confident hope that no reader will regard this series of studies as an attempt to revive, on a more limited scale, this inquisitorial scheme!

[8] N. G. Annan, *Leslie Stephen*, p. 14.

[9] *Culture and Anarchy*, p. 156.

... merge in Art my Christian fealty!
Through all the winsome sculptures of old Greece
Keep Thou an open walk for Thee and me!
No whiteness is like Thine, All-pure and good!
No marble weighs against Thy precious Blood.[10]

But indeed all secular literature was suspect even though it might be free from pagan taint. Edmund Gosse's mother believed "that to 'tell a story,' that is, to compose fictitious narrative of any kind, was a sin."[11] The more usual objection to novels was that at worst they were morally corrupting and at best a sinful waste of time. Pollok, no less censorious in verse than he intended to be in prose, describes them as

... oft cramm'd full
Of poisonous error, blackening every page;
And oftener still, of trifling, second-hand
Remark, and old, diseaséd, putrid thought;

. . .

Yet charming still the greedy reader on
Till, done, he tried to recollect his thoughts,
And nothing found but dreaming emptiness.[12]

Novelists who themselves would have been glad to deal honestly with their material found it expedient to truckle to that prudery which Evangelicalism had made a part of the Victorian code. "We must," says Thackeray, "pass over a part of Mrs. Rebecca Crawley's biography with that lightness and delicacy which the world demands. . . . A polite public will no more bear to read an authentic description of vice than a truly refined English or American female will permit the word breeches to be pronounced in her chaste hearing."[13]

Needless to say, the theatre was shunned as "the favorite haunt of sin."[14] For some saints, indeed, it was almost as reprehensible to read a play as to see one; but young Thomas Noon Talfourd, the future author of *Ion*, was allowed to feast his fancy on Hannah More's "Sacred Dramas."[15] Prejudice

[10] Charles Tennyson Turner, *Collected Sonnets*, p. 199. I am not sure that this poet would thank me for including him in the present chapter: he is more of a Churchman than the other poets whom I label as Evangelicals, including those of the Anglican communion. But after he conquers the drug-habit and begins to take his religion and his ministry seriously he appears as a strong Episcopalian Protestant whose Churchmanship is not High or Broad or Flat; hence on the whole I think he belongs here.

[11] Edmund Gosse, *Father and Son*, p. 22.

[12] *The Course of Time*, p. 149.

[13] *Vanity Fair*, pp. 230–231.

[14] Pollok, *The Course of Time*, p. 237.

[15] T. N. Talfourd, *Dramatic Works*, p. 6. I have not observed any Evangelical opinions concerning Charles Jeremiah Wells's *Joseph and His Brethren* (1824). This Biblical poetic drama was absurdly overpraised after its rediscovery by Rossetti, but it has a good deal of merit both dramatic and religious. Severely pious readers, however, probably found the quite unexceptionable scenes between Joseph and Potiphar's wife disquietingly realistic.

against the stage extended to musical instrumentalists and singers—even in some cases to so notably pious an artist as Jenny Lind. In 1847 eyebrows were raised when the Bishop of Norwich, A. P. Stanley's father, entertained her overnight at the episcopal palace after a concert.[16]

The greater the dramatist the greater the peril, even if he had been emasculated for family reading by Mr. Bowdler. As a writer in the *Christian Observer* declared, "It is scarcely possible for a young person of fervid genius to read Shakespeare without a dangerous elevation of the fancy. . . . It may be safer to entrust a pupil with Robinson Crusoe, than with Shakespeare."[17] Reading *The Merchant of Venice*, Charlotte Elizabeth Tonna "drank a cup of intoxication under which my brain reeled for many a year."[18] Frances Havergal looked into Shakespeare "that I might polish my own instruments for the Master's use. But there is so much that is entirely of the earth earthy, amid all the marvellous genius and even the sparkles of the highest truth which flash here and there . . . so much that is downward instead of upward; that it has crossed me whether I am not trusting an arm of flesh in seeking intellectual benefit thus." But since she really likes Shakespeare in spite of her better nature, she shrinks from a principle which "would throw over all means as to study and mental culture, and it does really seem as a rule as if God endorsed those means, and uses cultivated powers, and only very exceptionally uses the uncultured ones."[19]

We may be sure that when Miss Havergal writes in this reckless vein she is thinking of Shakespeare not as a man of the theatre but as a poet. It is significant that although Gosse's mother disapproved so rigidly of fiction that she refused to read Scott's verse-tales because they were not "true," she had no objection to lyric poetry if it was sufficiently edifying.[20] Probably, though her son does not mention the fact, she also tolerated those endless one-third-narrative, two-thirds-didactic sacred poems—theoretically Miltonic in inspiration but actually more like Young or Cowper—which were grounded too firmly on the Scriptures to be regarded as fictitious, such as Pollok's *The Course of Time* (1827), Robert Montgomery's *Satan* (1830) and *The Messiah* (1832), Heraud's *The Descent into Hell* (1830) and *The Judgment of the Flood* (1834).[21] The more cultivated Evangelicals were not unfriendly

[16] A. P. Stanley, *Letters and Verses*, pp. 111–113.

[17] Quoted by F. E. Mineka, *The Dissidence of Dissent: The Monthly Repository*, pp. 56–57. This seems to imply that Defoe is also a dangerous author, though less so than Shakespeare. Perhaps the latitudinarianism of Crusoe's theological colloquies with Friday was objectionable.

[18] N. G. Annan, *Leslie Stephen*, p. 119.

[19] E. Davies, *Frances Ridley Havergal*, p. 102.

[20] Edmund Gosse, *Father and Son*, p. 23.

[21] I date these poems to show that they belong to the closing years of the "interregnum" rather than to the Victorian period proper. They remained popular, however, among "serious" Victorian

to the seventeenth-century theory of religious poetry which had been handed down to them by such congenial mediators as Watts, Dennis, Blackmore, and Young.[22] If the bard wrote as a prophet deeply aware of the religious origin and end of all genuine poetry, he could count on being read and praised by all but the very dourest of the saints.

Hence although it can hardly be said that the Evangelical singers think poetically of religion, they certainly think religiously of poetry and of themselves as poets. Emma Tatham dedicates *The Dream of Pythagoras, and Other Poems* directly to God, begging Him to

> Hear me, and make me a pure golden harp
> For Thy soft finger. Might I be Thy bird,
> Hidden from all, singing to Thee alone.

But this is a little too quietistic: the poet should not praise God without remembering his God-given task of improving other men. Robert Pollok's invocation of the Holy Spirit has more of the right puritan energy. Spurning "The muse, that soft and sickly woos the ear/Of love," he asks the Paraclete for the power to utter

> The essential truth—Time gone, the righteous saved,
> The wicked damn'd, and Providence approved.
> Hold my right hand, Almighty! and me teach
> To strike the lyre, but seldom struck, to notes
> Harmonious with the morning stars . . .
>
> . . .
>
> That fools may hear and tremble, and the wise
> Instructed listen, of ages yet to come.[23]

The workings of Divine inspiration are described by Frances Havergal in a letter to a friend who has been teasing her for a poem on a particular occasion:

> I can never set myself to write verse. I believe my King suggests a thought and whispers me a musical line or two, and then I look up and thank Him delightedly, and go on with it. . . . The Master has not put a chest of poetic gold into my possession and said "Now use it as you like!" But He keeps the gold, and gives it me piece by piece just when He will and as much as He will, and no more.[24]

---

readers. So far as I know, the last pure example of this type is Edward Henry Bickersteth's *Yesterday, To-day, and For Ever*. It was published in 1866, but he tells us in his preface that it had been conceived "more than twenty years" earlier. Since the seventeenth edition appeared in 1885, it seems clear that this distinctively Evangelical type retained its readers longer than its writers.

[22] See the entries for "Poetry" in the topical indexes of *Religious Trends*, I and II.

[23] *The Course of Time*, p. 38.

[24] E. Davies, *Frances Ridley Havergal*, pp. 66–67.

Characteristically, Martin Tupper is less humble: he has discovered that the suicidal Mr. Smith's "two grand objects of concern" can be combined in the career of a successful author:

> Yea; how dignified, and worthy, full of privilege and happiness,
> Standeth in majestic independence the self-ennobled Author!
> For God hath blessed him with a mind, and cherished it in tenderness and purity,
> Hath taught it the whisperings of wisdom, and added all the riches of content.[25]

Even here, however, God receives a decent amount of credit.

But as there seemed to be fewer and fewer geniuses who wrote to elevate rather than to corrupt the soul, the literary aliment of Evangelicals was not only meagre but mainly retrospective. They read Bunyan and Quarles.[26] They read Milton, or talked as if they did, not suspecting that he "was of the Devil's party without knowing it."[27] They read Isaac Watts and Robert Blair and Edward Young. Henry Kirke White was not always beyond suspicion, but he had been a pious youth and had left behind him thirty-four Spenserian stanzas of a *Christiad*. "The gentle Cowper, dear to man and God,"[28] was a prime favorite: his piety conferred a blessing even upon *John Gilpin*, and the pathos of his delusion was irresistible to those who knew that they were saved. Mrs. Browning's *Cowper's Grave* is paralleled by Charles Tennyson's sonnets on *The Death-Smile of Cowper* and *Cowper's Three Hares*. For Anne Brontë, this "celestial Bard" speaks "the language of my inmost heart." If he should indeed be a lost soul, as he feared, "Oh! how shall *I* appear?"[29]

But Walter Bagehot exaggerates when he calls Cowper "the one poet of a class which have no poets."[30] As we have already seen, there were pious Victorians who expressed in verse the strong, deep convictions of Evangelical Christianity. Of their number, only Mrs. Browning and perhaps Charles Tennyson are remembered—and not for their most Evangelical effusions—by any but professional students of nineteenth-century poetry. The others are emotionally moved by their faith, but they are seldom moved to create

[25] *Proverbial Philosophy*, II, 30. Although, as we shall see, Tupper sometimes departed rather far from pure Evangelicalism, he maintained his popularity among the Evangelicals, who often called him "the Shakespeare of the Church," long after he had become (not wholly deservedly) a laughing-stock in more worldly circles. See Derek Hudson, *Martin Tupper*, pp. 40ff., 232, 245.

[26] Little Robert Browning's favorite picture book was the *Emblems*.

[27] Pollok and Montgomery were not infrequently compared to Milton; and as late as 1866 a reviewer in *The Globe* declared that "If any poem is destined to endure in the companionship of Milton's hitherto matchless epic, we believe it will be *Yesterday, To-day, and For Ever*." (Advertisement bound in with Bickersteth's poem.)

[28] Emma Tatham, *The Dream of Pythagoras, and Other Poems*, p. 62.

[29] *The Complete Works of Charlotte Brontë and Her Sisters*, IV, 317, 319.

[30] *Literary Studies*, I, 264.

poems. In their writings the puritan's dread of images and the poet's sensuousness usually cancel out, leaving them with nothing but a pious sense of obligation to versify the stock ideas and sentiments of their religion.[31]

Even in this group we may sometimes detect faint stirrings of latitudinarianism, but for the present let us ignore such symptoms and distill the essence of uncorrupted Evangelical Christianity. To some palates the wine may seem thin and sour, but its flavor can hardly be described as romantic. These poets are assuredly not champions of human self-sufficiency. "Crush pride into the dust"[32] is their unanimous exhortation; for

> Pride, self-adoring pride, was criminal cause
> Of all sin past, all pain, all woe to come.
> Unconquerable pride! first, eldest sin;
> Great fountain-head of evil.[33]

Bickersteth appears to think that the father of romanticism was not Rousseau but Satan. Meditating rebellion against God, the fiend soliloquizes:

> Why should I always please Him? Say, I choose
> To be my own eternal lord? What then?
> Oh, by those burning thoughts, those hopes that rise
> Within me subject to no will but mine,
> I ask, why are we made thus circumscribed?
> Are there not possibilities of being
> Higher and nobler far than those we see?
>
> . . .
>
> I know He is Almighty; but I see
> Another image of Omnipotence,
> The awful Power of self-determined choice.
> Suppose I choose to worship at that shrine,
> What hinders?[34]

We serve Satan rather than God, avers Emma Tatham, when the "proud heart" yearns:

> "O how much rather would I be the oak,
> With all its struggles and with all its storms,
> Than the unnoticed grass! a lofty lot
> Be mine, though perilous, for oh! it is

[31] As in my earlier volumes, I do not make myself responsible for any systematic discussion of hymns, but I glance at them occasionally when a so-called hymn may also be regarded as a religious lyric expressing the author's personal feeling.

[32] Anne Brontë, *The Complete Works of Charlotte Brontë and Her Sisters*, IV, 363.

[33] Pollok, *The Course of Time*, p. 89.

[34] *Yesterday, To-Day, and For Ever*, pp. 155–156.

A glorious thing to live without a father,
Even though broken; as the mountain top
Though lightning-blasted; never will I bend,
But self-sufficient stand, in torture proud
And mighty to endure." Yet, boasting dust!
What art thou? lo! the meanest worm that crawls
In passive service to its Maker's will
Is nobler—infinitely—than the height
Of intellect, when warring with its God.[35]

For the most perilous form of pride is the assertion of independent intellectual and imaginative power. Robert Montgomery sees it as the peculiar snare of the modern world. Knowledge not "tempered with a sanctifying tone" is merely "an ornamental curse." Such knowledge

In full omnipotence is reigning now;
Yet haply, with a spirit and a power
To breed an earthquake in the boastful heart
Of this free isle.[36]

In these days of progress through scientific invention, Tupper also gives warning that although

Man is proud of his mind, boasting that it giveth him divinity,
Yet with all its powers can it originate nothing.

God has withheld from man

... one special property, the grand prerogative—Creation.
To improve and expand is ours, as well as to limit and defeat;
But to create a thought or thing is hopeless and impossible.[37]

This warning is especially needed by poets, for more than most men they are prone to be "blinded into self-idolatry," forgetting that "Genius oft is mad Ambition's wing."[38] Byron, who both fascinated and shocked the Evangelical mind, is a prime example. Pollok credits him with a "capacious soul" and an almost unearthly poetic power. He could play upon all the human feelings,

Yet would not tremble, would not weep himself;
But back into his soul retired, alone,
Dark, sullen, proud: gazing contemptuously
On hearts and passions prostrate at his feet.

This titled, wealthy, famous, aspiring, greatly gifted man became

[35] *The Dream of Pythagoras*, p. 91.
[36] *Satan*, p. 252.
[37] *Proverbial Philosophy*, I, 109.
[38] Robert Montgomery, *Satan*, p. 122.

A wandering, weary, worn, and wretched thing;
A scorch'd, and desolate, and blasted soul;
A gloomy wilderness of dying thought—
Repined, and groan'd, and wither'd from the earth.
His groanings fill'd the land his numbers fill'd;
And yet he seem'd ashamed to groan. Poor man!
Ashamed to ask, and yet he needed help.[39]

Pure Evangelicalism, of course, gives no more direct encouragement to belief in natural goodness than to romantic titanism. Ever since the Fall—an event as historical as Waterloo—the heart of man has been corrupt and sinful. Our moral progress, like our material progress, is a delusion imposed upon us by the Tempter. In the sight of God, man is no better now than he ever was since he ate the fruit of that forbidden tree: his wickedness is merely a little more refined.

. . . The Past
Was roughened with a stormy wickedness;
The Present, with a smoother surface tempts
The judgment; 'tis a most diseaseful calm!
Beneath it, in their cool, collected power
The passions glide, all sinuous, but impure.[40]

It is of spiritual death in the Pauline sense that pious young John Ruskin is thinking when he writes:

Where the gentle streams of thinking,
Through our hearts that flow so free,
Have the deepest, softest sinking
And the fullest melody;
Where the crown of hope is nearest,
Where the voice of joy is dearest,
Where the heart of youth is lightest,
Where the light of love is brightest,
There is death.[41]

Ruskin's verses are entitled *The Broken Chain*. How is the chain to be mended? The "home Puritan religion" of Mark Pattison's boyhood (his father was an Evangelical clergyman) "almost narrowed to two points, fear of God's wrath and faith in the doctrine of the atonement."[42] At neither point would there seem to be a loophole for the entrance of self-sufficiency,

[39] *The Course of Time*, pp. 159–168 *passim*. For the same view of Byron see Montgomery, *Satan*, pp. 77–79.
[40] Montgomery, *Satan*, p. 118.
[41] *Poems*, p. 75.
[42] Mark Pattison, *Memoirs*, p. 326.

since of course Calvinistic soteriology excluded all human contribution to the process of salvation except the faith that

> . . . He that gave His blood for men
> Will lead us home to God again.[43]

All righteousness is God's, not man's. "What I do, God does; what I am, God is" would not appeal to Horatius Bonar, who sings:

> Not what these hands have done
> Can save this guilty soul;
> Not what this toiling flesh has borne
> Can make my spirit whole.
>
> Not what I feel or do
> Can give me peace with God;
> Not all my prayers, and sighs, and tears,
> Can bear my awful load.[44]

Nor would such poets deal in soothing puns about "at-one-ment." The Atonement is a bloody sacrifice offered by the Son to assuage the just wrath of the Father. God is no less loving than just, but his love becomes operative solely through the death agonies of the Lamb.

> No, not the love without the blood;
> That were to me no love at all;
> It could not reach my sinful soul,
> Nor hush the fears which me appal.
>
> . . .
>
> The love I need is righteous love,
> Inscribed on the sin-bearing tree,
> Love that exacts the sinner's debt,
> Yet in exacting sets him free.[45]

One Palm Sunday eve, Charles Tennyson dreams that he has lined the Crown of Thorns with soft protective down, only to be rebuked by his Lord:

> Without My wounds, the world remains undone;
> Why dost thou, then, forbid thy Lord to bleed?
> Why grudge mankind the Passion and the Creed?[46]

Even in the eighteenth-century phase of the Evangelical Movement, the rigor of predestination had been softened by the theory that conversion is sure evidence of Divine favor. After all, one could hardly be called unless

[43] Anne Brontë, *The Complete Works of Charlotte Brontë and Her Sisters*, IV, 314.
[44] *Hymns of Faith and Hope*, p. 184.
[45] *Ibid.*, p. 321.
[46] Charles Tennyson Turner, *Collected Sonnets*, p. 325.

one had been chosen.[47] The advantages of the New Birth were so immense that the inducements to suppose that one had received this boon were almost irresistible. Yet there were many scrupulous souls who suffered dread of damnation for long years before they could persuade themselves that they had experienced a genuine conversion. Born in 1836, Frances Ridley Havergal was the daughter of an Anglican Evangelical clergyman. She loved her pious rearing and could read the Bible at the age of four. Of course she was baptized and confirmed, and she grew up faithful in all the observances of the Established Church. She became an eminent writer of hymns and sacred lyrics, was active in charitable works, and in wholehearted surrender to Jesus lived so blameless and fruitful a life that unless her biographer is a liar she was something of a saint. But it was not until 1873, at the age of thirty-seven, that she received any assurance of "entire sanctification." Then at last she could write *Set Apart for Jesus:*

> Set apart for His delight,
> Chosen for His holy pleasure,
> Sealed to be His special treasure,
> Could we choose a nobler joy?
> And would we if we might?[48]

From such assurance may spring the spiritual—and physical—aberrations of antinomianism, the romanticism of the sectarian enthusiast. In the eighteenth century, the saints were often accused of taking very full advantage of the glorious liberty of the children of God; the charges, though malicious and hugely exaggerated, were not invariably without foundation.[49] But the main trend, among Methodists no less than among Anglican Evangelicals, moved steadily toward sobriety and discretion. The men who established the code of British respectability were eminently respectable. The sporadic antinomian eccentricities of little perfectionist coteries[50] are not reflected in the poetry of our period. Theoretically, the New Birth is a sure sign of election, and for the elect sin is impossible; but on the other hand immoral behavior after a supposed conversion is a sure sign that the conversion was spurious. For these Victorian Puritans no less than for Arnold, conduct is after all three-fourths of life. One is saved solely by faith, not works, but works are the best evidence for the possession of saving faith. This may be inconsistent, but it is salutary.

[47] Hence although Anglican Evangelicals were Calvinists while Wesleyans and a few other sects were Arminians, the actual difference is much less great than theological polemics would lead one to suppose.

[48] E. Davies, *Frances Ridley Havergal*, pp. 11ff., 157.

[49] See *Religious Trends*, II, 117–130.

[50] For examples of such behavior see R. A. Knox, *Enthusiasm*, pp. 549–577.

Such mysticism as may be observed in Victorian poetry deviates so widely from free-grace theology and often from Christianity of any sort that it has no place in this chapter. The group now under discussion grounds its beliefs not upon contemplative vision but upon a perfectly literal interpretation of the Bible—"The author, God himself." Constituting "Heaven's code of laws entire," it is

> ... the only star
> By which the bark of man could navigate
> The sea of life, and gain the coast of bliss.[51]

Nor do we observe any conscious wish to subject the authority of Scripture to the authority of the Inner Light. The Bible means what the Bible says.

The nearest approach to mysticism is a quietistic tendency which is more apparent in Evangelical poetry than in Evangelical mores and more prevalent among women than among men. Anne Waring

> ... would not have the restless will
> That hurries to and fro,
> Seeking for some great thing to do
> Or secret thing to know;
> I would be treated as a child,
> And guided where I go.[52]

As a humble wayside flower Sarah Williams speaks:

> I fain would give some sweetness out,
> Some bruisèd scent of myrrh;
> But Thou art close at hand, my Lord—
> I need not strive nor stir.[53]

Frances Havergal is of the same mind:

> I am not eager, bold, or strong,
> All that is past;
> I'm ready *not* to do,
> At last, at last.

But those lines were written after a long illness; her customary vein is that of *Shining*:

> Are you shining for Jesus, dear one?
> You have given your heart to Him;
> But is the light strong within it,
> Or is it but pale and dim?

[51] Pollok, *The Course of Time*, 73, 74, 75.

[52] *The Poets and the Poetry of the Nineteenth Century*, ed. by A. H. Miles *et al*, XI, 389. Hereafter this collection will be cited as *Miles*.

[53] *Ibid.*, IX, 199.

Can *everybody* see it,—
That Jesus is all to you?
That your love to Him is burning
With a radiance warm and true?[54]

Everybody could see Miss Havergal's light shining in missionary activities, the temperance movement, and so on. Nor would her less vigorous sister-poets feel that quiet self-surrender to Jesus conferred any exemption from Christian duty. They would all accept Tupper's repeated warning that subjectivism is the nurse of pride:

Fruitlessly thou strainest for humility, by darkly diving into self:
Rather look away from innate evil, and gaze upon extraneous good.

. . .

It is a good thing, and a wholesome, to search out bosom sins,
But to be the hero of selfish imaginings is the subtle poison of pride:

. . .

Well said the wisdom of earth, O mortal, know thyself:
But better the wisdom of heaven, O man, learn thou thy God:

. . .

Learn God, thou shalt know thyself.[55]

In short, all of these poets, male or female, believe in a God who has made them, not in a God whom they have made.

Otherworldliness is a marked characteristic of the group. Although here one must observe a considerable cleavage between Evangelical doctrine and Evangelical behavior, Arnold's Mr. Smith could have reconciled his "two grand objects of concern" by saying, and quite possibly believing, that he craved commercial success on earth solely as evidence of having been singled out for eternal bliss in heaven. So far as these poets are concerned, at all events, the purpose of the Christian's struggle against sin is not to contribute his mite to the redemption of the world but to demonstrate his personal qualifications for getting out of it upward rather than downward. Such titles as *Passing Through*, *Arise and Depart*, and *A Little While* indicate the favorite theme of Horatius Bonar, who exhorts his fellow-pilgrims:

Brethren, arise,
Let us go hence!
This is no home for us;
Till earth is purified
We may not here abide.

[54] E. Davies, *Frances Ridley Havergal*, pp. 93, 94.

[55] *Proverbial Philosophy*, I, 50, 90, 123–124. Tupper can be very absurd, but he is not such a fool as is supposed by those who rely on Calverley's parodies for their notion of him.

In this "serpent-world" the forgiven sinner is consoled only by the knowledge that

> Beyond the smiling and the weeping
> I shall be soon;
> Beyond the waking and the sleeping,
> Beyond the sowing and the reaping,
> I shall be soon.
> Love, rest, and home!
> Sweet hope!
> Lord, tarry not, but come.[56]

Bonar will not permit his readers to feel any enthusiasm about the Exhibition of 1851. They should think not of the Crystal Palace but of the glassy sea of heaven:

> From the crowd in wonder gazing,
> Science claims the prostrate knee;
> This her temple, diamond-blazing,
> Shrine of her idolatry.
> Heir of glory,
> What is that to thee and me?[57]

Even that much less uncompromising saint, Martin Tupper, complains that the Exhibition showed us nothing but "Triumphant Matter." It provided

> . . . not one drop of balm the heart to heal,
> One ray of peace the conscience to console!
> Oh! Man needs more than merchandise, to make
> His better nature quicken, and unseal
> His eyes from sinful slumber.[58]

Thus the otherworldliness of the Evangelicals permitted them to pass severe judgment upon the civilization which their own earnestness and practical energy had done so much to shape. Montgomery's Satan infers from the spectacle of England's industrial life that her real deity is Money. The nation has been corrupted by

> A lust of gain, that rankles into lies,
> Or fraudful means, or knavish arts; while Truth,
> Integrity, and Honour, are diseased,

[56] *Hymns of Faith and Hope*, pp. 25, 92.
[57] *Ibid.*, p. 18.
[58] Quoted by Derek Hudson, *Martin Tupper*, p. 105. Other poems by Tupper, to be sure, view the Exhibition more enthusiastically.

And die away in avaricious dreams
Of Mammon.[59]

The reform interests of the Evangelicals of this period are represented in their poetry, but less abundantly than one might expect. Satan regards slavery—not only on colonial plantations but in the factories where English men and women are exploited and English children abused—as a crime against the national ideal of liberty:

Why, what a hell-slave will this Commerce prove,
When life and feeling perish for her cause![60]

Jean Ingelow makes a social-minded parson tell his congregation of fishermen, who suppose that God cares only for the wealthy:

The day was, I have been afraid of pride—
Hard man's hard pride; but now I am afraid
Of man's humility. I counsel you,
By the great God's great humbleness, and by
His pity, be not humble over-much.[61]

On Judgment Day, says Pollok, such lowly ones will discover with joyful surprise the great truth of Christian democracy,

That men were really of a common stock;
That no man ever had been more than man.

But it is significant that this discovery will be postponed to the great Assizes. The social indignation of these poets pauses well on the safe side of radicalism. The Evangelicals had risen to power by showing England how to stave off revolution through religiously sanctioned reform—not too little of it, but also not too much. The more prosperous and respectable they became the less inclined they were to alter any conditions other than those so flagrantly evil that they threatened the onward march of progress. Reviewing the course of history, Pollok finds that

One passion prominent appears—the lust
Of power, which often took the fairer name
Of liberty, and hung the popular flag
Of freedom out.

[59] *Satan*, p. 251. The entire poem is a monologue delivered by Satan, who in order to express the poet's ideas is usually forced to talk as though he were William Wilberforce although he sometimes remembers to do a little sinister gloating over the evils he describes.

[60] *Ibid.*, pp. 61, 250–251.

[61] *Poetical Works*, p. 156.

Deceived by this disguise, men easily forgot that

> True liberty was Christian, sanctified,
> Baptized, and found in Christian hearts alone.[62]

In the same spirit Montgomery speaks of France as "too unholy to be free."[63] "Woe unto him whose heart the syren song of liberty hath charmed," says Tupper. "No station is degrading but it is ennobled by obedience." The notion of equality is "the lie that crowded hell, when seraphs flung away subjection." The child who is not controlled by firm parental discipline is liable to grow up "A scoffer about bigotry, a rebel against government and God." There are degrees of subordination even in the Holy Trinity, "For the Son, as a son, is subject; and to Him doth the Spirit minister."[64] On the whole the poems of this group are more calculated to quiet than to inflame the passion for liberty.

Simon-pure Evangelical poets were not greatly alarmed by the intellectual and spiritual revolution of their times, but they sometimes voiced their disapproval of it in tones which suggest a certain anxiety. Although they are not impressive in apologetics one may at least say for them that, despite some waverings to be noted later, they do not attempt to preserve their religion by turning it into something quite different. Bonar waxes heavily sarcastic against the unbelieving intellectuals:

> *They* are the thinkers, *we* the credulous;
> *They* have the mind, and can think out all truth,
> *We* dream and dote upon the fabulous.

> Man's high philosophy disdains Thy [God's] thoughts,
> And the proud voice of science scorns Thy word.

But nothing is really worth knowing except the will of God:

> To think HIS thoughts, is blessedness supreme;
> To know HIMSELF, the Thinker, is our life;
> To rest this weary intellect on His,
> Is the glad ending of mind's endless strife.[65]

Montgomery relies on old-fashioned physico-theology sharpened with the threat of hell-fire for those who remain unconvinced by the argument from design:

[62] *The Course of Time*, pp. 137, 141, 347.
[63] *Satan*, p. 88.
[64] *Proverbial Philosophy*, I, 35, 39, 40, 41. But Tupper hedges as regards the Trinity, adding that "these things be mysteries to man," and that "with these wondrous Persons abideth eternal equality."
[65] *Hymns of Faith and Hope*, pp. 347, 348.

If Nature fail, then Reason may despair;
The universe is stamp'd with God; who sees
Creation, and can no Creator view,—
To him Philosophy shall preach in vain:
A blinded nature, and a blasted mind
Are his; Eternity shall teach the rest.[66]

But James Drummond Burns deviates from the Paley tradition, preferring to rely on the obvious fact that nature furnishes evidence of God to people who believe in God. Reason is impotent to fathom the mysteries of the heavens, but faith beholds

God's name in starry cipher written fair,—
The vision of His Wisdom, Power, and Love,
Serenely throned these drifting mists above,
Revealed unto the upward glance of Prayer.[67]

The more up-to-date Tupper is quite willing that the operations of man's mind should be governed by the laws of nature if only the laws of nature are regarded as the thoughts of God:

He made and ordained necessity; he forged the chain of reason;
And holdeth in his right hand the first of the golden links.
A fool regardeth mind as the spiritual essence of matter,
And not rather matter as the gross accident of mind.

Evolution holds no terrors for him who knows that the universal process of causation originates in God:

Begin from the Maker, thou carriest down his attributes to reptiles,
The sharded beetle and the lizard live and move in Him:
Begin from the creature, corruption and infirmity mar thy foolish toil.[68]

In the eighteen-sixties Charles Tennyson is much less troubled by Darwinism than by the extension of scientific method to Biblical criticism and to the comparative study of religions. Many of his sonnets (but none of his best) attack Paulus, Strauss, Renan, Bunsen, Max Müller, and the deluded Broad Churchmen whose sophistry

. . . does not shrink
To substitute, for our sound faith in Christ,
A dreamy, hollow, unsubstantial creed.

Tennyson attempts no systematic refutation of the neologists, but he warns

[66] *Satan*, p. 145. As demanded by the absurd plan of the poem these edifying remarks are uttered by Satan, but of course they express the author's views.

[67] *Miles*, XII, 33.

[68] *Proverbial Philosophy*, I, 90; II, 34.

us that a mere code of ethics draped in unbelieved poetic myths about Renan's "sweet young Syrian" is no less spiritually impotent than intellectually dishonest. No real redemption without a real Redeemer.

> Mere harness will not pull us up to Christ,
> Without the strength of full and living creeds;
> These shiny morals are no match for sin.

To a Broad Church clergyman on Christmas morning, "Christ is born" can have no meaning but that of a pretty fable. The time approaches

> When priesthood in his own white robe shall stand
> Forsworn, among the faithful evergreens![69]

But Tennyson refuses to despair:

> For deep in many a brave, though bleeding heart
> There lurks a yearning for the Healer's face—
> A yearning to be free from hint and guess,
> To take the blessings Christ is fain to give:
> To all who dare not with their conscience strive,
> To all who burn for this most dear success,
> Faith shall be born! and, by her natural stress,
> Push through these dark philosophies, and live![70]

In all this there is not the slightest concession to subjectivism. Contrast his brother Alfred's "I have felt."

On the whole, however, the Evangelicals write with more zest and conviction when continuing an older struggle—that between the saints and the Scarlet Woman of Babylon,

> . . . the harlot-bride
> Of the world's Christ-hating King.
>
> Yet her day is near at hand,
> And her judgment lingers not;
> See the fierce-ascending smoke
> Of her vengeance, red and hot.
> See the mighty millstone flung
> By the glorious angel-hand;
>
> . . .
>
> She is sunk for evermore;
>
> . . .
>
> Let us then rejoice and sing;
> 'Tis the marriage of the Lamb;

[69] The allusion, of course, is to the traditional Christmastide decoration of the church.
[70] *Collected Sonnets*, pp. 166, 169, 173, 176.

And the Bride is ready; raise,
Raise the everlasting psalm![71]

As these apocalyptic lines imply, one must carefully distinguish between the spurious Bride and the genuine. The former is the Church of Rome; the latter is the Church of Christ, now poor and persecuted but destined to a glorious restoration when the Bridegroom comes to claim His own. In the Middle Ages, Bickersteth explains, the Tempter hatched his darkest, craftiest plot. He substituted a Satanic Trinity of himself, Baal, and Ashtaroth for the divine reality, and a false Bride for Christ's true Beloved.[72] The consequences of this sleight-of-hand need not be specified; even Satan, in Montgomery's poem, indignantly describes the Inquisition as "hellish."[73] The Reformers exposed the gigantic imposture, but the complete and final destruction of popery must await the Last Day.[74]

Pending her marriage with the Lamb, the true Bride remains a somewhat shadowy personification of the Protestant ideal, seldom invoked except for purposes of contrast with the Roman harlot. Your true Evangelical will not believe that any visible ecclesiastical institution, functionary, or rite is necessary for his soul's salvation:[75]

I need no priest save Him who is above;
No altar but the heavenly mercy-seat;

. . .

I need no blood but that of Golgotha;
No sacrifice save that which, on the tree
Was offered once, without defect or flaw,
And which, unchanged, availeth still for me.

. . .

I need no pardon save of Him who says,
"Neither do I condemn thee, go in peace;"

. . .

Forgiven through Him who died and rose on high,
My conscience from dead works thus purged and clean,

[71] Bonar, *Hymns of Faith and Hope*, pp. 350–351.

[72] *Yesterday, To-Day and For Ever*, pp. 273–275. Substantially the same story is told by Emma Tatham, *The Dream of Pythagoras, and Other Poems*, pp. 84–87.

[73] *Satan*, p. 70.

[74] In Newman's *Loss and Gain*, p. 147, a group of Evangelical Oxford students are almost too startled to be pleased by a report that the late Pope "seems to have died a believer." Not long before his death, at least, he had told a Protestant missionary "that it was his fervent hope that they two would not die without finding themselves in the same communion, or something of the sort. He declared, moreover, what was astonishing, that he put his sole trust in Christ."

[75] Anglican Evangelicals revered the Church of England as the nationally established form of Protestantism, but they did not suppose that they were saved because they were members of it. With many Nonconformists they also prized the Eucharist, but as a precious means of arousing and confirming right religious feelings rather than as the indispensable core of a Christian's life.

I serve the service of true love and joy;
And live by faith upon a Christ unseen.[76]

Essentially, then, the earthly life of the Evangelical Christian is a pilgrimage throughout which he relies solely upon his faith in the unseen Christ as revealed to him in God's Holy Word. The journey to the banks of Jordan is as Bunyan's hero found it—now hard and now easy, now joyous and now terrifying, now confident and now desperate. These poets are not, on the whole, a sour-faced lot—Pollok and Montgomery are exceptional in that respect. Perhaps Miss Havergal is rather more gushingly exuberant than the average when she writes:

The fulness of His blessing encompasseth our way;
The fulness of His promises crowns every brightening day;
The fulness of His glory is beaming from above,
While more and more we realize the fulness of His love.[77]

Jean Ingelow is more representative in that her gladness is more explicitly related to the Atonement:

Joy is the grace we say to God. Art tired?
There is a rest remaining. Hast thou sinned?
There is a Sacrifice. Lift up thy head,
The lovely world, and the over-world alike,
Ring with a song eterne, a happy rede,
THE FATHER LOVES THEE.[78]

But we cannot hope for heavenly union with Him who suffered for us unless we ourselves are willing to suffer. Gazing on her little godson, the future poet Philip Marston, Dinah Mulock quite mistakenly foresees for him royal triumphs in love and in action among men. But his head needs "a circlet rarer" than such earthly crowns—

A wreath not of gold, but palm. One day,
Philip my king,
Thou too must tread, as we trod, a way
Thorny and cruel and cold and gray:
Rebels within thee and foes without
Will snatch at thy crown. But march on, glorious,

[76] Bonar, *Hymns of Faith and Hope*, pp. 319–320. The stanza on the Lord's Supper shows that this poet's well-known hymn beginning "Here, O my Lord, I see Thee face to face" (*Ibid.*, pp. 68–69) does not imply the Real Presence but should be interpreted as a reverent and deeply felt expression of a Protestant view of the Eucharist as a commemorative service *reminding* us of Christ's sacrifice and "Giving sweet foretaste of the festal joy, / The Lamb's great bridal feast of bliss and love."

[77] E. Davies, *Frances Ridley Havergal*, p. 60.

[78] *Poetical Works*, p. 398.

Martyr, yet monarch; till angels shout
As thou sit'st at the feet of God victorious,
"Philip the king!"[79]

Our sins cannot bar us from such glory if only we genuinely repent of them;[80]

But is that heart of thine broken indeed?
Oh, it is broken hearts the Saviour calls
His bruised flowers; the sighs of penitence
Are fragrant in His presence. Kiss His feet;
Think, they were pierced for thee—how can they then
Reject thee![81]

The more difficult and painful our life, the surer we may be that we are walking in the Way of the Cross:

There is no curse in this my pain,
For He was crucified;
And it is fellowship with Him
That keeps me near His side.[82]

While the sheep struggle onward in sure and certain hope of an immortal crown, eternal damnation awaits the goats. On the Last Day, envisioned by the prophetic Pollok as already consummated, God

. . . lifted up his hand omnipotent,
And down among the damn'd the burning edge
Plunged; and from forth his arrowy quiver sent,
Emptied, the seven last thunders ruinous,
Which, entering, wither'd all their souls with fire.
Then first was vengeance, first was ruin seen!
Red, unrestrain'd, vindictive, final, fierce!

. . .

Nor ask if these shall ever be redeem'd.
They never shall: not God, but their own sin
Condemns them.[83]

From this scene let us turn to an elect Christian's deathbed as described by Bickersteth in *Yesterday, To-day, and For Ever.* There is no mention of priest or Sacrament (the poet is an Anglican), yet in his prayers the slowly dying man not only feels more keenly than ever before that he is "polluted

[79] *Miles*, VIII, 380.

[80] Only the elect are capable of genuine repentance, but this refinement is not insisted upon by the poets here discussed.

[81] Emma Tatham, *The Dream of Pythagoras, and Other Poems*, p. 113.

[82] Anne Waring, in *Miles*, XI, 394.

[83] *The Course of Time*, pp. 382, 384. As usual, in the last two lines the question of predestination is waived.

and undone" but obtains a livelier assurance that his sins are forgiven by virtue of his faith in the Crucified:

> I wash'd the dark stains of my travelling dress
> White in the fountain of His blood.

He and his wife talk happily of their two dead children and of relatives and friends who are waiting for him on the other side.

> . . . We were part
> Of the whole family in heaven and earth;
> Part of the mighty host whose foremost ranks
> Long since had cross'd the river, and had pitch'd
> Their tents upon the everlasting hills.
> How shrunken Jordan seemed!

His living children read to him the Scriptural promises of eternal life. As he grows weaker, they stand silently praying by his bed.

> . . . Never a word they spoke,
> But look'd their inexpressible love, till thoughts
> Of luminous stars, and large and loving eyes,
> Were strangely blended in a dream that came
> Enamell'd with rich pictures of my life,
> And floated like a golden mist away.

Now he is "more / Than ankle deep in Jordan's icy stream." The children cannot help imploring him to stay.

> My gentle wife, with love stronger than death,
> Was leaning over those cold gliding waves.

But he cannot return the pressure of her hands:

> . . . So rapidly the river-bed
> Shelv'd downward, I had pass'd or almost pass'd
> Beyond the interchange of loving signs
> Into the very world of love itself.

As the waters deepen to his loins he hears a Voice "like a silver trumpet, saying / 'Be of good comfort. It is I. Fear not.' " Safe on the farther bank he falls in abasement at the feet of Jesus, but

> He raised me tenderly, saying, "My child."
> And I, like Thomas on that sacred eve,
> Could only answer Him, "My Lord, my God."
> And then He drew me closer, and Himself

With His own hand, His pierced hand of love,
Wiped the still falling tear-drops from my face,
And told me I was His and He was mine,
And how my Father loved me and He loved.[84]

The foregoing remarks have been based upon an examination of the work of nineteen poets—a small but representative sampling. The reader would not thank me for a more exhaustive survey. The material is not, however, sufficient to justify any attempt to trace the chronological curve of Evangelical poetry as a whole. Although one would be inclined to guess that it is more abundant in the earlier than in the later decades of our period, the careers of seven of the nineteen continue into the 1880's, and of five into the 1870's. The long pseudo-Miltonic "sacred poem" as practiced by Pollok, Montgomery, and Heraud is short-lived;[85] but even after reviewers in the better periodicals no longer felt obliged to overpraise edifying trash there was apparently a public for Evangelical lyricism and writers (often female ones) to satisfy the demand. It is safe to say, however, that at the close of our period such verse appealed only to a specialized and rapidly shrinking circle; by that time most cultivated readers regarded it as subliterary.

Throughout the Victorian era not merely the creed but the puritanical moral code of the saints gradually relaxed in severity. During the fifties and sixties the domestic life and cultural ideals of many people who thought of themselves as Evangelicals were much less grim and barren than the preceding pages would indicate. We must also remind ourselves again that it is the indirect rather than the direct influence of Evangelical Christianity which is chiefly important for the study of Victorian literature. One could make out a case for the assertion that the Evangelical temper, in its original strictness, was a more prolific breeder of agnostics and extreme religious liberals than utilitarianism or scientific materialism. In later chapters we shall draw evidence of this fact from the poets. As for men of prose, the following were subjected to strong Evangelical influence in early youth: the three Bradleys (A. C., F. H., and G. G.), Stopford Brooke, Samuel Butler, Carlyle, Moncure D. Conway, George Eliot, W. J. Fox, J. A. Froude, Grote, Jowett, Kingsley, Macaulay, Harriet and James Martineau, James Mill, John Morley, Francis Newman, Mark Pattison, Romanes, Ruskin, Leslie and FitzJames Stephen, William Hale White.[86] But even when such

[84] *Yesterday, To-Day, and For Ever*, pp. 11–46 *passim*. This very favorable specimen of pure Evangelical poetry deserves to be compared and contrasted with Newman's *Dream of Gerontius*. Bickersteth also wrote the moving hymn, *Peace, Perfect Peace*.

[85] Bickersteth has been noted as exceptional.

[86] A merely illustrative list which could be expanded greatly. The reader is reminded of the broad

prodigal children of the saints abandoned all supernaturalistic religion they usually retained the best features of the Evangelical ethos—confident driving vigor, moral integrity, concern for practical goodness, sense of prophetic mission. In a way, the agnostics were the truest Victorian Puritans. They were never more loyal to the deepest impulses of Evangelicalism than when they used their private judgment in rebelling against it.

From any Evangelical home, however, roads of escape might run in more than one direction. They might lead to Roman or Anglican Catholicism. Francis Newman became a non-Christian theist, but John Henry did not.[87] If Hurrell Froude had lived longer he would probably not have gone the way of his brother. George Eliot's brother Isaac turned very "high," as did Mrs. Browning's sisters Henrietta and Arabella. To eighteenth-century Evangelicalism the Oxford Movement owed much; and rather curiously, as Annan observes, "It was the Evangelicals in the Oxford Movement such as Newman and Faber, who went over to Rome; the sons of High Churchmen, Pusey and Keble, remained firm. Among the Claphamites the Wilberforces seceded in droves. Three of the four sons of William Wilberforce and both his sons-in-law became Roman Catholics. Samuel alone remained in the Anglican Communion and lived to see his daughter and her husband go over to Rome."[88]

Unquestionably, however, the main spiritual highway outward from Evangelicalism ran to Broad Churchmanship and thence to more or less complete rejection of Christianity. Occasionally the wayfarer leapt directly from the first stage to the third; more frequently he moved from the first to the second without going further. Those who took this road were often merely rebelling against a parental discipline which defeated its own purpose by conditioning intelligent young people to reject a type of religion which proved especially vulnerable to the assaults of secularism. It must also be said, however, that Evangelicalism carried within its body the seeds of its

---

sense in which "Evangelicalism" is used in this chapter. Conway of course was an American, but he was so active in English religious liberalism for so many years that it seemed proper to include him. Froude and Pattison reacted not only against parental Evangelicalism but against the Tractarianism which they had briefly cultivated in its stead; after his *Nemesis of Faith* stage, furthermore, Froude returned to a fairly conventional Protestantism though not quite to his original faith. Romanes became a Broad Churchman after many years of unhappy disbelief. The inclusion of the Martineaus might be challenged, but the type of Unitarianism in which they were reared was no less harsh and narrow than Trinitarian Nonconformity. Their remoter ancestry was Huguenot. Matthew Arnold might be added on the ground that his father combined the theology of a Broad Churchman with the temperament of an Evangelical.

[87] Nor for that matter did the third brother, Charles, who became a completely unbelieving wastrel.

[88] N. G. Annan, *Leslie Stephen*, p. 121.

own decay. Its original doctrines are rooted in Christian objectivity and humility; so long as those beliefs are firmly held, Protestantism is no more romantic than Catholicism. But the Evangelical's supreme desire is to know that he is saved, a conviction which can be obtained only through a deeply personal and inward emotional experience. It cannot be easy to feel genuinely humble after you have discovered that you are one of the elect. In the saint's psychology, that wonderful subjective feeling of perfect goodness and perfect liberty inevitably becomes more important than any formal doctrine. Once the theology has grown soft and hazy, the feeling may continue to exist and may move in almost any direction. A very acceptable imitation of the assurance of election may be aroused by stimuli which have nothing to do with being washed in the Blood of the Lamb.

Even some of those poets on whom we have relied for our picture of pure and undefiled Evangelical Christianity occasionally express ideas for which they would have been liquidated—or rather, ignited—in Calvin's Geneva. It is all very well to say that a genuine conversion is satisfactory evidence of justification, but the notion that any man may be saved who wants to be saved pushes beyond the boundaries of anything that can be called Calvinism. That Tupper sometimes maintains the latter position (along with belief in the immortality of dogs) is not very surprising: although he always thought himself a strong Evangelical his views changed considerably with changing times.[89] But it is startling to hear Robert Pollok, who intended to measure all literature against the strictest Evangelical standards, declare as early as 1827 that on the Judgment Day of his vision all those were saved

> . . . who ever wish'd to go
> To heaven, for heaven's own sake; not one remained
> Among the accursed, that e'er desired with all
> The heart to be redeem'd: that ever sought
> Submissively to do the will of God.

Jehovah states that the damned are solely those who

> . . . refused to be redeem'd;
> For all had grace sufficient to believe,
> All who my gospel heard; and none who heard
> It not, shall by its law this day be tried.[90]

Of course one might argue that only the elect can *really* wish to be saved, but this would seem to be a shabby evasion of the original Calvinistic rigor.

[89] *Proverbial Philosophy*, I, 14; II, 94–95. For further evidence of his theological eccentricities see Derek Hudson, *Martin Tupper*, pp. 45, 67, 76–77.

[90] *The Course of Time*, pp. 350, 377.

The implication that pagans (and not necessarily virtuous ones) are exempt from Judgment is also curious. Something must be done with them. Where are they to go? In *A Word to the "Elect"*, meek little Anne Brontë rejects the familiar idea that one of the pleasures of heaven will consist in observing the agonies of the damned—"May God withhold such cruel joy from me!" She knows that no man deserves salvation, but she trusts that none will be damned "That have not well deserved the wrath of Heaven" and

> That even the wicked shall at last
> Be fitted for the skies;
> And when their dreadful doom is past,
> To life and light arise.[91]

Such unwillingness to believe in the eternity of hell-torment is a badge of Broad Churchmanship.

The popular hymns of Thomas Toke Lynch (1818–1871), a Congregationalist minister, were thought by precisians to be excessively tinged with nature-worship. To judge from the verses printed in Miles's collection, he is no pantheist; he merely likes to draw upon nature for symbols of divine wisdom and goodness, as Keble had often done in *The Christian Year*. Pious readers might, however, be justified in complaining that he more often makes them think about the azure sky than about the Cross. When he interprets the coming of spring to mean "Redemption draweth nigh" he looks back to James Thomson and forward to modernist preachers who base their Easter sermons on the fact that spring follows winter.[92]

The Free Kirk of Scotland originated in an Evangelical reaction against the looseness of the dominant "Moderate" party in the Established Church, but it emphasized internal evidence so strongly that it developed a sort of Presbyterian Broad Churchmanship. The views of the Free Kirk minister, Walter Chalmers Smith (1824–1908), are said to have grown progressively more heterodox as his career went on.[93] I am unable, however, to date his statement that

> . . . Faith's abode
> Is mystery for evermore;
> Its life to worship and adore,
> And meekly bow before the rod
> When the day is dark, and the burden sore.

[91] *The Complete Works of Charlotte Brontë and Her Sisters*, IV, 321.

[92] *Miles*, XI, 329. See also pp. 316, 320–321, 322.

[93] Horatius Bonar transferred his ministry from the Established to the Free Kirk in 1843, but having been born sixteen years earlier than Smith, he remained more strictly loyal to the creed in which he had been reared.

But all through Life I see a Cross,
Where sons of God yield up their breath:
There is no gain except by loss,
There is no life except by death,
There is no vision but by Faith,
No glory but by bearing shame,
Nor justice but by taking blame;
And that eternal passion saith,
"Be emptied of glory and right and name."[94]

These lines are rich in genuinely religious feeling. They show, however, that Smith is very unsure of the Crucifixion of Christ as a historical event but very sure of the crucifixion of all men as a fact diffused through the moral experience of the *sons* of God. Christ is a mystery, but we are all Christs.

The Evangelicals hold that salvation is by faith alone. But since the only evidence that one possesses such faith is a deep personal emotion there may be a tendency to ascribe to inward feeling some degree of power over the outward reality which was originally supposed to be the source of that feeling. "Verily," Tupper declares,

... evils may be courted, may be wooed and won by distrust;
For the wise Physician of our weal loveth not an unbelieving spirit;
And to those giveth he good, who rely on his hand for good;
And those leaveth he to evil, who fear, but trust him not.
Ask for good, and hope it; for the ocean of good is fathomless.

This goes a trifle beyond the truism that God is good only to those who believe in His goodness. It seems to anticipate the notion of popular "inspirational" psychology that we may produce evil by thinking evil and good by thinking good. The will of God varies in accordance with our emotional states. This interpretation is supported by a later passage of *Proverbial Philosophy* which insists that

... all thing stand by faith;
Albeit faith of divers kinds, and varying in degrees.
There is a faith towards men, and there is a faith towards God;
The latter is the gold and the former is the brass; but both are sturdy metal.

. . .

It is not for me to stipulate for creeds; Bible, Church, and Reason,
These three shall lead the mind, if any can, to truth.
But I must stipulate for faith; both God and man demand it:
Trust is great in either world, if any would be well.
Verily, the sceptical propensity is an universal foe.[95]

[94] *Miles*, XII, 118.

[95] *Proverbial Philosophy*, I, 16; II, 122, 125.

Believe in God and the next world if you can; if not, believe in man and this world. At all events believe *something*. Belief for belief's sake is more important than the object of belief.

Less robustly and confidently, Jean Ingelow also continues to "stipulate for faith" under conditions which render it difficult to "stipulate for creeds." In *The Middle Watch*, the immensity of the starry sky makes her feel small, weak, lonely. Where is God, and does He exist at all? But then she hears—

> O elder than reason, and stronger than will!
> A voice, when the dark world is still:
>
> Whence cometh it? Father Immortal, Thou knowest! and we,—
> We are sure of that witness, that sense which is sent us of Thee.

Here, as a later couplet shows, the inward witness is the voice of the God of the Scriptures, who has given us "a Ransome Divine." But in *Honors* her trust in the Bible has been shaken by Darwin and the Tübingen critics.[96] Thrown into a state of panic, she can only beg her contemporaries to "have the grace to wait":

> Wait, nor against the half-learned lesson fret,
> Nor chide at old belief as if it erred,
> Because thou canst not reconcile as yet
> The Worker and the word.

If we push on along the path of science, we may deprive ourselves of the God-feeling. For if God did not indeed "Give us the word, His tale of love and might," then we have no spiritual reliance at all. "We know not if He is."

> We sit unmoved upon our burial sod,
> And know not whence we come or whose we be,
> Comfortless mourners for the mount of God,
> The rocks of Calvary.
>
> . . .
>
> How wert thou bettered so, or more secure
> Thou and thy destinies!

It seems not to have crossed her mind that objective truths exist and that it is man's duty to discover them if he can and to live by them regardless of whether he likes them or not. All that really matters is that she should *feel*

[96] The poem purports to be a letter written by a university student who has failed to win an honors degree, but the dramatic mask is transparent.

bettered and secure rather than unowned and comfortless. The final stage is reached in a sonnet in which she asserts that though all great deeds were mere fables, though there were no God and no afterlife, and

> Though virtue had no goal and good no scope,
> But both were doomed to end with this our day—
> Though all these were not,—to the ungraced heir
> Would this remain, to live as though they were.[97]

This gospel of conduct feebly touched by emotions which are derived from a merely *als ob* conception of suprahuman values is closer to Matthew Arnold than to Wesley or Whitefield.

The ideas and feelings illustrated in the last five paragraphs cannot be described as romantic without stretching that epithet beyond reasonable limits. They betoken merely a slight blurring and slackening and subjectivizing of principles which, so long as they are held in full rigor, raise impregnable bulwarks against trust in human self-sufficiency. Genuinely Evangelical inwardness and emotionalism are held within Christian bounds by the objectivity of Reformation theology. The Bible is both the sole basis of that theology and the sole stimulus of all that is authentically Christian in the saint's emotional experience—the only means by which saving truth is mediated either to the reason or to the affections. Even the more mystical type of Evangelical would have nothing to feel mystical *about* except for the Bible. But the Bible was written very long ago by an Author who is very far away; and in the nineteenth century, for reasons too obvious to mention, belief in the inerrancy of its every syllable became increasingly difficult to maintain. As the cornerstone loosens, the doctrinal battlements collapse, leaving that sense of inward goodness, freedom, and power which had characterized the conversion-experience either to wither or to seek validation in other directions.

But the religious subjectivism to be studied in later chapters is by no means wholly an end-product of the decay of Evangelicalism in the Victorian period. It mainly represents a continuation of a much older romanticizing trend which the Evangelical Revival of the eighteenth century had attempted to check and reverse through a genuinely though limitedly Christian reassertion of the transcendence of God and the insufficiency of man. But in its loyalty to Reformation principles the Revival had ignored doctrines and practices which, whether right or wrong, seem in the long run to be the most potent psychological safeguards of Christian objectivity and humility.

[97] Jean Ingelow, *Poetical Works*, pp. 28, 267, 268, 461

Hence, even at the beginning of our period Evangelicalism is a crumbling dam in the great river of pride and despair which sweeps from the sixteenth century into the twentieth. Its moral and cultural influence on Victorian society is immense, but it wields that influence by entering into a compromise with the spirit of the age.

Chapter Three

MISS BARRETT AND MRS. BROWNING

EDWARD BARRETT MOULTON BARRETT did not long remain satisfied with the colorless and perfunctory Anglicanism of his childhood. At Trinity he responded to the influence of the Cambridge Evangelicals. By 1806, the year of Elizabeth's birth, he had gone further: he and his dutifully negligible wife now worshipped with the Wesleyan Methodists. His sectarianism, however, was not extremely rigid. He had only two grudges against the Church of England: not enough of its clergy had a firm grasp of saving truth, and in any case the idea of an officially established Church was repugnant.[1] Later, in the Wimpole Street days, he apparently regarded himself as an Independent; otherwise Elizabeth would not have said that he would never permit a daughter of his to marry "Even if a prince of Eldorado should come, with a pedigree of lineal descent from some signory in the moon in one hand, and a ticket of good behaviour from the nearest Independent chapel in the other."[2] But he never frequented such a chapel as the one described in Browning's *Christmas-Eve*. The type of Nonconformity which Mr. Barrett cultivated was barely distinguishable from the Anglicanism of the Clapham Sect—prosperous, cultivated, not very grim Evangelicals like William Wilberforce and Zachary Macaulay, pious men of affairs who knew how to make the best of both possible worlds.

Elizabeth and the other children at Hope End did not live in constant terror of the wrath to come. They seem to have enjoyed their religion as part of the general stir of imaginative vividness which characterized the household. In those early years, before business worries and family sorrows had aggravated the morbid side of his nature, Mr. Barrett's despotism was usually jolly and stimulating. He must never be crossed, but he was seldom so unpleasantly oppressive that a loving child would wish to cross him. Far from being opposed to secular culture, he was rather demoralizingly proud of the little bluestocking who had begun to study Greek at the age of eight. His indulgence conditioned the headstrong, willful girl to think of scholarship and poetry as the best means of getting her own way and satisfying her

[1] Dorothy Hewlett, *Elizabeth Barrett Browning: A Life*, p. 6. [2] Quoted, *ibid.*, p. 131.

intense craving for distinction. Once beyond the tomboy stage she too complacently accepted her father's stereotype of the dreamy, delicate, nervous female genius. Of course certain books were strictly prohibited, but with incredible carelessness Papa had shelved on the unforbidden side of his library Voltaire, Hume, Gibbon, Rousseau, Paine, Mary Wollstonecraft, and *Werther*. The adolescent Elizabeth read them as avidly as the adolescent Robert Browning read *Queen Mab*.[3]

But we are looking too far ahead. Little Elizabeth's nursery poems are mostly humorous family occasional pieces but sometimes dutifully echo the pious precepts of her rearing. Once at least she combined the spirit of the two *genres* in a song which contrives to be both jolly and edifying:

> Peter Quarry he called all his vices together
> To meet on the green field, or bright yellow meadow.
> Says he our acquaintance I fear will be short,
> For of going to virtue I've a great thought.
> Singing fal lal, etc.
>
> So you must be gone
> With your weeds and your bushes,
> And sweet virtue must come
> With her larks and her thrushes.
> Singing fal lal, etc.

An astonishing performance for a child of eight. Three years later she was aiming much higher with less agreeable results. She was only eleven when she began *The Battle of Marathon*, a frigid imitation of Pope's imitation of Homer which her proud father privately printed in 1820.

For *An Essay on Mind* (1826) her model is Pope as moralist, not as translator. But although the poem is ploddingly ethical rather than religious, there are a few indications that she has been reading more pious eighteenth-century poets—chiefly, we may conjecture, Mrs. Elizabeth Rowe.[4] She lauds "Divinest Newton" for having been

> Rich in all nature, but her erring side:
> Endow'd with all of Science—but its pride;

and she dreams of a heaven where pure minds, stripped of words no less than of flesh, will communicate ideas only through "voiceless intercourse." Two of the fourteen short pieces published with the *Essay* may owe their more explicit piety to her first serious illness in 1821. *The Prayer* explains

[3] Robert Browning and Elizabeth Barrett Barrett, *Letters*, I, 404. But what could the *forbidden* side of the library have contained? By this time Elizabeth has probably forgotten which side was which.

[4] For the piously sentimental Mrs. Rowe see *Religious Trends*, I, 134–140.

that the purpose of unhappiness is to prevent us from falling too deeply in love with this delightful world. In *The Dream* she has a vision of the whole sinful sweep of pre-Christian history, until at last

> . . . a God came to die, bringing down peace—
> "*Pan was not;*" and the darkness that did wreathe
> The earth, past from the soul—Life came by death!

Here is the first of several attempts to be as pleased about the death of Pan as she knows she should be. Nobody, however, would think of the 1826 volume as primarily a book of sacred poetry. Learned young Miss Barrett has not yet firmly combined her literary ambitions with her creed.

The pietistic element is much stronger in *Poems* (1833) and *The Seraphim and Other Poems* (1838). Despite hints of coming change to be noted later, the *Poems* of 1844 are also a body of religious verse. A close study of Elizabeth's writings in relation to the circumstances of her life would show that the poems become more urgently Evangelical as she becomes more saddened by family sorrows, more aware of the deterioration of her father's character, more oppressed by illness both physical and psychosomatic. In 1834 or thereabouts there is also some indication that she is sentimentally interested in a Nonconformist minister named George Barrett Hunter.[5] In that case her piety might to some extent be an expression of her need for love.

During this most emphatically religious stage of her career she gives an Evangelical twist to the Puritan theory of Christian poetry as it had been carried from the seventeenth century into the eighteenth by Dennis, Watts, and Blackmore.[6] In *The Dead Pan* she calls upon Christian poets to hymn the Crucified in refutation of Schiller's idea in *Die Götter Griechenlands* that the death of Pan means the death of poetry—"a doctrine still more dishonoring to poetry than to Christianity." It also blasphemes the Victorian faith in progress. Of course, she grants in *The Greek Christian Poets*, the modern world has had its pious versifiers. Also there are true poets who sing as if man had never fallen, and others who sing "as if in the first hour of exile, when the echo of the curse was louder than the whisper of the promise. But the right 'genius of Christianism' has done little up to this moment [1842], even for Chateaubriand. We want the touch of Christ's hand upon our literature, as it touched other dead things—we want the sense of the saturation of Christ's blood upon the souls of our poets, that it may cry *through* them in answer to the ceaseless wail of the Sphinx of our humanity."[7]

[5] Hewlett, *op. cit.*, pp. 57–58. [6] See *Religious Trends*, I, 127–131, 186–188, 189–194.

[7] Possibly she here translates into the language of Evangelicalism Shelley's words in *The Defence of Poetry*: "We want the creative faculty to imagine that which we know; we want the generous impulse to act that which we imagine; we want the poetry of life."

Although Elizabeth writes much better than other simon-pure Victorian Evangelicals, she is far from achieving a richly satisfying expression of "the genius of Christianism." In religious no less than in secular verse her considerable gift for making warmly emotionalized rhetoric move to incantatory rhythms is largely vitiated by her diffuseness, messiness, sentimentality, and lack of organic relation between thought and image. But as a sacred poet she is beset by additional handicaps. Her vocation as leader in a campaign to Christianize English poetry burdens her with a stultifying self-consciousness, tempts her to force her powers beyond their modest bounds. Even in asserting that poetry is essentially religious she is haunted by pious scruples about her craving to win fame through aesthetic creativity. She is quite enough of an artist to know that poetry is sensuous, but she does not see how she can be sensuous without succumbing to a soulless naturalism. Remembering her frigid *Essay on Mind,* she dreads being entrapped by the sensationalism and associationism of Locke, Hartley, and the Utilitarians. *A Sea-Side Meditation* asserts that the mission of the poet is to show men how to break the manacles of sense and soar into the world of the spirit. And yet, she continues, is there not too much of sinful pride in the poet's assertion of visionary power? Victory over the flesh is the gift of God, not the exploit of man. We must await that Final Day when "God's arm shall meet God's foe, and hurl him back!"

She cannot bear, however, to relinquish the belief that if angels may sing in heaven, poets may sing on earth:

> Sing, seraph with the glory! heaven is high;
> Sing, poet with the sorrow! earth is low:
> The universe's inward voices cry
> "Amen" to either song of joy and woe:
> Sing, seraph,—poet,—sing on equally!

"Equally" claims too much. On the other hand she feels that complete attainment of *The Soul's Expression* in poetry would be tantamount to death, for

> . . . if I did it,—as the thunder-roll
> Breaks its own cloud, my flesh would perish there
> Before that dread apocalypse of soul.[8]

She thinks too much *about* writing religious poetry.[9]

Although she would like to feel religious about nature she resists the

[8] Compare *Adonais*: "companionless / As the last cloud of an expiring storm, / Whose thunder is its knell."

[9] When I gave a course in verse-writing many years ago, a favorite theme of my less gifted students' verses was, "What fine poetry I would write if only I could write poetry!"

temptation. Once a beautiful scene drew her toward pagan animism, but she gathered up all her strength, expelled "the heathen dream" from her mind, and prophetically heard "Nature's death-shrieking" in that great day when the world will be nothing to us and Christ will be all in all. Vainly do we seek *The Image of God* in nature: He only is "like to God" who died that we might live. Sometimes, however, she concedes to the Christian, and to him alone, the right to praise Mother Earth because he knows that she has been granted a little of God's mercy:

> . . . Oh, beautiful
> Art thou, Earth, albeit worse
> Than in heaven is callèd good!
> Good to us, that we may know
> Meekly from thy good to go;
> While the holy, crying Blood
> Puts its music kind and low
> 'Twixt such ears as are not dull,
> And thine ancient curse!

"We want the sense of the saturation of Christ's blood upon the souls of our poets" because it is only the Blood that heals and saves. In *Sounds* she runs through a catalogue of the noises of Vanity Fair, including the chatter of a ritualistic priest who "disserts / Upon linen shirts." The hubbub muffles the voice of God murmuring in our souls:

> *I* am the end of love! give love to *Me*!
> O thou that sinnest, grace doth more abound
> Than all thy sin! sit still beneath My rood,
> And count the droppings of My victim-blood,
> And seek none other sound!

In *The Seraphim* (1838), two angels behold the Crucifixion from heaven and exclaim their way to the conclusion that henceforward man's love for God will outstrip their own. Seraphs indeed love, but

> . . . not with this blood on us—and this face,—
> Still, haply, pale with sorrow that it bore
> In our behalf, and tender evermore
> With nature all our own, upon us gazing—
> Nor yet with these forgiving hands upraising
> Their unreproachful wounds, alone to bless!

This is truly Christian and Evangelical; but when one angel tells the other that "Heaven is dull, mine Ador, to man's earth," the anticipation of the glory-of-the-imperfect doctrine of *Rephan* reminds us that Miss Barrett is destined to marry Robert Browning.

Much more ambitious is *A Drama of Exile* (1844), a full-dress Aeschylean lyrical drama in which the plan of redemption is revealed to Adam and Eve after their expulsion from Eden. Despite her almost too anxious insistence that Pan is dead, she had never wholly abandoned her beloved Greeks. Not only Hugh Stuart Boyd but Shelley had taught her to think of Prometheus as the forerunner of Christ. There was no incongruity in imposing the form of Aeschylus upon the matter of Milton, who himself had written not only a Christian classical epic but a Christian classical tragedy. We cannot blame her for failing to divulge a more immediate and a stronger influence—that of Byron's *Cain* and *Heaven and Earth.* In the dedication to her father she describes *A Drama of Exile* as "the longest and most important work (*to me!*) which I ever trusted into the current of publication." That is just the trouble. She is not equipped to compete with Aeschylus and Milton, or even with Byron, in a poetic drama whose characters are Jesus Christ, Adam, Eve, and Satan, with the Spirits of Organic and Inorganic Nature thrown in for good measure. That the result is neither absurd nor offensive is after all a high tribute. Here as elsewhere, also, she deserves praise for her intelligent and by no means wholly unsuccessful attempt to reconcile Evangelical Christianity with the traditions of humanistic culture. But she is a more appealing religious poet when she is less ambitious. Surely it is not only the Christian believer who still finds himself moved by some of her short lyrics of personal spiritual experience—*The Sleep, My Doves, Comfort,* and *Cowper's Grave.*

In the 1844 volume the sonnets placed just after *A Drama of Exile* are heavy with bitterness and self-accusation. At Torquay, four years earlier, had occurred the tragedy which haunted Elizabeth throughout the remainder of her life—her brother Edward's death by drowning. Quite irrationally, Mr. Barrett blamed her for the disaster: Edward would not have been sailing on that fatal day had Elizabeth not teased him to stay on with her at the seashore against her father's wishes. She accepted the burden of guilt and the pain of estrangement from the beloved parent who now became the man we loathe as Mr. Barrett of Wimpole Street. Elizabeth was thinking of herself when she said in a letter that the subject of *A Drama of Exile* was "especially the grief of Eve, under that reproach of soul which must have afflicted her with so peculiar an agony."[10] The first effect of this situation was to make

[10] Hewlett, *op. cit.*, p. 124. For the complicated circumstances of the drowning and their effect on the relations between Elizabeth and her father, see pp. 74–127 *passim.*

her cling to the Cross with the convulsive strength born of her misery and remorse; the ultimate effect was a weakening of her grasp as estrangement from her father brought estrangement from his religion.

The process was far advanced before she was willing to acknowledge the outcome. *A Drama of Exile* and some of its companion pieces represent the painful climax of her Evangelical fervor, not its decay. Nevertheless the 1844 *Poems* as a whole are somewhat less redolent of the chapel than the volume of 1838. Her Christian objectivity seems to be as solid as ever, but there is a less insistently technical emphasis on the atoning Blood. For the first time, such poems as *The Cry of the Children* and *The Cry of the Human* suggest the beginning of a trend away from Evangelical theology toward a slightly broadened Evangelical humanitarianism:

> The curse of gold upon the land
> The lack of bread enforces;
> The rail-cars snort from strand to strand,
> Like more of Death's White Horses.
> The rich preach "rights" and "future days,"
> And hear no angel scoffing,
> The poor die mute, with starving gaze
> On corn-ships in the offing.
> Be pitiful, O God.

In the darkened room at Wimpole Street her mind was much less secluded than her body. The letters of Miss Martineau and R. H. Horne, the visits of Kenyon and the rest, and the parliamentary Blue Books made her more up-to-date that she had been in less inactive years. Her father's no longer amiable tyranny prompted rebellious thoughts about the position of woman in society. In the year when this volume was published she had begun to plan a resolutely unconventional treatment of modern life: *Aurora Leigh* was stirring in her mind.

Thus even before the advent of her "rosy, rough rescuer" there are symptoms of approaching change. Those hints, however, are too obscure to prevent us from being startled as we move onward from the 1844 volume into the poems of her married life. Miss Elizabeth Barrett Moulton Barrett is an Evangelical poet; Mrs. Robert Browning is nothing of the sort. Even those who think her unworthy of close study for her own sake will grant that the fact is of some importance for interpretation of her husband's changing thought. It casts doubt upon the familiar notion that his movement away from chapel Christianity to subjectivist theism was retarded by her uncompromising Evangelicalism.

Mr. De Vane tells us that Browning was becoming distinctly heterodox when he began to court Elizabeth, but that "Miss Barrett stopped all that in no time, and the first poetic product of their union was *Christmas-Eve and Easter-Day*."[11] But we know that she was puzzled by the asceticism of the latter poem; and when we look back to the letters of 1845 and 1846 we find no evidence of desire to bind her lover to the foot of the Cross. She is quick to grant that "There is a narrowness among the dissenters which is wonderful; an arid, grey Puritanism in the clefts of their souls: but it seems to me clear that they know what the 'liberty of Christ' means better than those who call themselves Churchmen."[12] What she now values in the chapel is not its doctrinal purity but its freedom. A year later, discussing the question of where they are to be married, she declares herself "unwilling . . . to put on any of the liveries of the sects. The truth, as God sees it, must be something so different from these opinions about truth." She feels able to worship "anywhere and with all sorts of worshippers, from the Sistine Chapel to Mr. Fox's." In every denomination "there is a little to revolt, and a good deal to bear with." But she greatly prefers a chapel—of the sort "where the minister is simple-minded and not controversial." She is quite ready, however, to marry Robert anywhere—even at an Anglican church if the service is free from Puseyite embellishments. "After all, perhaps the best will be what is easiest." Browning warmly agrees with all this in a letter which adumbrates the theme of *Christmas-Eve*.[13]

As we have seen, the adolescent Elizabeth had read Voltaire, Gibbon, and Paine in her father's library. In maturity she confined neither her reading nor her friendships to the sphere of the Saints. During the years when she was writing her most fervently Evangelical poems she was corresponding with Harriet Martineau, an ex-Unitarian who now believed in nothing except Positivism and mesmerism, and with the highly unorthodox R. H. Horne. She had even planned to collaborate with the future author of *Orion* in a lyrical drama about the birth and growth of the soul. The scheme was abortive, but in 1844 they joined forces in a volume of critical essays, *A New Spirit of the Age*.

In 1842 she writes to Hugh Boyd, who has charged her with Calvinism: "I believe simply that the saved are saved by grace, and that they shall here-

[11] W. C. De Vane, "Browning and the Spirit of Greece," *Nineteenth-Century Studies*, pp. 193–194. Betty Miller, on the contrary, holds that in these poems Browning made "belated amends" to his dead mother "for the spirit of opposition which had drawn him from the Independent chapel of his boyhood." (*Robert Browning: A Portrait*, p. 173.) This hypothesis is also risky, but less so than De Vane's.

[12] Robert Browning and Elizabeth Barrett Barrett, *Letters*, I, 145.

[13] *Ibid.* II, 427, 434. They were, of course, married in the Anglican church of St. Pancras.

after know it fully; that the lost are lost by their choice and free will—by choosing to sin and die."[14] At this time and during the courtship she was deep in Carlyle and Emerson. She was reading novels, many of them French. Balzac she warmly admired and she preferred Hugo to Dickens. George Sand was then her ideal of emancipated creative womanhood—an illusion later damaged in Paris but never completely repudiated. She always liked the relaxed uncensorious atmosphere of Europe more genuinely than Robert did. "On the continent," she assures Henrietta, "you escape a quantity of Mrs. Grundyism, and can live as you like, nobody making you afraid."[15] In Italy she consorted happily with pagans like Landor, left-wing Unitarians like Miss Cobbe, and transcendentalists like Margaret Fuller. Probably she always remained a more definitely believing Christian than her husband eventually became, but we can hardly suppose that she did much to curb his growing heterodoxy during their life together.

In 1857 she writes Leigh Hunt: "I receive more dogmas perhaps . . . than you do. I believe in the divinity of Christ in the intensest sense—that he was God absolutely. But for the rest, I am very unorthodox. . . . In fact the churches do all of them, as at present constituted, seem too narrow and low to hold true Christianity in its proximate developments."[16] The proximate developments are spirit-rappings and the like. Although she is somewhat distressed by the vulgarity of Yankee mediums, she has been assured by a friend "that the mediumship in England will be of a higher character than in America by much."[17] Quite! Her spiritualism—which might well have disgusted Browning into clinging to his Christianity a little longer than he otherwise might have done—was the most absorbing of a cluster of neurotic fads which included homeopathic medicine, mesmerism, and Swedenborg—"I'm a Swedenborgian, you known, and believe in 'spheres,' 'atmospheres,' and 'influences.' "[18] Although she held that the spirits were at last conclusively demonstrating the truth of Christianity, she received no messages from the shades of departed Evangelicals. More appropriately it was "Dr. Channing's spirit (or one giving himself for such)" who told her that her sins were forgiven, that the veil between this life and the next is very thin, and that the spirit world is a place of "transcendent beauty."[19] It seems strange that the poems of her married years contain hardly a hint of this obsession. Perhaps she was unwilling to distress Robert, or perhaps Miss Marks is correct in supposing that spiritualism was not so much a part of her

[14] Quoted by Hewlett, *op. cit.*, p. 96.

[15] *Letters to Her Sister*, p. 122.

[16] *Letters of Elizabeth Barrett Browning*, II, 50.

[17] *Letters to Her Sister*, p. 258.

[18] *Ibid.*, p. 283.

[19] *Ibid.*, p. 311.

actual religious experience as it was a hysterical attempt to shake off the clutch of morphine.[20]

Although her Evangelicalism melted away with surprising rapidity after her marriage,[21] there is no need to doubt that it had been sincere while it lasted. What had always been fundamental in her nature was a loving heart, an abundance of warm, slack, diffused feeling, a desire to expand her personality by voicing that feeling in poetry, and a tendency to ascribe a kind of holiness to anything that pleasantly excited her. Between about 1828 and the receipt of Robert's first letter, Evangelical Christianity was the most exciting thing she knew and therefore the most propitious stimulus to self-expression. Its dominant mood was in keeping with the sorrow and illness and confinement which shadowed those years. Why should she question its truth so long as she could feel it as the supremely poetic subject? In her mundane extrapoetic life she had no great enthusiasm for the fine points of Puritan theology, still less for the mentality of the average chapel-goer. But when she donned her singing robes she was converted and reconverted by her own facile emotions, her own fluent rhythms; and then she sensed the saturation of Christ's blood upon her soul.

Robert Browning stopped all that in no time. He gave her something else to be excited about:

> . . . My own, my own,
> Who camest to me when the world was gone,
> And I who looked for only God, found *thee*!
> I find thee; I am safe, and strong, and glad.

Although the lines do not imply the complete substitution of Robert for the Deity, " only God" is not a phrase which William Wilberforce would have approved. This Pompilia is quite explicitly saying that she has found in her Caponsacchi a safety and strength and gladness which she has not derived from the Blood of the Lamb. The angel's words in *The Seraphim*, "Heaven is dull, / Mine Ador, to man's earth," have taken on new meaning.

Of course Mrs. Browning is not the woman to proclaim to the Victorian public that divinity is most potently revealed and mediated by whatever human being one loves most deeply. She will not say this unequivocally even

[20] Jeannette Marks, *The Family of the Barrett*, p. 625. But for general information as to the influence of laudanum and later of morphine in Mrs. Browning's life see also pp. 186, 474, 510–512, 516–517, 531, 534, 552, 619–624.

[21] As we have seen, there are slight hints of a change, or of desire for a change, even in the *Poems* of 1844. Conversely, the religious tone of several of the new pieces in the 1850 volume is that of a greatly diluted Evangelicalism. Thereafter, however, she must be classified as "Broad Church" if she is classified at all.

to her husband. *Sonnets from the Portuguese*, never intended by her for publication, barely nibbles at a theme which Robert was to treat more boldly. Clearer in this respect than any of her sonnets is the passage in *Aurora Leigh* which tells how the heroine's future father, attending Mass as a sightseer in Florence, first saw the girl who was to become his wife:

> A face flashed like a cymbal on his face
> And shook with silent clangour brain and heart,
> Transfiguring him to music. Thus, even thus,
> He too received his sacramental gift
> With eucharistic meanings; for he loved.

We are to infer that he thus discovers the truly human, and hence most deeply religious, meaning of "This is my Body, which is given for you."

If Miss Betty Miller's interpretation of Robert Browning's psychology is correct—and with some reservations it probably is—Elizabeth's enjoyment of this type of sacramental experience may after all have proved somewhat limited. Fortunately, at all events, her new life provided her with other sources of excitement. She responded to them with one eye turned toward heaven and the other cocked in the direction of George Sand, Victor Hugo, George Eliot, and Charlotte Brontë. She now attaches her religiosity chiefly to politico-social liberalism, humanitarianism, the gospel of service, feminism, and the mission of the poet to complement the work of the practical reformer by being eloquently idealistic on such topics. Her indignation sometimes strikes a prophetic note; she can cite Scripture for her purpose; she frequently invokes God and occasionally Jesus Christ. But the divine names are now primarily emotive symbols which gather up the man-made spiritual values of the social causes and ideals which her benevolism has espoused. In escaping from Wimpole Street she seems to have crossed the line which separates " God is love" from "Love is God."

Aurora Leigh shocked most of her old admirers but delighted Ruskin, Rossetti, and Swinburne. It is a courageous, high-minded, sentimental problem novel in verse. There are moments—not very many—when it is also a fine poem. The book is saturated in a spirituality which achieves its clearest expression in the closing lines:

> . . . The world's old,
> But the old world waits the time to be renewed:
> Toward which, new hearts in individual growth
> Must quicken, and increase to multitude
> In new dynasties of the race of men,—
> Developed whence, shall grow spontaneously

New churches, new œconomies, new laws
Admitting freedom, new societies
Excluding falsehood: HE shall make all new.
My Romney!—Lifting up my hand in his,
As wheeled by Seeing spirits towards the east,
He turned instinctively, where, faint and far,
Along the tingling desert of the sky,
Beyond the circle of the conscious hills,
Were laid in jasper-stone as clear as glass
The first foundations of that new, near Day
Which should be builded out of heaven, to God.

Men and women are to strive upward through higher and higher stages of individual development, the highest level being the identification of complete self-expression with complete social love. Before long there will be a whole race of creative and altruistic beings like Aurora and Romney, and then the brand-new world will automatically emerge. But the model and inspiration for the making of this world will be the Heavenly Jerusalem; and somehow all this human work, including the "new churches," will also be God's work. The question is whether the supernaturalistic element is organically essential to Mrs. Browning's social ideal or whether it is merely hitched onto that ideal to add a tinge of numinousness to her humanitarianism. To me the latter interpretation seems more probable. It is as if George Eliot, in some unguarded moment, had enlivened her gospel of the Choir Invisible with a bit of Swedenborg.

I shall not attempt to refute the anticipated rejoinder that Mrs. Browning is more *truly* Christian than Miss Barrett because she transcends the death-dealing letter and applies to contemporary problems the life-giving spirit of Love. It may be so. Let us be content to agree that she strikingly illustrates the failure of Evangelicalism to retain the loyalty of many of its most intelligent and gifted adherents. Whether she found something better or something worse is a matter of opinion. The type of religion which she cultivates during her married life will be illustrated so copiously in the next chapter that nothing more need be said about it here.

Chapter Four

SUBJECTIVE CHRISTIANITY

THE REFLECTIONS of non-Evangelical Protestantism in Victorian poetry are difficult to classify. My plan has been to include in this chapter the work of poets who can be regarded as fairly typical Broad Church Anglicans or liberal Nonconformists. In the next omnibus (Chapter VII) the passengers are to be livelier, more adventurous spirits, some of whom cultivate a purely home-made Christianity while others are so deeply romanticized that they spurn Christianity entirely. But even in the more conventional poetry of the present chapter the deviations from the historic Christian norm range all the way from "comparatively slight" to "very wide." At the outset we should also remind ourselves that the purpose of these general chapters is to study large clusters of ideas, not separate personalities, except when some acquaintance with those personalities becomes essential for an understanding of the ideas. Furthermore, a study based upon thirty-five poets, several of them read only in selections, will not enable us to plot an exact historical curve for the subjectivizing trend. Our task here is merely to examine one complex but relatively homogeneous state of mind which, although it hardly displays all its facets before about 1860, is at work alongside of other Victorian tendencies throughout the whole period.[1]

Since many readers will like the spiritual temper of these poets better than I do, I beg leave to say once more that I repudiate the religion of no person who believes in the insufficiency of man and the objective reality of God. I regard particular tenets favorably or unfavorably only when the course of history seems to indicate that they respectively promote, or derogate from, self-surrender to a transcendent Divine Being. In their theology, as a matter of fact, several members of this group are perplexingly ambivalent, uttering rampant heresies on one page and on the next expressing views to which the most orthodox reader would subscribe. Sometimes these inconsistencies are traceable to chronological changes in the individual's opinions: with the passing years his latitudinarianism may have grown more extreme or more

[1] Of course the *fundamental* tendencies involved are at least as old as Tillotson and Hoadly and perhaps as old as Pelagius.

moderate. At other times one suspects the author of adapting his views to the demands of different audiences or editors. But the great majority of these poets are honestly vacillating rather than insincere. If at times they express more Christianity than they actually believe, we must remember that none of them is sufficiently gifted to be able to find aesthetically effective ways of expressing novel insights; the old familiar groove is temptingly safe and easy. Then too, even the most radical of them have not completely detached their religious feelings from the traditional formulations. They retain a sentimental loyalty to impressions received in childhood; or, mindful of their moral obligation to their readers, they hesitate to deprive simple folk of the only embodiment of spiritual values which they could understand. Perhaps they fear that they themselves might be swept away into complete negation if the old reliable anchor were pulled up. A few of them value Christianity as a steadying socio-political influence. Probably most of them see no necessity for discarding impressive symbols which can now be interpreted to mean whatever one wants them to mean.

For one or more such reasons, these poets by no means always write as if God were the product of their emotions and Jesus Christ a personification of all that is best in man. Three members of the group produced hymns which are still sung by conservative congregations. It is not particularly surprising that Bishop How, a moderate sort of social-gospeler, should have written "For all the Saints who from their labours rest" and "O Jesu, Thou art standing." But who would suppose Sir John Bowring—brainy Unitarian, editor of the *Westminster Review*, friend of Bentham and the Mills—to have written not only "God is love! His mercy brightens" but "In the Cross of Christ I glory"? "Nearer, my God, to Thee" is the work of his fellow-Unitarian, Sarah Flower Adams.

As for nonliturgical poetry, all but a few passages of Mrs. Adams's drama of early Christian martyrdom, *Vivia Perpetua*, might have been written by a devout Trinitarian. Richard Barham is remembered only as a witty mocker of the medieval Church, but his *As I Laye A-Thynkynge* is a serious religious lyric which moved Christina Rossetti.[2] Other poets who will provide us with examples of more or less extreme liberalism can on occasion write as proponents of traditional belief. In *Palingenesis* the younger Lord Lytton ("Owen Meredith") reasons himself into temporary acceptance of the scheme of Redemption.[3] Any Evangelical might have uttered Thomas Cooper's cry:

[2] R. H. Barham, *Ingoldsby Legends*, pp. 380–382; Christina Rossetti, *Family Letters*, p. 9.
[3] *Poems*, pp. 255–256.

. . . Unbind my heavy chain
Of sin: release me, Saviour, with Thy good
And powerful hand: wash out my guilty stain
Of rebel pride in Thy atoning blood!
In brokenness of heart, I come—my Lord—my God![4]

The thought of William Walsham How's *The Two Worlds* would be wholly acceptable to a Catholic. The fact of the Incarnation, he reminds us, should prevent us from constantly bewailing "the trammels of this graceless flesh." The Almighty

In sacramental blessedness hath bound
Together outward sign and inward grace.

For in vast counterpart God only-wise
Outer and inner things alike hath planned,
That Man, through earthly type, with undazed eyes
The deeper things of God might understand.[5]

This group also illustrates the fact that Victorian poetry written to or about children is likely to be rich in nontechnical but unquestioningly traditional piety. Bennett is more than usually devout in poems with such titles as *On a dead Infant*, *The First Shoes*, *To a Lady I Know*, *Aged One*, and *Toddling May*.[6] In *Good-Night and Good-Morning*, the far from unsophisticated Richard Monckton Milnes describes a preternaturally good little farm-girl who rises merrily to her chores every morning because she says her prayers every night.[7] Charles Swain declares that nothing "more holy, more sublime" has been heard since the Incarnation than the first prayer of a little child.[8] And when Kingsley wrote his *Child Ballad* in 1847 he forgot all about "Cheap Clothes and Nasty":

Jesus, He loves one and all,
Jesus, He loves children small,
Their souls are waiting round His feet
On high, before His mercy-seat.[9]

There is the highest authority for respecting and emulating the faith of children. In reading Victorian poetry, however, one is often compelled to

[4] *Poetical Works*, p. 298. To be sure, *The Paradise of Martyrs*, here quoted, was written after he had abandoned his Chartist secularism for Christian Socialism, but these sentiments are more Evangelical than would be expected from a disciple of Kingsley. Just before this passage Cooper thanks God that even when he was a *doubting* Thomas he "never lost / Heart-worship for Thy Son."

[5] *Poems*, p. 179. This is probably the thought of Bishop Butler, who influenced Newman in the same way.

[6] William C. Bennett, *Poems*, pp. 5ff.

[7] *Miles*, IV, 248.

[8] *Poems*, p. 184.

[9] *Poems*, p. 200.

infer that belief in the actuality of God is something learned in childhood—and left there. The beautiful story which our mothers told us is remembered with wistful retrospective reverence. "But"—the old text takes on a new meaning—"when I became a man I put away childish things." The little child does not know whether his churchmanship is high, low, or broad. He is not shocked by the social callousness of institutional religion. No one has urged him to read *Tracts for the Times* or warned him not to read *Essays and Reviews*. He has never heard of Strauss or Darwin, Colenso or Feuerbach. In lesser degree rustics and "truly womanly" women are enviable for the same reason. But the poets of this chapter can claim no exemption from the obligations of intelligence. They are compelled

> From strange confusions to elicit peace;
> To blend with strength of ancient loyalty
> The impetuous forces of swift-rushing days;
> To weave the web of old historic power
> With woof of newer thoughts and fresher life.[10]

On the whole, despite such exceptions as have been noted, they prefer the new woof to the old web. They would say with Matthew Arnold that "at the present time two things about the Christian religion must be clear to anyone with eyes in his head. One is, that men cannot do without it; the other, that they cannot do with it as it is."[11]

These subjectivists can neither firmly repudiate God nor firmly believe in His objective reality. If we are to blame "science" for their predicament, we must stretch the term to include everything that Carlyle meant by "Juggernaut"—all manifestations of the machine-spirit in nineteenth-century philosophy, politics, industrial technology, economic theory and commercial practice, education, and of course the Higher Criticism. Nor should we forget that on one vitally important issue science and religion stand united against sentimental "spirituality": both assert that there is such a thing as truth and that it exists independently of human myth-making. This was Nietzsche's reason for refusing to regard the scientist as a genuine enemy of Christian asceticism: "These two phenomena, science and the ascetic ideal, both rest on the same basis . . . the over-appreciation of truth . . . and consequently they are *necessarily* allies, so that, in the event of their being attacked, they must always be attacked and called into question together."[12] It is not surprising, however, that religious liberals were blind

[10] William Walsham How, *Poems*, p. 127. [11] *God and the Bible* p, xi.
[12] "The Genealogy of Morals," *The Philosophy of Nietzsche*, p. 783.

to this fact at a time when the immense dogmatic authority of science asserted that the world of eye and ear was, if not the only reality, at least the sole world from which human reason could derive knowledge.

On the one hand, England's conception of the good progressive life increasingly depended on the identification of truth with the fruits of sense-perception. On the other hand, the idea of progress was suffused with unquenchable hankerings for "the things of the spirit." But such hankerings were blasphemies against Juggernaut. How could one believe in real imponderable values if the ponderable constituted the only reality which man could apprehend and use? Our poets can hardly be blamed for associating traditional beliefs with the fairy-tales of childhood—or for remembering, too, that there is no terror like the terror of a child who has lost its sureness. Confronted by the prospect of death, poor David Gray can do no better than pilfer from *In Memoriam*, comparing himself to "a child that in the night-time cries / For light."[13]

For although the official philosophy of these poets is optimistic, they frequently succumb to pessimism. It is hard to see anything outside the windows of a brightly lighted bus. In so clearly illuminating its own limited sphere, science enshrouded in darkness the profounder questions which lay beyond. Thomas Ashe is completely bewildered:

> Where is it I long to go?
>   Is it a prize I would gain?
> A kingdom I would inherit?
>   Should I find what I want there?
> What is fretting me so?
>   I would it were clear and plain!
>
> I, with the faith of a man,
>   With Fichte, Hegel, and all
> The mad philosophic kind
> Still am striving to find
>   What I for a minute may call
> A scheme of the Absolute.

He abandons his quest with the cry:

> But truth is hid, O truth is hid, somewhere;—
> In heaven, with God: and that is my despair.[14]

Why this fact should make him feel so desperate is hard to say.

"Oh let me die!" is the refrain of Arthur Hallam's *Lines Written in a*

[13] *Miles*, VI, 369.

[14] *Poems*, pp. 42, 58–59.

Great Depression of Mind. Elsewhere he laments his incapacity to feel those religious emotions which he knows to be "so sweet":

> Half in a craving want,
> And half in blank content,
> I hold my life of mind:
> An intellective thing
> I seem, of inward spring
> Devoid, a coreless rind.[15]

Emily Pfeiffer refuses to guess whether the bewildering changes of the age spell progress or deterioration: she is "a singer, and no seer." But she fears that the wisest of men could say no more than that life is an endless struggle between life and death, darkness and light, in which

> . . . all who live must draw unquiet breath,
> Hunger and agonise, or wholly cease;
> And for the hour, the soothest watchman saith
> He knoweth not if day or night increase.[16]

Owen Meredith would add that "in such dying age of time" our own nature is as mysterious to us as our environment. This aristocrat hankers to escape from the Babylon of "fashion and form" to share the better-adjusted life of "the tawny, bold, wild beast." For animals

> . . . appear to live
> To the full verge of their own power,
>
> . . .
>
> They do not their own lives disown,
> Nor haggle with eternity
> For some unknown Forever.[17]

He has been reading Whitman.

And yet the younger Lytton, with most of his fellow-wanderers, desires the Forever very deeply.[18] "If Jesus came to earth again," he says, we should all believe in Him and follow wherever He led. We need a new tangible revelation of "the living Word," who has become too far away and long ago to be alive in our imagination:

[15] *Writings*, pp. 29, 34. The poems quoted were written in 1828 and 1829, and their gloom is probably not unrelated to his frustrated love for Anna Wintour. He was soon to emerge from this stage into a more affirmative liberalism which included a good deal of authentic Christian feeling.

[16] *Under the Aspens*, p. 123.

[17] *Poems*, pp. 196–197, 220, 222.

[18] As a member of the English set in Mrs. Browning's Florence, he tried to satisfy this desire by dabbling in spiritualism. (Elizabeth Barrett Browning, *Letters to Her Sister*, p. 190.) I have not, however, observed any unmistakable signs of this interest in his poems.

I cannot bring Thee to my mind
Nor clasp Thee to my heart.[19]

The poem draws its title from Mark xvi: 6: "*Ye Seek Jesus of Nazareth Which Was Crucified: He Is Risen: He Is Not Here.*" The emphasis has shifted from the first part of the angelic declaration to the second: all one can be sure of is that "He is not here." Much the same feeling is voiced in Edward Dowden's *Emmausward*, which begs Christ to forgive our lack of faith;

. . . but ah! whoe'er Thou art,
Leave us not; where have we heard any voice
Like Thine? Our hearts burn in us as we go;
Stay with us; break our bread; so for our part
Ere darkness falls haply we may rejoice,
Haply when day has been far spent may know.[20]

Any sure knowledge of Our Lord must be sought in the future, not in the historic past. If the German critics are right, one cannot rely upon the Gospel; one cannot be certain that Jesus is more than a folk-myth. And for these poets the thought of His abiding sacramental presence is mere superstition.

The answer of Broad Church apologetics was that although Christ is not *there* in supernatural reality, He is nevertheless *here*. He is in our hearts, telling us that Love is God and that the Flesh can some day be made Word if only we are true to what is best in ourselves. He is present wherever men pour themselves out in service to their fellows. Let science deny that the Man-God is a historical fact; it cannot deny that He is an inward feeling which has shaped a beneficent thought. Though not literally born of the Virgin Mary, He was indeed conceived by the Holy Spirit—that is, by what Swinburne called "the Holy Spirit of Man." Thanks to Coleridge, Carlyle, Emerson, and the Germans, there were impressive arguments for the thesis that the reality of inward feeling was more real than the reality of sense-perception. In the light of this truth, the Darwinian struggle for existence could be transformed into a system of moral development or even into the unfolding of the Absolute. As for God the Father, Matthew Arnold explained that "*God* or *Eternal* is . . . really, at bottom, nothing but a deeply moved way of saying conduct or righteousness."[21] When our "morality" becomes strongly "touched with emotion," we produce God. To express such ideas without overtly rejecting the most rudimentary essentials of historic Christianity was a delicate task. All this would be much too deep

[19] *Poems*, p. 247. [20] *Miles*, VII, 97. [21] *Literature and Dogma*, p. 42.

for the rural churchwarden who told his rector that he admired the Sunday sermon with one slight reservation: "You see, sir, I think there be a God."[22]

Despite some hesitation, however, the poets of the present chapter adopt this mode of combining "the web of old historic power / With woof of newer thoughts and fresher life." Detailed exposition of the relation between their ideas and the technicalities of Broad Church theology would lead us too far from their poems into general intellectual background. Several of them had begun to speak their minds before the liberal gospel had been formulated by the clerics. In their writings, furthermore, the diverse elements of that gospel are so closely intertwined as to resist strictly systematic treatment. The poems are interesting to us chiefly because they express, in nontechnical, emotionalized language, the widely pervasive thoughts and feelings of which Broad Church theology was the more formal rationalization.

Conveniently, however, there are a few versifying parsons who provide personal links between liberal Christian theory and poetic practice. One of them was Dean Stanley, Thomas Arnold's biographer and his ideal sixth-former. As a theologian he never rivaled Maurice or even Jowett. The nature of his contribution to the Broad Church movement is indicated by a letter of Matthew Arnold to Fontanès: "Le Dean Stanley est le chef très brillant et très adroit de la minorité libérale du clergé anglican. Mieux que personne, il a l'instinct de la politique qu'il faut suivre, politique très réservée pour le fond des doctrines, très ferme pour tout le reste, et bien décidée à ne pas se laisser effrayer."[23] Stanley's private beliefs, as Arnold suggests, were probably more advanced than his discreetly vague official utterances would indicate. Carlyle was fond of saying that "he skated on the thinnest ice of any theologian he had ever heard of," but that "he has no misgivings about the part he is playing: he holds that there are fine things underlying all this."[24] Moncure D. Conway, an extreme left-wing "humanist," regarded Stanley as essentially an ally in the cause of rationalism. He opened the Jerusalem Chamber of the Abbey for the first series of Hibbert Lectures, established in honor of a highly rationalistic Unitarian. The inaugural lecturer was Max Müller, who stressed the usefulness of atheism as a corrective factor in the progressive enlightenment of religion. The lecturer for 1880 was Ernest Renan; the Dean entertained him at dinner in his official residence. Stanley was unable to attend the Channing Centenary in April of that year, but "he wrote two letters which were publicly read, expressing highest

[22] Leslie Stephen, "Are We Christians?" *Essays on Free-Thinking and Plain-Speaking*, p. 132.

[23] *Letters*, II, 101.

[24] William Allingham, *Diary*, p. 274.

homage to Channing, and begging that his absence might not be misunderstood."[25]

The hymns of so accommodating an Anglican priest should be instructive. We need not try to imagine their being sung by choir or congregation. Stanley seems to have thought of them as fragmentary contributions toward a Broad Church *Christian Year*. No mention is made of the saints in *The Traveller's Hymn for All Saints' Day*. It is an adaptation of Arndt's *Was ist des Deutschen Vaterland?* "Where is the Christian's Fatherland?" Not in Judaea or Greece or Ionia. Certainly not in "proud Rome." Not in Protestant Germany, Switzerland, or Sweden. Not "even" in England. No, it is

> . . . wheresoe'er
> Christ's Spirit breathes a holier air,
> Where Christ-like Faith is keen to seek
> What Truth or Conscience freely speak—
> Where Christ-like Love delights to span
> The rents that sever man from man.

Heedless of the traditional meaning of the season, the *Hymn for Advent* declares that "The Lord is come." He is already present

> . . . In ev'ry heart
> Where Truth and Mercy claim a part;
> In every land where Right is Might,
> And deeds of darkness shun the light.

In *Whitsunday*, Stanley has undertaken to translate the *Veni, Sancte Spiritus* in such a way as to bring out "the deeper meaning which belongs to the words, when considered in describing the purely spiritual aspect of Christianity." The rendering is reasonably faithful, but the hidden spirituality is occasionally revealed by the substitution of some vague moral platitude for the concrete simplicity of the original. According to Stanley's headnote, "*This Do in Remembrance of Me*" is "a Sacramental Hymn founded on the one common idea of commemoration which lies at the basis of all views of the Eucharist, whether material or spiritual, and to express this undoubted intention of the original institution apart from the metaphorical language by which the ordinance is often described." The poem says that the Eucharist is a good way of reminding ourselves that Christ wanted us to remember Him always. Such metaphorical language as "This is my Body. . . . This is My Blood" is so carefully avoided that there is no allusion to the words or

[25] M. D. Conway, *Autobiography*, II, 401, 402.

even to the idea. In the hymns for *Good Friday*, *Ascension*, and *Transfiguration* he similarly widens the clear, sharp Gospel focus until it becomes a soft benevolistic blur of "morality touched with emotion."[26]

This is what might be called the "wheresoe'er" technique. It matters little whether certain improbable events occurred in Palestine centuries ago, for all that is really important in Christianity becomes manifest "wheresoe'er" men live in accordance with the Christian ideal of conduct. The same approach is used in *A Christmas Carol* by Sebastian Evans:

> Needs no star nor Angel's word
> Now to guide us to our Lord.
> Bethlehem lies everywhere!
> Seek and find!—The Child is there![27]

It does not occur to him that Bethlehem would not now be everywhere unless it had once been somewhere. In *We are Seeking the Lord*, Thomas Hornblower Gill writes:

> O saints of old! not yours alone
> Those words most high shall be:
> We take the glory for our own;
> Lord! we are seeking Thee!

Another of his hymns rejoices in *The Glory of the Latter Days*:

> Doth not the Spirit still descend
> And bring the heavenly fire?

Neither of Gill's poems is necessarily inconsistent with the view that historic Christianity is still a going concern; but since he has been credited by his biographer with "distaste for all antiquarian and sacerdotal conceptions of Christianity" and "keen discernment of the spirit as opposed to the letter of scripture," we may conjecture that he is writing from wheresoe'eristic motives.[28]

Our liberals, though chiefly concerned with the good life for this world, do not entirely neglect the next; but they feel the need of justifying their hope of immortality on other than outmoded doctrinal grounds. Matter, argues Bowring, is indestructible. Why not also, a fortiori,

[26] A. P. Stanley, *Letters and Verses*, pp. 368–370, 373, 403. Stanley's conception of the Eucharist explains how, in 1870, he could conscientiously invite all the newly-appointed revisers of the New Testament to a special celebration of Holy Communion in Henry VII's Chapel. The group included several Scotch Presbyterians and English Nonconformists and one Unitarian. (William Blackburn, "The Background of Arnold's *Literature and Dogma*," *Modern Philology*, XLIII, 130.)

[27] *Brother Fabian's Manuscript and Other Poems*, p. 240.

[28] *Miles*, XI, 363, 367, 368.

Those elements of mind and thought,
Whose marvellous imaginings
Have the great deeds of progress wrought?[29]

Thomas Ashe relies upon a law of change which is both natural and "mystic." The sun moves; the snow melts. Similarly "Loves and lives still change, and creeds and words are as vapour." (He has been reading *Faust*.) Therefore, although perhaps the connection is not immediately obvious,

. . . There is no death. It is a dream, a delusion.
We shall still live on, with change and growth of existence.[30]

Owen Meredith would find evidence of heavenly perfection in earthly imperfection, thanking God "for the loss of all things here / Which proves the gain to be."[31] That we qualify for higher or lower degrees of bliss according to our deeds on earth is Bennett's opinion.[32] He does not mean that any of us will be barred entirely from heaven: it is all a question of "spheres." Indeed this group strongly disapproves of hell, especially as a place of *eternal* torment. The doctrine is assailed by Thomas Cooper as a corruption of the Galilean's gospel of love, a mere trick of priestcraft to frighten men into obedience.[33] Dean Stanley's expurgated version of the *Dies Irae* omits any hint of the possibility of damnation—a considerable feat.[34] In general the liberal poets like a muscular sort of heaven with plenty of upward striving and opportunity for service. Browning holds no monopoly on the theme. "Tell me, ye in Heaven," Swain demands,

Is perpetual rest
To your nature given?
Is your holy mission
Still eternal love?
Then there's work for angels
In that world above![35]

Tupper holds that we must not hope to find rest in heaven, "For sloth yieldeth not happiness: the bliss of a spirit is action." The very essence of immortality is a "deathless energy" which "spreadeth eagle-flight to the Sun of unapproachable perfection."[36] Eternal rest is also spurned by that passionate

[29] *Ibid.*, p. 153.
[30] *Poems*, p. 197.
[31] *Poems*, p. 164. This poem of 1859 may have been influenced by Browning; but it was in *La Saisiaz*, written in 1877, that the greater poet grounded his hope of immortality on the assurance "that loss so much the more exalts / Gain about to be."
[32] W. C. Bennett, *Poems*, pp. 365–366.
[33] *Poetical Works*, pp. 152–156.
[34] *Letters and Verses*, pp. 350–352.
[35] Charles Swain, *Poems*, p. 115.
[36] *Proverbial Philosophy*, I, 45. In Chapter II Tupper was found among the Evangelicals; but his thought was very fluid and he became much more liberal with the passing years. The poem provides many examples of the cult of energy.

striver, Lord Houghton. It can be desired neither by the practical reformer nor by the creative thinker. Perhaps, he conjectures, it is really the damned who spend the afterlife

> In dishonourable sleep;
> While no power of pause is given
> To the inheritors of Heaven;
> And the holiest still are those
> Who are furthest from repose.[37]

One thinks of the social-gospel curate in Sutton Vane's *Outward Bound* who is reconciled to the news of his salvation only by the further news that heaven will provide plenty of slums for him to work in.

Desire for celestial repose would be inconsistent with the basic tenet that religion is wholly a matter of doing, not of believing. "Be ye doers of the word, and not hearers only" was a favorite text of Victorian religious liberalism. In such works as Seeley's *Ecce Homo*, however, the text was interpreted to mean not that men who hold certain beliefs are obligated to behave in a certain way, but that if men behave in a certain way their beliefs are of no importance. Fundamentally there was nothing very advanced or novel in this position. The substitution of morality for religion had been common practice in eighteenth-century pulpits; the Evangelical Movement had been largely a reaction against the impotence of such preaching. But there is one important difference: whereas the latitudinarians of the eighteenth century are usually content to feel ethically about religion, those of the nineteenth are usually involved in a more difficult struggle to feel religiously about ethics. W. J. Fox tries to believe not merely that men should live virtuously, but that "Justice and faith are God in man."[38] "Ah! Pastor," William How advises a fellow-clergyman,

> . . . is thy heart full sore
> At all this sin and strife?
> Feed with the Word, but oh! far more
> Feed with a holy life.[39]

There is a great deal of genuine Christianity in Bishop How, but he would not hesitate to apply the epithet "holy" to any socially beneficent life, whether or not that life is supported by orthodox views of "the Word." His labors among the London poor have inclined him to agree with Owen Meredith's statement that

> . . . 'tis not the creed that saves the man:
> It is the man that justifies the creed.[40]

37 *Miles*, IV, 266. 38 *Ibid.*, XII, 301. 39 *Poems*, p. 145. 40 *Poems*, p. 254.

Since Christians hold no monopoly on human decency, noble conduct could justify other creeds than those of Christianity. Though the study of comparative religion as a branch of anthropology led some Victorians to think that all religions might be equally false, it led others to think that all might be equally true if they could be shown to be equally productive of altruistic behavior. Some poets of the present chapter regard the latter possibility with cautious friendliness. Julian Fane says that although the myth of the dying Baldur is "the fabric of an idol-faith," it is

> Yet fanciful and lofty; nay, I deem,
> Albeit Error heaped with hand uncouth
> The shapeless pile, She built upon the rock of Truth.[41]

At the close of our period Sir Edwin Arnold's *The Light of Asia* satisfied the hankering for spiritual exoticism without disloyalty to Broad Church essentials. He insisted that Buddhism is a religion of active love—"A third of mankind would never have been brought to believe in blank abstractions, or in Nothingness as the issue and crown of Being." The Buddha's personality "cannot but appear the gentlest, holiest, and most beneficent, with one exception, in the history of Thought." Observe especially "beneficent." In the bo tree's shade Gautama muses:

> 'Twere all as good to ease one beast of grief
> As sit and watch the sorrows of the world
> In yonder caverns with the priests who pray.[42]

So there is such a thing as muscular Buddhism.

Not only the sincere affirmations but the sincere negations of all good men should be regarded with tolerance. Those who assert most proudly the firmness of their faith, observes Bowring, are also the most easily angered and dismayed by the doubts of others. The injunction, "Prove all things," should have taught them that the actively seeking doubter is more truly spiritual than the smugly quiescent believer.[43] This idea is warmly endorsed by the *Angel Voices* which sing to William Bennett:

> To assurance doubt's the portal;
> Lies, through doubt, to faith the way;
> He who dreads to doubt, unblinded,
> Faith for him in fear shall end:
>
> . . .
>
> Work is worship; work for others;
> Toil in love, and doubt shall cease:

[41] *Poems*, p. 91. [42] *The Light of Asia*, pp. viii, xi, 123. [43] *Miles*, XI, 156.

On, for good, for men, thy brothers;
Self-abjurement brings thee peace.[44]

Doubt and serve, then; if you work hard enough for others, you will find that your doubt has become faith—faith in more service and in yourself as a worker.

It seems clear, then, that in emphasizing the response of these poets to large theological and philosophical concepts we must not underestimate the importance of the humanitarian factor. What, demands Bishop How, are Christians doing to ameliorate the miseries of the industrial poor?

Have ye bettered the poor man's narrowed span?
Have ye brightened the way he's trod?
Perchance, when he knows the love of man,
He may learn the love of God.

Indignation at the social callousness of institutional Christianity has reversed the order of the two great commandments of the Law. The same writer expressly answers Arnold's *Self-Dependence* in *A Starlit Night by the Seashore*. Not for him the stoical ataraxy of the stars: he desires to suffer with the suffering human world:

Let what grandeur crown the life of others,
Let what light on lone endurance shine;
I will set myself beside my brothers,
And their toils and troubles shall be mine.[45]

Despite many individual exceptions there was a good deal of evidence for the thesis that those Christians who were the most loyal to traditional orthodoxy were likely to be the most indifferent to the inequities of machine civilization. Hence a natural tendency on the part of the social-minded to deny the importance of " mere creeds and forms." Thomas Ashe warns some clerical friends who have asked him to write them a sermon in verse that if he should reveal the religion of his "inner heart"

Your breasts would flutter, ill at ease,
Beneath the snowy surplices.

. . .

You would not dare, be sure of it,
To read the folk my holy-writ;—

[44] *Poems*, p. 458. Has anyone observed how frequently Victorian poets, major as well as minor, are privileged to hear "voices"? Some graduate student should write a dissertation on "Auditory Hallucinations in Victorian Poetry."

[45] *Poems*, pp. 188, 192.

That man to man hold fast,
No matter if he bow before
A God the less or saint the more.

Put love for sects and rituals,
And lift up him or her who falls,
With love grown tenderer for their fate;

. . .

I do but preach the very thing
Christ preach'd, whom men heard, wondering.[46]

When Moncure D. Conway visited Germany in 1864, David Strauss told him that "He felt oppressed at seeing nearly every nation in Europe chained by an allied despotism of prince and priest. . . . He believed when writing the 'Leben Jesu' that in striking at supernaturalism he was striking at the root of the whole tree of political and social degradation."[47] In England, as contrasted with the Continent, prince and priest were neither so powerful nor so closely allied as to make aggressive secularism a major plank in the platform of the English radicals. Nevertheless the Anglican Church, seconded by the more comfortable members of the more "respectable" Nonconformist sects, did their poor best to retard the advance of politico-social reform. Victorian England offered the Visible Church a precious opportunity to win souls for Christ by making His gospel come alive in a civilization both religious and humane. But rather than loosen her clutch on her thirty pieces of silver she threw in her lot with the forces of repression, class privilege, and obscurantism.[48] Thanks largely to the heretics who had preached the gospel of brotherhood at a time when the orthodox had almost forgotten it, considerable improvement in this respect had been achieved by the close of the century. But irrevocable harm had been done: institutional Christianity had alienated both the thoughtful artisan and the freedom-loving intellectual.

Hence the earliest Victorian poetry of religious liberalism represents not the impact of science or German Bible-criticism upon traditional belief but the impact of social indignation upon the loveless competitive culture of which the Church was the spiritual arm. This poetry, a continuation into the thirties and forties of post-Waterloo reform agitations, is produced by

[46] *Poems*, pp. 284–285. [47] *Autobiography*, II, 14.

[48] To say this is not to deny the contributions to social welfare made by Anglican and Nonconformist Evangelicals before most of them consented to worship Ruskin's "Britannia of the Market-place." The value of Christian Socialism should also be recognized, although that movement was neither very Christian nor, except as regards the ideas imported from France by Ludlow, very socialistic.

members of the working class or by bourgeois humanitarian sympathizers. Their family background is normally Evangelical or Methodist. The anti-clericalism of some of these poets of protest led them onward into complete secularism; since *The Age of Reason* and *Queen Mab* were their favourite theological guides, they belong in later chapters. Others, however, called upon Christ the great reforming carpenter to bear witness for them against Tory Christianity.

Of this milder group, Ebenezer Elliott (1781–1849) and Samuel Bamford (1788–1872) are links between the romantic and the Victorian periods. Bamford remembers having been a founder and the secretary of a "Hampden Club" in the village of Middleton as early as 1816. The members "rented a chapel which had been given up by a society of Kilhamite Methodists. This place we threw open for the religious worship of all sects and parties." He believes that this was "the first place of worship occupied by reformers."[49] Thomas Cooper (1805–1892) is a later figure of the same general type. In his Chartist days he was a pretty aggressive secularist who simultaneously declared "I love the Galilean" and preached Strauss to his fellow-workers;[50] but Kingsley had made a hazily liberal Christian of him by 1856.[51] We may as well add William Cox Bennett (1820–1895) in one of his several guises. Although he worked for a time as a watchmaker he was primarily a liberal journalist and a purveyor of domestic heartthrobs who often vainly aspired to be a sort of British Béranger.[52]

In the famous *Corn-Law Rhymes* (1831) Ebenezer Elliott[53] insists that religion means nothing but being and doing good:

> They best serve God, who serve mankind:
> Christ bade us feed his little ones.

[49] *Passages in the Life of a Radical and Early Days*, II, 12, 13. Such clubs were precursors of the nonsectarian "Chartist Churches, where the spirit and teaching of early Christianity attracted large numbers of men and women who found Church and Chapel alike cold and unsympathetic." By 1843 they were an important influence "in Birmingham and the mining districts, where the preacher O'Neill, a prominent Chartist, seems to have become as great a power among the miners as Wesley himself had been a century earlier in Cornwall and Somerset." (J. L. and Barbara Hammond, *The Bleak Age*, p. 119.)

[50] Thomas Cooper, *Poetical Works*, p. 82; Margaret F. Thorp, *Charles Kingsley*, p. 74.

[51] Cooper was Kingsley's model for the shoemaker-poet of *Alton Locke*. We may observe in passing that *The Bad Squire*, Tregarva's social-protest ballad in *Yeast*, is precisely in the manner of this school. The squire is warned that when he dies "You will find in your God the protector / Of the freeman you fancied your slave." (Charles Kingsley, *Poems*, p. 203.)

[52] Thomas Hood is a little too early for notice in this volume, but we may remind ourselves that his social-protest poems had liberal religious implications.

[53] A fairly prosperous small manufacturer, not a workingman. He brought up two of his sons as Anglican clergymen, but when he wrote verse his tender heart was too much for his fundamentally conservative opinions.

The Evangelicals, he complains, are less interested in applying this injunction to England than to

> . . . gorgeous climes beneath the eastern sky.
>
> . . .
>
> Their Bibles for the heathen load our fleets;
> Lo! looking eastward, they inquire, "What news?"
> "We die," we answer, "foodless in the streets,"
> Oh, "they are sending bacon to the Jews!"

Dickens would like that. Very different is the spirit of *The Ranter*, an irregular field-preacher who, though still a Wesleyan, has broken away from Chapel "because the *spirit* thence is gone." In Jesus' own words, and invoking His example, he cries out to "the plundered poor" against the scribes and Pharisees of organized Christianity:

> What are the *deeds* of men called Christian, now?
> They roll themselves in dust before the great;
> Wherever Mammon builds a shrine, they bow,
> And would nail Jesus to their cross of hate,
> Should He again appear in *mean* estate.[54]

Like Mr. Lyons in *Felix Holt*, Elliott's father was both a Methodist and a radical; but as the century moved on this combination, fairly common between Peterloo and the passage of the Reform Bill, became much more difficult to maintain.

It is axiomatic with Elliott and his fellows that God is the common man's best friend, but that He is rather slow about manifesting that fact in contemporary society.

> When wilt thou save the people?
> Oh, God of Mercy! when?
> The people, Lord, the people!
> Not thrones and crowns, but men![55]

Readers of Mrs. Gaskell's *Mary Barton* may recall that when John Barton murders young Carson he uses for pistol-wadding a bit of a poem by Samuel Bamford, his fellow-weaver, entitled *God Help the Poor*. Up to the last stanza this refrain is merely an exclamation of despair, but the closing lines read:

> Shall toil and famine hopeless still be borne?
> No, GOD will yet arise and HELP THE POOR![56]

[54] *Poetical Works*, I, 230, 366–367, 369; II, 65, 188–189. [55] *Ibid.*, II, 203.

[56] Bamford, *Poems*, p. 101. For other examples, mostly too early for us, see pp. 33, 61, 69,

Bennett is equally sanguine:

> Yet God will right the people yet,
> Although the struggle's long;
> Yes, friends, we've faith that God will set
> The right above the wrong![57]

The doctrinal principles enjoined upon the worshippers of this God are necessarily few and simple. "They love not God, who do not hate man's foes."[58] There is no other theological requirement.

As we proceed, these poets of popular indignation will be drawn upon for further examples of the interplay of socio-political and religious liberalism, but except as regards the points already mentioned they are not distinctive enough to deserve treatment as a separate subgroup. It will be best to let them merge with the larger body of religiously "broad" poets from which they were briefly singled out for special attention. They do not monopolize, although they strongly feel, a more widely pervasive distaste for sacerdotalism as a force making for oppression and obscurantism. Anglican priestcraft receives its share of abuse, but the Roman Catholicism of the Continent provides a larger, more clearly defined target for such writers as Bennett. In his personal Utopia,

> My church's reverend priests should live,
> To unjust power, to titled vice,
> Not shrinking stern reproof to give.

England falls far below this dream. She possesses few such prophetic spirits as Kingsley,

> ... not eaten up with earthly greed,
> But with desire of Him the Cross who bore.

Nevertheless she is much better off than Europe, for Britons

> ... can scoff
> At this their priestly cry;
> We laugh their Jesuits off,
> And all their power defy.
> For England Wiseman sighs—
> To Rome the worst of sights;
> But all in vain he cries,
> "Put out—put out your lights!"

But thanks to secularistic revolutionary agitations, there is hope even for Europeans:

[57] *Poems*, p. 309. See also pp. 452–455.

[58] Ebenezer Elliott, *Poetical Works*, II, 61.

Freer of thoughts—the Tricolor;
Looser of lips—the Tricolor;
Souls and tongues shall be fettered no more
When thrones go down with the Tricolor.[59]

In 1845, writing as a Chartist, Cooper thinks of the Anglican clergy as priests in the blackest sense of that vile term. They inculcate reverence for "mystery" as a means of perpetuating tyranny. "Drudge on, in silent meekness!" is their command to the downtrodden toiler. But in 1873, less fiercely secularistic and more content with conditions in England, he turns his disapproval toward France, where the mummery of popish priests has caused an equally deplorable reaction toward atheism. It began with the revocation of the Edict of Nantes, after which

... nought was left to represent the faith
Of Christ, but mass idolatrous—the bread
Turned into Deity by the noisome breath,
Perchance, of some foul priest, and overhead
Held up for worship.[60]

W. J. Fox is more concerned with intellectual than with political liberty, though he would be quick to grant the close relation between the two. A hymn which he wrote for use in his Unitarian chapel declares that genuine religion can never die so long as young people, "though nursed in Superstition's chain," preserve the love of free enquiry.

Then, let not priest or tyrant dote
On dreams of long the world commanding;
The ark of Moses is afloat,
And Christ is in the temple standing.[61]

On the death of Cavour, Sebastian Evans, a more conservative thinker than Fox, fears that Italy will now be rent asunder by two bands of extremists: the wildly Utopian radicals who care nothing for "temperate Freedom," and the clericals who would revive

The dark, dishallowed priestcraft of dead creeds,
Who in the vineyards of God's heritage
Trampled the wine-vats, crushing human hearts,
Hopes, passions, aspirations, and thereout
Sucked horrible frenzy, drunkenness of lust,
And uttermost perdition![62]

[59] *Poems*, pp. 283, 297, 342, 517.
[60] *Poetical Works*, pp. 12, 131, 395–396.
[61] *Miles*, XII, 300.
[62] *Brother Fabian's Manuscript; and Other Poems*, pp. 243–244.

But the Honorable Julian Fane, son of the Earl of Westmorland, hardly needs to worry about such problems. In good eighteenth-century drinking club fashion he is content to associate "knaves in hoods and bands" with hypocrisy and spoilsport gloom:

> Come forth, the bowl is mantling high,
> We'll drink the death of every lie,
> The death of Cant until it die,
> Drowned deep in wine;
> We'll send the corpse to Curate Sly,
> That sleek divine![63]

This anticlericalism may be clarified by a side glance at a closely associated topic. Although their beliefs and disbeliefs would horrify a genuine Puritan, several poets of the present chapter proudly regard both their religious and their political liberalism as a heritage bequeathed to them by the Puritans of the seventeenth century.[64] Far be it from me to say that they were mistaken. At all events it is more than a coincidence that Bennett, Sebastian Evans, and Kingsley all wrote imitations of Macaulay's *Battle of Naseby*.[65] Elliott reveres

> The slander'd Calvinists of Charles's time;
> . . .
> With zeal they preach'd, with reverence they were heard;
> For in their daring creed, sublime, sincere,
> Danger was found, that parson-hated word!
> They flatter'd none—they knew nor hate nor fear,
> But taught the word of God—and *did* it here.

Where, he asks, is the spirit of Pym and Hampden today, when the Nonconformist has nothing to say but "Man, be circumspect and thrive!" The shades of Charles I and Laud must be smiling to see the triumph of their oppressive principles.[66] In *Our Glory-Roll*, a poem in praise of great Englishmen past and present, Bennett pays tribute to Latimer, Hooper, Ridley, Cranmer, and their descendants Pym and Hampden but describes the Laudians as "Popish prelates, fell as Rome's." Later, "bloody Claverhouse . . . preached the faith of Laud again with thumbscrew, boot, and sword."

[63] *Poems*, p. 49.

[64] "Among the disciples of Carlyle," said Walter Bagehot, "it is considered that having been a Puritan is the next best thing to having been in Germany." (*Literary Studies*, II, 213.)

[65] Bennett, *Poems*, pp. 194–195; Evans, *Brother Fabian's Manuscript*, pp. 205–206; Kingsley, *Poems*, pp. 221–222. But Evans is an elusive man, and his ballad may be partly ironic. He is stirred, but also perhaps repelled, by the pious bloodthirstiness of *The Puritan Militant*.

[66] *Poetical Works*, I, 263, 369–370.

But at last God sent William to us to save us from "the Romish Stuart, worst and last," and since then England has enjoyed continuous progress in "might and thought and wealth and rule."[67] This poem might easily have been written by an eighteenth-century latitudinarian Whig. Cooper's collection of heroes in Book VIII of *The Purgatory of Suicides* is even more interesting. He would honor

> ... each stalwart pioneer
> Of mental Freedom,—Wickliffe, Jerome, Huss,
> Luther, Melancthon, Cobham, Latimer!

But these, he adds, had noble descendants in the struggle for intellectual liberty: Herbert of Cherbury, Hobbes, Locke, Boyle, Hume, Godwin, Paley, Butler, Spinoza, Rousseau, Bayle, Voltaire, Fénelon, Erasmus (Cooper's order throughout, not mine), Pascal, Howard, Cartwright, Clarkson, Owen.[68] Again I feel no very strong impulse to deny that these worthies, in varying degree, represent the consequences of the Protestant Reformation. But in associating Voltaire with Luther, Cooper is not interested in the religion of either man: all he cares about is "mental Freedom."

There were other than socio-political motives for disapproving sacerdotal religion. Ironically enough, perhaps the most powerful stimulus to the emergence of a conscious and militant Broad Churchmanship was the Catholic Revival. From the first the Oxford Movement had disgusted and alarmed men like Thomas Arnold into formulating their intuitive distaste for dogma. After the 1845 secessions many others, who had been sympathetic observers or even disciples of Newmanism, recoiled from the brink of popery only to land in a morass of bewilderment through which they had to struggle as bravely and intelligently as they could. Their anti-Catholic feelings were aggravated in 1850 by the establishment of the Romanist hierarchy in England, by the ritualistic controversies of the sixties and seventies, and in 1870 by the promulgation of the dogma of papal infallibility and by the *Syllabus Errorum*, which controverted every article of the liberal creed.

For the "broad" Protestant, Catholicism was at the same time too otherworldly to be practically beneficent, too precise to be tolerant, and too sensuous, materialistic, and objective to be genuinely spiritual. But it was especially offensive for its loyalty to asceticism. With quietly ironic reverence Thomas Ashe recounts the legend of *St. Guthlac*—how, oppressed by sorrow

[67] *Poems*, pp. 126–130.

[68] *Poetical Works*, pp. 213–214. The poem was published in 1845, during his early phase of militant Chartism.

for his own sins and for those of others, the holy man retired to a hut in the fens and there slowly tortured himself to death, never finding spiritual peace but never ceasing his gloomy prayers and austerities. On the whole this unexpectedly good poem by a bad poet points rather delicately to the conclusion that Guthlac would have been a better Christian if he had served God by serving man in the active life. The contrast between the morbid devotee and the two muscular, happy, nature-loving Saxons who row him up the river to the scene of his hermitage is presented without comment. But there are a few broader hints, such as

> . . . So he racked himself the more
> With tortures, thinking to be purer-soul'd;

or "And being holy, prick'd himself with spikes." In another poem Ashe gently scolds one *Christine*, whose beauty and goodness have been an inspiration to her friends, for becoming a cloistered nun:

> Christine, for us face risk and loss,
> For only so you bear His cross.
>
> Come forth and gladden us again,
> And shine upon us with your beams;
> Make holier the hearts of men,
> And leave your ecstacies and dreams:
> And charm us to be pure and clean
> And good, when we behold Christine.[69]

For Charles Kingsley, Christine's vows would be an offense not so much against the gospel of service as against the holiness of the heart's affections. His poetic drama, *The Saint's Tragedy*, represents celibacy as the most detestable of all popish perversions of the true spirit of Christianity. St. Elizabeth of Hungary is "a type of two great mental struggles of the Middle Age; first, of that between Scriptural or unconscious, and Popish or conscious purity: in a word, between innocence and prudery; next, of the struggle between healthy human affection, and the Manichean contempt with which a celibate clergy would have all men regard the names of husband, wife, and parent." Later in his preface he reproaches the Puseyite clergy, "those miserable dilettanti, who in books and sermons are whimpering meagre second-hand praises of celibacy . . . nibbling ignorantly at the very root of that household purity which constitutes the distinctive superiority of Protestant over Popish nations." [70]

[69] *Poems*, pp. 77, 46–56.

[70] *Poems*, pp. 12, 15. I regret that limitations of space forbid my showing how the text of this interesting work illustrates the principles set forth in the Preface.

Detestation of such evils was not inconsistent with literary exploitation of medieval strangeness and glamor. A rigorously non-Catholic poet might imitate old ballads and tales of chivalry—even pious ones, if their piety was regarded as quaintly or thrillingly superstitious. It is quite possible to feel romantic about Catholicism if one is a Protestant. Irrational beliefs which might be rather touching in a child might also be harmlessly exciting when attributed to imaginary adults of less enlightened times. And although Kingsley, in his *Invitation*, tells Tom Hughes that "High Art" is "popish stuff," Broad Church admirers of "mournful Ruskin"[71] could feel quite reverent toward a painted Madonna in the Uffizi.[72]

Or the medieval Church might be treated with not unkindly humor by liberals whose disapproval of Catholicism was tempered by antiquarian enthusiasm. Everybody knows Barham's immortal *Jackdaw*; its companion-pieces are almost equally funny in their broadly extravagant style, so like that of his friend Thomas Hook.[73] But there are moments when he abandons ecclesiological burlesque and gives us a glimpse of his real feelings. Just when *The Auto-da-Fé* seems about to reach its appropriate climax of merely comic horror, he switches from his rollicking anapaests to iambic couplets and delivers a serious attack upon the Inquisition:

> God! that the worm whom thou hast made
> Should thus his brother worm invade!
> Count deeds like these good service done,
> And deem THINE eyes look smiling on!!

Similarly in *The Lay of St. Aloys*, Barham interrupts a humorous description of the elaborate ceremonial at the funeral mass of Count Stephen to tell us that he personally prefers a humble committal service in a rural churchyard, where the village pastor,

> . . . in simplest vestment clad,
> . . . speaks, beneath the churchyard tree,
> In solemn tones—but yet not sad—
> Of what Man is—what Man shall be![74]

According to the poet's son, *Ingoldsby Legends* was not devoid of serious purpose. Barham was "firmly and conscientiously opposed to avowed Popery, and not less so to that anomalous system [Tractarianism] which

[71] *Ibid.*, p. 247.

[72] See for example Emily Pfeiffer, *Under the Aspens*, pp. 120, 121.

[73] With Sydney Smith, another of his friends, Barham was a survivor of the eighteenth-century type of High Churchmanship: that is, he was a strong Church-and-State Protestant Episcopalian who cared very little what people believed so long as they subscribed to the Establishment.

[74] *The Ingoldsby Legends*, pp. 169, 266.

means Popery if it means anything." He "could not view with indifference the propagation of opinions which he believed to be erroneous, harmful in many ways, and especially tending to dissipate religious feeling upon a multitude of ceremonial trivialities rather than to concentrate it upon the conduct of life."[75]

Sebastian Evans is a more refined writer and a more complicated man. *Brother Fabian's Manuscript* is a wittier monastic burlesque than Barham could have produced. In her fish pond the worthy Prioress of St. Wigbald keeps a pet pike which she feeds with the most luxurious meats

> Except indeed on Fridays, when the fare
> Was only rye-bread manchet, soaked in milk.
> She had her faults, good dame,—for who is free?
> But none can ever say she gave her fish
> Flesh on a Friday.

This is characteristic. But *The Three Kings of Cologne* and *Judas Iscariot's Paradise* mingle comic antiquarianism with so much genuinely sympathetic insight into the spirit of medieval faith that one is inclined to call Evans an *anima naturaliter Catholica* who cannot forgive the sins of the Visible Church as he sees it at work in the nineteenth century. Pio Nono has made a Broad Churchman of him. When he is not poking half-wistful fun at the Middle Ages he thinks that "Bethlehem lies everywhere" and that "the Creed may die but the Christ lives through."[76]

For a thorough-going liberal, Catholicism, both Roman and Anglican, represented a view of life which was inconsistent with the desire to associate spiritual values with material progress. Kingsley spurns the "popish" scenery of the Apennines in favor of

> . . . the vale of Windsor,
> England's golden eye.
> Show me life and progress,
> Beauty, health, and man;
> Houses fair, trim gardens,
> Turn where'er I can.[77]

Martin Tupper marvels at "how great a thing it is, how glad," to live in times

> When science and invention bless the world,
> Banishing half our pains and woes far hence;

[75] R. H. Dalton Barham, *Life and Letters of the Reverend Richard Harris Barham*, p. 238.
[76] *Brother Fabian's Manuscript*, pp. 14–15, 37ff., 60ff., 270. See also above, pp. 70, 79.
[77] *Poems*, p. 247.

When Right is Might, and Reason holds her own;
O, happy day! for prophets, priests and kings
Have longed in vain to see such glorious things.[78]

It is fitting that these lines should have been written in 1851.[79] As everyone knows, the Crystal Palace Exhibition of that year was regarded by large sections of the British public as a great festival of technological world brotherhood and as a fit occasion for rendering thanks to God for the accomplishments of nineteenth-century man. The less famous Exhibition of 1862 could still arouse the same feelings in Charles Tennyson Turner:

. . . The man
Ardent, competitive, and large of plan,
Brings all his spirit to such marts as these.

. . .

O Art and Commerce, set the nations free,
And bid the rites of war's proud temples cease.
O power of steam! for ever may'st thou be
A rolling incense in the house of peace!
And all these vast consignments but increase
Our sense of brotherhood and charity![80]

Ebenezer Elliott, who knows much more about steam than Tennyson Turner, is even more strongly inclined to image it as incense ascending in the temple of peaceful competitive progress. In *Steam at Sheffield*, a factory shows

. . . that man hath found
Redemption from the manacles which bound
His powers for many an age. A poor man's boy
Constructed these grand works! . . .

. . .

Engine of Watt! unrivall'd is thy sway.
Compared with thine, what is the tyrant's power?

It might be well to recall here that Elliott was a small manufacturer, not a laborer; but most intelligent and ambitious artisans of the period would doubtless have agreed with him. Not merely technology but the commerce which technology implemented held out hopes for the aggrandizement of the common man—unless he was too weak or lazy or ignorant to compete with his fellows. Elliott's Methodist field-preacher is a propagandist against

[78] Quoted by Derek Hudson, *Martin Tupper*, p. 125.

[79] But see above, p. 32, for evidence that Tupper in his Evangelical vein can view the Exhibition as a display of soulless materialism.

[80] *Collected Sonnets*, p. 126. This poet was assigned to Chapter II, but his type of Evangelicalism is not inconsistent with such aspirations.

the Corn Laws. Once they are abolished, freedom, prosperity, and world peace will be at hand.

> Yes, world-reforming Commerce! one by one
> Thou vanquishest earth's tyrants. . . .
>
> . . .
>
> Then o'er th'enfranchised nations wilt thou shower
> Like dew-drops from the pinions of the dove,
> Plenty and peace; and never more on thee
> Shall bondage wait; but, as the thoughts of love,
> Free shalt thou fly, unchainable and free;
> And men, thenceforth, shall call thee "Liberty"!

Before we say that abolition of the Corn Laws has nothing to do with religion let us read two stanzas from another poem by Elliott:

> Free Trade, like religion, hath doctrines of love,
> And the promise of plenty and health;
> It proclaims, while the angels look down from above,
> The marriage of Labour and Wealth.
>
> . . .
>
> The hall of our fathers, with heav'n for its dome,
> And the steps of its portals the sea—
> Of labour and comfort will then be the home,
> And the temple where worship the Free.[81]

What, while the angels look down from above, will free men worship? Labour, and his spouse Wealth. Tupper would add that the best of it all is that the more charitable you are the wealthier you will become. "Wouldst thou be rich, give unto the poor;—thou shalt have thine own with usury." Honesty is equally productive of tangible rewards,

> For honesty of every kind, approved by God and man,
> Of wealth and better weal is found the richest cornucopia.[82]

But it was impossible to achieve success in the world of getting and spending without a considerable amount of knowledge, technological or commercial or both. Also when one became rich one should live like a gentleman; and a gentleman not only kept a gig but had some acquaintance with books and pictures and music, though of course not so much as his womenfolk. The Victorian cult of progress is therefore closely involved with the popular education movement, especially for liberals who took a

[81] *Poetical Works*, I, 356–357; II, 120.

[82] *Proverbial Philosophy*, I, 104; II, 132. For eighteenth-century foretokenings of this quasi-religious glorification of money-making see the topical index of *Religious Trends*, II, under "Commerce and industry."

lively interest in reform. The more orthodox clergy, allied with the more conservative politicians, regarded the movement suspiciously. They wanted the common people to be schooled but feared that purely secular education would make them materialistic and, still worse, subversive. It was important that they should be able to read the Bible; it was even more important that they should not be able to read Tom Paine. Most defenders of the traditional faith, with their characteristic gift for antagonizing intelligent freedom-loving men, made it clear that they had no use for national schooling except as a medium for sectarian indoctrination. Hence almost all the genuine champions of popular education were either complete secularists or more or less extreme latitudinarians.

Writing in 1845, Thomas Cooper calls knowledge "the new-born world's great heroine / That shall be." Already kings and priests quake to behold the slogan "Knowledge is Power" inscribed on the banner of the toilers.[83] As a member of the Education Commission of the London Council, William Cox Bennett had a stake in this problem. His allegory, *The Cry of the Lawful Lanterns,* is "Humbly Dedicated to the Opponents of National Education." The first stanza will show the obvious symbolism:

A people dwelt in darkness,
In gloom and blinding night,
Till some grew tired of candles
And dared to long for light;
When straight the establish'd lanterns
Were stirr'd with hate of day,
And loud the lawful rushlights
In wrath were heard to say,
"O have you not your lanterns,
Your little shining lanterns,
What need have you of sunshine?
What do you want with day?"[84]

Few American readers will find it hard to understand how Victorian liberals can regard education as good not merely for the brain but for the soul. What, asks Bennett in *A Cry for National Education*, is

More worth man's culture than the mind of man?
Oh what an unknown glory then would wear
The coming years the future towards us leads,
If man to stir the unnurtured mind would care
With the perfection the soul's culture breeds![85]

[83] *Poetical Works*, pp. 67, 68. [84] *Poems*, p. 248. [85] *Ibid.*, p. 446.

In much the same spirit Charles Swain writes:

Oh, the gift of Mind is greater
Than the gift of land could be,
Nothing from our kind Creator
Breathes so much of deity;
. . .
Scarce an angel's comprehension
Spans the vastness of its power!

But of course it is only "through cultivation / That the living Mind expands." Elsewhere Swain assures the altruistic reader that self-cultivation is by no means selfish, for

He who seeks the Mind's improvement
Aids the world, in aiding Mind!
Every great commanding movement
Serves not one, but all mankind![86]

Devoted as he is to steam engines, Elliott would not restrict the artisan's education merely to technics. He invites us to enter *The Home of Taste* and admire

The proud mechanic there,
Rich as a king, and less a slave,
Throned in his elbow-chair!
Or on his sofa reading Locke,
Beside his open door!
Why start?—why envy worth like his
The carpet on the floor?

Too many artisans, however, are still so lacking in taste that they prefer to dwell in "the home of sluttery."

O lift the workman's heart and mind
Above low sensual sin!
Give him a home! the home of taste!
Outbid the house of gin!

Have we strayed too far from anything that could be called religion? Elliott would not think so, for he continues:

O give him taste! it is the link
Which binds us to the skies.[87]

In *Poetry and the Poor*, Bishop How protests against the idea that to give the

[86] *Poems*, pp. 170, 211. [87] *Poetical Works*, II, 115.

poor some glimpse of beauty would merely be to render them desperate with envy. Appreciation of what they cannot possess is better

> Than thraldome to the sense, and heart of stone,
> And horrible contentment with the night.
>
> Oh! bring we then all sweet and gracious things
> To touch the lives that lie so chill and drear
> That they may dream of some diviner sphere,
> Whence each soft ray of love and beauty springs.

Two years later, however, he doubts that aesthetic cultivation in itself can do anything to make men more religious. He respects the motives of the wealthy young men of the "*University Settlements*" *in East London*, who hope that "where love and beauty go before, / Some path may open for an Angel's feet." But the slum-dwellers refuse to be drawn to the beauty of holiness through the holiness of beauty. Perhaps the order should be reversed:

> Ah! what if Angel feet best lead the way,
> And thoughts of God wake men as from the dead,
> Dreams of new beauty visit souls that pray,
> And Art but follow whither Faith hath led?[88]

Broad as he is, good Bishop How retains a firmer hold on Christian objectivity than most of his fellows.

Yet it cannot be said of the poets of this chapter that even those who are most indifferent to traditional doctrines have lapsed into complete subjectivism. Their romantic impulses are diluted by the uncertainty of their ideas and the feebleness of their emotions. Fortunately also those impulses are bent in a potentially religious direction by their devotion to humanitarian service. They aspire to make goodness practically operative in that very world which is the world of all of us—an ideal in which self-assertion is considerably chastened by self-abnegation. But although it would be absurd to describe any of these writers as a thoroughgoing romanticist, it would be equally absurd to ignore the romantic element in their thought. Their romanticism becomes most obvious precisely at the point where they begin to assert that they possess not merely an ethics but a religion—that goodness, in short, is not merely goodness but God.

Whence does this belief derive its authority? Almost wholly from the

[88] *Poems*, pp. 133, 167.

revelation of the Inner Light. At the very beginning of our period, W. J. Fox represents the spirit of true religion as saying to man,

> . . . Look within;
> God is in thine own heart—
> His noblest image there, and holiest shrine.
> Silent revere—and be thyself divine.[89]

And in the 1870's Cooper berates the High Church ritualists for their attempt

> To re-enthrone old Priestcraft. Do ye dream
> That ye can veritably restore to life
> The dead putrescence? 'Midst the whirl of steam,
> The speed of telegraphs, and the lightning-gleam
> Of knowledge which proclaims the reign of Law,
> Will toiling men a truth your bold tale deem
> That ye can make your Maker?

But science, which has destroyed objective supernaturalism, has left subjective supernaturalism all the freer to assert its purer, more spiritual truths. The Puseyites should abandon their superstitious mummery and

> . . . strive to lead
> The toiling crowd to reverence and enshrine
> The Real Presence of the Lord Divine
> Within their hearts.[90]

If God is certainly revealed in the heart of man, and not at all certainly revealed anywhere else, when these poets say that they believe in God they must mean that they believe in the truth and goodness and creativity of their personal feelings. This is what I have called "the romantic faith." It is true, as Professor Buckley has emphasized, that the Victorians often reproach the poets of the romantic generation for having been too dreamily idealistic, too indifferent to workaday realities and immediate social obligations.[91] The devotion of our Victorian liberals to objective ethical activities is obviously strong. Nevertheless the sole *spiritual* sanction of their humanitarianism derives from a pretty complete subjectivity. More strongly than the romantic poets they want to be good practical Christians, but they satisfy that desire by romanticizing Christianity.

Occasionally the poets of this group reveal their admiration for the poets of the Romantic Period or for contemporary thinkers who were setting

[89] *Miles*, XII, 300.
[90] *Poetical Works*, pp. 300–301.
[91] J. H. Buckley, *The Victorian Temper*, pp. 14–40.

forth a romantic philosophy. Arthur Hallam, in his Apostles Club days, thinks Wordsworth both a great mystic and a great moral teacher. In the same spirit he hails Shelley as a

> . . . spirit of light and love,
> Creative emanation from the Mind,
> Which in its wondrous solitude doth move
> All things and thoughts that are.

To judge from *Timbuctoo*, Hallam had attended one or more of Coleridge's metaphysical *soirées* on Highgate Hill, where he

> . . . saw a face whose every line
> Wore the pale cast of Thought; a good old man,
> Most eloquent, who spake of things divine.
> Around him youths were gathered, who did scan
> His countenance so grand and mild; and drank
> The sweet, sad tones of Wisdom.[92]

Except for Thomas Ashe, who describes himself as seeking the Absolute "with Fichte, Hegel, and all," I have observed in this group no unmistakable signs of the influence of German transcendental idealism. Until about the middle of the century the subjectivism of the average religious liberal was more likely to be grounded upon the naïve intuitionalism of the Common Sense school. Those who wanted something deeper were usually satisfied with Coleridge, Carlyle, and Emerson.[93] Kingsley's admiration for Carlyle is well known. Stanley fears that Carlyle's conception of Christianity has too much in common with Strauss but "cannot help hoping that he may be the means of reviving a true Christian feeling, or at least preparing the way for it."[94] Few if any of these poets would be inclined to smile at Leigh Hunt's statement that the distinguishing quality of Emerson's writings "is that of an *aroma*: something which is less definable than perceptible, less manifested, than felt."[95] For Bennett, Emerson provides sufficient evidence that prophets yet walk the earth.

> O that my soul might from his living tongue
> Drink wisdom![96]

But these scattered indications of indebtedness or admiration are less important than the frequent appearance, throughout the writings of this

[92] *The Writings of Arthur Hallam*, pp. 5, 42–43, 72. For Shelley, see also Emily Pfeiffer, *Under the Aspens*, pp. 115–116.

[93] Hallam knew something about the German philosophy but thought it inconsistent with Christian principles.

[94] *Letters and Verses*, p. 48.

[95] *The Religion of the Heart*, p. 201.

[96] *Poems*, p. 537. See also Thomas Ashe, *Poems*, p. 273.

group, of ideas and states of feeling which any reader would associate with romanticism. Fundamentally, despite all their uneasy hesitations and compromises, these poets want to believe in the independent goodness and power of man's natural energies. Kingsley explains that Walter of Varila, a boisterous Gratiano-like character in *The Saint's Tragedy*, "represents the 'healthy animalism' of the Teutonic mind, with its mixture of deep earnestness and hearty merriment. His dislike of priestly sentimentalities is no anachronism. Even in his day, a noble lay-religion, founded on faith in the divine and universal symbolism of humanity and nature, was gradually arising, and venting itself, from time to time . . . through chivalry, through the minne-singers, through the lay inventors, or rather importers, of pointed architecture, through the German school of painting, through the politics of the free towns, till it attained complete freedom in Luther and his associate reformers."[97] Whether or not modern romanticism is the historical product of Protestantism, it seems clear that Victorian Broad Churchmen like to speak of the Protestant tradition in romantic language. It is also significant, and a little ominous, that Kingsley, Carlyle, Ruskin, and Browning should think of the energy-cult as "Teutonic."

These poets desire heroes. Thinking of Garibaldi, Bennett bids the earth

> Rejoice . . . thou hast not lost
> The God-like of thy earlier time
> When nation-makers' mighty shadows cross'd
> The radiance of thy prime,
> And with their grandeur made thy years sublime;
> High let their names be toss'd,
> Toss'd and retoss'd upon the thunderous voice,
> Who in their deeds, grow greater in each clime,
> Feeling themselves, through them, of nobler worth.[98]

Thus the function of heroes is not to make us feel humble but to make us feel vicariously "God-like." Such hero-worship tends toward self-worship. More cynically but shrewdly, Owen Meredith observes that heroes are very scarce in these days when "the men are so many and small;"

> And since we seek vainly (to praise in our songs)
> 'Mid our fellows the size which to heroes belongs,
> We take the whole age for a hero, in want
> Of a better; and still, in its favor, descant
> On the strength and the beauty which, failing to find
> In any one man, we ascribe to mankind.[99]

[97] *Poems*, pp. 13–14. [98] *Poems*, p. 421. [99] *Poems*, p. 20.

The better we think of mankind, the better we think of ourselves. Love of neighbor, divorced from the love of any God except the divinity of one's own emotions, may produce a very egoistic sort of altruism.

Glance back for a moment to the eighteenth century, where in James Thomson's *Castle of Indolence* the insufferable Knight of Arts and Industry lectures the inmates of the castle:

> Toil and be glad! let Industry inspire
> Into your quickened limbs her buoyant breath!
> Who does not act is dead; absorpt entire
> In miry sloth, no pride, no joy he hath:
> O leaden-hearted men, to be in love with death!
>
> Resolve! resolve! and to be men aspire!
> Exert that noblest privilege, alone
> Here to mankind indulged; control desire;
> Let godlike reason from her sovereign throne
> Speak the commanding word *I will!* and it is done![100]

Compare a stanza from Charles Swain's *Work*:

> Pause not in fear;
> Preach no desponding, servile view,—
> Whate'er thou will'st thy Will may do!
> Strengthen each manly nerve to bend
> Truth's bow, and bid its shaft ascend!
> Toil on![101]

The Victorian gospel of work is not so unromantic as it sounds, for it is inseparable from this notion of the autonomy of the will and the inflation of personality. When Carlyle scorned Coleridge as an impractical dreamer, the pot was calling the kettle black.

For a student of the great romantics, the medley of scientific, Christian, and romantic views of external nature in these Victorian poets is especially interesting. Nowadays most orthodox Christians would say that science is impotent to disturb a supernaturalistic religion because it concerns itself solely with natural appearances, but that for the same reason science makes it almost impossible to maintain a religion of nature in the absence of belief in the supernatural revelation. It is therefore surprising to find the opposite situation prevailing among the poets of this chapter.[102] Science severely

[100] *Religious Trends*, I, 532–533, where the passage is described as pre-Victorian.

[101] *Poems*, p. 213.

[102] Later chapters will recognize exceptions and complications. Nevertheless, outside of the Evangelical and the Catholic groups, the majority of the whole body of Victorian poets find it easier to feel religious about nature than to feel religious about God.

damages their belief in Christian doctrine, but leaves relatively unscathed their belief in the numinousness of nature. The reason for this paradox is probably to be sought in the substitution, by liberal theology, of immanence for transcendence. God is *primarily* immanent in the good heart of man, but if He were not also immanent in nature man would have nothing to worship but himself. This, except for a disciple of Feuerbach, would be going too far. Science or no science, divinized man needs a divinized nature in which to feel reverently but proudly at home. Why not satisfy the claims of science by including man within nature and then interpret evolution as the progressive unfolding of mind?

These poets have their qualms, of course. Despite his enthusiastic acceptance of Darwinism, Kingsley thinks with horror of

> . . . that wild war,
> In which, through countless ages, living things
> Compete in internecine greed.—Ah God!
> Are we as creeping things, which have no Lord?

In another poem, however, such feelings do not prevent him from addressing nature as "Great Mother" after winning her attention with a thrice-repeated Shelleyan "Oh hear!" He mentions "The Father" four lines later, but without meaning to imply that God is nature's husband.[103] Similarly Edward Dowden feels himself to be living in times when

> . . . spectral faiths contend, and for her course
> The soul confused must try,
> While through the whirl of atoms and of force
> Looms an abandoned sky.

But the spectacle of a child sleeping in perfect animal relaxation is enough to convince him that

> . . . Peace abides, of earth's wild things
> Centre, and ruling thence,
> Behold, a spirit folds her budded wings
> In confident innocence.[104]

The materials of this chapter are so variegated that we can arrange a sequence running all the way from definitely Christian to definitely romantic types of nature-experience. Bishop How's *Hymn of Praise, On the Appearance of the Northern Lights* simply glorifies the Creator for this marvelous manifestation of His power:

[103] *Poems*, pp. 198–199, 268.

[104] *Miles*, VII, 91.

My heart is full of praise I cannot speak:
O! if its song be inarticulate,
Yet be it, God, as true to Thee as Night's,
Who in her stillness praiseth Thee the most,
With her fair earnest face turned full on Thee,
All senses lost in one deep speechless worship![105]

This gives a slightly novel but not a heterodox twist to the familiar theme of nature and man joining in worship of God.[106] In a more Newtonian but still a thoroughly Christian spirit, John Stuart Blackie loves onward past the sun to that "Father of Lights . . . Whose thought is order, and whose will is law."[107]

God may be revealed not only in the rationality but in the beauty of His world. For Ebenezer Elliott, the plates of Audubon's *Birds of America* represent a higher religion than that of the bigot. Through them God addresses us:

This beauty is my language! . . .
. . .
These are my accents. Hear them! and behold
How well my prophet-spoken truth agrees
With the dread truth and mystery of these
Sad, beauteous, grand, love-warbled mysteries![108]

Here the Scriptures are not rejected, but the implication is that *Birds of America* provides a satisfactory equivalent. *Vogel als Prophet*. Firsthand contact with nature has even greater spiritual potency. One Sunday morning Edward Dowden, finding of course no solace in church for his "secret ache," slipped out into the woods,

And sought this brook, and by the brookside stood
The world's Light, and the Light of Life of me.
It is enough, O Master, speak no word!
The stream speaks, and the endurance of the sky
Outpasses speech.[109]

In Owen Meredith's *Lucile* natural objects, especially the sun, have a redemptive function. The Duke is repentant but despairing. Lucile exhorts him to pull himself together in a long inspirational lecture which ends:

[105] *Poems*, p. 31. See also p. 57.
[106] For the same fundamental theme see Thomas Ashe, *Poems*, p. 279, and lines by Frances Anne Kemble in *Miles*, VIII, 261.
[107] *Miles*, IV, 278.
[108] *Poetical Works*, II, 70.
[109] *Miles*, VII, 96. But the following sonnet implies that twilight is a better time for this sort of revelation.

"Cease the sin with the sorrow! See morning begin." The rising sun clinches the effect of her words:

> As the stream to its first mountain levels, elate
> In the fountain arises, the spirit in him
> Arose to that image [the sun]. The image waxed dim
> Into heaven; and heavenward with it, to melt
> As it melted, in day's broad expansion, he felt
> With a thrill, sweet and strange, and intense,—awed, amazed—
> Something soar and ascend in his soul, as he gazed.[110]

A similar empathetic melting into nature has been enjoyed by Thomas Ashe:

> O sweet communion of the hills,
> Lulling the soul to peace!
>
> . . .
>
> As in the glens I rove,
> Nature she is my love;
> The heavens down to me lean:
> My life melts like a mist
> Into the amethyst
> Of skies that brood above,
> Or peer the hills between.[111]

To several of our poets such experiences seem unfavorable to belief in a transcendent personal deity. It is easier to believe, with John Westland Marston, that

> . . . still, as taught bards' earliest lays,
> A spirit-life in Nature dwells,
> And mystic power the soul doth raise
> When sunset fades or ocean swells.[112]

In *The Luggie*, David Gray bows before an

> . . . All-beholding, All-informing God
> Invisible, and ONLY through effects
> Known and belov'd. . . .
> Soul of the incomplete vitality
> In atom and in man! Soul of all Worlds![113]

Observe the drift from "beholding" to "informing" and then to the World

[110] *Poems*, pp. 121, 124–125. See also p. 147 for another instance of this solar mysticism.

[111] *Poems*, p. 273.

[112] *Dramatic and Poetical Works*, II, 361.

[113] *Miles*, VI, 363. In *The Luggie*, Gray desires to express what he called "the pure, beautiful theology of Kingsley." (Harriet Jay, *Robert Buchanan*, p. 75.) Here, however, he sounds more like Thomson's *Seasons*.

Soul. Belief in a divine vitality which can be known and loved only in its works inevitably leads to pantheism. Thus the nature into which we observed Ashe melting a moment ago speaks:

I am war and peace,
I am life and death,
All bears my yoke:
I, in a night,
Touch the green rice with blight;
. . .
Yet me to kindness stirs
My puny man:
His heart is great,
To bear the strokes of fate:
. . .
With arctic cold
I temper him
And tropic heat.
Juggling is vain:
Me God or Nature call,
The thing is plain:
All's I, and I am all.

This mixture of Emerson's *Brahma* and Swinburne's *Hertha* would indeed be plain enough did not Ashe immediately plunge us into bewilderment by adding:

On Him I lean, in Him I live:
She [Nature] cannot hide my God away.—
Nature, I ponder all you say;
You such wise lessons give.[114]

Whatever nature's lessons may be they do not, for this group as a whole, do much to curb man's drive toward boundlessness. Nature usually makes him feel important. Bennett addresses the ocean:

World-girdler, how the earth's great hearts
 Their awful greatness win from thee!
Lo! to what height their stature starts,
 They who have been thy brood, O Sea![115]

And here is William How in the Alps:

Oh! man's desire is of the infinite:
And here is greatness which flings back the bounds
Ev'n to the farthest that may be on earth.
. . .

[114] *Poems*, pp. 280–281. This poem, *Bettws-Y-Coed*, is dated 1879.

[115] *Poems*, p. 449.

Say'st thou the might of these stupendous things
Makes thee feel little? Scorn upon thy feeling!
It is the very pinnacle of greatness
To sit upon the mountain-throne, and grasp
The might and grandeur of these grandest forms,
And make them all thine own.[116]

One thinks of Byron: "Ye elements! in whose ennobling stir / I feel myself exalted." The divinity of man outstrips the divinity of nature. His "royal task," says poor John Sterling, is to develop the silent, hidden forces of nature into full strength and beauty.[117] Why, Leighton asks, should we feel insignificant when we gaze upon the stars? They have no memory, no sense of right and wrong, no emotion or aspiration. We must not merely believe but "*know* and *feel*" in our very blood that

... this that sees and comprehends
Is greater than that seen and comprehended.[118]

Science, then, has not prevented these poets from using a quasi-religious kind of nature-experience as a channel for the outrush of man's spirit toward boundlessness. There are many other channels. The official favorite, as we have seen, is the form of self-expansion known as "serving mankind," which mingles so ambiguously with Christian charity. Another is the attempted sanctification of commercial progress in an atmosphere of intense individualistic competition. Closely related to the foregoing is nationalistic pride and its culmination in warfare. Bennett addresses England:

So great thou art; so greater thou shalt grow,
Doing the will of Him who bade Thee be
Foremost among the nations.[119]

For subjectivists like Bennett, the surest way in which Englishmen can discover God's will in such matters is to consult their own patriotic hearts. John Westland Marston condemns war of "conquest, gain, or hate," but declares that God, "Being Lord of Justice, still is Lord of Hosts." In a *just* war, then, we may

Strike down even man for what makes man divine,
Nor disobey the God to save the shrine.[120]

The historic faith does not deny the possibility of a just war. But to the extent

[116] *Poems*, p. 17. These lines were written in 1846. How's habit of dating all his poems makes it possible to say that he moves from a romantic to a Christian view of nature, and finally to a gospel of human service in which nature is of little or no importance.

[117] *Miles*, IV, 183.

[118] *Ibid.*, V, 83.

[119] *Poems*, p. 432.

[120] *Dramatic and Poetical Works*, II, 347.

that the Lord of Hosts becomes merely a pugnacious feeling in man's heart the criterion of justice becomes subjective.

The substitution of immanence for transcendence may also romanticize the Christian view of sexual love. When Arthur Hallam was courting Anna Wintour in Italy he relieved his feelings in a Christian-Platonic love-mysticism derived mainly from *La Vita Nuova*. He believes "that Woman's Love was sent / To heal man's tainted heart, and chasten him for Heaven."[121] But what if man's heart, far from being tainted, is itself heavenly? In that case sexual love loses its potentially sacramental quality and becomes "spiritual" per se as a means of satisfying the drive toward personal infinitude. We have already observed a passage in *Aurora Leigh* which seems to point in this direction.[122] Although later chapters will provide clearer and more numerous examples, we may infer from *The Saint's Tragedy* that Kingsley detests celibacy, not because he thinks it contrary to the will of God, but because it denies the essential divinity of human nature.

For a poet, however, the most cherished means of personal enlargement, and the one which he is most eager to regard as essentially religious, is poetry itself. Of course the poet, like any good Victorian, should work for his fellow-men; but the benefits which he confers upon them are so immense as to mingle his altruism with a strong infusion of pride. What some of these little men say about the office and function of the bard would make Shelley himself blush. "Poor, despised, the Poet knows himself God-chosen great on earth."[123] Let no one scorn him as a purveyor of idle fictions:

> . . . Fiction! Poetry
> Lives but by truth. Truth is its heart. Bards write
> The life of soul,—the only life.

"Poets and Sages"—there is not much difference—enjoy a kind of immortality to which no ordinary man can aspire, for they

> . . . perpetuate
> Their being in the words that, age by age,
> Fulfil their lofty ends! Their speech sublime,
> Inspires the general heart; their beauty steals
> Brightening and purifying, through the air
> Of common life . . .
>
> . . .

[121] *Writings*, p. 20.
[122] See above, p. 59.
[123] W. C. Bennett, *Poems*, p. 191.

. . And thus the Sons
Of Genius have prerogative to stand
Exempt from Time's decree.[124]

Gazing hopefully into the future, Bennett exhorts his infant son:

Walk thou a poet among men,
A prophet sent of God,
That hallowed grow the common ways
Of earth which thou hast trod;
That truth in thy eternal words
Sit throned in might sublime,
And love and mercy, from thy tongue,
For ever preach to Time.[125]

The poet, then, is a prophet in the specifically religious sense of the term. He is also, according to Emily Pfeiffer, a priest, who

Builds with his breath a house of high repute,
Wherein he chants the office, for the mute
Appealing ones, who at his feet are bowed.[126]

With a scornful glance at the less ennobling sort of sacerdotalism, Thomas Ashe also affirms the priesthood of the poet:

Him the Academy
Of heaven's elect—him, least,—
Sets above rules, and seeks.
He is, too, priest;
And marriage bands he knits;
His infant baptisms
And hands on the young head,
His requiems for the dead,
Are real, not shams.
On throne episcopal he sits;
He blesses wine and bread.
. . .
Idle? He toils as few:
His heart is stout:
He lives for you,
For you he daily dies;
And who comes to him buys
Red wine and milk, without
Money and without price.[127]

Interpreted in relation to the sacramental symbolism of the passage, the last

[124] J. W. Marston, *Dramatic and Poetical Works*, II, 335, 337.
[125] *Poems*, p. 21. [126] *Under the Aspens*, p. 111. [127] *Poems*, p. 281.

five lines broadly hint that the poet's function is not merely priestly but divine.

Our embarrassment at such bumptiousness is intensified by the fact that of the thirty-five poets glanced at in this chapter not one can be credited with high accomplishment and not more than five or six with tolerable competence. The contrast between their toplofty notion of what it is to be a poet and their inability to write poetry is glaring. To be sure, they are merely trying to embody the contemporary stereotype of what a poet should be. Thousands of Victorian readers hoped to find in "idealistic" verse a substitute for the faith which they were losing. That Bennett, Swain, and Ashe were hugely popular in their day is a shocking fact from the literary if not from the religious point of view, but it betokens a hunger for something better. Among subjectivist Christians there was need for a poet of real imaginative power and finished craftsmanship who could both preach and sing, rebuke the evils of his time and flatter its complacency, express the humanitarian aspirations of Englishmen but not (like the social-protest poets) imperil the *status quo*, present contemporary problems so eloquently as to create an illusion of having solved them, and above all satisfy the romantic impulse as richly as it could be satisfied without overt hostility to the Christian tradition. We are about to remind ourselves that the one poet who almost perfectly fulfilled these requirements was Tennyson. Browning, who also claims a separate chapter, gave similar satisfaction to a smaller body of readers in a more subtle and ambiguous way. He will provide a transition from the relatively mild subjectivists of this group to the bolder spirits of Chapter VII.

Chapter Five

TENNYSON

IT IS NOT EASY to recapture the precise quality of enthusiasm which Tennyson aroused in his more intelligent Victorian readers. "The best and bravest of my contemporaries," said James Anthony Froude,

> determined to have done with insincerity, to find ground under their feet, to let the uncertain remain uncertain, but to learn how much and what we could honestly regard as true, and to believe that and live by it. Tennyson became the voice of this feeling in poetry, Carlyle in what was called prose. . . . Tennyson's Poems, the group of Poems which closed with *In Memoriam*, became to many of us what *The Christian Year* was to orthodox Churchmen. We read them, and they became part of our minds, the expression, in exquisite language, of the feelings which were working in ourselves.[1]

Although Froude might not wish these words to be applied to the poems of later years, one doubts the possibility of dismembering Tennyson into "real" and "laureate," or "early" and "late." Even in his querulous and disappointed old age his fundamental beliefs and aspirations were those of his youth. He was always a loyal though often a discouraged alumnus of the Apostles Club. Essentially, what Froude admired in him was the attempt to be confused earnestly and hopefully, to regard incertitude not as a source of despair but as a challenge and an inspiration. This spirit is as strong in *Merlin and the Gleam* as in *Ulysses*.

It is strong also in *The Voyage*, a poem of the 1864 volume. Here the basic metaphor is that of a shipload of idealists sailing in pursuit of a constantly elusive "fair Vision" which they imagine sometimes as Fancy and sometimes as Virtue, or Knowledge, or Heavenly Hope, or Liberty. The endless, fruitless, undefined quest leads them through the flowery tropics into "colder climes":

> Now mate is blind and captain lame,
> And half the crew are sick or dead,
> But, blind or lame or sick or sound,
> We follow that which flies before;
> We know the merry world is round,
> And we may sail for evermore.

[1] Quoted by Amy Cruse, *The Victorians and Their Reading*, p. 187.

In *Locksley Hall*, that railway-train world which is to "spin forever down the ringing grooves of change" has no destination, Ulysses in the great monologue neither knows nor cares where he is going, and the young mariner in *Merlin and the Gleam* has no idea of what he is being exhorted to chase.[2] But in these poems the quest at least moves horizontally, not round and round and round the merry world as in *The Voyage*. To many Victorians, however, this circularity would seem noble rather than pathetic or absurd. F. T. Palgrave called *The Voyage* "a brilliantly descriptive allegory" of "Life as Energy, in the great ethical sense of the word,—Life as the pursuit of the Ideal"; and when Henry Sidgwick read the poem he exclaimed, "What growth there is in the man mentally! How he has caught the spirit of the age!"[3]

Sidgwick generalized too sweepingly: *The Voyage* by no means expresses the spirit of Newman, or Mill, or Arnold, or Swinburne. On the whole, however, Tennyson's poems do indeed reflect the dominant central trend of the thought of the period on religious as on most other matters. They provide, says Frederic Harrison, "exquisitely graceful restatements of the current theology of the broad-Churchmen of the school of F. D. Maurice and Jowett."[4] If we make due allowance for Tennyson's personal peculiarities and for the looseness and variability of Broad Churchmanship, we may profitably use Harrison's statement as an interpretative clue. For Tennyson, the deepest religious thinkers of the age were such men as Maurice, Jowett, Stanley, Robertson, Martineau. With them, he felt strong if somewhat uneasy admiration for Carlyle. The leading religious liberals were Tennyson's personal friends and the warmest champions of his wisdom. For Kingsley, *In Memoriam* was "the noblest Christian poem which England has produced for two centuries;"[5] and Robertson found in it "the most satisfying things that have ever been said on the future state." Jowett, who thought Tennyson an intuitive Hegelian, perceived in the German seer's *Philosophy of History* "just 'the increasing purpose that through the ages runs' buried under a heap of categories."[6]

At other times Jowett felt that poets were even wiser than metaphysicians, for "Poetry may solve the riddle of the Universe. Philosophy and science never can."[7] In the preceding chapter we observed that subjectivist Christians

[2] The fact that Tennyson defined the Gleam as "the higher poetic imagination" corroborates rather than refutes this statement.

[3] P. F. Baum, *Tennyson Sixty Years After*, p. 258.

[4] *Tennyson, Ruskin, Mill, and Other Literary Estimates*, p. 10.

[5] Baum, *op. cit.*, p. 132.

[6] Hallam Tennyson, *Alfred Lord Tennyson: A Memoir*, I, 298*n*, 425. Hereafter this book will be cited as *Memoir*.

[7] Charles Tennyson, *Alfred Tennyson*, p. 279.

magnified the prophetic functions and powers of the poet, whose creative imagination grasps eternal truths which transcend the man-made formularies of theology. At Cambridge, Tennyson imbibed this congenial doctrine from the Apostles, especially from Arthur Hallam, and in 1830 he proclaimed it in *The Poet*. On this point, however, Tennyson was divided against himself. Should he give his golden apple to Pallas or to Aphrodite? (The claims of Hera were never formidable.) He felt strongly drawn toward sensuous beauty, but unlike Paris in *Oenone* he felt even more strongly drawn toward helpful wisdom. He was never a thoroughgoing aesthete in the art-for-art's-sake sense. When in 1869 he condemned that cult as "truest Lord of Hell" he was not utterly denying any of his early hankerings. He had always believed that the highest aim of poetry is to do people good. Nevertheless he would have been glad, especially at the outset of his career, to persuade himself that pure noninstrumental loveliness was socially beneficent, and that the artist can best serve his fellows by giving them shapes of beauty, imaginative creations unsullied by vulgar preachment. And yet the distinction between social-minded and wickedly irresponsible aestheticism was difficult to maintain. In *The Hesperides* the golden apple—clearly the symbol of art—is its own excuse for being,

> Holy and bright, round and full, bright and blest,
> Mellowed in a land of rest;

whereas in *Oenone* it is very wrong of Paris to give the apple to Venus. In the same spirit Tennyson felt compelled to revise *The Lotos-Eaters* moralistically by adding that Lucretian chorus in which the happy aesthetes betray their selfish indolence.

Lecky seemed to remember that "Among nineteenth century poets he placed Keats on the highest pinnacle," but Hallam Tennyson reports his father as saying: "One must distinguish Keats, Shelley and Byron from the great sage poets of all time, who are both great thinkers and great artists, like Æschylus, Shakespeare, Dante, and Goethe."[8] Both recollections are probably accurate. On one side of his nature, Tennyson would have been well content to be a "landscape-lover, lord of language," serving mankind through the delight of images and melodies; but like Keats he was torn between the "philosopher" and the "versifying pet lamb," between Ulysses and the lotos-eaters. His soul would gladly luxuriate in *The Palace of Art*, yet she cannot do so without feeling like "a glorious devil." "Trench said to me, when we were at Trinity together, 'Tennyson, we cannot live in

[8] *Memoir*, II, 287.

art.' . . . 'The Palace of Art' is the embodiment of my own belief that the Godlike life is with man and for man."[9] It will not do to say that the aesthetic impulse was fundamental and the didacticism a reluctant concession to environmental pressure. The drive toward preachment came from within as strongly as from without; it was his "own belief" and inseparable from his artistry. Despite some wavering and reluctance, Tennyson devoted his career to the song of "the Godlike life."

This song included all the characteristic notes of Broad Churchmanship. The poems amply corroborate his son's recollections: "His creed, he always said, he would not formulate, for people would not understand him if he did. . . . He thought, with Arthur Hallam, 'that the essential feelings of religion subsist in the utmost diversity of forms;' that 'different language does not always imply different opinions, nor different opinions any difference in *real* faith.' "[10] Tennyson holds that Love is God rather than that God is Love. His religion is wholly an expression of his personal feelings; all the evidence is internal. Since Christianity is the most beautiful and ethically potent way in which man can express all that is highest in himself, it deserves adherence. "There's more in Christianity than people now think," he assured Allingham.[11] Nevertheless, like all religions and all philosophies it provides no more than partial glimpses of the unknown truth; hence dogmatic formulations of its insights should be opposed by "honest doubt." Any creed should be respected to the extent, and only to the extent, that it expresses "the essential feelings of religion." There is much to be said for Taoism (*The Ancient Sage*) and for the more enlightened sort of Mohammedanism (*Akbar's Dream*). But the former poem makes Lao-tze speak in the accents of Benjamin Jowett, and in the latter Akbar, with his vision of a universal creedless church, is a mixture of Lessing and Dr. Thomas Arnold.

In short, "Tennyson loves the spirit of Christianity, but hates many of the dogmas." He maintains an obscure reverence toward Jesus Christ but shrinks from asserting that He possesses any divinity other than that of "the Highest Human Nature." He repudiates predestination and eternal punishment. Though his horror of the latter doctrine was deeply serious, he "had a story of a Lincolnshire farmer who said, when he came out of church—'burned for ever and ever! I don't believe that: no constitution could stand it.' "[12] Equally characteristic of the liberal position are his efforts to authen-

[9] *Ibid.*, I, 118–119. [10] *Ibid.*, p. 309.

[11] William Allingham, *A Diary*, p. 163. Hereafter this book will be cited as *Allingham*.

[12] *Ibid.*, pp. 149, 328, 378.

ticate religion by interpreting evolution as a scheme of moral and spiritual progress.

Despite a fondness for mulling over the mysteries of the spirit, Tennyson also resembles most members of the Broad Church party in subordinating "the first and great commandment" to the second. Religion existed for the sake of practical goodness; spiritual union with God was less important than serving mankind. In *The Golden Year*, old James finds Leonard's poem about bringing in the millennium by fulfilling "the mission of the Cross" too visionary,

> . . . but well I know
> That unto him who works, and feels he works,
> This same grand year is ever at the doors.

It is the gospel of Carlyle and Kingsley. Maurice is hailed as one of "that honest few / Who give the fiend himself his due;" but when he visits Farringford he will talk with Tennyson not of liberal theology but first of the Crimean War and then of

> . . . dearer matters,
> Dear to the man that is dear to God,—
>
> How best to help the slender store,
> How mend the dwellings of the poor,
> How gain in life, as life advances,
> Valor and charity more and more.

The sermon preached before the haughty squire in *Aylmer's Field* combines Tennyson's personal Vere-de-Vere complex with the indignation of a Christian Socialist.

The humanitarian element in Tennyson's thought may seem to conflict with his love of the past and his dread of all sudden and violent change. There is indeed a wide chasm between such lyrics as *You Ask Me Why* and the opening section of *Maud*. On the whole, however, both Tennyson's liberalism and his Toryism are comfortably contained within that Victorian Compromise of which Broad Churchmanship is the religious expression. In political and social matters Tennyson usually found himself at the extreme right of a group whose extreme left was cautiously melioristic rather than radical.[13]

On occasion the Broad Churchman can be extremely narrow in opposing

[13] There are sharply radical implications in the work of the social-protest poets described in the preceding chapter, but the compromisers were able to absorb the humanitarianism of these rebels and screen out the potentially explosive elements.

religious views which are more precise than his. Tennyson's disapproval of Catholicism, both Roman and Anglican, is intense. An antiritualist, he does not like to hear

> The snowy-banded, dilettante,
> Delicate-handed priest intone.

Rascally King Pellam in *Balin and Balan* is a proto-Puseyite: in his chapel one "scarce could spy the Christ for Saints." The original scheme for the entire *Idylls* was a sort of latitudinarian *Faerie Queene* in which King Arthur stood for "Religious Faith" and the Round Table for "liberal institutions." There were to be two very different Guineveres, a good one representing primitive Christianity and a bad one representing Roman Catholicism.[14] The final work, though of course much less systematically allegorical, remains loyal to the general spirit of the early plan. In *The Holy Grail*, the quest is treated with deep reverence: Tennyson is far too imaginative to be incapable of feeling what mystical experience must mean to mystical people. The essential thought of the poem, however, is that the grail-quest is a corrupting influence because it diverts the knights from their proper task of human service just when the Round Table has begun to crack:

> . . . How often, O my knights,
> Your places being vacant at my side,
> This chance of noble deeds will come and go
> Unchallenged, while you follow wandering fires
> Lost in a quagmire!

Arthur himself is far too busy to indulge in so visionary an adventure. While his knights are taking their impossible vow he himself is hard at work smoking out a nest of bandits who have been outraging maidens. Macaulay, at whose request the Duke of Argyll persuaded Tennyson to write *The Holy Grail*, would have liked most of it had he lived to read it.

This poem illustrates Tennyson's distaste for Christian asceticism, which he associates chiefly with Catholicism. The emotions of the holiest character, Percivale's cloistered sister, are merely the result of thwarted human love. Though priggish as regards sex, Tennyson rivals Kingsley in his detestation of celibacy. As for asceticism in a more general sense, *St. Simeon Stylites* may be read as a legitimate and acute study of that most insidious of Christian snares, the pride of humility. Pretty certainly, however, the poet regarded the imagined speaker as a typical representative of Catholic sainthood.

We are again reminded of Kingsley by Tennyson's fondness for using the

[14] *Memoir*, II, 123.

past as a means of commenting upon the religious disputes of the present. The theme of his trilogy of historical dramas is the struggle between Papal Rome and England, instinctively Protestant by a sort of prevenient grace even when nominally Catholic. The poet explains that in *Queen Mary* "are described the final downfall of Roman Catholicism in England, and the dawning of a new age; for after the era of priestly domination comes the era of the freedom of the individual." According to the stage directions, typical *Protestant Murmurs* are "What sort of brothers then be those that lust / To burn each other?" while typical *Catholic Murmurs* are "Liar! dissembler! traitor! to the fire!" In *Harold*, of course, both the contending forces are technically Catholic; but the Normans are a tricky Ultramontane lot, strong for the Pope, saints, relics, and all such frippery, while the Saxons are good muscular Christians. The fact that Edward the Confessor is half Norman explains why he is superstitious and much *too* saintly, in the Tractarian manner of King Pellam. His piety is selfish—"A conscience for his own soul, not his realm." Stigand, the Saxon Archbishop, is a ruggedly comic, this-worldly old fellow, a sort of Friar Tuck or Fra Lippo Lippi. No believer in the Apostolic Succession, he delights in his uncanonical consecration derived from an Antipope. Harold himself declares that he "ever hated monks," and he bequeathes to future generations of Englishmen "a legacy of war against the Pope." He speaks as a precursor of nineteenth-century latitudinarianism:

> O God! I cannot help it, but at times
> They seem to me too narrow, all the faiths
> Of this grown world of ours, whose baby eye
> Saw them sufficient.

In that consciously Browningesque monologue *Sir John Oldcastle, Lord Cobham*, the brave old heretic talks Lollardry in the accents of a Victorian liberal who has been disturbed by the reestablishment of the Roman hierarchy in England, *Quanta Cura*, the *Syllabus Errorum*, Infallibility, and the crypto-Popery of Anglican ritualists. He repudiates that "hard celibacy, / Sworn to be veriest ice of pureness," which melts into fornication or such practices as St. Paul blushed to specify. Rather than bow down before the "dead wood" of a wayside Calvary, he will worship the living wood of the "green boscage, work of God," or the "living water" of the mountain spring which says in honest English, not in Latin, "He that thirsteth, come and drink." But for him there is a tree more sacred than those of the forest. He remembers the heresy-trial at which

> ... I anger'd Arundel asking me
> To worship Holy Cross! I spread mine arms,
> God's work, I said, a cross of flesh and blood,
> And holier.

Thus he appeals from unholy Church to holy Nature and yet holier Man. As for penance, "What profits an ill priest / Between me and my God?" He would not confess his sins even to an Apostle. He denies the full doctrine of Transubstantiation, interpreting the Eucharist to mean that

> He veil'd Himself in flesh, and now He veils
> His flesh in bread, body and bread together.

Tennyson's own reverence for "that mystery / Where God-in-man is one with man-in-God" excluded any taint of popery. His son describes what seems to have been the poet's last Communion, some three months before his death: "On June 29 [1892] the Rector of Freshwater, Dr. Merriman, administered the Sacrament to us all in my father's study. The service was very solemn. Before he partook of the Communion he quoted his own words, put into Cranmer's mouth [in *Queen Mary*]:

> It is but a communion, not a mass:
> No sacrifice but a life-giving feast;

impressing upon the Rector that he could not take it at all, unless it were administered in that sense."[15] Dr. Merriman made no objection to this enrichment of the Liturgy.

But Tennyson's hostility to Catholicism was not maintained unwaveringly throughout his career. In such early poems as *Saint Agnes' Eve*, *Sir Galahad*, and the original version of *Mariana in the South*, he tentatively savors the Tractarian mood. In old age his dread of spiritual chaos enhanced his appreciation of the firm, definite faith and heartfelt spirituality of such Roman Catholic friends as Aubrey de Vere and W. G. Ward, "most generous of Ultramontanes." The latter he admired not only as "loyal in the following of thy Lord" but as a deft polemic fencer against materialism who claimed to have logical reasons for those beliefs toward which Tennyson's feelings vainly groped. The old poet disapproved of the expulsion of the religious orders from France: even popery might be better than complete unbelief and "the red fool-fury of the Seine." "People must have some religion. . . . I have often thought the day of Rome would come again," he said in 1872.[16] But reflections of this milder attitude in the poems are rare and

[15] *Memoir*, II, 412.

[16] *Allingham*, p. 215

insignificant.[17] They are heavily outweighed by the innumerable cases in which, throughout his career, he displays the familiar liberal illiberality.

Beset on the one side by Rome and Oxford and on the other by complete infidelity, subjectivist Christians would have been glad to maintain an offensive-defensive alliance with that stricter Protestantism from which they had deviated. Outwardly at least it was often possible to do so. The theology of cultivated Evangelicals was becoming more and more latitudinarian. Most of the leading Broad Churchmen were themselves ex-Evangelicals; when confronted by a Newman or a Mill, they remembered the pious language of their parents. That they attached new meanings to the old words was a fact easily ignored for the sake of Protestant unity. As for Dissenters, all but those liberal brainy ones who were essentially members of the Broad Church party could be dismissed as intellectual noncombatants. On the whole, however, there was more antagonism than friendship between the older and the newer Protestantism. Both groups were moving in the same direction, but at such different speeds that their fundamental kinship was considerably obscured. To a genuine Evangelical no less than to a genuine Puseyite, Maurice, Jowett, Colenso, or Stanley hardly deserved the name of Christian. The liberals in turn felt hindered in their efforts to subjectivize religion by the fundamentalism of the Saints.

Tennyson's attitude toward the Evangelicals reflects the ambiguity of this situation. When forced to become a clergyman, his unfortunate father seems to have lost whatever religion he may have possessed; but the poet's mother was a gently pious Evangelical, and his aunt, Mrs. Bourne, a very strict Calvinist whose influence may explain the fact that his contributions to *Poems by Two Brothers* show some concern about original sin. In the *Supposed Confessions of a Second-Rate Sensitive Mind* he wistfully longs to regain the faith which he learned at his mother's knee. This desire must have been felt even in later years; at all events his dread of complete negation occasionally impels him to use language more technically pious than his actual beliefs would otherwise justify. The deathbed of *The May Queen* is redolent of Evangelicalism, and nothing suggests that the author disagrees with the imagined speaker.

Tennyson's most characteristic religious poetry is of course implicitly hostile to strict Evangelicalism, and his theology was sometimes criticized adversely by rigid Protestants. On one occasion even his moral standards were impugned. A temperance society objected because his patriotic song

[17] See for example *The Wreck* (1885)—"I cling to the Catholic Cross once more, to the Faith that saves"; and *The Sisters* (1880)—"They found her beating the hard Protestant doors."

Hands All Round began with the words, "First drink a health." His son Hallam was commissioned to explain in the press "that the common cup has in all ages been the sacred symbol of unity, and that my father only used the word 'drink' in relation to this symbol."[18] Nevertheless, Tennyson's remarkable gift for enveloping unorthodox ideas in a solemnly edifying atmosphere rendered his "message" acceptable to all but the most precise. By 1860 he had convinced his mother, who by this time was reading hardly anything but the Bible and Dr. Cumming's *Prophecy*, that God had answered her prayers of many years "to urge thee to employ the talent he has given thee, by endeavouring to impress the precepts of his Holy Word on the minds of others."[19]

From about 1880 onward, however, Tennyson displays a slight tendency to regard infidelity as a regrettable but natural reaction against the narrow and cruel bigotry of Evangelical Protestantism. A stout Churchman of his own sort, he prefers to attack Nonconformity rather than Anglican Evangelicalism when writing in this vein. In *Despair*, the most striking example, a man addresses the Calvinistic Dissenting minister who has resuscitated him after an attempt to drown himself. The speaker and his wife had once been pillars of this same minister's chapel, "nursed in the drear nightfold of your fatalist creed." Horrified at last by such teachings, they renounced *all* creeds,

> And we broke away from the Christ, our human brother and friend,
> For He spoke, or it seem'd that He spoke, of a hell without help, without end.

They stuffed themselves with the "horrible infidel writings" of "the new dark ages . . . of the popular press," but they found stark unbelief even worse than Calvinist belief: "We had past from a cheerless night to the glare of a drearier day." And so "we poor orphans of nothing" made a suicide pact, "Knowing the love we used to believe everlasting would die." The woman drowns, but the man is swept ashore. He tells the minister that he has sometimes glimpsed a more loving God than that of the chapel, "But the God of love and of hell together—they cannot be thought." Despite this glimmer of insight he has no real hope, scorns the preacher's efforts to console him, and promises to attempt suicide again at the next opportunity.

The mother in *Rizpah* appeals from Calvinistic theology to what the Bible tells her of the loving God, the merciful Saviour:

> Election, Election and Reprobation—it's all very well,
> But I go tonight to my boy, and I shall not find him in hell.
> For I cared so much for my boy that the Lord has look'd into my care,
> And He means me I'm sure to be happy with Will, I know not where.

[18] *Memoir*, II, 265. His father, of course, enjoyed his port very much. [19] *Ibid.*, I, 265, 452.

In *The Northern Cobbler*, a Methodist shoemaker tells how he conquered the liquor habit, not through the inconsistent teachings of the chapel, but through the forgiving love of his wife, whom he had kicked in drunken rage:

> An' Muggins 'e preäch'd o' hell-fire an' the loov o' God fur men,
> An' then upo' comin' awaäy Sally gied me a kiss ov' 'ersen.

But Tennyson does not make much use of this device for simultaneously rebuking unbelief and old-fashioned Protestantism.

Thus far we have considered Tennyson primarily as the bard of an ecclesiastical party. When we call a Victorian a Broad Churchman, however, we of course describe his religious position much less specifically than when we call him an Evangelical or an Anglo-Catholic. We know a good deal about Tennyson's opinions, but his spiritual center still eludes us. What did he actually believe as a modern man in search of some sort of positive suprapersonal reliance? Let us abandon at the outset any hope of finding a precise answer to that question. His ideas as well as his moods are different in different poems, and the inconsistencies appear in each of the "periods" into which students have vainly tried to divide his career. He would have us respect him as a thinker, but when we ask him *what* he thinks he answers, "You must remember that I am a poet." In many of the poems most important for interpretation of his thought he speaks through the lips of imagined characters; and it is when the mask seems thinnest, as in *Maud*, that he insists most urgently on the dramatic character of the piece. Wholly to accept these disclaimers is to abandon all hope of getting at his beliefs; wholly to reject them is to forget that Tennyson, uncertain of his own ideas, sometimes wonders how he would look when costumed in the ideas of others. Probably no one would hesitate to infer that in the two *Locksley Hall* poems, despite the figment of a story, the poet speaks for himself. If we avoid the common error of supposing that the famous optimistic prophecy in the earlier poem represents the hopes of 1842 rather than a vision of the Cambridge days which the speaker is now vainly trying to recapture, we may say that both poems represent much the same attempt to preserve the obligatory progress-cult in the face of discouragement, but that the pessimism of the later piece is more embittered and querulous. Having reached this conclusion, we turn to the *Memoir* and read: "My father said that the old man in the second *Locksley Hall* had a stronger faith in God and in human goodness than he had had in his youth; but he had also endeavoured to give the moods of despondency which are caused by the decreased energy of life."[20] If *Locksley Hall Sixty Years After* is more optimistic than *Locksley Hall,* and seems more pessimistic merely because the senile poet is deliberately trying, as a dramatic experiment, to sound a little senile, one is tempted to throw down one's cards and rise from the table, protesting that it is impossible to play the game of criticism with so slippery a man.

In Memoriam, central for our inquiry, may seem free from such ambiguities. Here at least he speaks his own mind in response to the most significant experience of his life. And yet Tennyson, reading the poem to Knowles, said: "It is a very impersonal poem as well as personal. There is more about myself in 'Ulysses.' . . . The different moods of sorrow as in a drama are dramatically given. . . . 'I' is not always the author speaking of himself, but the voice of the human race speaking through him."[21] Even in this work, then, he thwarts the reader's inclination to suppose that he seriously means what he says. In XXXVII, after an important group of lyrics on the relation between private faith and revealed religion, Melpomene apologizes to Urania for having "darkened sanctities with song":

> For I am but an earthly Muse,
> And owning but a little art
> To lull with song an aching heart,
> And render human love his dues.

Similarly in XLVII, after rejecting absorption into "the general Soul" in favor of personal immortality, he reminds us that these lays are merely

> Short swallow-flights of song, that dip
> Their wings in tears, and skim away.

The familiar sequence on the doubts raised by evolutionary science is anxiously broken off in LVII:

> Peace; come away: the song of woe
> Is after all an earthly song.
> Peace; come away: we do him wrong
> To sing so wildly: let us go.

He dodges every vital issue that he raises, yet would have us believe that "Like Paul with beasts, I fought with death."

"It's too hopeful, this poem, more than I am myself," said Tennyson to Knowles. "I think of adding another to it, a speculative one, bringing out the thoughts of the 'Higher Pantheism' and showing that all the arguments are about as good on one side as another, and thus throw man back more on

[20] *Memoir,* II, 329. [21] *Ibid.,* I, 304–305.

the primitive impulses and feelings."[22] It is probably safe to assume that we come closest to Tennyson's real thought when he is not thinking—when he is least systematically argumentative about theology and metaphysics and relies most completely on his subjective emotions. His creed begins and ends in "I have felt."

He told Allingham that "his belief rested on two things—'a Chief Intelligence and Immortality.'" For him the latter was by far the more important, but a God was needed to validate the conviction "that death will not end my existence." Although he sometimes toys with notions of metempsychosis ending in ultimate absorption into a reservoir of undifferentiated spirit, his real desire was for endless personal survival. "What I want is assurance of immortality. . . . If I ceased to believe in any chance of another life, and of a great Personality somewhere in the Universe, I should not care a pin for anything. . . . I could not eat my dinner without a belief in immortality. If I didn't believe that, I'd go down immediately and jump off Richmond Bridge."[23]

> . . . The Good, the True, the Pure, the Just,
> Take the charm "For ever" from them, and they crumble into dust.

Confronted by the possibility that mortal existence may after all be meaningless, he shakes off the morbid fear with a desperate effort:

> What is it all, if we all of us end but in being our own corpse-coffins at last,
> Swallowed in Vastness, lost in Silence, drowned in the deeps of a meaningless Past?
>
> What but a murmur of gnats in the gloom, or a moment's anger of bees in their hive?—
> Peace, let it be! for I loved him, and love him for ever: the dead are not dead, but alive.

We should not, however, infer from *Vastness*, *In the Valley of Cauteretz*, or even *In Memoriam* that Tennyson's craving for immortality was chiefly the consequence of his love for Arthur Hallam. Even if his friend had never existed, the master-passion would have been no less intense. The tragedy at Vienna provided a means of expressing his hopes and fears on a question of almost obsessive importance to himself. It also, however, confirmed him in the feeling that the right answer to this question was to be found by believing in the eternity of love.

We do not know why his desire for immortality was so passionate. Perhaps it was his strongest belief because it was also his deepest dread. His mind

[22] *Ibid.*, p. 317. [23] *Allingham*, pp. 62, 185, 215, 329. See also *Memoir*, II, 35.

did not dwell upon union with God in a state of celestial bliss: the afterlife was necessary in order to make this life bearable. Nevertheless belief in immortality and belief in a loving God were interdependent:

> The wish, that of the living whole
> No life may fail beyond the grave,
> Derives it not from what we have
> The likest God within the soul?

To paraphrase, is not the desire of eternal life—not only for ourselves and our beloved dead, but for the whole human race—authenticated by the fact that it is an expression of love, the divine principle of the universe? But the question is circular: the only unimpeachable evidence for cosmic love is human love. Let us trace Tennyson's thought through the climactic sequence of *In Memoriam*. "Love is and was my lord and king." By deifying the noblest feeling of his own breast he feels able to believe that "all is well." (CXXVI.) This faith is identified with the official Victorian faith that "social truth shall spread, / And justice," despite the revolutionary upheavals of 1848. Hallam, smiling down upon the tumult from the abode where the eternal are, confirms our confidence that "all is well." (CXXVII.) Next, this love which impels belief in social progress is identified with the love which conquers death and thus confers an eternity of human improvement. (CXXVIII.) But the basis of both these loves, we find in CXXIX, is Tennyson's love for Hallam,

> Known and unknown, human, divine;
> Sweet human hand and lip and eye;
> Dear heavenly friend that canst not die,
> Mine, mine forever, ever mine;
>
> Strange friend, past, present, and to be;
> Loved deeplier, darklier understood;
> Behold, I dream a dream of good,
> And mingle all the world with thee.

These lines suggest a tendency to confuse Hallam with the Second Person of the Trinity. The thought is continued into the final lyric of the sequence, where Hallam's spirit—now not unlike the Third Person—is felt as immanent in nature, giving Tennyson assurance of an all-pervasive divine Love.

Clearly, then, Tennyson's belief in a loving God and in immortality derives from those inward feelings which were given their sharpest focus by Arthur's death. He knows that this belief cannot be supported by rational proof. "We have but faith: we cannot know." This faith, however, is by no means passive or quietistic: it demands a strong effort of the will. He who seeks confirmation of all that is best in himself through spiritual communion with the dead must be "with divine affections bold." Does "divine" imply that these affections are given us by God, or that divinity consists of our highest human volitions? The reader is not sure, and neither is the poet. If we are to believe in the extrapersonal existence of a God who hears us and works with us to establish those truths which in this life "never can be proved," the "living will" must, he says in CXXXI, "rise in the spiritual rock." The poet explained that he was referring to "that which we know as Free-will, the higher and enduring part of man."[24] Bradley, however, adds that " 'Rise from the spiritual rock' can hardly mean 'rise in our natures,' but must imply that the will to rise in them springs from a divine source."[25] He might have instanced Enoch Arden, who is helped by "Prayer from a living source within the will." But since human nature provides the only evidence for a divine element working *through* human nature, the distinction is tenuous.

Tennyson's will was not, however, strong enough to keep his faith sure and steady. From boyhood to old age he was quite as much a doubter as a believer; and his doubts were rooted in that morbid side of his character which stubbornly resisted his desire to be optimistic and edifying.

> What find I in the highest place
> But mine own phantom chanting hymns?

The implications of this question could be evaded only by discovering a more presentable answer than an absolutely unqualified "I have felt." There must be some way of convincing himself and others that his feelings gave him knowledge not merely of what he wanted but of what really existed.

Perhaps those feelings, at their purest and most intense, could be regarded as flashes of mystical insight.

> Speak to Him, then, for He hears, and Spirit with Spirit can meet—
> Closer is He than breathing, and nearer than hands and feet.

According to Bradley, "The language used of these [mystical] feelings and experiences is such that one is compelled to ask why, after all, the poet should declare that 'We have but faith, we cannot know;' . . . since the immediate certainty claimed for those feelings would appear to be, or to

[24] *Memoir*, I, 319. [25] A. C. Bradley, *A Commentary on Tennyson's In Memoriam*, p. 237.

justify, something more than faith or a believing of what we cannot prove. Perhaps he distrusted what he could not suppose to be the common possession of mankind."[26] More probably he distrusted what he could not suppose, in any but a few exceptionally self-confident moments, that he himself possessed. The most striking instance of what might seem to be a mystical experience is *In Memoriam*, XCV—"By night we lingered on the lawn." As he read Arthur's letters,

> The dead man touched me from the past,
> And all at once it seemed at last
> The living soul was flashed on mine,
>
> And mine in this was wound, and whirled
> About empyreal heights of thought,
> And came on that which is, and caught
> The deep pulsations of the world.

But the original readings were "*His* living soul . . . And mine in *his*." In revising, Tennyson tried to make the experience sound more traditionally mystical, explaining in the notes to the Eversley Edition that this was the soul "perchance of the Deity"—or as he said more colloquially to Knowles, "the Deity, maybe." Professor Baum demands too much when he protests that the poet should have known whether he was communing with Hallam or with the Almighty.[27] Probably all that really happened was that for a moment the letters brought his dead comrade very close to him in a way not peculiar to mystics.

Speaking through the lips of *The Ancient Sage*, Tennyson informs the young sceptic that

> . . . more than once when I
> Sat all alone, revolving in myself
> The word that is the symbol of myself,
> The mortal limit of the Self was loosed,
> And past into the Nameless, as a cloud
> Melts into heaven.

His son explains that Tennyson could induce trances like the "weird seizures" of the hero in *The Princess* by repeating his own name ("The word that is the symbol of myself") a sufficient number of times. The resultant weakening of the sense of personal identity seemed to justify the assertion that "There are moments when the flesh is nothing to me, when I feel and know the flesh to be the vision, God and the spiritual the only real and true."[28]

[26] *Ibid.*, p. 65.
[27] P. F. Baum, *Tennyson Sixty Years After*, p. 308.
[28] *Memoir*, I, 320; II, 90.

This feeling-knowledge is a valuable antidote for his dread of materialism. If he can transform the phenomenal world into a hazy sort of illusion, nothing prevents him from saying,

> But in my spirit will I dwell,
> And dream my dream, and hold it true.

By pronouncing any word again and again we can destroy its relation to the thing it symbolizes; and since our life among things is so largely a life among words, this sense of unreality is readily transferred from the word to the thing. If we wish to enshroud the harshness of actuality in an emotional blur, we may call the result of this device a spiritual experience. By thus repeating his own name, Tennyson was able to lose it in the Nameless. But haziness about the material produces no certitude about the immaterial. "Mystic" and "misty" are not perfect synonyms.

"I can sympathize with God in my poor way," said Tennyson. "The human soul seems to be always—in some way, how we do not know—identical with God."[29] But if the human soul is identical with God, contemplation of God is hard to distinguish from contemplation of self. *In Memoriam*, XCII, repudiates the materialistic pseudomysticism of the table-tipping séance, but in his old age he was rather more fascinated than repelled by spiritualism, telepathy, and mesmerism—not because of their preternatural flavor but because of their claims to be empirical. Though his brother Frederick's spiritualism "had too much flummery mixed up with it," he was "inclined to believe there is something in it."[30]

Heaven for Tennyson is not an ultimate peace, but a continuation of the strivings of mortal life. The spirit of Hallam continues to struggle and advance, following the gleam even after he has seen his Pilot face to face. His efforts will be aided by the spirit of the Duke of Wellington, of whom the *Ode* declares:

> We doubt not that for one so true
> There must be other nobler work to do
> Than when he fought at Waterloo,
> And Victor he must ever be.

Masterman is surely right: "The knowledge of God does not come to him as a direct intuition . . . but as a secondary deduction." He posited God as "necessary for the satisfaction of the demands of the human race."[31] The loving Deity is never contemplatively experienced; but He must exist if

[29] Charles Tennyson, *Alfred Tennyson*, p. 360. [30] *Memoir*, II, 343.
[31] C. F. G. Masterman, *Tennyson as a Religious Thinker*, pp. 50–52, 129, 169.

there is to be immortality, and immortality must be true if life on this earth is to have any moral significance.

What profit lies in barren faith,
And vacant yearning, tho' with might
To scale the heaven's highest height,
Or dive below the wells of death?

. . .

I'd rather take what fruit may be
Of sorrow under human skies.

We must conclude that Tennyson was not a mystic but an emotional pragmatist.

He is more successful in using nonmystical Christianity as a means of validating his feelings. His personal belief in immortality, free will, and a God of love was a vestigial remnant of the Christian faith, and it could be expressed through a judicious selection of the language and imagery of the tradition from which it derived. "The cardinal point of Christianity," he informed Bishop Lightfoot, "is the Life after Death."[32] For him, this would merely be another way of saying that Christianity placed love at the center of the universe and made it the guiding principle of human life. Jesus was the most compelling, though perhaps not the unique, exemplar of this principle. "The highest, holiest manhood," he could be worshipped as "Strong Son of God, immortal Love."

The concretizing and personalizing of those unspeakable truths which lie "deep-seated in our mystic frame" might be mere myth-making, but there was much to be said for myths on grounds both ethical and aesthetic. Tennyson knew the power of images. Although he felt superior to all sects and creeds, he was never more sincere than when he said, "I dread the losing hold of forms." "Truth embodied in a tale" could be understood and shared as a moral force by all men, both wise and simple. "And so," as a product of this practical human need, "the Word had breath," or at least has been *given* breath by our imaginations. Christianity was especially valuable as a bulwark against "the faithless coldness of the times," a means of keeping Arthur's realm, or Albert's, from reeling back into the beast. "This is a terrible age of unfaith," he often said to his son. The fact alarmed him because he felt that complete unbelievers were usually complete villains, like Philip Edgar in *The Promise of May*. In answer to Lord Queensberry's protest againt this "abominable caricature" of a freethinker, Lionel Tennyson was commissioned to explain through the press that his father had not

[32] *Memoir*, I, 321.

intended to imply any inevitable connection between Edgar's beliefs and his behavior. It is difficult, however, to credit the sincerity of this disclaimer. Ethical principles needed the support of communal religious emotion. He told Browning that Christian morality, "without the central figure of Christ, *the* son of Man, would become cold, and that it is fatal for religion to lose its warmth."[33] Even the most enlightened religion of pure inwardness incurred the risk of this lowering of temperature:

See thou, that countest reason ripe
In holding to the law within,
Thou fail not in a world of sin,
And even for want of such a type.

On this basis Tennyson was able to write the last stanza of *Crossing the Bar* and to utter that *Human Cry* which he wrote at Jowett's request as an anthem for Balliol College Chapel:

Hallowed be Thy name—Hallelujah!
Infinite Ideality!
Immeasurable Reality!
Infinite Personality!
Hallowed be Thy name—Hallelujah![34]

One cannot say, however, that the Christian faith was the primary and fundamental force in his religion. He was never able to regard it as an expression of objective truth but accepted it with the reservation that he had the right to interpret it to suit himself. Christianity as a way of transforming human nature through self-surrender to the redeeming Son of God held little or no meaning for him. Although he frequently deplores the sinfulness of the times he does not conceive of sin as alienation from God, but merely as human misconduct and disorder. Adultery, by far his favorite sin, is wrong as an offense against Arthurian or Victorian respectability. Feeling that God is unknowable, "he had some sympathy with those who would speak of a Divine Mind rather than of a Divine Personality, but at the same time he insisted that in order to keep morality warm God must be more or less anthropomorphic."[35] Yet although he "dreaded the losing hold of forms," he dreaded even more the subjection of his formless emotions to "the knotted lies of human creeds."[36] He never thought of the Incarnation as the

[33] *Ibid.*, I, 309, 325–326; II, 267–268, 421.
[34] "Did you ever?" inquired Matthew Arnold of his sister on reading this poem. (*Letters*, II, 195.)
[35] *Memoir*, I, 311.
[36] So reads the original 1830 version of *To* —— (William Blakesley, his "Clear-headed friend")—later softened, characteristically, to "The knots that tangle human creeds."

supreme historical fact. For him, Jesus was never a reproach and a crisis and a judgment, but simply a model of human conduct not very clearly distinguishable from Arthur Hallam; the personification of human love, not its divine source; "the Christ that is to be" as the culmination of the progressive development of mankind, the dimly-conceived Omega but not the Alpha.

In order to rationalize this version of Christianity, subjectivist theologians leaned heavily on German mind-over-matter metaphysics. Their fundamental spiritual impulse, as Professor Marchand well expresses it, was toward "a non-dogmatic, non-theological religion of humanism based on intuition and reason harmonized and made one by transcendental philosophy."[37] Tennyson liked the intuitional side of this combination much better than the rational. Deeply as he craved to know that he would live forever, he feared that intellectual analysis might confute rather than validate his never very confident longings. It was better to let one's emotions determine in advance what *should* be thought and then dutifully think it.

> Hold thou the good, define it well;
> For fear divine Philosophy
> Should push beyond her mark, and be
> Procuress to the Lords of Hell.

Systematic knowledge is "earthly of the mind," while the wisdom of our highest aspirations is "heavenly of the soul." "Cut from love and faith," knowledge is "But some wild Pallas from the brain / Of demons."

Tennyson saw, however, that transcendental idealism, with its analytical and systematic side minimized and its "shaping-spirit-of-imagination" side maximized, could lend intellectual authority to his feelings. What friends like Carlyle, Maurice, and Jowett told him *about* the wise Germans sounded very encouraging. It might actually be true, then, that the material world of knowledge was an illusion and the spiritual world of wisdom was real. Read at first hand, however, metaphysics was less satisfying. In about 1853, largely under the influence of Jowett, he "began to study . . . Spinoza, Berkeley, Kant, Schlegel, Fichte, Hegel, and Ferrier,"[38] but his son does not believe that any of these thinkers "particularly influenced him." "I have but a gleam of Kant, and have hardly turned a page of Hegel," reads a letter of later years.[39] Avid source-hunters may find in his poems many passages which might be derived from knowledge of transcendental philos-

[37] L. A. Marchand, *The Athenaeum*, p. 247*n*.

[38] Charles Tennyson, *Alfred Tennyson*, p. 279.

[39] *Memoir*, I, 308; II, 158.

ophy; but most of these are more easily explained by remembering that such philosophy was a rationalization of the impulses which Tennyson felt most strongly, and that he depended on the latter much more than on the former.

The importance of his founding membership in the Metaphysical Society should not be exaggerated. He dimly hoped that out of the clash of learned and candid minds some answer to his doubts might emerge, but there is no reason to suppose that the papers and discussions did more than bewilder him. His only contribution was *The Higher Pantheism*, read at the first regular meeting by Knowles. The author was not present to explain it, and there were no comments from the respectful but puzzled audience. Of the one hundred meetings of the Society held between April 21, 1869, and his resignation on December 9, 1879, he attended only eleven, all but one of them during the first four years. According to Grant Duff (a member), Tennyson had nothing to say on these occasions, but James Martineau more generously remembered that he was "usually . . . a silent listener, exceptionally interposing some short question or pregnant hint."[40] Tennyson's beliefs were not the product of his slight acquaintance with technical philosophy. That those beliefs derived some encouragement from the general atmosphere of transcendental idealism in his environment is probable enough.

In *The Two Voices*, Tennyson can find no rational arguments with which to resist the voice which urges him toward suicide.[41] What silences the tempter and allows the "hidden hope" of the second voice to be heard is the spectacle of a model Victorian family—the gravely smiling husband, his "prudent partner," and their "little maiden"—on their way to Morning Prayer and Sermon. The poet, however, does not follow them to church. Instead,

> . . . forth into the woods I went,
> And Nature's living motion lent
> The pulse of hope to discontent.
>
> . . .
>
> I wondered, while I paced along;
> The woods were filled so full with song,
> There seemed no room for sense of wrong.

In *Maud*, on the contrary, the woods have plenty of room for wrong. They support the first voice, not the second:

[40] *Ibid.*, p. 170; A. W. Brown, *The Metaphysical Society*, p. 159.

[41] The poem, begun shortly after Hallam's death, was originally intended to present the wholly pessimistic *Thoughts of a Suicide*. The happy ending was a discreet afterthought.

For nature is one with rapine, a harm no preacher can heal;
The Mayfly is torn by the swallow, the sparrow speared by the shrike,
And the whole little wood where I sit is a world of plunder and prey.

The existence of evil in nature was a serious threat to Tennyson's belief in a God of love. "Are God and Nature then at strife?" Allingham remembers him as saying: "An Omnipotent Creator who could make such a painful world is to me *sometimes* as hard to believe in as to believe in blind matter behind everything. The lavish profusion too in the natural world appals me, from the growths of the tropical forest to the capacity of man to multiply, the torrent of babies."[42]

This poet's uneasy relations with science, especially with the theory of evolution, have received so much expert attention that our consideration of the topic may take a good deal for granted. Peering through the microscope he would say, "Strange that these wonders should draw some men to God and repel others. No more reason in one than in the other."[43] When he felt like a confident Victorian seer, science bore witness to that

... one far-off divine event,
To which the whole creation moves;

when he felt morbid, he seized upon science as objective material to be morbid *about*, likening the stars in *Maud* to

Innumerable, pitiless, passionless eyes,
Cold fires, yet with power to burn and brand
His nothingness into man.[44]

These varying moods, however, suggested an ambiguity in the term "reason." Microscope-reason was the reason of knowledge; the reason which drew men to God was the reason of wisdom. In Tennyson's mind, as in his intellectual environment, the two reasons seemed to be at strife.

He had done his hardest worrying about evolution before the publication of *Origin of Species*. The book disturbed him, of course, but its chief effect was to increase his need of the solution at which he had already arrived. Since he cared little about dogma and was anything but a literalist in his view of the Bible, the supposed impiety of Darwinism was not for him an important issue. He was alarmed by evolutionary theories, both pre-Darwinian and Darwinian, not because they threatened traditional Christianity but because they threatened the romantic view of nature and the romantic view of man.

[42] *Allingham*, p. 96. [43] *Memoir*, I, 102.
[44] But of course the most famous examples of this mood are *In Memoriam*, LIV, LV, LVI.

One of Tennyson's earliest poems is a fragment entitled *Armageddon* (the germ of his prize-poem *Timbuctoo*), which contains the following lines:

> I wondered with deep wonder at myself:
> My mind seem'd wing'd with knowledge and the strength
> Of holy musings and immense Ideas,
> Even to Infinitude . . .
>
> . . .
>
> I was a part of the Unchangeable,
> A scintillation of Eternal Mind,
> Remix'd and burning with its parent fire.
> Yea! in that hour I could have fallen down
> Before my own strong soul and worshipped it.[45]

Self-deification and all, here is that romantic faith of which the gospel of "I have felt" is a dilution. But it is important that romantic self-assertion should be projected outward into nature and echoed back from the heart of the universe to the heart of man. When "Nature, red in tooth and claw" answers our "immense Ideas" with indifference or even scorn, our confidence collapses into loneliness and fear. "O life as futile, then, as frail!" The first of *The Two Voices* was right when it said of man,

> That type of Perfect in his mind
> In Nature can he nowhere find.

But there was an even more disturbing possibility. What if the mind itself were merely a part of the mechanism of the loveless, soulless nature depicted by science? "No evolutionist," he said to John Tyndall, "is able to explain the mind of man or how any possible physiological change of tissue can produce conscious thought."[46] This he said, however, in deepest fear that he might be wrong. Even in his Cambridge prize-poem of 1829 he had felt that the subjection of romantic mind to antiromantic nature meant the death of poetry's power

> . . . to sway
> The heart of man: and teach him to attain
> By shadowing forth the Unattainable.

The "brilliant towers" of Timbuctoo, says the personified spirit of creative imagination, have already begun to dwindle:

> O city! oh latest throne! where I was raised
> To be a mystery of loveliness

[45] Quoted by Charles Tennyson, *Alfred Tennyson*, p. 38.
[46] Quoted by Lionel Stevenson, *Darwin Among the Poets*, p. 95.

> Unto all eyes, the time is well-nigh come
> When I must render up this glorious home
> To keen Discovery.

Sixty years later, in *Parnassus*, he is still struggling with the same dread:

> What be those two shapes high over the sacred fountain,
> Taller than all the Muses, and huger than all the mountain?
>
> . . .
>
> Poet, that evergreen laurel is blasted with more than lightning!
> These are Astronomy and Geology, terrible Muses!

If at times Tennyson thought of nature as cold and mechanical, at other times he thought of it as a seething ferment of cruel bestiality, the world of the struggle for existence. Very strong was his sense of the conflict, in himself no less than in other men, between spirituality and animality. The evolutionary hypothesis was all the more intolerable because it lent scientific support to the feeling that there were apes and tigers within his own breast.

He seems to have found little or no consolation in that revived physico-theology of the *Bridgewater Treatises* type which dominated the scientific instruction of his Cambridge days. At a meeting of the Apostles he voted "No" on the question, "Is an intelligible first cause deducible from the phenomena of the universe?"[47] The tactics which he preferred may loosely be described as those of romantic transcendentalism. First of all it was necessary to protect the human spirit from science by placing man and nature in a dualistic relationship in which the former would be elevated over the latter. This could be achieved, after a fashion, by emphasizing the distinction between knowledge and wisdom, identifying truth with man's noblest wishes, and especially by cultivating a dreamy scepticism as regards the reality of matter. "I believe we never see Matter," he said to Allingham. "What we count the material world is only an appearance. . . . I think Matter more mysterious than Spirit." When A. R. Wallace told him (as early as 1884!), "I conceive Matter not as substance at all, but as *points of energy*," the poet answered that "this was something like his own notion." He was also impressed by the quasi-scientific vitalism of James Hinton's *Life in Nature*.[48] Any idea was welcomed that dematerialized the world of appearances sufficiently to enable him to say:

> The Peak is high, and the stars are high,
> And the thought of a man is higher.

[47] *Memoir*, I, 44.

[48] *Allingham*, pp. 183, 186–187, 294, 334.

A deep below the deep,
And a height beyond the height!
Our hearing is not hearing,
And our seeing is not sight.

As regards the next step Tennyson is uncertain. Sometimes he feels it safer to keep his humanity separate from even so spiritualized a nature, maintaining toward science an attitude of uneasy superiority—"What matters Science unto men?" More often, however, he exploits the transcendental privilege of imposing upon nature those ideas of love, freedom, progress, and immortality which the mind has attained by withdrawing itself from the phenomenal world. Through becoming resolutely contranatural we win the right to tell nature what she really means. The lesson of *The Higher Pantheism* is that if we could see and hear with our souls instead of with our eyes and ears, to behold the physical universe would be to behold God. In the light of this truth, evolution is transformed into a system of moral and spiritual progress. Thus regarded, science encourages even our hope of immortality, for if love is lord and king of the universe it is inconceivable that the ascent of man should be truncated by death. The unbroken upward sweep of humanity is imaged by the tiers of sculptured figures in Merlin's hall in *The Holy Grail*:

... In the lowest beasts are slaying men,
And in the second men are slaying beasts,
And on the third are warriors, perfect men,
And on the fourth are men with growing wings.

In this way Tennyson, despite his fear of materialism, was able to convince a large section of the Victorian public, and sometimes even himself, that he had weighed the facts of science and drawn from them rational and inspiring conclusions which corroborated the official cult of progress and the tenets of Christianity. This paradox will bewilder us unless we remember that the evidence for his more optimistic view of evolution was provided not by science but by his wishful heart.

And so, after examining Tennyson's relations with mysticism, Christianity, transcendental philosophy, and science, we circle back with him to *In Memoriam*, CXXIV, where the irreducible core of his faith is expressed:

That which we dare invoke to bless;
Our dearest faith; our ghastliest doubt;
He, They, One, All; within, without;
The Power in darkness whom we guess,

I found Him not in world or sun,
Or eagle's wing, or insect's eye,
Nor thro' the questions men may try,
The petty cobwebs we have spun.

If e'er when faith had fallen asleep,
I heard a voice, "believe no more,"
And heard an ever-breaking shore
That tumbled in the Godless deep,

A warmth within the breast would melt
The freezing reason's colder part,
And like a man in wrath the heart
Stood up and answered, "I have felt."

This seems a slender basis for a reputation as a great philosophical poet. Perhaps it is all that a believing man can honestly say, although personally I do not think so. At all events it makes a huge difference whether our feelings lead us to belief in our feelings or to belief in an objective reality beyond them. In the former case we are no more likely to feel faith than to feel doubt. Conway avers that "Many were made sceptics by Tennyson's 'In Memoriam.' "[49] This "rationalist" is a deeply prejudiced witness, but one cannot say that even for Tennyson himself "I have felt" expresses any deep victorious sureness. His dearest faith and his ghastliest doubt were the two sides of a single coin. "Sometimes I have doubts, of a morning," he said in 1867; and in the same year, "Sometimes I have a kind of hope."[50]

In his old age—say from 1880 onward—Tennyson thought that England was disintegrating into social and spiritual chaos. Unwilling to grant that he himself was a prime representative of this disintegration, he sometimes took refuge from the evil times in relatively "pure" poetry, sometimes cried out hysterically against them, and sometimes reaffirmed the Victorian faith in "the Vision of the world, and all the wonder that would be." The dominant mood was one of bewildered discouragement tempered by an unquenchable hope which was equally sincere.

... Ah! If I
Should play Tiresias to the times
I fear I might but prophesy
Of faded faiths and civic crimes,
And fierce transition's blood-red morn,

[49] M. D. Conway, *Autobiography*, II, 38.

[50] *Allingham*, pp. 148, 151.

> And years with lawless voices loud,
> Old vessels from their moorings torn,
> And cataclysm and thundercloud;
> And one lean hope, that at the last
> Perchance—if this small world endures—
> Our heirs may find the stormy past
> Has left their present purer . . .[51]

"I am afraid I think the world is darkened," he said to the Queen in 1883; "I dare say it will brighten again."[52]

Dark world or bright, he must do his duty as Poet Laureate, congratulating Victoria at her Jubilee on

> Fifty years of ever-broadening Commerce!
> Fifty years of ever-brightening Science!
> Fifty years of ever-widening Empire!

Even on such official occasions the note of doom is heard, but it is resolutely muffled:

> Are there thunders moaning in the distance?
> Are there spectres moving in the darkness?
> Trust the Hand of Light will lead her people,
> Till the thunders pass, the spectres vanish.

Whatever the Gleam may be, Victoria's Merlin inspiringly exhorts the young poet-mariner to follow it.

The increasing looseness of moral standards made him insist more earnestly than ever on the calorific importance of Christianity, but he became even less willing to commit himself as to what Christianity means.[53] The wisdom of *The Ancient Sage* is delivered to the brash young sceptic a thousand years before the birth of Christ, and it embodies all that Tennyson had ever truly believed. For once, indeed, he was willing to say that the poem was "very personal."[54] If you go in to the altar of your deepest self, declares the Sage, you may

> . . . learn the Nameless hath a voice,
> By which thou wilt abide, if thou be wise,
> As if thou knewest, for thou canst not know.

[51] Unpublished version of the prefatory lines of *Tiresias*, quoted by Charles Tennyson, *Alfred Tennyson*, p. 483.

[52] *Memoir*, II, 457.

[53] He liked to quote Dean Stanley's remark, "So far from being effete, Christianity is as yet undeveloped." (*Memoir*, II, 231.)

[54] *Memoir*, II, 497.

And if, using the wisdom gained by introspection, you then send your "free soul" out into the universe, you will even see Him.[55]

The existence of the Nameless cannot be proved, but neither can anything else—not even the reality of the world which you seem to behold.

> Thou canst not prove thou art immortal, no,
> Nor yet that thou art mortal . . .
>
> . . .
>
> . . . Wherefore be thou wise,
> Cleave ever to the sunnier side of doubt,
> And cling to Faith beyond the forms of Faith!

Some hold that "none but gods" could have made this fair world, but the beauty of nature must remain

> A beauty with defect—till That which knows,
> And is not known, but felt thro' what we feel
> Within ourselves is highest, shall descend
> On this half-deed, and shape it at the last
> According to the Highest in the Highest.

Be the master, not the slave, of the illusion of time: for the Nameless, everything is one "Eternal Now."

> My words are like the babblings in a dream
> Of nightmare, when the babblings break the dream.
> But be thou wise in this dream-world of ours,
> Nor take thy dial for thy deity,
> But make the passing shadow serve thy will.

The world seems to be full of evil, but "Who knows but that the darkness is in man?" Perhaps the so-called night of death will confer upon us the light which now we lack—

> . . . the last and largest sense to make
> The phantom walls of this illusion fade,
> And show us that the world is wholly fair.

The Sage draws personal confirmation of this faith from Wordsworthian intimations of immortality experienced in boyhood[56] and from the fact that repetition of his own name gives him a sense of the Nameless.[57] But all these high matters are inscrutable mysteries; meanwhile there is work to be done.

[55] I use "Him" for convenience, but a remarkable feature of this poem is that throughout its considerable length the Nameless is never referred to by any pronoun—masculine, feminine, or neuter.

[56] Tennyson to Allingham in 1866: "In my boyhood I had *intimations* of Immortality—inexpressible! I have never been able to express them. I shall try some day." (*Allingham*, p. 137.)

[57] See above, p. 117.

"Let be thy wail, and help thy fellow-men." Be charitable, and not for human praise; shun avarice, gluttony, anger, cruelty. But remember also to "think well," for good deeds spring from good thoughts and *vice versa*:

> An evil thought may soil thy children's blood;
> But curb the beast would cast thee in the mire,
> And leave the hot swamp of voluptuousness,
> A cloud between the Nameless and thyself,
> And lay thine uphill shoulder to the wheel,
> And climb the Mount of Blessing.

Thus Tennyson tries to establish the rights and powers of romantic transcendentalism on the basis of an absolute scepticism. Since the foundation is shifting sand, the structure collapses into a fumbling moralistic pragmatism. Right working is the grand desideratum; but he acknowledges that there can be no right working without right thinking, and he does not know what to think except that it is important to "curb the beast." He had always had a strange way of writing about the lower animals as if their badness were the badness of evil men. The poor sinless creatures live in "the hot swamp of voluptuousness." *By an Evolutionist* is his final pronouncement upon this subject:

> I have climbed to the snows of Age, and I gaze at a field in the Past,
> Where I sank with the body at times in the slough of a low desire,
> But I hear no yelp of the beast, and the Man is quiet at last
> As he stands on the heights of his life with a glimpse of a height that is higher.

Apparently one privilege of old age is freedom from the beastliness of youth. But mere subsidence of animal vitality can hardly be that

> . . . one far-off divine event
> To which the whole creation moves.

What he actually felt concerning evolution in these closing years is shown more frankly in *Locksley Hall Sixty Years After*:

> Is there evil but on earth? or pain in every peopled sphere?
> Well, be grateful for the sounding watchword "Evolution" here,
>
> Evolution ever climbing after some ideal good,
> And Reversion ever dragging Evolution in the mud.

"Chaos, Cosmos! Cosmos, Chaos!" Visited by Jowett near the end, he begged the wise man "not to consult with him or argue with him, as was his wont, on points of philosophy or religious doubt." It was better to smoke his pipe among quiet old peasants, "from whom he always tried to ascertain their thoughts upon death and the future life."[58] Some consolation might also be drawn from the faith of the young. He asked Sophia Palmer, the adolescent daughter of his Anglo-Catholic friend Lord Selborne, what she would think if she saw the bodies of her parents rotting in the grave. She replied that she would feel they were yet living. "'You are sure?' he pressed her; and on her repeating her assurance, 'Ah well!' he said, with rather pathetic relief, 'Yes, I do hold it so. I have tried to say it—to show it—that the body is the husk—the shell. But at times these new lights, this science wearies and perplexes me; yet I know they cannot reach, cannot explain . . .' "[59] He was greatly pleased when Darwin himself assured him that "Evolution does not make against Christianity."[60] And yet one knew nothing, and the bright vision of the Cambridge Apostles glimmered faintly and very far away.

> All the world is ghost to me, and as the phantom disappears,
> Forward far and far from here is all the hope of eighty years.

But even in *Locksley Hall Sixty Years After* the truth of the "dream of good" is reaffirmed: "Love will conquer at the last."

No clergyman prayed at Tennyson's bedside during his last moments, but a few hours after he had crossed the bar the Vicar of Lurgashall "came . . . to see him lying, grand and peaceful, in death. 'Lord Tennyson,' said the old man, standing with upraised hands at the bedside, 'God has taken you, who made you a Prince of men.' "[61] The Vicar probably thought, with the majority of cultivated Victorians, that the lord of language who now lay so silent had been the century's supreme singer of Christian faith and wisdom.

[58] *Memoir*, II, 211, 418.
[59] Charles Tennyson, *Alfred Tennyson*, p. 460.
[60] *Memoir*, II, 57. The incident occurred in 1868, but it illustrates the incertitude which grew even more oppressive in his last years.
[61] *Memoir*, II, 429.

Chapter Six

BROWNING

ABOUT 1875 Edward Berdoe, a physician and surgeon of repute, lost his Christian faith "after a long course of reading the works of Agnostic teachers" and became a complete unbeliever except for vague leanings toward Buddhism. Providentially, however, he chanced to hear "a brilliant and powerful lecture by Mr. Moncure Conway at South Place Chapel, Finsbury, on Robert Browning's *Sordello*."[1] At once he began to read the poems for himself, "and the feeling came over me that in Browning I had found my religious teacher." He joined the Browning Society, got further light from its papers and discussions, "and by slow and painful steps I found my way back to the faith I had forsaken."[2]

The Browning Society, says Berdoe, constituted "a platform on which all could meet—Christians, both Protestants and Catholics, atheists, agnostics, and indifferents—and each find something in Browning which appealed to the best that was in us." Even "Mr. James Thomson, the atheist," read a paper on "The Genius of Robert Browning" which expressed admiration for his ability to believe in Christianity on a rational basis despite his sympathetic understanding of contemporary doubt. At any of the meetings, indeed, "the unbeliever must have felt that there was something in Christianity after all, when such a genius as Browning could accept it as devoutly as a medieval saint; and the Christian no doubt often felt that the all-embracing love of the poet was a good deal wider and much more divine than the narrow bounds of some of our creeds."[3] At the first meeting of the Society, F. J. Furnivall, its cofounder with Miss Hickey, had struck the keynote. "Browning," he declared, "is the manliest, the strongest, the lifefullest, the deepest, the thoughtfullest living poet, the one most needing earnest study, and the one most worthy of it."[4] Most of the papers presented at subsequent sessions bore more or less directly on the poet's spiritual

[1] Conway, the biographer of Thomas Paine, had become minister of this originally Unitarian but now "Ethical Society" chapel after the death of W. J. Fox, Browning's early friend and literary mentor. Browning was on rather intimate terms with Conway. See Conway's *Autobiography*, II, 18, 21, 24; and *New Letters of Robert Browning*, pp. 155, 157–158, 185.

[2] Edward Berdoe, *Browning and the Christian Faith*, pp. vii–ix.

[3] *Ibid.*, pp.x–xi.

[4] *New Letters of RobertBrowning*, p. 280*n*.

message. "In Browning," wrote J. B. Bury, "are the germs of a religion that transcends ecclesiastical Christianity and Comte's Positivism, and includes the soul of both." The Reverend John Kirkman, however, found it sufficient to call Browning "the greatest Christian poet we have ever had. Not in a narrow dogmatic sense, but as the teacher who is as thrilled through with all Christian sympathies as with artistic or musical." This disciple names "Browning, Isaiah, Carlyle" as bold spirits whose ruggedness is needed "in these oily days of minds as well as railway-trains advancing without friction." "A prophet whom God has given to our storm-tost age!" cries Dorothea Beale; and Mrs. Turnbull "can only say in humility and gratitude, 'Let us thank God for our great poet and teacher!' "[5]

Such enthusiasm was not confined to the inner circle of disciples. Berdoe relates that "A student at one of our [Nonconformist] theological colleges once consulted the divinity lecturer as to the best books on modern theology which he could present to a clerical friend. The answer came promptly and decisively—'Give him a set of Browning.' "[6] *The Athenaeum* described *The Ring and the Book* as "the most precious and profound spiritual treasure that England has produced since the days of Shakespeare. . . . Its intellectual greatness is as nothing compared with its transcendent spiritual teaching."[7]

To that teaching American bosoms were gratifyingly responsive. In 1885, Browning was pleased to find himself the outstanding figure in a work on *The Higher Ministries of Recent English Poetry* by the Reverend George Wakefield Gunsaulus of Chicago. Lecturing on Browning at the Chicago Theological Seminary, this Congregationalist minister concluded his remarks by saying, "I know of no discovery for which he will not prepare the soul—I know of no experience for which his lines will not equip the minds of modern men."[8] Professor Hiram Corson of Cornell, honorary member of the London group and founder of the first Browning Society in America, hailed in the poet "the most quickening spirituality of the age. . . . Browning is the most essentially Christian of living poets."[9] Even today the Corsonian tradition survives in American universities, though it has become less popular than a closely related admiration for the wisdom of Wordsworth and Shelley. As generations of Yale students can testify, William Lyon Phelps revered Browning as a great religious teacher. In 1911 Professor Gingerich was only a little old-fashioned when he asserted that Jesus arose

[5] *Browning Studies*, pp. 6, 16, 43, 79, 144. [6] *Browning and the Christian Faith*, p. xiii.
[7] Quoted by Frances T. Russell, *One Word More on Browning*, p. 129.
[8] *New Letters of Robert Browning*, pp. 362–363, and *n.* [9] *Browning Studies*, pp. 47, 53.

> out of all the fatalistic philosophies of the ancients ... declaring once for all the soul's worth and asserting its supreme power of making its own free choice. Out of the heart of the nineteenth century civilization there rose a figure, stalwart and vast, that struck ringing blows for the soul's worth on the new and modern basis of the world's incompleteness and man's imperfections. And perhaps since the days of Christ there has been no one who has more persistently and dauntlessly asserted the energy and power and freedom and central importance of the soul of man than Robert Browning.[10]

Thus Jesus, despite his unfortunate ignorance of man's imperfections, preached the gospel that the Victorian poet enunciated in his more modern way.

Few if any of Browning's Victorian disciples would have asserted categorically that Browning was a Christian because Christ was a Browningite. Apparently, however, they tended to draw an emphatic distinction between Christian spirit and Christian creed and to value the poet because in transcending the latter so boldly he manifested the former so compellingly. He was, they said, "essentially Christian," but "not in a narrow dogmatic sense." Julia Wedgwood writes him that his belief in immortality is all the more convincing to her because she knows how strongly he is "opposed to all authoritarian forms of traditional belief."[11] "Strict orthodoxy," Berdoe explains, "is rapidly dying out, but strict orthodoxy and vital Christianity are by no means synonymous."[12] What Browning offers is Christianity at its most vital.

When we emerge from this bath of inspirational treacle with the intention of discovering what Browning actually says about religious problems we find a bewildering mixture of traditional Christianity, subjectivized Christianity, and outright romanticism. The general trend, accelerating rather markedly after the death of his wife, moves from a broad sort of Evangelicalism toward attitudes which Berdoe would describe as "vital." But no perfectly precise curve can be plotted: there is plenty of heterodoxy in earlier poems and an occasional glimpse of old-fashioned Christian objectivity even in later ones. I shall probably be expected to add that the difficulty of interpreting his thought is aggravated by his use of the dramatic method in so many important poems. It seems to me, however, that in Browning's monologues the positive or negative relationship of the speaker's ideas to the poet's is even more obvious than in the case of Tennyson. Nobody has ever supposed that Browning agreed with Caliban or disagreed

[10] S. F. Gingerich, *Wordsworth, Tennyson, and Browning: A Study in Human Freedom*, pp. 218–219.
[11] *Robert Browning and Julia Wedgwood*, p. 9. [12] *Browning and the Christian Faith*, p. xv.

with Fra Lippo Lippi. If there is the slightest danger that the casuistries of a Blougram or a Sludge might demoralize the reader, the poet adds an epilogue telling him what to think of the shifty rascal.[13]

But precisely because these disguises are almost always so diaphanous they set us wondering why Browning should have been so fond of them. Why this persistent attempt to achieve self-expression through self-concealment, this desire for simultaneous publicity and privacy, this strange mixture of boldness and timidity? In this as in other respects there was something insecure about the man's personality, something not quite sound or genuine. No one who is really strong and confident makes so much noise about it. His robustious poetry contrasts embarrassingly with his sedentary, unadventurous, nineteenth-century-bourgeois life. In the matter of the elopement, to be sure, he lived up to the spirit of his poetry; but Miss Miller has made out a strong case for her thesis that what he always sought, in Elizabeth and in other women before and after her, was not a mate but a mother.[14] This singer of "the value and significance of flesh" was abnormally priggish about his body.

The reader often suspects that Browning is trying to rise above a cold sluggishness of temper by executing a war dance which might inflame his anxious respectability into factitious ardor. In conversation with Tennyson, Allingham "called Browning a *vivid* man, to which T. assented, adding, 'How he did flourish about when he was here!' "[15] The implication is that he was a little *too* vivid to be quite a gentleman. Kingsley says of Browning in a letter of 1853 that "though he is a good fellow nothing will take the smell of tallow and brown sugar out of him. He cannot help being coarse and vulgar and is naïvely unaware of the fact. However, if he had been either a gentleman . . . or a hard handed workman in contact with iron fact he might have been a fine poet."[16] In some measure, the bluster of Browning's poetry may be an effort to rise above his self-consciousness in matters of social stratification. A genius would not need to be a gentleman. On the other hand, to shout too noisily in his own person might betray a vulgarity of self-exposure which could be avoided by the dramatic method. And of course when he dined out with the best people he must take care not to give the impression that his distinction depended on his success in the poetry *business*; he must try to behave like a man of the world.

[13] See H. N. Fairchild, "Browning the Simple-Hearted Casuist," *University of Toronto Quarterly*, XVIII (1949), 234–240.

[14] Betty Miller, *Robert Browning: A Portrait.*

[15] William Allingham, *A Diary*, p. 65.

[16] Una Pope-Hennesy, *Canon Charles Kingsley*, p. 153. Kingsley's father was a clergyman of minor country gentry descent.

But snobbery will not provide a complete explanation of his use of poetry to create a substitute personality. He has passed beyond the reach of the "deep analysis" which his case demands. We may conjecture, however, that Browning was overcompensating, and trying not to *seem* to overcompensate, a sexual enfeeblement induced by excessive mothering. The same malady afflicted Ruskin, but of course much more severely. As men go, Browning was normal enough; he simply needed to convince his fellows that he was considerably more "stalwart and vast" than he actually was. He tried so strenuously to do so that the "mask" element, not merely in the dramatic monologues but in all his poetry, is probably very large.[17]

But if the Freudians are right, all artistic creation is a mask, all outward personality a *persona*. Perhaps, then, the preceding paragraphs have said no more than that Browning's mask fitted him somewhat more loosely than those of most other poets of comparable power. For our purpose, at all events, what we call "Browning" is the poetry that he wrote. Its religious implications are difficult enough to understand without indulging in guess-work as to the human mystery behind the words. We must take the mask for the face and be content to describe what we see.

The sculptor Hiram Powers, who dabbled also in phrenology, found that Mrs. Browning's organ of ideality was larger than her husband's, but that Robert possessed "the biggest bump of reverence he ever saw."[18] Bump or no bump, Browning often impresses us as more genuinely religious than Tennyson in desiring to believe in a spiritual reality external to himself. The dying poet in *Pauline* speaks for him when he expresses "a need, a trust, a yearning after God;" and so does Caponsacchi when he defines faith as "The feeling that there's God, he reigns and rules / Out of this low world." We need not lament or dread change, says Juan in *Fifine at the Fair*, if we believe in the Divine Permanence: "We come and go, outside there's Somebody that stays." Almost at the end of Browning's career, wise old Ferishtah exhorts a disciple:

> Never enough faith in omnipotence,—
> Never too much, by parity, of faith
> In impuissance, man's—which turns to strength,
> When once acknowledged weakness every way.

Browning, in short, knew the meaning of religion.

[17] The ideas expressed in this section were formulated before I had found confirmation of several of them in Betty Miller's biography and in R. D. Altick's penetrating article, "The Private Life of Robert Browning," *Yale Review*, XLI (1952), 247–262.

[18] W. H. Griffin and H. C. Minchin, *Life of Robert Browning*, pp. 50, 161.

More specifically, he seems also to have known the meaning of Christianity. The speaker in *Pauline* hungers not only for God but for God incarnate in Jesus Christ. The bewildered Sordello in Book VI gropes toward some

> . . . outward influence,
> A soul, in Palma's phrase, above his soul,
> Power to uplift his power,—such moon's control
> Over such sea-depths.

He tries to find his "moon" in a merely ethical ideal of humanitarian service, but he must be lifted above himself before he can lift others. He needs, says Browning in his own person, an "utterly incomprehensible" transcendent Power; but he needs even more a human embodiment of that Power—

> . . . its representative,
> Who, being for authority the same,
> Communication different, should claim
> A course, the first chose but this last revealed—
> This Human clear, as that Divine concealed.

That representative, as He appears in *Christmas-Eve* and *Easter-Day*, is no Arthur Hallam, no personification of human love: He is the Being whom Christina Rossetti calls "The Lord God Almighty Jesus Christ." He does not say to man,

> . . . Believe in good,
> In justice, truth, now understood
> For the first time.

Rather, as one having authority, He demands,

> . . . Believe in me,
> Who lived and died, yet essentially
> Am Lord of Life.

He is the guarantor of that immortality for which the pagan Cleon despairingly longs. Karshish cannot believe that He raised Lazarus from the dead, and yet—and yet,

> The very God! think, Abib; dost thou think?
> So, the All-Great, were the All-Loving too—
> So, through the thunder comes a human voice
> Saying, "O heart I made, a heart beats here!
> Face, my hands fashioned, see it in myself!
> Thou hast no power nor mayst conceive of mine,

> But love I gave thee, with myself to love,
> And thou must love me who have died for thee!"
> The madman saith He said so: it is strange.

Some of the poems, indeed, sound so aggressively Christian that if they had been taken literally—as of course they were not—they would have made the more advanced members of the Browning Society wince. For example, the close of the ugly story of *Gold Hair*:

> The candid incline to surmise of late
> That the Christian faith proves false, I find;
> For our Essays-and-Reviews debate
> Begins to tell on the public mind,
> And Colenso's views have weight:
>
> I still, to suppose it true, for my part,
> See reasons and reasons; this to begin:
> 'Tis the faith that launched point-blank her dart
> At the head of a lie—taught Original Sin,
> The Corruption of Man's Heart.[19]

The Pope—one of Browning's thinnest disguises—laments that men do not live the Christianity which they profess; but how, he presciently asks, would they live if they professed nothing but the validity of their heart's impulse? For a moment, the speaker in *Christmas-Eve,* like a good Broad Churchman, luxuriates in the pride of his own tolerance, praising

> A value for religion's self,
> A carelessness about the rest of it,
> Let me enjoy my own conviction,
> Not watch my neighbour's faith with fretfulness,
>
> . . .
>
> Better a mild indifferentism,
>
> . . .
>
> Better pursue a pilgrimage
> Through ancient and through modern times
> To many peoples, various climes,
> Where I may see saint, savage, sage
> Fuse their respective creeds in one
> Before the general Father's throne!

But at this very moment, symbolically, "the horrible storm began afresh," and the robe of Jesus was torn from the dreamer's hand. This tolerance had

[19] But some ambiguity may lurk behind even this apparently explicit statement. Conway reports that when he objected to these lines Browning "thought I had missed his meaning." (*Autobiography*, II, 21.) The poet did not, however, go on to explain what his meaning was.

been the fruit not of Christian charity but of sentimental "indifferentism." His cry of penitence restores him to his own religious tradition,

> For scarce had the words escaped my tongue,
> When, at a passionate bound, I sprung
> Out of the wandering world of rain,
> Into the little chapel again.

The little chapel is important for an understanding of Browning. His Nonconformist background largely accounts for that authentically religious objectivity with which we have credited him. The same background, however, also helps to explain more ambiguous features of his religion which are yet to be examined. For although Browning was reared a Dissenter, the York Street Congregational Chapel which he attended with his parents was a vastly more refined, prosperous, theologically moderate place of worship than the plebeian and rampantly fundamentalist meetinghouse of *Christmas-Eve*. The more cultivated bourgeois Congregationalists of the period had not forgotten their seventeenth-century heritage, but they had already begun to transform it into something quite different. They were anything but wild-eyed enthusiasts or grimly Calvinistic Puritans. On the whole they were more liberal than most Evangelical Anglicans.

At the dame-school, to be sure, the Ready sisters used to sing Watts's hymns as they brushed the children's hair, and little Robert's favorite picture book was Quarles's *Emblems*. Such pabulum was suitable for young children. The atmosphere of his home, however, does not appear to have been oppressively pious. Both Robert's parents adored him, spoiled him, thought that he could do no wrong. His dreamy-headed father, to judge from his quietly noble life and beautiful death, seems to have had the makings of a saint, but dogmatic beliefs were never of great importance for him.[20] He was born and reared an Anglican, and according to Sarianna he returned to his original fold "many years before his death."[21] It is symptomatic that he had joined with other liberal Dissenters and with a good many secularists as a founding subscriber of nonsectarian London University. He is said not only to have liked W. J. Fox as a man but to have sympathized with his very advanced opinions.[22]

The poet's mother was mild-tempered, delicate, a lover of flowers and music. German on her father's side but Scotch on her mother's, she had been

[20] Since on occasion saints can behave very foolishly, I do not think that the old man's humiliating entanglement with Mrs. von Müller need deprive him of this praise. But see Betty Miller, *Robert Browning*, pp. 168, 172.

[21] Alexandra Orr, *Life and Letters of Robert Browning*, p. 17.

[22] *New Letters of Robert Browning*, p. 119*n*.

brought up as a Presbyterian. Probably her Presbyterianism was of the "Moderate" variety, for she became a Congregationalist in 1806. She could not, however, persuade her husband to join her until 1820, when Robert was eight years old. Thereafter the whole family went to chapel on Sunday mornings, but for the evening service they regularly attended an Anglican church to hear "the preaching of the Rev. Henry Melvil (afterwards Canon of St. Paul's), whose sermons Robert much admired."[23] We must also remember the intimacy of the family with Sarah and Eliza Flower, and its friendly acquaintance, through these Unitarian sisters, with W. J. Fox, whose heterodoxy was too flamboyant even for his Socinian congregation. A close friend of John Stuart Mill, he combined a creedless humanism with Philosophic Radicalism and Saint-Simonianism, listing Socrates, Christ, and Bentham as the three great teachers of Utilitarian morality.[24] That Fox helped the young poet at the outset of his career is well known.

These facts are far from indicating that the Nonconformity of Browning's early environment was aflame with sectarian ardor. Indeed, they render it difficult to accept the theory which Betty Miller has proposed in her valuable biography. She contends that Robert's brief adolescent flare-up of aggressive unbelief was bitterly opposed by his mother. The pious matriarch insisted that her son abandon such wicked notions and return to the fold. He surrendered his reason to her will, and spent the rest of his days in feeling ashamed of having done so. Hence all his insecurity, his timid reliance on dramatic disguises, his "life-long obsession with the psychology of the charlatan, the quack, the second-rater and the 'apparent failure.' "[25] This hypothesis can neither be proved nor disproved by solid evidence, but it seems inconsistent with what we know of Robert's lordly status in the family circle and of the religious temper of the household.

As the reader is already aware, I am even more sceptical of Mr. De Vane's opinion that the breakdown of the poet's Evangelicalism was temporarily arrested by his wife.[26] Elizabeth's death in 1861, to be sure, made all the fundamental religious questions especially urgent and difficult for the widower. Returning to England, he found intellectual circles seething with disputes about Darwin, Colenso, Mill's *Liberty*, and *Essays and Reviews*. He felt both a private and a public obligation to think about these matters, and he did so with curious results. It is unlikely, however, that

[23] Orr, *op. cit.*, p. 18.

[24] A few of Fox's poems were cited in Chapter IV.

[25] *Robert Browning*, pp. 10ff. I have already indicated my substantial agreement with her general interpretation of Browning's psychology. (See above, p. 135.) My scepticism applies only to her claim to have discovered a specific traumatic experience.

[26] See above, pp. 56–59.

during their married life Elizabeth had done much to retard the broadening and loosening of his religion. If the poems of the Italian years are on the average somewhat more orthodox than those written before his marriage and after his bereavement, the reason is probably that the happy husband felt no need to quarrel with his not very rigorous inherited faith. Nor does the heterodoxy of the post-1861 poems betoken a complete severance from every aspect of the religious tradition of his boyhood environment. His brief attack of Shelleyan unbelief was itself an exaggerated outburst, appropriate to romantic adolescence, of one essential factor in the ethos of Dissent. If the disease never returned in so acute a form, it never wholly disappeared from his bloodstream. When he later became an admirer of Emerson and a friend of Carlyle, Stanley, and Jowett, a "vital" Christian but not a "dogmatic" one, he had not sundered himself from the Puritan spirit. He had simply moved onward with its natural current.

Browning joins Tennyson, the Spasmodics, and several other Victorian poets in exhibiting a rather definite pattern. First there is a rampant assertion of the romantic faith, emphasizing especially the rights and powers of genius and displaying a scornful attitude toward traditional religious self-surrender. This defiant grandiose aspiration, however, is accompanied by feelings of frustration and guilt. The poet sees that he cannot have the moon after all. He rebukes his own pride, acknowledges that he should think less of personal greatness and devote his life and his art to the humble service of his fellow-men. This reaction pushes him back in the direction of Christianity so sharply that when the first youthful ferment subsides he may, as a sort of penance, express himself in terms which sound quite orthodox. As his career continues, however, one sees that he has by no means completely renounced the craving for self-trust and self-expansion. By subjectivizing his Christianity he achieves a compromise which permits him to be *almost* as romantic as he had pictured himself in his boyish dreams, but without overt defiance of the dominant religious tradition of his culture. If something of the original Titanism has been sacrificed, what remains of it is safe, respectable, and edifying.

The starting point, then, is the yearning of the Shelleyan young poet in *Pauline* for

> . . . self-supremacy,
> Most potent to create and rule and call
> Upon all things to minister to it;

his lust to "be all, have, see, know, taste, feel, all." Despite a penitential impulse which bids him surrender his pride to God, " I cannot chain my soul." Nevertheless these aspirations, the similar "vast longings" of Paracelsus, and the selfish ambitions of Sordello are chastened and Christianized as the three early poems develop. But has the *Pauline*-poet really recovered, as he asserts, from the fever of egotism? John Stuart Mill, in that remarkably perceptive critique, did not think so:

> The self-seeking and self-worshipping state is well described—beyond that, I should think the writer had made, as yet, only the next step, viz. into despising his own state. I even question whether part even of that self-disdain is not assumed. . . . If he could once muster a hearty hatred of his selfishness it would *go*; as it is, he feels only the *lack of good*, not the positive evil. He feels not remorse, but only disappointment. Meanwhile he should not attempt to show how a person may be *recovered* from this morbid state,—for he himself is hardly convalescent, and "what should we speak of but that which we know."[27]

Mr. De Vane and Mr. Altick believe that these strictures made Browning turn from overt self-revelation to objective and dramatic poetry.[28] But *Pauline* itself is supposed to be dramatic: it is merely an immature performance in what was to become Browning's favorite genre. Furthermore he never recovered from the ailment which Mill diagnosed so unerringly, although he learned to avoid such artless display of its more extravagant symptoms by creating a more credible *illusion* of objectivity. Juan, admiring the gypsies in *Fifine*, is less "idealistic" than the speaker in *Pauline*, but equally romantic:

> . . . My heart makes just the same
> Passionate stretch, fires up for lawlessness, lays claim
> To share the life they lead: losels, who have and use
> The hour what way they will.

Of several mutually inconsistent conceptions of poetry and of art in general in the work of Browning's maturity, one is the familiar romantic glorification of

> . . . that brave
> Bounty of Poets, the only royal race
> That ever was, or will be, in this world!
> They give no gift that bounds itself and ends
> I' the giving and the taking: theirs so breeds
> I' the heart and soul o' the taker, so transmutes
> The man who only was a man before,

[27] W. C. De Vane, *A Browning Handbook*, p. 12. The italics are Mill's. The misquotation is from Pope's *Essay on Man*.

[28] *Ibid.*, p. 13; R. D. Altick, "The Private Life of Robert Browning," *Yale Review*, XLI (1952), 253–254.

> That he grows godlike in his turn, can give—
> He also: share the poet's privilege,
> Bring forth new good, new beauty, from the old.

The godlike poet makes his readers godlike by sharing with them his shaping power. Abt Vogler, extemporizing, achieves the miracle of a chord:

> Consider it well: each tone of our scale in itself is nought;
> It is everywhere in the world—loud, soft, and all is said:
> Give it to me to use! I mix it with two in my thought:
> And, there! Ye have heard and seen: consider and bow the head!

Bow the head before God, but also before the artist who has manifested "a flash of the will that can." As the *Essay on Shelley* bears witness, Browning never ceased to be a disciple of the Sun-treader in his sense of the divinity of poetic imagination.

Far from being wholly abandoned, indeed, Browning's romantic impulse remained strong enough to break down the religious objectivity which was a genuine part of his original character and to substitute for it a reliance on the Inner Light so nearly complete that it caused him to part company, implicitly and very nearly explicitly, from the Christian tradition. His personal religion has been described by Pigou, Jones, Dowden, Berger, Phelps, De Vane, Raymond, and a host of other interpreters. Without threshing the whole mass of straw for the fiftieth time we may single out those features which seem especially pertinent to the theme of the present study.

Alongside of those poems which, as we have already observed, seem faithful to the firmer elements in his Nonconformist background may be placed others which suggest distaste for traditional Protestant theology. *Johannes Agricola in Meditation* exposes the psychology of Antinomianism. The Zeus defied by Ixion, the Setebos dreaded but envied by Caliban, are thoroughly Calvinistic. More important for us, however, are the numerous pieces which, though ostensibly they preach Christianity, deviate very widely from the fundamental Christian beliefs which in other poems—and sometimes elsewhere in the same poem—seem to be so stoutly held. So striking are these deviations that we are sometimes constrained to wonder whether the passages which any Christian reader would regard as fully orthodox should not, after all, be interpreted in some esoteric sense. "The sole death," avers St. John in *A Death in the Desert*, occurs when we attempt to argue that the power and love of God are mere projections from the human mind. Yet the same speaker wonders what can be done to convert the man who,

> . . . owning his own love that proveth Christ,
> Rejecteth Christ through very need of him.

If Christ's love, as in Tennyson, is proved by human love, it can only be described as the product of man's emotion, and the "sole death" of the other passage becomes the source of spiritual life. St. John, not in this poem, said something quite different: "Beloved, if God so loved us, we ought also to love one another." That very beautiful and moving poem, *Saul*, perfectly illustrates what Browning means by "owning his own love that proveth Christ," for the Incarnation is here the product of David's love rather than of God's. "Would I suffer for him that I love? So wouldst thou—so wilt thou!" The great miracle seems to imply the assumption of divinity by human weakness quite as much as the invasion of human weakness by divine power:

> 'Tis the weakness in strength that I cry for! my flesh that I seek
> In the Godhead! I seek and I find it. O Saul, it shall be
> A Face like my face that receives thee; a Man like to me
> Thou shalt love and be loved by for ever: a Hand like this hand
> Shall throw open the gates of new life to thee! See the Christ stand!

Does this passage mean, "The Word was made flesh," or "My flesh is made Word"? David and Jesus seem very nearly identical, for the difference between "Face" and "face," "Hand" and "hand," is largely typographical. Here again, at all events, God's love is summoned into being by man's love.

So far, one would be inclined to say that Browning the Evangelical has become Browning the Broad Churchman—a familiar Victorian development. That statement, however, is hardly applicable to the conception of Christ expressed nine years later in the *Epilogue* of *Dramatis Personae*. The First Speaker, "as David," describes Temple-worship under the Old Testament dispensation, but Browning probably wishes us to think of the sacerdotal pomp of Roman and Anglican Catholicism.[29] The Second Speaker, "as Renan," declares that the Deity worshipped in these elaborate rites has become utterly unreal to our minds:

> The music, like a fountain's sickening pulse,
> Subsided on itself; awhile transpired
> Some vestige of a Face no pangs convulse,
> No prayers retard; then even this was gone,
> Lost in the night at last.

[29] W. O. Raymond, *The Infinite Moment and Other Essays in Robert Browning*, p. 49.

But the Third Speaker, Browning in his own person, insists that the Face has not vanished: it can always be found in nature and in the heart of man. Hence

> . . . where's the need of Temple, when the walls
> O' the world are that? What use of swells and falls,
> From Levites' choir, Priest's cries, and trumpet-calls?
>
> That one Face, far from vanish, rather grows,
> Or decomposes but to recompose,
> Becomes my universe that feels and knows.

"That Face is the Face of Christ. That is how I feel him," said Browning when he read the poem to Mrs. Orr.[30] But this is not the Jesus of the York Street Congregational Chapel or of any other expression of Christianity, broad or narrow.

Why did Browning trouble to apply the name of Christ to the universe of romantic pantheism? Partly because, like most Victorians, he wanted to think of himself as a Christian no matter what he believed. Due weight should also be given to M. D. Conway's observation: "Browning was not conventionally orthodox, but it was a necessity of his genius to project a divine drama into the universe. He hated to give up anything scenic, even a day of judgment."[31] Probably, however, the motives were chiefly moral and pragmatic. In conversing with Mrs. Orr, Browning granted that Christianity "may be a fiction. But I am none the less convinced that the life and death of Christ, as Christians apprehend them, supply something which their humanity requires, and that it is true for them." There are, he continued, abundant signs of divine power in the world, but not many signs of divine love. "That love could only reveal itself to the human heart by some supreme act of *human* tenderness and devotion; the fact, or fancy, of Christ's cross and passion could alone supply such a revelation."[32] But since the revelation of God's love through the Cross is quite possibly a man-made fiction, the evidential value which Browning assigns to it is not very formidable.

He is unable to regard this pragmatically desirable fact or fancy as a unique historical event. The Incarnation is the eternal identification of man and God in one spirit of loving sacrifice which is manifested in all its power

[30] Alexandra Orr, "The Religious Opinions of Robert Browning," *Contemporary Review*, LX, 880.

[31] *Autobiography*, II, 30.

[32] Alexandra Orr, "The Religious Opinions of Robert Browning," *Contemporary Review*, LX, 879.

whenever a good man and a good woman, like Robert and Elizabeth, are deeply in love. In *The Ring and the Book*, that

> . . . lyric Love, half angel and half bird,
> And all a wonder and a wild desire,
>
> . . .
>
> Yet human at the red-ripe of the heart

is she who had once so delighted Browning by praising the "veined humanity" of his own pomegranate heart.[33] But some readers have supposed the love here invoked to be the love of Christ; and in a sense they are right—or if they are wrong, their confusion is faithful to the confusion of Browning's mind. Caponsacchi and Pompilia do not quite deify each other, but they explicitly canonize each other as embodiments of that perfect human love which is indistinguishable from divine love. Caponsacchi has seen in "the perfect soul Pompilia"

> The glory of life, the beauty of the world,
> The splendour of heaven.

He speaks as one who,

> Priest and trained to live my whole life long
> On beauty and splendour, solely at their source,
> God,—have thus recognized my food in her.

She is the Sacrament. He tells his judges

> That I assuredly did bow, was blessed
> By the revelation of Pompilia.
>
> . . .
>
> . . . For Pompilia, be advised,
> Build churches, go pray!

In her gentler way, Pompilia says as much for him. After she is dead,

> If God yet have a servant, man a friend,
> The weak a saviour, and the vile a foe,
> Let him be present, by the name invoked,
> Giuseppe-Maria Caponsacchi!

Her final words to the court are especially meaningful:

> . . . Through such souls
> God stooping shows sufficient of his light
> For us i' the dark to rise by. And I rise.

[33] See H. N. Fairchild, "Browning's Pomegranate Heart," *Modern Language Notes*, LXVI (1951), 265-266.

Such love as theirs, then, is all that is necessary for salvation. It is the equivalent of "the fact, or fancy, of Christ's cross and passion." The love of Caponsacchi and Pompilia is very beautiful and good, but much that Browning says of its betokens some confusion as to the difference between man and God.

Browning, like Tennyson, is able to derive from a subjectivist interpretation of the New Testament materials with which to corroborate his personal intuitions. But he was displeased with Robert Buchanan for referring to him in the dedication of *The Outcast* as "an essentially Christian teacher and preacher." When Buchanan asked him, "Are you not, then, a Christian?" he "immediately thundered, 'No.' "[34] He was not, of course repudiating what *he* meant by Christianity, but refusing to commit himself to what he suspected Buchanan meant by it.[35] Browning could never feel sure about Christianity because he did not believe in feeling sure about anything. For him incertitude was precious because certitude implies finality. He repudiated historic Christianity because it claimed to possess eternal and perfect and absolute truth. "What's whole, can increase no more. . . . What's come to perfection, perishes."

The fundamental tenets of Browning's personal religion were precisely those of Tennyson's: immortality, free will, and the divinity of what is best in man—in other words, love as God. The great thing, of course, was love:

> I know nothing save that love I can
> Boundlessly, endlessly.

Far more surely than Gospel or creed, this knowledge is sufficient to establish the existence of a loving God:

> So let us say—not "Since we know, we love,"
> But rather, "Since we love, we know enough."

The comparison with Tennyson must be qualified in one important respect: for Browning the best love is sexual love regarded as a sort of Caponsacchi-Pompilia or Perseus-Andromeda or Robert-Elizabeth incarnation. It is very important for Browning that the Word should be made *flesh*—so important that in the erotic union of human and divine the fleshification of spirit is sometimes more obvious than the spiritualization of flesh. In one of the lyrical interludes of *Ferishtah's Fancies* he refuses to offer a love which is all soul:

> Take Sense, too,—let me love entire and whole—
> Not with my Soul!

[34] W. H. Griffin and H. C. Minchin, *Life of Robert Browning*, p. 296.

[35] He need not have been so suspicious since, as we shall see, Buchanan was not a Christian at all.

So far, so good; human love needs physical roots as well as spiritual flowers. But he continues:

> Make, Love, the universe our solitude,
> And, over all the rest, oblivion roll—
> Sense quenching Soul![36]

Soul proved by quenching soul? Only in the *Epilogue* of the same volume does this paradox seem to make him uneasy. After speaking of those moments when the thought of heroic personalities in history gives him highest confidence in the greatness of human nature he adds:

> Only, at heart's utmost joy and triumph, terror
> Sudden turns the blood to ice: a chill wind disencharms
> All the late enchantment! What if all were error—
> If the halo irised round my head were, Love, thine arms?

The question involves more than one layer of ambiguity. Rather than become mired in psychiatric speculations we have been trying hard to think of Browning's mask as identical with his face. But when a poet writes about love it becomes impossible not to think of him as a human being, and what recent studies have taught us about this man's life and character renders the aggressive virility of his love-gospel a little embarrassing.

A good many conjectures have been made as to Browning's sources in formal philosophy, Hegel being by long odds the favorite. But although he certainly knew the general positions of Hegel and of many other philosophers he depended so completely on his personal insights that inquiries into this problem are not likely to be fruitful. To Mrs. Orr "He was emphatic in his assurance that he knew neither the German philosophers nor their reflection in Coleridge. . . . Miss Martineau once said to him that he had no need to study German thought, since his mind was German enough—by which she possibly meant too German—already."[37] He did not know Jowett until 1865, by which time he had written many poems that have been regarded as expressions of the purest Hegelianism. The extent of his firsthand knowledge of German Bible-criticism and of the controversies which it aroused in France and England is also uncertain; but from such poems as *Christmas-Eve*, *A Death in the Desert*, *Gold Hair*, and the *Epilogue* to *Dramatis Personae* it is clear that he took a warm if somewhat muddled interest in these questions. His feelings were divided. He welcomed any-

[36] See Betty Miller, *op. cit.*, pp. 286–288 for the biographical background of these lines.

[37] Alexandra Orr, *Life and Letters of Robert Browning*, p. 100.

thing that would make Christianity so broad and loose and uncertain that he could identify it with his private religion; he disliked any cocksure systematic attempt to destroy illusion. But on this topic Professor Raymond has said all that needs to be said.[38]

Browning was less worried by evolution than Tennyson because he never conceived of it as a physical process. He saw no difficulty in identifying it with his belief that "progress is / The law of life." Writing to Furnivall in 1881, he denies that he is an enemy of Darwinism: "In reality, all that seems *proved* in Darwin's scheme was a conception familiar to me from the beginning." He had, he continues, stated the evolutionary principle in *Paracelsus* and *Cleon*. "But go back and back, as you please, *at* the back, as Mr. Sludge is made to insist, you find (*my* faith is as constant) creative intelligence acting as matter but not resulting from it."[39] What Sludge actually said was,

> We find great things are made of little things,
> And little things go lessening, till at last
> Comes God behind them.

The concept of "creative intelligence acting as matter" is explicitly stated only in *Paracelsus*, V, where Browning refers to the subject of evolution for the first time. Here man is the product of a life-force of joy and love surging upward from the lowest to the highest. Its aspiration is never attained, but for that very reason it will never stop.

This idea is probably a heritage from the romanticized vitalistic science which was popular in the opening years of the century, but if Browning had developed it he might be considered an important precursor of the quasi-scientific pantheism of Swinburne and Meredith. Ascending development in the individual and society is always one of his favorite doctrines. He does not, however, again address himself to the specific problem of evolution until after the publication of *Origin of Species*.[40] By that time the changing intellectual climate had made his views on the subject less romantic. Without invoking the life-force concept, he is content to think of evolution as an upward movement originating in God's concern for the development of distinctive human personalities.

There is a hint of Spencerian influence in Hohenstiel-Schwangau's assertion that man "tends to freedom and divergency / In the upward progress." More interesting, however, is the Prince's feeling that the concept of

[38] W. O. Raymond, *The Infinite Moment*, pp. 19–51. [39] *Letters of Robert Browning*, p. 189.

[40] *Caliban upon Setebos* may have been suggested by Darwin's work, but there is no very compelling reason to suppose that it was. See, however, W. C. De Vane, *A Browning Handbook*, p. 265.

evolution gives him a place in the continuity of nature, a sense of summing up within himself the entire process of growth. If there is a subhuman heritage in his humanity there must also be a human potentiality in the subhuman. He feels

> . . . many a thrill
> Of kinship, I confess to, with the powers
> Called Nature: animate, inanimate,
> In parts or in the whole, there's something there
> Manlike that somehow meets the man in me.

Hence evolution does not mean that he lives on a lofty pinnacle, but "that I recognize mankind / In all its height and depth and length and breadth." This would seem to be a more earthy and realistic version of the *Paracelsus* idea. In *Prince Hohenstiel-Schwangau* this view of evolution is introduced to support Browning's doctrine that although man should aspire, he should aspire in a concatenation of ascending actions. He should work, not dream; climb, not leap. He must begin at the bottom if he is to rise.

> Mankind i' the main have little wants, not large;
> I, being of will and power to help, i' the main,
> Mankind, must help the least wants first.

The wisest social service reflects the evolutionary process. Later we shall find that this "begin-at-the-beginning" idea is often used by Browning to prevent the broken arcs of this world from interfering with the perfect round of the next.

Similar views appear in two of the *Parleyings*, where the author speaks in his own person. Just once, in *A Song to David*, Christopher Smart hit upon the way poetry must be written and the way life must be lived—that is, by beginning with concrete realities. Nowadays the favorite method is just the reverse: "Master the heavens before you study earth." This is utterly wrong:

> I say, o'erstep no least one of the rows
> That lead man from the bottom, where he plants
> Foot first of all, to life's last ladder-top:
>
> . . .
>
> . . . Friends, beware lest fume
> Offuscate sense: learn earth first ere presume
> To teach heaven legislation. Law must be
> Active in earth or nowhere.

The evolutionists, Francis Furini is made to say, begin at the top with man and look downward. Hence (but I do not quite understand why) they see nothing but a whirl of atoms and are unable to account for the moral nature of man. Furini (Browning), on the other hand, would begin at the bottom and look upward. Not at the bottom of physical nature, but at the bottom of himself. There he finds two basic facts: "my self-consciousness" and "my Cause—that's styled / God." In the light of these primary awarenesses evolving nature becomes the process which gradually flowers into human wisdom and goodness. To pose as a champion of earthy realism and describe the scientists as a set of impractical dreamers was polemically ingenious. But it is Browning, rather than the evolutionists, who begins at the top: his starting-point is his own fully-evolved humanity, and he begs the question of how that humanity has been produced. Evolution is not for him a biological hypothesis: it is simply one more illustration of *Life in a Love.* He and Darwin are not talking about the same thing.

This glimpse of Browning's attitude toward science chiefly serves to remind us again how completely his ideas on all subjects depend upon faith in his personal feelings. "Law must be / Active in earth or nowhere," but the only law he recognizes is the fiat of his heart. In his bolder, ruggeder way, he repeats the Tennysonian "I have felt."

> I trust in my own soul, and can perceive
> The outward and the inward, nature's good
> And God's.

As with Tennyson also, this creed may be equated with Christianity or it may operate quite independently. It has no *necessary* connection with the Christian tradition.

The feeling-faith remains constant throughout his career. Many of his best earlier poems assume it without incongruously arguing for it; we can read them as expressions of a temperament which is exempt from rational criticism because it does not attempt to be rational. After the death of Elizabeth, however, he more and more succumbs to the urge to convince and edify, with results which are aesthetically and philosophically damaging. Close study of his rationalizations is unrewarding, since he himself invariably repudiates them and falls back upon what Tennyson calls "the primitive impulses and feelings," saying:

> . . . I have one appeal—
> I feel, am what I feel, know what I feel;
> So much is truth to me.

This self-reliance is confirmed by his belief in the essential divinity of human love: to feel nobly is to know God and to share His knowledge. And yet man neither can nor should be perfectly sure that he possesses such knowledge, for certitude is the enemy of growth and struggle and the adventure of moral choice. To insist on the inevitability of human ignorance is also a valuable means of protecting faith against the threats of science.

> You must mix some uncertainty
> With faith, if you would have faith *be*.

It is true by definition that faith never possesses logical or scientific certainty. But the idea of *mixing* uncertainty with faith suggests the deliberate compounding of an antidote against the sort of knowledge that might contribute to unbelief. In order to be "very sure of God" we must take care to be very *un*sure of the validity of perception and rational inference. That assurance achieved, we may proceed to philosophize quite recklessly. One shares Jones's opinion that

> it is a little difficult to show why, if we are constrained to doubt our thought when by the aid of causality it establishes a connection between finite and finite, we should regard it as worthy of trust when it connects the finite and the infinite. In fact, it is all too evident that the poet assumes or denies the possibility of knowledge, according as it helps or hinders his ethical doctrine.[41]

But even man's knowledge of God, though more reliable than his knowledge of the visible world, was purely subjective and personal. At least as early as *Rabbi Ben Ezra* (1864), Browning conceded that his intuitions were valid only for himself:

> Now who shall arbitrate?
> Ten men love what I hate.

The individual is the only arbiter, and his only realm of authority is his own mind. The little chapel of *Christmas-Eve* shrinks to a private chamber. Thenceforward Browning becomes increasingly anti-intellectual, sceptical, and solipsistic. Necessarily, too, the connection between his personal religion and Christianity grows more and more tenuous.

In *La Saisiaz*, the sudden death of Miss Egerton Smith raises the question of immortality.

> I will ask and have an answer,—with no favour, with no fear,—
> From myself.

Purely from myself. There is no appeal to Christian dogma or even to

[41] Henry Jones, *Browning as a Philosophical and Religious Teacher*, pp. 261–262.

specifically Christian sentiment. This feature of the poem is ascribed by De Vane to the influence of a symposium on "The Soul and Future Life" in *The Nineteenth Century*, which, as Browning states in the poem, he and his friend were discussing shortly before her death. "*La Saisiaz*," says this authority, "may be said to be Browning's contribution to this debate. His argument, like those of most of the contributors to the *Symposium*, deliberately left on one side the question of the authority of the Christian revelation. . . . He spoke, then, according to the rules of the *Symposium*."[42] But when we glance at Volume I of *The Nineteenth Century* we find that there were no rules which necessitated abstention from Christian arguments, and that out of ten contributors to the symposium at least six and possibly seven (one case is debatable) base their belief in immortality on the promises of Christ.[43] More probably, then, Browning ignored Revelation in *La Saisiaz* because by 1878 Christian belief no longer played any vital part in his religious thought. As early as 1864, indeed, on the death of Miss Wedgwood's brother, he wrote her that "the rare flashes of momentary conviction that come and go in the habitual dusk and doubt of one's life" are enough to make him believe in immortality "in spite of a temper perhaps offensively and exaggeratedly inclined to dispute authoritative tradition, and all concessions to the mere desires of the mind." He is rather surprised at the strength of his belief in a future life, for it is "a very composite and unconventional one."[44]

In *La Saisiaz* he finds that the question of immortality cannot be answered—can hardly even be asked—without positing the existence of a soul and of a God. Thus what requires to be established is assumed in advance. He grants that these presuppositions are not susceptible of rational proof; but he cries, in an astonishing burst of intellectual irresponsibility, "Prove them facts? that they o'erpass my power of proving, proves them such." To deduce immortality from the existence of God and the soul may, he continues, be "mere surmise, not knowledge"; but this surmise comes from "my own experience," and "that is knowledge, once again." All knowledge, the argument runs, is the fruit of experience, and all my feelings are experiences. Hence any feeling I may happen to possess is a source of real knowledge. This is the sort of wisdom that gave Browning his reputation as a profound thinker. To be just, however, we must observe that all this is truth solely

[42] *A Browning Handbook*, pp. 376–377.

[43] See H. N. Fairchild, "*La Saisiaz* and *The Nineteenth Century*," *Modern Philology*, XLVIII (1950), 104–111.

[44] *Robert Browning and Julia Wedgwood*, p. 7. But no man was ever more willing to make "concessions to the mere desires of the mind" than Robert Browning.

for Browning: he emphatically disclaims any knowledge of how other men think or feel.

Soon there follows a long debate between Fancy and Reason:

> ... Take, thou, my soul, thy solitary stand,
> Umpire to the champions Fancy, Reason, as on either hand
> Amicable war they wage and play the foe in thy behoof!
> Fancy thrust and Reason parry! Thine the prize who stand aloof.

Whoever wins the contest, the umpire, his solitary soul, will run off with the prize. Hence it seems unnecessary to trace the windings of this not very formidable *estrif*. Reason makes the most obliging concessions to Fancy, but gives up in despair when confronted by the dilemma of fate *versus* free will. Browning breaks off the shadow-boxing by saying that we have arrived at the point from which we started. "So, I hope—no more than hope, but hope—no less than hope." Many people, he concludes, have abandoned their religion on the authority of such great infidels as Voltaire, Rousseau, Gibbon, Byron. He hopes that some readers may be helped in their doubts by this example of a poet who "at least believed in Soul, was very sure of God." That many were so helped is a fact no less incontestable than bewildering. It is enough for us to observe that in its final stage Browning's faith, like Tennyson's in *The Ancient Sage*, owes its "sureness" to an absolute scepticism as regards reason and knowledge.

Having seen that Browning's personal religion is solely a matter of subjective feeling, we may now consider some of the directions in which his feelings led him. His cult of the glory of the imperfect—reach exceeding grasp, the endless quest of an ever-receding goal, the joy of aspiring failure—has provided material for too many inspirational calendars to require description here. It may be worth observing, however, that the glory-of-the-imperfect doctrine was a useful instrument in the romanticizing of Christianity. On the one hand, it had a flavor of Christian humility; on the other hand, its scorn of finality encouraged limitless expansion. At a time of deep uncertainty as to life's ultimate aim, the transference of value from the thing sought to the mere seeking provided a potent emotional lift. Since one did not know what the prize was, it was heartening to be assured that "The prize is in the process." The thing to be done, since it never *is* done, must be less important than the courage and vigor of the doing.

"Boys," the headmaster of my boarding school used to tell us at morning chapel, "it doesn't much matter what you do, so long as you do it with all your might!" This professional corrupter of youth associated such wisdom with Theodore Roosevelt, but it is also Browning's:

> Let a man contend to the uttermost
> For his life's set prize, be what it will.

The doctrine tends to obscure the fact that some prizes are better worth striving for than others. The consequent lack of aesthetic, ethical, and spiritual discrimination largely justifies Santayana's celebrated condemnation of Browning's "barbarism."[45] The fastidious Latin regards him much as the Duke in *My Last Duchess* regards the intolerable bride for whom "'twas all one."[46]

And yet the wife of James Lee shows no lack of discrimination when she says,

> If you loved only what were worth your love,
> Love were clear gain, and wholly well for you.

Although the main trend of Browning's work seems one boisterous negation of this principle, Santayana should have recognized that the glorification of the imperfect is in some measure an attempt to compensate for a frustrated yearning toward perfection. On this point *James Lee's Wife* is centrally important. In the last five stanzas of Part VI the fact of mutability ("Nothing can be as it has been before") denies the unquenchable longing "To draw one beauty into the heart's core, / And keep it changeless." That is what we want, and that is what we never get. How then is this "old woe o' the world" to be confronted? With a courage so robust that it seems to turn defeat into victory:

> . . . Rejoice that man is hurled
> From change to change unceasingly,
> His soul's wings never furled!

But however bravely we may try to rejoice in our lack of joy, the fact remains that

> Nothing endures: the wind moans, saying so;
> We moan in acquiescence: there's life's pact,
> Perhaps probation—do *I* know?
> God does: endure his act!

[45] George Santayana, *Interpretations of Poetry and Religion*, pp. 188–216.

[46] The remainder of this chapter draws heavily, with the kind permission of the editors of the respective journals, on two articles of mine: "Browning's Heaven," *Review of Religion*, XIV (1949), 30–37; and "Browning's 'Whatever Is, Is Right,' " *College English*, XII (1951), 377–382.

And yet this acceptance of God's inscrutable will can never assuage man's feeling that it is

> ... bitter not to grave
> On his soul's hands' palms one fair good wise thing
> Just as he grasped it![47]

For one who believed so passionately in a future life the solution seemed obvious: there must be a heavenly perfection to make up for the imperfection of this life. In *La Saisiaz* he writes:

> Only grant a second life, I acquiesce
> In the present life a failure, count misfortune's worst assaults
> Triumph, not defeat, assured that loss so much the more exalts
> Gain about to be.

Faith in divine wisdom and goodness cannot be reconciled with the world as it is

> If you bar me from assuming earth to be a pupil's place,
> And life, time,—with all their chances, changes,—just probation-space.

Heaven implies attainment of

> ... the ultimate, angel's law,
> Indulging every instinct of the soul,
> There where law, life, joy, impulse are one thing.

Abt Vogler sums it up in a single line: "On the earth the broken arcs; in the heaven, a perfect round." Imperfection here and perfection hereafter. The fullness with which we attain the latter depends on how manfully we grapple with the former.

But since our imperfect mortal life is the gift of that love which is God, it is *Life in a Love*. It "means intensely, and means good." Its inadequacies are not curses, but challenges to noble striving and failing and striving again. For Browning, the strongest argument for the existence of the next world was the badness of this. A badness which authenticates immortality can be, must be, experienced as goodness. The more robustly one glorified imperfection here, the more one assured oneself of perfection hereafter. The price of victory was defeat. One passed God's earthly examination by flunking it:

> For thence,—a paradox
> Which comforts while it mocks,—
> Shall life succeed in that it seems to fail.

[47] See Isaiah l: 16, where God says to personified Zion, "I have graven thee upon the palms of my hands."

The earth-heaven contrast is after all, then, a contrast not between evil and good but between two radically inconsistent conceptions of goodness—the goodness of broken arcs and the goodness of the perfect round. But although Browning's nature included an earnest desire for the latter, he turned more and more in the direction of the former. The goodness of the perfect round became a vague dream as he lost the Christian foundation for belief in it, while the goodness of the broken arcs remained real and vivid. He found it difficult to believe in heavenly flesh without believing also in fleshly heaven, for if one commits oneself wholeheartedly to the glory of the imperfect as regards this life, one may end by applying even to the heavenly life the principle that "What's come to perfection, perishes."

For Browning, heavenly perfection seldom if ever implies any essential difference in *kind* of activity between this world and the next: there will simply be an opportunity to carry on more satisfyingly the human work which has fallen short of its goal. "Nothing has been which shall not bettered be / Hereafter." The emphasis is on projection of an improved human life beyond the grave rather than on a radical transformation of being. Only in this sense does the Grammarian say that it is "God's task to make the heavenly period / Perfect the earthen." For the old scholar, the value of immortality lies in the promise of unlimited time for the annotation of classical texts. Similarly in *Old Pictures in Florence* the obscure failures feel no envy of the painters who have won fame on earth:

> We are faulty—why not? we have time in store.
>
> . . .
>
> Things learned on earth we shall practise in heaven.

There is nothing here, or in *Andrea del Sarto,* to indicate that this celestial continuation of human work is ever to attain the bliss of finality.

In fact *Old Pictures in Florence* shows that Browning, as an artist who delights in the rich diversity of appearances, shrinks from an afterlife in which the human countenance could express

> . . . no more play and action
> Than joy which is crystallized for ever,
> Or grief, an eternal petrifaction.

He is, on the contrary, attracted by the notion

> That, when this life is ended, begins
> New work for the soul in another state
> Where it strives and gets weary, loses and wins:
> Where the strong and the weak this world's congeries

Repeat in large what they practised in small,
Through life after life in unlimited series;
Only the scale's to be changed, that's all.

The penultimate line suggests that he is talking about transmigration rather than about a peculiarly strenuous heaven. What is important for us in the passage is Browning's insistence on the value of imperfection even after death. In the next stanza, however, he partly retracts this extravagance:

Yet I hardly know. When a soul has seen
By the means of Evil that Good is best,
And, through earth and its noise, what is heaven's serene,—

. . .

Why, the child grown man, you burn the rod,
The uses of labour are surely done;
There remaineth a rest for the people of God:
And I have had troubles enough, for one.

This half-whimsical recognition of the desirability of a little peace and quiet beyond the grave is rare in Browning. Much more characteristic is his explicit repudiation of static bliss in *Rephan*. Here an angel who has been granted the high privilege of dwelling among men describes his existence "When my home was the Star of my God Rephan."[48] In that starry life there was neither too much nor too little of anything, no growth or change, no awareness of better or worse, no hope or fear—nothing but unruffled serenity. No Browning angel could long endure such a place. Soon he yearns for variety, movement, incompleteness, aspiration, stimulating failure:

Oh, gain were indeed to see above
Supremacy ever—to move, remove,

Not reach—aspire yet never attain
To the object aimed at!

In response to this desire, the voice of a higher God than Rephan addresses the angel:

. . . So wouldst thou strive, not rest?

Burn and not smoulder, win by worth,
Not rest content with a wealth that's dearth?
Thou art past Rephan, thy place be Earth!

[48] Rephan is mentioned by the prophet Amos, v: 26, as "the star of your God, which ye made to yourselves." The name also occurs in Acts vii: 42–43.

Now, happy on earth, the angel rather puzzlingly reproaches man for his lack of faith:

> Have you no assurance that, earth at end,
> Wrong will prove right? Who made shall mend
> In the higher sphere to which yearnings tend?

Apparently earthly struggle may win a better heaven than that from which the angel has escaped, but how this "higher sphere" will differ on the one hand from Rephan's star and on the other from mortal life is impossible to say. One can only be sure that there will be plenty of vigorous activity.

If the perfect round of Browning's heaven sometimes shattered into broken arcs there were, conversely, moments on this side of the grave possessing a peculiarly satisfying quality which transcended the probationary struggle and muddle. The "good minute"—the phrase is drawn from *Two in the Campagna,* but the idea frequently appears elsewhere—is not a glimpse of peace wholly detached from the flux, but rather a concentrated spurt of vital energy so intense that it gives the illusion of being better than it needs to be for any instrumental purpose and, therefore, a pure good in itself. It is that flash of complete self-expression

> When a soul declares itself—to wit
> By its fruit, the thing it does!

The good minute may be provided by creative achievement in art or by patriotic self-sacrifice. Preeminently, however, it is associated with physical love: the *Summum Bonum,* as everyone knows, is "the kiss of one girl." *Now* more boldly implies that the good minute par excellence is, or ought to be, the sexual act.

But the bliss of *Now* is shadowed by the question, "How long such suspension may linger?" Not very long, as we see in the less explicit *Two in the Campagna:*

> . . . I kiss your cheek,
> Catch your soul's warmth,—I pluck the rose
> And love it more than tongue can speak—
> Then the good minute goes.

One might almost say that the good minute never actually occurs—"Never the time and the place and the loved one all together"—but that existence sometimes throws out a hint as to what it might be like. And yet this aspiration must somehow, somewhere, be satisfied. Might there not be a better immortality than a mere continuation of earthly effort?

How long such suspension may linger? Ah, Sweet—
The moment eternal—just that and no more—
When ecstasy's utmost we clutch at the core
While cheeks burn, arms open, eyes shut and lips meet!

As early as 1855, in *The Last Ride Together*, he had begun to conceive of a heaven which would be an infinite prolongation of the good minute:

What if we still ride on, we two,
With life for ever old, yet new,
Changed not in kind but in degree,
The instant made eternity,—
And heaven just prove that I and she
Ride, ride together, forever ride?

Although the confusion which we have been examining runs from almost the beginning to the very end of Browning's career, if space permitted it would be possible to show that this good-minute immortality becomes a favorite solace of his old age. Thus a lyrical interlude in *Ferishtah's Fancies* (1884) declares that if he had never known love's rapture,

. . . how should I conceive
What a heaven there may be? Let it but resemble
Earth myself have known! No bliss that's finer, fuller,
Only bliss that lasts, they say, and fain would I believe.

The same feeling is strong in Browning's last volume, *Asolando* (1889). These poems, however, also provide clear evidence that he has espoused the doctrine of chase and struggle too completely to be satisfied with an endless good minute. On earth, the special quality of the experience is inseparable from the vigorous quest of it, the almost but not quite getting it, the brave adventure of trying to get it again. Would not these values be lost if the consummation were eternally complete and unimperiled? Would not such a heaven prove as wearisome as Rephan's star, which this volume contemns? In *Speculative* he says that, although "Others may need new life in Heaven,"

I shall pray: "Fugitive as precious—
Minutes which passed,—return, remain!
Let earth's old life once more enmesh us,
You with old pleasure, me—old pain,
So we but meet nor part again!"

He wants the good minute, but he wants it entangled in the hurly-burly of "earth's old life"—the pain as well as the pleasure of it.

But he cannot eat his cake and have it too. Heaven cannot simultaneously provide *both* the broken arcs and the perfect round. The Reaper is at the door, and he must make his final choice. In the *Epilogue* of *Asolando*, his farewell to mankind, he casts his vote for an eternity of struggle and strife. In heaven no less than on earth he would be

> One who never turned his back but marched breast forward,
> Never doubted clouds would break,
> Never dreamed, though right were worsted, wrong would triumph,
> Held we fall to rise, are baffled to fight better,
> Sleep to wake.

That is to be the final glimpse of Robert Browning—eternally falling and rising, striving and thriving, speeding and fighting toward a goal which, if it ever were attained, would thereby lose its power to stimulate his appetite for boundlessness. He had wished to think of heaven as a state in which the probationary struggle would be rewarded by the gift of "one fair good wise thing," but he had committed himself so recklessly to mere energy-worship that at last he was impelled to project life's turmoil beyond the gates of death.

The collapse of the perfect round of heaven into the broken arcs of the earthly struggle would seem to imply the complete victory of the romantic passion for infinitude. In the last analysis, one is tempted to conclude, he cannot bear stoppage on either side of the grave. And yet this statement is too definite to reflect the confusion of his spirit. Before bidding him farewell we must bewilder ourselves by observing that his passion for boundless outrush is always safely contained within the stockade of the Victorian compromise. The face—here the difference cannot be ignored—was not quite so romantic as the mask. His romanticism was curbed not only by a surviving tincture of Christian objectivity but more potently by a cynically pragmatic, cautious common sense which seems alien to all aspiration, Christian or romantic. There is a side of him which prefers Blougram to Gigadibs, Hohenstiel-Schwangau to Sordello, Ogniben to Caponsacchi. And it is only when, weary of overcompensating his inferiority-feeling, he deflates illusion with shrewd but rather ignoble casuistry that he becomes a poet of much intellectual interest.

His "begin-at-the-beginning" view of evolution, as we have seen, not only supports faith in progress but provides a safeguard against progressing too fast and too far. If we begin at the *very* beginning and skip no rung of the ladder, the upward climb will be so greatly prolonged that the unattainability of our ideals will be ensured. This attitude is often applied not merely to evolution but to human life in general. *Pisgah-Sights* illustrates a type of optimism astonishingly like that of Pope's "Whatever is, is right":

> How I see all of it,
> Life there, outlying!
> Roughness and smoothness,
> Shine and defilement,
> Grace and uncouthness:
> One reconcilement.
>
> . . .
>
> All's lend-and-borrow;
> Good, see, wants evil,
> Joy demands sorrow,
> Angel weds devil!
>
> "Which things must—*why* be?"
> Vain our endeavour!
> So shall things aye be
> As they were ever.
> "Such things should *so* be!"
> Sage our desistence!
> Rough-smooth let globe be,
> Mixed—man's existence!
>
> . . .
>
> Only a learner,
> Quick one or slow one,
> Just a discerner,
> I would teach no one.
> I am earth's native:
> No rearranging it!
> *I* be creative,
> Chopping and changing it?

Here the champion of strife and struggle and ceaseless forward movement disclaims the slightest desire to alter the benignly static chiaroscuro of life.

Pisgah-Sights first appeared in 1876. Although a large amount of characteristic work was still to come, it represents the later Browning. Similar expressions of acquiescence in the cosmic *status quo* are confined almost wholly to poems published after 1870. It is only natural, one might say, that with advancing years Browning should have wearied of chasing the unattainable and should have relaxed into a benign serenity. But this simple solution is not satisfactory, for in the later period expressions of what might be called the *Pisgah-Sights* theme are mingled with precisely the same emphasis on the glory of struggle which characterized his earlier work. We already know that in his valedictory volume of 1889 his enthusiasm for the good endless chase remains so strong that he hopes to continue it even in heaven. Furthermore, the fact that the *Pisgah-Sights* theme is rare in poems published before 1870 does not necessarily imply that it is inconsistent with the *Andrea del Sarto* theme of "Ah, but a man's reach should exceed his grasp." Mood and tone are different, but it may be shown that the basic philosophy is the same. In what is usually regarded as Browning's gospel the goal of a man's striving must never be attained in this life. "So the chase takes up one's life, that's all." If the chase resulted in catching anything, man would become that most pitiable of all objects, a "faultless painter."

So far as our mortal existence is concerned we are exhorted to lead lives of dauntless activity which neither can nor should bear fruit in any final accomplishment. Thus Browning's passion for movement protects, rather than militates against, his distaste for essential change. He has been misunderstood by those who have interpreted his gospel of action as a call to build a better world. Fundamentally, the world is already just what it should be—an exciting ferment of energies. Since struggle is good, evil must be struggled against; but for precisely the same reason evil must not be destroyed: "Good, see, *wants* evil." His deliberately unselective aesthetic doctrine is in keeping with his ethics. "*I* be creative?" The lynx-eyed corregidor in *How It Strikes a Contemporary* sets down everything he sees; Fra Lippo Lippi would have the artist

> ... paint these
> Just as they are, careless what comes of it.
> God's works—paint any one, and count it crime
> To let a truth slip.

Practically speaking, of course, life's heroic bustle must be bustle about something. Browning regards himself as a good liberal; the atmosphere of service and sacrifice and championship of freedom agrees with his kind heart. Noble actions performed *ad hoc*, like those of Pheidippides, Hervé Riel, and Caponsacchi, provide him with favorite subjects. His liberalism, however, is restricted by the fact that all high goals are beyond reach. To the very limited extent that the world needs to be improved at all, the task is to be done by taking one short, realistic, empirical step after another. This view, sensible as it may be, does not betoken any very impatient ardor for the transformation of society: no matter how many such steps one takes, one can be perfectly sure of not arriving. The one-step-at-a-time idea first appears in *Sordello*, where the hero, disheartened by his failure to revive the spirit of ancient Rome, is asked

> . . . Why count as one
> The first step, with the last step? What is gone
> Except Rome's aëry magnificence,
> That last step you'd take first?—an evidence
> You were God: be man now! Let those glances fall!
> The basis, the beginning step of all,
> Which proves you just a man—is that gone too?

Here the realism involved is partly that of Christianity, but in later years the Christian element shrinks almost if not quite to the vanishing point.

One must not accept at face value many of the arguments offered in that sinuous piece of casuistry, *Bishop Blougram's Apology*. Nevertheless it is hard to believe that Browning does not sympathize with the Bishop's comparison of idealistic young Gigadibs to a steamship passenger who brings along absurdly bulky luggage, all of which the angry captain throws overboard. The prelate likens himself to the experienced traveler who snugly furnishes his cabin with just the right amount of impedimenta. The moral:

> . . . See the world
> Such as it is,—you made it not, nor I;
> I mean to take it as it is,—and you,
> Not so you'll take it,—though you get nought else.

Although Blougram perverts this teaching to base ends, the idea is thoroughly characteristic of one side of Browning.

It has already been granted, however, that in Browning's poetry up to about 1870 the emphasis on the good endless chase is so strong as to have convinced many readers that he is an apostle of progress and creative change. The later poems must chiefly be relied on for correction of this fallacy. *Prince Hohenstiel-Schwangau* (1871) is wholly a defense of the one-step-at-a-time doctrine. The speaker grants that his record reveals

> . . . no novelty, creativeness,
> Mark of the master that renews the age;

but this apparent deficiency was merely a sign of his ability

> . . . to perceive that God
> Knew what he undertook when He made things.
> Ay: that my task was to co-operate
> Rather than play the rival, chop and change
> The order whence comes all the good we know.

He adds that since good comes out of evil, complete destruction of evil would entail destruction of good. A similar passage in *Fifine at the Fair* insists that despite the "chop and change" (a favorite pejorative phrase) of unbelieving philosophy, man's religious nature remains unshaken. From something higher than logic-chopping Juan has learned

> . . . how from strife
> Grew peace—from evil, good—came knowledge that, to get
> Acquaintance with the way o' the world, we must not fret
> Nor fume, on altitudes of self-sufficiency,
> But bid a frank farewell to what—we think—should be,
> And, with as good a grace, welcome what is—we find.

Here is the gospel of Bishop Blougram, now (1872) espoused without the slightest reservation in favor of poor dreaming Gigadibs.

The relationship in Browning's thought between glorification of effort and acquiescence in things as they are is clearly shown by a passage in *Pacchiarotto* (1876). The hero is cured of his itch for reforming the world by an embarrassing adventure which convinces him that

> Man's work is to labour and leaven—
> As best he may—earth here with heaven;
> 'Tis work for work's sake that he's needing:
> Let him work on and on as if speeding
> Work's end, but not dream of succeeding!
> Because if success were intended,
> Why, heaven would begin ere earth ended.

Work is a pure good in itself, but it must be carried on *as if* it were directed toward some attainable purpose. On the other hand there must be no real hope of achievement, for the result of success would be a breaking-down of the dichotomy of earthly frustration and heavenly fruition.

Such passages show us how to interpret Browning's continued expression of the *Andrea del Sarto* theme during his later period. He writes in *Red Cotton Night-Cap Country*:

> . . . Aspire, break bounds! I say,
> Endeavour to be good, and better still,
> And best! Success is nought, endeavour's all.
> But intellect adjusts the means to ends,
> Tries the low thing, and leaves it done, at least.
> No prejudice to high thing, intellect
> Would do and will do, only give the means.

Aspire to the heights, of course; but since success is less noble than endeavour, avoid the peril of success by confining positive action to "the low thing." The last two lines are a half-hearted attempt to scramble back to loftiness: Browning has no real fear that "the means" will be provided.

In *Asolando* the old poet attempts to reassert the nobility of struggle and strife. The rather pathetic robustiousness of the volume need not cause us to revise our view of Browning's acquiescence in things as they are; for we have seen that even in the earlier poems man's heroic bustle is not expected to produce any substantial change in the divinely ordained medley of good and evil. Thus, although the *Epilogue* shows the poet fighting the good fight even after death, we need not suppose that his endless onward drive will "chop and change" the celestial economy.

His romanticism, then, was too much for his Christianity, but his psychic insecurity, combined with the pressure of the Victorian compromise, was too much for his romanticism. Perhaps, however, he owed his success as a nineteenth-century prophet to his ability to combine the *Andrea del Sarto* and the *Pisgah-Sights* themes in a single gospel of vigorous inactivity. By means of the former he satisfied the Victorian desire for earnest moral effort, confident vitality, progress, service, muscular drive toward "ideals." By means of the latter he soothed the Victorian dread of any really fundamental change. There was a ringing challenge to be up and doing—with no danger of disturbing the constituted order. As if they were riding a mechanical horse in a gymnasium, his disciples could enjoy plenty of virile exercise without the disquietude of going anywhere in particular.

Probably, however, their recognition of his essential safeness was mainly subconscious. His unromantic frigidity was like an inner voice in a string quartet, hardly heard in itself but subtly influencing the total effect. What his admirers consciously heard was what they wanted to hear—a fortissimo of vitality, very bold but somehow completely wholesome too. How advanced he was in his scorn of creeds, how reassuring in his belief in immortality! How brave of him to wish to aspire and fail and struggle onward, "There as here!"

Rebuking Mrs. Orr for her disapproval of the *Asolando* epilogue, Frederic Kenyon relates that "A remarkable testimony to its inspiring quality was borne by the troops in South Africa during the [Boer] war. A chance quotation of some lines from it during an entertainment in camp produced an instant demand for its repetition, and over three hundred men stayed behind to take it down verbatim from dictation."[49] These soldiers did not

[49] Alexandra Orr, *Life and Letters of Robert Browning*, p. 406*n*.

deliberately wish to continue fighting even after death. But they responded to the courage, the noise, the virile rhythm, the confident talk of heaven and duty from the lips of a famous, wise poet; and so the poem gave them an illusion of spiritual uplift. Thus it was with many other Victorian readers—the multitude being very great, and having nothing to eat.[50]

[50] Mark viii: 1.

Chapter Seven

SEERS AND SEEKERS

THE THREE foregoing chapters seem to corroborate A. W. Benn's opinion that the Broad Churchmen and liberal Nonconformists "occupied the extreme right of a much vaster intellectual movement whose left wing stood outside Christianity altogether."[1] The phrase "extreme right" might be questionable were not Benn thinking of the more conservative liberalizers. Even they, however, are recognized as allies by that ardent foe of supernaturalism, the scientist W. K. Clifford. He is less inconsistent than he seems in disclaiming any hostility toward latitudinarians who have abandoned priestcraft but cling to the illusion of a Divine Helper:

> No such comradeship with the Great Companion shall have anything but reverence from me, who have known the divine gentleness of Denison Maurice, the strong and healthy practical intelligence of Charles Kingsley, and who now revere with all my heart the teachings of James Martineau. They seem to me, one and all, to be reaching forward with longing anticipation to a clearer vision which is yet to come—*tendentesque manus ripae ulterioris amore*. For, after all, such a helper of men, outside of humanity, the truth will not allow us to see. The dim and shadowy outlines of the superhuman deity fade slowly away from us, and as the mist of his presence floats aside, we perceive with greater and greater clearness the shape of a yet grander and nobler figure—of Him who made all Gods and shall unmake them. From the dim dawn of history, and from the inmost depth of every soul, the face of our father Man looks out upon us with the fire of eternal youth in his eyes, and says, "Before Jehovah was, I am!"[2]

By the close of the present chapter the outlines of the superhuman deity will have become very shadowy indeed, and we shall clearly behold the face of our father Man. But as the uneasy whimsicality of my heading may suggest, the twenty poets who will provide us with material are an even more miscellaneous lot than those of Chapter IV. They are not a group, but an interwoven cluster of groups; also, to an extent which so compact a

[1] *History of English Rationalism in the Nineteenth Century*, I, 356.

[2] "The Ethics of Religion," *Lectures and Essays*, II, 244–245. The passage is fundamentally Comtian, but one thinks also of Swinburne's "great god Man, which is God." The essay on "Cosmic Emotion" is heavily sprinkled with allusions to and quotations from Swinburne and Whitman, for which see *Ibid.*, pp. 275, 277, 287, 288, 292, 294, 296.

sketch cannot satisfactorily exhibit, each of these groups is a cluster of special cases.

It may be said, however, that the poets of this chapter are distinguishable from the Subjective Christians by one or more of the following characteristics: (1) Although several of them come of Evangelical stock, they differ from the subjective Christians in being psychologically related to Protestant enthusiasm rather than to Protestant Bible-reading and sermon-hearing. Their appropriate seventeenth-century ancestors would be Seekers or Ranters or Familists or antinomian "mystics" of some sort, not the soberer, more extroverted sectarians or the Anglican Puritans. (2) As the preceding statement implies, they provide more unmistakable evidence that the religion of their heart's desire is the romantic faith. (3) Although they make some use of subjectivized Christianity, they are more inclined to satisfy their desire for self-expansion through various substitute religions: for example, the religion of humanity, Spiritualism, nature-mysticism, and the cult of genius. (4) On the average, excluding Tennyson and Browning from consideration, they possess considerably higher intrinsic literary merit than the subjectivists of Chapter IV. (5) Chronologically, as the following table will show, the poets of this chapter arise slightly later:

Decade of Birth	*Subjective Christians*	*Seers and Seekers*
1780–89	3	0
1790–99	1	0
1800–09	9	3
1810–19	9	4
1820–29	8	9
1830–39	5	2
1840–49	0	1
1850–59	0	1
	—	—
	35	20

The tendencies represented by the Seers and Seekers are at least as old as those represented by the Subjective Christians, but their free and full expression is somewhat retarded until the Victorian compromise begins to waver. The difference, however, is not very significant. Several of these men were flourishing in the thirties or forties.

Not all of the poets to be considered here exhibit all of the listed characteristics. I have included a few who express their religious aspirations in the language of historic Christianity. Perhaps they do not belong in this chapter, but where else could they be placed? They are not Evangelicals; they are not "Broad" in the usual sense; they are not Catholics, although occasionally they sound as if they were. Fundamentally, it seems to me, they are irregular mystics who want to write religious poetry and who find in Christian symbolism the most adequate vehicle for externalizing their spiritual experience. Although their use of such symbolism is not consciously insincere, their objectivity lies mainly in imagery rather than in creed. On the other hand their Christian commitments are too strong to justify the assertion that they are mere aesthetes, toying with the trappings of a religion in which they do not believe.

One such poet is the brainy and advanced Mrs. Augusta Webster (1837–1894), a political liberal and a champion of national education. Christina Rossetti admired her work but refused to join her in agitating for woman suffrage.[3] In her day she was sometimes called "the female Browning," not only because she was very deep but because she liked to use blank-verse dramatic monologues and epistles as devices for self-expression.[4] More explicitly, she has taken over Browning's trick of making pagans talk in such a way as to indicate a dim reluctant awareness of the truth of Christianity. Some time after the Crucifixion, Pilate soliloquizes:

> . . . We live now,
> And life means a great hurrying on to death;
> And then we die, and death means nothingness.
>
> . . .
>
> This Jesus, now—How strangely he has seized
> Upon my mind! . . .
> . . . He seemed to wear
> A quiet on him, as if he *did* rest,
> As if he somehow would have given rest
> To those who learned of him.[5]

In *The Manuscript of Saint Alexius*, Mrs. Webster relates with apparently complete sympathy a medieval legend of a youth who deserts his bride and his parents in order to devote himself utterly to the love of God. But the precise reason for her approval of his asceticism is suggested by another monologue, *The Inventor*. The speaker is a failure; his wife and children

[3] Christina Rossetti, *Family Letters*, pp. 97, 175.

[4] Far from imitating Browning's *manner*, her style is almost excessively calm and chastened. Nevertheless she is not only an intelligent woman but a true poet—one of those forgotten Victorians who deserve to be dug up and reinspected more carefully than I am able to do here.

[5] *Selections from the Verse of Augusta Webster*, pp. 28–29. The same method is used in *With the Dead*, *Ibid.*, pp. 3–14.

are starving. Much as he loves them, he feels that he must go on with his chosen work—partly because it will benefit mankind, but chiefly because he conceives it to be God's will that he should obey his creative impulse regardless of any other obligation.[6] This is probably what justifies the conduct of Saint Alexius in Mrs. Webster's eyes: he gives himself wholeheartedly to his personal ideal, and that, as in Browning, is what matters.

Although Dora Greenwell (1821–1882) was something of an intellectual, she was a softer, dreamier person than Mrs. Webster. Her contemporaries found her verse "touched with something of a religious mysticism"[7] which reflected her struggles to rise above persistent ill health. Christina Rossetti, who knew her well, liked her "large-mindedness"[8]—a quality illustrated by the fact that she wrote sympathetic biographies of both Lacordaire and John Woolman. Her interest in philanthropy provided the common denominator. Miss Greenwell's religious inclinations, however, seem more Catholic than Quakerish. *Gone* suggests approval of prayers for the dead. *The Man With Three Friends,* drawn from the *Gesta Romanorum,* tells an allegorical story much like that of *Everyman.* An incident in Calderón's *Los Dos Amantes del Cielo* is the source for *Daria*: a much-courted young girl, sick of her suitors' extravagant conceits, declares that she will be the bride of Jesus, the only lover who really has died for her. More impressive, and equally Christian though less peculiarly Catholic in flavor, is *The Eternal Now.* In God's mind her old sin, which she has comfortably forgotten, is *now.* Yet in lamenting this fact, she joyfully recognizes that He is *now* forgiving her. That faint, blurred grief for some sorrow of long ago is quick and keen *now* in His heart. His love never drifts away into the past. With Him everything, bitter or sweet, is fresh and living and immediate.[9]

Since James Smetham (1821–1889) was the son of a Wesleyan minister,[10] it is no surprise to find him continuing the old-fashioned practice of writing psalm-paraphrases and Biblical narratives. Even when he sticks less closely to Scripture his poems sometimes have a mildly Evangelical flavor. But he was also a devotee of William Blake, about whom he wrote a poorish adulatory essay. In one poem he reveals his admiration almost too patently by speaking of "the omnific power / Which wraps Eternity within an hour."[11] The

[6] *Ibid.*, pp. 48ff., 90.
[7] Memoir by Alexander H. Japp, *Miles,* VIII, 341.
[8] *Family Letters*, p. 51.
[9] *Miles*, VIII, 348, 349, 350, 357.
[10] He was an unsuccessful painter—not officially a Pre-Raphaelite but a friend of Ruskin, Rossetti, and Madox Brown. Most of his writings are critical essays. None of his scanty poems was published in his lifetime and none is dated later than 1869. His mind collapsed in 1877 because of his failure as an artist.
[11] It is much less certain that "omnific power" is drawn from Coleridge's *Religious Musings*, but Smetham may have borrowed from two poets in a single couplet.

embodiment of that power is Jesus. Smetham longs to find in heaven the fulfillment of the broken gleams of beauty, wisdom, and goodness vouchsafed to us in this life. But being something of a mystic he believes that even here it is possible to contemplate this perfection in "the quiet depths of Love." He also believes, however, that *In Memoriam* is a great religious poem.[12]

Perhaps I am wrong in feeling that the Christianity of Mrs. Webster, Miss Greenwell, and Smetham is not quite securely anchored. There seems to be clearer justification for including in this chapter the poems of Henry Septimus Sutton (1825–1901). He was strongly influenced by Emerson, who in turn admired his work and became his personal friend. Bronson Alcott thought him "a profound religious genius, combining the remarkable sense of William Law with the subtlety of Behmen and the piety of Pascal."[13] Alcott was referring to such prose works as *The Evangel of Love* (1847) and *Quinquenergia* (1854), where Sutton enwraps the "Love is God" doctrine in Neoplatonism, Behmenism, and nature-mysticism. The poems are puzzling because while they sometimes express his religious philosophy more or less directly, they almost as often use Christianity for an exoteric means of imaging esoteric truths.[14] Hence they could be enjoyed for quite different reasons by Emerson and by Christina Rossetti.[15]

Too supernaturalistic to be a Broad Churchman, too much the mystic to be an Evangelical, too "inward" and crotchety to be a Catholic, he must be regarded as a sort of spiritual Ishmaelite. But he was fundamentally a religious person. More than once he expresses a deeply unromantic dread and detestation of pride and a strong sense of the reality of sin.[16] *Rose's Diary*, the imaginary spiritual journal of a pious young girl, ranks high in the devotional poetry of the period. Each part derives much of its value from the whole, but the following lines are representative:

What mean these slow returns of love; these days
Of withered prayer; of dead unflowering praise?
These hands of twilight laid on me to keep
Dusk veils of holy vision? This most deep,
Most eyelid-heavy, lamentable sleep?

. . .

[12] *Literary Works*, pp. 256–257, 269, 273, 277, 285.

[13] Quoted by W. G. Horder in his memoir of Sutton, *Miles*, XII, 152. It is symptomatic that James Martineau also regarded him as a profound religious thinker. Before his conversion to Catholicism Patmore corresponded with Sutton on religious questions.

[14] No less ambiguous for the literary critic than for the historian of ideas, they range from merest doggerel to poetry of some distinction.

[15] *Miles*, XII, 152–153.

[16] *Poems*, pp. 29, 33, 69.

Wake, wake me, God of love! and let Thy fire
Loosen these icicles and make them drop
And run into warm tears; for I aspire
To hold Thee faster, dearer, warmer, nigher,
And love and serve Thee henceforth without stop.[17]

It seems incongruous that *Rose's Diary*, which St. Theresa might have read with pleasure, should first have appeared in conjunction with the occultist muddle of the "Proposals for a New Practical Theology" of *Quinquenergia*. The fact helps to explain why Sutton, despite strong Christian feelings, was never able to find a fully satisfying spiritual home within historic Christianity. By 1857 he regarded himself as a disciple of Swedenborg. Most of his Swedenborgian propaganda was embodied in prose treatises, but there are several poems in which he speaks prophetically of "the grand organic manhood" and of

The promised Cubic City, full of light,
E'en now descending from God's heavenly height [18]

In a later section of this chapter we shall find that Sutton, like several other Swedenborgians of this period, was not hindered by his visionary beliefs from dalliance with the romantic religion of nature.

Sutton knew George MacDonald (1824–1905) and is said to have exerted some influence upon him.[19] The Scottish seer deserves respectful treatment at our hands if only because one of the most distinguished present-day interpreters of orthodox Christianity has acknowledged a debt to him. Meeting him in the heaven of *The Great Divorce*, C. S. Lewis tells him that a copy of *Phantastes*, bought at the age of sixteen,

> had been to me what the first sight of Beatrice had been to Dante: *Here begins the New Life*. I started to confess how long that Life had delayed in the region of imagination merely: how slowly and reluctantly I had come to admit that his Christendom had more than an accidental connection with it, how hard I had tried not to see that the true name of the quality which first met me in his books is Holiness.[20]

In MacDonald's poems as well as in his mystical tales there is indeed a holiness which might have been helpful to a youth who was groping his way into the Christian faith. When the groping youth became a believing man,

[17] *Ibid.*, pp. 150–151.
[18] *Ibid.*, pp. 197, 200.
[19] MacDonald's inclusion may be questioned because so much of his work appeared after 1880 and because he expressed his religious thought more fully in prose. But he was publishing poems as early as 1855, and they are useful for our purposes.
[20] *The Great Divorce*, p. 61.

his gratitude might well incline him to forget that the early guide whose spiritual insight had pushed him toward Christianity had himself been moving away from it.

If Carlyle's tenderness had been on the outside rather than on the inside, the result would have been a man much like George MacDonald. Substitute the Highlands for the Lowlands, and Aberdeen for Edinburgh University, as the scene of the Everlasting No, and their histories are similar. The strict Calvinism in which young MacDonald had been reared collapsed for a time into utter scepticism. His version of the Everlasting Yea was found in a mixture of Broad Church immanentist theology, Inner Light mysticism, romantic nature-poetry, Browning, Carlyle, and most of all the Germans. Unlike Carlyle, however, he did not waste much time in further romanticizing the thought of Goethe, Kant, and Fichte: instead, he went directly to such pure romantics as Novalis (his prime favorite), Tieck, and Fouqué. But if in this amalgam his romanticism transformed the Gospel into something like *Undine*, what remained of his Christianity transformed *Undine* into something like the Gospel. His angels were fairies but his fairies were also angels.

It would be absurd to attempt to unravel his ambiguities in the page or two to which the scale of this book restricts me. The reader must judge for himself the validity of these few generalizations. In my opinion, his Christianity is by no means romanticized to the vanishing point. He is perhaps more of a sentimentalist than a mystic, and such mysticism as he possesses is not harmoniously adjusted either to his love of nature or to his warm humanitarianism. What one thinks about him shifts, as he shifts, from poem to poem. *Consider the Ravens* is beautifully Franciscan, a poem of Christian self-surrender if ever there was one. But the "Love is God" theme has seldom been obscured more verbosely than in *Somnium Mystici*, his "Microcosm in Terza Rima," which suggests damaging comparisons with Dante. If the whole body of his work exhibits any general trend, it moves toward the empty dreaminess of

> Oh, the dews and the moths and the daisy-red,
> The larks and the glimmers and flows!
> The lilies and sparrows and daily bread,
> And the something that nobody knows![21]

George MacDonald began, as Professor Lewis ended, in the knowledge of what that something was.

[21] *Poems*, p. 67.

One or two other poets of this chapter exhibit a somewhat similar mixture of Christian and romantic elements; others pass through an early phase of relatively objective Christianity on their way to other positions. In the Spasmodics, on the contrary, a hot youthful flame of romanticism usually subsides into the Broad Church compromise. But only in the poets who have thus far been considered can Christianity be regarded as a factor of major importance.

At one time or another, however, most of our Seers and Seekers pay tribute to that religion of benevolence which was so prominent among the Subjective Christians. Naturally it is emphasized in the verse of two social-protest poets who share the indignations and hopes of Elliott, Cooper, and Bennett. But for Gerald Massey and Ernest Jones the relation between the gospel of service and the Christian faith becomes even more tenuous.[22] In their verses Christ is less often appealed to, and even the term "God" is little more than a symbol of that humanitarian sympathy to which the adherents of "creeds and forms" are so indifferent.

Massey, a more representative humanitarian poet than Jones,[23] wants a religion of deeds, not of pious words:

> We pray, "*Thy Kingdom Come*," But not by prayer
> Can it be ever built of breath in air.
> In life through labour, must be brought to birth
> The Kingdom; as it is in heaven, on Earth.[24]

He is more consistently sanguine than Jones, who often emphasizes with almost despairing gloom the dehumanizing influence of machine civilization on the mind and soul of the worker. The factory, says Jones, "has stilled the laughter of the child." Youth is

> Trampled by thy fierce steam-horses,
> England's mighty Juggernaut.[25]

But Massey derives some consolation from the death of a workhouse child:

> No room for little Willie,
> In the world he had no part;
> On him stared the Gorgon-eye,
> Through which looks no heart.

[22] Joseph Skipsey, another champion of the worker, might also be mentioned in this connection; but he says almost nothing of religious pertinence until he takes up Spiritualism.

[23] Most of what needs to be said about Jones will appear later, since from the first he mingles his socio-political indignation with the cult of nature.

[24] *My Lyrical Life*, I, 78.

[25] *The Battle-Day: and Other Poems*, pp. 84, 87, 92, 94.

Come to me, said Heaven;
And, if Heaven will save,
We will grieve not, though the door
Was a Workhouse Grave.[26]

The sovereign remedy is the enlightenment of the toiler through education. Massey prays:

Bless, bless, O God! the proud intelligence
That now is dawning on the People's forehead.[27]

On this theme Jones is no less hopeful than his fellow-reformer:

Needs but one timeworn prejudice be given to the wind,
And soon successive truths will pass the gateway of the mind;
For fallacy is ever placed upon perdition's brink,
And sinks the ground beneath her feet, when men begin to think.

Even more than political tyranny, the chief obstacle to perfectibility through education is "priestcraft's curse."[28] Massey heartily concurs:

Trust not the Priests, whose tears are lies, and hearts are hard and cold;
Who lead you to sweet pastures, where they fleece the foolish fold!
The Church and State are linked and sworn to desolate the land:
Good people, 'twixt these Foxes' tails, we'll fling a fiery brand.

Elsewhere he exempts Maurice, foe of bigotry and defender of the poor, from his condemnation of the clergy.[29]

But the enlightenment which Massey desires for the toilers is more than mere logic-chopping. It is not enough that the trade unionists should call themselves the Knights of Labour. To deserve that title they must "true workers be / In Labour's Knightlier Chivalry." Their struggles for better working conditions must be motivated by delicate moral sensibility and refined aesthetic taste:

Come let us worship Beauty: she hath subtle power to start
Heroic word and deed out-flashing from the humblest heart!

. . .

O blessed are her lineaments, and wondrous are her ways
To picture God's dim likeness in the faded human face!

. . .

Come let us worship Beauty with the Knightly faith of old,
O Chivalry of Labour toiling for the Age of Gold!

He is trying to give Chartism something of the flavor of Kenelm Digby and

[26] *My Lyrical Life*, I, 253.
[27] *Ibid.*, II, 232.
[28] *The Battle-Day*, pp. 110, 173.
[29] *My Lyrical Life*, II, 79, 249.

the Young England movement. Whether the strange feminist *mystique* which accompanies his championship of woman suffrage is an outgrowth of his chivalric beauty-worship or a symptom of the influence of Comte is hard to tell. At all events he has very lofty notions of the *Ewigweibliche*:

> My fellow-men, as yet we have but seen
> Wife, Sister, Mother and Daughter, not the Queen
> Upon her Throne, with all her jewels crowned!
>
> . . .
>
> She is the natural bringer from above;
> The Earthly mirror of Immortal Love;
> The chosen Mouthpiece for the Mystic Word
> Of Life Divine to speak through; and be heard
> With human Voice, that makes its Heavenward call
> Not in one Virgin Motherhood, but all.[30]

Observe his application to the Virgin Mary of that "wheresoe'er" technique which was so popular in Chapter IV.

Not that humanitarian religiosity is monopolized by the bards of Chartism. George MacDonald's sense of obligation to serve his fellows is almost as strong as his longing for contemplation. The Spasmodic heroes, after having had their Faustian fling, discover that they should think less of themselves and more of others. "How I wish," cries Bailey's Festus,

> I could love men! for amid all life's quests
> There seems but worthy one—to do men good.
>
> . . .
>
> . . . Man is one:
> And he hath one great heart. It is thus we feel,
> With a gigantic throb athwart the sea,
> Each others' rights and wrongs; thus we are men.[31]

Thomas Gordon Hake appeals from "Christian" civilization to the neglected spirit of Christian charity in simple tales of village life which demand our pity for *The Cripple*, *The Blind Boy*, and a lowly maiden called *The Lily of the Valley*. R. H. Horne's interesting attempt to combine humanitarianism with a genuinely humanistic philosophy of life must also be set aside for the present.

No poet of this chapter, however, is wholly content with a religion of "Love thy neighbor." They all desire not merely ethical but spiritual values, and sooner or later they all recognize that mere good will, no matter how

[30] *Ibid.*, I, xxv; II, 221, 278, 281.

[31] *Festus*, pp. 14–15.

actively manifested, will not give them everything they need. In several cases they seek a solution of their problem in Spiritualism. The appeal of this cult lay in its apparent power to provide empirical support for the longing to be assured of eternal life and to experience something like the Communion of Saints through messages from one's beloved dead.[32] Mrs. Browning thought such communications fully consistent with her liberalized Evangelicalism, and many of her contemporaries held the same view. Others regarded Spiritualism as a way of transcending the superstitions of "popular" Christianity without ceasing to be "essential" Christians. The majority position probably lay somewhere between these extremes. Spiritualism might be unorthodox, but at least—as Mr. Sludge himself had argued—it provided an antidote against complete unbelief. A friend told Mrs. Browning "that twenty or thirty persons *of his own acquaintance* have been brought to abjure atheism and materialism by these manifestations." Kirkup the artist reported that he himself had been won over from a negative agnosticism. "It is certainly true," he affirmed. "There is a spiritual world—there is a future state. . . . I am convinced at last."[33] The mediums had succeeded where William Blake, his early mentor, had failed. In view of such results, surely it was a trifle illiberal of Tennyson to wonder why, "according to Wallace, none of the Spirits that communicate with men ever mention God, or Christ."[34] Victorian Spiritualism was intertwined with trends at once more "experimental" and more excitingly occult than the jejune mysteries of orthodoxy—mesmerism, animal magnetism, mental telepathy, clairvoyance, and (about the close of our period) oriental-flavored theosophy. The Swedenborgian element is particularly strong. The visions of the eighteenth-century seer lent authority to the table-tippings and helped to purify them from any materialistic taint—except when the mediums were caught red-handed.[35]

The cult of beauty and the chivalric ideal of trade unionism are not sufficient to satisfy the aspirations of Gerald Massey (1828–1907).

[32] Purely scientific study of the problem held little or no appeal for the poets. Not much came of the "Ghostly Guild" founded at Cambridge in 1851 to investigate psychic phenomena. F. W. H. Myers, one of the figures to be considered in this section, was a member of the group which founded the Society for Psychical Research in 1882, but to judge from his poems his attitude towards the subject was hardly one of disinterested experiment.

[33] Elizabeth Barrett Browning, *Letters to Her Sister*, pp. 190, 208, 212.

[34] William Allingham, *A Diary*, p. 339.

[35] The thought of Swedenborg, as we shall see later, was also a potent factor in the nature-mysticism of the period. It has not, however, seemed desirable to undertake a study of the influence of his specific doctrines. The Seers and Seekers drew from him what they wanted—spirits in the life beyond, spirits in the earth, and a spirit in the breast of man.

Hardly has the Chartist movement collapsed[36] when he becomes aware that

As after death, our Lost Ones grow our Dearest,
So, after death, our Lost Ones come the nearest:
They are not lost in distant worlds above;
They are our nearest link in God's own love—
The human hand-clasps of the Infinite!

But he remains anxious to be thought of as a man of cool, sober reason:

I ought to explain that the kind of Spiritualism, Gnosticism, or Neo-Naturalism to be found in my poetry is no delusive Idealism derived from hereditary belief in a physical resurrection from the dead! . . . My faith in our future life is founded upon facts in nature and realities of my own personal experience; not upon any falsification of natural fact. These facts . . . have given me proof palpable that our own human identity and intelligence do persist after the blind of darkness has been drawn down in death. The Spiritualist who has plumbed the void of death . . . *cannot be bereaved in soul!* And I have ample testimony that my poems have done welcome work, if only to destroy the tyranny of death, which has made so many mental slaves afraid to live.[37]

Yet the palpable facts on which this considerable claim is based do not seem to be completely objective, for we are told that

The Near or Far is in our depth of love
And height of life: We look WITHOUT, to learn
Our lost ones are beyond our human reach:
We feel *Within*, and find them nestling near.

Are spirit-rappings the product of the Inner Light? Apparently, in some measure, they are:

Eternity is not beyond the stars—
Some far Hereafter—it is *Here*, and *Now*!
The Kingdom of Heaven is within, so near
We do not see it save by spirit-sight.
We shut our eyes in prayer, and we are *There*
In thought, and Thoughts are spirit-*things*—
Realities upon the other side.

In *The Haunted Hurst, a Tale of Eternity* the poet is assured by a ghost that reality is spiritual on *both* sides of the grave;

Soul's no mere shadow that gross substance throws;
Our passions are not pageantary shows,

[36] In the preface of *My Lyrical Life*, I, xx, he says that he has been a convinced Spiritualist for forty years. The book appeared in 1889.

[37] *My Lyrical Life*, I, xx–xxi, 79.

Exhaled from Matter, like the cloud from cape,
They are the life's own lasting final shape.

. . .

What you call Matter is but as the sheath,
Shaped, even as bubbles are, by spirit-breath.

. . .

Spirit is lord of substance, Matter's sole
First cause, formative power, and final goal.[38]

This is the mystical side of Spiritualism. What might be called the sacramental side is represented by the séance. As the ghost goes on to explain,

Spirits may touch you, being, as you would say,
A hundred thousand million miles away.
Those wires that wed the Old World with the New,
And do your bidding hidden out of view,
Are not the only links mind lightens through!

"Sacramental" is my word, not Massey's; but it is surely applicable to "*They Sang a New Song*," where the medium's stock property is likened first to the Atlantic Cable and then to the altar:

Gather round the Table,
    When the day is done;
Lay the Electric Cable,
    That weds two worlds in one.
We have found the passage
    Past the frozen pole;
We have had the Message
    Answering soul to soul.

. . .

Gather round the Table;
    By knowledge faith is fed!
Ours the fact they fable;
    Presence is the Bread.[39]

Although the mediumistic revelation is as up-to-date as the Atlantic Cable, it is also as old as the pyramids. Jesus is only one of its symbolic embodiments, and not the earliest:

The light of Asia was of Afric born;
Africa, dusky Mother of the Morn;
She bore the Babe-Messiah meek and mild,
The Good Lord Horus, the Eternal Child:
The unhistoric Saviour,—hence divine—
Buddha in India; Christ in Palestine!

[38] *Ibid.*, pp. 48, 49, 304–305.

[39] *Ibid.*, pp. 269, 343.

The implications of "unhistoric—hence divine" are worth pondering. "Comparative Religion" has convinced Massey that the Christian heaven is simply a late variant of the *Egyptian Elysium*, where

> We shall see the good Osiris and his son the Word-made-True,
> Who died and rose—the Karest—in the Aah-en-Ru.
>
> He who daily dies to save us, passing Earth and Hades through,
> Lays his life down for a pathway to the Aah-en-Ru.
>
> Lo, the Cross of life uplifted in the region of Tattu,
> With its arms outstretched for welcome to the Aah-en-Ru![40]

But all the Babe-Messiahs, Palestinian or Egyptian, are merely man-made symbols of the otherwise inexpressible truth that

> A luminiferous motion of the soul
> Pervades the universe and makes the whole
> Vast realm of Being one.

From this medley of broken-down Christianity, anthropology, spirit-rappings, pseudo-science, subjective idealism, and romantic pantheism, Massey derives even more sanguine hopes for the future than those which had been nourished by his earlier faith in political reform and popular education. These are days of rapid and perplexing change, but

> We are English yet, my friends, we are English yet.
> We are standing in the shadow of some sublime
> Wide-winged Angel of the coming time.

He is especially eager to convince *young* Englishmen that

> This is no winter-withered earth to you.
> Love comes, and life is deified anew!
> And hearts grow larger than their fortunes are.
> The horizon lifts around, sublime and far,
> With god-like breathing-space—an ampler scope
> In loftier life, and glorious ground for hope.[41]

When Joseph Skipsey (1832–1903) was a young collier with a small but authentic poetic gift, he wrote like this:

> "Get up!" the caller calls, "Get up."
> And in the dead of night,
> To win the bairns their bite and sup,
> I rise a weary wight.

[40] *Ibid.*, pp. 82, 83–84.

[41] *Ibid.*, pp. 74, 75, 344.

My flannel dudden donn'd, thrice o'er
My birds are kiss'd, and then
I with a whistle shut the door
I may not ope again.

Surely Housman had read him? But once the poor fellow had been taken up by the literati and made curator of Shakespeare's birthplace and an editor of the *Canterbury Poets* series, it occurred to him that he should have an inspiring outlook on life, and then he wrote like this:

I'm the spirit Emmalina, thy guardian angel, and
Drawn hither by a subtle law but few can understand—
The golden chord of sympathy, I leave the summer-land,
Thy aching brows with lilies to entwine.

We need not linger for more than a moment over his group of "Psychic Poems"; they say nothing that Massey does not say better. Perhaps, however, Skipsey shows even more clearly the strength of the subjective element in Victorian Spiritualism when he cries:

I thank my God I ever lived to see the blessed day,
When the spirit's immortality to me is rendered clear;
Not by a logic might be made some other time to play,
But by a flash of inner light too keen for doubt to bear.

The inward authentication of psychic phenomena is apparently very essential. And by processes obscure to the uninitiated, Skipsey draws from Spiritualism the highly romantic inference that man is

A more than soul Titanic, . . . who still
Can make the very death-forged bolts of heaven
To dance attendance on his potent will.

. . .

A victor o'er the elements, a victor
E'en over self he moves, till lo! appears
Upon the earth he treads the very picture
Of what can be in the seraphic spheres.[42]

The spirits are not likely to convey messages of humility to one who has been so deeply impressed by the last act of *Prometheus Unbound*.

The romantic motivation of the Spiritualism of Frederick William Henry Myers (1843–1901) is particularly clear. His *Collected Poems*, read in conjunction with the prefatory "Autobiographical Fragment," provide an almost complete clinical history. From earliest childhood he had been

[42] *Carols from the Coal-Fields; and Other Songs and Ballads*, pp. 108, 227–228, 232, 252.

horrified by the idea of death as complete extinction of being. Ultimately he is able to rise above this dread by asserting: "I believe in a progressive moral evolution, no longer truncated by physical catastrophes, but moving continuously towards an infinitely distant goal." It is essential for him, as for Browning, that the goal should be infinitely distant, for what he wants is not the goal but the sense of personal expansion obtained from pursuing it: "I know that my nature imperatively craves . . . a personal, an unbounded, an endless career of life and joy. . . . We need, as I have elsewhere said, 'a summons to no Houri-haunted paradise, no passionless contemplation, no monotony of prayer and praise; but to endless advance by endless effort, and, if need be, by endless pain.' Be it mine, then, to plunge among the unknown Destinies, to dare and still to dare!"[43] Browning with a dash of *Manfred.*

Not inappropriately, his clerical father was a pioneer Broad Churchman, a stout champion of internal evidence. He was incumbent of St. John's, Keswick. The family knew and revered the aged Wordsworth, and the son's study of the poet is still of some use. Trinity made an accomplished classical scholar of young Frederick. He did not reject the loosely formulated faith in which he had been reared, but his first deeply satisfying religious feelings were kindled by Plato, Virgil, and Marcus Aurelius. Their teachings did not, however, prevent him from lapsing, by 1864, into a state which he compares to Teufelsdroeckh's "Centre of Indifference." After about a year the philanthropist Josephine Butler reconverted him to Christianity "by an inner door; not to its encumbering forms and dogmas, but to its heart of fire." This seems a little unfair to his father, who was anything but a formalist. It is possible also that Myers, looking back on this phase from his final enlightenment, is too eager to emphasize the heterodoxy of the poems which he then produced: they sound hardly less loyal to the letter than to the spirit of Christianity. In *Saint Paul,* for example, he writes that Jesus came not to the rich and great,

> . . . but to her who with a sweet thanksgiving
> Took in tranquillity what God might bring,
> Blessed him and waited, and within her living
> Felt the arousal of a Holy Thing.[44]

Perhaps, however, such passages illustrate what he means by saying that during his Christian phase he had felt "the need of an inward make-believe." At all events his faith soon melted away "from increased knowledge of history and of science, and from a wider outlook on the world." He "passed

[43] *Collected Poems,* pp. 5–6, 18, 19, 20.

[44] *Ibid.,* pp. 7–12 *passim,* 119.

through various moods of philosophical or emotional hope," his chief reliance, to judge from his poems, being the Wordsworthian religion of nature. We shall illustrate this stage of Myers's development in the next section of the chapter. Before long it collapsed into cómplete despair, and he uttered *A Last Appeal*:

> O somewhere, somewhere, God unknown,
> Exist and be!
> I am dying; I am all alone;
> I must have Thee![45]

This was in 1872. But in November of the previous year he had begun to take some interest in Henry Sidgwick's psychical investigations, and his hopes gradually rose. In 1873 he "came across my first personal experiences of forces unknown to science." Thereafter all was plain sailing. In the light of this final solution, Christianity

> looks to me now like a mistaken short-cut in the course of a toilsome way.... The Christian scheme is not cosmical.... Yet I cannot in any deep sense *contrast* my present creed with Christianity. Rather I regard it as a scientific development of the attitude and teaching of Christ. I look upon Christ as a Revealer of Immortality absolutely unique.... But his work grows more and more remote.... A New discovery is needed—to be made by no single Columbus, but by the whole set and strain of humanity.... And such an inquiry must be in the first instance a scientific and only in the second instance a religious one. Religion, in its most permanent sense, is the adjustment of our emotions to the structure of the Universe; and what we now most need is to discover what that cosmic structure is.

There is room for only one example of his own poetic contribution to this enterprise. In *A Cosmic Outlook* he writes:

> The inward ardour yearns to the endless goal,
> The endless goal is one with the endless way;
> From every gulf the tides of Being roll,
> From every zenith burns the indwelling day;
> And life in Life has drowned thee and soul in Soul;
> And these are God, and thou thyself art they.[46]

For better or worse, Spiritualism has shown Myers how to satisfy that craving for boundlessness and self-deification which Christianity had denied.

Fundamentally, Frederick Tennyson (1807–1898) was a deeply sceptical man who tried to stave off uneasiness by writing purely aesthetic poetry more or less in the manner of Landor. He was always hostile to formulated

[45] *Ibid.*, pp. 12, 17, 220. [46] *Ibid.*, pp. 12, 13, 14, 17, 390.

creeds and ecclesiastical institutions.[47] But he did not *want* to be an unbeliever: he detested materialism and hungered for some sort of supernatural reliance. In *Past and Future* he honors whoever can be termed the first prophet, first lawgiver, first poet, and so on. "But," he continues,

> . . . thou shalt be more glorious than all these,
> Who shalt subdue despair by any art,
> Whose hand shall cope the pyramid of Peace,
> And heal again sad Nature's breaking heart;
>
> Shall make Man walk, as if his God were near,
> Stirr'd in the winds and lighten'd in the sky;
> And pale Guilt trembling with a sudden fear
> Whisper unto his fellows—"He is by!"[48]

In the late 1850's this shy, disappointed, fastidious, crotchety man was an almost fanatical member of the Florentine table-tipping coterie; but as the cult developed an orthodoxy of its own he grew suspicious of it. Gradually he became a mainly theoretical Spiritualist, a more ardent disciple of Swedenborg than of Home. In his lonely retirement on the island of Jersey he developed new eccentricities without abandoning the old ones. He took up astrology and was deeply versed in the arcana of Freemasonry. Almost none of the poems published within our period reflect his occult interests, but the Greek mythological tales comprising *Daphne and Other Poems* (1891) are incongruously sprinkled with Swedenborgian lore. Perhaps their late date may excuse us from troubling ourselves with these crushingly tiresome pieces. From his manuscripts were posthumously drawn a few shorter and earlier poems which serve to illustrate the quality of his Swedenborgian Spiritualism. In *A Prophecy*, an angel appears on Mt. Sinai to announce the imminence of the New Jerusalem. Another poem tells how, when he was listening to music on a sunny May morning,

> An inner voice came to me from the sky:
>
> "There is a glory which thou canst not see,
> There is a music which thou canst not hear;
> But if the spaces of Infinity
> Unrolled themselves unto thine eye and ear,
> Thou wouldst behold the crystal dome above
> Lighted with living splendours, and the sound

[47] In the closing years he became less aggressive in this respect because he felt that although all positive religions were equally false they might also be equally true as symbolic expressions of the inexpressible.

[48] *Shorter Poems*, p. 68.

Of their great voices uttering endless love
Would sink forever thro' the vast profound.

. . .

"Behold, by the free winds the clouds are blown
Into vast shapes, and glorified with light;
The sound with wonders peoples all that sight;
But 'tis thy Spirit blends all these in one;
And that same Spirit free from fleshly thrall
Henceforth shall pasture its immortal bliss
On all things lovely gathered out of all
The sunless worlds, as from the parts of this."[49]

Observe the bewildering relation between subjective and objective in "An *inner* voice came to me *from the sky*," and the fact that it is the privilege of the poet's spirit to wield the esemplastic power which imposes unity upon the otherwise discrete wonders of earth and even of heaven.

Such passages indicate that we take no wild illogical leap in turning from Spiritualism to the romantic religion of nature as exemplified by several poets of this chapter. For Massey, the phenomena of the séance validate, and are validated by, the belief that matter is simply a bubble blown by Spirit. God is "that luminiferous motion of the soul" which "Pervades the universe, and makes the whole / Vast realm of being one." In proclaiming his faith in "progressive moral evolution," Myers might have appealed to so eminent a scientific authority as A. R. Wallace, who thought that Spiritualism, as a religion of "Eternal Progress," was "much superior to Christianity."[50] The basis of the position is more or less Spencerian, but Massey's idea that progressive evolution is somehow identical with Man implies a kind of Unknowable quite unknown to Spencer. Both Massey and Skipsey regard the Inner Light as the final arbiter of all such truths, and Frederick Tennyson seems to think that the poet's imaginative power is the force which welds cosmic diversity into cosmic unity.

According to the spirit who instructs Massey in *The Haunted Hurst*,

The veriest atoms, even as worlds above,
Are bridal-chambers of creative Love,
Quick with the motion that suspends the whole
Of matter spiral-spinning toward Soul.

. . .

There is a Spirit of Life within the Tree
That's fed and clothed from Heaven continually,
And does not draw all nourishment from earth.[51]

[49] *Ibid.*, pp. 60–61, 169.

[50] William Allingham, *A Diary*, p. 339.

[51] *My Lyrical Life*, I, 346, 347.

Behind such utterances there is more than can be accounted for in terms of Spencer or even of Hegel. To the facts already adduced this chapter adds abundant evidence that science did not make it impossible for Victorian poets to maintain, with Wordsworth in *Nutting*, that "There is a Spirit of Life within the Tree." If vitalism ever disappeared from scientific speculation, which may be doubted, it was certainly revived by James Hinton, whose *Life in Nature* (1862) and similar works blend a considerable amount of sober science with a vitalistic conception of nature suffused with mysticism, romantic pantheism, and a theory of cosmic sexual energy.

Several of these poets appear to believe in the World Soul as confidently as if they had never heard of materialism. Myers holds that a man should live "With the one soul of all things in his eyes."[52] Ellison speaks of "the universal soul / Pulsing through each part and whole," believing that

> . . . in Nature's every form
> . . .
> One spirit still is hovering nigh,
> The soul of all her poesy.[53]

The soul of the universe, as in Wordsworth, is a poet's soul, and evolution is the growth of a poet's mind. The budding poet in Sutton's *Eugene* entered into his birthright as he learned to hear the "beautiful continual hymn" of "that poetic soul / Majestical that vivifies the whole," and "Caught glimpses of the Deity that lies / Creative under all." A few lines later, Eugene himself is called "This creative creature."[54] The World Soul is not only poetically creative but morally and spiritually beneficent. "I know," writes Call,

> . . . that the soul that eternally weaves
> The garments of worlds, never fails or deceives.

Those who possess this knowledge lead "The joyful life in the great Life of Things." They may pray:

> O, Life, that ever lives in the sky,
> That throbs in the star, that flows in the sea,
> That still lives on when all things die,
> Power, Love, or God, live, live in me,
>   Like music or fragrance or morning light.[55]

This life, as the foregoing lines suggest, is life everlasting. Before his conversion to Spiritualism, Myers draws consolation from the thought:

[52] *Collected Poems*, p. 181.
[53] *Miles*, XI, 268.
[54] *Poems*, pp. 1, 2, 3. When Pope rhymed "whole" and "soul" he became responsible for a great deal.
[55] Wathen Mark Wilks Call, *Golden Histories*, pp. 169, 213, 240.

And here indeed might death be fair,
If Death be dying into air,—
If souls evanished mix with thee,
Illumined Heaven, eternal Sea.[56]

To a resolute mind, Constance Naden's *The Pantheist's Song of Immortality* is even more bracing:

Yes, thou shalt die: but these almighty forces
That meet to form thee, live for evermore:

. . .

Be calmly glad, thine own true kindred seeing
In fire and storm, in flowers with dew empearled;
Rejoice in thine imperishable being,
One with the essence of the boundless world.[57]

We may derive a sense of expansion from the prospect of absorption into a universe of infinite vitality. Myers experiences this feeling as he lies on the beach at night, his ears beaten by the boom of the surf:

Then half-asleep in the great sound I seem
Lost in the starlight, dying in a dream
Where overmastering Powers abolish me,—
Drown, and thro' dim euthanasy redeem
My merged life in the living ocean-stream
And soul environing of shadowy sea.[58]

He that loseth his life in the illimitable Whole shall find it.

Whatever the ultimate sources of such ideas may be, their indebtedness to the nature-experience of the great romantics, and especially of Wordsworth, is clear enough. Beneath the immediately audible sounds of nature Ellison hears

A music of far far diviner power;
A choral burst from out the sanctuary,
The touching music of Humanity;
Which at the heart still of all Nature lies,
The deep bass now of all her harmonies.[59]

Not yet a Spiritualist, Myers attends the Oberammergau Passion play in 1870. The "feigned Jerusalem" of the performance is to him a symbol of the unreality of Christian belief for the modern world. But he lifts up his eyes from the stage-play of faith unto the surrounding hills. From them cometh

[56] *Collected Poems*, p. 223.
[57] *Miles*, IX, 390.
[58] *Collected Poems*, p. 212.
[59] *Miles*, XI, 283. The allusion to *Tintern Abbey* is obvious.

help in the form of a recollection of his childhood in the Lake Country, where once

> . . . upon my infant head
> His blameless hands the Priest of Nature spread,
> Spake fitting words, and gave in great old age
> The patriarch's blessing and the bard's presage.

Wordsworth's way to God is better than the Way of the Cross:

> To such a life, embosomed and unfurled
> In the old unspoken beauty of the world,
> Might Nature with a sweet relenting show
> More of herself than men by knowledge know.[60]

Shelley was also helpful to Myers on his pilgrimage toward Spiritualism. He propounds the arresting theory that

> . . . not like ours that life was born,
> No mortal mother Shelley knew,
> But kindled by some starry morn
> Lit by a snow-flake from the blue.[61]

But Allingham, who knew Sir Bysshe and Lady Shelley and the poet's sisters, was puzzled by the resemblance of the cenotaph to a pietà—"odd jumble of ideas." Nevertheless he was distressed by Carlyle's scorn of the great romantic, for "Shelley is a star in my sky."[62] Wathen Call is grateful to Shelley for an unexpected reason:

> First Byron wrought in me a deep distress;
> Then Shelley made me weep, smile, love, adore.
> And feeling as he felt, I learnt to see
> What grace, what poesy, what wisdom crown'd
> The mystical sweet spirit and profound
> Of the melodious Seer of Galilee.[63]

References to other romantic poets are fairly frequent, but too sporadic to deserve analysis. We should note, however, the importance of Swedenborg as a link between the Spiritualists and the devotees of nature. He was one of Allingham's guides, and Henry Sutton became something like a practicing Swedenborgian in 1857. Emerson, Sutton's lifelong friend, exerted a strong influence on several other poets of this chapter. Allingham, who knew the American romantic slightly and corresponded with him, valued him as an interpreter of Swedenborg and, more surprisingly, of Plato.

[60] *Collected Poems*, pp. 175–176, 180–181.
[61] *Ibid.*, p. 34. [62] *A Diary*, p. 242. [63] *Golden Histories*, p. 256.

Entries in Allingham's diary for April, 1850, are revelatory: "Abbey River, Whirlpool: sit under shadow of ruined house with back to a rock, reading Emerson on Plato, to the tune of running water. . . . Read Emerson on Swedenborg, high and pleasant thoughts; look over the Atlantic to America and to Emerson. Thought of a tragedy. Evening—'Flowers and Poets' "[64]—that is, the actual fruit of his meditation was not a tragedy but a characteristically trivial lyric so titled.

As regards our present theme no firm dividing line can be drawn between these poets and several of the Subjective Christians of Chapter IV; but the general drift away from Christian views of the natural revelation toward romantic pantheism is unmistakable. The former view of nature, however, occasionally appears. As the westering sun shines through a bush, Ellison recalls the burning bush beheld by Moses. Then he broadens the symbol:

> Yea, this whole world so vast, to Faith's clear eye,
> Is but that burning Bush full of His Power,
> His Light, and Glory; not consumed thereby,
> But made *transparent*: till, in each least flower,
> Yea! in each smallest leaf, she can descry
> *His* Spirit shining through it visibly![65]

The deity similarly apprehended in the stars by Sutton and Alexander Smith seems to be the God of Christianity.[66]

But as the first two volumes of this series have reminded us, belief in the supernatural revelation atrophies when the natural is too exclusively emphasized. Ernest Jones, already cited as a poet of social protest, views nature as an eighteenth-century sentimental deist rather than as a full-fledged romantic. It is not Christ the reformer but the God of Nature whom he invokes against the alliance of tyranny and priestcraft. For the old-time English peasant, orchards and cornfields are "altars where he worships God." But the factory workers are "Perishing from want of *Nature*!" Their prayer is

> Take us back to lea and wild wood,
> Back to nature and to Thee!
> To the child restore his childhood—
> To the man his dignity!

Rejecting the Czar's claim of divine right, the Russian serf appeals to "God's book of nature: its writings read not thus." No, Nature bespeaks

[64] *Diary*, pp. 57, 58. [65] *Miles*, XII, 293.
[66] H. S. Sutton, *Poems*, pp. 17–19; Alexander Smith, *Poetical Works*, pp. 106–107.

the will of Nature's God that all have an equal right to enjoy the beautiful world which He has given them.[67]

Then as divine immanence more and more supplants divine transcendence, the God of Nature is gradually transformed into the God that is *in* nature and nowhere else. In this process not only God but nature itself loses the objectivity which moves the true scientist to regard the physical universe with potentially religious feelings of self-abnegation. For it is only in the mind of man, nature's culmination, that the "sense sublime / Of something far more deeply interfused" becomes fully conscious, spiritual, creative. In their apparent devotion to numinous nature, very few of the poets whom we are now considering feel any reverence toward powers other than their own. On one occasion Sutton is unusually outspoken:

> Man doth usurp all space,
> Stares thee in rock, bush, river, in the face.
> Never yet thine eyes beheld a tree;
> 'Tis no sea thou seest in the sea,
> 'Tis but a disguised humanity.
> To avoid thy fellow, vain thy plan;
> All that interests a man is man.[68]

Romantic naturalism is seldom so unabashedly humanistic. Usually, as we have seen, these writers prefer to derive a sense of boundlessness from the affinity between the soul of the poet and the less articulately poetic soul of the world. Sutton himself declares that to be a poet

> . . . is to give back Nature's each true feature,
> And glass her surfaces by the control
> Of that which shapes them—their interior soul.[69]

According to Ellison,

> Of all Nature's harmonies
> The corresponding key-note lies
> In man's soul, and every part
> Hath an echo in his heart;
>
> . . .
>
> The moral world and physical,
> The outer and the inner, all
> Form one vast and perfect whole
> And the highest poet he
> Who of the vast machinery
> At the centre stands, and sees

[67] *The Battle-Day*, pp. 88, 95, 103. [68] *Poems*, p. 44. [69] *Ibid.*, pp. 95–96.

Creation rise by due degrees;
And with Wisdom's master-key
Unlocks the soul of harmony.[70]

In *The Poet's Prayer to the Evening Wind*, a barefaced imitation of Shelley's ode, Ernest Jones tells the wind that he aspires to be "A bard, as thou, brave, fetterless, and free."[71] But we need not suppose that he depends on the forces of nature for the attainment of this ambition. What the wind means for him, as for Shelley, is produced by "the incantation of this verse." His real belief is expressed in *Corayda*:

While the mind still reigns in its kingly dome,
While the heart in the breast beats still,
There is nothing so stubborn, wherever we roam,
But must yield to the conquering will.[72]

Massey images the poet as *The Bridegroom of Beauty*. He

. . . is greater than a King.
He plucks the veil from hidden loveliness.

. . .

All things obey his soul's creative eye;
For him earth ripens fruit-like in the light.

But he concerns himself with profounder matters than the revealing of sensuous beauties:

The shows of things are but a robe o' the day,
His life down-deepens to the living heart.

. . .

The soul of all things is invisible,
And nearest to that soul the Poet sings.[73]

Four of the devotees of nature whose poems we have been citing deserve some attention as individuals either because of some strongly marked idiosyncrasy or because of the complicated way in which the nature-cult mingles in their work with other trends. What remains to be said of Henry Ellison (1811–1880) is that the common denominator of his poems is a rather extreme transcendentalism. Although he expresses the utmost reverence for something called "nature," he really cares nothing about objects. Probably he considers himself a Platonist. In *Season-Changes* he avers that any gloomy feelings roused by the spectacle of transitoriness and decay in nature can easily be banished,

[70] *Miles*, XI, 268.
[71] *Poems*, p. 127.
[72] *Corayda: A Tale of Faith and Chivalry*, p. 6.
[73] *My Lyrical Life*, I, 223–224.

. . . for here below
What are such things but idle show;
Whose whole worth in thyself doth dwell
Created by thy magic spell.

. . .

Lies not life's true worth in thought?
Are not hence its best hues caught?
Can we not in soul pass in
To the promise-land, and win
Even to reality
Some shadow of that purer sky?

. . .

Is it not enough to think
And as with a Lethe-drink
Gnawing sorrows melt away,
In the warmth of Faith's full ray.

"Faith" means faith in the magic spell that dwells in yourself. One advantage of his position, to be sure, is that he can switch back and forth between a hazy transcendentalized naturalism and a hazy supernaturalism. In *To Psyche* he even speaks of "The Presence and the Throne of the Most High,"[74] but probably that throne is situated within the heart of man. A strong point in Ellison's favor, indeed, is that he does not seem to expect us to regard him as a Christian.

Although Wathen Mark Wilks Call (1817–1890) published *Golden Histories*, his last volume of verse, in 1871, none of the poems which it contains "save a bit of translation" had been written later than 1859[75]—an early date for the rather advanced spiritual deliquescence that he represents. As we already know, Shelley aroused his love for "the melodious Seer of Galilee." Coleridge's theological writings convinced him that he could receive Holy Orders without disloyalty to his conscience. But Eternal Punishment was too much for him. His denial of this dogma gradually drew him into denial of all others, and he "quietly retired from the English Church."[76] He was a friend of Moncure D. Conway and married the no less heterodox widow of Charles Hennell.

To turn from these facts to his poems is to be reminded of the obscure but tenacious relationship between the dry or rationalistic and the sweet or

[74] *Miles*, XI, 276, 280, 291.

[75] Author's letter of presentation to Alexander J. Ellis, pasted into a copy in the Cornell University Library. In 1876 Call published a revised edition of *Reverberations*, which first appeared in 1849. In revising it he may have added a few poems written later than any of those in *Golden Histories*, but the point is not important for us.

[76] M. D. Conway, *Autobiography*, II, 154.

romantic types of unbelief. *Golden Histories* is a group of seven tales drawn from Greek and Roman legend with intent to show that all the so-called Christian virtues may be possessed by men and women who know nothing about Christianity.

More interesting to us is a section of the volume subtitled "Romantic Poems"—102 pages of shortish lyrics in which the most persistent theme is nostalgic longing for the nature-experience enjoyed in childhood days when he played Robin Hood and Maid Marian with little Miss Brabant, his future wife:

> Ah! sweet days of my youth!
> Are ye vanish'd for aye?
> O Beauty! O Truth!
> Did ye die in your May?
>
> I was young, I was young,
> When the clouds spoke of God,
> When the trees as they swung,
> Seemed to nod to his nod.

Such insights have not irrevocably vanished: even now they return "When I feel like a child." He himself is the grown-up *Little Boy Blue* of whom he writes:

> O the Nymphs and the Graces
> Still gleam on his eyes,
> And the kind fairy faces
> Look down from the skies;
>
> . . .
>
> A winding and weaving
> In flowers and trees,
> A floating and heaving
> In sunlight and breeze;
>
> And a striving and soaring,
> A gladness and grace,
> Make him kneel, half adoring
> The God in the place.[77]

The fairy-tale "mysticism" of these poems forbids us to think of Wordsworth as a major influence. Like MacDonald, who says this sort of thing better, Call depends chiefly on German sources—observe also his favorite meter. But while MacDonald thinks primarily of Novalis, the horn blown by this Little Boy Blue is *Des Knaben Wunderhorn*.

[77] *Golden Histories*, pp. 145, 147, 150.

Call's identification of the romantic impulse with the egocentricity of childhood is disarmingly frank. As a child he dreamed of a bird who sang that the universe was made expressly for him:

> All, all is thine! thou, thou alone art king,
> Fair, good, and wise!

He continues to believe in this message:

> I dreamt it once, perchance as childhood dreams,
> When life began;
> I dream it now nor think it less becomes
> The time-taught man.

(Here, to be sure, he must be thinking of the Wordsworthian rainbow.) In this nostalgic faith, amusingly enough, he rebukes the nostalgia of the medievalists:

> Knighthood, noble action, simple faith,
> Regal Church and soldier King delight you;
> But a royal life and knightly death,
> Even in this age of prose invite you.

Cease to bewail the passing of "the old forms" and cleave to "the enduring spirit":

> Trust the soul that dwells in every soul,
> Into one brave friendship let men enter;
> All the stars and planets as they roll
> Find in one great sun their common centre.[78]

In short, come blow your horn.

Call is ever so spiritual, but although his poems do not usually abound in sensuous luxuries they suggest a slightly excessive interest in children's flesh. Among various elevating *Influences* he mentions

> The children that about us play,
> With golden hair and soft white flesh,
> Smooth as magnolia flowers.

Elsewhere we read:

> When I am smothered under children's faces,
> Dazzled by floating hair and warm blue eyes,
> And catching glimpses, mid their wild embraces,
> Of delicate white limbs that scorn disguise,
> I praise thee, World.[79]

[78] *Ibid.*, pp. 190, 241.

[79] *Ibid.*, pp. 198, 209.

The debt to Longfellow is obvious, and the poem is entitled *Hymn*, but somehow one does not like "catching glimpses."

William Allingham (1824–1889) was also fond of fairies (vaguely Irish rather than German), but he did not learn so much from them. If the Protestantism of his native Ulster ever meant anything to him it soon faded from his mind, leaving a confusion which he was never able to resolve despite the help of Plato, Swedenborg, Blake, Shelley, and Emerson. All students of the period are gratefully aware how anxiously he pesters Carlyle, Tennyson, and Browning for statements of their religious ideas. To the diary which records these interviews he confided in 1882 a sort of creed. The question of the existence of God, he says, is certainly vital,

> but this does not justify dogmatism upon it. . . . I will have nothing to do with the Church of Rome, or indeed with any form of Christianity . . . because I know the structure is built on false dogmas. No verbal Revelation of any date, in any tongue, has the least authority with me. . . . We cannot in the least describe, or comprehend, or even think Deity. And yet we can believe in Deity, and that belief is not fantastic, but natural, sound, and reasonable. There is to me no conception of the Universe possible save as the dominion of Power and Wisdom, unfathomably great, yet in sympathy with my own intelligent nature, a greatness presenting itself to me (when I dare at all to shape it) as a true Personality . . . *Almighty God*, —to whom turns my soul, sharing, I know not how, the mystic divine nature. . . . Logic has no hold here. Rhetoric is out of place.[80]

To judge from his poems, however, these words were written in an exceptionally confident mood. Besides, a man who has rejected the dogmatic principle is compelled to find reasons of his own for his personal religion, and this Allingham was never able to do. He knew that such faith as he possessed was of the sort which vanishes under rational scrutiny:

> A charm, most spiritual, faint,
> And delicate, forsakes our breast,
> Bird-like, when it perceives the taint
> Of prying breath upon its nest.[81]

He might have been happier if, like his friends of the aesthetic group, he had used his facile lyricism for expressing the cult of beauty; but something forced him to try to think and feel beyond the limits of his mediocrity. It is unfortunate that his personal charm admitted him to the society of so many men who were bigger than he. "When the main road of dogma has become a quagmire," he told Carlyle, "people will get back to Religion by byways, as it were. Domestic love will not fail. The love of Nature, too, I own I think

[80] *Diary*, pp. 317–318.

[81] *Songs, Ballads, and Stories*, p. 61.

a powerful help to religious feeling."[82] Domestic love was granted him, but there is no indication that he made much use of it as a byway to God. Nature was a little more helpful in his quest. When he looks at the starry skies he feels himself expanding with

> An Infinite Universe lighted with millions of burning suns,
> Boundlessly fill'd with electrical palpitant world-forming ether,
> Endlessly everywhere moving, concéntrating, welling-forth pow'r,
> Life into countless shapes drawn upward, mystical spirit
> Born, that man—even we—may commune with God Most High.[83]

In his case, however, the cosmic process fell short of its final goal. He must console himself as best he can with the reflection that all men march to the *General Chorus* of "Life, Death; Life, Death." He does not know what it means, but he finds it somehow inspiring:

> On with the rest, your footsteps timing!
> Mystical music flows in the song,
> (Blent with it?—Born from it?)—loftily chiming,
> Tenderly, soothing, it bears you along!
> *Life, Death; Life, Death;*
> Strange is the chant of human breath![84]

This is the best wisdom that he can derive from nature or from anything else, but he does not think that it is all he needs to know.

Thomas Gordon Hake (1809–1895)[85] is an interesting poet and a baffling personality; I find no other Victorian quite like him. In his *Memoirs* he writes: "To keep those in order who believe too much, Nature has issued a series of minds that believe too little, and I am one of them." He confesses this cheerfully, since he holds that "Good little boys and girls are never very well." He is anticlerical and antitheological. "A well-educated scientific man would decide a religious question in five minutes which would take five hundred years for all the doctors of divinity to get to the bottom of."[86] We must not infer, however, that the scientist's answer will surely be negative; for Hake dearly loves paradoxes and puzzles, and science as he conceives of it is by no means restricted to surface phenomena.

His humanitarian strain has already been noted. In such poems as *Old Souls* and *New Souls* this tendency combines with his contempt for desiccated and impotent ecclesiastical institutions, leading him to contrast Christ (purely as a

[82] *Diary*, p. 215. [83] *Songs, Ballads, and Stories*, p. 99. [84] *Ibid.*, p. 113.

[85] A successful physician with a strong interest in what would now be called psychiatry, he tended Rossetti in his mental disorder and became a valued friend.

[86] *Memoirs of Eighty Years*, pp. 1, 7, 35.

man) with Christianity.[87] His best and queerest poems, however, attach themselves to a nature-occultism which in some ways predicts that of D. H. Lawrence. What haunts him is the dark blood-brotherhood between external nature and what we should now call the subconscious. This bond is so close that man cannot distinguish between the me and the not-me, so close that he cannot stand away from it and judge it good or bad. It arouses a kind of religious dread only because it so inscrutably and compulsively *is*.

He is aware that the bond grows tightest when volitional control over our associations is loosest.

> Dread under-life whose dreams
> Along the midnight rush,
> Poured out like cavern-streams
> That from the darkness gush,
> A murderous thought has issued forth to flood
> A maiden's sleep in blood.

The subjective-objective nexus is present also in reverie, as when another maiden

> . . . leans across the castle parapet
> Trolling for visions where swift waters flow;
> . . .
> And all appear the river's voice to know
> While there she listens to its playful fret,
> Her soul held captive in the bliss around,
> The full-leaved boughs that rustle in the glare
> Her fellow-prisoners in the witching sound,
> Stretching and purring in the sunny air:
> So her fixed look is in the vision bound
> That with unwary eyes she sought to snare.

That such entanglement may be no less sinister than delightful becomes apparent in a remarkable poem entitled *The Snake Charmer*. An old Hindu snake-charmer, about to die, feels drawn toward the hideous jungle swamp where he used to catch his cobras. He knows the end is near,

> Yet where his soul is he must go:
> He crawls along from tree to tree,
> The old snake-charmer, doth he know
> If snake or beast of prey he be?
> Bewildered at the pool he lies,
> And sees as through a serpent's eyes.

[87] *Poems*, 3ff., 75ff.

Conversely, the eyes of the actual serpent which now confronts him

> Grow human, and the charmer's seek.
> A gaze like man's directs the dart
> Which now is buried at his heart.
>
> The monarch of the world is cold:
> The charm he bore has passed away;
> The serpent gathers up its fold
> To wind about its human prey.
> The red mouth darts a dizzy sting,
> And clenches the eternal ring.[88]

The ring is presumably that familiar mystical symbol, the circle of destiny.

Hake's desire to penetrate such mysteries "scientifically" sometimes leads him to dabble in the Swedenborgian doctrine of correspondences and in preexistence, metempsychosis, astrology, and so on. However, he has no real hope that nature will yield up her secret in response to any such desperate though fascinating guesses, still less that she will submit herself to his transcendental will. He "cannot recall the time when I did not feel myself the subject of destiny against which I had no instinct of resistance."[89] What he struggles to resist is not destiny, but identification of destiny with mere mechanism. *The Angel of Nature* is

> The messenger of joy and sorrow,
>
> . . .
>
> Unto all hearts she is akin;
> She laughs, she grieves, though not within.
>
> . . .
>
> Where the moon's changing aspects break,
> Her face looks up, though not to think.

She accepts man's gifts, returning joy to some, pain to others, a mixture of both to most. She sings prophetically,

> But few who hear her legends feel
> The dreaded meanings they reveal.

Many love her,

> But she no glance of love returns,
> Though at the full her passion burns.

She is not omniscient: there is some deeper secret behind her which even she cannot unriddle. If she knew everything,

[88] *Poems*, pp. 81, 86–87, 145; *Legends of the Morrow*, p. 104.

[89] *Memoirs*, p. 17.

> . . . her heart would break,
> And crave for its eternal sleep;
> And shed the tears that mortals weep.
>
> Then would she feel as poets feel
> And never turn her love aside;
> They know her and they still appeal
> To their exalted virgin bride,
> Who to the last their love denies
> To the long yearning of their eyes.[90]

If even poets cannot consummate the marriage, Hake's only source of romantic pride would seem to be that the mystery of man is itself the deepest mystery of nature.

If C. S. Lewis's Screwtape were asked how to make a Spasmodic poet (the project would interest him) he might provide the following recipe. Take one English or Scottish child, preferably bourgeois or upper-proletarian. Endow him with an unusually strong romantic ambition and a sense of inferiority so painful as to demand extravagant overcompensation. Have him reared in a Nonconformist or Evangelical family, sufficiently rigid to make him feel restricted and rebellious but sufficiently enthusiastic to incline him to confuse his Christianity with his romanticism. See that he obtains just enough education to whet but not to satisfy his hunger for knowledge, beauty, "culture." The grand object is to set up a conflict within him between the awareness of being hopelessly *borné* and the craving for limitless expansion. Convince him that this inner conflict is a microcosm of the age, which he himself is therefore destined to interpret to his contemporaries. From the first he should feel guilty about wanting to be so big, but he must be prevented from making fruitful use of this guilt-feeling by the notion that it is a mark of distinction. Fill him with inordinate desire to achieve fame, not exactly by *writing* poetry but by being recognized as a great poetic genius. He should have sufficient talent to be tempted to abuse it in pretentious thinking, overstrained feeling, bombastic style, inchoate structure. That he may be helpless to resist this temptation, all power of self-criticism and all sense of humor must be withheld. Literary models of the sort that will flatter his weaknesses should be held before his eyes. Let him read *Faust* in the light of *Manfred* and *Cain*—accepting all the "Faustian" rant and ignoring all the sound human wisdom. The Promethean Shelley will also furnish a delusive consciousness of power. Lead him to admire Keats's

[90] *Legends of the Morrow*, pp. 3–10 *passim.*

hunger for fame, but blind him to the qualities which justified it. *Paradise Lost* will provide a disastrous model of sublimity; he should be in no doubt as to who is the hero. Thanks to his religious background, this literary heritage can easily be vulgarized not only by his own nature but by memories of Young's *Night Thoughts* and Montgomery's *Satan*. Intoxicate him with confidence of success; then crush him with the world's derision and let him relapse into a second-rate popular versifier or sentimental prose essayist.

"Spasmodic" ideas and stylistic qualities frequently appear in the work of Victorian poets who do not satisfy all the requirements of the norm. This is true of the early Tennyson, and occasionally of the later. *Pauline* and *Paracelsus* are Spasmodic poems. Lionel Trilling, in fact, thinks that "Browning might not unjustly be called a Spasmodic poet who managed to be good."[91] The flavor has been detected in *Aurora Leigh*, *Dipsychus*, *The City of Dreadful Night*, and *Wuthering Heights*.[92] It is not so easy, however, to draw up the roster of the Spasmodic School proper. Let us restrict our attention to Philip James Bailey (1816–1902), Sydney Thompson Dobell (1824–1874), and Alexander Smith (1829–1867). Some rigorists would exclude Bailey because his *Festus* (1839) sticks more closely to the German model in action and setting, whereas Dobell's *Balder* (1853) and Smith's *A Life-Drama* (1852) are confined to the world of contemporary human beings and stress the genius-theme more strongly than does Bailey's work. Nevertheless *Festus* is so clearly the Spasmodic fountainhead that we cannot do without it. It would be a waste of time to concern ourselves with John Westland Marston's *Gerald* (1842),[93] William Bell Scott's *The Year of the World* (1846), and John Stanyan Bigg's *Night and the Soul* (1854), feeble and slightly less authentic specimens of the same type. The socio-political liberalism of *The Roman* (1850), Dobell's closet-drama of the *risorgimento*, sets it apart, but it is otherwise rich in Spasmodic qualities.

Since the works in question are all nominally dramatic it is fair to ask how far the authors may be identified with their heroes. In a "Prefatory Note" to the second edition of *Balder*, Dobell warmly protests against any such assumption, although he does not pretend to be "altogether free from some of the sins of my hero," for " 'Balderism' in one form or another is a predominant intellectual misfortune of our day."[94] Nevertheless "objectivity"

[91] *Matthew Arnold*, p. 149.

[92] One might suggest that such solemnly over-ambitious historical painters as Haydon and Martin are essentially Spasmodists.

[93] The elder Marston was included among the Subjective Christians of Chapter IV, and on the whole that is where he belongs.

[94] *Poetical Works*, II, 4–5.

is the last term one would think of applying to him or to his fellows. Unquestionably their heroes are the mouthpieces of the poets' own aspirations and frustrations.[95]

Our three Spasmodics use the name of God very freely, but they will not commit themselves to any fixed creed. Clara, the heroine of *Festus*, delights her lover by declaring that "True faith nor biddeth nor abideth form!" On the Day of Judgment, Christ denies Satan's claim to Festus's soul:

> Spirit, depart! this mortal loved me.
> With all his doubts, he never doubted God:
> But from doubt gathered truth, like snow from clouds,
> The most, and whitest, from the darkest.[96]

But Bailey is much more interested in theological questions than Dobell or Smith, and not merely because his closer imitation of Goethe entails the use of supernatural machinery. Somewhere or other in the almost six hundred pages of *Festus* many religious problems are discussed in language of such turgid obscurity that they become more inscrutable than ever. Bailey appears to believe in predestination without disapproving of his hero's extreme romantic self-will, a fact in keeping with my notions concerning the historical nexus between Calvinism and romanticism.[97] That they are linked by antinomianism is suggested when Festus's Guardian Angel assures him:

> The soul once saved shall never cease from bliss,
> Nor God lose that He buyeth with His blood.
> She [the soul] doth not sin. The deeds which look like sin,
> The flesh and the false world, are all to her
> Hallowed and glorified. The world is changed.
> She hath a resurrection unto God,
> While in the flesh, before the final one,
> And is with God. Her state shall never fail.

When Lucifer obtains permission to tempt Festus, God gives him fair warning that this mortal is one of the elect. The information fails to discourage Lucifer, but not because he has any hope of reversing the divine decree. From the very outset of the poem he himself is a repentant sinner, a lover of God and an object of God's love:

[95] Alexander Smith, in fact, used *A Life-Drama* as a receptacle for several poems which he had previously written in his own person.

[96] *Festus*, pp. 70, 556. Tennyson, who admired *Festus*, may have remembered the latter passage when he wrote, "There lives more faith in honest doubt," etc. For a clearer case of Tennyson's indebtedness to Bailey, see H. N. Fairchild, "'Wild Bells' in Bailey's *Festus*?" *Modern Language Notes*, LXIV, 256–258.

[97] See especially *Religious Trends*, I, 545–548.

God! for thy glory only can I act,
And for thy creature's good. When creatures stray
Farthest from Thee, then warmest towards them burns
Thy love.[98]

Consequently, Lucifer's efforts to corrupt Festus are no less half-hearted than futile. He often abandons them entirely in order to give the hero such edifying instruction that the Guardian Angel hardly seems necessary.[99]

Bailey, who has read *Queen Mab* with care, sometimes transforms predestination into a determinism more Shelleyan than Calvinistic. Festus addresses a prayer to the

Soul of the world, divine Necessity,
Servant of God, and master of all things!

Lucifer, with no insidious intent, assures him that

Some souls lose all things but the love of beauty;
And by that love they are redeemable;
For in love and beauty they acknowledge good;
And good is God—the great Necessity.[100]

But if love and beauty are goodness, and goodness is God, and God is Necessity, and Necessity is the World Soul, the World Soul cannot be the *servant* of God.

The most clearly definable religious position maintained by Bailey is a thoroughgoing Universalism. Hell simply performs the function of Purgatory:

It is a fire of soul in which they burn,
And by which they are purified from sin.

All the spirits of the damned will be transferred to heaven at the Final Judgment. On one occasion Jesus even offers the damned *immediate* release from torment if they will believe and repent; many take advantage of the boon. This offer is not extended to Satan, but he will be saved on the Last Day in agreement with God's declaration:

It suits not the eternal laws of good
That evil be immortal.

Bailey is able to deal thus cavalierly with the mysteries of eschatology because he really believes in nothing but the importance of feeling benevolent

[98] *Festus*, pp. 8, 472.

[99] This absurdity probably derives from Montgomery's *Satan*. See above, p. 33*n*. Another queer complication is that Lucifer is deeply and tenderly in love with Clara, Festus's sweetheart.

[100] *Festus*, pp. 21, 435.

and enlarged. Salvation for him is a sentiment, and his conception of heaven is wheresoe'eristic:

> ... Heaven is no place;
> Unless it be a place with God, allwhere.
> It is the being good—the knowing God—
> The consciousness of happiness and power.[101]

The two later Spasmodics arrive at much the same position with less pretentious fuss. A friend of Dobell assured John Nichol that the poet had "a living Faith, at once deeply reverent and enlightened, in God and Christ," but that he was far too religious to adhere to any particular creed.[102] Nichol's own opinion is that "his sympathies probably lay more with the broadest section of the broad Church of England than with any other denomination."[103] But Samuel Thomson, Dobell's maternal uncle, had founded the sect of Freethinking Christians, who scorned the Unitarians for their enslavement to sacerdotalism. They would believe in nothing that they could not find in the Bible, and they did not find very much. They were opposed to public prayer, to preaching, to any sort of outward observance or institutional control. Dobell's parents were devoted members of the sect and intended their son to be one of its ministers.[104] In his late teens he himself was an enthusiastic disciple, and although he gradually lost his taste for the special tenets of the group he retained something of its temper. Amy, Balder's wife, asks him for instruction about God. He responds that he does not pretend to "know the Absolute." He can only give her "my blind man's dream." Man cannot see God in this life, nor will he do so even "in the eternity to come." We know God only in the sublimity of His works, reverencing which we receive a foretaste of what angels feel when they behold Him face to face. This response to the majesty of the creation is the only worship that God wills for us.[105]

On this point the Spasmodics sometimes join hands with the nature-worshippers of the preceding section; we have already observed that Alexander Smith sees God in the stars.[106] By the age of seventeen he seems to have lost all definable belief in losing the Presbyterianism of his native Kilmarnock. First Byron and Wordsworth, then Shelley, and finally Keats and Tennyson "became his chief teachers."[107] Occasionally, however, some vestiges of Christianity lend sanction to his sentimental optimism. When he

[101] *Ibid.*, pp. 37, 38–39, 406, 408–412 *passim*, 553, 557.
[102] Sydney Dobell, *Poetical Works*, pp. xxxii–xxxiii.
[103] Dobell, *Thoughts on Art, Philosophy, and Religion*, p. xvii.
[104] "E. J." [i.e., Emily Jolly], *Life and Letters of Sydney Dobell*, I, 52ff., 64ff.
[105] *Balder*, pp. 162–163. [106] See above, p. 190. [107] *Poetical Works*, pp. ix–x.

hears his bewildered contemporaries crying, "Let us hide from Life, my Brothers," he retorts:

> Like a mist this wail surrounds me; Brothers, hush; the Lord Christ's hands
> Even now are stretched in blessing o'er the sea and o'er the lands.
> Sit not like a mourner, Brother! by the grave of that dear Past,
> Throw the Present! 'tis thy servant only when 'tis overcast,—
>
> . . .
>
> I see long blissful ages, when these mammon days are done,
> Stretching like a golden ev'ning forward to the setting sun.[108]

Despite all such poking at the dead ashes of supernaturalism, what the Spasmodic hero most earnestly wants to believe in is the limitless power of the human mind. He is impatient to experience every possibility that life can offer. When Walter, hero of *A Life-Drama*, is advised by a friend to "be calm and still" he replies:

> . . . I'd be as lieve
> A minnow to leviathan, that draws
> A furrow like a ship. Away! away!
> You'd make the world a very oyster-bed.
> I'd rather be the glad, bright-leaping foam,
> Than the smooth sluggish sea. O let me live
> To love and flush and thrill—or let me die![109]

Festus is disconsolate because he has no life to lead but his own. He would think the thoughts and do the deeds of *all* men:

> I feel no bounds. I cannot think but thought
> On thought springs up, illimitably, round,
> As a great forest sows itself; but here
> There is nor ground nor light enough to live.
> Could I, I would be everywhere at once,
> Like the sea, for I feel as if I could
> Spread out my spirit o'er the boundless world,
> And act at all points: I am bound to one.
> I must be here and there and everywhere,
> Or I am nowhere.[110]

Let me play the lion too.

In accordance with his Goethean ancestry, what Festus wants is infinite expansion of personality through the exercise of his intellectual faculties. The aspiration of Walter in *A Life-Drama* is more specialized: like Keats,

[108] *Ibid.*, pp. 23, 25. The reviewers who accused him of plagiarizing from Tennyson were apparently right.

[109] *Ibid.*, p. 74.

[110] *Festus*, p. 46

he hopes to achieve boundlessness through poetic fame. He feels this desire no less deeply for fearing that he cannot attain it:

> O Fame! Fame! Fame! next grandest word to God!
> I seek the look of Fame! Poor fool—so tries
> Some lonely wanderer 'mid the desert sands
> By shouts to gain the notice of the Sphynx,
> Staring right on with calm eternal eyes.

However, he has his more confident moments:

> Ye are my menials, ye thick-crowding years!
> Ha! yet with a triumphant shout
> My spirit shall take captive all the spheres,
> And wring their riches out.
>
> God! what a glorious future gleams on me;
> With nobler senses, nobler peers,
> I'll wing me through Creation like a bee,
> And taste the gleaming spheres![111]

Balder stands somewhere between Festus and Walter: he wants poetic fame, but he wants it for the sake of Faustian power:

> . . . Not Fame but Power.
> Or Fame but as the noise of Power, a voice
> That in the face is wind, but in the ear
> Truth, Knowledge, Wisdom, Speculation,
> Hope, Fear, Love, Hate, Belief, Doubt, Faith, Despair,
> Every strong gust that shifts the souls of men,
> And so far worth the utterance; Fame the paid
> Muezzin on the minaret of Power,
> Calling the world to worship; . . .
> . . .
> . . . Not Fame but Power.
> Power like a god's and wielded as a god!

He has the mad notion that he can somehow conquer death by expressing the grim specter's essence in imperishable verse:

> . . . That I should do it,
> And be the king of men, and on the inform
> And perishable substance of the Time
> Beget a better world, I have believed
> Up thro' my mystic years, since in that hour
> Of young and unforgotten ecstasy
> I put my question to the universe,
> And overhead the beech trees murmured "Yes."

111 Alexander Smith, *Poetical Works*, pp. 5, 9.

This, we may interject, is the true romantic motive for interrogating nature. But he continues:

> Therefore I grew up calm as a young god,
> Having in well-assured serenity
> No haste to reach and no surprise to wear
> The inevitable stature; nor thought strange
> To feel me not as others, to pursue
> Amid the crowd a solitary way,
> And take my own in the o'erpeopled world,
> And find it no man's else.[112]

All one really needs to know about Dobell is that he had memorized every word of *Manfred* by the age of seventeen.[113]

But these are *Victorian* romantics who must convince themselves that their Titanism will not only satisfy the lust for infinitude but benefit mankind. Festus prays that with the march of progress all gifted men may realize that their powers are of God and use them for His glory and for

> . . . lifting up the mass of mind
> About them . . .
>
> . . .
>
> Fine thoughts are wealth, for the right use of which
> Men are and ought to be accountable.[114]

Walter, a little self-consciously, tells his sensible friend Edward that the age needs a great genius,

> A mighty Poet, whom this age shall choose
> To be its spokesman to all coming times.
> In the ripe full-blown season of his soul,
> He shall go forward in his spirit's strength,
> And grapple with the questions of all time,
> And wring from them their meanings.[115]

Balder no more hesitates to assume this lofty function than will Nietzsche's Zarathustra in his more amiable moods:

> . . . I will arise and reign;
> As God contains the world I will contain
> Mankind, and in the solvent of my soul
> The peopled and unpeopled ages . . .
>
> . . .

[112] *Balder*, pp. 10, 15.
[113] Jolly, *Life and Letters of Sydney Dobell*, I, 54.
[114] *Festus*, p. 63.
[115] Smith, *Poetical Works*, pp. 17–18.

. . . Mine hour is come,
The earthquake has yawned by me, I have seen
The seething core of nature, both these ears
Are deaf with voices, I am blind with light,
My heart is full of thunder! In the form
Of manhood I will get me down to man!

. . .

And merely walking through them with a step
God-like to music like the golden sound
Of Phoebus' shouldered arrows, I will shake
The laden manna round me as I shake
Dews from the morning tree. And they shall see
And eat, and eating live, and living know,
And knowing worship.[116]

Such benevolence, like that of Paracelsus before he knows better, is only a tool of self-aggrandizement.

What is Dobell's own opinion of the rant which he makes his hero utter? He thinks it is gorgeous, and he thinks it is reprehensible. We should not forget that only Part I of *Balder* was ever completed. The entire work, Dobell explained in the Prefatory Note to the second edition (1854) of Part I, was to consist of three parts, showing "the Progress of a Human Being from Doubt to Faith, from Chaos to Order. Not of Doubt incarnate to Faith incarnate, but of a doubtful mind to a faithful mind. In selecting the type and condition of humanity to be represented, I chose, for several important reasons, the poetic type and the conditions of modern civilization." His hero was so portrayed "as to indicate the absence of faith rather by the states and proportions of the other qualities than by a more distinct and formal statement of the differential defect." It is useless to complain, he retorts against the reviewers, that Balder is an unbelieving egotist, for "This is precisely the impression which I wished the reader of this volume to receive."[117]

Although one feels that Dobell sympathizes with his hero's Titanic balderdash much more strongly than he is willing to admit, his statement is not consciously insincere. The hostile reviews provide a sufficient reason for his failure to carry out the whole scheme. Even Part I can be so read as to substantiate his apologia. Balder's ambition to conquer death through the force of genius is mocked by the loss of his child. The blow deranges the mind of Amy, his wife, but he only rants the more wildly. When for a time she seems to have recovered, his happiness tempts him to indulge in the

[116] *Bald* pp. 142–143.

[117] *Poetical Works*, II, 3–4.

notion of "serving" the world by ruling it as a poet-god. Nemesis again rebukes his *hybris*: Amy relapses even more deeply into madness. He himself becomes manic-depressive. Now he recognizes despairingly the existence of a divine force more powerful than he. Finally he meditates killing his wife to spare her further misery, but he cannot decide whether God would approve or condemn the action. The muddled verbiage at the end of Part I is too impenetrable to permit us to guess what finally happens, but some scattered posthumous fragments intended for use in the sequel indicate that he spares Amy's life, nurses her back to health, and allies himself with her in service to God through service to mankind.[118]

It is doubtful, however, whether these developments would have entailed a radical transformation of Balder's original nature. In the Prefatory Note to Part I, the author insists that his hero should not be identified with Sydney Dobell, "the author of 'The Roman,' a book of faith, patriotism, and self-sacrifice."[119] Now the protagonist of *The Roman* (which had been warmly admired) believes in nothing *except* patriotism and self-sacrifice: his "faith" is politico-social liberalism and sentimental humanitarianism. The faith of the redeemed Balder would probably have been of the same sort, though more conservative because he is English rather than Italian. And *The Roman* contains plenty of Spasmodic mouthing. It is usually on the theme of patriotism and self-sacrifice, but not always. The reformer complacently describes the type of humanity which he strives (not unsuccessfully) to represent:

> He who takes counsel with the things which yet
> Are not, and answers with his kindling eye
> Questions ye cannot hear; he who is set
> Among us pigmies, with a heavenlier stature
> And brighter face than ours, that we must leap
> Even to smite it,—that man, friends, must have
> The self-existence of a God.[120]

We need not suppose, then, that Balder's late-found self-sacrifice would have been wholly unmingled with the old self-assertion.

None of Dobell's later works is of any importance for us. After public disapproval and ridicule made him abandon *Balder* he tried, like the more or or less Spasmodic hero of *Maud*, to find emotional relief in the Crimean War. But he had shot his bolt. *Sonnets on the War* (1855), written in collaboration with his friend Alexander Smith, contains a good deal of pacifistic sentiment which entails a few humanitarian references to God and Christ.

[118] Dobell, *Thoughts on Art, Philosophy, and Religion*, pp. 255ff.
[119] *Poetical Works*, II, 5.
[120] *Ibid.*, I, 154–155.

England in Time of War (1856), entirely his own work, is considerably more conservative and nationalistic, as if he were experimenting with jingoism as a vehicle for what little remained to him of the Spasmodic urge. Two years later his health began to fail,[121] the doctors warned him that any prolonged onset of the *furor poeticus* would be too much for him, and he passed the rest of his life as a successful man of business.

Since *A Life-Drama* is a complete work, the reformation of its hero is actually presented to us. Smith, however, was too much of a bungler to establish any clear connection between Walter's poetic megalomania and the course of the story. The young genius is jilted by an aristocratic girl who feels compelled to make a better match. Later he seduces a sweet young thing named Violet and suffers verbose agonies of remorse and gloomy cynicism. "He told me once," one of his friends informs another,

> The saddest fate that can befall a soul
> Is when it loses faith in God and Woman.

But the interlocutor predicts that

> He will return to the old faith he learned
> Upon his mother's knee. That memory
> That haunts him, as the sweet and gracious moon
> Haunts the poor outcast Earth, will lead him back
> To happiness and God.

So indeed it proves, granting that Walter's mother (we do not meet her) must have been a woman of large views. Violet at last forgives him and restores his faith by telling him that

> Religions change, and come and go like flame.
> Nothing remains but Love . . .
> . . . Walter! dost thou believe
> Love will redeem all errors? Oh, my friend,
> This gospel saves you! doubt it, you are lost.

Walter accepts the saving gospel and promises to become a better man with Violet's help:

> I will go forth 'mong men, not mailed in scorn,
> But in the armour of a pure intent.
> Great duties are before me and great songs,
> And whether crowned or crownless, when I fall

121 "His chest," John Nichol explains, "had suffered by the delivery to the members of the [Edinburgh] Philosophical Institution of a lecture, remarkable for its comprehensive view of the subject, on the Nature of Poetry"—a theme on which Dobell had always been inclined to overstrain himself. (*Ibid.*, I, xxiv.)

It matters not, so that God's work is done.
I've learned to prize the quiet lightning-deed,
Not the applauding thunder at his heels
Which men call Fame.[122]

But the coupling of "great duties" with "great songs" suggests that Walter has not wholly forsworn the cult of genius. At heart Smith, like Dobell, prefers the poet-hero's early pride to his late-found meekness. The romanticism of *A Life-Drama*, however, is more superficial than that of *Balder*. One suspects that Smith was motivated chiefly by the hope that he might be taken for a great poet if he talked enough nonsense about the glory of being one. This hope was promptly destroyed by Aytoun's *Firmilian*. Not quite willing to give up, Smith wrote some insignificant poems in which the critics detected too many borrowings from Tennyson. In 1863 he turned to prose and became the pleasant familiar essayist known to readers of *Dreamthorp*.

Festus requires no reformation: as one of the elect he is incapable of sin and can do as he pleases. Bailey was fortunate in that he produced his poem before the Victorian compromise had crystallized. At a time when English poetry was in the doldrums, so grandiloquent an attempt to rival Goethe was not to be scrutinized too meticulously. The pompous theological muddle and "idealistic" sententiousness of the work encouraged the notion that Bailey was a true genius. Anxious not to disillusion the public on this point, Bailey devoted the rest of his career chiefly to revising and enlarging *Festus* for subsequent editions.[123] He survived until 1902 as a member of that privileged group of Victorians whose reputation was based on the fact that they had written one important but forgotten poem many years ago.[124]

It is easy to dismiss the Spasmodics as a group of early-Victorian mooncalfs who, after sowing their literary wild oats, adapt their mediocrity to the more sensible standards of the changing age. We may be grateful to them, however, for revealing with such absurd clarity that romantic lust for infinitude which so many of their contemporaries and successors expressed with more ambiguous discretion. Dobell was quite right: "Balderism in one

[122] *Poetical Works*, pp. 129, 136–137, 138.

[123] He did, to be sure, separately publish two similar but less ambitious works—*The Angel World* (1850) and *The Mystic* (1855), both of them with some negligible shorter pieces. But these two poems were essentially appendixes to *Festus*, and by 1889 most of what they contained had been incorporated into the *magnum opus*.

[124] Even today, however, Bailey has not lost his charm for a certain kind of reader. One of the test passages used by I. A. Richards for his famous experiment in *Practical Criticism* was a typically bumptious speech from *Festus*. Several of his guinea-pigs thought it very "noble"—a favorite epithet in their answers—and two of them aptly compared it to Browning. (*Practical Criticism*, pp. 20ff.)

form or another is a predominant intellectual misfortune of our day"; and even those who regarded it as a misfortune could derive a strange pride from being so unfortunate. Aytoun smashed the school, but not its aspirations.

Nor can it even be said that Dobell and Smith, in making their proud heroes submit to the Victorian ideal of service, were completely renouncing the Faustian dream of power. Does not Faust himself at last obtain the most richly satisfying self-enlargement from becoming a drainer of marshes and a highly aggressive and dominant servant of his people?[125] The liquidation of Baucis and Philemon was unfortunate, but it did not prevent Faust's soul from being admitted to a heaven—complete with Virgin Mary, saints, and choirs of angels—in which Goethe no more believed than did his Victorian imitators.

Extremely different from Hake, Richard Henry (later Hengist) Horne (1803–1884) resembles him in one respect: he is in a class by himself.[126] Those who have called him a Spasmodic have misunderstood him, or the Spasmodics, or both. His philosophy of life is reasoned, consistent, and as elevated as any philosophy can be which falls short of the religious level. On his own premises he achieves a genuine synthesis. *Orion* (1843) is not a closet-drama but an allegorical narrative conveying the author's ideas through an original and interesting myth. The author too often intrudes as interpreter of the action, but he is much more objective than Bailey and his kindred. The poem tells a good story. The style, though far from exciting, is pure, manly, simple, and dignified. There are refreshing glints of humor and some excellent topical satire.

In reading Goethe, Horne has valued the humanistic wisdom more highly than the romanticism. *Orion*, a sort of Hellenic *Bildungsroman*, is closer to *Wilhelm Meister* than to *Faust*.[127] At the outset the hero, not a poet but an adolescent giant dwelling in the forest with his two extremely different

[125] After abandoning poetry, Dobell was active in all good works as a leading citizen of Gloucester. In his business he was no less benevolent than successful: he introduced a sort of profit-sharing scheme for his employees. (*Poetical Works*, I, xxiv–xxv.)

[126] The following remarks are based solely on *Orion*, his only work which retains the slightest importance for a student of Victorian poetry. I have also read *Prometheus the Fire-Bringer* (1866), a close imitation of Greek tragedy which uses the familiar myth as a vehicle for the ideas which are more effectively expressed in *Orion*.

[127] Both in *Orion* and in *Prometheus the Fire-Bringer*, Horne expresses indebtedness for the advice of Dr. Leonhard Schmitz, a German scholar resident in England. Schmitz was an entrepreneur of German classical and historical scholarship. He published Greek and Latin grammars, translated copiously from Niebuhr, compiled elementary Greek and Roman histories of his own (the former avowedly based on Thirlwall), and edited a periodical, *The Classical Museum*. The nature and extent of his influence on Horne is conjectural; but probably he was more helpful as an expert on ancient mythology than in connection with the basic philosophy of *Orion* and *Prometheus*.

brothers, is a crude ignorant young cub, but good-natured and full of eagerness to experience and learn and act.[128] He achieves fully developed humanity by passing through ascending levels of love. First his mooncalf adoration of Artemis chastens his roughness, develops his intellect, gives him noble dreams of good. But love of the unattainable virgin huntress is too Platonically fleshless and bloodless; it lacks roots in reality. The second phase is his passion for the mortal Merope—a love with plenty of reality and therefore genuinely educative, but too sensual and too selfish. He thinks of nothing but his craving to possess her loveliness. Hence—the moral symbolism is obvious—he is blinded by henchmen of Merope's swinish father, King Oinopion.

But this disaster, since he uses it nobly, becomes another upward step in his *Bildung*. His desire for Merope,

> . . . being less than his true scope,
> Had [would have] lowered his life and quelled aspiring dreams,
> But that it led to blindness and distress,
> Self-pride's abatement, more extensive truth,
> A higher consciousness of efforts new.

He is rewarded for his courage by the restoration of physical and spiritual sight. Rich in sympathy for mankind because of his sufferings, he dwells at last in perfect love with the dawn-goddess Eos, symbol of man's trust in progress:

> 'Tis always morning somewhere in the world,
> And Eos rises, circling constantly
> The varied regions of mankind. No pause
> Of renovation and of freshening rays
> She knows, but evermore her love breathes forth
> On field and forest, as on human hope,
> Health, beauty, power, thought, action, and advance.

From her Orion draws even higher ideals than from his worship of Artemis; and from his own disciplined humanity he draws the will to bring those ideals down to earth and use them for the betterment of his fellows. At last the jealous Artemis slays Orion, but Zeus grants him immortal life as a constellation so that men whose ears are attuned to the music of the spheres may evermore hear his message:

> The human spirit is a mountain thing,
> But ere it reach the constellated thrones,

[128] His character as it develops is much like that of Browning's Herakles. Browning, who like his wife knew Horne well, may have owed something to the earlier work in that respect.

It may attain, and on mankind bestow,
Substance, precision, mastery of hand,
Beauty intense, and power that shapes new life.
So shall each honest heart become a champion,
Each high-wrought soul a builder beyond Time.

. . .

And thus, in the end, each soul may to itself,
With truth before it as its polar guide,
Become both Time and Nature, whose fixed paths
Are spiral, and when lost will find new stars,
Beyond man's unconceived infinities,
And in the Universal Movement join.[129]

Horne is not quite unique but certainly very unusual among Victorian poets in that, like Orion at the final stage of his development, he embodied in the action of a liberal politician and reformer the ideals which he professed as a poet. Mrs. Browning was moved to write *The Cry of the Children* by his report on the mines and factories. More importantly for us, he differs from all the other humanitarians considered in this chapter and in Chapter IV as a humanist who never attempts to associate service and progress with any sort of supernaturalistic religion and as a naturalist who asserts no transcendental dominance of mind over matter. In these respects he suggests comparison with Hake, but he has no tincture of occultism. A friend of Conway and Clifford, he was a convinced freethinker.[130] Looking back at his major work in 1872, he is happy to think that "If the superstitious asceticism of ancient dogmas and legends still holds out in its old stone fortress, 'Orion' has nevertheless starred the rock, and let in some clear rays of healthy light."[131] He was born early enough to interpret the Victorian belief in "the march of mind" not in terms of a subjectivized Christian gospel but as an extension, strengthened by fresh scientific evidence, of that eighteenth-century doctrine of necessitated perfectibility which found in supernatural religion its most detested enemy. His closest associates in the cause of reform were heirs of the Encyclopedist tradition—rationalists, Philosophic Radicals, secularistic strayers from the Unitarian fold like Miss Martineau and W. J. Fox.[132]

Yet he was anything but a mere logic-chopper. If he sounds Godwinian when he speaks of "belief in the pre-arranged and constant progress of man," he sounds no less romantic when he speaks of "man's inconceived infinities." *Queen Mab*, so Godwinian and so romantic, may have helped to reconcile

[129] *Orion*, pp. 105–106, 121, 157–158. [130] M. D. Conway, *Autobiography*, II, 295.
[131] *Orion*, p. xii.
[132] He succeeded Fox for two years (1836–1837) as editor of the very advanced *Monthly Repository*.

his incredulous brain and his illusioned heart; at all events his phrase, "perfection's germ," was probably borrowed from Shelley's poem.[133] On the other hand, although his romantic impulse is unquestionably strong it is tempered by what seems to be a genuinely self-abnegating love of man and a genuinely objective reverence for the universe and its laws.[134] The good giant is first the product and finally the ally of nature, never its creator or master. His loyalty to the inorganic, the instinctive, the fleshly grows all the stronger as he follows the unbroken path of cosmic development toward the organic, the rational, and the humanly spiritual. Although Horne feels in 1872 that evolutionary science has done much to substantiate this philosophy since he first set it forth in 1843,[135] his original inspiration was probably derived from the less romantic, more authentically naturalistic and humanistic side of Goethe's Hellenic paganism. At all events, *Orion* is a remarkable attempt to draw the highest ethical values from a resolutely nonreligious philosophy.

[133] *Orion*, pp. xxiii, 27.

[134] For evidence on the latter point see *Ibid.*, pp. 26, 32, 75, 139.

[135] *Ibid.*, pp. xv–xvi.

Chapter Eight

BUCHANAN AND NOEL

ALTHOUGH several of the Seers and Seekers are writers of some literary as well as historical interest, none of them occupies so important a position on the main highway of English poetry as to deserve a separate chapter. Two of them, however, are so rewarding to the student of spiritual pathology that they are worth particular attention. It will not be inappropriate to couple the names of Robert Williams Buchanan (1841–1901) and Roden Berkeley Wriothesley Noel (1834–1894).[1] They were personal friends and sympathetic interpreters of each other's work.[2] To some extent both were continuators of the Spasmodic tradition—Buchanan more obviously than Noel.[3] They both tried to write authentic poetry and sometimes succeeded. Noel did so more frequently than Buchanan or at least abused his gift less wantonly. As regards religion they followed related though not identical paths of thought and arrived at much the same conclusions.

They differed markedly, however, in background and personality. Buchanan was the son of a freethinking Glasgow tailor who left his trade to become an editor of obscure socialist journals. The son obtained a Glasgow B.A. but never knew enough to justify his intellectual pretensions. He was neurotic and sickly. Although he possessed a good deal of sentimental generosity, the "Fleshly School" imbroglio bears witness to his jealousy, bad temper, and professional irresponsibility. Noel, son of the Countess of Gainsborough, seems to have been a rather noble person by nature as well as by birth. Buchanan, reared in an atmosphere of radicalism and aggressive secularism, nevertheless developed religious aspirations which he was unable to satisfy. Noel intended to take Orders after receiving his Trinity M.A.; but German philosophy and foreign travel broke down his orthodoxy, and

[1] Although their careers run considerably beyond the terminus of this volume they are Victorian poets in the sense in which I am using that term. Both began to publish verse in 1863 and were steadily productive thereafter.

[2] Noel wrote an essay on *Robert Buchanan's Poetry*; Buchanan edited, with a substantial "Prefatory Notice," a volume of selections from Noel's poems for the Canterbury Poets series.

[3] But although Buchanan more frequently reminds us of his close friend Sydney Dobell, Noel's *A Modern Faust* (1888) is distinctly Spasmodic in theme if not in style.

his service as Groom of the Privy Chamber to Queen Victoria may have helped to make him a republican with socialistic leanings.

Noel was an almost pure romantic who, except in occasional moments of despairing scepticism, was able to regard himself as a Christian by identifying Christianity with the romantic faith. Buchanan's case-history is more complicated. Within the straitened limits of this chapter it is impossible to give a full account of the constantly veering philosophical and religious views revealed by the two stout volumes—small print and double columns—of his *Complete Poetical Works.* He was a perfect specimen of the Victorian believing unbeliever. If you asked him to believe anything in particular he would talk like the village atheist. If you asked him to deny the existence of God and the hope of immortality he would talk like an enraptured seer. He felt no less at home with Leslie Stephen, Lecky, and Lewes than with Dobell and Noel. He wished to resemble his picture of Goethe—a poetical sceptic, a mystical positivist.[4] Hardly less antagonistic to the rampant infidel than to the orthodox Christian, he attacks materialism and rejoices in the death of Nietzsche:

> Poor gutter-snipe! Answer'd with his own prayer,
> Back to primeval darkness he has gone;—
> Only one living soul can help him there,
> The gentle human god he spat upon!

That even Nietzsche may hope for the human god's pardon is suggested by *The Ballad of Judas Iscariot,* one of Buchanan's most effective poems, where Christ admits the soul of the humbled, repentant Judas to communion with Him in heaven. In his softer moods this positivist can credit Christianity with "the higher truth of poesy divine" and apostrophize *Pilgrim's Progress*:

> O fairy Tale Divine! O gentle quest
> Of Christian and the rest!
> What wonder if we love it to the last,
> Tho' childish faith be past,
> What marvel if it changes not, but seems
> The loveliest of dreams?[5]

Several of Buchanan's more ambitious works—*The Book of Orm, Balder the Beautiful, The City of Dream*—suggest a comparison with Bunyan in being allegories of man's quest for God. But the difference is far greater than the similarity, for the deity sought in these poems is not the Hebraic Jehovah, nor any god of the Greeks or Teutons or Hindus,

[4] *The Drama of Kings,* p. 470.

[5] *Complete Poetical Works,* I, 287, 494ff.; II, 52, 380.

. . . nor the Man Divine,
The pallid rainbow lighting Palestine;
Nor any lesser of the Gods which Man
Hath conjured out of Night since time began.
I mean the primal Mystery and Light,
The most Unfathomable, Infinite,
The Higher Law, Impersonal, Supreme,
The Life in Life, the Dream within the Dream,
The Fountain which in silent melody
Feeds the dumb waters of Eternity,
The Source whence every god hath flown and flows,
And whither each departs to find repose.

This God, he says in *The Book of Orm*, has hidden Himself behind the veil of the sky, which He has woven for that purpose. Our constant longing to behold His face is therefore constantly thwarted.

Yet mark me closely!
Strongly I swear,
Seen or seen not,
The Face is *there*!

But if the veil were lifted the revelation would be unbearably terrifying. For Buchanan all intellectual clarity is associated with unbelief, and all belief with inscrutable mystery. God owes His very existence to the fact that He is "the Dream within the Dream." Our only justification for seeking Him is the certainty that He can never be found. For this very reason, however, there is something to be said for all man-made religious symbols:

No creed is wholly false, old creed or new,
Since none is wholly true.[6]

But Buchanan's inherited rationalism forbids him to cultivate the sentimental latitudinarianism which this relativistic position would otherwise have encouraged. He remains quite enough of a freethinker to insist that men should not call themselves Christians unless they affirm the doctrines of Christianity. To the genuine secularist, nothing is more infuriating than the refusal of self-styled believers to specify their beliefs. Hence this Gilbertian chorus from *The Devil's Sabbath*:

To all us literary gents the future life's fantastical,
And both the Christian Testaments are only "wrote sarcastical;"
They're beautiful, we all know well, when viewed as things poetical,
But all their talk of Heaven and Hell is merely theoretical.

[6] *Ibid.*, I, 257, 280–284; II, 52.

But we are Christian men, indeed, who, striking pious attitudes,
Raise on a minimum of creed a maximum of platitudes!
For this is law, and this we teach, with grace and with urbanity,
That whatsoever creed men preach, 'tis essential Christianity![7]

Despite his nostalgic affection for Bunyan's fairy-tale, the same honesty makes it impossible for him to profess any serious belief in the historic faith. He is a little perplexed that so genuinely Hellenic a pagan as Noel should also be "a true Christian." Eager not to misrepresent his friend he hastens to explain:

Not that I conceive for one moment that he accepts the whole impedimenta of Christian orthodoxy—he is far too much of a pagan still ever to arrive at that. But he believes, as so many of us have sought in vain to believe, in the absolute logic of the Christian message: that logic which is to *me* a miracle of clear reasoning raised on false premises, and which to others is false premises and false reasoning all through.[8]

The peculiarities of Noel's interpretation of the Christian message will emerge gradually as we proceed, but his address to Byron may serve as an introductory sample:

A fierce, glad fire in buoyant hearts art thou,
A radiance in auroral spirits now;
A stormy wind, an ever-sounding ocean,
A life, a power, a never-wearying motion!
Or deadly gloom, or terrible despair,
An earthquake mockery of strong Creeds that were
Assured perversions of calm earth and sky,
Where doom-distraught pale souls took sanctuary,
As in strong temples. The same blocks shall build,
Iconoclast! the edifice you spilled,
More durable, more fair: O scourge of God,
It was Himself who urged thee on thy road;

. . .

May all the devastating force be spent?
Or all the godlike energies be shent?
Nay! thou art founded on the strength Divine:
The Soul's immense eternity is thine!
Profound Beneficence absorbs thy power,
While Ages tend the long maturing flower.[9]

As we see, Noel is moved not only by Byron's "fierce, glad fire" but by

[7] *Ibid.*, II, 411. The penultimate line suggests that he is glancing at Matthew Arnold.
[8] Roden Noel, *Poems*, p. xix (Buchanan's "Prefatory Notice"). [9] *Ibid.*, pp. 310–311.

his "terrible despair." The Victorian poet feels a Byronic melancholy when he gazes upon a storm at sea:

> O hymn sublime, confounded, infinite
> Of Tempest, how the chaos in my soul
> Responds to your appeal, and drifts with cloud!
> I too am worn with many moods at war,
> Wind thwarting tide; stern duty, passion, love,
> Wrestle while, unresolved to harmony,
> They urge me blindly, violent, confused.

He has read not only *Childe Harold* but *Morte d'Arthur* and *Stanzas from the Grande Chartreuse*, for he adds:

> The old-world order passeth, and the new
> Delaying dawns, one crimson, loud with voices
> We know not, with wild wars in earth and heaven;
> The fountains of the great deep are broken up,
> Threatening deluge; our firm earth goes under.

At such times nature seems merely to deride "the ideals of our childhood." The caves in a sea cliff look like huge church windows

> Which Time, the old Iconoclast,
> While the centuries rolled by,
> Slow-fashioned there in irony
> Of Gothic minster, Gothic creed,
> Human worship, human need.

Our life is like *The Merry-Go-Round* revolving at night on the shaky old pier at Fowey, "Over all the silent stars! beyond, the cold grey wave." It whirls round and round "To a loud monotonous tune that hath a trumpet bray." This bright spot in the darkness is meaningless and transitory:

> I know that in an hour the fair will all be gone,
> Stars shining over a dreary void, the Deep have sound alone.
> I gaze with orb suffused at human things that fly,
> And I am lost in the wonder of our dim destiny.[10]

Noel's darker moods are shared by Buchanan. A Hardyesque passage in *The Drama of Kings* portrays his *deus absconditus* as too completely self-hypnotized by His contemplation of the passage of time to care anything about His world. The glories of heaven blaze all around Him, yet

> He heeds them not, but follows with eyes yearning
> The shadow men call Time.

[10] *Ibid.*, pp. 41–42, 84, 89.

Some problem holds Him, and He follows dreaming
The lessening and the lengthening of the shade.
Under His feet, ants from the dark earth streaming,
Gather the men He made.

. . .

How should He care to look upon such creatures,
Who lets great worlds go by?[11]

A world without death, says Buchanan, would be unbearable, since in such a world man's painful quest of the Absolute would be endless. Orm therefore blesses God "for Sleeping, and for Silence, and Corruption." Three pages later, however, he thinks that death releases the soul from the flesh-prison which prevents it from uniting in love with other souls. But eighteen pages further on, death is associated with absorption into external nature rather than with benevolism, for Orm prays:

In the time of transfiguration,
Melt me, Master, like snow;
Melt me, dissolve me, inhale me
Into thy wool-white cloud;

. . .

And melt and dissolve me downward
In the beautiful silver Rain
That drippeth musically,
With a gleam like Starlight and Moonlight,
On the footstool of Thy Throne.

In *The City of Dream*, grim old Death, who has dogged the footsteps of the hero throughout life's pilgrimage, turns at last into a "radiant child" who seems to promise that all the great questions will be answered. But Satan, in *The Devil's Case*, admits:

Death alone I cannot vanquish—
Death and God, perchance, are One!

Yet throughout the pretentious muddle of his speculations on death Buchanan never quite lost the hope expressed in the lines which he chose to print last of all among his collected poems:

Forget me not, but come, O King,
And find me softly slumbering
In dark and troubled dreams of Thee,
Then, with one waft of Thy bright wing,
Awaken me![12]

[11] *The Drama of Kings*, pp. 257, 259. The comparison with Hardy is not aimless. See my article in *PMLA*, LXVII (1952), 43–64, which identifies the *Drama* as "The Immediate Source of *The Dynasts*."

[12] *Complete Poetical Works*, I, 269, 272–273, 290; II, 158, 273, 432.

Either of these men might have written:

> Ah! for a vision of God! for a mighty grasp of the real,
> Feet firm based on granite in place of crumbling sand!

But in this case the poet is Noel, whose longing to solve the mystery of life and death was sharpened by the loss of his little son. The early primrose budded while the child lay ill; he hoped he would be up to see it open, but he died on the very day it bloomed.

> I wonder if he saw it,
> Saw the flower open,
> Went to pay the visit
> Yonder after all!
> I know we laid the flower
> On a stilly bosom
> Of an ivory image;
> But I want to know
> If indeed he wandered
> In the little garden,
> Or noted on the bosom
> Of his fading form
> The paly primrose open;
> How I want to know![13]

The power of some bad poems to move us is one of the anomalies of literary criticism.

In groping toward answers to such questions Noel's chief support is a romantic pantheism which should be studied not only in his poems but in his highly revealing critical essays. "I believe," he declares,

> that Rousseau, Wordsworth, Byron, Shelley, Keats, Coleridge, were verily prophets, to whom a new revelation was entrusted. In a time when . . . the angels of Faith and Hope seemed to be deserting forever the desecrated shrines of mankind —then it was that these Prophet-Poets, as very ministers of Heaven, pointed men to the World-Soul, commanding them once more to veil their faces before the swift subtle splendour of Universal Life. . . . "The light that never was on sea or land, the consecration and the poet's dream," is indeed a new revelation, made peculiarly in the modern poetry of true spiritual insight, and of this Poetry of Nature Wordsworth is the High Priest. . . . In seeking for a *note* of this peculiar modern nature-worship, I think we must set down as a principal one, *Pantheism*, either overt or implicit. For it is a *worship*—precisely as the Scandinavian and Greek Mythologies are *worships*—only in a modern form.[14]

One is tempted to say that Noel is more like John Middleton Murry than anybody but John Middleton Murry.

[13] *Poems*, pp. 99, 343.

[14] *Essays on Poetry and Poets*, pp. 1–2, 4, 88.

The Wordsworthian nature-faith is "modern," Noel insists, even in the sense of being strictly up-to-date. Mechanistic science has by no means destroyed it: the notion that nature can be known "correctly" only by the scientist is giving way before the realization that "Spiritual Imagination alone knows Nature." By the use of this faculty James Hinton has reconciled science with a pantheism which is consistent with a deeply religious awe. Noel admiringly cites Hinton's theory

> that, as atoms we name inorganic are compelled, by some unknown power, to resist the law of chemical affinity and combine into vital organisms—into human bodies, whereunto pertains consciousness and thought, so these world-atoms of the void yonder, together with this our own world-atom, may form greater living organisms endued with grander thought. Then we should ourselves be to these as the living monads of our own blood, as the parasites of our tissues to us.

With sanguine feelings which we now find difficult to share, he appeals also to

> recent investigations into the nature of ultimate elementary atoms by Thomson, Clerk-Maxwell, and Clifford; how these hypothetic entities pulsate and radiate, whirl and travel, just like planets and suns. May not these too be worlds with life and thought in them, if one could only comprehend? . . . What rational vital unity then pervades solid granite rocks, the Atlantic that rebels against their boundary, solar systems yonder, and ourselves who wonder!

Such a vitalistic interpretation of the universe is further encouraged, and somehow harmonized with essential Christianity, by Hegel and Robert Browning. *A Grammarian's Funeral* teaches us that

> Things are not in their momentary appearances . . . they are fulfilled in their disappearances even, and their living again in richer form. . . . "That which thou sowest is not quickened except it die: and God giveth it a body as it hath pleased Him." So a rather discredited old book says. Three great writers see and teach this very distinctly—Hegel, Hinton, and Browning.[15]

Noel's attitude toward nature is not without a tincture of genuinely religious objectivity and humility. He does not *consciously* wish to think of man as master of the physical universe. For him, nature-worship would not be a religion unless it entailed *worship*. One thinks of Spinoza when Noel says: "He who loses his own personality in Nature, who lays down before her . . . his own private wrongs and griefs and fevered aspirations, hereby redresses the balance so unduly weighted with the self-will and momentary longings of one restless man." Not without some confusion between two

[15] *Ibid.*, pp. 4, 279, 343, 344. For Hinton see above, p. 187.

meanings of the term "law," he declares that in nature "the harmony of inviolable laws appears coöperant to an end. But I think that this inevitableness of a universal order involves the idea of rightness, that of some fulfilled obligation tinged with morality, or what is akin to it. I know this cannot be proved, but I think it may be felt." He himself feels it so strongly that except in a few unusually despairing moments he cannot believe that nature is completely alien to human aspirations. "All that is profound, eternal, impersonal in us, goes forth to wed with the profound, eternal, impersonal Heart of all. It is beyond our good and right, more than our ideal, yet justifies, sanctions, transcends, absorbs it."[16]

Thus when he sees huge waves thundering fiercely into a cave he asks:

> Of Demiurgic Powers, afar from the man and the woman,
> Are these dim echoing chambers the mystical veiled thought,
> Indifferent, aloof, or enemy to the human?
> How, then, are they a haven for minds and hearts o'er-wrought?
> Ah! many and many an hour in your sublime communion
> I pass, O Gods unknown, of ocean, wind, and cloud;
> I find profound repose, refreshment flow from the union.

But even this communion with the human though more than human Heart of all is not sufficient when Noel "wants to know" what has become of his little son. He is thinking of the dead child in *A Southern Spring Carol*:

> Ah! Nature never would have power
> To breathe such ecstasy of flower,
>
> . . .
>
> If *he* were turned to common earth!
> If a child so fair, so good,
> Were a waif on Lethe's flood,
>
> . . .
>
> She [Nature] would reel dissolved, and faint
> With deep dishonour of the taint!
> The very girders of her hall
> Crushed, her stately floor would fall.
> Ourselves are the foundation-stone;
> If thought fail, the world is gone.

Needless to say, thought does *not* fail. In response to the incantation of this verse the vernal landscape reveals all its latent humanity:

> Nature rises on immortal wings!
> And soaring, lo! she sings! she sings!

[16] *Ibid.*, pp. 2, 3.

There is no death!
She saith.
O Spring! O Spring! O Southern Spring!
What a triumphal song you sing![17]

In Noel's opinion such flights of imagination are authenticated by philosophy and even by science. In his essay, *The Poetic Interpretation of Nature*, he declares that "since Berkeley, Kant, and modern physiology, it is no longer permissible to doubt that . . . what we call 'laws of nature' are merely the interpretation which our sensible and mental constitution enables us to put upon the language of the Kosmos."[18] This is a drier version of his statement that "Spiritual Imagination alone knows Nature." And so the inviolable laws which we are to regard with such deep self-surrendering reverence are after all the product of our own minds. "Ourselves are the foundation-stone." The worshipper of nature is the maker of nature, and the circularity of the romantic faith—from man to nature to man—is once again made manifest.

On this theme Buchanan is much less fruitful. As we shall see later, he feels a theoretical reverence for evolving nature as the matrix of Man's loving heart; but since he can conceive of no religion (other than the religion of humanity) which is more than mere emotional guesswork about unfathomable mystery, his dabbling in nature-worship is inconsistent and half-hearted. Unlike Noel, he seldom tries to philosophize about nature because, though he wants to believe, he associates reason exclusively with unbelief. In the thirty-four *Coruisken Sonnets* he begins by lamenting that he can find God neither in the city, where human misery seems to deny His existence, nor in the country, where we are like children waiting in a fair house for a father who never comes. If God really *is* present in the hills about Loch Coruisk, He should be ashamed of Himself: He should be in London helping the poor. Since He seems to care nothing for suffering men, He Himself should be judged at the Last Day. The beautiful hills are changeless and impassive and indifferent to humanity—like God. It would be better to be unhappy and imperfect and passionate than to be a mountain-peak deity. But the little brook which "murmurs 'God made me!' " reminds Buchanan of "the happy hearts of Earth," and he asks God to forgive him for his fretfulness. In the last sonnet a rainbow appears—"Art thou a promise?" This is feeble stuff compared to Noel. In *The Book of Orm*, "Earth the Mother" had beheld God's face in the days before He hid it behind the veil of the sky, but now the senile crone hardly remembers how

[17] *Poems*, pp. 79, 119–120.

[18] *Essays on Poetry and Poets*, p. 5.

He looked. Feeling that she knows the great secret, men question her, but they get either no answer or an answer which makes them deny God's existence. Again there is a rainbow, however. As the poem continues, Orm not only enjoys nature but sometimes detects beneath its beauty "An understream of sober consecration." These Wordsworthian intimations, however, are disappointingly evanescent:

> Yet nought endured, but all the glory faded,
> And power and joy and sorrow were interwoven;
> There was no single presence of the Spirit.

Later on, Orm declares that he will worship God when the mountains and rivers and clouds do so—which they obviously don't.[19] In short the super-God, "the Dream within the Dream," is not to be found in nature. It is axiomatic with Buchanan that He is not to be found at all.

Let us return to Noel. Despite his reverence for the romantic poet-prophets, some of his most seriously philosophical nature-poetry is more deeply indebted to the Greeks than to Wordsworth. There was of course nothing incongruous in using Greek mythology as a vehicle for romantic pantheism: Wordsworth himself, not to mention Shelley and Keats, had done the same. The great romantics, according to Noel, were the revivers, not the inventors, of the true faith. Of course he has no literal belief in the symbols of pagan myth, but he holds that the Greeks "were not far from the truth when they formulated their conviction that our spiritual kinship with Nature testifies to some spiritual beings like ourselves behind the phenomena of Nature—the elements, and so-called inanimate objects, being only their expression, body, or vesture. . . . Modern Nature-poetry is reverting . . . to this primal conception of the ancients." And quite rightly, since no other religion is fit for a true poet: "For as Science . . . affords no help to the poetic feeling of life and spirit in Nature,[20] so neither does a theology which teaches that there is a God external to the world, who once made, and still possibly sustains it. Poetry demands God immanent in Man and Nature." After quoting Wordsworth's "I'd rather be a pagan" sestet he pays one of his tributes to the wise Germans: "But the philosophy of idealism supplies for the logical faculty the conception needed to lift it into some harmony with the vision of children, poets, and the more primitive, less sophisticated races."[21] It is interesting that he should value transcendental idealism as a rationaliza-

[19] *Complete Poetical Works*, I, 248ff., 259–260, 277.

[20] He means unenlightened *materialistic* science. A moment later he cites Hinton as providing scientific support for the vitalistic-pantheistic faith. The romantic may either fight science head on or reinterpret it romantically and then stand forth as its champion.

[21] *Essays on Poetry and Poets*, pp. 7, 8, 9.

tion of the intuitive wisdom of childhood. The gap between romantic primitivism and romantic transcendentalism is not so wide as Professor Lovejoy would have us think.

The long poem entitled *Pan* is Noel's contribution to the widespread and rather tedious debate, initiated by Miss Barrett's retort upon Schiller, as to whether Pan is dead or alive. Noel of course supports the latter thesis:

> Pan is not dead, he lives for ever!
> Mere and mountain, forest, seas,
> Ocean, thunder, rippling river,
> All are living Presences.

Science (of the wrong sort) is impotent to tell us "whence all the vision flows." It flows from a Pan-spirit at the heart of everything.[22] The poem reaches the conclusion that Christ came not to destroy Pan but to fulfill him—a point which must be reserved for later examination.

Buchanan admires his friend's Neo-Hellenic paganism but seldom emulates it: his myths are usually homemade or, as in *Balder the Beautiful*, Scandinavian. Nevertheless he also writes a *Pan*. It advances the heterodox idea that Pan is dead in his old rural haunts but still alive in the city, where his spirit gives our drab existence "the gleam of some forgotten life."[23]

The two poets, however, stand shoulder to shoulder as humanitarians and advanced socio-political liberals who associate their views with spiritual values. We have already noted that Buchanan disapproves of God's indifference to social service. The poet's sympathies embraced the lower animals as well as man. Like Tennyson, Browning, Christina Rossetti, and many other eminent Victorians, he opposed vivisection. He belonged to the Humanitarian League, among whose members his *Song of the Fur Seal* was much admired.[24] The aristocratic Noel's *Poor People's Christmas*, contrasting the message of the herald angels with the actual life of the poor, might have been written by one of the plebeian social-protest poets. In *Livingstone in Africa* the great missionary desires to manifest the spirit of Christ by rescuing the blacks from the horrors of the slave trade rather than by "saving souls" in the ordinary sense.

Noel's personal tragedy made him especially sensitive to the sufferings of children, for

> Where'er there comes a little child,
> My darling comes with him.

[22] *Poems*, pp. 65, 68.

[23] *Complete Poetical Works*, I, 185.

[24] See the special chapter on Buchanan as a humanitarian in this narrower sense contributed by Henry S. Salt to Harriet Jay, *Robert Buchanan*, pp. 144–152.

A display of toys in an arcade makes him love outward from his lost son to other men's living children:

> I will be a minister
> The fountain of their joy to stir,
> In such resorts, and by such measures,
> As were wont to yield him pleasures;
> Or where little hearts may ail,
> Love's yoke-fellow, I will not fail,
> Where are tears and visage pale,
> To quell the tyranny of Fate,
> Or man, that renders desolate:
> And I deem he will approve
> In the bowers of holy Love,
> Near and nearer to me move.

His memories of that little boy drew him to the verge of Christianity, but he could never bring himself to take the leap. In *The Children's Grass,* he juxtaposes the children of the poor and of the rich, bitterly asking,

> Are not these thy children, Father?
> These—or only those?
> Are we not all orphans rather
> Of whom—none knows?[25]

Buchanan could look back to boyhood days when the home of his father, disciple of Robert Owen both as atheist and as socialist, was visited by the pioneer French socialists, Blanc and Caussidière. The mature poet subscribed to no fixed political or economic creed but retained a warm affection for the French people and for the ideals of the Revolution. Victor Hugo influenced him strongly. *The Drama of Kings* (1871) was an outburst of indignant sympathy for France and an attack on the German pretense of fighting "in the name of the Lord." But the first part of this work deals with Bonaparte, the pretended champion and real betrayer of fair Liberty. At last he is overthrown by the "Titan," Liberty's faithful lover, the "Spirit of Man," for

> The legions of the conqueror are weak
> Against the strength of the Free Thought of Man.

Now, in 1871, the martyrdom of man[26] is being repeated, with Bismarck in

[25] *Poems,* pp. 144, 345, 350.

[26] The jumble of negation and affirmation, pessimism and optimism, in Buchanan's thought reminds us of Winwood Reade's *Martyrdom of Man.* It was not published until the year after the *Drama,* but Buchanan knew Charles Reade and may have had opportunities to converse with his nephew.

the oppressor's rôle. But the poet's hopes are revived by the deposition of Napoleon III and the proclamation of the Third Republic. At last he permits the Chorus to predict that the liberated Spirit of Man will eventually establish the "perfect State":

> 'Tis where the home is pure,
> 'Tis where the bread is sure,
> 'Tis where the wants are fewer,
> And each want fed.
> Where plenty and peace abide,
> Where health dwells heavenly-eyed,
> Where in nooks beautified
> Slumber the dead.[27]

Noel also sympathizes with France in her struggle with Germany and believes that England and America should enter the war on her side. This is no time to prate of international amity:

> Arm, England, arm! The halcyon hour must wait
> When Love and Righteousness shall vanquish Hate.
> Jesus of old was royal hailed in scorn:
> Now the world crowns Him—still it is with thorn!
>
> . . .
>
> Fair is our dream of universal peace;
> But there be wolves, and lambs of tender fleece.

Economic competition—compare Tennyson's *Maud*—is in itself a kind of war, and a baser kind than an armed crusade for liberty. Noel's long socialistic poem, *The Red Flag* (1872), rebukes the nominally Christian world in the name of the Crucified Carpenter, to whom he prays:

> Friend of the lowly, fainting on the wood,
> Behold thy poor upon a golden rood!

He tells those decorous well-fed churchgoers who are shocked by *The Origin of Species* that their own behavior exemplifies the struggle for existence:

> Lift up your pious eyes at Darwin's creed;
> And try to prove him right about your breed,
> Dear fellow-Christians! who live as though
> Not even yet you'd struggled from below.
> For beasts of prey with all their savage strife
> Are still the cherished models of your life.
>
> . . .

[27] *The Drama of Kings*, pp. 75, 272.

Ah! what if some unshamed iconoclast,
Crumbling old fetish-remnants of the past,
Rouse from dead cerements the Christ at last?
What if men take to following where He leads,
Weary of mumbling Athanasian creeds?

The same religious-revolutionary hope is expressed in *Poor People's Christmas*, where the widow of a man who has been goaded to suicide by economic injustice has a vision of Jesus in the guise of "a common workman." He consoles her, saying:

My servants fashion even now
Justice for the commonweal;
From toilers with the hand, the brow,
Idle men no more may steal;
My servants seek; I whisper how
They may find the remedy,
Save my little ones who cry:
For I am poor Myself, you know;
The Poor are Mine, and I will heal!—
Already dawns millenium;
Soon My holy reign will come.[28]

The connection between Noel's pantheism and his religion of social reform is clearly revealed by *The Spirit of Storm*, a poem which manages to be both Shelleyan and Spencerian:

I send my spirit adrift upon the storm,
Careering along the triumph of the blast,
Exultant! well I know the living God,
God the creator, for destroyer too;
Who purifies by hurricane, evolves
From birth-throes of rebellion, fraught with fear,
Perplexity and pain, the common weal,
Raised to a higher excellence.

Out of the evolutionary-revolutionary turmoil symbolized by the storm arise, as Spencer taught, organisms not only more complex but more altruistic and cooperative. The final outcome will be "the nobler type of Man," Noel's version of the Tennysonian "Christ that is to be." Mother Nature is a good Utopian Socialist:

Lo! the World-Soul commandeth to emerge
From dead, resolved, more simple forms the higher

[28] *Poems*, pp. 31, 34, 138, 145–149 *passim*.

Through pain, defeat, death, folly, sorrow, sin,
Compelleth all to be themselves, through all.
From thee, O mystic Mother, deeply dark,
From thee, O mother Nature, impulse floweth,
Urging mankind to launch, like wintering bird,
Upon the unknown dim airs, by faith to find
Fair undiscovered realms beyond the dawn![29]

For reasons already explained, Buchanan's faith in the ultimate triumph of the Spirit of Man is less deeply rooted in nature-mysticism. Even for him, however, that triumph is the result of the evolutionary process. He is more of a positivist than Noel. *The Drama of Kings* is dedicated "To the Spirit of Auguste Comte" as "this Drama of Evolution." Buchanan is by no means an orthodox worshipper in the temple of the Great Being—he was never an orthodox anything. Nevertheless he represents that looser, vaguer, more sentimental reverence toward Collective Humanity which most Englishmen associated with the name of Comte. It provided a link between the unbelieving and the believing sides of Buchanan's nature, enabling him to spurn the illusions of supernaturalism and yet to bow his head before the concept of *God Evolving*:

No God behind us in the empty Vast,
No God enthroned on yonder heights above,
But God emerging, and evolved at last
Out of the inmost heart of human Love.[30]

Noel has much the same idea, but he steeps it more deeply in romantic pantheism and tries harder to identify it with Christianity. "Pan is not dead," he answers Mrs. Browning, "save in this sense—that God manifest in Nature is now, since the revelation of our Blessed Lord Jesus Christ, felt to be less worshipful than God manifest in Divine Humanity."[31]

Such language is too pious for Buchanan's taste, but he knows that his friend means no harm by it. He and Noel, he says, fully agree that "The atheist and the Christian, the believer and the unbeliever, meet on the platform of a common beneficence. Faith in Love is all-sufficient, without faith in any supernatural or godlike *form* of love." He credits Noel with a "fully reasoned-out faith in the divine destiny of Man."[32] Despite some verbal differences, then, both poets worship the Divine Humanity—the God of William Blake. What we mean when we say "God" is simply "Mercy, Pity, Peace, and Love," the highest qualities of perfected Man. Man is God

[29] *Ibid.*, pp. 91–92.

[30] Quoted by Harriet Jay, *Robert Buchanan*, p. 151.

[31] *Essays on Poetry and Poets*, p. 8.

[32] Noel, *Poems*, pp. xx, xxiv (Buchanan's "Prefatory Notice").

because man loves and Love is God. God does not yet fully exist, for the absolute identity of Man and Love is still to be achieved; but He *will* exist when completely loving Man emerges as the final product of the evolving universe. God, then, depends on Man. Does not Man in turn depend upon the laws of nature? Yes, in a sense—that is what makes it all so "scientific." But we must remember Noel's statement that "what we call 'laws of nature' are merely the interpretation which our sensible and mental constitution enables us to put upon the language of the Kosmos."[33] It is from Man's love that nature derives her power to produce loving Man—again the romantic circularity. Man is the Alpha and the Omega. In worshipping God, as Feuerbach taught, he worships only himself.

Thus in the *Ode to the Spirit of Auguste Comte* prefixed to *The Drama of Kings*, Buchanan declares that

> . . . God is multiform,
> Human of heart and warm,
> Content to take what shape the Soul loves best;
> Before our footsteps still
> He changeth as we will—
> Only—with blood alone we gain Him, and are blest.

The idea that humanity assumes divinity through martyrdom may be a Christian heresy or, as has already been suggested, a reflection of Reade's *Martyrdom of Man*. It reappears in lines which support the latter hypothesis:

> The creeds I've cast away
> Like husks of garner'd grain,
> And of them all this day
> Does never a creed remain;
> Save *this*, blind faith that God
> Evolves, thro' martyred Man.

The Last Faith, says Buchanan, is faith in man, the one faith without which we perish:

> Hate Man, and O, thou hatest, losest God;
> Keep faith in Man, and rest with God indeed.
> And what if, after all, the God thou seekest
> Were here, not yonder,—God in act to be,
> To find and know Himself for evermore.

Orm's closest approach to fulfillment of his quest occurs when

> At last in a Garden of God
> I saw the Flower of the World.

[33] See above, p. 225.

This Flower had human eyes,
Its breath was the breath of the mouth.[34]

And in *The Drama of Kings* the Chorus is sustained by the belief that when at last we behold the face of God we shall find it to be none other than the face of perfected Man.[35]

Noel, as we have seen, is not thoroughly satisfied with faith in man unless he can associate human love either with the love of Christ or with the love which permeates both the World Soul and the Spirit of Man and binds them together. The latter sort of love is celebrated in the lines:

Find the birthplace of sweet Love;

. . .

Find his nest within the grove
Of mystic manifold delight,

. . .

Discover hidden paths of Love!
Explain the common miracle,
Dear abundant treasure-trove,
Celestial springs in earthly well,
In human vase Heaven's ænomel!

Like so many men who completely discard divine transcendence in favor of divine immanence, he is rather vague as to the distinction between *eros* and *agape*. His proneness to confuse the two is aggravated partly by his Neo-Hellenic paganism and partly by his admiration for Hinton's theory that the all-pervasive cosmic energy is sexual. *The Secret of the Nightingale* is the bird's "holy love" for its mate:

Behold the chosen one, the bride!
And the singer, he singeth by her side.
Leap, heart! be aflame with them! loud, not dumb,
Give a voice to their epithalamium!
Whose raptures wax not pale or dim
Beside the fires of seraphim.
These are glorious, glowing stairs,
In gradual ascent to theirs:
With human loves acclaim and hail
The holy love of the nightingale!

Elsewhere two lovers fail to cooperate with nature by seizing upon what Browning would call their "good minute":

[34] *Complete Poetical Works*, I, 280; II, 382, 432.

[35] *The Drama of Kings*, pp. 5–6.

Spring confused her lovers all,
Each obeyed the sacred call;
Only we refused to fall,
Surely, calmly, self-incurled
'Mid such sweet madness of the world!

. . .

And we are still apart, alone!
Might our clashing kindle Hell?
Ask no more, I cannot tell;
Was it well? was it well?

Noel's answer is obvious enough. But such a poem as *Passion* is less Browningesque than Swinburnian:

O pale my lady, and were you death,
Kissing away the soul's own breath,
I would follow, for all cold Reason saith,
Even where Ruin raveneth![36]

Remembering Buchanan's attack on "The Fleshly School," we shall not expect his conception of love to be so concrete and full-blooded. He tenderly cared for his invalid wife, but he seems to have been more deeply devoted to his mother, who lived far too long for his good.[37] Thinking perhaps of the conclusion of *Faust* and perhaps of Comte, he sometimes rationalized his fixation into a doctrine of salvation through womanhood and especially through motherhood. He tells the Virgin Mary that if he could worship at any Christian shrine it would be at hers, since

Holiest and best of all things, holier far
Than Godhead, is eternal Motherhood![38]

In the essay *On Mystic Realism* appended to *The Drama of Kings* (1871) he writes of himself that "The personal key-note of all his work is to be found in 'The Book of Orm,' and most of all in 'The Man Accurst.' "[39] This concluding section of *Orm* (1870) presents a vision of Judgment. Everybody has been saved except one utterly vile, defiantly unrepentant man. As a last resort God asks if any of the redeemed is willing to leave heaven and share the wretch's exile. There are two volunteers—his mother and his wife, both of whom he had treated basely. The man weeps, whereat God admits him. *Orm* is an early though thoroughly characteristic work, but in one of his last poems Buchanan asserts:

[36] *Poems*, pp. 8, 9, 18, 21, 159.
[37] Harriet Jay, *Robert Buchanan*, p. 2.
[38] *Complete Poetical Works*, II, 300.
[39] *The Drama of Kings*, p. 467.

I reverenced from the first
The Woman-Soul divine
(Mother, that faith was nurst
On that brave breast of thine!)
Pointing the heavenward way,
The angel-guide of man,
She seems to me today
As when my faith began![40]

Some readers may be reluctant to accept the conclusion that these poets represent the complete submergence of Christianity in romantic nature-worship and man-worship. Does not Noel profess belief in "the revelation of our Blessed Lord Jesus Christ"? Must we demand of so ardent a lover of mankind any *particular* interpretation of those words? And do not *The Man Accurst* and *The Ballad of Judas Iscariot* suggest that Buchanan was mistaken in thinking that he was not a Christian? Both poets cherished the *Christ-ideal*, and that is what really matters. It may be so. Instead of debating the point let us examine more closely what these men actually say concerning Jesus Christ.

"To me," says Buchanan, "the historical Christ, the Christ of popular teaching, is a Phantom, the Christ-God a very Spectre of the Brocken, cast by the miserable pigmy Man on the cloudland surrounding and environing him. I conceive only the ideal Christ, as an Elder Brother who lived and suffered and died as I have done and must do; and while I love him in so far as he is human and my fellow-creature, I shrink from him in so far as he claims to be Divine."[41] Jesus, then, is a nonhistorical ideal personification of loving and suffering humanity. But despite Buchanan's frequent use of the "martyrdom of man" idea, Orm shudders when he beholds a vision of God in heaven with the bleeding Lamb at His feet:

All the while it cried for pain,
It could not wash away the stain.

Orm is relieved to awaken from "that pale Dream of Pain." For Buchanan, furthermore, Christ is by no means a unique symbol of loving self-sacrifice. In *Balder the Beautiful* he explicitly compares the relations between Odin and Balder to those between God the Father and God the Son. Balder prays to Odin:

As the blood of a sacrifice is shed,
Let me die in my brethren's stead.

[40] *Complete Poetical Works*, I, 290–294; II, 431.
[41] Noel, *Poems*, p. xix (Buchanan's "Prefatory Notice").

He would be "Thy Son who dies that men may live." Meeting Christ at the close of his wanderings, Balder hails Him as "elder Brother." Christ in turn greets Balder as one of "The golden Sons of Gŏd." There are, he explains, many other "Paracletes," such as Buddha, Prometheus, and Hiawatha;

> And whosoe'er loves mortals most
> Shall conquer Death the best,
> Yea, whosoe'er grows beautiful
> Shall grow divinely blest.

The unexpected lugging in of beauty might be a reminiscence of *Hyperion*, though the first two lines suggest Coleridge's "He prayeth best who loveth best." Essentially, however, Christ is at most one of various man-made symbols of George Eliot's "Choir Invisible." Walt Whitman apparently qualifies for membership in this company: in one poem he is told that there is "something Christ-like in thy mien," and in another he is described as a Christlike iconoclast who believes in Man.[42]

In a very late poem entitled *A Catechism*, Buchanan summarizes his beliefs. Asked if he is a repentant sinner, he answers:

> ... If Sin be blent
> Into my nature as its element,
> Then 'tis my God's as surely as 'tis mine;
> But since I know my Father is Divine,
> I know that all which seemeth Sin in me
> Is but an image and a mystery.

To the question "*Who is God?*" his response is especially revealing:

> ... He is I;
> Impersonal in all that seems to be,
> He first and last grows personal in me.

"*Hath He no Being, then, apart from thee?*" "None," responds the catechumen. "*Yet abideth through Eternity?*" "As *I* abide." "*Yet is He Lord of Death?*" "Yea, and if I should perish, perisheth." "*Is He not more than thou?*"

> ... He is the Whole
> Of which I am the part, yet this my Soul
> Is He, and surely through this sight of mine
> He sees Himself, and knows Himself Divine.

[42] *Complete Poetical Works*, I, 279, 425, 471, 476–477, 479; II, 395ff. While traveling in America Buchanan saw something of Whitman in Camden and Washington. For other poems to or about Whitman see I, 380; II, 398.

Asked to list God's attributes, Buchanan insists that His only attribute is Love, which is manifested "In me, / And in mine other self, Humanity." Asked if he believes in Jesus Christ, the Son of God, he responds:

> In Him, and in my Brethren every one:
> The child of Mary who was crucified,
> The gods of Hellas fair and radiant-eyed,
> Brahm, Balder, Gautama, and Mahomet,
> All who have pledged their gains to pay my debt
> Of sorrows . . .
>
> . . .
>
> . . . the wise, the good,
> Inheritors of Nature's godlike mood;
> In these I do believe eternally,
> Knowing them deathless, like the God in me.

"*How many sacraments hath God ordained?*"

> None; since all sacraments in Man are blent,
> And I myself am daily sacrament.[43]

Particularly important for us is Buchanan's insistence that although the Divine Humanity is greater than any single man, the difference is more quantitative than qualitative. The divinity of Collective Humanity is the sum total of the divinity of individual men: the Great Being would not be God unless Buchanan, along with every one of his fellows, were godlike. "He is I . . . He first and last grows personal in me." One sees how easily a cult of humanity, divorced from belief in objective godhead, can be used to satisfy the romantic desire for self-deification.

Noel is of course more ambiguous. He has a more religious nature than Buchanan and takes fuller advantage of the circumstances which enabled a poet of his generation to identify with Christianity any sort of nonmaterialistic attitude toward nature and any sort of enthusiasm for the welfare of mankind. Buchanan, we know, regards him with some surprise as an authentic Christian who "embraces in full affluence of sympathy and love that ghostly godhead [Christ] and credits *him* with all the mercy, all the knowledge, all the love and power which we [Buchanan] believe to be the common birthright of Humanity,—the accumulation of spiritual ideals from century to century."[44] Several of Noel's poems, considered in isolation from the general drift of his thought, could be used to support this description of him. For example, these lines from *Suspiria:*

[43] *Ibid.*, II, 302–305.

[44] Noel, *Poems*, p. xix (Buchanan's "Prefatory Notice").

'Tis only a little we know; but ah! the Saviour knoweth;
I will lay the head of a passionate child on His gentle breast,
I poured out with the wave, He founded firm with the mountain;
In the calm of His infinite eyes I have sought and found my rest.
O to be still on the heart of the God we know in the Saviour,
Feeling Him more than all the noblest gifts He gave!
To be is more than to know; we near the Holy of Holies
In coming home to Love; we shall know beyond the grave.[45]

What more could be demanded of any Christian poet?

But the further we read in his work the more it becomes apparent that for him "Christ" is merely a passionate, imaginative, personalized way of expressing that love which is the essence of the pantheistic World Soul. In *Pan*, Jesus is identified with the love-goddess

... who is the heart of all,
Uranian Aphrodite, whom
The world laid in a Syrian tomb
Under the name of Jesus.

For Venus and Pan and the other gods of Greece are not truly dead: it is only that Jesus more worthily embodies the holy truth which they symbolized before His coming. The principle involved is precisely that of *Hyperion*:

For while the dawn expands, and lightens,
Greater Gods arrive to reign,
Jupiter dethrones the Titans,
Osiris rules the world again,
But in a more majestic guise;
Sinai thunders not, nor lightens,
Eagle, sun-confronting eyes
Veils before mild mysteries!
Balder, Gautama, full-fain
Pay humble tribute while they wane;
All the earlier Beauty prone is
Before a lovelier than Adonis!

We are not to suppose, however, that Christ is the final goal of the evolution of love. The purpose of the World Soul will not be attained

Till even the Person of our Lord
In yonder daylight of the Spirit,

. . .

[45] *Ibid.*, p. 103. See also pp. 121–122 for another apparently heartfelt expression of belief in the Christian Saviour.

Will fade in the full summer-shine
Of all grown Human, and Divine,
And every mode of worship fall,
Eternal God be all in all;
Pan lives, though dead![46]

Eternal God can only be the Divine Humanity, which has nothing to worship but itself, and Christ is a provisional man-made symbol of that ideal. Spiritual progress consists in learning to get along without Him. Meanwhile He derives solely from human love whatever temporary sacredness He may possess. Noel, who shared Buchanan's admiration for Whitman and devoted an essay to him, quotes these lines from the American romantic's *To Working Men*:

We consider Bibles and religions divine—I do not say they are not divine;
I say that they have all grown out of you, and may grow out of you still;
It is not they who give the life; it is you who give the life.

"Does it not breathe the very spirit of Christ?" demands Noel.[47]

"Christianity" is a noise produced by the organs of speech, and there is nothing to prevent any man from using that noise in connection with any conceivable affirmation or denial. But our efforts to engage in rational discourse with one another are considerably hindered when we insist on using the same noise as a means of pointing toward referents which are not merely different but incompatible. Whatever semantic signs we adopt, the fact remains that the religion of Noel and Buchanan is approximately the same religion as that of Mr. Middleton Murry. It is a quite different religion from that of George Herbert, of Christopher Smart, of Gerard Hopkins, of T. S. Eliot. Perhaps more clearly than any other poet whom we have yet considered, Noel and Buchanan illustrate the chasm which separates what I choose to call Christianity from what I choose to call the romantic faith. Although my own preference is glaringly obvious, nothing in this series of studies necessitates the conclusion that either religion is "truer" than the other. I insist only that they are radically different, and that the difference is important for the history of ideas. Perhaps the contrast will become even more obvious if we now turn to a group of poets who say, with Leslie Stephen's rustic churchwarden, "You see, sir, I think there be a God."[48]

[46] *Ibid.*, pp. 70, 73–74.

[47] *Essays on Poetry and Poets*, p. 325.

[48] See above, p. 68.

Chapter Nine

CATHOLIC CHRISTIANITY

MAN is but Man at last; and God is God."[1] After our long immersion in the poetry of inwardness, the elder De Vere's truism startles us like some daring paradox. The preceding chapters have displayed a movement from objectivity to subjectivity, from transcendence to immanence, from trust in God to trust in man—in short, from traditional Christianity to a romanticized reinterpretation of that religion and sometimes to an overtly non-Christian proclamation of the pure romantic gospel. The body of verse now to be examined points in the opposite direction. It supports my preliminary attempt to refute the popular idea that the Catholic Revival was merely a special aspect of the Romantic Movement.[2]

The Catholic poets often expressly repudiate the romantic reliance on independent human power. In *A Tale of Modern Times*, Aubrey de Vere the younger makes a saintly old man tell his life-story. In his Byronic youth,

> Strength without bound in spirit, body, and soul
> I felt, and in my rapture mocked control.

Following wherever his aspiring passions led, he saw many lands and studied all arts and sciences,

> . . . murmuring in my mirth
> That text, "Be thou, O Man, the Lord of Earth."
> . . .
> . . . I sought within
> For God, and there alone; and recked not of my sin.

Meanwhile everyone thought him wise and good, for he was a benevolist of the self-regarding sort: "I loved my kind—but more their acclamations." Needless to say, it is on a mountain peak that his pride reaches a climax of blasphemously mystical rapture in which he feels himself "A worshipper no longer but a God!" From this moment, however, he is haunted by a shadowy

[1] Aubrey de Vere, the elder, *A Song of Faith, Devout Exercises, and Sonnets*, p. 20.

[2] See above, pp. 10–14. I must also repeat the reference to my article, "Romanticism and the Religious Revival in England," *Journal of the History of Ideas*, II, 330–338. It contains a good deal of matter complementary to the present chapter.

form which he takes to be that of some mysterious enemy. His fear impels him to scrutinize his real nature—"Then my disease I knew, but not the cure." In terror he flies here and there, relentlessly dogged by the ominous shadow. But when at last he renounces pride in genuine penitence, the pursuer reveals Himself as Jesus.[3] Speaking more obviously for himself, Frederick William Faber tells of moods in which he longs to mingle his wildness with the wildness of a tempest in the woods. "There is in me," he continues,

> At times a hot and fierce desire to see
> And realize my immortality:—
> When it would be relief to me to heave
> A huge unnatural weight of rock, and leave
> The mass on some hill-top, for aye to prove
> That there is nought man's spirit may not move.

Such Spasmodic longings, being prompted by Satan, cannot be subdued by unaided human nature.

> These are the spirit-wasting moods, yea, these
> The fever, restlessness, and weak disease
> Of one who prays too seldom: at dead night
> Doth the strange spirit come with unstayed might,
> Until our open souls grow large and swell
> With the influx of a dark, invisible
> And dire possession, that doth quickly drench
> Our powers in sin, and fain our souls would wrench
> From the good Cross, which like a floating mast
> Unto the shipwrecked, is our first and last
> True hope:—and our hands bleed in holding fast.[4]

These poets can be called dupes of superstition, but they cannot be called romantics unless romanticism can be dissociated from reliance on human self-sufficiency.

I have not attempted to discover whether these two poems were written before or after the conversion of De Vere and Faber to Roman Catholicism in 1851 and 1845 respectively. For me the question is unimportant. Having irritated Protestants elsewhere in this series of studies, I must now irritate readers who would restrict the term "Catholic" to Christians in communion with the see of Rome. Accepting my own interpretation of romanticism,

[3] Aubrey de Vere, the younger, *Irish Odes and Other Poems*, pp. 205–212 *passim*. Francis Thompson probably read this poem, though its theme is too familiar to justify identifying it as a source of *The Hound of Heaven*. Hereafter the name "De Vere" will refer to Aubrey Thomas de Vere (1814–1902) except when his father Sir Aubrey de Vere (1788–1846) is specified.

[4] *Poems*, pp. 364–365.

they may well challenge me to deny that there is a strong tincture of romantic self-will in refusing to recognize the Church of Rome, speaking through the Pope,[5] as the infallible authority on faith and morals. Against this dogma, against some practices arising from it, and against the spiritual and intellectual rigidity which it tends to generate, the Anglo-Catholic is literally "protestant" in the interests of what he believes to be an authentic and enlightened conception of the Catholic faith. This recalcitrance, however, implies no glorification of independent human power, no reluctance to submit his will to the will of an absolutely transcendent God. To a Church which manifested the complete perfection of the Mystical Body of Christ he would joyfully surrender every faintest stirring of private judgment. Even the Visible Church as it actually exists receives from him a degree of reverence and obedience which no Protestant would accord it. The Anglo-Catholic affirms that it is a divinely instituted, divinely guided extension of the Incarnation, and that its bishops and priests are apostolic mediators of the grace historically brought down among men by the Word who is eternally made Flesh.

But since free will seems to be the inescapable condition established by God for all His dealings with men, the Anglo-Catholic cannot believe that God would abrogate it even for the sake of the Church. If individuals remain capable of sin after receiving the Holy Ghost in Baptism, one hesitates to insist that the same precious aid has rendered the Church absolutely incapable of error. Though recognizing that the Church is divinely guided to a degree which no individual can claim, the Anglo-Catholic sees tragically abundant evidence that she has also been granted freedom to stray from her Guide. He cannot ascribe infallible authority a priori to an institution in whose development stupid and sinful men have been allowed to play so large a part. This unwillingness arises not from Pelagian pride but from a thoroughly unromantic and Christian distrust of human nature.[6] The ambiguity of the Anglo-Catholic position is the inevitable ambiguity of the Christian's terrestrial state. A Church Militant founded upon such a rock as Peter, so faithless though so faithful, must in some measure be a Church Errant. Belief in an infallible Church is a strong anchor against the drift towards naturalistic humanism, but those who find the price of this

[5] Or, as a more rigorous Ultramontanism would have it, the Pope speaking to the Church.

[6] In speaking of human nature here and elsewhere I refer to man's nature in his fallen state and, of course, without denying that even in that state he retains a natural tendency to seek God. Such remarks as the above imply not the total corruption of man but the insufficiency of his unaided goodness. Similarly, when I speak unsympathetically of "faith in man" I do not mean Christian faith in man as a believing and penitent child of God.

safeguard too heavy are not necessarily more romantic than those who are willing to pay it. It would be difficult to prove that Newman was any closer to Carlyle before 1845 than after. For these reasons, be they valid or invalid, I include both Anglican and Roman Catholicism within the Catholic Revival as a single force opposed to romanticism.

It would otherwise be difficult to treat the literary side of the movement, since except for a handful of Irishmen every poet in this and the two succeeding special chapters is either an Anglican or an ex-Anglican convert to Rome. Why this should be the case I cannot say. Perhaps Anglo-Catholicism was necessary for restoring the broken relationship between the English literary tradition and the Catholic faith; perhaps also the adventure of reviving that faith was more stimulating to the imagination than the calmer satisfactions of inherited assurance. Naturally the poetry of the Revival sometimes reflects the issues involved in the Rome-Canterbury cleavage, but as regards the fundamental opposition between historic Christianity and the dominant trend of nineteenth-century religious thought the differences which separate the two branches of the Church are less important than the similarities. We shall therefore ignore the distinction between Anglican and Roman Catholicism except in the few instances when it will force itself on our attention.

For every poet in this chapter, no matter whether he writes as Anglican or Romanist, the deadliest sin is pride and the most Christlike virtue is humility. In a poem by De Vere, Saint Francis tells Brother Leone that "Perfect Joy" would be to endure a night of extreme pain and humiliation with a mind so full of the sufferings of Christ upon the Cross that no thought of one's own misery has room to enter.[7] At the very core of humility, however, lurks the snare of pride. *Ambitious Repentance* is Faber's warning to a "poor sinful heart" (perhaps his own) which, having tasted the joy of penitence, perversely longs for more and bigger occasions for God's forgiveness. We must be content with our own shabby little sins:

> Ah! there is store of bitter honey yet
> Deep in these scentless flowers.
>
> Covet no more: from these few pangs thou must
> Enough for penance earn;
> And wait and work: faith's last hard lesson learn,
> Calmness in self-distrust.[8]

[7] *Selections*, p. 204. [8] *Poems*, p. 223.

Profitably to distrust yourself is to trust in God, as Newman discovered on the Mediterranean:

> I loved to choose, and see my path, but now
>   Lead Thou me on.
> Keep Thou my feet: I do not ask to see
>   The distant scene: one step enough for me.[9]

This humble sense of day-by-day dependence on spiritual rations provided by God is equally strong in Keble:

> New every morning is the love
> Our wakening and uprising prove;
> . . .
> New mercies, each returning day,
> Hover around us as we pray;
> New perils past, new sins forgiven,
> New thoughts of God, new hopes of Heaven.[10]

Give us this day our daily bread.

Hence for these poets the most repugnant feature of nineteenth-century liberalism is its confidence in drawing spiritual power not from God but from the sinful heart of man. Faber does not fear that Christianity will be destroyed by materialism and Mammon-worship, since

> These have no moral soul within them swelling,
> No spirit-pulse, no passionate indwelling.

The danger lies rather in a pseudo-religion of human self-reliance,

> . . . lest quickened times should bring
>   Guesses and notions, clothed in earnest dress,
> And men, from this reformed self-worshipping,
>   Should make an idol of their earnestness,
> Counting unreal love of moral beauty
> Coin that may pass for simple-hearted duty.[11]

In other words the great liberal-romantic heresy is that of Pelaglus. Against it the Catholic poets constantly assert the sinfulness of man, the necessity of the Atonement, the certainty of a Judgment which will mean eternal damnation for the unrepentant.[12]

They seldom impress us as self-righteous: they draw evidence of human weakness from their own hearts no less than from observation of other men.

[9] *Verses on Various Occasions*, p. 156.

[10] *The Christian Year*, pp. 3–4.

[11] *Poems*, pp. 111–112.

[12] See for example Edward Caswall, *The Masque of Mary, and Other Poems*, pp. 120, 211–215.

To his friend, Newman may seem to be "a type . . . Of holy love and fear," but his Guardian Angel knows better. No less remorsefully than gratefully this poet bows his head at the name of Jesus,

> . . . for 'tis the sign
> Of awful mercy towards a guilty line,
> Of shameful ancestry, in birth defiled,
> And upwards from a child
> Full of unlovely thoughts and rebel aims
> And scorn of judgment-flames.
>
> . . .
>
> And so, albeit His woe is our release,
> Thought of that woe aye dims our earthly peace;
> The Life is hidden in a Fount of Blood.[13]

We live, says Richard Chenevix Trench, "Under a canopy of love," but in agreement with Newman he adds that Christian love is inseparable from Christian suffering. Jesus was "the Man of Griefs" *because* He was "the Man of Love." But this knowledge is so hard to bear that we constantly try to evade it:

> If there had anywhere appeared in space
> Another place of refuge, where to flee,
> Our hearts had taken refuge in that place,
> And not with Thee.[14]

Although there *is* no other refuge, Isaac Williams feels that in these days we have become more eager than ever to accept any creed that will exempt us from following the Way of the Cross.[15] Advent reminds Keble that we hate the truth which we profess, and that the Lord whose approach it heralds comes not only as our Redeemer but as our Judge. On the first of January the joy of Christmastide is shadowed by the Circumcision:

> The year begins with Thee,
> And Thou beginn'st with woe,
> To let the world of sinners see
> That blood for sin must flow.[16]

The Christian Year is of course not always so somber and minatory. Jesus, Keble reminds us in another poem, called Levi the publican

> That we might learn of Him lost souls to love,
> And view His least and worst with hope to meet above.

[13] *Verses on Various Occasions*, pp. 72, 155.

[14] *Miles*, IV, 200, 202; XI, 226. Perhaps Trench's position was too moderate to justify regarding him as an Anglo-Catholic; but he was no Evangelical or Broad Churchman, and he associates himself with the poets of this chapter on most of the fundamental issues.

[15] *The Cathedral*, p. 32.

[16] *The Christian Year*, pp. 7, 23.

God's saving grace is at work in the present-day cave of Mammon—"No mist that man may raise, shall hide the eye of Heaven." But even in the exercise of Christian charity this poet detects a danger that charity may detach itself from the Cross and become a luxury of self-esteem. Why did Jesus, on healing the deaf stutterer (Mark vii: 34), look up to heaven and sigh? Because He knew how many sinners would reject His love. If for our Lord the doing of good was mingled with sorrow,

> ... shall the heirs of sinful blood
> Seek joy unmix'd in charity?
> God will not let love's work impart
> Full solace lest it steal the heart;
> Be thou content in tears to sow,
> Blessing, like Jesus, in thy woe.[17]

Even Adelaide Procter, a Roman Catholic so unusually soft and cheery that most of her poems delighted the readers of *Household Words*, thanks God not only because life is joyous but because

> ... all our joy
> Is touched with pain.
>
> . .
>
> I thank Thee, Lord, that here our souls,
> Though amply blest,
> Can never find, although they seek,
> A perfect rest,—
> Nor ever shall, until they lean
> On Jesus' breast![18]

And even then Jesus will show us the wounds in His hands and His side.

Believing most ardently in baptismal regeneration as opposed to the Evangelical emphasis on conversion, these poets are troubled by the fact that very few professed Christians behave as if they had been regenerated. "O let not all your dreams be bright," Keble warns the parents of a baptized infant:

> From the foul dew, the blighting air,
> Watch well your treasure, newly won.
> Heaven's child and yours, uncharm'd by prayer,
> May prove Perdition's son.[19]

To avoid staining one's christening robe is no easy matter, for the Tempter is busy and ingenious. Faber goes so far as to assert that "All human feeling

[17] *Ibid*, pp. 120–121, 177.

[18] *Poems*, pp. 80–81.

[19] *The Christian Year*, p. 249.

grown to be intense / Comes nigh to sin."[20] The blessedness of monastic withdrawal from temptation is a common theme,[21] but even monks and nuns are sinners. According to Robert Stephen Hawker the surest way to keep unspotted is to die very soon after baptism.[22] If this boon is withheld, our only hope lies in clinging tight to the Cross.

There is no assurance of election: the possibility of damnation exists up to the last breath:

> The grey-hair'd saint may fail at last,
> The surest guide a wanderer prove;
> Death only binds us fast
> To the bright shore of love.[23]

The dying Gerontius does not know that he will be granted the blissful pain of Purgatory, nor do the friends who pray about his bed:

> From the perils of dying
> From any complying
> With sin, or denying
> His God, or relying
> On self, at the last;
> From the nethermost fire;
> From all that is evil;
> From the power of the devil;
> Thy servant deliver
> For once and for ever.[24]

Even John Middleton Murry, who describes the Oxford Movement as merely a belated sacerdotal perversion of "the spiritual awakening of Keats and Shelley, Coleridge and Wordsworth,"[25] might hesitate to apply the term "romantic" to the type of religious sensibility which the preceding paragraphs have illustrated. The poets thus far cited, and others to be drawn upon later, sometimes respond also to the tenderer, more joyful aspect of Christianity, but they never relax their detestation of "relying on self." On the whole, except when enfeebled by nostalgic aestheticism, the temper of the Catholic poetry produced within this period is markedly austere and ascetic. The fact may surprise those who have been told by Catholic proselytizers

[20] *Poems*, p. 56. This hard and ugly saying may be less monstrous than it sounds if Faber means, as he probably does, that all very strong human feeling except feeling about God and His gifts is liable to take on a self-sufficient quality which may tempt us to forget that all goodness is God's goodness.

[21] For a few of many examples see Edward Caswall, *The Masque of Mary*, p. 129; Aubrey de Vere, *Poetical Works*, p. 173; John Manners, *England's Trust*, pp. 34–35; Newman, *Verses on Various Occasions*, pp. 49–50.

[22] *Poetical Works*, p. 66.

[23] Keble, *The Christian Year*, p. 115.

[24] Newman, *Verses*, p. 326.

[25] *Things to Come*, pp. 99–100.

that Catholicism is a religion of love, joy, and beauty while Protestantism is a religion of fear, gloom, and ugliness; that Protestants think dourly of the Atonement while Catholics think merrily of the Incarnation; and so on. This trick falsifies both the faith of properly instructed Catholics and that of civilized modern Protestants. There is nothing un-Catholic in the severity of the poetry which we are examining.

Whether this poetry is *fully* Catholic is another question. If the goal of Catholicism is to make manifest every element of Christian belief and experience in balanced harmony of light and shade, one may fairly object that the poetry of the Revival overemphasizes the ascetic prerequisites of Christian gladness and says too little about the gladness itself. Newman's statement, "The Life is *hidden* in a Fount of Blood," is not quite true: the Blood does not hide the Life but reveals and imparts it. The influence of Evangelicalism, very strong in Newman and hardly less so in several other Tractarian pioneers, has been blamed for this lack of completeness and equilibrium. That explanation has some validity, but another cause is probably more important. In the nineteenth century the chief defect of Protestantism, from the traditional Christian point of view, was not its dwindling grimness but its rapidly increasing subjectivity and sentimentalism. Hence the poets of this chapter lay heavy corrective stress upon the sterner aspects of Christianity. That one lopsidedness should breed another is natural but unfortunate.

Like all human beings, however, these poets have their romantic impulses; and like all Victorian poets they are more or less strongly influenced by the great writers of the preceding period. For obvious reasons Scott would have considerable appeal for admirers of Digby's *Broad Stone of Honour*. De Vere thinks of Coleridge as a profound seer whose poems were

> But preludes to some loftier rhyme
> That would not leave the spheral chime.[26]

In his *Recollections* he lists Coleridge with Bacon and Aquinas as one of the three "uninspired writers" who were chiefly instrumental in his conversion. Coleridge had said of the Catholic Church that "nearly all her doctrines affirmed great Ideas, but had condensed those ideas into idols. That seemed to me his rhetorical way of saying that Catholicism was a religion, and not a mere philosophy." The poet-metaphysician also helped De Vere to surmount Locke's sensationalism by showing him "that the so-called philosophical charges against the Church were but cavils proceeding from . . . 'the Under-

[26] *Poetical Works*, III, 412. See also I, 206–207.

standing,' " and that those charges could be refuted by an appeal to that higher Reason whose powers had earlier been proclaimed by Plato and Augustine.[27]

Not at all surprisingly, the author of *Cain* is condemned or studiously ignored. Nor do our poets say anything of interest about Shelley with the exception of De Vere, who seems more eager than his fellows to harmonize his Christian commitments and his love of romantic poetry. His *Lines Composed Near Shelley's House at Lerici, on All Souls' Day, 1856* describe Shelley as a great genius and lover of mankind whose noble ideals had no roots in revealed truth.

> Visions that hour more fair, more false, he saw
> Than those the mythologic heaven that throng;
> Mankind he saw exempt from Faith and Law
> Move godlike forth, with science winged and song;
> He saw the peoples spurn religious awe,
> Yet tower aloft through inbred virtue strong.
> Ah, Circe! not for sensualists alone
> Thy cup! it dips full oft in Helicon!

Shelley's doctrine of "All things in common; equal all; all free!" ignored the fact that man is a sinner:

> Convents have all things common: but on Grace
> They rest. Inverted systems lack a base.
>
> The more obedience to a law divine
> Tempers the chaos of man's heart, the less
> Becomes the need of outward discipline
> The balance of injustice to redress.

Liberty becomes mere anarchy, however, when the brotherhood of man is asserted and the fatherhood of God denied. But De Vere's poem, written on All Souls' Day, ends with reflections appropriate to the feast. Something like invincible ignorance may be pleaded for Shelley. He was the victim of the Protestant Reformation, which tore him from the bosom of his holy mother the Church. De Vere, who has been a Roman Catholic for five years, takes a fling at Anglicanism when he tells Shelley:

> No heart hadst thou, from Faith's sole guide remote,
> With statutable worship to adore,
> Or learn a nation-licensed creed by rote.

[27] *Recollections*, p. 315.

We may pray for Shelley, then, as a potentially religious heretic deprived by English schism of any full opportunity to learn the truth:

> O Cross! sole hope that dost not woo to mock!
> Some, some, that knew thee not thou liv'st to save.[28]

Toward everything *essentially* romantic in the thought of the romantic poets the Catholics turn a face of flint. Wordsworth provides no exception to this statement, but he introduces some complications and raises the whole question of the Catholic Revival attitude toward external nature. Keble, Faber, and both the De Veres knew Wordsworth personally in his later years and had been deeply moved by the very scenes which had inspired him. They revered him as man and as poet; the style, subject matter, and thought of their poems sometimes bear his impress. We must remember, however, that the Wordsworth admired by these poets is not the romantic who worshipped his genius in nature but the reverent old High Anglican Tory connoisseur of the productions of the divine landscape gardener.[29] By the time they reach maturity, indeed, they distinguish more sharply between romantic and Christian nature-feeling than Wordsworth was able to do even in his most conservatively pious moments.[30]

It has been said that the poets of the Romantic Period were somehow Catholic, and the Victorian Catholic poets somehow romantic, in that both groups exemplified the "sacramental" conception of nature. Since I cannot dissociate belief in symbolically given Grace from belief in a personal, objective, and transcendent Giver, I do not think that the epithet "sacramental" can be applied to the romantic religion of nature without making it mean something radically different from what it means to an orthodox Christian. It does, on the other hand, provide an analogy useful for explaining how a Catholic can respond religiously to nature without supposing that natural objects have any inherent spiritual potency or that their function is to provide material for his own imaginative exploits. When the mind of man is prompted by the mind of God to apprehend as numinous any good or beautiful action or thing, a situation exists which may be compared to the giving and receiving of a sacrament. Catholics enjoy this type of religious experience because they believe in the Seven Sacraments and especially in the Eucharist, not because they suppose that everything is on the same level of

[28] *Poetical Works*, III, 359–362.

[29] Sara Coleridge rightly complained that De Vere was too fond of Wordsworth's later poems to be "a true Wordsworthian." (De Vere, *Recollections*, p. 197.)

[30] For an analysis of the later Wordsworth's religious thought which may help to explain this statement see *Religious Trends* III, 204–262.

holiness or can be placed on the same level by man's autonomous will. Thus safeguarded, the sacramental principle may be extended to nature without incurring the dangers of pantheism.

Keble's love of nature and of Wordsworth's poetry should not be permitted to obscure his unwavering supernaturalism. Like all orthodox Christians he believes in the natural revelation; and like all orthodox Christian poets who are responsive to the beauty of nature he says a good deal about it. He is not a Paleyan teleologist. With some encouragement from Butler's *Analogy*, he holds that what God tells us through the Creation *symbolically* corresponds to the doctrines of revealed Christianity. This does not imply that the natural revelation stands on an even footing with the supernatural. The former simply corroborates the latter through what might be called physical parables.

> There is a book, who runs may read,
> Which heavenly truth imparts,
> And all the lore its scholars need,
> Pure eyes and Christian hearts.
>
> The works of God, above, below,
> Within us and around,
> Are pages in that book to show
> How God Himself is found.

The text for this poem, *Septuagesima Sunday*, is Romans i : 20: "The invisible things of Him from the creation of the world are clearly seen, being understood of the things that are made." But according to Keble we need "Christian hearts" if we are to make the visible world symbolize the invisible truths of Christianity. When it comes to embodying this idea in poetry, all that his own Christian heart can find in nature is a cluster of tritely edifying metaphors such as

> The glorious sky embracing all
> Is like the Maker's love.[31]

It is like the Maker's love, however, only for those who believe in the Maker. Let no critic accuse me of praising Keble's pious nature-poetry because it is so unromantic: I think it is rubbish.

Faber also is anything but a great Christian nature-poet, but he is more interesting in this connection than Keble. "Come, then, into the mountains," he invites a careworn friend,

[31] *The Christian Year*, p. 42.

. . . for God's decrees
Are wrapped about them like a mantle: they
Whom He foreknew, perchance may lift the veil,
And see His depths within the blessed light
Which kindles love and yet doth not increase
Our knowledge. Come, then, to this trickling spring,
It will remind thee of thy morning dew.
Let the huge mountains throw their rugged arms
Around thee, while their virtue goeth out
Into thy heart with hidden sacraments![32]

Faber uses "sacraments" metaphorically without implying that a mountain is a vehicle of Grace in anything like the same sense as Holy Communion. The foreknown—those whom God thinks of as Christians no matter what they think of themselves—may sometimes be privileged to experience nature as an outward and visible sign of God's blessing. Contrary to Keble's overstrained notion they obtain no "knowledge "of Christian doctrine, but they come into contact with a Love which enlarges their capacity for loving. In this important though loose and incomplete sense the spring "reminds" us of the baptismal font and the mountains seem to say "This is my Body."

To this extent, nature for Faber is "Mistress of Christian symbols":

All over doth this outer earth
  An inner earth enfold,
And sounds may reach us of its mirth
  Over its pales of gold.[33]

But he acknowledges that such metaphors are too stiff and literal to image the complexity with which

. . . matter lies forever in the lap
Of spirit, and their subtle boundaries
Fade, and revive, and quiver like the light,
In most intelligent confusion . . .

. . .

Matter and spirit pressing on each other,
Stealing and borrowing each the other's place,
With sweet encroachments.[34]

Although even our senses give us faint glimmerings of this relationship, full awareness of it demands an intuitive spiritual power which has been cor-

[32] *Poems*, p. 126.

[33] With "pales of gold" compare "piece-bright paling," Hopkins's metaphor for the stars in *The Starlight Night*.

[34] *Ibid.*, pp. 97, 98, 129–130.

rupted by sin. We can revive that faculty only to the extent that we revive our Christian faith.[35]

Edward Caswall similarly holds that the world of eye and ear is externally physical but internally spiritual:

> Nature! deign to drop thy veil,
> For a little moment's space;
> Well I know, its folds conceal
> Many a miracle of grace.

But again like Faber, he does not picture matter and spirit as two layers of a cake or two drawers of a bureau. He regards all "Powers of the Universe" as manifestations of the power of God. They include the powers of the angels in their traditional degrees; of Mary and all the saints in heaven; of Holy Church, "consociate with Peter's central throne"; of the state; of the human mind; of the physical laws of nature.

> All these, and many more yet unreveal'd,
> Or in the book of Nature or of God,
> Each within each involv'd,
>
> . . .
>
> All these where'er they be,
> Are Thy great work, O Lord;
> And here or in far space,
> Or in the far infinity beyond,
> Not of themselves,
> But in Thee only, and for Thee exist,
> Dread emblems of Thyself, who hast all made![36]

Despite De Vere's admiration for romantic poetry, no Hebrew prophet would include him among those who inflame themselves with idols under every green tree.[37] He writes that in the majestic Apennines

> . . . the Good looks piercingly down through the Fair!
> No form material is here unmated,
> Here blows no bud, no scent can rise,
> No song ring forth, unconsecrated
> To meaning or model in Paradise!

But this Plato-flavored awareness of the spirituality of the material is a privilege restricted to Christians. Unless beheld through the eyes of faith, nature remains as in pagan times "a sorceress still." The same principle

[35] Faber gradually arrived at this position after a good deal of youthful dalliance with more romantic views of nature. Those who wish to trace this development should see especially *The Senses*, *Heidelberg Castle*, and *Thirlmere*.

[36] *The Masque of Mary, and Other Poems*, pp. 95, 142.

[37] Isaiah lvii: 5.

extends to all those human energies which work with materials provided by nature:

> The earth was shaped for myriad forms of greatness,
> As Freedom, Genius, Beauty, Science, Art,
> Some extant, some to be. Such forms of greatness
> Are, through God's will, greatness conditional.
> Where Christ is greatest, these are great; elsewhere
> Great only to betray.[38]

For these poets nature never represents a permanent ideal of perfection which man has deserted. On the contrary the sacramental view is sometimes modified, if not contradicted, by the idea that nature herself fell with Adam and now struggles dumbly toward redemption. As De Vere says,

> A serpent o'er her bosom crept:
> A serpent stung her while she slept:
> A serpent's poison taints her blood.[39]

Romans viii: 19–22 provides the text of Keble's lines for *Fourth Sunday after Trinity*: "For the earnest expectation of the creature waiteth for the manifestation of the sons of God. . . . For we know that the whole creation groaneth and travaileth in pain together until now." Holy Writ

> . . . bids us see in heaven and earth,
> In all things fair around,
> Strong yearnings for a blest new birth
> With sinless glories crown'd.[40]

Caswall addresses the flowers:

> For Adam's sake the world a curse doth wear,
> And in his fall ye share.
> O, partners in one doom.
> Betwixt your race and ours let friendship be;
> Give us of your bright blooms
> To deck our tombs,
> And we in your short lives will honour ye.[41]

But no matter whether the Creation reminds them of God's love or of His wrath, the nature-feeling of these poets remains vitally different from that of the romantics.

As for Newman, he never attempted to harmonize his love of nature with his religion. He was far too orthodox to *deny* that every man may know the

[38] *Poetical Works*, III, 374; *Selections*, p. 211.
[39] *Poetical Works*, I, 122.
[40] *The Christian Year*, p. 105.
[41] *The Masque of Mary*, p. 93.

existence of God solely by the light of natural reason, but this was one of the few dogmas that he did not *like*. "I know," he says,

> that even the unaided reason, when correctly exercised, leads to a belief in God, in the immortality of the soul, and in a future retribution; but I am considering it actually and historically; and in this point of view, I do not think I am wrong in saying that its tendency is toward a simple unbelief in matters of religion.

He himself believed in God only because something within him impelled him to do so.

> Were it not for this voice, speaking so clearly in my conscience and my heart, I should be an atheist, or a pantheist, or a polytheist when I look into the world. I am far from denying the real force of the arguments in proof of a God; but these do not warm me or enlighten me; they do not take away the winter of my desolation.[42]

To an extent which would be perilous for most people, Newman confirmed his sense of the objectivity of God by cultivating a deep scepticism toward all other objectivities. He never, to be sure, seems to have denied the existence of a real external world: what he denied was the reality of the phenomena. To put it crudely, things looked material but actually were spiritual. The relation between appearance and reality was analogous to that subsisting between a sacramental symbol and the Grace for which it stands.[43] In this, as in the idea that some prevenient awareness of the supernatural revelation is necessary if the natural reason is to be "correctly exercised," he is at one with Keble, Faber, De Vere, and Caswall. But Newman differs from them in that, being more sensuous than they, he was forced to regard nature more suspiciously in order to attain his goal. For him all outwardness save that of dogmatic religion was a snare. In the woods it was only too easy to delight in the senses for their own sake, forgetting Berkeley and Butler and sacramental correspondences. Well he knew what Isaac Watts calls "the hazard of loving the creatures," and he refused to risk it.

As early as 1827, in *The Trance of Time*, he refers in a quite Wordsworthian vein to childhood days—so blissfully long, so intoxicatingly rich in the illusion of mastery—when

> . . . the summer
> Bade me gaze on, and did not fade;
> Even suns o'er autumn bowers
> Heard my strong wish, and stay'd.

[42] *Apologia Pro Vita Sua*, pp. 217, 219.

[43] *Ibid.*, p. 36. But here the sacramental analogy is even more than usually imperfect; for in a Christian sacrament the outward and visible sign is no less real than the inward and spiritual Grace.

But now he knows the transitoriness of nature and the vanity of all delight in it.

> Then what this world to thee, my heart?
> Its gifts nor feed thee nor can bless.
> Thou hast no owner's part
> In all its fleetingness.
>
> The flame, the storm, the quaking ground,
> Earth's joy, earth's terror, nought is thine,
> Thou must but hear the sound
> Of the still voice divine.

By 1831, as *The Pilgrim* shows, he has wholly renounced nature in the interests of ascetic discipline.

> There stray'd awhile, amid the woods of Dart,
> One who could love them, but who durst not love.
> A vow had bound him, not to give his heart
> To streamlet bright, or soft secluded grove.
> 'Twas a hard humbling task, onwards to move
> His easy captured eyes from each fair spot,
> . . .
> Yet kept he safe his pledge, prizing his pilgrim-lot.

Thereafter the temptation, if it continued to be felt at all, was too trivial to be worth notice. But in *The Elements*, composed in 1833 on the Mediterranean tour, he grimly concedes that nature has one important spiritual function: to show man his utter dependence upon God by thwarting his craving to understand her divinely ordained mysteries.[44]

Newman's attitude toward nature is one aspect of the larger paradox which baffles anyone who seeks to fathom him. At heart this leader of the Catholic reaction against romanticism was a deeply romantic man. He championed religious objectivity on grounds almost wholly subjective. The enemy of Locke was extremely empirical. The great antisentimentalist *felt* his way to Rome. "Both Callista and Charles Reding," Professor Baker correctly observes, "seem to know what they ought to believe before they believe it, a complex psychological condition which may help us to understand Newman's own development."[45] But is not this condition, after all, peculiar in degree rather than in kind? If nobody sensed what he ought to believe before he believed it, nobody would ever believe anything of much importance for human life. Why do some men seem inwardly impelled to surrender their inwardness to a suprapersonal externality? One must choose

[44] *Verses*, pp. 24, 61, 189.

[45] J. E. Baker, *The Novel and the Oxford Movement*, p. 65.

between two answers—that of Feuerbach and that of Christian theology. According to the former, the surrender is an illusion, since faith in God is merely the most potent device for affirming faith in ourselves. According tc the latter, it is the inward power, not the outward, which is illusory. The apparently subjective process derives its initiating impulse from Grace: something within us responds, often without our awareness of what has been granted, to something quite beyond us. Then, mingling reasoning and feeling in proportions which vary with the individual, we move our spirits outward toward the externality which has illumined our inwardness. Why this happens to some people and not to others we do not know.

As we observed in Chapter II, strict unromanticized Evangelicalism appears to be no less objectively theocentric, no less firmly opposed to reliance on human self-sufficiency, than Catholicism. How then account for the fact that the former proved much more vulnerable to subjectivizing influences than the latter? At first glance the advantage might seem to lie with those who sought salvation wholly through faith rather than through an interweaving of faith and works. Possibly the explanation lies in T. S. Eliot's irritating words, "The spirit killeth, but the letter giveth life." For although forms without faith are barren and worse than barren, a faith which will not pour itself outward into specific forms—dogmatic, ecclesiastical, sacramental, aesthetic—is liable to become mere faith in feeling. Of course the Evangelicals had the letter of the Scriptures, but that was a form too malleable to resist either the force of the Inner Light or the force of science. Hence although Newman drew from the Evangelical Movement much of what was purest and most vital in his Christianity, he found it necessary to move onward. More than most men, he needed many strong anchors against the drift of sentimental liberalism. Whether at last he paid too high a price for his moorings is a debatable question. By this means, at all events, he succeeded in curbing his romantic impulse and in directing it toward the Christian faith.

Most of the Catholic poets who flourish within this period are conscious of their position as pioneers in a revival of beliefs and practices which were sharply opposed to the spirit of the age. Granting the inevitable differences, Anglicans and Romanists are equally eager to champion that stronghold of religious objectivity, the doctrine of one Holy, Catholic, and Apostolic Church. The elder De Vere was one of those orthodox Anglicans who paved the way for the Oxford Movement by reviving the tenets of seventeenth-century Anglo-Catholicism. His *Song of Faith* (1842) reminds us of

Bishop Ken and may well have been written in emulation of his theological poems.[46] De Vere hails the Church as "a holy Creature; Daughter of God" and as "Pure Spouse of Christ! Mother of Christendom!" Thanks to her Apostolic heritage, she is sole possessor of "The supernatural truths revealed in Christ" and of "The sacraments and holy ceremonies" which convey those truths to men. Her authority deserves obedience, for

> . . . Sacerdotal powers, with functions meet,
> Are hers, the visible Exponent given
> Of the Invisible—Guardian of the Keys,
> And consecrated Vicar in those towers
> That stand upon the Rock, and point to Heaven.[47]

This conception of the Church is implicit and often explicit in the Catholic poetry of the period.

For a mixture of political, ecclesiastical, and genuinely religious reasons, the fathers of the Oxford Movement laid great stress upon the Apostolic Succession. The complexion of public affairs made it necessary to validate the threatened authority of the Church of England on a non-Erastian basis. For Keble, in that sermon on *National Apostasy* which Newman regarded as the opening gun of the campaign, the suppression of the Irish sees implies "that the Apostolical Church in this realm is henceforth only to stand, in the eye of the State, as *one sect among many*, depending, for any preeminence she may still appear to retain, merely upon the accident of her having a strong party in the country." Such statements should not, however, lead us to suppose that the Tractarians emphasized the *Successio* merely to protect the interests of their caste. Although we shall see later that the worldly motive was damagingly strong, Keble is perfectly sincere when he asks in the same sermon: "How, consistently with our present relations to the State, can even the doctrinal purity and integrity of the MOST SACRED ORDER be preserved?"[48] Certainly these clerics wanted to save their professional skins, but they also wanted to restore England to the Catholic faith. For that faith the concept of Holy Church was central, and the Church Visible possessed no holiness other than that derived from Christ through the Apostles and their successive generations of heirs. Newman is a factional strategist, but much more than that, when in *Lyra Apostolica* he tells the "poor wand'rers" who shrink from the Church that Jesus

[46] For William Ken, much honored among Victorian Anglo-Catholics, see *Religious Trends*, I, 98-106.

[47] *A Song of Faith*, pp. 65, 67, 69, 71–72.

[48] *The Christian Year*, pp. 541, 542.

... saw of old, and met your need,
Granting you prophets of His creed,
The throes of fear to swage;
They fenced the rich bequest He made,
And sacred hands have safe conveyed
Their charge from age to age.[49]

Those hands, of course, are the hands of bishops, whom Isaac Williams glorifies as

... fountains of benison,
Which Christ, the mighty Sea of love, supplies;
Visible angels lighting human skies;
How may we praise—how style you; called alone
To sit in sackcloth on Christ's earthly throne,
Channels of living waters? Golden ties
From Christ's meek cradle to His throne on high?
Bright shower-drops sparkling from God's orb of light?[50]

In reading such effusions we must try hard not to think of any particular prelate whom we may be privileged to know. "Sackcloth" makes it especially difficult to isolate episcopal function from episcopal personality. Rightly or wrongly, however, these poets believe in the sacredness of bishops and find in that belief another bulwark against self-will. The bishop who administered Confirmation at R. S. Hawker's church in 1840 may have been a saint or a worldling; Hawker may have admired or despised him as a human being. Theologically, nothing matters but that

He lifts the appointed hand! He breathes the tone
That none but Apostolic lips may own;
Yea! in yon fane by hallowing footsteps trod,
He claims and binds the eternal troth of God.[51]

Not bishops alone, but through episcopal ordination the entire priesthood, possesses and imparts apostolic grace. "Good Meäster Collins," the village parson of Barnes's poems, is a very unremarkable little man.[52] Nevertheless he is God's priest: he can administer the means of grace, can bind and loose. His power excels that of any monarch; for kings, as Isaac Williams reminds the Almighty, are divinely commissioned to wield temporal authority, "But in Thy Priesthood Thou Thyself art here." Listening to a sermon,

[49] *Verses*, p. 78. [50] *The Cathedral*, p. 47. [51] *Poetical Works*, p.

[52] Barnes was no less a Catholic Christian for having steered clear of factional disputes. His poems present an almost perfect model of the function of the church, and of the Church, in a rural Parish. They are pervaded by a strong, simple, quietly assured sacramentalism.

We sit with lov'd disciples round Thy feet;
Or, as the growing bread Thy love supplies,
From Apostolic hands we take and eat.[53]

What all this reverence for bishops and priests fundamentally means is that Holy Church is eternally holy in being eternally impregnated and guided by the Holy Ghost—a more reliable source of spiritual authority, these poets believe, than the reformed parliament of 1832. Hence John William Bowden refuses to be daunted by the dark immediate *Prospects of the Church*:

Nay, Bride of Heaven! thou art not all bereft,
Though this world's prince against thy power rebels;
By thrones, dominions, wealth, and honours left,
Within thee still the ETERNAL SPIRIT dwells,
Thy pledged possession.[54]

Fortified by the same assurance, the Anglican Newman's voice rings out confidently to unbelievers and half-believers:

Wand'rers! come home! obey the call!
A Mother pleads, who ne'er let fall
One grain of Holy Truth;
Warn you and win she shall and must,
For now she lifts her from the dust,
To reign as in her youth.[55]

What Holy Church undertakes to teach is traditionally orthodox Christianity. To illustrate the fact at any great length would be to labor the obvious. So far as basic beliefs are concerned, Catholics never have anything original to say. Gerontius does not employ his last moments in devising a religion of his own; he simply paraphrases the Creed:

Firmly I believe and truly
God is three, and God is One;
And I next acknowledge duly
Manhood taken by the Son.
And I trust and hope most fully
In that Manhood crucified;

. . .

And I hold in veneration,
For the love of Him alone,
Holy Church, as His creation,
And her teachings, as His own.

Soon his departed spirit hears the angels, with equal lack of originality, singing the same dogmas in their ceaseless "Praise to the Holiest":

[53] *The Cathedral*, p. 45. [54] *Lyra Apostolica*, p. 155. [55] *Verses*, p. 79.

O loving wisdom of our God!
When all was sin and shame,
A second Adam to the fight
And to the rescue came.

O wisest love! that flesh and blood
Which did in Adam fail,
Should strive afresh against the foe,
Should strive and should prevail.[56]

A completely undiluted Trinitarianism is of course to be expected from these poets. In contrast with much that has gone before we are struck by their refusal to transform the Holy Ghost into a depersonalized synonym of the Inner Light.[57] Similarly Jesus Christ is not Arthur Hallam, or the hero of an edifying myth, or a personification of human benevolence, but literally and historically Incarnate God. In three successive stanzas of *Requests*, Digby Dolben vainly asks for Peace, for Truth, for Love. But in the last stanza he shifts from abstract virtues to a Divine Person:

I asked for Thee—
And Thou didst come
To take me home
Within Thy Heart to be.

This source of peace, truth, and love, he reminds us elsewhere, is the Baby in the manger:

Tell us, tell us, holy shepherds,
What at Bethlehem you saw.—
"Very God of very God
Asleep amid the straw."

And He is also the triumphant victim of the Eucharistic Sacrifice:

Tell us, tell us, all ye faithful,
What this morning came to pass
At the awful elevation
In the Canon of the Mass.—
"Very God of Very God,
By whom the worlds were made,
In silence and in helplessness
Upon the altar laid.[58]

[56] *Verses*, pp. 327, 363.
[57] See Edward Caswall, *The Masque of Mary*, p. 254, for a particularly complete statement of the traditional view of the Third Person.
[58] *Poems*, pp. 40, 73.

The keystone of God's redemptive plan is the miraculous birth, incarnate life, reconciling death, resurrection, ascension, and eternal sacramental presence among us of His Son—the Incarnation in the most inclusive sense. Hence the highest—and aesthetically the least manageable—theme of Christian poetry is "The Word was made Flesh, and dwelt among us." For Richard Watson Dixon,

> . . . This doth outshut
> All infinites, that Christ left His,
> Yet brings it to His sacrifice,
> (O mystery of mysteries,
> Leaving His infinities,
> And entering into space and time,
> The Godhead!) this transcends sublime,
> That through man's nature He transfused
> What soul and corpse alike renews,
> The perfect God and perfect Man![59]

Thanks to the Incarnation, Caswall is not troubled by the evolutionary hypothesis. God could as easily have created the world "Through the slow growth of million million ages" as "by one sheer act."

> Wherefor howe'er the work was wrought,
> All praise be Thine, who hast all made;
> All praise be Thine, who all hast bought,
> With the price thy Lifeblood paid;
> What time descending from the empyreal height,
> Thou who creation with thy finger framest,
> Begotten God of God, and Light of Light,
> The uncreated Word, created flesh becamest![60]

Some orthodox readers may wish that the poets of this chapter had shown fuller recognition of the complete humanity which existed in conjunction with the complete divinity of the Incarnate Lord. Dolben's much-admired *Homo Factus Est*[61] would be a welcome exception did not our knowledge of his personal peculiarities render his love poem to Christ the Man a little disquieting. The Catholics may be forgiven for a slight lopsidedness on this point in a period when belief in Christ's divinity was ebbing. At such a time the doctrine of His humanity might too easily be detached from the whole fabric of Christology and perverted to the service of Socinianism or of sentimental humanism.

To the extent that a man believes in the Incarnation not as a fairy tale

[59] *Christ's Company and Other Poems*, p. 52.
[60] *The Masque of Mary*, p. 83.
[61] *Poems*, pp. 1–3.

but as a miraculous historical event he will feel, and will express in his religious practice, deepest reverence for her whom Wordsworth called "Our tainted nature's solitary boast," the Mother of God.

> He at a mother's breast was fed,
> Though God's own Son was He;
> He learnt the first small words He said
> At a meek mother's knee.[62]

The stanza forms part of a leaflet printed for the little ones of Hawker's church school, but Dolben is not writing for children when he speaks of

> . . . God and man made one in Mary's kiss
> Bending in rapture o'er the manger bed.[63]

Not in the theological tenets but in the devotional practices and the personal religious experience of many Roman Catholics, the cult of Mary may develop excesses and aberrations which Anglicans deplore. Some of the early Tractarians, eager to claim for the Church of England a purer Catholicism than that of Rome, hesitate to praise the Virgin without warning the reader that she is a mere mortal; that she is to be loved and honored but not worshipped or adored; that we are not to rejoice in her but in the God-Man whom she bore.[64] But gradually the Anglo-Catholics make less of these scruples, having found in Mary the surest guide to a Christ-centered faith. Even Keble, always so anxious to be Catholic without being popish, comes to believe that

> . . . unforbidden may we speak
> An Ave to Christ's Mother meek:
>
> . . .
>
> Inviting so the saintly host above
> With our unworthiness to pray in Love.[65]

A stanza from Hawker's *The Lady's Well* reads as first published in 1840:

> And Mary was her blessèd name,
> Though not by men ador'd;
> Its sound some thoughts of love should claim
> From all who love their Lord.

But in 1843 and in subsequent editions we find:

[62] R. S. Hawker, *Poetical Works*, p. 65.

[63] *Poems*, p. 13.

[64] See for example De Vere, the elder, *A Song of Faith*, p. 24; Keble, *The Christian Year*, p. 161 Isaac Williams, *The Cathedral*, pp. 234–235.

[65] *The Christian Year*, p. 519.

And Mary was her blessèd name
In every land adored:
Its very sound deep love should claim
From all who love their Lord.[66]

This revision illustrates the dominant Anglo-Catholic trend.

That Our Lady is a favorite theme in Catholic Revival poetry goes without saying. Faber addresses her as

... whitest Flower! O ever-blessed Mary!

. . .

Mother of God! chaste Lily of the earth!
Lead us to Jesus, Mother! for us part
The veils that hang before the Sacred Heart.
All prayers are to thine honour, which we pray
To Him who, God and Man, within thee lay,
Thy womb His Road, who is Himself our Way![67]

De Vere's *Mater Christi* brings home to us that God the Son, as a member of the Holy Family, assumed the limitations not only of humanity but of childhood:

As tapers 'mid the noontide glow
With merged yet separate radiance burn,
With human taste and touch, even so,
The things He knew He willed to learn.

But she from whom He willed to learn knew that this obedient child was the source of all knowledge:

One only knew Him. She alone
Who nightly to His cradle crept,
And lying like the moonbeams prone,
Worshipped her Maker as He slept.[68]

Not only Mary, but in lesser degree all her fellow-saints, are honored by these poets. In verse as in worship their feasts are commemorated; their lives, miracles and all, are related with affection; their intercession for us and for our beloved dead is invoked. Keble thinks of them as heavenly allies of the Oxford Movement.[69] As an Oratorian, the post-1845 Newman delights to praise St. Philip Neri for the faithfulness with which he emulated the considerate mildness of Jesus. The same writer's charming *Valentine to a Little Girl* gently introduces her to the concept of martyrdom. Is she looking for someone to be her Valentine? Mary, "the Mother undefiled,"

[66] *Poetical Works*, p. 124 and *n*.

[67] *Poems*, p. 327.

[68] G. B. Woods (ed.), *Poetry of the Victorian Period*, p. 392.

[69] *The Christian Year*, p. 534.

will tell her that Valentine is a martyr-saint, one of many such in heaven who stand

> Round their warrior God and King,—
> Who before and for them bled,—
> With their robes of ruby red,
> And their swords of cherub flame.

Any of these heroes will gladly receive her love and return his own:

> And beneath the eternal sky,
> And the beatific Sun,
> In Jerusalem above,
> Valentine is every one;
> Choose from out that company
> Whom to serve, and whom to love.[70]

In a way still more incomprehensible to liberated minds, our poets believe in the objective reality of angels. Sometimes even the orthodox reader could wish that they did not. Adelaide Procter lugs in an angel whenever she wants to pluck at our heartstrings. Also, like many otherwise well-instructed Christians, she appears to think that departed human spirits, especially those of little girls with ringlets, are transformed into angels.[71] Newman knows better, of course. He thanks his Guardian Angel for having toiled to bring about his conversion and prays that at last the unseen friend may bear his soul to purgatory. So it is with the soul of Gerontius, whose angel sings:

> My work is done
> My task is o'er,
> And so I come
> Taking it home,
> For the crown is won,
> Alleluia,
> For evermore.[72]

The fundamental postulate of this book is that the *sine qua non* of religion is belief in an objectively real transcendent Divine Being whose nature and will in no way depend upon what men think and feel. The preceding chapters have not, however, sufficiently recognized a serious difficulty which this view entails. How can we enter into life-giving relationship with an infinitely remote and inaccessible *deus absconditus*? By reading a book

[70] *Verses*, pp. 290–292, 298. [71] *Poems*, pp. 3–5, 245–246.

[72] *Verses*, pp. 301, 334, See also pp. 369–370 for the concluding song of the Guardian Angel to Gerontius.

which, however devoutly we affirm its literal truth, is inevitably refracted by our fallible minds? By agreeing and disagreeing with sermons? By consulting our consciences—that is, our personal feelings? By straining in prayer or mystical meditation to project our minds out of space and time, only to fall back in frustration on our own petty dreams and cravings? In reaction from such unbearable loneliness we may wholly succumb to subjectivism; or, if we wish to continue to regard ourselves as Christians, we may reinterpret Christianity in terms of a more or less completely immanentist theology. In either case the result is much the same. The more remote God is, the more necessary it is that He should reach down and touch us in order that we may reach up and touch Him. Hence of course the sovereign importance of the Incarnation. It is not enough, however, that this should occur only once. A religion grounded upon a unique event in the world of space and time has the advantage of definiteness, concreteness, objectivity. But there is the corresponding danger that the spiritual impact of the event may grow slacker and feebler through the years, like the running down of a clock. What was once a living fact may become an old story in a book. We may repeat the story and affirm belief in it, but its reality gradually fades from the mind and our religion becomes a thing of words. Or we may say that the factual truth of the story is less important than its beautiful loving savor—with the result that we end in worshipping our beautiful loving selves. How to satisfy the need of immanence without losing hold on transcendence? How to make one particular revelation of God's love a never-dwindling spiritual force so that today, no less surely than in Palestine centuries ago, we may touch the hem of Christ's garment and be healed?

Caswall believes that the Church knows the answer to both questions:

> He who in awful Godhead sits
> Upon His throne on high,
> This morning enter'd my abode,
> In His Humanity!
>
> He, who for me, a trembling babe
> On Mary's heart reclin'd,
> This morning in my heart and flesh
> His Deity enshrin'd![73]

Whether the sacramental system is religious or superstitious; whether its symbolic structure is man-made, God-made, or a mixture of both; whether its obvious liability to abuse is inherent in itself or in the human weakness

[73] *The Masque of Mary*, p. 272.

of those who try to live by it—these are topics which may endlessly and fruitlessly be debated. Here we need only observe, in a pragmatic and historical spirit, its immense psychological potency as a means of bringing God into the mind and body of the worshipper without diminishing the sense of His outwardness and otherness. As we have already seen, the principle of grace-conferring symbolism may be interpreted very broadly. But the underlying thrust which integrates the manifold richness and complexity of Catholicism is centripetal. The core of the whole sacramental system consists of seven great symbolic actions among which the Eucharist is pre-eminent. If we learn what these poets feel about the Sacrament of the Altar we shall understand their religious sensibility more clearly than if we attempted to illustrate every aspect of sacramentalism from their work.

Keble and Caswall appear to have somewhat different reasons for believing that Holy Communion provides a closer, surer experience of God than can be attained through private prayer. For the Anglican poet, the Sacrament is the daily bread of the soul:

> Prayer shall not fail, but higher He would lead thee:
> His bosom-friend ate of that awful Bread:
> So will He wait all day to bless and feed thee;—
> Come thou adoring to be blest and fed.[74]

For the Roman Catholic, it is the Holy Sacrifice:

> For me is immolated still,
> Again and yet again,
> In the pure Host, the very Lamb
> On Calvary's altar slain.[75]

Faber, Caswell's fellow-convert, adds that in this sacrifice Christ is priest as well as victim.[76] At first the Tractarians thought of the Eucharist as received, while the Romanists thought of it as offered; but toward the close of our period Anglo-Catholics were turning toward the latter position, which on the whole characterizes them today. The difference, however, is a matter of relative degrees of emphasis, not of sharply opposed alternatives. Each conception implies its fellow. Another poem of Keble's shows that he regards the two views as interdependent:

> Fresh from th'atoning sacrifice
> The world's Creater bleeding lies,
> That man, His foe, by whom He bled,
> May take Him for his daily bread.[77]

[74] *The Christian Year*, p. 221.
[75] *The Masque of Mary*, p. 269.
[76] *Poems*, p. 326.
[77] *The Christian Year*, p. 187.

And we have just heard Caswall say, on good liturgical authority, that the daily sacrifice of the Mass is celebrated "for me."

Regardless of where the emphasis rests, the Catholic view of Holy Communion implies the Real Presence of Christ in the Bread which is His Body and the Wine which is His Blood. It will always remain impossible to express what actually occurs in a miracle so far beyond human words without using language too materialistic for some believers or too vague for others. If during this period, as perhaps at other times, Roman Catholics risked the former inadequacy for the sake of clarity and precision, Anglican Catholics tended toward the latter, their English distaste for sharp formulations combining with their awareness that a sacrament is an action performed *because* its meaning transcends verbal expression. But no poet of this chapter, Romanist or Anglican, doubts the actual nonmetaphorical truth of the celebrant's words, "Behold the Lamb of God." For none of them is the Eucharist a memorial service devised by Christians to intensify their feelings about an event which happened long, long ago. They would admit—some of them reluctantly—that for any individual the efficacy of the Sacrament is largely conditioned by the firmness of his faith and the purity of his intention. Nevertheless they believe that the grace and virtue of the Sacrament are *out there* for the communicant to take and use no matter whether he does so or not; they are presented *to* him, not made *by* him. Their operation within his soul hinges on what he thinks and feels about Almighty God, not about himself. It is at the altar rail that the deepest inward emotion is most unromantically dependent upon objective divinity.

All this was so difficult for non-Catholics to believe that the present volume is chiefly devoted to illustrating the historical consequences of not believing it. For the sake of contrast we may recall Clough's *The New Sinai*, a typical product of Victorian religious liberalism which asserts that, since Christianity is obsolete, we need a fresh revelation of God imparted to us by some contemporary Moses. Digby Dolben answers Clough in a serious parody entitled *The Eternal Calvary*. We Christians, he says, do not ground our faith upon any human prophet of any age, but upon Incarnate God. And since Jesus abides eternally among us in the Blessed Sacrament, we required no new revelation.

> Not so indeed shall be our creed,—
> To wait a new commission,
> As if again revealed to men
> Could be the heavenly Vision;
> The priceless thing He died to bring

From out the veil, to miss,
While Host and Cup are lifted up
On countless Calvarys.
"Among the dead," an angel said,
"Seek not the living Christ."
The type is done, the real begun,
Behold the Eucharist!
The curse is spent, the veil is rent,
And face to face we meet Him,
With chanting choirs and incense fires
On every altar greet Him.

Receive it then, believe it then,
As childlike spirits can;
Receive, believe, and thou shalt live,
And thou shalt Love, O man![78]

The issue between Clough and Dolben is clear-cut; we must take our choice. Those who side with the latter are not, however, thereby committed to agree with everything that the Catholic poets say, still less to admire the way in which they say it. To hold the truth is not to use it wisely or express it effectively. That Catholic Revival poetry is a little unbalanced in its asceticism has already been suggested. We may also feel that its spirit is too narrow and intolerant to provide a faithful reflection of the Catholic ideal. The chief weakness of the Catholic Revival is that it was a *revival.* In order to transform England into a Christian nation it seemed necessary to assert everything that the age denied and deny everything that it asserted. The Catholics thought that the best way of redeeming the modern world was to show how violently they disapproved of it. In the long run they might have had a better chance of achieving their purpose if they had calmly and lovingly exemplified the wholeness of Catholic truth and left the heretics to draw their own conclusions; but they were pushed off balance by their detestation of the errors which they strove to correct. They had a war on their hands; and although Christians are sometimes compelled to fight they can never do so without some detriment to their Christianity. They become too spleenful, intense, loveless. They try to conquer the enemy by adopting so much of his tactics that they injure their own cause.

In the sermon on *National Apostasy,* Keble deplores

> the growing indifference in which men indulge themselves, to other men's religious sentiments. Under the guise of charity and toleration we are come almost

[78] *Poems,* pp. 42–43.

> to this pass, that no difference in matters of faith is to disqualify from our approbation and confidence, whether in public or domestic life. . . . Do not parents commit their children to be educated, do they not encourage them to intermarry, in houses on which Apostolical Authority would rather teach them to set a mark, as unfit to be entered by a faithful servant of Christ?[79]

This tendency to "set a mark" appears not only in *The Christian Year*[80] but in several of Newman's Anglican poems. In earlier times, he says, believers were zealous "Christ's tokens to display"; but now

> Each stands alone, Christ's bonds in sunder torn;
> Each has his private thought, selects his school,
> Conceals his creed, and lives in closest tie
> Of fellowship with those who count it blasphemy.[81]

It is possible to think that such utterances embody real unpalatable truths without admiring their rigidly Pharisaic tone. There is no human habitation which is "unfit to be entered by a faithful servant of Christ." Jesus did not "set a mark" on the publican's door: to the dismay of the High Churchmen of His day, He invited Himself to dinner. If one is orthodox enough to believe that there is no salvation outside the Church, one had better be orthodox enough to add that only God knows who is *within* the Church; that the wind bloweth where it listeth; that Christ has other sheep which are not of this fold but whom He intends to save; that in the mind of God many sinners who call themselves Protestants are better Christians than many sinners who call themselves Catholics. The spirit displayed in these quotations is not likely to win souls for Christ. The immediate need, Keble and Newman would have said, was to organize an uncompromisingly militant ecclesiastical party; Christian charity must wait. It is still waiting.

Meanwhile the champions of Holy Church, so hot in their abhorrence of heresy, were divided among themselves. The Roman Catholics, many of whom were converts, regarded all Anglicans of whatever altitude as no less completely Protestant than Particular Baptists or Plymouth Brethren. At first the protagonists of the Oxford Movement engaged in a double combat —on the one side against Protestant latitudinarianism and on the other against "popish corruptions." Later not a few of them developed Romeward hankerings which sometimes led to their conversion and sometimes not. In 1833 Newman exclaims:

[79] *The Christian Year*, p. 548.
[80] *Ibid.*, p. 420, for example. But see above, p. 245, for a reminder that Keble is not always so harsh.
[81] *Verses*, p. 166.

Oh that thy creed were sound!
For thou dost soothe the heart, thou Church of Rome,
By thy unwearied watch and varied round
Of service, in thy Saviour's holy dome.[82]

Twelve years later, the impregnable soundness of that creed seemed to him as plain as day. It was probably just after Newman's submission that Faber wrote him:

O pray for me!—thou knowest what prayer I need!
What is it to be one in whose weak heart
Two faiths are lodged, while thought and feeling blend
In the wild war; yet neither will depart?
What is it to be one, spell-drawn to stay
For the completing of his nature, trembling
Between two different characters each day,
And seem to his harsh friends to be dissembling?[83]

Young Lord John Manners, unlike his friend Faber, did not accept Newman's solution. When he visits Geneva he cannot condemn it as "foul heresy's fair home" without adding an equally severe reference to Roman "errors." But when he reaches Rome on his travels he reproaches her for excluding him from Holy Communion; and in Spain he feels himself an "outcast":

Three Sundays now have passed since we
On Spanish land first trod;
And never have I dared to seek
The presence of my God.

. . .

I seem, midst sights and sounds of prayer,
That o'er these mountains swell,
To be—it is a fearful thought—
An outward infidel.[84]

Many Anglicans were untroubled by such qualms, but the more firmly they were assured of the authenticity of their Catholicism the more poignantly they felt the bitterness of the fact that the Church of England was a Protestant denomination not only for Romanists but for the large majority of its own members. It was a branch of the Apostolic Church in which most bishops did not know what a bishop is. Roman Catholics had their own cross to bear in the suspicion and dislike of all but a small proportion of the English people. We cannot expect that a movement so

[82] *Ibid.*, p. 153. [83] *Poems*, p. 247.
[84] *England's Trust, and Other Poems*, pp. 122–123, 136, 145.

harassed by opposition from without and so torn by dissension within, a movement so many of whose adherents bore deep psychic scars from the struggles through which they had passed, should fully have succeeded in holding up before the world the seamless garment of Christ.

The Irish problem did nothing to simplify matters. Keble speaks wistfully of Ireland as

> . . . a distant isle, where Faith is fresh of hue,—
> Where Memory tarries, to reprove our cold irreverent age,
> In churches set like stars around some saintly hermitage;—
> Where old Devotion lingers beside the granite Cross,
> And pilgrims seek the holy well, far over moor and moss.[85]

But for him and his fellow-Tractarians the suppression of the Anglican sees in Ireland was the most flagrant example of "national apostasy," and they strongly opposed the political as well as the religious liberty of Hibernian Catholics. Nor did the old landholding Roman Catholic families of England, appalled by the flood of ragged vulgar immigrants, feel much sympathy with their Irish coreligionists. But the Anglo-Irish Aubrey de Vere cried out against the Irish Establishment and the oppression with which it was linked. Pointing to Christ Church Cathedral in Dublin he asks:

> Who built it? Who endowed it?
> Why kneel the natives there no more
> While grooms and courtiers crowd it?
>
> . . .
>
> How soon shall Freedom spurn the weight
> Of centuries dead and gory?
> How long the eighth Henry maculate
> Victoria's grace and glory?
> Against our honor and the Queen's
> We deem this mockery:—end it!
> Disloyal is the pen that screens,
> The bayonets that defend it![86]

During our period a considerable number of native Irish poets composed in English or translated from the Gaelic lyrics of nationalistic indignation and self-pitying nostalgia. They sing of old Erin as she was in happier days

> . . . when bells were tinkling,
> Clergy preaching peace abroad,
> Psalms a-singing, music ringing
> Praises to the mighty God.
>
> . . .

[85] *The Christian Year*, p 243.

[86] *Irish Odes and Other Poems*, pp. 18, 21.

Oh! the hardship, oh! the hatred,
Tyranny, and cruel war,
Persecution and oppression,
That have left you as you are![87]

These writers are still fighting the Battle of the Boyne and glorying in the exploits of Rory O'More. Mangan, the best poet of the lot, was a gifted drunkard and drug addict who veered back and forth between a philosophic-libertine scepticism[88] and a remorseful fideism, both of which sprang from the same distrust of reason. He sometimes succeeds in reminding us that the tradition which he represents bore good poetic fruit at the turn of the century:

Let us pray to Him who holds life's issues in His hands,
Girdling them with seas and mountains, rivers deep, and strands,
To cast a look of pity upon Kathaleen Ny-Houlahan.[89]

But on the whole we must say of these Irish lyricists that their politics embitters and cheapens their religion quite as much as their religion spiritualizes their politics. John Keegan's *Irish Reaper's Harvest Hymn* to the Virgin is a fair sample:

But sure in the end our dear freedom we'll gain,
And wipe from the green flag each Sassenach stain,
And, oh! Holy Mary, your blessing we crave!
Give hearts to the timid, and hands to the brave;
And then, Mother Mary!
Our own blessed Mary!
Light Liberty's flame in the hut of the slave![90]

Doubtless Our Lady is quick to pray for all oppressed and suffering men, but the assumption that she is an ardent Fenian is too hasty. The distinction between her and Kathleen ni-Houlihan is sharper than these poets realize. At times, too, their enjoyment of martyrdom becomes excessive. When the hope of victory seems impracticable they fall back upon the consoling thought that Ireland is far, far too spiritual to care for earthly triumphs. Mangan, quite bellicose in *Dark Rosaleen*, elsewhere addresses Erin:

Look not, nor sigh, for earthly throne,
Nor place thy trust in arm of clay—
But on thy knees
Uplift thy soul to God alone.

. . .

[87] Samuel Ferguson, *Dublin Book of Irish Verse*, pp. 220, 222.

[88] Long before FitzGerald he drew from Turkish and Persian poetry a very similar type of fatalistic Epicureanism.

[89] *Dublin Book of Irish Verse*, pp. 137–138.

[90] *Ibid.*, p. 186.

Embrace the patient Crucifix,
And seek the path of pain and prayer
Thy Saviour trod![91]

This theme is not uncongenial to the interests of Anglo-Irish landlords. Even so true a friend of Ireland as De Vere hopes that the Irish, in resisting English tyranny, will not let themselves be corrupted by a radicalism both spiritually *and* politically subversive:

Wait thou the end; and spurn the while
False Freedom's meretricious smile!
Stoop not thy front to anticipate
A triumph certain! Watch and wait!
The schismatic, by birth akin
To Socialist and Jacobin,
Will claim, when shift the scales of power,
His natural place. Be thine that hour
With good his evil to requite;
To save him in his own despite;
And backward scare the brood of night![92]

De Vere's title, *Against False Freedom*, reminds one of those American commencement addresses which inform the graduates that there is an immense difference between liberty and license, and that they should cleave to the former and spurn the latter. The listener, without denying that such a distinction exists, sometimes hesitates to trust the notable on the rostrum to draw the dividing line. Ideally speaking, it should be possible to distinguish true freedom from false in the light of the Christian faith. In practice, however, the concept of Christian liberty is sharply refracted by the fallible minds of believers who attempt to apply it to the specific conditions of their day. As we now return from the Irish to the English scene, we shall find that the poetry of the Catholic Revival too abundantly illustrates this fact. It reveals its weakest side when it touches upon social and political issues.

These poets believed, and not infrequently affirmed, the doctrine of the equality of all souls before God. The elder De Vere expresses it in one of his sonnets:

The brotherhood with Christ! Now face to face
With God we stand. With Him disparity
Of love, proportioned to man's earthly state,
Exists not: right of eldership is none
Where all with Christ are heirs. The Low, the Great,
The Wise, the Simple, gather round His throne

Ibid., p. 131.

[92] *Irish Odes and Other Poems*, p. 53.

In heaven, one equal boon to supplicate:—
God's sons confest! the Brethren of the Son![93]

This is the truth which might have redeemed nineteenth-century liberalism. But Catholics closed their eyes no less tightly than most other Christians to its implications for contemporary life. Adelaide Procter, to be sure, finds the courage to write:

For each man knows the market value
Of silk or woollen or cotton;
But in counting the riches of England
I think the poor are forgotten.

Our Beasts and our Sheaves and our Chattels
Have weight for good or for ill;
But the Poor are only His image,
His presence, His word, His will;—
And so Lazarus lies at our doorstep,
And Dives neglects him still.[94]

Such Christian indignation, however, is extremely rare in the poetry of Victorian Catholics; it is voiced much more frequently by reformers who do not believe in Christ at all.

Speaking merely for myself, I rejoice that nineteenth-century Catholics uncompromisingly opposed liberalism in so far as it was a naturalistic and humanistic movement hostile to Christianity. But I lament their lack of sympathy for liberalism as a struggle for political and intellectual freedom, and I deny that it would have been impossible to encourage the good in it without condoning the evil. One of the snares in which Catholics are liable to be trapped is the fallacy that any obedience is better than any disobedience, any order better than any disorder. I have not forgotten the manifiold charitable activities of Roman and Anglican Catholics during this period, the admirable slum-parishes, the cooperation of High Churchmen with other Anglicans and with Dissenters in supporting the Ten Hours Bill, the social-mindedness of Cardinal Manning, the short-lived liberalism of Pius IX, the Christian-democratic humanitarianism of Lamennais and his associates, the high though impractical politico-social ideals of Young Englandism and of Catholic medievalism in general. Nevertheless I do not see how any candid person can assert that nineteenth-century Catholicism as a whole manifested a sufficient Christian concern for the freedom of man's body and mind.[95]

[93] *A Song of Faith*, p. 265.

[94] *Poems*, p. 247.

[95] I have already paid my respects to Victorian Protestantism in this connection. See above, p. 75.

Most Catholic readers will prefer C. F. Harrold's kindlier statement:

> It was not liberalism in the deepest sense that the Tractarians opposed, but a secular liberalism which looked to a millennium based on the spirit-denying, Philistine proposition that to make men perfect is no part of mankind's objective, but to make imperfect men comfortable. We shall see that the Tractarians attacked liberalism, and its bourgeois world, because for them it meant the ultimate victory of secularism.[96]

Assuredly it was secularism, both positivistic and romantic, that the Tractarians primarily combated. One can hardly believe, however, that they would have extended their opposition to every aspect of the liberal movement if the motives which actuated them had been wholly religious. When Newman writes of the 1832 crisis, "The vital question was how we were to keep the Church from being liberalised,"[97] he means first and foremost that the vital question was how the sacred truths of Christianity were to be protected. But he *also* means that the vital question was how the vested interests of the Anglican clergy could be upheld and—an important corollary—how Oxford could be preserved as a clerical institution. The motives of the Tractarians, though far from unworldly as human motives go, were not quite pure enough for their religion. In *Lyra Apostolica* Isaac Williams cries:

> Heard ye? the unerring Judge is at the door!
> The curse of God is on thee, hapless Age,
> Binding thy brows with deadly sacrilege;
>
> . . .
>
> O full-sailed bark! God's Curse thy bearing wind,
> And Sacrilege thy freight. Strange pregnant scene,
> While boldness mocks at judgment, and behind
> Rises an Awful Form! May I be clean![98]

What hideous spiritual aberration could have occasioned this prophetic outburst? The sonnet is entitled *Withholding of Tithes*.

Despite its deep Tory tinge, however, *Lyra Apostolica* displays one hint of uncertainty as to the political program best calculated to further the interests of the Established Church. Hurrell Froude's *The Exchange. Farewell to Feudalism* (entitled *Farewell to Toryism* in his *Remains*) suggests that at a time when thrones are tottering the Church might benefit from an alliance with radicalism.[99] The purport of this somewhat gingerly poem would be cloudy did we not know from external sources that Froude—less from social

[96] "The Oxford Movement: A Reconsideration," *The Reinterpretation of Victorian Literature*, pp. 36–37.

[97] *Apologia*, p. 52.

[98] *Lyra Apostolica*, pp. 143–144.

[99] *Ibid.*, p. 170.

sympathy than from desire to free the Church from Erastian domination—had been impressed by the Christian democracy of Lamennais. Largely under Froude's influence, Newman himself was attracted by this policy during the latter half of 1833. In two letters of this period he says that in past ages the power of the Church was derived not from the aristocracy but from the common people. "Tory as I am, theoretically and historically, I begin to be a Radical practically . . . for this simple reason, *because* the State has deserted us, and we cannot help ourselves." But before the year is out he has abandoned this strategy. "I have left off being anti-aristocratical," he informs Froude. "I do not feel the time has come."[100] He means that despite the rebellious stirrings of the democratic spirit the Church will still derive stronger practical advantage from "aristocratical" than from radical affiliation. There can be no doubt that he arrives at this conclusion with relief: he does not *want* to feel that the time has come.

Newman's final choice had already been made for him in 1815 at the Congress of Vienna.[101] In adopting a socio-political program too Christian to be merely brutal but too reactionary to be fully Christian the Victorian Revival reflected, as closely as English constitutional liberties permitted, the mind of European Catholicism under the Holy Alliance. The Anglo-Catholics are by no means to be excepted from this statement. They did not possess the power of Rome, but they thirsted after such power and would have made similar use of it if they could have obtained it.[102] In *The Broad Stone of Honour*, published before his submission to Rome, Kenelm Digby buttresses his theory of Christian chivalry with many references to the politico-ecclesiastical writings of reactionary Continental Catholics. De Vere had become a Romanist by the time he wrote

> Now, now, ye kings and princes of the earth,
> Lift up your eyes unto the hills eterne,
> Whence your salvation comes;[103]

[100] Quoted by Ruth Kenyon, "The Social Aspect of the Catholic Revival," *Northern Catholicism*, p. 373.

[101] "Final" is, I think, approximately correct. In 1871, to be sure, when he cautiously and non-committally answers Matthew Arnold's query on this subject, he says: "Perhaps la Mennais [*sic*] will be a true prophet after all. . . . It may be in the counsels of Providence that the Catholic Church may at length come out unexpectedly as a popular power." But he views the possibility with no great confidence or enthusiasm, for "Of course the existence of the Communists makes the state of things now vastly different from what it was in the Middle Ages." Providence is therefore unlikely to do anything precipitate in this matter. The same letter shows that Newman has forgotten, or chooses not to remember, how very practical had been the motives of his "radicalism" in 1833. (*Unpublished Letters of Matthew Arnold*, pp. 57–61.)

[102] I shall not quarrel with anyone who chooses to extend this remark to the Protestant sects, but at the moment I am talking about Catholics.

[103] *Poetical Works*, I, 200.

but the Anglo-Catholic Young Englanders feel as he does. Manners admires Don Carlos and his followers as champions of the old chivalric spirit of Catholic Spain.[104] His friend George Smythe makes a pious loyalist of the Vendée speak of Paris,

> Where Fraud, and Crime, and Marat reign, and the Triple Colours wave
> O'er the Churches of Our Lady, and the Blessed Geneviève;
> Where Agnus, Pix, and Crucifix, are made the wanton's spoil,
> And the bells which called to vespers, now call to blood and broil.

A footnote informs us that "The Vendéan peasants always said their prayers before engaging, and most of them signed the Cross every time they fired." In an even more abysmal ballad of Smythe's each stanza begins:

> O never yet was theme so meet for roundel or romance,
> As the ancient aristocracy and chivalry of France.[105]

Our Catholic poets were not Tories in the sense of being satisfied with the *status quo*. Their supernaturalism affirmed that the kind of life called "everlasting" must form its buds in this world if it is to bloom in the next. The ugly, selfish, soulless, machine-ridden world of Industrial Revolution secularism must indeed be reformed, but not by trust in human self-sufficiency. Against the nostrums of contemporary liberalism they advocated a Christianized sociology. Unfortunately, however, most of them played into the hands of a less enlightened sort of Toryism by identifying Christian civilization with the feudal system.

Their program is clearly set forth in *England's Trust* (1841), a very bad but historically precious poem by Lord John Manners (Disraeli's Coningsby). He laments the passing of the good old days when the peasant, rightly proud of his place in a God-given social order, gladly served the gentry who so gladly served him. That happy, trustful, cooperative peasant has now been replaced by the disgruntled factory worker, slave of the competitive society which prates of liberty.

> Oh! would some noble dare again to raise
> The feudal banner of forgotten days,
> And live despising slander's harmless hate,
> The potent ruler of his petty state!
> Then would the different classes once again
> Feel the kind presence of the social chain,
> And in their mutual wants and hopes confess
> How close allied the little to the less.

[104] *England's Trust, and Other Poems*, p. 7.

[105] *Historic Fancies*, pp. 33, 173, 177*n*.

The only alternative is bloody revolution, for the modern theory of government by checks and balances cannot long

> Restrain the pent-up violence of man,
> If by our selfishness we once destroy
> The sole pure fountain of a nation's joy,
> And show the poor a yawning gulf between
> The noble's castle and the village green.[106]

In the same spirit De Vere calls upon the English nobles, "undeposed as yet," to

> . . . Awake!
> Hold fast your birthright for the people's sake:
> Let high and low discharge their mutual debt.
> Things hollow must collapse; effete decay;
> But that which stablished first Nobility—
> Honour and Truth—if these abide, her stay,
> While live the nations she can never die.
> Be true to England: to yourselves be true:
> And England shall work out her furthest fates by you.[107]

Needless to say he does not mean that the solution lies in the merely secular sway of the gentry. They must be controlled and guided by that Christian faith which was the mother of chivalry. In the organic unity of knightly valor and Catholic truth, of State and Church, the highest function of the former was to implement the teachings of the latter. In olden times, says Manners, nobles and monarchs possessed great power, but if they wielded it unjustly

> God's priest was there to do his Lord's behest,
> And haughtiest kings have stooped to kiss the rod
> Wielded by some poor minister of God.

Our hopes of reform through benevolent aristocratic paternalism will be

> Vain, unless freed from those, her galling chains,
> The Church her lost expansiveness regains,
> And unrestrained by mortmain's jealous laws,
> May dare to advocate her own good cause;
> Unless in her a power divine we own,
> And worship humbly at her altar-throne.[108]

One may share the desire of these poets to restore the Church to a central position in society without sharing their notion of what that society should

[106] *England's Trust*, pp. 16, 32–33.
[107] *Poetical Works*, I, 315.
[108] *England's Trust*, pp. 16, 33.

be like. They wanted a state of affairs which the Middle Ages had never succeeded in establishing except in brief sporadic instances. Even if such happy conditions had been the rule rather than the exception, the chances of reviving them in the nineteenth century were nil. The real question was not how to restore Christian feudalism, but how to Christianize the existent industrial society by developing the religious implications of democracy. This task they evaded not merely because it was more difficult than dreaming but because they did not at heart believe in human freedom.

"The Princely sceptre and the Priestly gown," says De Vere, "Are symbols of eternal Power serene." They work together to preserve

> . . . that peace by Heaven bestowed
> Upon the Holy Order of the Poor;
> That genuine peace which can alone endure
> While men are trained to mark the hand of God
> Alike in all things; doing each his part,
> In low estate or high, with an untroubled heart.[109]

Now it may well be argued that all legitimate and justly used secular power stands in a sacramental relationship to divine power. It is also true that man does not live by bread alone, that some people will always be much poorer than others, and that Christianity will enable them to find peace and joy in conditions which might otherwise be intolerable. Furthermore we have the highest authority for believing that poverty possesses definite spiritual advantages in its freedom from the distractions and temptations of wealth. These facts do not imply, however, that the poor should make no individual or collective efforts to ameliorate their lot and should submit themselves to the domination of those who selfishly resist such efforts. Men are often miserable not merely because of their own sins but because of their oppressors'. Translated into plain English, De Vere's high-sounding words mean that there is a Holy Order of the Rich and a Holy Order of the Poor. The Christian obligation of the latter is to stay precisely where they are and obey the Rich. The Christian obligation of the Rich is to treat the Poor decently enough to keep them quiet and to persuade them that this permanent stratification represents the will of God. For the furtherance of their common interests, Princes and Priests should unite to enforce this pleasing arrangement. The most objectionable feature of the mocking Communist slogan, "You'll have pie in the sky by and by," is the disquieting truth which it embodies. There can be no doubt that De Vere sincerely wants to save souls. But how many souls has this pious Toryism ever won for Christ?

109 *Poetical Works*, I, 225.

How many has it estranged from Holy Church, from Christianity of any sort, from all belief in a loving God?

Dean Church remembers that in his Oxford days "There was a good deal of foolish sneering at reason" and "silly bravado about not caring whether the avowed grounds of opinions taken up were strong or feeble."[110] This is not the place for a discussion of the formal apologetics of the Catholic Revival: our concern is with the poets. Even the most sympathetic student of their writings must grant that they sneered at reason too persistently in times when the philosophical credentials of the Church need to be emphasized with especial vigor if intellectual life was not to be monopolized by unbelievers. Nor is it too cynical, in view of the socio-political temper of the Revival, to suspect that the motives of this pious irrationalism were not exclusively spiritual. The snare of obscurantism is a special aspect of the snare of obedience. It is important that the Holy Order of the Poor should not be mentally equipped to cross the boundary which separates them from the Holy Order of the Rich. If men are to be duly subservient to the Visible Church and to the secular institutions which support it they had better not think too much or possess too much knowledge to think with. The surest way of guarding them from the infection of wicked ideas is to discourage them from having any ideas at all. It is hard for all persons who possess strong feelings of certitude in religious matters to recognize the possibility that the self-surrender most acceptable to the divine Giver of free will may be the self-surrender of men who have been granted complete liberty to give or to withhold their allegiance and whose minds have not been insulated from the arguments in favor of the latter course.

Our poets hold a quite different view. "The mysteries divine of Love and Goodness," says the elder De Vere, "Are dim to Reason's microscopic eye."[111] His son advises a sceptic:

> Our life is finite, let the mind be so;
> And therefore bound the Spirit's appetites:
> Some things we cannot, some we should not know;
> Wisdom there is that weakens, lore that blights.[112]

From the example of Charles I and Laud, Manners hopes to learn "How to despise bold Reason's ceaseless din." He thinks wistfully of those bygone times

> . . . when faith, through ignorance, could hear
> The voice divine, and own a Godhead near.[113]

[110] R. W. Church, *The Oxford Movement*, p. 257.
[111] *A Song of Faith*, p. 108.
[112] *Poetical Works*, I, 141.
[113] *England's Trust*, pp. 4, 13.

We must suppose, then, that full knowledge would make it impossible to believe in God. Religion is an island of nonsense steadily eroded by the encroaching waves of reason and education.

Such "faith through ignorance" is possessed by the Swiss boatmen whom Faber hears praying for clear weather in their hymn to the Virgin and St. Nicholas. Some may deem them superstitious, but

> Alas! how oft hath science made
> The heart obtuse, the eye untrue,
> Obscuring providential tracks
> With veils a woodman's faith sees through.
>
> . . .
>
> The men of Linz see into Heaven,
> Where sages but detect its law;
> Judge which the better wisdom is,
> And who hath holier love and awe.[114]

Miss Procter addresses *An Appeal* to the Irish Church Mission for Converting the Catholics. She fears that secular education will corrupt the unreflecting faith of the Irish peasantry,

> For in learning and in science
> They may forget to pray,—
> God will not ask for knowledge
> On the great judgment day.[115]

In an allegorical vision Caswall beholds

> The light of modern days,—
> The light of Intellect, false reason's ray!
> Upward from earth it came,
> Not downwards from on high:
> And lo, beneath its pale and haggard beam
> Sweeps boisterously along
> A democratic rout;
> Uproar and anarchy set loose from chains.
> O woe was me, what blasphemies I marked!
> Science run mad;
> Mammon in triumph borne;
> And nature's law set up in place of God.[116]

Notice the association of democracy with the false, earthborn, blasphemous sort of reason. Inferentially, the reason which comes "downwards from on high" bears with it the sacred truths of Toryism.

In all this we are again confronted not by utter falsehood but by a truth

[114] *Poems*, p. 443. [115] *Poems*, p. 209. [116] *The Masque of Mary*, p. 127.

from which vital elements have been excluded on subconscious grounds which are less than purely religious. Certainly it is better to be stupid and saved than to be intelligent and damned. But if you tell intelligent people over and over again that religion is not for them but for superstitious peasants they are likely to take you at your word. Probably the Last Judgment will not include anything like a doctoral examination, but it might conceivably entail an enquiry into the extent to which we have developed our individual share of God's gifts, intelligence not excluded. Of course the whole problem of the relations between reason and faith bristles with difficulties beyond the scope of this study. We must confine ourselves to the obvious fact that these poets give a misleadingly limited notion of the richness and power of Catholic thought. Eager to save souls *and* eager to stave off democracy, they leave reason to the subversive positivists, utilitarians, and scientists. And then Catholics often wonder why so many freedom-loving intellectuals should have turned against the Church.

Kenelm Digby, whose *Broad Stone of Honour* profoundly influenced most of these poets, exclaims:

> Oh, the vain pride of intellectual ability. How worthless, how contemptible, when contrasted with the riches of the heart. . . . What is the understanding, the hard dry capacity of the brain? a mere dead skeleton of opinions, a few dry bones tied up together without flesh or sinews. . . . "There are truths," says the Count de Maistre, "which man can only attain by the spirit of his heart (*mente cordis*)."[117]

This passages raises several objections. Pride in intellectual ability, like all pride, is vain; but intellectual ability in itself is not vain at all, nor do those who possess it inevitably succumb to the sin of pride. People who talk about the riches of the heart are no less likely to be prideful than those who try to use their brains as far as they will go. Genuine intelligence is not hard and dry. It is significant that Digby, in his championship of the heart, should have cited the rampantly reactionary De Maistre. Finally I recall with some embarrassment that Leigh Hunt's *Religion of the Heart*[118] preaches the most extreme non-Christian sentimental subjectivism. One may plead that for Digby and De Maistre, as the context indicates, "heart" means the heart which has been impelled by Grace toward acceptance of the Christian absolutes. They are thinking of that outward-looking inwardness which we observed in Newman, not, like Leigh Hunt, of the Savoyard Vicar's "Consultons la lumière intérieure." But even granting (rather uneasily) that

[117] *The Broad Stone of Honour*, I, 40–41.

[118] First published in 1832 as *Christianism.* Enlarged and republished in 1853 as *The Religion of the Heart.*

they themselves are sufficiently guarded against romantic infiltration at this point, what of the Victorian liberals whom they hoped to wean from their reliance on the Inner Light? Was not Tennyson using his *mens cordis* when he answered "I have felt"? Heart-Catholicism, too widely sundered from brain-Catholicism, is not the most effective antidote for heart-romanticism. The campaign of these poets against subjectivism was weakened by their distrust of free intelligence.

The poets of the Catholic Revival also expose themselves to romantic influence when, as frequently occurs, the impracticability of their socio-political program forces them to seek consolation in retrospective nostalgia. If the romantics drew their choicest materials for the renascence of wonder from a highly unrealistic picture of the Middle Ages, the Catholics derive their ideal of pious feudalism from the same source. There remains a vital difference between dreaming of times when it was easier to be a Christian and dreaming of times when it was easier to be a romantic; nevertheless at this point there is a good deal of overlapping in theme and mood. To a considerable extent the medievalism of Catholic Revival poetry bears witness to the fact that Catholicism is the most historical-minded form of Christianity. Professor Graham Hough reminds us, however, that by no means all of the literary medievalism of the Romantic and Victorian periods exemplifies the rise of the historical spirit and method. Much of it, on the contrary, represents a desire to free the imagination from a too rapidly changing world of space and time.

> By the middle of the nineteenth century the sense of change has reached the level of general consciousness, and there are few Victorian readers in whom the awareness, enthusiastic or dismayed, of being rapidly bustled along by science and history is not constantly evident. . . . The eager search for new revelations is one pole of romantic literature; but the other pole is this huge nostalgia for a timeless and unchanging order.

In the nineteenth century, as he rightly observes, the Middle Ages were often used for satisfying this desire with the aid of historical materials but not in a genuinely historical spirit.[119] Hough's remarks are probably no less applicable to the poets of this chapter than to the romantics from whom I have been trying so hard to distinguish them. Professing a faith grounded upon the invasion of a real world of time by the Timeless, they employ the Middle Ages as a means of escaping from the time-world or of arresting its

[119] *The Last Romantics*, pp. 117–119.

headlong course. It is not so much that they falsified the Middle Ages as that they fabricated a period which had never existed.

Sometimes we feel, as we did in reading the Irish lyricists, that actual realization of their aims in modern society would be no more delightful to them than the melancholy pleasure of dreaming about those glorious old times which were so deeply buried in unreality that they could never be tarnished by fact. What E. A. Robinson has taught us to call the "Miniver Cheevy" mood is very strong. Musing in St. Alban's Cathedral, Manners loves to

> Turn my tired gaze to some time-hallowed page
> That sadly tells us of a nobler age,
> When men of stalwart hearts and steadfast faith,
> Shrank from dishonour rather than from death;
>
> . . .
>
> When Mother-Church her richest stores displayed,
> And Sister-State on her behalf arrayed
> The tempered majesty of sacred law.[120]

De Vere, though much less of a mooncalf, strikes the same note:

> Dead is our Arthur; dead the Cid of Spain;
> Alfred and Charlemagne.
> Where now are England's wise and holy kings
> "With whom old story rings"?
> Where now the mitred martyrs of the Faith,
> Martyrs in life and death?
> Meek sages, courteous lovers, bards devout,
> Scorning the world's vain shout?[121]

Faber, however, usually resists the allurements of this debilitating mood. He urges that if the past possessed real spiritual truth, this truth must be fought for as a present need, not merely dreamed of in defeatist fantasy:

> I cannot live on dreams my whole life long,
> I cannot gaze on ruined arch, and aisle,
> And altar desolate, and then beguile
> My weary soul with some old loyal song,
> Or tale of English honour.

Compared with Manners, Smythe, and De Vere he is less bedazzled by Kenelm Digby, whose influence should not so persistently be regarded by Catholic students as an unmixed blessing to the Revival. In a triptych of sonnets on *Chivalric Times*, Faber begins with the usual glorification of those

[120] *England's Trust*, p. 3.

[121] *Poetical Works*, I, 75.

"Beautiful times! times past!" But the second sonnet condemns the days of chivalry as

> Unlovely times! times past! when it was thought
> That peer and peasant were of different earth;
> When it was not believed that God had wrought
> In both one human heart of equal worth,
> One equal heart, which by the Saviour's birth
> And Passion, at the selfsame price was bought.

Finally the third sonnet states the real truth—that the Age of Chivalry, like any other period in history, was a mixture of good and evil, an awesome spectacle of "the adverse circles of the Church and World." In two other sonnets he takes an equally balanced view of *The Poor in the Middle Ages*.[122]

The Catholic poets were prone to forget such facts not because of their religion but because of the sentimental Toryism which infected their socio-political thinking. Their dream of the Middle Ages had to be insulated against a democracy which was no dream at all. The Anglicans—not of course the Romanists—made somewhat similar use of Caroline England. But although they regarded it nostalgically, they also drew from it ammunition to be used in those reforming efforts which frustrated, and in turn were frustrated by, their desire for a timeless dream. In the reign of Charles I they find what they think the nineteenth century needs—an interfusion of Anglo-Catholicism and Toryism in which piety sanctifies politics and politics enforces piety. The fanatics and levellers who shattered the Caroline harmony were precursors of the contemporary enemies of Throne and Steeple. When he looks at his own times Coningsby's prototype sees

> Portents with which our English air was rife
> What time religion and philosophy
> Cut off a sainted monarch's blameless life.
> The sick and fierce affection to be free
> From all restraints of Church and monarchy;
> The haughty confidence of power, that springs
> From our dull years of cold indifference,
> And weighs and counts the cost of holiest things,
> Asking the use of prelates and of kings,
> And views high mysteries with eyes of sense,—
> Warns us that England once again may hear
> The shouts of Roundhead and of Cavalier.[123]

The Oxford Movement Cavaliers glorify the Stuarts, sometimes in-

[122] *Poems*, pp. 210, 519–520, 523.

[123] Manners, *England's Trust*, p. 89.

cluding the eighteenth-century Pretenders.[124] They affirm the divine right of kings, good or bad—the Young Englanders were avid readers of Filmer—and they seldom think of kings without thinking of bishops and *vice versa.* Charles I is "the Royal Martyr";[125] Archbishop Laud, though less frequently, the prelatical one.[126] This trend does not, to put it mildly, exhibit Victorian Anglo-Catholicism at its best: the nexus between institutional Christianity and reactionary politics here becomes too repellently obvious. I firmly believe that Charles I died a martyr; but he was otherwise a weak though amiable man and an extremely bad king. Before he gave his life for his faith he had succeeded, with the help of Laud, in making that faith repugnant to thousands of religious freedom-loving men. A Christian should have the honesty to say so.

In short the religion of the Catholic Revival poets does not prevent them from writing as half-polemic, half-nostalgic reactionaries and obscurantists when confronted by the social and political issues of their day. Lord Acton's celebrated dictum is too temperate: not merely power, but even the desire for it, exerts a corrupting influence upon the spirit. To some extent the pressure of contemporary problems may also be a factor in the *aesthetic* inadequacy of this body of poetry. Here we are thinking only of the material included in the present chapter. Christina Rossetti and Coventry Patmore are later to receive the separate attention which they deserve. Although some would say that he had reached full stature before 1880, Gerard Manley Hopkins has been reserved for treatment in a turn-of-the-century volume along with Francis Thompson and other Catholic poets of high merit. But the poets cited in this chapter, generally speaking, are either too eager to reform their world by preaching at it or too eager to escape from it into the Never-Never Land of a timeless past. Much the same dilemma confronted all Victorian poets no matter what they believed or disbelieved; one merely observes that the Catholics were by no means exempt from it. The historical trend, on the whole, shifts from the former deficiency to the latter, but in most of these poets didacticism and escapism mingle in varying proportions.

Of the preachment we have already had a sufficient dose. In a large majority of the passages which have been quoted to illustrate this idea or that, the writer has been moved by no other desire than to versify edifying

[124] For expressions of Jacobite sympathies see *Ibid.*, p. 87, and George Smythe, *Historic Fancies*, pp. 106–111.

[125] See, for a few out of many examples, Keble, *The Christian Year*, p. 204; Isaac Williams, *The Cathedral*, p. 28; Manners, *England's Trust*, p. 4; George Smythe, *Historic Fancies*, p. 59.

[126] As in *England's Trust*, p. 30, and R. S. Hawker, *Poetical Works*, pp. 137–138.

truths; he has not been trying to write poetry. Sometimes, to be sure, the intensity of his conviction has excited him, and the excitement has produced rhythms more organic and images more vital than those of merely conventional bedizenment. The result, if not exactly poetry, is rather like it. Such charity may here and there be extended to Faber, perhaps to Keble and Caswall, more confidently to Newman at his best. But of the poets now in the dock only Barnes, Hawker, De Vere (in one particular type of work), Dixon, and Dolben show any realization that to write a poem is to make a beautiful and significant object. The others express their beliefs feebly or eloquently according to their rhetorical gifts, but they make no real attempt to synthesize religious and aesthetic sensibility in shaping works of art.

William Barnes (1801–1886) specializes in a partly nostalgic theme—the rural culture which, though already much corrupted by the world of getting and spending, retains enough of its pristine innocence to remind the poet of what it had been in his childhood. Again we recognize a familiar preromantic and romantic subject, and again there is an essential difference. For although Barnes is a Christian lover of nature, his Dorsetshire peasants derive their spiritual sustenance not from something deeply interfused in the fields and woods, but from the parish church whose bells

> . . . be good vor sound,
> An' liked by all the naïghbours round.

Their tolling often speaks of grief as well as of joy,

> But still 'tis happiness to know
> That there's a God above us;
> An' he, by day and night, do ho [take thought]
> Vor all of us, an' love us,
> An' call us to his house, to heal
> Our hearts, by his own Zunday peal
> Of bells a-rung
> Vor wold an' young,
> The bells of Alderburnham.

Vo'k A-Comen into Church present "a touchèn zight," for

> . . . there, wi' mild an' thoughtful feäce,
> Wi' downcast eyes, an voices dum',
> The wold an' young do slowly come,
> An' teäke in stillness each his pleäce,
> A-zinkèn slowly,
> Kneelèn lowly,

Seekèn holy thoughts alwone,
In pray'r avore their Maker's throne.

Those thoughts are of

. . . Him that shed
His blood vor us, an' still do spread
His love upon the live an' dead;
An' how He gie'd a time an' pleäce
To gather us, an' gie us greäce,—
The Church an' happy Zunday.

The context shows that "gie us greäce" is to be interpreted sacramentally. The blessing thus received sweetens the week-day toil of these simple-hearted believers and imparts a quality of gentle but merry Christian goodness even to such purely secular pieces as *Blackmwore Maidens* and *The Surprise*. We need not suppose that rural Dorset, even in its least sophisticated days, presented so perfect a model of the right relationship between the Church and the people; Barnes after all is a parson. Since he is also an amiably sentimental conservative, the "pie in the sky" element is a little too obtrusive, as when a farmer who has thatched a new roof is made to say:

Then, wi' my heart a-vill'd wi' love
An' thankfulness to God above,
I didden think ov anything
That I begrudg'd o' lord or king.[127]

Nevertheless Barnes does a fair amount of his preaching in and through modestly authentic poetry. He makes us feel that Christianity is the normative factor in a way of life which he depicts with a motive different from that of a propagandist.

Robert Stephen Hawker (1803–1875) was an eccentric, superstitious, posturing egotist who drew most of his poems from a piously imaginative and imaginatively pious passion for the Middle Ages.[128] Almost as fully as the old traditions of village life survived in Barnes's wholesome cheerful Dorset, so did the atmosphere of the Middle Ages survive in Hawker's strange wild Cornwall. Both men live very much in the past, but enough of their respective pasts was still present to keep them from being mere nostalgic mopers. Hawker had better evidence than most antiquarians for exclaiming:

[127] *Poems of Rural Life in the Dorset Dialect*, pp. 69, 140, 170, 298.

[128] He was an Anglican priest up to his final illness, when, barely if at all conscious of what was going on, he was received into the Church of Rome at the request of his Roman Catholic wife. There is, however, some reason to believe that she did without authorization what he would have wished her to do. See Margaret F. Burrows, *Robert Stephen Hawker*, pp. 81–83.

Let not the Dreamer-of-the-Past complain—
The Saints, the Sanctuaries, the Creed, this very day remain!

Morwenstow ("The Stow, or the Place, of St. Morwenna," he explains) teemed not only with pagan barrows and cromlechs but with legends of Celtic saints, ruined abbeys, anchorites' cells, ancient wayside crosses, holy wells. His own "Saxon shrine," an ecclesiologist's dream, still served a Christian parish. Those who erected it had built for the centuries—"The vision of their hope was long."[129]

Read in their entirety, Hawker's collected poems are disappointing. He is too deeply tinged with the pious pedantry of the Camden Society. Much of his verse is parish-magazine stuff. An uneasily self-conscious man, at other times he tries too hard to be literary. As the region's professional bard—a Celtic tradition which impresses him unduly—he writes too many occasional pieces for weddings and birthdays of local gentry. But here and there, notably in *King Arthur's Waes-Hael* and *The Quest of the Sangraal*, he shows remarkable power to recreate, with barely a hint of preachment, the rugged savagery and heartfelt faith of the early Middle Ages. The former poem, a devotional drinking-song, is based on the custom of closing the pierced lid of the wassail bowl and sucking the wine through reeds in commemoration of the infant Jesus at Mary's bosom.

Waes-hael! thus glowed the breast
  Where a God yearned to cling;
Drink-hael! So Jesu pressed
  Life from its mystic spring;
Then hush, and bend in reverent sign,
  And breathe the thrilling reeds for wine.

The Quest of the Sangraal, similarly un-Tennysonian in the absence of mere prettiness and in the presence of Christianity, again depicts the Knights of the Round Table as

... thorough men,
Built in the mystic measure of the Cross:—
Their lifted arms the transome, and their bulk,
The Tree, where Jesus stately stood to die.

And of course the Grail is no "Gleam," but very specifically

The Vessel of the Pasch, Shere Thursday night,
The self-same Cup, wherein the faithful Wine
Heard God, and was obedient unto Blood.[130]

[129] *Poetical Works*, pp. 47, 48, 50.

[130] *Ibid.*, pp. 165, 173, 175.

The high quality of the last two lines is sustained almost unflaggingly in *Aisah Schechinah*, a poem which is not "medieval" at all unless the Christian religion is a picturesque old legend. "The Woman Numinous" is Hawker's translation of the Hebrew title. Here Mary appears as Queen of Heaven without ceasing to be the handmaid of the Lord. This transmutation of Christian dogma into a work of art with the appropriate aid of Jewish mysticism deserves to be quoted entire:

A shape, like folded light, embodied air,
Yet wreath'd with flesh and warm;
All that of heaven is feminine and fair,
Moulded in visible form.

She stood, the Lady Schechinah of earth,
A chancel for the sky;
Where woke, to breath and beauty, God's own birth,
For men to see Him by.

Round her, too pure to mingle with the day,
Light, that was life, abode;
Folded within her fibres meekly lay
The limbs of boundless God.

So link'd, so blent, that when, with pulse fulfill'd,
Moved but that infant hand,
Far, far away His conscious Godhead thrill'd,
And stars might understand.

Lo! where they pause, with intergathering rest,
The Threefold and the One!
And lo! He binds them to her orient breast,
His manhood girded on.

The Zone, where two glad worlds for ever meet,
Beneath that bosom ran:
Deep in that womb, the conquering Paraclete
Smote Godhead on to man!

Sole scene among the stars, where, yearning, glide
The Threefold and the One:
Her God upon her lap, the Virgin-Bride,
Her awful Child, her Son.[131]

This, in my opinion, is one of the great English religious poems.

[131] *Ibid.*, pp. 161–162.

To the literary critic, Aubrey de Vere (1814–1902) displays a dual personality. Some Catholic scholars have tried to admire his efforts to sprinkle the moribund Wordsworth's nature-poetry with holy water, but in this vein he is a crushing bore. Whenever he writes in his own person he is fundamentally a didactic versifier who aspires to sound poetical without really trying to write poetry.[132] Although he plainly fancies himself as a lyricist, his gifts in that field are slight. On the other hand he becomes an interesting poet when, usually through the lips of a fictitious spokesman, he relates objectively some old Irish legend.[133] His best tales illustrate the not quite completely transforming impact of Christianity upon the aboriginal paganism. *The Children of Lir* is too long and complicated for our present purposes but the reader who turns to it will find it a beautiful thing.

Oiseen and Saint Patrick, though much less ambitious and serious, pleasantly imparts a sense of the cultural continuity of Ireland. The pagan bard dwells with the saint as an honored guest. They passionately disagree about religion but understand and love each other. Patrick, for all his desire to save Oiseen's soul, likes to hear him sing of the old, free, wild, unbelieving days. *The Bard Ethell*, subtitled "Ireland in the Thirteenth Century," is good enough to establish De Vere as an ancestor of the early Yeats:

I am Ethell the son of Conn;
  Here I bide at the foot of the hill;
I am kinsman to Brian and servant to none;
  Whom I hated I hate: whom I loved love still,
Blind am I. On milk I live,
  And meat, God sends it, on each Saint's-Day,
Though Donald MacArt—may he never thrive—
  Last Shrovetide drove half my kine away!

Vividly the blind bard sees in memory

The wild duck, a silver line in wake
  Cutting the calm mere to far Bunaw;

and although he has grown deaf he seems to hear the sounds of hunting and of battle as he heard them in passionate youth. Well he remembers King Malachi, his pious and warlike patron of long ago:

From his nurse's milk he was kind and brave;
And when he went to his well-wept grave

[132] His *Mater Christi* is one of the rare exceptions. See above, p. 264.

[133] He also handles acceptably Roman and English traditions of the early Church; but he is much more successful with Irish sagas although some of the full-dress ones, notably *Cuchullain*, are too much like *Idylls of the King* to seem quite genuine.

Through the triumph of penance his soul uprose
To God and the Saints. Not so his foes.

Ethell honors the memory of Saint Patrick,

But Patrick built not on Iorra's shore
That convent where now the Franciscans dwell:
Columba was mighty in prayer and war;
But the young monk preaches as loud as his bell
That love must rule and all wrongs be forgiven,
Or else, he is sure, we shall reach not heaven!
This doctrine I count right cruel and hard:
And when I am laid in the old churchyard
The habit of Francis I will not wear.[134]

A finely objective study of the confrontation of Christianity and human nature.

In their very different ways Barnes, Hawker, and De Vere remind us that imaginative exploitation of the past seldom seems damagingly nostalgic or unreal when its traditions have descended to the poet as a personal birthright. Richard Watson Dixon (1833–1900) lacks this advantage. His medievalism illustrates, on the contrary, the tendency of a good deal of Catholic poetry, from about 1860 onward, to submerge its religious impulse in the artiness of the Aesthetic Movement. More must be said of this topic in the next volume, but it is sufficiently important for the present one to deserve a few remarks.

So far nothing has been said of the peculiarly insidious snare which is expressed by the term "ritualism."[135] This corruption of the sacramental outwardness with which the Liturgy unites God and man is exhibited chiefly, though far from exclusively, by "high" Anglicans[136] and by converts to Rome rather than by born-and-bred Catholics.[137] Worshippers who are not habituated to rich and elaborate forms may become so enthusiastic over

[134] *Poetical Works*, I, 337, 338, 339, 342.

[135] "Ceremonialism" would be more accurate, and I shall sometimes use it although it is probably a waste of time to struggle against popular usage. Ritualistic worship is the performance of a sacramental *rite*. The evils associated with "ritualism" arise when the ceremonies of the rite are valued for antiquarian or aesthetic rather than for religious reasons.

[136] The temper of the Tractarian pioneers was much more dogmatic than aesthetic; ceremonial for its own sake held little interest for them. But after 1845 ritualism developed markedly among the Puseyites and had become their main distinguishing feature by 1860.

[137] Such early Victorian converts as Digby and Pugin were much more ritualistic than the Tractarians. They were distressed, however, to find that their aesthetic enthusiasm was not shared by those ultramontane clerics of the Wiseman-Manning type who dominated Roman Catholicism in England after the reestablishment of the hierarchy in 1850.

vestments and candles and incense that they associate the Holy Sacrifice with "the elegance of sanctity."[138] Of course it is all a question of equilibrium. For raising the hearts of men toward God, substance without form is as impotent as form without substance. In this world it is only in the absence of spirit that the letter killeth, and chiefly through the letter that the spirit giveth life. The corruption lies not in recognizing the high religious importance of ceremonial, but in valuing it as an end rather than as a means. In the sphere of worship, beauty is never its own excuse for being.

But in the nineteenth century as in the twentieth, the aesthetic appeal of the Liturgy persuaded many cultivated and imaginative drifters, and many affected and neurotic ones, that they simply must become Catholics in order to enjoy the full flavor of so enchanting an experience. This applies to Roman as well as to Anglican Catholicism, though probably the un-English atmosphere and the tighter discipline of the former screened out a larger proportion of mere thrill-seekers. Fortunately not a few of those who came to see the show remained to pray: the soul may be touched through the senses. On the whole, however, ceremonialism weakened the spiritual force of the Catholic Revival by adding too many incense-sniffers and connoisseurs of needlework to the roll of its nominal adherents. There were even men who became priests because High Mass gave such fine opportunities for a tenor, the rose vestments for Mid-Lent Sunday were so fetching, and "Father" fell so sweetly from the lips of young ladies or perhaps from "ces voix d'enfants chantant dans la coupôle." The breed still exists to try our faith in the Apostolic Succession. Sundered from the dogmatic and ascetic aspects of religion, ritualism had another unfortunate result: it enabled non-Christian aesthetes to obscure the confrontation of belief and unbelief by using the atmosphere and trappings of liturgical worship as part of the studio paraphernalia of art for art's sake. If the Catholic Revival produced Newman and Christina Rossetti, it was also partly responsible for Pater and Dante Gabriel.

Dixon's position in relation to this trend is not easily defined. He was born too late to experience the ardors of the Oxford Movement proper.[139] At the university he consorted with Morris, Swinburne, and Burne-Jones, shared their admiration for Rossetti, and took a hand in the ill-fated project of the Union frescoes. His friends, of course, soon abandoned their inclination toward picturesque priesthood in favor of "pure" art; but Dixon refused to

[138] Walter Pater, *Marius the Epicurean*, p. 336. Not only the religious but the social implications of the phrase are ominous.

[139] His first poems were published in 1861, his last in 1896. But according to Robert Bridges, "very little of his verse can be dated as begun after 1881." (Bridges's Memoir in *Poems*, p. xxvii.)

give up either his religion or his desire to be a poet. He became a quite un-picturesque, hardworking, insufficiently appreciated Anglican priest who did his duty by his flock and wrote a good history of the Church of England. A conservative High Churchman, he never stood forth as an aggressive partisan of Anglo-Catholicism or identified himself with advanced ritualistic practices. His ceremonialism was manifested in his poetry rather than in his churchmanship. His original ambition was to sound like a thoroughly Christianized Keats. He felt that the best Christian poetry was Catholic, but like his Oxford friends he associated Catholicism with aestheticism. Neither his religious impulse nor his creative gift was strong enough to prevent him from being drawn into the Pre-Raphaelite orbit.

I said above that he tried to write genuine poetry, not that he succeeded in doing so. *Christ's Company* (1861), his first volume, is both pious and technically accomplished, but somehow labored and stagey. Why it appealed so strongly to Hopkins is a mystery. The agony of *The Holy Mother at the Cross* is submerged in over-ingenious concettism. *St. John* becomes a pseudo-medieval poet who beholds in vision

> A glorious lady standing in meek pride,
> Upon whose front, "called out of Misraim,"
> I read, written in blood: "I am the Bride
> Won by my knight Christ with the sword of wood,
> The thorns, the nails, the spear." She spoke, and her
> Two hands fell round the cross, her ransomer.
>
> Upon the lotus of her face I stood
> Long meditating; while I scanned her robes
> Of whitest samite, striped with stripes like blood,
> And partly soiled with ashes, sad as Job's
> Whom Satan did reprove with many a stroke;
> And all the seam was wrought with little crosses
> Of brightest flame, which pierced little bosses
>
> Of hearts that seemed like eyes, and wept and spoke.

The little crosses and bosses do not wholly obscure the fact that Dixon believes in Christ and His Church, but when he writes of *St. Mary Magdalene* we can hardly tell her from Elizabeth Siddal:

> Kneeling before the altar steps,
> Her white face stretched above her hands;
> In one great line her body thin
> Rose robed right upward to her chin;

Her hair rebelled in golden bands,
And filled her hands;
Which likewise held a casket rare
Of alabaster at that tide;
Simeon was there, and looked at her,
Trancedly smiling, sick and fair;
Three parts the light her features tried,
The rest implied.[140]

Religion provides materials for this Pre-Raphaelite word-painting, but not its motive. *Eunice* and *The Soul's World* are more thoughtful, but the thought is very elusive. It is hard to say precisely what they mean; but to me they suggest, like several of his later poems, that at times he regarded Christianity as an exoteric body of symbols which did not quite perfectly represent the esoteric truths of a private mysticism which he was unable to formulate in terms intelligible to himself or to anyone else.

Judging from subsequent volumes, Dixon finally solved his aesthetico-religious problem by putting his priesthood in one box and his art in another. *Mano* (1883) and *The Story of Eudocia and Her Brothers* (1888) are spineless, bloodless, endless tales like parodies of William Morris's verbal tapestries. Christianity does little more than provide "atmosphere." He also—Morris again—likes to write Neo-Hellenic idylls and eclogues in Wardour Street lingo. The *Lyrical Poems* of 1887, with one or two trivial exceptions, might have come from a man who was not a Christian at all. In a flat, subdued, well-bred tone, Dixon raises, and refuses to answer, the familiar questions about life and death and love and nature. Those questions do not seem greatly to interest him except as opportunities for fabricating wistfully melancholy verses. The precarious equilibrium between his faith and his artistry has been lost. Nothing remains but a despiritualized (though quite harmless) and very dull aesthetic ceremonial.

The spiritual and aesthetic emptiness of Catholicism-for-art's-sake is seldom illustrated by Digby Dolben (1848–1867), but *He Would Have His Lady Sing* is a prime example. He asks his lady—not that he ever had one—to sing to him of the Heavenly City,

And all the fair pleasance
Where linkèd Angels dance,
With scarlet wings that fall
Magnifical, or spread

[140] *Christ's Company and Other Poems*, pp. 23, 42.

Most sweetly over-head
In fashion musical
Of cadenced lutes instead.

Sing me the town they saw
Withouten fleck or flaw,
Aflame, more fine than glass
Of fair Abbayes the boast,
More glad than wax of cost
Doth make at Candlemas
The Lifting of the Host.

. . .

Where Mother Mary walks
In silver lily stalks,
Star-tirèd, moon-bedight;
Where Cecily is seen,
With Dorothy in green,
And Magdalen all white,
The maidens of the Queen.[141]

Robert Bridges thinks that in this poem Dolben "transcended anything of the kind that was ever done by a modern medievalist."[142] It is assuredly a very tasty bonbon, but it represents all that is most debilitating in ceremonialism. Some would say that it is none the worse poetry for that, but mere delight in frippery can never produce good art.

In Dolben's work this pseudo-Catholic decorativeness is rare. When it does appear, it is probably a symptom of a more fundamental difficulty. His father was an aggressive Protestant, but through the influence of a maternal aunt the lad was already an ardent Puseyite when he entered Eton. Here he was overpowered, not by a boyish "crush," but by a serious homosexual passion for a schoolmate.[143] There is no reason to suspect any causal relation between his religion and his abnormality.[144] For him the two were deadly enemies engaged in a struggle which forms the principal theme of his poems.

We are speaking of a boy who was drowned at the age of nineteen. What

[141] *Poems*, pp. 102–103. In the last stanza quoted he has remembered *The Blessed Damozel*: "Cecily, Gertrude, Magdalen, / Margaret, and Rosalys."

[142] *Ibid.*, p. liv*n*.

[143] Bridges, *ibid.*, pp. xxiff., is explicit on this point. Dolben was his fag at Eton. The most conclusive evidence, however, is provided by the poems themselves. Though Dolben's desires were frustrated by "Archie" Manning's friendly uncomprehending normality, it will not do to say that they were "merely ideal."

[144] The statement would be absurdly supererogatory had not Mr. Geoffrey Faber, in his *Oxford Apostles*, attempted to demonstrate such a connection in Newman and Hurrell Froude, whom he regards as homosexuals. His argument will be convincing only to those who share his basic assumption that celibacy implies sexual abnormality. There are other reasons for not marrying.

would have become of him if he had been granted a longer life no one can say; he might well have achieved complete victory over his weakness. Earlier in this chapter we have drawn from his poems expressions of the highest type of Catholic religious sensibility.[145] There can be no doubt that his faith was sincere; he used it, quite legitimately, for sublimation but not as a cloak. He became a tertiary, and later a secondary, of the Anglican Benedictine order. But in his need for an absolute control he felt strongly drawn toward Rome, and shortly before his death he had told his disapproving father that once he had graduated from Oxford he would delay no longer in making his submission.

Dolben, in short, was a seriously religious person. The fact lends pathos to the numerous poems in which the struggle is almost too much for him. He does not wish to believe that his devotion to so beautiful and noble a being as Archie is sinful. Sometimes he tries to give it traditional dignity by associating it with an ancient Greece which is full of

> ... boys, with hair as golden
> As Queen Cytheréa's own is.

He dreams of a reconciliation between Hellenism and Christianity in which Jesus, the thorn-crowned God of Love, will somehow identify Himself with Apollo, the masculine God of Beauty. Once, despairing of any such compromise, he speaks as a monk who wishes he were a Greek watching the stars in an olive grove amidst "The boyish laughter and the paean songs"; or lying in the thyme by the Cephissus hearing tales of "all those ancient victories of love," of Sappho, and Echo, and Helen,

> Or that fair legend, dearest of them all,
> That tells us how the hyacinth was born;

or listening to Socrates among "Young eyes that glistened and young cheeks that glowed."

> O sunny Athens, home of life and love,
> Free joyous life that I may never live,
> Warm glowing love that I may never know,—
> Home of Apollo, god of poetry.
>
> . . .
>
> I weary of this squalid holiness,
> I weary of these hot black draperies,
> I weary of the incense-thickened air,
> The chiming of the inevitable bells.

[145] See above, pp. 261, 263, 268.

He would escape from the reproachful eyes of "the great wan Christ" on the Crucifix, but where can he turn?

> Is there no place in all the universe
> To hide me in? no little island girt
> With waves, to drown the echo of that cry:
> "Behold the Man, the Man of Calvary!"

He is unconsciously answered by a fellow-monk who walks across the cloister singing,

> Sweetest Jesu! Thou art He
> To whom my soul aspires;
> Sweetest Jesu, Thou art He,
> Whom my whole heart desires.[146]

If he could forget the bloodstained Cross and simply fall in love with the sweetness of the human Jesus, the chasm between Greece and Palestine would be narrowed; Pan might not be dead after all.

Here, however, lurked the most insidious of the snares which beset the poor youngster—the temptation to behold the lineaments of Archie in the face of Incarnate God and then, still thinking of Archie, to say,

> The world is sweet, but He is sweeter far,
> The Boy of Nazareth.

This is, I fear, the real theme of *Homo Factus Est*. In a poem disquietingly entitled *Osculo oris sui osculetur me*, he tells Christ that even complete union with Him in heaven would not be able to quench "The soft remembrance of those human eyes" he had loved at Eton. Yet he begs the Lord to "stay me with the Apples of Thy love" and burn all baser passions from his heart. In another poem, however, he speaks of purgation in this life as a means of joining Archie in the next:

> So only, only, may I win
> Some pardon for my youthful sin,—
>
> . . .
>
> So only may I stand with him
> When suns have sunk and moons grown dim;
> And see him shining in the light
> Of the new Heaven's sinless white.[147]

At least twice he runs away from Christ and Apollo and Archie to his mother's arms—or, to be thoroughly up-to-date, towards her womb. She occupies *The Shrine* within whose portals

[146] *Poems*, pp. lii, 4–7 *passim*, 29.

[147] *Ibid.*, pp. 15, 21 35, 36.

The mists of time are backward rolled,
And creeds and ages are no more;
But all the human-hearted meet
In one communion vast and sweet.

(This Benedictine tertiary will even try a little Broad Churchmanship if only it will help him to elude the Hound of Heaven.)

I enter—all is simply fair,
Nor incense-clouds, nor carven throne;
My mother—ah! whom should I see
Within, save ever only thee?[148]

But in this direction there is no hope of escape. Indeed the gentle lady, as often happens, may be partly to blame for her son's inability to feel like an adult.

A difficult case—whether a desperate one or not is no business of ours. But Dolben seems never to have given up trying to be a Christian, and nothing more is demanded of any sinner. In the following *Prayer* there is no confusion between Archie and the Saviour:

From falsehood and error,
From darkness and terror,
From all that is evil,
From the power of the devil,
From the fire and the doom,
From the judgement to come—
Sweet Jesu, deliver
Thy servants for ever.[149]

I have not been able to regard the poets of this chapter as enthusiastically as might have been expected. In my opinion their reaction against the age was too extreme to permit them to maintain the serenity, balance, and wholeness which are essential to the Catholic ideal. Where religion impinges upon social or political problems, the subspiritual motivation of their cult of obedience and of their anti-intellectualism is distasteful to one who denies that to be a Catholic is to be a reactionary or an obscurantist. I feel that very few of them are interested in making poems, and that those who attempt to do so too easily sacrifice religious conviction in favor of empty ceremonies of technique. When they write as propagandists for sentimental Toryism or as aesthetic medievalists they betray some superficial symptoms of the romanticism to which their fundamental beliefs are so strongly opposed. Yet when I compare their religious thought with that of the Evangelicals,

[148] *Ibid.*, pp. 81–82. See also p. 22 for the same theme.

[149] *Ibid.*, p. 52.

the Liberals, or the Seers and Seekers, much of my shaken respect for them is restored. With all their limitations, they hold the Christian faith in a form highly resistant to subjectivizing influences. They toy with the trappings of romanticism, but they are not romantics. None of them supposes that Jesus Christ is a warm feeling in the heart or that God is a product of human imagination. None of them deifies man. None of them says, with Parolles in *All's Well*, "Simply the thing I am shall make me live." They believe in the insufficiency of man and the transcendent objectivity of God. They irritate me profoundly, but they seem to possess a truth which I find nowhere else and without which I cannot live.

Chapter Ten

CHRISTINA ROSSETTI

CHRISTINA ROSSETTI's poems, most of which concern some aspect of historic Christianity, have been admired by many capable critics who do not share her beliefs. No need to argue, then, that she is a poet of intrinsic literary merit. On the other hand Catholic Christians must guard themselves against a natural temptation to overpraise her work. Few poets owe so much of their fame to the anthologist: she wrote an immense amount of rubbish. Even in her best poems she has very few things to say and says them over and over again. Her imagery reflects the conflict in her nature between sensuousness and asceticism. Occasionally she tries too hard to load every rift of her vein with ore; at other times one could wish for a little more gold. Her impersonal, officially "sacred" verse can be mechanical and perfunctory; it is when she thinks of herself in direct or indirect relation to her faith that she most fully comes alive. Even in such moments, however, she does not always come alive as an *artist.* A less meticulous craftsman than Gabriel, she is a better poet because she writes with her heart's blood rather than with ink. But occasionally she succumbs to the danger which shadows this advantage—that of being so deeply moved by personal experience that she supposes the feeling itself to be a poem rather than the material for one. In a few other poems she veers toward the opposite extreme, borrowing from the aesthetic set with whom she was so closely associated some elaborately tricky pattern which seems to lack organic relationship with the content. To say all this is merely to suggest why she is very good rather than great. The fact remains that she is the most accomplished orthodox Christian writer of authentic poetry between Vaughan and Hopkins.

The home of Gabriele and Francesca Rossetti pulsated with intellectual, aesthetic, and spiritual stimulation to which each of their children responded differently. William Michael accepted only the intellectual element; Dante Gabriel, the aesthetic, with perhaps a very little of the spiritual. Maria, who was to become an Anglican nun, would have nothing but the spiritual. Christina took both the aesthetic and the spiritual in full measure, but very little of the intellectual. Her father was sometimes an esoterically antipapal

Catholic and sometimes a freethinker of the sort who can find no religious institution sufficiently "spiritual" for his believing but crotchety temper. At the time of Christina's birth in 1830 her mother was an Evangelical; but she soon responded to the Oxford Movement to the extent of becoming "high" without ceasing to think of herself as a Protestant. William Michael insists that Mrs. Rossetti was "devout but not . . . sanctimonious;"[1] but according to Miss Zaturenska, she was "apt to be too intense, too fanatical when her religious emotions were touched"[2] although in all other respects she maintained remarkable poise and calm. It was doubtless she who set the religious pattern for the girls, leaving the boys to such guidance as might be supplied by her erratic husband. Her own father, Gaetano Polidori, had reared his sons as Roman Catholics and his daughters as Protestants.

Both little girls were pious, but in early as in later years Christina was too ready to regard her sister as a perfect model of sanctity. Christina is the Laura, and Maria the Lizzie, of *Goblin Market*. Maria Rossetti was sickly, nervous, overintense but shallow, lacking in tenderness. She tried to compensate for these deficiencies by donning the armor of extreme holiness, precision, and confident self-righteousness. She seemed so sure of salvation, and on such convincing grounds, that she may have made her adoring sister less confident of her blessedness than she might otherwise have been.

Christina knew little and cared less about systematic theology. It never crossed her mind that dogmas needed to be proved: one might as well argue about the air one breathed. Nor did ceremonial for its own sake appeal to her: she preferred a Low Mass, the simpler the better. On the other hand, even in her most mystical moments she remained a faithful communicant of her parish. William, a dry rasp of impatience in his throat, speaks of "her perpetual church-going and communions, her prayers and fasts, her submission to clerical direction, her oblations, her practice of confession. . . . I have often thought," he adds, "that Christina's proper place was in the Roman Catholic Church, yet I never traced any inclination in her to join it, nor did she ever manifest any wish to enter upon the conventual life—I think she held herself unworthy of attempting it." He suggests that she may have remained an Anglican out of loyalty to her mother, "who, though gradually conforming to the external practices of the High Church section, was far indeed from wishing to Romanize."[3] His explanation of why Christina did not take the veil is probably correct, though a sense of obligation to care for her mother, and later for the ailing old aunts, perhaps entered into the

[1] Christina Rossetti, *Poetical Works*, p. xlvii (W. M. R.'s *Memoir*).

[2] Marya Zaturenska, *Christina Rossetti*, p. 2.

[3] *Poetical Works*, p. lv.

situation. If we must ask why she remained an Anglican, her father's detestation of the papacy may have added some weight to her mother's loyalty to the Establishment.

But since Christina felt that she could believe and practice Catholic Christianity within the Anglican Communion, her failure to abandon it is not at all surprising. In her own parish she could find frequent communions, feasts and fasts, clerical direction, the confessional, and everything else that her heart desired. On *Whitsun Day* she remembered that the Apostles

> . . . chose death for their life and shame for their boast,
> For fear courage, for doubt intuition of faith,
> Chose love that is strong as death and stronger than death
> In the power of the Holy Ghost.

That power, she believed, had descended straight into the hands of her rector. When she wrote the following lines she was conscious of no alienation from that holy community of the faithful which was to become the Bride of Christ in the New Jerusalem:

> Who is this that cometh up not alone
> From the fiery-flying-serpent wilderness,
> Leaning upon her own Beloved One?
> Who is this?
>
> Lo, the King of kings' daughter, a high princess,
> Going home as bride to her Husband's Throne,
> Virgin queen in perfected loveliness.
>
> Her eyes a dove's eyes and her voice a dove's moan,
> She shows like a full moon for heavenliness:
> Eager saints and angels ask in heaven's zone,
> Who is this?

In her poetry, as in her parish church every twenty-fifth of March, she joyfully commemorated the Annunciation of the Blessed Virgin Mary:

> Herself a Rose, who bore the Rose,
> She bore the Rose and felt its thorn.
>
> . . .
>
> Christ's mirror she of grace and love,
> Of beauty and of life and death:
> By hope and fear and faith
> Transfigured to His Likeness, "Dove,
> Spouse, Sister, Mother," Jesus saith.

She glories not only in Mary but in all the other saints,

> Strong as the lion, pure as the dove,
> With open arms and hearts of love.
>
> . . .
>
> Out of great tribulation they went
> Home to their home in Heaven content.

With the saints her devotion rises to Him whom they adore:

> Light beyond light, and bliss beyond bliss,
> What words cannot utter, lo, who is this?
> As a king with many crowns He stands,
> And our names are graven upon His hands.
> As a priest with God-uplifted eyes,
> He offers Himself in sacrifice;
> As the Lamb of God for sinners slain,
> That we too may live He lives again.

He continues to offer Himself to us and for us through His sacramental presence in the Eucharist. In short the need of "Romanizing" never occurred to Christina Rossetti. These passages also serve to remind us that her indifference to formal theology implies no indifference to fundamental doctrine. Love for her is the essence of Christianity solely because the Love who "came down at Christmas" to lie as a babe in a manger was and is "The Lord God Almighty Jesus Christ."

Although anything but a social-gospeller, she was mindful of the second great commandment. She wrote reams of deliberately inartistic devotional and hortatory prose for adults and children; sent letters to the newspapers against child labor—also, alas, against vivisection and woman suffrage; sacrificed herself for friends and relations; worked beyond her strength among factory girls and fallen women. This she did, not because she enjoyed it, but because she did not.

> Yea, Lord, I will serve them by Thy grace;
>   Love Thee, seek Thee, in them; wait and pray;
> Yet would I love Thyself, Lord, face to face,
>   Heart to Heart, one day.

Her view of the social mission of the Church does not go much beyond the palliative kindness expressed in one of her poems for children:

> The dear old woman in the lane
>   Is sick and sore with pains and aches;
> We'll go to her this afternoon,
>   And take her tea and eggs and cakes.

This limitation, however, shields her religion from the reactionary prejudices which distress us in too many other Catholic poets. As her brother William observes, a special aspect of her charity appears in "a love of animals, and especially such animals as are frequently regarded as odd or uncouth, rather than obviously attractive."[4] He is thinking of the "feeble nation" of the conies and particularly of the wombat who "prowled obtuse and furry" from Cheyne Walk into *Goblin Market*.

Almost fanatically severe in what she demanded of her own belief and conduct, she was tolerant of others, maintaining, without the least sacrifice of principle, generous-hearted friendship with persons who had different standards. She felt quite sure they were wrong, but her great humility forbade her to think of herself as anything more than a fellow-sinner who had her own ideas on these matters. To her unbelieving brothers she was a perfect sister. She and Swinburne respected each other as human beings and fellow-artists. He sent her all his volumes. She read them rather than commit the sin of writing him untruthfully that she had done so, but she pasted strips of paper over the passages which she must not read again.

As this anecdote suggests, her scrupulosity sometimes went to extremes. She abandoned theatre-going because it gave her too much pleasure, not because she thought it corrupting to the spectator; also, having heard that stage-folk led immoral lives, she believed that if there were no actors the sum total of immorality would be reduced. She gave up chess because she so dearly loved to win. In her closing years she picked up every scrap of paper on the street lest the Holy Name, which might conceivably be printed or written on it, be trodden upon by her or some other passer-by. It is a tribute to her genuineness as an artist that these eccentricities are never carried over into her poems.

Her work, however, is so heavily freighted with self-accusation and morbid fears that to many readers her piety seems overstrained and unhealthy. They have sought a cause in the frustration of her youthful passion for John Collinson and of her less avid but tenderer and maturer love for Charles Bagot Cayley. She rejected both men on religious grounds: Collinson, because he could not make up his mind as to whether he was a Roman Catholic or an Anglican; Cayley, because he was an agnostic. No one can fail to observe the scars left upon her spirit by these renunciations.

> Hope in dreams set off a-straying,
>   All his dream-world flushed by May;

[4] *Poetical Works*, p. ix.

While unshrinking, praying, weighing,
Love said nay.

. . .

Youth gone and beauty gone, what doth remain?
The longing of a heart pent up forlorn,
A silent heart whose silence loves and longs;
The silence of a heart which sang its songs
While youth and beauty made a summer morn,
Silence of love that cannot sing again.

. . .

I cannot tell you what it was;
But this I know; it did but pass.
It passed away with sunny May,
With all sweet things it passed away,
And left me old, and cold, and grey.

It would be rash, however to attach specifically biographical significance to such passages. The meaning of her pain, not the actual circumstances of it, is what matters. Deep beneath the everyday surface of her life brooded a grim spiritual drama. She loved the world, condemned that love as sinful, renounced the world, was made unhappy by her renunciation, condemned that unhappiness as sinful. In the two abortive love affairs this inward tragedy approached the status of outward tragedy, assumed a pattern of words and actions, and made itself available for art. Sometimes she seizes upon this material and uses it with the freedom which any other poet would claim. In relation to her spiritual experience Collinson and Cayley are symptoms, not causes. It will not do to say that whenever she voices a longing for Jesus what she really wants is union with a man. Assuredly she had much to sublimate, and the task was not easy for her. But she was only seventeen at the outset of the Collinson affair. If she had not already determined to set the love of Jesus above all other loves she could have captured the wavering milksop easily enough. To the question whether the pious scruples which caused her to reject Collinson and Cayley had any real connection with the love of Jesus one can only answer that for her the scruples and the love of Jesus were interdependent.

In the preceding chapter I expressed the opinion that Catholic Revival poetry, regarded as a body of verse produced by a fairly well-defined group, failed to provide a balanced representation of the whole truth about historic Christianity. But to raise this complaint against any individual writer would be absurd. Especially in a culture which possesses no strongly dominant spiritual consensus, religious poetry will often move us most deeply when its lack of equilibrium suggests that the poet's faith is hard-won and maintained with difficulty against hostile pressure from without and from within.[5] It is a waste of time to scold Christina for not having been as cheerful as Adelaide Procter. What may justly puzzle us is not that she is so somber, but that she is so somber although, as Keats would say, she seems "calculated for" a more joyous apprehension of Christianity than she usually permits herself to express.

We cannot, of course, be sure that she was mistaken in thinking that her sensuousness would collapse into sensuality if she gave it free rein. Rightly or wrongly, at all events, she tried desperately hard to escape from the flesh by means of mysticism:

> Wisest of spirits that spirit which dwelleth apart
> Hid in the Presence of God for a chapel and nest,
> Sending a wish and a will and a passionate heart
> Over the eddy of life to that Presence in rest:
> Seated alone and in peace till God bids it arise.

She must think of no joys but the joys of heaven;

> And if that life is life,
> This is but a breath,
> The passage of a dream,
> And the shadow of death;
> But a vain shadow
> If one considereth;
> Vanity of vanities,
> As the Preacher saith.

Yet if no one ever distrusted Goblin Market more profoundly than Christina, no one ever beheld its marvels with more delighted eyes. Loving it too much she vainly tried not to love it at all, like her perfect Maria.

> "Lie close," Laura said,
> Pricking up her golden head:
> "We must not look at goblin men,
> We must not buy their fruits:
> Who knows upon what soil they fed
> Their hungry thirsty roots?"
> "Come buy," call the goblins
> Hobbling down the glen.
> "Oh," cried Lizzie, "Laura, Laura,
> You should not peep at goblin men."

[5] "Lack of equilibrium" can only be a deduction from the poet's work as a whole. Since all art implies selection, no single work of art can ever give us the whole truth about anything.

But Laura peeped, and would thereby have damned her soul to hell except for Lizzie's aid. The ironic contrast between "Pricking up her golden head" and the rest of the passage represents Christina's possibly correct judgment of her own nature.

No, she must take the road that leads "up-hill all the way," carrying her burden, the love of goblin fruit, like Christian's pack of sins in *Pilgrim's Progress*. She must not peep at that broad, easy, delightful downward road, the way of *Amor Mundi*:

> "Turn again, O my sweetest,—turn again, false and fleetest:
> This beaten way thou beatest, I fear is hell's own track!"
> "Nay, too steep for hill mounting; nay too late for cost counting:
> This downhill path is easy, but there's no turning back."

The tension between what she was and what she thought she should be exhausted her. Physical as well as spiritual distress played its part: throughout most of her life she was a sick woman. Try as she might to rejoice in disfigurement as a bulwark against pride, this lover of beauty did not enjoy being brown-skinned, bloated, flabby, bulge-eyed, prematurely old. In a disquietingly large number of poems, she longs for rest so intensely that she thinks of death as blessed oblivion rather than as blessed gateway:

> Rest, rest; the troubled breast
> Panteth evermore for rest:—
> Be it sleep or be it death,
> Rest is all it coveteth.

Here she succumbed to a temptation perhaps graver than those which she had wearied herself in fleeing:

> I am full of heaviness.
> Earth is cold, too cold the sea:
> Whither shall I turn and flee?
> Is there any hope for me?
> Any ease for my heart-aching,
> Any sleep that hath no waking,
> Any night without day-breaking,
> Any rest from weariness?
>
> Hark the wind is answering:
> Hark the running stream replieth:
> There is rest for him that dieth;
> In the grave whoever lieth
> Nevermore hath sorrowing.

This is uncomfortably close to Swinburne's *Garden of Proserpine*. Not that she doubts for one moment the certainty of life after death; but it is that wonderfully long interval of slumber in the grave while she awaits the resurrection of the body which attracts her:

> Life is not good. One day it will be good
>   To die, then live again;
> To sleep meanwhile . . .
>
> . . .
>
> Asleep from risk, asleep from pain.

In order to enjoy this boon, however, it was necessary to die, and she was terribly afraid of dying. Her over-sensitive imagination was appalled by the physical ghastliness of it, but also by the possibility that she might die, unlike the joyful saint Maria, in a state of unforgivable spiritual torpor. How would it be possible to feel the approach of the Bridegroom at a time when one could feel nothing at all? And if she did not greet Him, would He greet her? The following lines were written late in her career but at least ten years before the onset of her final illness:

> I have dreamed of Death:—what will it be to die
>   Not in a dream, but in the literal truth,
>   With all Death's adjuncts, ghastly and uncouth,
> The pang that is the last and the last sigh?
> Too dulled, it may be, for a last good-bye,
>   Too comfortless for any one to soothe,
>   A helpless charmless spectacle of ruth
> Through long last hours, so long while yet they fly,
> So long to those who helpless in their fear
>   Watch the slow breath and look for what they dread;
> While I supine with ears that cease to hear,
> With eyes that glaze, with heart-pulse running down
>   (Alas! no saint rejoicing on her bed),
> May miss the goal at last, may miss a crown.

"Charmless spectacle" is pathetically revelatory of the *Amor Mundi* which she dreaded.

It would have been easy for Christina to wallow in self-pity, to seek relief in the perverted thrill of posing as a lost soul, or to relapse into acedia. She did nothing of the sort. Her poems exhibit no steady ascent from the depths to the summit: what they reveal is the fact that she never gave up. She would have been glad, of course, to evade the necessity of struggling. The long slumber of the grave offered one means of escape, but its attractions were spoiled by the fear of dying and the fear of Judgment. She must live, then. But how could she live without some compromise between her flesh and her spirit—a compromise which, she felt sure, would end in the subjection of the latter to the former? For the true mystics, the symbol of earthly life was not an up-hill climb but one joyous leap, here and now, into the arms of the Almighty Lover. This she greatly desired; such rest would be even better than the rest of the tomb. But did she love Jesus deeply, purely, passionately enough to be worthy of it? She *believed in* loving Him, but that was not at all the same thing. Worse still, could she be sure that He loved her, the barren fig tree? In the abasement of *Ash Wednesday* she remembers that He is no less just than tender:

> Thy justice hath a sound:
> "Why cumbereth it the ground?"
> Thy Love with stirrings stronger
> Pleads, "Give it one year longer."
> Thou giv'st me time: but who
> Save thou shall give me dew,
> Shall feed my root with blood
> And stir my heart for good?—
> Oh by thy gifts that shame me
> Give more lest they condemn me.
> Good Lord, I ask much of Thee,
> But most I ask to love Thee:
> Kind Lord, be mindful of me,
> Love me and make me love Thee.

On most lips this prayer would be unexceptionable, but in her heart of hearts Christina suspects the motive which has made her utter it. She is asking Jesus to woo her into mystical love of Him not as the final reward of struggle against the flesh but as a substitute for that struggle. She wants the Crucified to assure her that she need not climb her personal Calvary. In her best moments, however, she knows that she is not to be let off so easily. What then could she do? The answer must be given as far as possible in her own words, for to paraphrase would be to preach a trite little sermon on the Way of the Cross. From her "perpetual church-going and communions, her prayers and fasts, her submission to clerical direction, her oblations, her practice of confession," she gained firmer assurance of Christ's love than from begging Him for special privileges and exemptions. Leaping to the top of the hill at a single bound was out of the question. She must begin with the remorse and dread in which she now actually stood and toil upward from it, painful step by painful step.

If not with hope of life,
  Begin with fear of death;
Strive the tremendous life-long strife
  Breath after breath.

Bleed on beneath the rod;
  Weep on until thou see;
Turn fear and hope to love of God
  Who loveth thee.

But how may she know that God loves her? Simply by remembering that He loves everyone and died for everyone—it was as banal as the Catechism. In the dialogue *Dost Thou Not Care?* she asks her obsessive question and receives the answer of the Christian faith:

"I love and love not: Lord, it breaks my heart
  To love and not to love.
Thou veiled within Thy glory, gone apart
  Into Thy shrine which is above,
Dost Thou not love me, Lord, or care
  For this mine ill?"—
"I love thee here or there,
  I will accept thy broken heart—lie still."

"Lie still, be strong, today; but, Lord, to-morrow,
  What of to-morrow, Lord?
Shall there be rest from toil, be truce from sorrow,
  Be living green upon the sward,
Now but a barren grave to me?
  Be joy for sorrow?"
"Did I not die for thee?
  Do I not live for thee? Leave Me to-morrow."

She saw that quiet, patient trust was what she needed, not hysterical clamor after love or despairing self-accusation. If she truly repented of her sins and relied on God's power to wash them away, to confess them should make her ashamed but not gloomy or fearful:

Can peach renew lost bloom,
Or violet lost perfume,
Or sullied snow turn white as overnight?
Man cannot compass it, yet never fear:
The leper Naaman
Shows what God will and can.
God who worked there is working here;
Therefore let shame, not gloom, betinge thy brow.
God who worked then is working now.

The title of this poem is *Go in Peace*; she is thinking of her confessor's formula, "Go in peace. The Lord hath put away all thy sins." God is working now in His Church.

In 1872, when Gabriel was alarmingly ill, she wrote to William: "I know not . . . what to hope, but with my whole heart I commit our extremity to Almighty God."[6] If she could thus firmly trust in Him, everything that had been worth loving in Goblin Market might some day be restored to her a hundredfold. "Sick with hope deferred," she is encouraged by the words:

"But Christ can give thee heart Who loveth thee:
Can set thee in the eternal ecstasy
Of His great jubilee;
Can give thee dancing heart and shining face,
And lips filled full of grace,
And pleasures as the rivers and the sea.
Who knocketh at His door
He welcomes evermore:
Kneel down before
That ever-open door
(The time is short) and smite
Thy breast, and pray with all thy might."
"What shall I say?"
"Nay, pray.
Though one but say, 'Thy will be done,'
He hath not lost his day
At set of sun."

To Lucy Brown, William's betrothed, she writes: "May love, peace and happiness be yours and his together in this world, and together much more in the next; and, when earth is an anteroom to heaven (may it be so, of God's mercy, to us all), earth itself is full of beauty and goodness."[7] Even before sunset, then, a Christian's life was not vanity of vanities.

On *Good Friday Morning* she reflects that Jesus carried His Cross up-hill alone, but that in her toilsome ascent she has Him for companion and guide and support:

Upon my hill of sorrows
I, Lord, with Thee,
Cheered, upheld, yea carried
If a need should be:
Cheered, upheld, yea carried,
Never left alone,
Carried in Thy heart of hearts
To a throne.

[6] *Family Letters*, p. 36.

[7] *Ibid.*, p. 39.

In this faith she sets forth upon her pilgrimage, determined not to evade suffering but to use it:

> These thorns are sharp, yet I can tread on them;
> This cup is bitter, yet He makes it sweet:
> My face is steadfast toward Jerusalem,
> My heart remembers it.
>
> Although to-day I walk in tedious ways,
> To-day His staff is turned into a rod,
> Yet will I wait for Him the appointed days,
> And stay upon my God.

In climbing her own small Calvary she was sometimes, but very rarely, refreshed with glimpses of the bliss that awaited her at the end of the journey. Such an experience is suggested by *A Birthday*, where she feels that "my love is come to me."[8] Almost always, however, she had no other reliance than those which any ordinary Christian possesses—private prayer, the Word of God, public worship, the Sacrament of the Altar. These were the weapons with which she fought off despair.

Again and again, like all other communicants of her parish, she retraced the drama of the Christian Year, expressing in poems which are sometimes stereotyped but sometimes among her best the feelings which she shared with them. Advent sounded its solemn warning of that final day when the Lord will return to earth as its Judge:

> Let us wait the end in peace, for truly
> That shall cease which was before:
> Let us see our lamps are lighted, duly
> Fed with oil nor wanting more:
>
> . . .
>
> Yea, the end of all is very near us:
> Yea, the Judge is at the door.
> Let us pray now, while we may:
> It will be too late to pray
> When the quick and dead shall all
> Rise at the last trumpet-call.

This is not Christina's personal morbidity but simply the Christian midnight

[8] W. M. Rossetti's footnote in the *Poetical Works* reads: "I have more than once been asked whether I could account for the exuberant joy evidenced in this celebrated lyric; I am unable to do so." Of course, he adds, it may be "a mere piece of poetical composition . . . but I am hardly prepared to think that." Nor is anyone else. Probably the poem represents an exceptionally strong mystical awareness of the presence of God—vouchsafed to her perhaps in Holy Communion, perhaps in meditation, perhaps in washing the breakfast dishes.

which precedes the Christian dawn. The Nativity mood, though inseparable from Advent penitence, was very different:

Enough for Him, whom cherubim
  Worship night and day,
A breastful of milk
  And a mangerful of hay.

. . .

Angels and archangels
  May have gathered there,
Cherubim and seraphim
  Thronged the air;
But only His mother
  In her maiden bliss
Worshipped the Beloved
  With a kiss.

What can I give Him,
  Poor as I am?
If I were a shepherd
  I would give a lamb,
    If I were a Wise Man
      I would do my part,—
    But what I can I give Him,
      Give my heart.

Such was the healing agitation, the troubled peace, which Christina found as a member of Holy Church. From youth to old age she fought to keep it central in her mind. Not always with success. She lost it, regained it, lost it, clutched at it—with what final result is beyond our knowledge. On May 20, 1892, she tells William that she must probably undergo an operation for "something brooding in my health . . . demanding sharp treatment. . . . I beg prayers of every one who will pray for me. And, dear William, do not worry yourself about me: you see this is not an avowed certainty as yet, and come what will I am in Better Hands than either yours or my own; I desire to realize and to rest in this."[9] But her brother reports that she was unable to maintain this trustful spirit. She rallied temporarily from the operation for cancer, but soon relapsed and died in December, 1894. The previous August she had taken to her bed "in a calm and resigned mood, but, as the time advanced, with tremulous agitation, both of the spirit and of the bodily frame. Not that she was ever abashed by pain, or craven-hearted—far indeed from that; but the terrors of her religion compassed her about, to

[9] *Family Letters*, p. 185.

the overcoming of its radiances. At the close of a week of collapse and semi-consciousness, she died without a struggle, in the act of inarticulate prayer."[10]

This testimony is not lightly to be brushed aside. The agnostic William impresses us as an honest man. He loved his sister deeply and within his limitations understood her very well. One could wish, however, for supplementary evidence from an observer less inclined by subconscious motives to make the most of "the terrors of her religion." William might have interpreted expressions of wholesome penitence as outcries of despair. At such a time, too, neither he nor anyone else could be sure how much of her misery was spiritual and how much merely physical. Nor, even if we accept his report as perfectly accurate, need we suppose that a merciful God attaches more importance to the deathbed babblings of a sinner under extreme torture than to a lifetime of desperate perseverance.

Her brother does not know, nor do we, anything about those very last moments of "inarticulate prayer" which were granted her when the actual struggle was over. We are entitled to hope that she was trying to say something like this:

Leaf from leaf Christ knows;
Himself the Lily and the Rose;

Sheep from sheep Christ tells,
Himself the Shepherd, no one else.

. . .

Grain by grain, His hand
Numbers the innumerable sand.

Lord, I lift to Thee
In peace what is and what shall be:

Lord, in peace I trust
To Thee all spirits and all dust.

[10] *Poetical Works*, p. liv.

Chapter Eleven

PATMORE

WHEN Patmore is not intolerably bad he can be very exciting. He would, however, be the first to insist that the merit of his writing cannot be considered separately from the merit of what he says. The sense of vatic mission is strongest in the *Odes*, but even in *The Angel in the House* he wears the prophet's mantle:

> . . . Of Heav'n I ask,
> May I, with heart-persuading might,
> Pursue the Poet's sacred task
> Of superseding faith by sight,
> Till even the witless Gadarene,
> Preferring Christ to swine, shall know
> That life is sweetest when it's clean.
> To prouder folly let me show
> Earth by divine light made divine;
> And let the saints, who hear my word,
> Say, "Lo, the clouds begin to shine
> About the coming of the Lord!"

He would have been enraged by A. E. Housman's remark: "Nobody admires his best poetry enough, though the stupid Papists may fancy they do. But I should say as little as possible about his nasty mixture of piety and concupiscence."[1] His best poetry, he would have insisted, embodied that love-doctrine which his critic describes so unsympathetically. True, Patmore sometimes writes excellent poems without riding his special hobby—*Winter*, *The Toys*, *The Azalea*, *Departure*—and it may well have been such pieces that made the famous little chill run up and down Mr. Housman's spine. It would seem perverse, however, to say that Patmore writes good poetry only when he is *not* expressing the ideas which are supremely important for him and which he thinks should be supremely important for everyone. A reasoned evaluation of Patmore's work must depend very largely on whether his religious philosophy actually *is* "a nasty mixture of piety and concupiscence." If so, he was not the sort of poet that he aspired to be.

[1] Quoted by F. L. Lucas, *The Decline and Fall of the Romantic Ideal*, p. 97.

Let me confess at the outset that I do not understand Patmore. This chapter can offer no more than a sharing of bewilderment. The more I read of what has been said about him, the more convinced I become that he is not to be explained in terms of pagan mythology, Plato, Aristotle, Bernard, Aquinas, Dante, John of the Cross, Theresa, Calderón, Swedenborg, Butler, Coleridge, Hegel, Emerson, or Marie Lataste. In using these and doubtless other "sources," he screened out whatever was uncongenial to him and interpreted the residuum as an expression of the gospel according to Patmore. What he read is much less important than what he himself was. And what he was is very difficult to discover.

The psychologists have taught us to doubt the virility of a man who is constantly talking about sex, but in Patmore's case no such suspicions are justified. He married three times and begot several children, the last of them at the age of sixty. Derek Patmore explains, "His first marriage with Emily Andrews was of such felicity and harmony that he spent the rest of his life trying to repeat it." Before the death of his second wife in 1880 he had already fallen in love with Harriet Robson, who was to become his third as promptly as the conventions permitted. We are told that his letters to Harriet during their married years "display how even as an ageing man he could play the part of husband and lover. Here is the sensualist, the Eastern lover who demands complete surrender, a being who shocks by his almost unnatural exultation in the joys of the marriage bed." In his seventies a "Platonic" devotion to Alice Meynell collapsed into a physical though senile passion which forced her to break off their friendship. Derek Patmore also reports that "Hidden away behind the shelves in the library at Heron's Ghyll was a complete set of the *Eroticon Biblion Society*—reprints of the forbidden masterpieces of the world's erotic literature, which showed him the dangers of passion."[2] We are permitted to doubt, however, that he used them solely as a solemn warning. He was a close friend of Monckton Milnes, whose large collection of erotica was interesting to Swinburne.

Quite regardless of his love-mysticism, Patmore's poems are not those of an ascetic. "If I come where ladies are," he says in a familiar passage, he feels refreshed and quickened. The conclusion of the wife's letter in *The Azalea* could hardly have been written by one who lacked joyous experience of the physical side of marriage:

> Parting's well-paid with soon again to meet,
> Soon in your arms to feel so small and sweet,
> Sweet to myself that am so sweet to you!

[2] *The Life and Times of Coventry Patmore*, pp. 3, 148, 205.

Wind and Wave—it will not do to be mealy-mouthed about this poet—is a remarkable symbolic rendering of the sexual act, outwardly less explicit than Browning's *Now*, but behind its veil of metaphor much bolder. We may feel sure that no matter how spiritual Patmore's conception of love may have been, the mystic flowers could never have been detached from their earthy roots.

Coitus was precious to him chiefly because it gave fullest satisfaction to an impulse even more fundamental in his nature than sexuality per se—the desire for dominance. He worshipped Woman, but not women: the complete subjection of the female to the male was an essential article of his personal creed. "Ah, Child," the sage old Pythoness cries to the bewildered Psyche in *Natura Deorum*,

> Ah, Child, the sweet
> Content, when we're both kiss'd and beat!

He ruled the roost (here at least "roast" would be incorrect) not merely in bed but throughout the household.

As a violent antifeminist he loathed woman suffrage, his desire for mastery extending beyond the domestic sphere into the political. He has been described as "a combination of Catholic mystic and Colonel Blimp."[3] His hatred of democracy was a pure reactionary passion untinged by any Young England nonsense about the chivalric obligations of the gentry. Disraeli, who championed the ideals of Manners and Smythe when they suited his purposes, had betrayed the aristocracy in the Reform Bill of 1867. Now the victorious rabble

> Bray of their full-blown rights and liberties,
> Nor once surmise
> When each man gets his due the nation dies.

It is bitterly hard for a poet to sing

> In the year of the great crime,
> When the false English Nobles and their Jew,
> By God demented, slew
> The Trust they stood twice pledged to keep from wrong.

Gentlefolk can only withdraw from politics and pray for God's mercy on the dying nation. They must not hope that their way of life will survive:

> Know, 'twas the force of function high,
> In corporate exercise, and public awe
> Of Nature's, Heaven's, and England's Law
> That Best, though mixed with Bad, should reign,

[3] F. L. Lucas, *The Decline and Fall of the Romantic Ideal*, p. 81.

Which kept you in your sky!
But, when the sordid Trader caught
The loose-held sceptre from your hands distraught,
And soon, to the Mechanic vain,
Sold the proud toy for nought,
Your charm was broke, your task was sped,
Your beauty, with your honour, dead.

To complete the familiar pattern of authoritarianism, antifeminism, and anti-Semitism, he held "That war's the ordained way of all alive."

Hearing him in this vein, one would suppose that his father had been a belted earl rather than a hack journalist. During the poet's first marriage, when he worked as a minor employee of the British Museum, the life of a "gentleman" was merely the unattainable ideal depicted in *The Angel in the House*. His second marriage changed all that, for Marianne Byles was an heiress.[4] Now he left the Museum and became so successful a gentleman-farmer that after eight years he sold the estate at a profit which enabled him to live thenceforward as a man of leisure. With increasing prosperity his love of dominance increasingly expressed itself in the stereotypes of social superiority. His pride in being an English gentleman was so intense that it went beyond its mark and made him almost a Spanish hidalgo in his fierce punctilious regard for honor and ceremony. He could be class-conscious even as a lover:

Let love make home a gracious Court;
There let the world's rude, hasty ways
Be fashion'd to a loftier port,
And learn to bow, and stand at gaze.

He could also be class-conscious as a Catholic. Believing that Catholicism is the only fit religion for a gentleman, he regretted that English opposition to the decrees of the Vatican Council forced an alliance between the Catholic gentry and the Irish, who are "Discrediting bright Truth with dir and brogue." But Protestants were even worse than bog-trotters: they did not know that it was bad form to address Jesus directly. Patmore tells Ou Lady that in praying to her Catholics obtain

. . . a reward and grace
Unguess'd by the unwash'd boor that hails Him to His face,
Spurning the safe, ingratiant courtesy
Of seeing Him by thee.

This is carrying gentility a little too far.

[4] He was not aware of the fact until after she had accepted him.

The biographers of Patmore agree that he was a rampant egotist. Basil Champneys, who knew him well, tells us that although among close friends he could be tender, winning, and modest, he was usually "haughty, arrogant, austere in mien, dictatorial and unsympathetic in his utterances. He was in fact self-centered."[5] An aphorism in *The Rod, the Root, and the Flower* reads: "If you wish to influence the world for good, leave it, forget it, and think of nothing but your own interests." On the nuptial couch, he states elsewhere in the same volume, "The external man and woman are each the projected simulacrum of the latent half of the other, and they do but love themselves in thus loving their opposed likenesses."[6] His personal intuitions constituted pure reason, immediate perception of absolute truth. Those who perceived different truths were fools, rascals, unwashed boors. Champneys believes it was Patmore's intuitional philosophy that made him so dictatorial.[7] This puts the cart before the horse. A trait of character can be rationalized, but never created, by a metaphysical system. Patmore merely permitted transcendental idealism to tell him what he knew in the first place—that he was right.

He savored his crotchets and was tempted both by his pugnacity and his sense of fun to display them in misleadingly extravagant paradoxes. It is not easy to tell at a given moment whether he is absurd unintentionally or deliberately. And with all his faults he had courage, imaginativeness, high seriousness, a noble aspiration. Thus far, however, both the debits and credits indicate that he was an extremely romantic man. Did he become a Catholic to conquer his craving for self-assertion, or to satisfy it? Not consciously for the latter purpose, we may be sure. The surface facts tell us little about the subconscious motives, but we must use them for what they are worth.

At the time he married Emily Andrews, in 1847, he was a sort of Emersonian-Swedenborgian Anglican with Catholic hankerings the strength of which is problematical. His wife, the daughter of a Congregational minister, was, Patmore relates, "terrified from her cradle by the hideous phantom which Puritanism conjures up when the Catholic religion is named."[8] In the spiritual autobiography which he wrote out for Hopkins in 1888, he seeks to give his friend the impression that he was at heart a Catholic throughout his first marriage and would have made his submission

[5] Introduction to Patmore, *Poems*, p. xxxvii.

[6] *Rod, Root, Flower*, pp. 25, 103.

[7] Basil Champneys, *Memoirs and Correspondence of Coventry Patmore*, II, 12. This work will be referred to hereafter as *Champneys*.

[8] *Ibid.*, p. 53.

much sooner had it not been for Emily's restraining influence. But Champneys (a Protestant) feels "convinced that in the retrospect . . . the leaning towards Rome seemed to him to have been stronger and the variance from his wife's position greater than it actually was."[9] This is likely enough, but the point hinges upon the elusive question of what Patmore meant by "Catholic."

Not long after Emily's death his friend Aubrey de Vere, who had long been at work on him, persuaded him to visit Rome. There, after some wavering, he entered into communion with the Holy See in 1864. In Rome also he fell in love with Marianne Byles, who had been won over from Anglicanism by Manning. Patmore assures Hopkins that he was untroubled by doubt after his conversion, "though it was not until the autumn of the year 1877 that my faith became the controlling power which for five and thirty years I had longed and prayed to find in it." This assertion is startling in view of the fact that by the end of 1877 Patmore had written practically all of his poems.[10] He goes on to explain that he had felt himself "hopelessly out of harmony with the feelings and practice of the best Catholics with regard to the Blessed Virgin. . . . I could not abide the Rosary. . . . I resolved to make an external profession of my acceptance of the Church's mind by a pilgrimage to Lourdes." There he rose from his knees "with a tranquil sense that the prayers of thirty-five years had been granted."[11] He means, I believe, that at Lourdes he experienced an overwhelming conviction that the Virgin of the Rosary and the Virgin of his erotic mysticism were one and the same. Having made a pilgrimage to demonstrate the subjection of his mind to that of the Church, he discovered that the two minds were in perfect harmony.

But we are not yet ready to examine Patmore's Mariology. Instead let us pause to observe that this poet, in both of the major phases of his spiritual history, presents us with striking examples of a genuinely religious sensibility. There are puzzling passages in *The Angel in the House*; but when the poem is read in itself, without peeking ahead at the *Odes*, it appears to be a legitimate if slightly peculiar interpretation of the Christian view of marriage. Patmore's contemporaries did not find it alarming; many of them, indeed, did not find it alarming enough. Furthermore, Book I of *The Unknown Eros, and Other Odes* includes several religious poems quite unrelated to his erotico-spiritual obsession. Their dominant theme is that we cannot hope

[9] *Ibid.*, I, 125.

[10] It is also startling because 77 minus 35 leaves 42. Patmore must be referring to the total period of his quest for spiritual truth, not merely to his experience as a professed Roman Catholic.

[11] *Champneys*, II, 56.

to keep unspotted in this world, that we must nevertheless strive to become better than we are, and that God will forgive us at last if we have tried hard enough. *The Toys*, a familiar anthology-piece, reminds us that men, like children, often find their intensest pleasure in mere playthings. Perhaps God will say of us, as Patmore has said of the sleeping child whom he had punished, "I will be sorry for their childishness." *Let Be* warns the unco' guid not to feel too sure of their superiority to the struggling sinner. Perhaps they have never fallen merely because they have never tried to climb, whereas

> Haply yon wretch, so famous for his falls,
> Got them beneath the Devil-defended walls
> Of some high Virtue he had vow'd to win.

But in "*Faint Yet Pursuing*" he abandons his youthful straining for "heroic good," content to be thankful for small graces. He has learned

> That less than highest is good, and may be high.
> An even walk in life's uneven way,
> Though to have dreamt of flight and not to fly
> Be strange and sad,
> Is not a boon that's given to all who pray.

All will be well with him if he perseveres in fighting his sins,

> Because the good of victory does not die,
> As dies the failure's curse,
> And what we have to gain
> Is, not one battle, but a weary life's campaign.
>
> . . .
>
> Yea, though I sin each day times seven,
> And dare not lift the fearfullest eyes to Heaven,
> Thanks must I give
> Because that seven times are not eight or nine,
> And that my darkness is all mine,
> And that I live
> Within this oak-shade one more minute even,
> Hearing the winds their Maker glorify.

This proud man can be humble. Were it not for the testimony of these poems, indeed, I should have been tempted to outrage some Roman Catholic readers by including Patmore among the Seers and Seekers of Chapter VII.

There is also a good deal of biographical evidence that after his conversion Patmore tried to be a dutiful son of what he conceived to be the one true Church. He desired to think with its mind, and assiduously sought good Catholic authority for his personal views. Champneys never heard him say anything "which gave me the slightest impression of his feeling any dissatisfaction with or failing in full loyalty to the Church which he had joined." But Champneys remembers two statements which point in directions so antipodal that they suggest an irreconcilable conflict. On at least one occasion the poet told his friend that he accepted the authority of the Catholic Church because "no other seemed to him to teach or produce so complete a surrender to the Divine Will." Three pages earlier, however, the biographer recalls that "He *often* said to me, 'I could never be happy in any Communion but my own. There is no other which would allow me to think and say so exactly what I choose'."[12]

A third remark recorded by Champneys will increase our bewilderment: "I believe in Christianity as it will be ten thousand years hence."[13] Here he may have had in mind something like Newman's idea of the development of doctrine. Much more probably, however, the statement means that it will take the Church ten thousand years to discover that her *real* message is the message of Patmore—a position more like Coleridge's than like Newman's. It is not easy to pin him down on such questions, since he extended the term "Catholic" to embrace not only Keble (whom he considered a truer Catholic than Newman) but Crébillon Fils and the Venus de Milo. Anything—Romanist, Anglican, Protestant or pagan—was Catholic if it spoke to him of goodness, truth, beauty. And nothing possessed goodness, truth, or beauty unless it could somehow be made to illustrate his preoccupation with sex.

The Catholicism of an Italian peasant is extremely different from that of, say, Jacques Maritain. It is dangerous to underestimate the differences in an attempt to preserve the outward unity of the Church on a basis of ignorance, superstition, and sentimental vulgarity. It is no less dangerous, however, to exaggerate the differences in order to secure special privileges for a spiritual élite.[14] Just as empty ceremonial is the peculiar snare of the aesthete, so this is the peculiar snare of the mystic. Not all mystics, of course, are caught in it. There are avowed Catholics, however, who think of the formal teachings and devotional practices of the Church as a façade of exoteric symbols which reveal to them, while they screen from the unenlightened majority of the faithful, an esoteric meaning which sometimes seems to be rather tenuously related to the Catholic faith. The more fully they possess the secret, the less important become the outward symbols, although one had

[12] *Ibid.*, II, 18, 21. Italics mine. [13] *Ibid.*, p. 29.

[14] M. Maritain exemplifies the intelligent and learned Catholic who does *not* exaggerate the differences.

better be content to use them in public rather than present a stumbling block to the uninitiated. If these privileged spirits are to be called Catholics, one must admit that they have discovered a way of being Catholic and romantic at the same time. What demands self-surrender from their fellow-believers confers boundless self-expansion upon them. They are sometimes especially eager to make full use of the glorious liberty of the children of God in matters of sex. Patmore himself observes that "Popular esotericism—and esotericism is becoming popular—means conscientious wenching, or worse."[15] There is, then, an esotericism even deeper than what ordinarily passes as such.

Patmore had a most unpopular temperament and he did not practice or advocate wenching, but he was emphatically an esotericist. He presents all the familiar symptoms. "The holier and purer the small aristocracy of the true Church becomes, the more profane and impure will become the mass of mankind."[16] That rabble did not consist wholly of avowed heretics, for ordinary modern Catholics were "the most ignorant of all people." He saw no particular advantages in belonging to the Church unless one used it as a gateway to mysticism. The Scriptures and the Liturgy interested him only in so far as he could interpret them in accordance with his deeper insight. "Even in later days," says Champneys, "if I visited with him some Roman Catholic church, I seemed to detect in the manner of his genuflexions a moral as well as a physical effort. On the other hand he loved to expatiate on the inner meaning of the Church's ritual." Not a man who liked to bend the knee, he was "bitterly hostile to any abuse of priestly authority," and not slow to detect instances of such abuse.[17]

To the best of my recollection, *The Standards* is the only poem which suggests the slightest interest in the Church as an institution at work among human beings in the modern world. "This piece was written," Patmore's note explains, "in the year 1874, soon after the publication of an incendiary pamphlet by Mr. Gladstone against the English Catholics occasioned by the Vatican Council." In this time of trial, all true believers must stand shoulder to shoulder. The old Catholic landholding families are warned not to lapse into heresy (few of them liked Infallibility) and not to shrink from alliance with the dirty Irish and with the flatterers of priests. Even here, however, where the tactical motive for affirming unity is so strong, the esoteric note is sounded. Those who require a "cage," sneers Patmore, may find one in the infallible Church. He would rally to the fray not the automatically submissive but those

[15] *Rod, Root, Flower*, p. 48. [16] *Ibid.*, p. 51. [17] *Champneys*, II, 25, 28, 87.

> Who adore, in any way,
> Our God by His wide-honour'd name of YEA,
> Come up; for where ye stand ye cannot stay.
>
> . . .
>
> Come who have felt, in soul and heart and sense,
> The entire obedience
> Which opes the bosom, like a blissful wife,
> To the Husband of all life!

For these true mystics Infallibility is no cage, but a joyful swooning in the arms of the Almighty Lover. The circle of adepts excludes many avowed Catholics but also, as "in any way" implies, includes many avowed heretics who have experienced this kind of Everlasting Yea. The latter are urged to join the Church and submit themselves to Pio Nono as the only sure way of obtaining and preserving this rapture. They will soon understand why Patmore told Champneys that no other spiritual allegiance "would allow me to think and say so exactly what I choose."

The esoteric principle applies not merely to Infallibility but to all other dogmas of the Church. Patmore thinks of them as "only the seeds of life. The splendid flowers and the delicious fruits are all in the corollaries, which few, besides the Saints, pay any attention to. . . . The work of the Church in the world is, not to teach the mysteries of life, so much as to persuade the soul to that arduous degree of purity at which the God Himself becomes her teacher. The work of the Church ends when the knowledge of God begins." The Church is necessary merely because in this life such knowledge is only for the few. Patmore cites Aquinas: "The Ark of the Covenant was a symbol of mysteries of the faith which must not be unveiled but to those who are advanced in holiness." The postgraduates, however, enjoy a freedom which a seventeenth-century Calvinistic sectarian might envy: "When the state which the theologians call 'Perfection' is attained, and life is from good to truth instead of from truth to good," our slogan may be " 'Love and do what you like.' 'Habitual grace' knows how to suck the baits off the hooks of the Devil, and can take up adders without being bitten."[18]

When Patmore says that he was essentially a Catholic before his submission to Rome he means that he already knew these secrets, though not yet quite completely, when he wrote *The Angel in the House.* The prefatory poem of Book X declares that wisdom "must be glad as well as good," since "Beauty and joy are hers by right." Such wisdom is possessed by a few choice spirits,

[18] *Rod, Root Flower*, pp. 39, 46, 83, 84.

Oases in our waste of sin,
Where everything is well and fair,
And Heav'n remits its discipline;
Whose sweet subdual of the world
The worldling scarce can recognise.

. . .

Nay, continence and gratitude
So cleanse their lives from earth's alloy,
They taste, in Nature's common food,
Nothing but spiritual joy.

These *schöne Seelen* soar far above the

. . . new-made saints, their feelings iced,
Their joy in man and nature gone,
Who sing, "O easy yoke of Christ!"
But find 'tis hard to get it on.

Far from chastening this Antinomianism, Patmore's life as a Roman Catholic brought it to full bloom. We find perhaps the most explicit statement of it in *The Rod, the Root, and the Flower*:

To some, not necessarily, perhaps, the greatest saints, Christ is actually and perceptibly risen. He has turned the water of nature into the wine of the Marriage Feast, though "His time is not yet come," and to the Sacrament of the Real Presence, He has added a Sacrament of the Manifest Presence. For souls thus favoured, the Church's teaching and rites are but a scaffolding which has fulfilled its purpose. The Temple is built and occupied. "Felix quem Veritas per se docet . . . Taceant omnes doctores."[19]

In saying that such saints are "not necessarily, perhaps, the greatest," he sounds a little too self-consciously modest. To be fair, however, Patmore never claimed for himself uninterrupted enjoyment of the Sacrament of the Manifest Presence. He asserts only that he has sometimes received it, and with a joy which he longs, however vainly, to express to others in prophetic numbers. In the past, according to the eleventh of the *Odes*, he has glimpsed the "Beautiful habitations, auras of delight." But too often, now that age comes on, when he dreams of "that realm of Love," he can see only "a dove / Tangled in frightful nuptials with a snake"—fitting image of "The heart where good is well perceived and known, / Yet is not will'd." But the high vision was not granted in vain, for

Often in straits which else for me were ill,
I mind me still

[19] *Ibid.*, p. 63.

I *did* respire the lovely auras sweet,
I *did* the blest abodes behold, and at the mountains' feet,
Bathed in the holy Stream by Hermon's thymy hill.

The Sacrament of the Manifest Presence and the Marriage Feast are clearly one and the same. Furthermore, a great many passages in his poems, footnoted by what we know of his passionate nature, imply that the Marriage Feast is simply sexual intercourse between husband and wife who are able to find spiritual meaning in physical delight. In the last two lines quoted above, the Scriptural geography could easily be translated back into the anatomical terms which for Patmore it symbolizes. On the other hand, an equal if not a larger number of passages seem to say that the full sacramental grace of the Marriage Feast is reserved for wedded lovers who, all the while burning with desire for each other, *refrain* from carnal intercourse.

Hence the central question to be asked about Patmore may be framed in the words of Sir Andrew Aguecheek to Maria: "What is *pourquoi*? Do, or not do?" I have already confessed my inability to reach any conclusive answer, but I can at least try to show what the problem is by examining the *Odes* in the light provided by *The Rod, the Root, and the Flower*[20] and by what we know concerning his unfulfilled plans for *The Marriage of the Blessed Virgin* and for *Sponsa Dei*. The early lyrics are of no importance for us, and *Tamerton Church-Tower* is almost equally negligible. As regards *The Angel in the House* (with its sequels) we shall concentrate on the respects in which it seems to predict Patmore's fully matured views.

In the *Angel*, Patmore prays that the "Spirit of Knowledge" may grant him

A simple heart and subtle wit
To praise the thing whose praise it is
That all which can be praised is it.

The "thing" of course is love, later to be hymned as *The Unknown Eros*. The essence of all value, it permeates everything that men think of as good, true, fair; but it reveals itself most potently, comes to clearest focus, in the love of husband and wife. That love in turn is present in all the everyday circumstances of wedded life, but it finds its center in the sanctified sexual act, the greatest of sacraments.

Especially in the *Angel*, the connubial sacrament is sometimes interpreted

[20] Since we are studying the religious thought of Patmore's poetry, it may be felt that this prose work is cited too frequently. Surely, however, full use should be made of a document which so often explains what he was trying to say in the less explicit language of the poems.

more or less Platonically: the purpose of wedded love is to raise our minds to the love of God. But no poem of Patmore's, early or late, gives the slightest warrant for supposing that he uses the language of human passion as an imperfect but necessary means of expressing a purely spiritual desire for union with God—a yearning radically different from earthly love not only in degree but in kind. He may be right in insisting that his Eros is "not Amor," but it is certainly not Agape or even a symbol of it. His mature thought, moreover, is thoroughly un-Platonic in its Blake-like detestation of the abstract and the infinite. Wedded love is no faint transitory shadow of ineffable reality. It is that which the ineffable needs in order to become real—real to us and, one may almost say, real to itself.

> "The Infinite." Word horrible! at feud
> With life, and the braced mood
> Of power and joy and love.

"Religion has no real power until it becomes natural. . . . You may see the disc of Divinity quite clearly through the smoked glass of humanity, but no otherwise."[21]

> Have you not seen a bird's beak slay
> Proud Psyche [butterfly] on a summer's day?
> Down fluttering drop the frail wings four,
> Missing the weight which made them soar.
> Spirit is heavy nature's wing,
> And is not rightly anything
> Without its burden, whereas this,
> Wingless, at least a maggot is,
> And wing'd, is honour and delight
> Increasing endlessly with height.

The marriage-bed would at least be something without Eros; Eros would be "not rightly anything" without the bed. That is why he burns to mate with Psyche. The function of the wife is to be "the continent of the infinite, making it conscious and powerful by limitation."[22] From the very beautiful poem entitled *Beata* we learn that the Virgin Mary was blessed among women in being privileged to fulfill this function in relation to God:

> Of infinite Heaven the rays
> Piercing some eyelet in our cavern black,
> Ended their viewless track
> On thee to smite
> Solely, as on a diamond stalactite,
> And in mid-darkness lit a rainbow's blaze,

[21] *Rod, Root, Flower*, pp. 42, 54. [22] *Ibid.*, p. 55.

> Wherein the absolute Reason, Power, and Love,
> That erst could move
> Mainly in me but toil and weariness,
> Renounced their deadening weight,
> Renounced their undistinguishable stress
> Of withering white,
> And did with gladdest hues my spirit caress,
> Nothing of Heaven in thee showing infinite,
> Save the delight.

Mary prevented God from being a cosmic bore. The poem inverts a famous passage in *Adonais.* Loathing what he elsewhere calls "the ghastly boundlessness of space," Patmore thinks the white radiance of eternity spiritually impotent without the dome of many-colored glass which renders it sensible.

God feels as Patmore does. Hence the Incarnation. It was "independent of the idea of Redemption,"[23] a necessary consequence of the fact that God is not merely Love but a lover. In the *Angel* we are told that

> Female and male God made the man;
> His image is the whole, not half;
> And in our love we dimly scan
> The love which is between Himself.

These lines are explained in *The Rod, the Root, and the Flower* when Patmore appeals to the Thomistic definition of God as "an *Act*—the Act of love, the 'embrace' of the First and Second Persons, and their unity is the thence proceeding Spirit of Life, 'Creator Spiritus,' the Life and Joy of all things. . . . This 'dry doctrine' of the Trinity, or primary Act of Love, is the keynote of all living knowledge and delight. God Himself becomes a concrete object and an intelligible joy when contemplated as the eternal felicity of a Lover with the Beloved, the Ante-type and very original of the Love which inspires the Poet and the thrush."[24] Love is all one homogeneous passion, from the Trinity to the nuptial bed. Why then did St. Paul take so grudging a view of the latter? Because the saint possesses within his own masculine-feminine nature something very like the love which exists between the First and Second Persons of the Trinity. Hence "The external womanhood is a superfluity and even a hindrance to the Saint. He sees in her only the projected shadow of one half of his own personality, and she is an obstacle to his peace and well-being in the society of the reality. But this

[23] Quoted by Frederick Page, *Patmore*, p. 133, from Patmore's notes for *The Marriage of the Blessed Virgin.*

[24] *Rod, Root, Flower*, p. 117. The text reads "Anti-type," obviously not what Patmore intended.

thought need not trouble us, who are not Saints, in our domestic felicities."[25] The last sentence clearly implies that these felicities consist preeminently of what ordinary human beings mean by sexual intercourse. The second of the two title-page mottoes of *The Rod, the Root, and the Flower* is "My covenant shall be in your flesh." Its full meaning is prepared for by the phallic symbolism of the first motto: "There shall come forth a rod out of the root of Jesse, and a flower shall rise up out of his root."[26] Elsewhere in this volume we are reminded that not all saints have been as ascetic as Paul: "If we may credit certain hints contained in the lives of the Saints, love raises the spirit above the sphere of reverence and worship into one of laughter and dalliance."[27]

We have digressed a little. Let us return from the dalliance of the saints to that of God. "The love which is between Himself" cannot fully satisfy Him because in its abstract perfection it violates the principle, fundamental in Patmore's thinking, that "Spirit craves conjunction with and eternal captivity to that which is not spirit; and the higher the spirit the greater the craving. God desires depths of humiliation and contrast of which man has no idea; so that the stony callousness and ignorance which we bewail in ourselves may not impossibly be an additional cause in Him of desire for us." God made Himself man not because our weakness needed Him, but because He needed our weakness. "In His union and conjunction with Body, God finds His final perfection and felicity."[28] Redemption was the natural result, not the purpose, of the Almighty Lover's craving for "eternal captivity to that which is not spirit."

"There are some sorts of love which are permitted only to God. He alone, for instance, may love and worship images graven by His own hands."[29] He used this privilege in loving, yes, and worshipping, the Virgin Mary,

> Life's cradle and death's tomb!
> To lie within whose womb,
> There, with divine self-will infatuate,
> Love-captive to the thing He did create,
> Thy God did not abhor,
> No more
> Than Man, in Youth's high spousal-tide,
> Abhors at last to touch
> The strange lips of his long-procrastinating Bride.

In making a love-captive of God, who would otherwise have been "not

[25] *Ibid.*, p. 117. [26] Isaiah xi: 1. But Patmore and the prophet do not mean the same thing.
[27] *Rod, Root, Flower*, p. 32. [28] *Ibid.*, pp. 61, 132. [29] *Ibid.*, p. 38.

rightly anything," Mary becomes, as is said in *The Child's Purchase*, "Our only Saviour from an abstract Christ." She is the

> Desire of Him whom all things else desire!
>
> . . .
>
> Neither in His great Deed nor on His throne—
> O, folly of Love, the intense
> Last culmination of Intelligence,—
> Him seem'd it good that God should be alone!
> In season dire, on His sweet-fearful bed,
> Rock'd by an earthquake, curtain'd with eclipse,
> Thou shar'd'st the rapture of the sharp spear's head,
> And thy bliss pale
> Wrought for our boon what Eve's did for our bale;
> Thereafter, holding a little thy soft breath,
> Thou underwent'st the ceremony of death;
> And now, Queen-Wife,
> Sitt'st at the right hand of the Lord of Life,
> Who, of all bounty, craves for only fee
> The glory of hearing it besought with smiles by thee!

This gallant infatuated nobleman cannot refuse His lady anything when she smiles at Him.

The Virgin Mary was a woman, but for Patmore she is also Womanhood —the eternal feminine. "*Woman*, according to the *Salve Regina*, is 'Our Life, our Sweetness, and our Hope.' God is so only in so far as He is 'made flesh,' i.e. Woman. 'The Flesh of God is the Head of Man,' says St. Augustine. Thus the Last is indeed the First. 'the lifting of her eyelash is my Lord.' . . . Heaven becomes very intelligible and attractive when it is discerned to be—Woman."[30] Even when due allowance is made for the "poetic license" of mysticism and for Patmore's delight in paradox, one cannot but feel that his conception of the Incarnation, and therefore of the whole sacramental principle, is out of balance. Transcendence here not merely uses immanence but is made to depend upon it. The Lord is the servant of the handmaiden. The Creator is merged in the creation, the substance in the symbol. One might as well say of the Eucharist: "God's desire to save sinners becomes very intelligible and attractive when it is discerned to be—eating bread and drinking wine."

What then of the Crucifixion? Patmore asserts that "The great prophecy, 'Man shall be compassed by a woman,' was fulfilled when Jesus Christ made the body, which He had taken from Mary, actually divine by the subdual of

[30] *Ibid.*, pp. 38, 39. The *Salve Regina* is, of course, a prayer addressed to the Virgin Mary, not to the *Ewigweibliche.*

its last recalcitrance upon the Cross. The celestial marriage, in which, thenceforward, every soul that chose could participate, was then consummated"[31]—in the pain which is ever inseparable from love's delight. As the Pythoness tells little Psyche,

> Love is not love which doth not sweeter live
> In having something dreadful to forgive.
>
> . . .
>
> Sadness is beauty's savour, and pain is
> The exceedingly keen edge of bliss.

"The 'reconcilement of the highest with the lowest,' though an infinite felicity, is an infinite sacrifice. Hence the mysterious and apparently unreasonable pathos in the highest and most perfect satisfactions of love. The Bride is always 'Amoris Victima.' The real and innermost sacrifice of the Cross was the consummation of the descent of Divinity into the flesh and its identification therewith; and the sigh with which all creation heaved in that moment has its echo in that of mortal love in the like descent."[32] Here the Cross becomes a phallic symbol for Christians no less than for pagans. "It is finished!" sighs the satiated mortal husband, the recalcitrance of his flesh subdued for the time being. If the analogy is offensive to some of my readers I can assure them that it is offensive to me.

"I only report," says Patmore in the Preface of *The Rod, the Root, and the Flower*, "the cry which certain 'babes in Christ' have uttered: 'Taste and see that the Lord is sweet.' "[33] Thus far, the esoteric secret seems reasonably clear: human beings apprehend the Lord's sweetness most completely in nuptial union. Felix discovers

> . . . that the mind and heart of love,
> Which think they cannot do enough,
> Are truly the everlasting doors
> Wherethrough, all unpetition'd, pours
> The eternal pleasance.

Love's mind and heart attain reality only through the body, apostrophized in well-known lines as

> Creation and Creator's crowning good;
> Well of infinitude;
> Little, sequester'd pleasure-house
> For God and for His Spouse;
> Elaborately, yea, past conceiving, fair,
>
> . . .

[31] *Ibid.*, p. 61. [32] *Ibid.*, p. 196 [33] *Ibid.*, p. 20.

Form'd for a dignity prophets but darkly name,
Lest shameless men cry "Shame!"

Patmore abhors the prurience of the pious, insisting that we "must not be afraid to follow the doctrine of the Incarnation into all its *natural* consequences. . . . The Catholic Church itself has been nearly killed by the infection of the puritanism of the Reformation." It has so persistently represented "the greatest of all graces and means of grace" as impure that "the doctrine of the Incarnation has been emasculated and deprived of its inmost significance and power."[34] In all fairness he might have remembered that this sort of puritanism was not invented by the Puritans. Nor was it always advocated, let alone practiced, by them. At times there is something very Miltonic about Patmore: he would certainly subscribe to "He for God only, she for God in him."

The Platonic lover is told that although he is better than the gross sensualist he

. . . should not boast of being least;
And if to kiss thy Mistress' skirt
Amaze thy brain, scorn not the Priest [of Love]
Whom greater honours do not hurt.
Stand off and gaze, if more than this
Be more than thou canst understand,
Revering him whose power of bliss,
Angelic, dares to seize her hand,
Or whose seraphic love makes flight
To the apprehension of her lips;
And think, the sun of such delight
From thine own darkness takes eclipse.
And, wouldst thou to the same aspire,
This is the art thou must employ,
Love greatly; so shalt thou acquire
Unknown capacities of joy.

Self-conscious straining to be deeply spiritual in wedded love is less fruitful than

. . . sweet and regular
Use of the good in which we are.

. . .

So let your Grace with Nature chime.
Her primal forces burst, like straws,
The bonds of uncongenial laws.

. . .

[34] *Ibid.*, pp. 68, 197.

Be this your rule: seeking delight,
Esteem success the test of right;
For 'gainst God's will much may be done,
But nought enjoy'd . . .

. . .

Jehovah's mild magnificence
Smiles to behold His children play
In their own free and childish way,
And can His fullest praise descry
In the exuberant liberty
Of those who, having understood
The glory of the Central Good,

. . .

Take in love's innocent gladness part
With infantine, untroubled heart,
And faith that, straight t'wards heaven's far Spring,
Sleeps, like a swallow, on the wing.

But the innocent carnal play of "private charity" will bear rich spiritual fruit. Love to God gradually develops from the realization that the male bears the same relation to Him as the female to the male and must therefore submit himself to the courtship of the Divine Wooer. First the husband feels, as he embraces his wife, that his real desire is to possess not her, but a maiden more ideal and remote. Then dawns the question:

What if this Lady be thy Soul, and He
Who claims to enjoy her sacred beauty be,
Not thou, but God; and thy sick fire
A female vanity,
Such as a Bride, viewing her mirror'd charms,
Feels when she sighs, "All these are for his arms!"
A reflex heat
Flash'd on thy cheek from His immense desire,
Which waits to crown, beyond thy brain's conceit,
Thy nameless, secret, hopeless longing sweet,
Not by-and-by, but now,
Unless deny Him thou!

"What a Lover sees in the Beloved is the projected shadow of his own potential beauty in the eyes of God. The shadow is given to those who cannot see themselves in order that they may learn to believe the word, 'Rex concupiscet decorem tuum.' "[35]

Patmore is quite right, then, in distinguishing his esotericism from that of "conscientious wenching." He certainly believes in an ascent from flesh to

[35] *Ibid.*, p. 43.

spirit. But his thought is circular, for if flesh yearns toward spirit, spirit, as we have seen, yearns toward flesh and is "not rightly anything" until that yearning is satisfied. "The Highest has found His ultimate and crowning felicity in a marriage of the flesh as well as the Spirit; and in this infinite contrast and intimacy of height with depth and spirit with flesh He, who is very love, finds, just as ordinary human love does, its final rest and the full fruition of its own life." Consequently we "must not be afraid to follow the doctrine of the Incarnation into all its *natural* consequences."[36] In the sequence of odes consisting of *Eros and Psyche*, *Natura Deorum*, and *Psyche's Discontent*, the divine Eros is more ardently carnal than the mortal Psyche, who cries

> Enough, enough, ambrosial-plumed Boy!
> My bosom is aweary of thy breath.
> Thou kissest joy
> To death.

Puzzled by this strangely unspiritual deity, she seeks advice from the Pythoness, who reassures her:

> Gods, in the abstract, are, no doubt, most wise;
> But in the concrete, Girl, they're mysteries!
> He's not with thee,
> At all less wise nor more
> Than human Lover is with her he deigns to adore.

Thus Patmore was never less Platonic than when he wrote:

> There comes a time in the life of every one who follows the truth with full sincerity when God reveals to the *sensitive* Soul the fact that He alone can satisfy those longings, the satisfaction of which she has hitherto been tempted to seek elsewhere. Then follows a series of experiences which constitute "the *sure* mercies of David." The Enemy, who can assault us only through the flesh, has had his weapon taken out of his hands. The sensitive nature is, from day to day, refreshed with a sweetness that makes the flesh-pots of Egypt insipid; and the Soul cries "Cor meum et caro mea exultaverunt in Deum vivum."[37]

If we interpret these words in the light of what we already know of Patmore we may infer that coitus fulfills its function as "the greatest of all graces and means of grace" when husband embraces wife with keenest physical rapture, reminding himself the while, "What this really *means* is that God, with the same sort of delight, is now embracing *me*." This must be a difficult psychological feat.

[36] *Ibid.*, pp. 68–69.

[37] *Ibid.*, p. 65.

Several passages in the original *Angel* and in *The Victories of Love* suggest that a sexless heaven is hardly less repugnant to Patmore than a sexless earth.

> "In heaven none marry." Grant the most
> Which may by this dark word be meant,
> Who shall forbid the eternal boast
> "I kiss'd, and kiss'd with her consent!"
> If here, to Love, past favour is
> A present boast, delight, and chain,
> What lacks of honour, bond, and bliss,
> Where Now and Then are no more Twain!

Earth's embraces will become forever warm and still to be enjoyed in being transferred to the timeless. There is another way of evading the doctrine that there will be no marriage in the hereafter:

> What if, in heaven, the name be o'er
> Because the thing is so much more?
> All are, 'tis writ, as angels there,
> Nor male nor female. Each a stair
> In the hierarchical ascent
> Of active and recipient
> Affections.

Perhaps we are to become neither male nor female, but both male *and* female, our primal hermaphroditism restored to us. In that case we could, as female, love upward, and as male love downward, in the celestial scale. At all events heaven will be a great surprise to the puritan. There,

> . . . fools shall feel like fools to find
> (Too late inform'd) that angels' mirth
> Is one in cause, and mode, and kind
> With that which they profaned on earth.

In the *Odes*, Patmore regards this problem somewhat differently, but what he says of it there should be considered in relation to the more fundamental difficulty with which we must now bemuse ourselves.

For non-esoteric Catholics, the indispensable core of spiritual experience is the Eucharist. Individuals vary in the frequency with which they can mos profitably receive the Blessed Sacrament; but there is general agreement that, granting proper preparation and a right state of mind, a faithful Catholic should come up to the rail regularly and often. No priest would tell his flock that it is essentially holier not to receive the Sacrament than to receive it. So it is, one would suppose, with Patmore's sacrament of the Marriage

Feast. Everything that he has said to us thus far implies that it demands "sweet and regular / Use of the good in which we are." If his symbolism bears any relation to his real thought and his real character, he means quite literally that a man most fully experiences God's love of him when he makes love to his wife. To refrain from the sexual act would be to lose the grace and virtue of the sacrament. One must be able to say, "Consummatum est."

All this seems clear enough, no matter whether we like or dislike it. What is far from clear is how Patmore can also affirm the precisely contrary position that the man who most deeply feels the love of God is he who passionately desires his wife's body without doing anything much about it. The inconsistency runs all through Patmore's work. The doctrine of "not do" is more prominent in the *Odes* than in the *Angel*; but the *Angel* makes a good deal of it, while conversely the erotic language of the later work is franker and more intense than that of the earlier.

Patmore's sensuality was not untinged by the puritanism which he condemned so violently—a familiar combination, of course. Though never a true ascetic, he sometimes feared that his enjoyment of the physical pleasures of sex was too earthy. Such scruples appear to have been especially active at the time of his first marriage. Precisely because his love for Emily had spiritual flowers as well as physical roots, he accused himself of neglecting the former in favor of the latter. Some letters written to Henry Septimus Sutton during the first year of married life show uneasiness about this problem.[38] In *Tamerton Church-Tower*, his first long poem,[39] the hero loves his bride too carnally and is punished by her death. The *Angel*, and on a more mystical plane the *Odes*, seek to transcend the conflict not by condemning the joys of the body but by sacramentalizing them. As we are about to see, however, this solution was not wholly satisfactory. Although he took pleasure in parenthood, he was not the man to identify coition with reproduction. His status as a Catholic encouraged him to interpret the former in the light of the sacramental principle, but it raised a practical problem as regards the latter.

Yet even before his conversion his scruples about carnality led him to say in the *Angel* that

> Strong passions mean weak will, and he
>   Who truly knows the strength and bliss
> Which are in love, will own with me
>   No passion but a virtue 'tis.

[38] Frederick Page, *Patmore*. p. 52.

[39] Not published until 1853, but written 1848–49

This is a corollary of the general principle which in his Catholic days he expressed in the words, "True goods are peacefully desired, sought without eagerness, possessed without elation, and postponed without regret"[40]—a statement so contrary to human experience that one finds it hard to suppose that Patmore believes it. Quite truly, however, he says that attraction is the warp and reverence the woof of the marriage-garment. The craving for unity must not blind us to the fact of duality. The husband, in his desire for dominance, should

> . . . reverently understand
> How the two spirits shine remote;
> And ne'er to numb fine honour's nerve,
> Nor let sweet awe in passion melt,
> Nor fail by courtesies to observe
> The space which makes attraction felt;
> Nor cease to guard like life the sense
> Which tells him that the embrace of love
> Is o'er a gulf of difference
> Love cannot sound, nor death remove.

This is both perceptive and noble, and it demands our recognition of the true gentleness which enters into Patmore's concern for gentility. The fourth line, however, is somewhat overstrained. If awe *never* melted into passion, Malthus would have had nothing to worry about; in fact he himself would not have existed.

But when Patmore is in this vein the only passion on which he sets any high value is "the passion of refusal."

> Nothing more clearly proves that love between man and woman is "a great sacrament" than the sense of infinite non-desert and infinite poverty of capacity for its whole felicity, which those who are most deserving and most capable of its joy, feel in the presence of its mysteries. From this sense of incapacity for an infinite honour and felicity proceeds the tender passion of refusal, which is the first motion of perfect Love.[41]

Many years earlier, he had said the same thing in *The Victories of Love*:

> Love's inmost nuptial sweetness see
> In the doctrine of virginity!
> Could lovers, at their dear wish, blend,
> 'Twould kill the bliss which they intend,
> For joy is love's obedience
> Against the law of natural sense;

[40] *Rod, Root, Flower*, p. 45.

[41] *Ibid.*, p. 109.

And those perpetual yearnings sweet
Of lives which dream that they can meet
Are given to us that lovers may
Be not without sacrifice to lay
On the high altar of true love.

The passage is puzzling. Undoubtedly marital intercourse, on any but the basest level, includes desire for a more complete union of personalities than it ever quite achieves, and the resultant sense of incompleteness may confer a spiritual benefit by reminding us that married love means much more than the physical gratification which nevertheless plays so vital a part in it. But it is a *non sequitur* to infer that since coitus is insufficient, husband and wife should sacrifice its pleasures "Against the law of natural sense" and seek love's highest joy in complete virginity. Wedded lovers should be chaste in the best sense of that abused term, but they have no business to be virginal. Having chosen a way of life which the Church cordially blesses, they should not behave as if they had been called to a different way of life. Virgin marriage between two persons who are capable of performing the sexual act and who—as Patmore invariably implies—intensely yearn to do so is psychologically, morally, and spiritually perverse. The wholesome attitude is voiced by the Queen of Sheba in Yeats's poem: "Oh Solomon, let us try again!"

Patmore holds that "All men are led to Heaven by their own loves; but these must first be sacrificed."[42] Yet the sacrifice is somehow ambiguous. He wants to eat his cake and have it too, as if rejection of sensuality provided the most delicious kind of sensual titillation: "Refuse it, mortal, that it may be yours!" Psyche, at first delighted, is at last distressed by the carnality of her divine lover, but when at last he is willing to go she begs him to stay. When Eros asks what in the world she *does* want, she replies:

I cannot guess the good that I desire;
But this I know, I spurn the gifts which Hell
Can mock till which is which is hard to tell.
I love thee, God; yea, and 'twas such assault
As this which made me thine; if that be fault;
But I, thy mistress, merit should thine ire
If aught so little, transitory and low
As this which made me thine
Should hold me so.

Ruefully and half teasingly, Eros blesses her renunciation:

Yea, palate fine,
That claim'st for thy proud cup the pearl of price,

[42] *Ibid.*, p. 45.

And scorn'st the wine,
Accept the sweet, and say 'tis sacrifice.

"The 'rapture of refusal' of virgin love," says Patmore, "includes no self-denial, and is therefore a part of the joy of the highest holiness."[43] The easiness of the yoke is shown in *Deliciæ Sapientiæ de Amore*. In that ode the blest inhabitants of heaven are not disappointed by their sexlessness, for even on earth they had obscurely felt that sexless love would be best if only they could manage it. Now at last they

. . . wear the crown
Of which 'twas very heaven to feel the want.

Swooning and palpitating with "the tender passion of refusal,"

. . . each to the other, well content,
Sighs oft,
"'Twas this we meant!"

. . .

For lo, the Elect
Of generous Love, how nam'd soe'er, affect
Nothing but God,
Or mediate, or direct,
Nothing but God,
The Husband of the Heavens.

On earth, Patmore contentedly grants in his more realistic moments, the impracticability of *direct* enjoyment of God's embraces "need not trouble us, who are not Saints, in our domestic felicities." But when he is trying to scale the height of his great argument he insists that virgin marriage is an ideal which should at least be striven toward. And it is not an inconceivable ideal, for it was realized by Mary and Joseph. Their "spousals high" were to have been held up as the model of Christian marriage in a partly narrative, partly dramatic, partly lyrical poem on *The Marriage of the Blessed Virgin*. Patmore projected it in the winter of 1876 and abandoned it two years later; hence he was thinking about it when writing most of the *Odes*. "The love expressed in 'Eros,' " he declares, "is the love of Mary and Joseph."[44] Some of the *Odes*, in fact, are choruses snatched from the wreckage of the *Marriage*. Otherwise nothing remains but some memoranda and disjointed fragments, which are, however, sufficient to show what Patmore intended.

The poem was to tell how a virgin birth resulted from a virgin marriage.

[43] Quoted by Page, *Patmore*, p. 138.

[44] Quoted by Page, *Ibid.*, p. 134. For Patmore's memoranda about the *Marriage* and for valuable interpretative comments on them I draw upon pp. 129ff. of Page's book.

Mary was a girl of sixteen; Joseph, no graybeard, but a forty-five-year-old carpenter. They were not betrothed, but husband and wife: he "the most virile of men" and she "the most womanly of women." Nevertheless he offered Mary virgin love and was accepted as a husband on that basis. "The poem," says one of Patmore's notes, "should confine itself to the days preceding the Annunciation. The consciousness of her glories shown in the Magnificat proves her too high at this time for poetry." But Joseph must somehow have foreseen the reward of their rapture of refusal, for he was to say to Mary:

> Emmanuel, God with us, and by you;
> Slowly I begin to understand.
> Mother of God—O my dear little girl.

And Mary was to answer, "O, Joseph, but that will be grand!" She would have been represented as the handmaid of Joseph, not of the Lord. "If she was to be a model to women, *the* perfect woman, she must be a model in woman's chief state, marriage; and she must have loved God in Joseph rather than in Himself. *This is the theme of the Poem.*"

Not surprisingly, Patmore decided that "All allusion to Christian doctrine should be avoided. Christianity lies in this marriage like the white germ between the lobes of the lupin seed." In his own strange way, Patmore holds that Love is God quite as firmly as the broadest of Broad Churchmen. Mary and Joseph, he believes, brought the Timeless into time by loving each other passionately without consummating their marriage. "The birth of our Lord was the natural result of the virgin marriage in its perfection, and Jesus would probably have been born of Eve had she and Adam persevered—for the Incarnation was necessary, and independent of the idea of Redemption, and there would have been no reason for four thousand years delay, but for the sin of Adam and Eve."[45] Of Mary he says: "She alone is what all lovers mean when they love; and thus the likeness of all Christian women to her love is no longer extravagant." That is why the spirits of husbands and wives sing in heaven, " 'Twas this we meant!"

Patmore abandoned *The Marriage of the Blessed Virgin* because he feared that such high matters could not, after all, be handled without profanation. But he could not help thinking about them. The virgin-marriage idea was also the principal theme of the prose *Sponsa Dei*, begun probably in 1881 and burned in 1887 largely because of Hopkins's disapproval.[46] The sacrifice

[45] *The Contract* (No. II of the *Odes*) shows how Adam and Eve, by breaking an agreement to confine themselves to "virgin spousals," lost their chance of producing Jesus, "of proud virgin joy the appropriate birth."

[46] Aubrey de Vere, we might add, had vainly urged Patmore to suppress the "Psyche" odes.

was not quite complete, for the basic ideas of *Sponsa Dei* were included among the aphorisms of *The Rod, the Root, and the Flower*. Even had he printed everything that he wrote, he would probably not have enabled us to understand him any better than we now do. When he died in 1896, and was buried (with debatable appropriateness) in the habit of a Franciscan, he left behind him an apparently insoluble enigma.

Mr. Champneys finds that in all of Patmore's work from the *Angel* onward "is intimated that root idea of his philosophy of love, that passion and purity are in direct, not in inverse ratio one to the other."[47] True, but the root seems to branch off in two very different directions: toward the doctrine of sacramental coitus, and toward the doctrine of "the tender passion of refusal." Possibly these are not coordinate, but represent two layers of significance, the former being esoteric in relation to conventional Catholicism but exoteric in relation to the latter, which is always (or perhaps only after his conversion) what he *truly* means. In that case, however, we should be forced to conclude that Patmore's deepest spiritual message is inconsistent not only with what he often says but with everything we know about his life and character. Granting that there really are two conflicting doctrines on the same level of meaning, is there any way in which they can be harmonized, or, failing that, any point at which their lines intersect? Having already been very unpleasant in this chapter, I regret that I must now become even more so. It would be more agreeable, though absurd, to treat Patmore as a Victorian John of the Cross; but since in the *Odes* no less than in the *Angel* he is concerned with the religious bearings of the actual circumstances of married life, that is the problem to which we must continue to address ourselves.

In "the tender passion of refusal," that which is sacrificed on the altar of "love's obedience / Against the law of natural sense" must be something real, delightful, avidly desired, and good though not quite good enough. Furthermore we must experience its joy if we are to know the costliness of what we are offering up. Virgin marriage does not, apparently, imply complete abstention from physical contact; up to a certain point it is very fleshly indeed. Shall men and women be less carnal than God, who "has found His ultimate and crowning felicity in a marriage of the flesh as well as the Spirit"? Patmore writes in *The Rod, the Root, and the Flower*:

> Perfect, easy, and abiding control over the senses is the fundamental condition of perceptive knowledge of God, and this control consists, not in the destruction of

[47] Introduction to Patmore, *Poems*, p. xxxii.

> the senses and in the denial of their testimonies, but in the conversion of them from smoky torches into electric lights. "He who leaves all for my sake shall receive a hundredfold *in this life*" of the same felicities which we can only obtain by abandoning the pursuit of them.[48]

To glory in the senses, but to sanctify them by keeping them under perfect spiritual control. To obtain the felicities of union by pursuing them—and then abandoning the pursuit. To "take up adders without being bitten." How was that to be managed? Remembering Patmore's fondness for using Scriptural phrases like "Consummatum est" in a private erotic sense, "He who leaves all for my sake" might conceivably mean, "He who engages in sexual intercourse but withdraws from it before its climax." From this practice he might have derived an illusory sense of reconciliation between what he was and what he thought he should be, between frank passion and an Eros who is "not Amor." Were these "the sure mercies of David"?

But one hesitates to believe that the deepest secret of Patmore's esotericism was anything so shabby as *coitus interruptus*. We had better let the mystery remain mysterious, repeating, as we part company from this very peculiar Catholic, our unanswered question, "What is *pourquoi*? Do, or not do?"

[48] *Rod, Root, Flower*, p. 129.

Chapter Twelve

AESTHETICISM

ALTHOUGH we now return to the highway of our theme after a detour into historic Christianity, the transition from the Catholic poets to those included in the present chapter is in some respects less abrupt than I could wish. The kinship between ceremony for ceremony's sake and art for art's sake was noted in Chapter IX, and more must soon be said of it. In a different way Patmore blunts the edge of the contrast, for like the aesthetes he was a thwarted romanticist. His Catholicism was strong enough to prevent him from being a pure romantic, but his romanticism was strong enough to make him an extremely ambiguous Catholic.[1] In studying him we have already moved so far from the central trend of Catholic Revival poetry as to prepare ourselves for complete abandonment of it.

The title of this chapter is more categorical than its contents. We are to draw a few inferences from the work of nine poets who, relatively to the dominant temper of Victorian literature, may be characterized as "arty."[2] They do not constitute a homogeneous school. Not all of them would have been called Pre-Raphaelites by their contemporaries, loosely as the term was used. Vagueness on that point was natural enough, since even the original Brotherhood of painters soon discovered that mere revolt against academicism could not unite men whose conceptions of art differed so radically as those of Rossetti and Hunt.

Although the tendencies which our nine poets represent were at work before the end of the eighteen-forties, the main bulk of their writing runs from the late sixties through the eighties. For better or worse, the Aesthetic Movement in England does not disclose its full implications either for art or for religion until after the close of the period with which the present volume

[1] Another link is provided by Patmore's early personal association with the Pre-Raphaelites, who admired his first lyrics as "thoughts toward nature." It will be remembered that he contributed to *The Germ*. But the point does not deserve emphasis, since the poems in question have neither the qualities of his own mature work nor those of full-blown Pre-Raphaelitism.

[2] A tenth, Dante Gabriel Rossetti, will receive separate treatment in the following chapter although he must sometimes be glanced at in this one. In Swinburne and a few other poets, "aesthetic" traits commingle with trends which are more important for our purposes. Consequently, such hybrids will be treated in other connections.

is concerned. Louise Rosenblatt defines *l'art pour l'art* as "la foi dans l'indépendence de l'art, rejetant en conséquence toute fin didactique, morale, ou sociale en littérature et présentant souvent aussi l'effet artistique de l'œuvre d'art comme l'unique critérium pour juger de son succès ou de son échec."[3] In reaction against the prevalent hostility to "pure" art, our poets are moving toward this doctrine at various rates of speed, but they do not yet firmly grasp it as a theory or consistently body it forth in practice.[4] Hence they furnish only limited opportunities for studying the ultimate consequences of the Aesthetic Movement. Although some of them are clearly precursors of the *fin-de-siècle* decadence they should not indiscriminately be lumped together with Wilde, Beardsley, and Dowson. The "Conclusion" of *Studies in the History of the Renaissance* appeared in 1873, but not until well into the eighties was there any large-scale attempt to write, paint, and live in accordance with its perhaps misunderstood teachings—teachings which, in any case, Pater himself had by that time considerably though vainly revised. In short, the present chapter can do no more than begin a story which must be finished in the next volume of this series.

Professor Rosenblatt has traced *L'Idée de l'art pour l'art* back to its origins in romantic metaphysics, critical theory, and creative practice.[5] Usually from a less philosophical point of view and from a shorter historical perspective, many other students of the Victorian period have emphasized the romantic affiliations of the Aesthetic Movement. We have had Welby's *The Victorian Romantics*, Doughty's study of Rossetti as *A Victorian Romantic*, and Hough's *The Last Romantics*—an admirable book with a misleading title. A glance at our own times would have reminded Professor Hough that nineteenth-century aestheticism is by no means the last manifestation of the romantic spirit. He might, one feels, have done more to dispel the popular impression that English romanticism died about 1830 but was resuscitated in 1848 by a group of painters who, since their inspiration was largely literary, stimulated in turn a brief final reappearance of romanticism in poetry. Assuredly the aesthetes in general and the Pre-Raphaelites in

[3] *L'Idée de l'art pour l'art dans la littérature Anglaise pendant la période Victorienne*, p. 9.

[4] Among related figures not included in this chapter, Rossetti as practicing painter and poet was an almost pure aesthete, but he had no taste for theorizing about art. I shall argue later that Swinburne used the art-for-art's-sake gospel as a means of defending work which was motivated chiefly by non-aesthetic aims. Whistler both preached and practiced the gospel in all its fullness; but the fundamental issue between him and Ruskin was not clearly drawn until the libel suit of 1878, and the "Ten O'clock" lecture was delivered in 1885. In any case Whistler's views were more easily applicable to painting than to poetry.

[5] *Op. cit.*, pp. 9, 53ff.

particular wanted to be romantic; assuredly they were much influenced by Blake, Coleridge, and Keats. But they are by no means the sole or the most significant Victorian exponents of the tradition. Their romanticism is nerveless, attenuated, and superficial. They use the old magic not to transform the world but to shut it out. When they do more than play with the stock properties of romance their wistful attempts to recapture the high vision of their forebears turn morbid and begin to rot. In Roden Noel, Blake and Shelley would recognize an authentic disciple, but they would scorn the Morris of *The Earthly Paradise*.

For all that was most alien to the Victorian temper, the cult of art for art's sake drew from Continental rather than from English sources. The frustrated and decadent romanticism of France was the hive from which the celebrated "poisoned honey" was chiefly imported. Up to the close of our period the traffic in this commodity was not very heavy, nor had it, except in the case of Swinburne, exerted its full effect on the English mind. It is interesting to note, however, that among the poets of this chapter the most nearly pure aesthetes are those who show symptoms of the French influence. Arthur O'Shaughnessy pays his respects to Baudelaire and translates from Verlaine, Henri Cazalis, Catulle Mendès, and others. John Payne dedicates his *New Poems* (1880) "To the Beloved Memory of Théophile Gautier" and in *A Funeral Song* honors him as "our poet in the front of faith."[6] In an elegiac sonnet on the death of Corot in 1875, Payne explains that the painter was weary of life but could not die in the spring because he loved it so much; hence he waited until the following February, when he "went where Gautier lies."[7] Like several other poets of this group, Payne abounds in proudly labeled French "fixed forms" such as the ballade, rondeau, and villanelle.[8] Among his many incompetent translations are several from Villon, a favorite among the aesthetes because he showed that pure poetry could use material which most Victorians regarded as impure.

But Payne is a late figure.[9] Until Swinburne told them about Gautier and Baudelaire, the Pre-Raphaelite pioneers knew little or nothing about French aesthetic theories. The romantic trend which influenced them most strongly was medievalism, the most superficial aspect of the English Romantic

[6] *Selections*, p. 115. [7] *New Poems*, p. 36.

[8] Henry Austin Dobson, who cultivated such forms but specialized chiefly in eighteenth-century French "atmosphere," has been omitted from this chapter partly because his graceful verses are completely sterile as regards religion and partly because he is a little too late for us.

[9] Perhaps too late for inclusion in this study, since he lived until 1916 and was productive through 1909. But he published five characteristic volumes within our period, and on the whole it seems best to use him here and have done with him.

Movement and therefore the easiest to cultivate at a time when the shaping spirit of imagination was so sharply challenged by materialism and mechanism. If a Victorian found it impossible to assert human boundlessness without feeling like a fool, he could at least recapture some faint flavor of the interfusion of natural and supernatural by realizing the strange and strangeifying the real in imitations of medieval painting and poetry. But between the Pre-Raphaelites and the poets of the 1780–1830 period stood the Catholic Revival, which enriched nineteenth-century medievalism but also complicated and confused it. I have insisted that romanticism and Catholicism are fundamentally antipodal; but I have granted that the Romantic Movement and the Catholic Revival considerably overlap on the surface, and it is with surfaces that we are now chiefly concerned. The difference between ceremonies of religion and ceremonies of art, when both are cultivated with too much regard for the pattern and too little for the carpet, becomes tenuous. In either case the phrase "empty forms" is applicable.

It is not surprising, then, that outwardly aestheticized Catholicism and outwardly Catholicized aestheticism should perplexingly intertwine in the Gothic Revival. Pugin is a clear example of this relationship. The initial success of the Morris firm was in ecclesiastical, not domestic, decoration. One of its first customers was Father Mackonockie of the aggressively ritualistic parish of St. Alban's, Holborn.[10] The interior of another leading Anglo-Catholic church, All Saints, Margaret Street, was decorated by the painter and musician William Dyce, a prominent High Church layman. Though not a member of the Pre-Raphaelite Brotherhood he worked in the same general style. Unlike Evangelicalism, Catholicism was friendly to art. Unlike Broad Churchmanship, it expressed itself in concrete symbols which, whatever they might mean, were lovely and gracious.

Matthew Arnold preferred the "style" of Catholicism to that of Protestantism.[11] To that style Pater was of course more notably responsive. As a boy he was so devout a little acolyte that he thought of becoming a priest. As a Brasenose don he attended chapel regularly, thought that all students should be compelled to do so, and was very reverent about the Eucharist. For a few years before writing *Marius the Epicurean* he frequently visited the Anglo-Catholic monastery of St. Austin's, Walworth. To what extent he finally recovered the faith of his childhood is hard to say. Religion for him meant performing beautiful actions with beautiful objects in beautiful places. To Catholic Christianity thus misdefined he was almost, though never quite, willing to surrender himself for the sake of the sweetness

[10] J. W. Mackail, *Life of Willian Morris*, I, 151. [11] *Essays in Criticism. First Series*, p. 141.

to be derived therefrom. Rather surprisingly, moreover, *Marius* suggests that Pater was developing a new appreciation of the communal side of worship, the joy of believing togetherness. If the pleasures of worship were intensified when shared with others, there might after all be some objective sharable reality, some Beauty-Truth beyond the clutter of private momentary luxuries which he had originally supposed to be all we know and all we need to know. This change was one aspect of the partial shift of his aesthetic philosophy from Heraclitus toward Plato. He could not, however, uproot his profound distrust of abstractions: his mind was too deeply immersed in the nineteenth-century relativistic flux, which he had preached so tellingly in the seventies, to permit him to become either a complete Platonist or a complete Christian.

But we are looking too far ahead. The original Pre-Raphaelite Brotherhood represents a more rudimentary phase of the aesthetico-spiritual confusion. It also exhibits an internal cleavage: those of its members who liked the atmosphere of medieval Catholicism were considerably less religious than those who did not. Hunt and Millais, under strong Ruskinian influence, stood for "childlike submission to Nature"[12] in a spirit of liberalized but still fervent Protestant piety. They disapproved of that "Early Christian" style, which, although it had earlier been imported from Germany by such painters as Herbert and Dyce, was chiefly associated with the name of Ford Madox Brown. They feared lest their own program of reverent naturalism be given a Gothic Revival twist at the hands of Rossetti, Woolner, Stephens, and Collinson. So far as Rossetti was concerned such fears were amply justified. In one breath he declared himself in agreement with Hunt's view that "the radical want in modern art was a stricter study of Nature," and in the next breath identified Pre-Raphaelitism with the aims of the "Early Christian" school.[13] Paintings like *Ecce Ancilla Domini* and *The Girlhood of Mary Virgin*, though not wholly false to the ideals of Hunt and Millais, were much closer to those of Ford Madox Brown. Brown, though never officially a Pre-Raphaelite, through his influence on the young Rossetti did much to bend the movement toward a piously-flavored medievalism. While working in Italy he had been deeply impressed by Overbeck and Cornelius, the leaders of a group of German "Early Christian" painters who called themselves "The Nazarenes." Loyal to the spirit of Wackenroder and Novalis, they lived in a pseudo-monastic community where they produced pseudo-Catholic paintings in an artfully artless pseudo-primitive style.

[12] W. Holman Hunt, *Pre-Raphaelitism and the Pre-Raphaelite Brotherhood*, I, 91.
[13] *Ibid.*, pp. 98, 104.

Brown emulated them; Rossetti emulated Brown; some of the lesser Pre-Raphaelites and their unofficial associates emulated Rossetti.

But the minute verisimilitude which characterizes a good deal of fifteenth-century (especially Flemish and Dutch) painting was not discordant with the Ruskinian code of fidelity to nature. Hence in working up the details of their canvasses the disciples of Brown were sufficiently faithful to the standards of Hunt and Millais to incur—quite unjustly—the charge that they treated holy things with blasphemous realism. On the other hand, the Nazarene element in their work caused them to be accused of crypto-popery. Ruskin, even when defending them in his 1851 letters to *The Times*, shook a reproving finger at their Puseyite, if not definitely Romanist, predilections. The critics need not have been alarmed on this score. Probably no authentic work of art on a subject freighted with inescapable moral or religious implications can be created without some degree of imaginative sympathy with the meaning of its symbols. But the hollow, factitious, self-consciously literary piety of Pre-Raphaelite medievalistic painting does not suggest that these artists were strongly moved even by the vicarious faith of the craftsman. Rossetti spoke of *Ecce Ancilla Domini* as "the blessed white daub"[14]—a teasing technical problem. His sensuousness soon drew him toward a much more luscious style which would have been no less offensive to Overbeck than its literary equivalent was to Robert Buchanan. Brown, so active not only in religious painting but in church decoration, was a freethinker.[15] Pious canvasses were for him a subvariety of the historical genre. They demanded, to be sure, a special kind of effect which was sometimes hard to capture. Dissatisfied with *Christ and Peter*, he notes in his diary that "Four of the other apostles require more *religious feeling*, which must be done—William and Gabriel Rossetti [who had posed as models] require more veneration to be added to them."[16] They did indeed, and so did Brown.

Soon after the dissolution of "P. R. B.," Morris, Burne-Jones, and (more dubiously) Swinburne, as students at Oxford, combined a similar enthusiasm for the decorativeness of medieval piety with a religious feeling which, had it not proved so evanescent, could be described as genuine. Swinburne had much less of it and retained it even more briefly than his fellows, but the influence of John Nichol and of his own nature did not immediately obliterate the teachings of his Anglo-Catholic parents. Morris and Burne-Jones came from Evangelical homes; but Morris had become an

[14] W. M. Rossetti (ed.), *Præraphaelite Diaries and Letters*, p. 29.

[15] M. D. Conway, *Autobiography*, II, 134.

[16] *Præraphaelite Diaries*, p. 116.

Anglo-Catholic at Marlborough, a "high" public school, and Burne-Jones had been won over to similar views by Father John Goss, a Puseyite veteran of the Oxford Movement with whom he became acquainted while visiting a friend in Birmingham at the age of fifteen. Their Catholicism, while it lasted, was more than a nostalgic pose. The wish to be precisely like the hero of Charlotte Yonge's *Heir of Redclyffe* included the wish to be a believing and practicing Christian, albeit a priggish one. If they read Malory and Digby's *Broad Stone* and Fouqué's *Sintram* they also read, faithfully though less zestfully, the Fathers, Milman's *Latin Christianity*, *Tracts for the Times*, and Archdeacon Wilberforce's treatises on Baptism, the Eucharist, and the Incarnation. If they dreamed rather idly of forming an aesthetico-pietistic community on the Nazarene pattern, they also quite seriously intended to become Anglo-Catholic priests. For a time, indeed, Morris felt strongly inclined to make his submission to Rome.

Of course it was a queer mixture of reality and unreality. Why did the reality so quickly evaporate, leaving only the notion that Catholic Christianity, along with other aspects of medieval glamour, was aesthetically fetching? Their admiration for Rossetti was doubtless a potent factor, but Anglo-Catholic ceremonialism must assume a large share of the blame. If the Tractarians had made it too hard to be a Christian, the Ritualists, in their desire to save souls (the old snare) had made it too easy to be one—and to cease to be one. If you were sensitive to aesthetic values the path of ceremonial might lead you from the studio to the church; but no less smoothly it might also lead you from the church to the studio.

In 1855 Morris informs his friend Cormell Price: "I don't think that even if I get through Greats I shall take my B.A., because they won't allow you not to sign the 39 Articles unless you declare that you are 'extra Ecclesiam Anglicanam' which I'm not, and don't intend to be, and I won't sign the 39 Articles." It is not clear whether he objects to the Articles because they are too orthodox or because (despite *Tract 90*) they are too Protestant. At this time, in any case, he has given up the idea of taking Orders and is trying to reconcile his mother to his plan of becoming an architect.[17]

A poem of the same year enclosed in a letter to Price suggests that his difficulties went deeper than any scruples about the Articles. The verses have no title but are dated "Tuesday in Holy Week." The kiss of Judas (in the Gospel for the preceding day) has made him dream of other kisses:

[17] *Letters to His Family and Friends*, pp. 14, 15–16.

Lover's kiss beneath the moon,
With it sorrow cometh soon:
Juliet's within the tomb:

Angelico's in quiet light
'Mid the aureoles very bright
God is looking from the height.

. . .

There beneath the angel rows
With the light flame on his brows,
With his friend, the deacon goes:

Hand in hand they go together,
Loving hearts they go together
Where the Presence shineth ever.

Kiss upon the death-bed given,
Kiss on dying forehead given
When the soul goes up to Heaven.

. . .

Willow standing 'gainst the blue,
Where the light clouds come and go,
Mindeth me of kiss untrue.

Christ, thine awful cross is thrown
Round the whole world, and thy Sun
Woeful kisses looks upon.

. . .

I cannot say the things I would,
I cannot think the things I would,
How the Cross at evening stood.

Very blue the sky above,
Very sweet the faint clouds move,
But I cannot think of love.[18]

What is one to make of this medley of apparently genuine religious feeling, irrelevant artiness, the longing to express something inexpressible, and the Cross as a personal symbol of frustrated sexuality? What sort of mind is it that can begin with the kiss of Judas and end with "But I cannot think of love"? That last line, taken in conjunction with the faintly Dolbenish triplets about the affectionate deacon and his friend, does not conflict with Henderson's guardedly expressed thesis that Morris had a homosexual streak which made him incapable of satisfying Jane Burden.[19]

[18] *Ibid.*, pp. 6–7.

[19] *Ibid.*, p. xxiv (Philip Henderson's Introduction).

Morris did, as a matter of fact, take his B.A. in 1856. Whether he then declared himself "extra Ecclesiam Anglicanam" I have not attempted to discover. The question is immaterial, since within a year or two he had moved not merely outside the Anglican Church but outside any sort of supernaturalistic religion. He found some relief from the melancholy which shadowed his life, some equivalent of religious objectivity, in his delight in craftsmanship and, finally, in his attempts to make a world where all workers could share that delight. Even in his most affirmative moments, however, he can do no more than urge a bereaved friend "to think that life is not empty nor made for nothing, and that the parts of it fit one into another in some way; and that the world goes on, beautiful and strange and dreadful and worshipful."[20] But although the world might be worshipful, he would not worship it or anything else. Throughout his maturity he seems to have been spiritually tone deaf. In 1882 Allingham went walking with him. "We talked, among other things, of believing or not believing in a God, and he said 'It's so unimportant, it seems to me,' and he went on to say that all we can get to, do what we will, is a form of words."[21] Indifferent to such forms as an individual, he became, as a socialist, necessarily hostile to the religious opiate. "I want to get mumbo-jumbo out of the world," he muttered on his deathbed.[22]

The spiritual history of Burne-Jones does not concern us. Long after the Oxford days Moncure D. Conway found him painting a saint for a church window. "And I almost a nihilist!" he said smilingly to his rationalist friend. Conway adds the interesting comment: "It was precisely that which made him so happy in such work. When a man gets entirely out of all creeds and superstitions he can see them with an impartial eye as varied expressions of human nature. They become folk-lore, mythology, variegated fauna and flora of the human heart and imagination."[23] Discounting Conway's characteristic inability to tell an artist from an anthropologist, we may apply this remark to the spirit in which our poets treat medieval religious material. It is aesthetically appealing stuff, and since they do not believe in it they feel all the freer to use it as they please.

Not one of the nine poets is a Roman or Anglican Catholic. Two of them manage to be enthusiastic medievalists in some poems and overtly anti-Catholic in others. The painter-poet William Bell Scott's *Bede in the Nineteenth Century* represents Wiseman as attempting to revive that Gothic

[20] Quoted by J. W. Mackail, *Life of William Morris*, I, 337.

[21] William Allingham, *A Diary*, p. 316.

[22] *Letters*, p. lxvi (Henderson's Introduction).

[23] *Autobiography*, II, 132.

darkness which Bede, exceptional in his day, had vainly tried to illumine. But in *Anthony* and *Saint Margaret* respectively, the same poet exploits the macabre-grotesque and the decorative-pious aspects of the tradition which he has contemned, while in *Four Acts of St. Cuthbert* he sounds like a completely reverent hagiologist.[24]

The inconsistency of Eugene Lee-Hamilton is even more striking. In *Poems and Transcripts* (1878) a gargoyle-like dwarf carries the poet's mind back to

> . . . those black times
> When prowled the monk, the leper, and the witch
> Amid the rubbish of a nobler world;
> When blunted was the mind by ignorance
> And dull despair, and much the body, too,
> Was stunted, and misshapen, and debased
> By centuries of famine, when mankind
> Were but a herd of mean and trembling slaves,
> Beneath the lash of heaven, and their voice
> A litany unceasing.

The Middle Ages had almost wholly forgotten the world's "golden youth,"

> . . . when, in Greece, the sculpter loved to mould
> The youth still sprinkled with Olympic dust;
> When Phidias and Praxiteles had clothed
> Immortal Gods in Man's most beauteous shape.[25]

But in *Gods, Saints, and Men* (1880) this Neo-Hellenist presents twelve tales all but two of which relate medieval legends of miracles. Lee-Hamilton's attitude toward this material is ambiguous. *The Fiddler and the Slipper*, a variant of the "Jongleur de Nôtre Dame" story, is broadly comic with an undercurrent of hostility, in the manner of *Ingoldsby* with a touch of *Hudibras*. It takes place

> Somewhere in the Middle Ages—:
> That happy time of long-shanked pages,
> Of troubadours and ladies fair,
> With hawk on wrist and golden hair;

but also the not-so-happy time

[24] *Poems*, pp. 35–36, 44ff., 147ff. Scott (1811–1890) tried to satisfy his youthful admiration for Shelley by writing in the Spasmodic vein. (See above, p. 201.) Failing in this attempt he fell back upon an easier sort of romanticism and began writing and painting in a somewhat Pre-Raphaelitish way a little before the formation of the Brotherhood. At last he was contentedly drawn into the orbit of Rossetti, Morris, and Swinburne.

[25] *Poems and Transcripts*, pp. 3–4.

Of monks and nuns with morbid cravings,
With visions and ecstatic ravings,
Of heretics' and witches' trials,
Of recantations and denials;
That kindly period which exhibits
So many forms of chains and gibbets,
Of thumbscrews, racks, and Spanish shoes
To alter men's religious views,
Or touch the hearts of stingy Jews;
Those good old days so picturesque,
So hungry, pious, and grotesque.[26]

But there is nothing to indicate that the other tales in this volume are intended satirically. The miracles are related with no hint of opposition. One would never suspect from, say, *The Witness* or *The Emperor on the Ledg* that Lee-Hamilton detested the faith of the Middle Ages.

People for whom certain things are sacred do not like to see them fingered by poets for whom they are merely quaint or glamorous. They must try to remember that an infidel like John Payne is fully entitled to write:

I pray thee, sir priest, to christen my babe
With bell and candle and psalter;
And I will give up this bonny gold cup
To stand on the holy altar.[27]

Why should he not try to enlarge his imaginative experience by pretending to be a medieval Catholic writing a ballad in which the characters naturally talk like Catholics? From the critical point of view the only objection is that in the complete absence of intellectual agreement the highest degree of dramatically emotional sympathy is needed for a convincing poem about people who have religious convictions. Payne is deficient in this quality, and so are most of his fellows. They have some of the words, but they do not know the tune. There are a few striking exceptions. Parts of O'Shaughnessy's *Chaitivel* ring true. Scott's *Anthony* is mostly spurious, but perhaps not these lines:

Thou wood of the cross of the agony,
Ye nails that fixed Him to the tree,
Sponge that held the last bitter draught,
Lift, support, and strengthen me!

Drops of His sweating that eased His pain,
Drops of blood, the parched world's rain,
Tears that brought us man's second spring,
Cleanse, absolve, absolve and sain.

[26] *Gods, Saints, and Men*, pp. 32–33. [27] *Selections*, p. 173.

Mary's most holy eyes then lifted up,
Angels' most holy hands holding the cup,
And Spirit most holy that then came down,
Make my soul with ye to sup![28]

Almost the whole of the *Defence of Guenevere* volume is a remarkably credible evocation of the grimmer, less chivalrous side of the Age of Chivalry, with religion as a minor but dramatically appropriate element in the picture. In these early pieces Morris sees the Middle Ages, not whole but at least steadily, as a period in the actual history of Europe. This praise cannot be extended to the medieval tales in *The Earthly Paradise*, where like the other aesthetes he is merely trying to escape from the ugly time-world into a timeless dream where religion, with everything else, is faint and misty.

Even at their best, however, the aesthetic medievalists think of Catholicism not as a faith but as a flavor. In one way or another it helps them to obtain the interfusion-thrill of Novalis's "Die Welt wird Traum, der Traum wird Welt." Lee-Hamilton likes the naïve literalness of the superstitions which he scorns. Scott, preferring Gothic-gooseflesh spookery, writes ballads of witchcraft with long silly refrains. O'Shaughnessy fancies a more delicate and suggestive preternaturalism. Repeatedly we are reminded of the close relation between poetry and painting in the Aesthetic Movement. Scott, a better painter than poet, sometimes tries to paint in verse. Here is *Saint Margaret* dying on her knees before the altar:

Slowly a moonshine breaks over the glass,
The black and green witchcraft is there no more;
It spreads as it brightens, and out of it pass
Four angels with glorified hair,—all four
With lutes, and our Lord is in heaven's door.
Margaret! they hail thee.

The next stanza seems to combine Rossetti's *Beata Beatrix* with Keats's *Eve of St. Agnes:*

Her eyes are a-wide to the hallowèd light,
Her head is cast backward, her bosom is clad
With the flickering moonlight pale purple and white;
Away to the angels her spirit hath fled,
While her body still kneels—but is she not dead?
She is safe, she is well![29]

A highly picturesque form of *bona mors*.

Morris's verbal Pre-Raphaelite canvasses are more original and striking,

[28] *Poems*, p. 54.
[29] *Ibid.*, p. 36.

but sometimes they make us too conscious of the artist himself as he prepares his palette, poses the sitter, and arranges the drapes. On hearing of her husband's violent death, Lady Harpdon prays:

> Christ! I have been a many times to church,
> And, ever since my mother taught me prayers,
> Have used them daily, but today I wish
> To pray another way; come face to face,
> O Christ, that I may clasp your knees and pray.
>
> . . .
>
> Let us go, You and I, a long way off,
> To the little, damp, dark Poitevin church;
> While you sit on the coffin in the dark,
> Will I lie down, my face on the bare stone
> Between your feet, and chatter anything
> I have heard long ago, what matters it
> So I may keep you there, your solemn face
> And long hair even-flowing on each side,
> Until you love me well enough to speak
> And give me comfort; yea, till o'er your chin,
> And cloven red beard the great tears roll down
> In pity for my misery, and I die
> Kissed over by you.

"Kissed *over*" as applied to Jesus Christ has a special offensiveness which must be spoken of later. At present my point is that we are made aware of the picture, red beard and all, to an extent which prevents us from believing in Lady Alice as a bereaved wife who turns to Christ for consolation. Similarly Guenevere, in her hour of trial, thinks she sees

> A great God's angel standing, with such dyes,
> Not known on earth, on his great wings, and hands
> Held out two ways, light from the inner skies
> Showing him well, and making his commands
> Seem to be God's commands, moreover, too.[30]

We appreciate the pose and recall Morris's later efforts to make his dye vats produce the right colors, but we forget Guenevere and God. "Showing him well" epitomizes the inherent falsity of this whole pseudo-religious trend.

Morris also provides clear examples of the fascination exerted upon some of these poets by the cruelty and violence of the Middle Ages—not, goodness knows, because they themselves were cruel, violent men but because, being too bloodless, they thirsted for a little vicarious blood. The mingling of piety and savagery provides a pleasing ambiguity. In *Shameful Death* the

[30] *The Defence of Guenevere . . . and Other Poems*, pp. 4, 68–69.

narrator concludes his story of murder and vengeance, in which he himself has played a bloody part, with the tag:

And now, knights, all of you
I pray you pray for Sir Hugh,
A good knight and a true,
And for Alice, his wife, pray too.

The Judgement of God begins:

"Swerve to the left, son Roger," he said,
"When you catch his eyes through the helmet-slit,
Swerve to the left, then out at his head,
And the Lord God give you joy of it."[31]

In those lines the irony becomes so obvious as to make us wonder whether Morris's motive here may not be partly satirical as well as dramatic. This, he would at least not object to our observing, is what Christianity amounted to in the lives of these devout believers.

Stranger ironies and ambiguities might be drawn from the supposed relations, in the Middle Ages, between heavenly and earthly love. The dichotomy is oversimplified, for at least five colors could be teased into various shades on the palette: carnal passion, idealistic *amour courtois*, erotic mysticism, the cult of the Virgin Mary, and the cult of "stunners" like Elizabeth Siddal and Jane Burden. The subject, however, is too remote from our main concern to justify close analysis of its complexities. A few random examples will suffice. With an eye cocked in the direction of *The Blessed Damozel*, Payne makes Isobel address her lover from the grave:

No harm can reach me in Death's deep:
It hath no fear for me;
God sweetens it to lie and sleep,
Until His face I see;

He makes it sweet to lie and wait,
Till we together meet
And hand-in-hand athwart the gate
Pass up the golden street.[32]

Conversely O'Shaughnessy, in the striking song in *Chaitivel* beginning "Hath any loved you well, down there," makes a living woman challenge the claims of any rivals whom her dead lover may have met among the tombs.[33] The Virgin Mary and some mortal stunner intermingle in Morris's

[31] *Ibid.*, pp. 103, 105. [32] *New Poems*, p. 110. [33] *Lays of France*, pp. 126–129.

Praise of My Lady. Her cheeks, of course, are "Hollow'd a little mournfully," and

> Her forehead, overshadow'd much
> By bows of hair, has a wave such
> As God was good to make for me.
> *Beata mea domina!*
>
> . . .
>
> Her lips are not contented now,
> Because the hours pass so slow
> Towards a sweet time: (pray for me),
> *Beata mea domina!*

A similar jumble of flesh and spirit appears in *King Arthur's Tomb* when Guenevere asks Jesus whether in judging her He will take account of the fact

> That I am beautiful, Lord, even as you
> And your dear Mother? why did I forget
> You were so beautiful, and good, and true,
> That you loved me so, Guenevere? O yet
>
> If ever I go to hell, I cannot choose
> But love you, Christ, yea, though I cannot keep
> From loving Launcelot; O Christ! must I lose
> My own heart's love? see, though I cannot weep,
>
> Yet am I very sorry for my sin;
> Moreover, Christ, I cannot bear that hell,
> I am most fain to love you, and to win
> A place in heaven some time—I cannot tell—
>
> Speak to me, Christ! I kiss, kiss, kiss your feet;
> Ah! now I weep![34]

The gamy thrill imparted to sexuality by the zest of flirting with damnation, suggested in the lines just quoted, is of course a favorite theme with Swinburne. O'Shaughnessy's *Bisclavaret,* though Swinburnian in this respect, is not a mere imitation of the master. The poem takes its originating hint, but not its substance, from the celebrated werewolf *lai* of Marie de France. O'Shaughnessy imagines a special race of men, outwardly like other people but inwardly set apart by a rebellious animality and a defiant-despairing hatred of the God who forbids their lusts. At night they go about doing no end of mysteriously dreadful things, the thought of which fills harmless little O'Shaughnessy with a Cheevyish longing to share in

[34] *The Defence of Guenevere . . . and Other Poems*, pp. 20–21, 146–147.

Their unknown curse and all the strength
    Of the wild thirsts and lusts they know,
The sharp joys sating them at length,
    The new and greater lusts that grow.

The werewolves would have no fun at all if they were simple atheists rather than blasphemers. They howl:

We hunt the chosen of the Lord;
    And cease not, in wild course elate
Until we see the flaming sword
    And Gabriel before His gate!

We hold high orgies of the things,
    Strange and accursèd of all flesh,
Whereto the quick sense ever brings
    The sharp forbidden thrill afresh.

And far away, among our kin,
    Already they account our place
With all the slain ones, and begin
    The Masses for our soul's full grace.[35]

It does not follow that these poets were not religious at all merely because they had no belief in the medieval Catholicism which they exploited for artistic purposes. We must consider the possibility that they had found spiritual reliances which released them from obsolete superstition but left them free to play with it as a policeman's child might play with his father's handcuffs. *My Beautiful Lady*, a worthless poem by the Pre-Raphaelite sculptor Thomas Woolner, relates the hero's conversion from beauty-worship to a Carlyle-Kingsley doctrine of duty and service which he associates with Christianity. John Addington Symonds's *Antinomianism* is extremely uncharacteristic of him in advocating humble reliance on the will of God.[36] Scared by the Paris Commune, Alfred Austin appreciates those village church bells which help to explain *Why England Is Conservative* by chiming so "sweet and safely."[37] W. B. Scott, in a sonnet sequence entitled *Outside the Temple*, wishes that he were inside but finds the problem too

[35] *Poems*, pp. 19, 21.

[36] *New and Old*, p. 221. The title is misleading, for the theme of the poem is rather a sort of quietism.

[37] *Lyrical Poems*, pp. 116–117. Of course Austin was not a genuine aesthete or a genuine anything. He did not, however, develop his jingoistic line until he became poet laureate on the death of Tennyson. The lyrics which he wrote during our period and in the 1880's suggest that he often thought of art for art's sake as a fashionable tendency which it might be well to cultivate. Hence I draw a few examples from him without leaning on him at all heavily.

difficult to justify anything more than a half-hearted pantheism.[38] None of these poets, in short, writes as a firmly convinced Protestant Christian.

They are somewhat richer in the quasi-religious by-products of romanticized Christianity which have become so familiar to us. We are dealing with *Victorian* aesthetes who are not quite ready to "live merrily and trust to good verses." Pre-Raphaelites like Rossetti adored Keats as a poet of pure non-instrumental beauty of phrase and form. But here is Holman Hunt preaching to Millais what he conceives to be the true Pre-Raphaelite gospel: "Revivalism, whether it be of classicism or of medievalism, is a seeking after dry bones. Read, my dear fellow, the address of Oceanus in Keats' *Hyperion*, and you will see how the course of life on creation's lines is inevitably progressive, and only under debasing influences retrogressive."[39] Thus in the age of Victoria, as in our own, there were those who valued Keats as a poet of fortifying ideas. Not all such persons shared Hunt's unusually fervent Broad Church piety, but it is safe to say that all of them were responsive to the message of that ex-Evangelical romantic, John Ruskin. Something of his spirit is present whenever these poets attempt to associate art with romantic nature-feeling, with a semireligious sense of the spiritual mission of beauty, or with social reform through creative joy. On these themes, however, our aesthetes (the later Morris excepted) are too weak and wavering to be classified as thoroughgoing Ruskinites.

"It cannot be too clearly asserted," Hunt vainly insists, "that Pre-Raphaelitism in its purity was the frank worship of Nature, *kept in check by selection and directed by a spirit of imaginative purpose*."[40] This is the basis on which Ruskin himself championed the Pre-Raphaelites. Primarily it represents the ideal of Hunt and Millais: but it was not rejected by the Nazarene faction, for the "imaginative purpose"—that of phenomenalizing the supernatural and supernaturalizing the phenomenal—was applicable both to romantic naturalism and to romantic medievalism. It is, however, the naturalistic interfusion which W. B. Scott had in mind when in 1851—the year of Ruskin's letters to *The Times*—he wrote his sonnet *To the Artists Called P.R.B.*:

> I thank you, brethren in Sincerity,—
>
> . . .
>
> For you have shown, with youth's brave confidence,
> The honesty of true speech and the sense
> Uniting life with "nature," earth with sky.[41]

[38] *Poems*, pp. 73ff.
[39] *Pre-Raphaelitism and the Pre-Raphaelite Brotherhood*, I, 61.
[40] *Ibid.*, II, 357. Hunt italicizes the qualifying clause lest his readers be alarmed by "frank."
[41] *Poems*, p. 183.

Some of our poets would like to think of themselves as the offspring of this union. Even that malicious little fribble Alfred Austin, Browning's Pacchiarotto, insists that

> My virgin sense of sound was steeped
> In the music of young streams;
> . . .
> And so it is that still to-day
> I cannot choose but sing,
> Remain a foster-child of May,
> And a suckling of the Spring:
> . . .
> That though my verse but roam the air
> And murmur in the trees,
> You may discern a purpose there,
> As in music of the bees.[42]

John Addington Symonds is a much less absurd representative of the Wordsworthian tradition. For a time his love of the Alps was merely sensuous (Tintern Abbey in 1793), but gradually he found a higher meaning in

> The solitary voices of the floods,
> Flowers, and deep places of primeval woods;
>
> These wrought the change; for these from childhood's dawn
> Had nurtured me; through these, as through the rites
> Of due initiation, I was drawn
> Into communion with those sacred heights
> On which God's glory broodeth as a cloud,
> Which with the voice of very God is loud.

But for Symonds the apprehension of God in nature implies the divinization of man, or at least of the artist. Witness his *Lines Written on the Roof of Milan Cathedral.* The cathedral is man's work; Monte Rosa, seen from its roof, is God's work. But thesis and antithesis (he may well be thinking of Hegel) find their synthesis in the fact that

> . . . God on man's work here
> Hath set His signature and symbol clear—

not because the duomo is a religious edifice but because it is so "divinely" beautiful; while conversely the mountain would be "cold and dumb and bare" did not "man's soul" impart spiritual life to it. Hence

[42] *Lyrical Poems*, p. 3.

God is man's soul; man's soul a spark of God:
By God in man the dull terrestrial clod
Becomes a thing of beauty; thinking man
Through God made manifest, outrival can
His handiwork of nature. Do we dream,
Mingling reality with things that seem?
Or is it true that God and man appear
One soul in sentient art self-conscious here,
One soul o'er senseless nature stair by stair
Raised to create by comprehending there?[43]

One soul in all things, from clod to cathedral, a creative soul in which God and man participate. This poet is probably not worshipping anything external to himself when he writes *At Amalfi*:

Dread Pan, to thee I turn: thy soul
That through the living world doth roll,
Stirs in our heart an aching sense
Of beauty, too divinely wrought
To be the food of mortal thought,
For earth-born hunger too intense.[44]

Symonds is not the only member of this group who would be a romantic pantheist. Philip Marston, to be sure, has crotchety scruples about the second half of the noun. His epigram, *Atheist to Pantheist*, reads:

What you call God, I nature name, and hence
Am Atheist; but where the difference?[45]

Where indeed? Pebbles in a stream—permanence within flux—give Scott an intimation of the *Oneness of All*:

Could I but find the words that would reveal
The unity in multiplicity,
And the profound strange harmony I feel
With these dead things, God's garments of to-day;
The listener's soul with mine they would anneal,
And make us one within eternity.

But he insists that natural objects, and the works of man's mind as well, are merely

. . . types and symbols: earth and heaven
Each other interpenetrate: all creeds

[43] *New and Old*, pp. 143, 171.
[44] *Ibid.*, p. 166. By this time aesthetes are beginning to get this feeling more easily in Italy than a home.
[45] *Collected Poems*, p. 328.

And churches crowning the hill-tops of time,—
Pillars of fire by night, of cloud by day,
Are but attempts to touch the symbolized.[46]

There were strong motives for trying to view nature mystically at a time when belief in the reality of appearances would subject poetic imagination to the tyranny of scientific materialism. The aesthete's characteristic incompetence in scientific matters often renders him liable to accept quite naïvely the notion that science has somehow "disproved" the religion of nature along with all other faiths. That is why Austin so nervously shields his nature-experience from the assaults of reason:

Confess this is not bookish lore;
'Tis feeling only, and no more.
Poets lack what you learning call,
And rustic poets most of all.
Why from the plain truth should I shrink?
In woods men feel; in towns they think.
Yet, which is best?[47]

For him the question is rhetorical, but this attempt to revive the least mature form of sentimental anti-intellectualism is a feeble bulwark against Darwin. More intelligently, Scott tries the familiar device of regarding evolution as a law of spiritual as well as of physical development:

Anon the bird screamed—then the furred beast creeps
Growling; then Adam speaks erect and strong.
Shall there not rise again from Nature's deeps
One more whose voice shall be the perfect song?

Yet he grants in the next sonnet of his *Outside the Temple* series that this prospect is too remote to satisfy us who now live and who know that we shall die. Contemplation of the infinite universe of "revolving firmaments" shrivels us with a sense of "blind fatality":

No rest is there for our soul's winged feet,
She must return for shelter to her ark—
The body, fair, frail, death-born, incomplete.

We cannot know whatever truth may lie beyond the wall of our flesh. Hence except in his feebly mystical vein the only advice which Scott receives from nature is like the stoical message of Arnold's *Self-Dependence*:

Gain faith and courage through self-harmony,
And live your lives, nor only live to die.[48]

[46] *Poems*, pp. 88, 116. [47] *Lyrical Poems*, p. 18. [48] *Poems*, pp. 78, 84, 86, 87

One of Arnold's less bracing moods is echoed by Lee-Hamilton:

> Nature for me has most charm in what is her moment elegiac;
> When she brings home to the mind all that is fleeting and fair;
>
> . . .
>
> When the mind that is calm is possessed by the beauty of Nature,
> Yet is aware of a voice telling of mutable things."[49]

In the material drawn upon for this chapter I find only one attempt to combine, somewhat in the Swinburne-Meredith manner, a harshly Dionysian variety of romantic pantheism with the struggle-for-existence nature depicted by evolutionary science. In Arthur O'Shaughnessy's *Colibri* (1881) a disillusioned European plunges into the forests of the upper Amazon, where he finds happiness with a girl who is nominally an Indian but essentially a nature-spirit and sister of the birds like Hudson's Rima.[50] The man's psychic healing is brought about by uncorrupted passionate love through which he develops a sense of kinship with nature in general. The concluding lines:

> . . . Oh, last night,
> The great voice of the universal soul
> Seemed to be speaking to me from the height
> And from the depth, bidding me rise up whole,
> Blasting my weakness in the scornful roll
> Of thousand-throated thunder. Every tongue
> Of fair infuriate creature, gracious, strong,
> Uttered or roared or sang the frenzied song
> Of its appalling self. . . .
> . . . And I, like one
> Roused by some vast resuscitating voice
> From death's drugged lethargy, watched with delight,
> Against the jaggèd blue, the faultless poise
> And sheer intrepid leap or violent run
> Of ounce or jaguar—hearkening while the noise
> Of all that hurricane of life and strife
> Roared and rolled on terrific through the leagues
> Of shaken woodland, till a loftier life
> Of great primeval passions and fatigues
> Rose and grew mine—a long exuberant breath
> Of pauseless life to end in dreamless death.[51]

It is interesting to see that our old friend the "universal soul" can be

[49] *Poems and Transcripts*, pp. 76, 77.
[50] See H. N. Fairchild, "Rima's Mother," *PMLA*, LXVIII, 357–370
[51] *Songs of a Worker*, pp. 165–166.

associated with life and strife and primeval passions. But the other poets of this group insist on trying to be Wordsworthian, and their efforts are unconvincing because they cannot quite believe in what they are saying.

Ruskin himself gradually discovered that his philosophy of art could less congenially be united with Wordsworth's naturalism than with a humanitarianism somewhat like Carlyle's. The pre-1880 aesthetes were not wholly unreceptive to Ruskin's ideas on the social mission of beauty. For all their escapism they knew that they had to live in the world of the Industrial Revolution, and they wanted to make that world less intolerable for themselves. Even the most self-centered of them recognized that this aim could not be achieved in a society which denied the joy of making and appreciating—and buying—beautiful things to all but a minute proportion of its members. They were easily convinced that social reform demanded aesthetic reform, and conversely a few of them could see that aesthetic reform demanded social reform.

If such a relationship existed, questions about the moral obligations and opportunities of the artist could not be brushed aside as irrelevant. Poems and paintings which palpably *tried* to preach at you were contemptible, but good art did you good precisely because of its noninstrumental beauty. When Pater, in the last phase of his career, asserted the substantial identity of moral and aesthetic values he was returning to Plato through Ruskin. "Ruskin's is the first theory that I know of," writes Professor Ladd, "to suggest that in the activity of art itself there lay the ultimate social value, the means to the end of good living. He did not merely relate art more closely to living than former theorists, but suggested that art was itself a good life. This was his genuinely modern contribution." Ladd also recognizes that Ruskin believed in the moral sense,[52] which Shaftesbury, under Platonic and Neo-Platonic influence, had identified with aesthetic taste. But Ruskin was indeed a trail-blazer not only in asserting more explicitly than Shaftesbury that art was a good life but in asserting that it was a good life for everyone.[53]

The aesthetes were not much interested in Ruskin's later, more specifically sociological works. It was as a social-minded art critic that he affected their thinking. Although his philosophy of art is a kind of substitute-religion, his distrust of creedal formulas made him associate it with morality rather than with any supernaturalistic faith. His religious development is so instructive

52 Henry Ladd, *The Victorian Morality of Art*, pp. 161, 339.

53 Even Shaftesbury, however, cannot quite make up his mind as to whether the aesthetico-moral sense is a special privilege of the virtuoso or a universal endowment.

that we may remind ourselves of its main trend. He was, of course, the too anxiously reared child of strict Evangelical parents. Their puritanical morality and detestation of Catholicism are strong—stronger than their theology—in the first two volumes of *Modern Painters*, in *Seven Lamps of Architecture*, and in *Stones of Venice*. He reconciled his anti-Catholic prejudice with his love of the Middle Ages in the paradox that Gothic architecture is Protestant in its essential spirit. As the parental creed grew hazier and hazier he increasingly identified the spirit of Protestantism with the spirit of nature. His naturalism moved onward from a piously flavored physico-theology of the *Bridgewater Treatises* type to romantic pantheism, and later (by 1858) to a rampantly non-Christian glorification of animal force expressed in mystical-sounding language. But soon, with Carlyle's transcendental energy-worship as the connecting link, he developed a shapeless theistic humanitarianism which many readers identified with Christianity because of his prophetic manner and his fondness for Biblical phrases. To his friends, however, he made it clear that he accepted no revelation save that of his own insight. During the final phase, from 1874 onward, he was reconverted to belief in immortality by spiritualism. He also came to think of himself as a Catholic, with the proviso that the Church should agree with him rather than he with the Church. He became so devoted to St. Francis as to feel that he was, in some indefinable way, a tertiary of the Franciscan order. Patmore, De Vere, and Manning expected to hear of his conversion any day, but he was only going mad.

Ruskin at his best was a genuine lover of art. He *wanted* to say that beautiful things were good because they were beautiful. But for reasons chiefly associated with his Evangelical background he could not preserve his doctrine of the morality of art from being corrupted by the dominant Victorian idea that the artist should eschew the "unpleasant" and concern himself with edifying themes. These apparently antithetical conceptions of art might have been restated and synthesized on a Christian basis; but Ruskin, as we have seen, had attempted to divorce his aesthetico-moral theory from religion. Although the separation was incomplete, the only strong links between the two were at precisely those points which were likely to bring about confusion rather than reconciliation. He cast aside the Christian belief that all beauty is God's beauty but retained the Evangelical sense of prophetic vocation and the Evangelical distrust of the sensuous. The latter tendency was especially strong because his mother had saddled him with an impotent loathing of sex combined with an inability to stop thinking about it.

In the early gropings of the Aesthetic Movement, one might profess the higher side of Ruskin's art-gospel only to be drawn, by its lower side, back toward that prudery and didacticism which one had hoped to surmount. Holman Hunt, a by no means contemptible painter, avers that the *true* purpose of the Pre-Raphaelite reform "was to make art a handmaid in the cause of justice and truth." He is eager to show "how in a quite childlike way we at the beginning set ourselves to illustrate themes . . . connected with the pathetic, the honest, the laudable, and sublime." He was distressed to find so little evidence of such intentions when he visited the galleries of Paris with Rossetti in 1849. "There was nothing to make intelligible the axiom that 'art is love.' " Delacroix and Géricault painted as if they believed "that art is hatred, war, murder, lust, pride, and egoism." Delaroche was a partial exception. "He had, it is true, indulged a taste for bloodshed and murder unworthy of a man of genius, but in 'The Children of Edward IV' he had aroused sympathy for the imprisoned brothers by the pathetic sign that their only guardian was the vigilant but helpless spaniel."[54] This is exactly like Ruskin's praise of *The Old Shepherd's Chief Mourner*, dog and all.

Rossetti did not fully agree with these judgments: Hunt sadly reports that his companion "declared an admiration for Delacroix which I could not endorse."[55] But some poets whose views of art approached Rossetti's more closely than Hunt's can on occasion pay tribute to the "Victorian" aspect of Ruskin's teachings. In *Any Sculptor to Any Model*, Symonds makes the sculptor say to the nude girl:

> Yea, it is mine by Art, the hierophant
> Of myriads when these moving lips are dumb,
> To find thy meaning, and to speak it forth
> Through marble and through bronze that shall not fade;
> Making thy moulded shape—not face alone,
> But hands, breast, lifted arms, firm limbs, that tell
> Of service, strength, will, conquest, energy—
> One service for the minds of those that know.[56]

If the artist is to render the model's "shape—not face alone," he should do so in order to give men elevating ideas about service, energy, and so on. Even stronger anxiety to find extra-aesthetic justification for aesthetic creativity is shown in O'Shaughnessy's *Song of a Fellow-Worker*. The poet insists that he is no less a toiler than the humble artisan whom he addresses:

[54] *Pre-Raphaelitism*, I, 118, 129–130; II, 361.

[55] *Ibid.*, I, 130.

[56] *New and Old*, p. 18. The title recalls Browning's *Any Wife to Any Husband*, but Symonds is thinking of Jules's speech to Phene in *Pippa Passes*. "Find thy meaning," however, may be a reminiscence of *Fra Lippo Lippi*.

> I carve the marble of pure thought until the thought takes form,
> Until it comes before my soul and makes the world grow warm;
> Until there comes a glorious voice and words that seem divine,
> And the music reaches all men's hearts and draws them into mine.[57]

In the last line, note the use of benevolism as a means of self-enlargement.

William Morris took no interest in the moralistic aspect of Ruskin's theory of art, but, as he himself repeatedly declares, he was profoundly affected by its sociological implications. At Oxford, he says, the Anglo-Catholicism which he had brought from Marlborough was soon "corrected by the books of John Ruskin which were at the time a sort of revelation to me; I was a good deal influenced by the works of Charles Kingsley, and got into my head therefrom some socio-political ideas which would have developed probably but for the attractions of art and poetry."[58] What especially impressed him was the chapter on "The Nature of Gothic" in *Stones of Venice*. He reprinted it in 1892 at the Kelmscott Press with a Preface in which he said: "The lesson which Ruskin teaches here is that art is the expression of man's pleasure in labour; that it is possible for man to rejoice in his work, for, strange as it may seem to us to-day, there have been times when he did rejoice in it."[59]

Those times were of course the Middle Ages. In his Oxford days Morris was by no means insensitive to the politico-social side of Victorian medievalism. Digby's *Broad Stone* taught him that the ideals of *Alton Locke* and *Yeast* had actually been realized in the Age of Chivalry.[60] Pugin, in his *Contrasts*, placed side by side the great monuments of Gothic art produced by free and happy craftsmen and the hideous fabrications of nineteenth-century slave labor. But as Morris's Puseyite enthusiasm faded he became less and less willing to believe with Digby and Pugin that medieval society had been able to produce good art solely because it was a Catholic society. Carlyle's *Past and Present*, on the other hand, could show him the sociological, but not the aesthetic, possibilities of a non-Catholic medievalism. Ruskin, who had himself been taught by Pugin that the art of any period is the fruit of that period's conception of the good life, provided Morris with the aesthetico-social ideal which he needed. According to *Stones of Venice*, Gothic is an

[57] *Songs of a Worker*, p. 4.

[58] *Letters to His Family and Friends*, p. 185.

[59] Quoted by Mackail, *Life of William Morris*, II, 289.

[60] Though Kingsley himself would not have drawn this inference. Christian Socialism and Young Englandism shared a good deal of common ground. Witness the sympathetic treatment of young Lord Vieuxbois in *Yeast*. He wants all the right things although he relies too much on maypoles as a means of achieving them.

expression of the Protestant spirit, which in turn is an expression of "nature."[61] The medieval craftsman was a free man, enslaved neither by the machine nor by the Pope. Glorying in the imperfect, he poured forth his creative energies heedless of all stultifying absolutes, aesthetic or spiritual.

Unless we assume that Morris in his final phase retrospectively exaggerates his youthful enthusiasm for Ruskin, we shall find it difficult to understand why his medievalistic poetry should be hardly less devoid of social sympathy than of religious conviction. Yet there is much to be said for the thesis that he was always a lover of his fellows. He wanted them to share the delight which he himself found in making beautiful things. But since this communal joy in handiwork was denied by the machine-world, what more could a poet do than protect himself from ugliness by writing as "The idle singer of an empty day"? If he sang beautifully enough of a day which had *not* been empty, his work might not be completely idle after all. People might take his poems into their houses along with his chairs and chintzes, thus experiencing vicariously a little of his creative pleasure.

During his aesthetic period his only spiritual stay seems to have been a rather bleak version of the religion of humanity. Perhaps it might more accurately be described as a cult of manhood. He believed in courage, endurance, sympathy and respect for other wanderers in the dark, and in the immortality of being remembered as having possessed those virtues. In *Jason*, Orpheus sings to the sea:

> So, if thou hast a mind to slay,
> Fair prize hast thou of us to-day;
> And if thou hast a mind to save,
> Great praise and honour thou shalt have;
> But whatso thou wilt do with us,
> Our end shall not be piteous,
> Because our memories shall live
> When folk forget the way to drive
> The black keel through the heaped-up sea.[62]

This spirit was prominent in the Old Norse sagas which he began to translate and imitate in 1869. Considering the strong "Nordic" element in the theory of Gothic set forth in *Stones of Venice*, it is not altogether surprising that Morris should have returned to Ruskin by way of Iceland.[63] Under the rugged Norse influence he regains the vitality which had sunk

[61] Kingsley, to whom Morris expresses indebtedness for "some socio-political ideas," also associated Protestantism with romantic naturalism.

[62] *The Defence of Guenevere . . . and Other Poems*, p. 218.

[63] This idea, rather faintly suggested by Mackail, is fully and convincingly developed by Margaret Grennan in *William Morris, Medievalist and Revolutionary*. See especially pp. 37–45.

to so low an ebb in *The Earthly Paradise*, and with it the hope of making a society of happy craftsmen. In a letter of 1874 he praises the tale of *Burnt Njal* because "all men's children in it, as always in the best of the northern stories, [are] so venerable to each other, and so venerated." On the preceding page he tells Mrs. Howard: "Do you know, when I see a poor devil drunk and brutal I always feel, quite apart from my aesthetical perceptions, a sort of shame, as if I myself had some hand in it."[64] The man who wrote those two sentences had an excellent chance to become a Christian. But he preferred the myth of Ragnarok, the death of the gods, which would be followed by a new world to which we ourselves might contribute something. If we failed we might at least be remembered, like the heroes of the Icelandic Choir Invisible, for our courage in having tried.[65]

Sigurd the Volsung (1877) brought Morris's aesthetic period to a close. In that year he began to preach to popular audiences the Ruskinian doctrine "that art is the expression of man's pleasure in labour." In 1883, having convinced himself that a capitalistic society inevitably denied this boon to all but a few unjustly privileged individuals, he joined the Social Democratic Federation. Except for their obvious negative implications, the writings of his socialistic period are of no interest to a student of religious ideas. Only by uprooting every trace of supernaturalism could the social revolution hope to realize that ideal of brotherhood which Christianity had betrayed. All gods must be consumed in the flames of Ragnarok, leaving men to shape a better world with their own free hands. For Morris, however, that new world would rather closely resemble the Ruskinian Middle Ages, when the craftsman rejoiced in his work.

Not much need be said of the less radical humanitarianism which sporadically crops up in a few other poets of this group. We have already noted the social-gospel element in Woolner's *My Beautiful Lady*.[66] Scott's *In the Valley* describes a rural village in which Poverty is an old woman feeding crumbs to the birds, Faith the hospitality which offers "the bench beneath the trees," and Charity the local lady bountiful.

> Jesus then the white bread bears,
> And naked John the water shares
> In a white cup to everyone
> Resting from the mid-day sun.[67]

The point is that everything real in Christianity may be found in good human life. Symonds, who seems to have been reading Browning's *Paracelsus*,

[64] *Letters*, pp. 64, 65.
[65] *Mackail*, I, 343–344.
[66] See above, p. 360.
[67] *Poems*, pp. 171–172.

rebukes *Intellectual Isolation* in a sequence of seven sonnets which set "humble fellow-service" above "lonely pride."

Arthur O'Shaughnessy's final volume, *Songs of a Worker* (1881), owes its title and some of its contents to a mood induced by the death of his wife and two children within the space of six months.[68] Hitherto an unusually pure aesthete for this period, he now wants to be a "worker" in the sense of making some contribution to human welfare. I have already quoted his plea to be regarded as a servant of his fellows through the creation of beauty.[69] The humble stonecutter with whom he is talking feels no jealousy toward the sculptors who work with stone on their higher plane,

> For though the common stones are mine, and they have lofty cares,
> Their work begins where this leaves off, and mine is part of theirs.
>
> And 'tis not wholly mine or theirs I think of through the day,
> But the great eternal thing we make together, I and they;
> For in the sunset I behold a city that Man owns,
> Made fair with all their nobler toil, built of my common stones.

In another poem of this volume, *Christ Will Return*, O'Shaughnessy cries out against the Church of "the rich men and the priests" for forgetting that "Christ is very poor." He will return not to them, but to the suffering many who truly love and long for Him and to all those of every class who serve humanity:

> . . . These are of Thee,
> Pure, fearless young Reformer![70]

Even in this exceptional mood, however, O'Shaughnessy succeeds no better than his fellows in convincing us that the gospel of service lies very close to his heart.

Perhaps I have been laboring the obvious in showing that these poets are not Catholics, or unsophisticated Protestants, or confidently romantic pantheists, or (except for Morris in his post-aesthetic phase) wholehearted adherents of the religion of humanity. Why should an aesthete be any of these things, since presumably he is a worshipper of pure noninstrumental Beauty? We have observed, however, that the aestheticism of these poets is rudimentary and uncertain. Furthermore, the sort of artist who devotes

[68] But several of the poems relapse into mere artiness; and the second part of the volume, the uncompleted "Thoughts in Marble" on which he was working when he died, expresses an aggressively pagan aestheticism.

[69] See above, p. 369.

[70] *Songs of a Worker*, pp. 7–8, 11, 17.

himself to lovely images, melodies, and patterns in reaction against the Victorian appetite for " messages " is of all men the least likely to be captivated by an abstract Platonic ideal of Beauty with a capital *B*. For him, as for Keats in *Endymion*, it is more delightful that Cynthia should turn out to be the Indian Maid than that the Indian Maid should turn out to be Cynthia. What really interests him is not Beauty, but objects which for one or more inexplicable reasons he calls "beautiful." But in poetry, beautiful objects are made with words; and since outside the realm of nonsense it is difficult to use words without expressing or suggesting ideas, poetry provides more ambiguous material for a quasi-religion of "pure" Beauty than painting or sculpture, let alone music. To be sure, one of the most popular nineteenth-century concepts was that poetry is somehow religious and religion somehow poetical, but those who said so almost never meant that poetry embodies a spiritual good independent of the truths which it utters. If they were more or less tender-minded they might mean that poetry is the most pleasurable form of orthodox preachment; or a body of myth impressively though imperfectly symbolizing the *essential* message of Christianity; or a vehicle for romantic insights more inspiring than those of traditional religion, however broadly conceived; or ethically fortifying humanistic culture as a superior substitute for supernaturalism; or the sole remaining way of talking about "the things of the spirit" when one could no longer believe anything in particular. All of these attitudes imply a more didactic conception of poetry than a genuine aesthete could stomach. Tough-minded positivists thought that poetry resembles religion in being nonsense. In this idea poets could find protection from a crassly instrumental view of their art, but only at the expense of conceding that poetry was no less absurd and futile than Christianity. They were seldom willing to pay so stiff a price, for they could not bear to abandon the Shelleyan faith that their dreaming was of supreme importance for the world from which they shrank.

> We are the music makers,
> And we are the dreamers of dreams,
> Wandering by lone sea-breakers,
> And sitting by desolate streams;—
> World-losers and world-forsakers,
> On whom the pale moon gleams;
> Yet we are the movers and shakers
> Of the world for ever, it seems.[71]

They must have it both ways.

[71] O'Shaughnessy, *Poems*, p. 39.

Torn as they were between the desire to feel like romantic geniuses and the dread of being instructive, their efforts to extract some sort of spiritual sustenance from their fondness for beautiful things were not very successful. They offer, however, some interesting clinical material. W. B. Scott, who is by no means satisfied with his disbelief, still hopes that poetry will give him *Contentment in the Dark.* The old legendary illusions are not wholly lost:

> Nay, even these are ours, but only found
> By Poet in those fabulous vales, due east,
> Where grows the amaranth in charmèd ground;
> And he it was thenceforth became the Priest,
> And raised Jove's altar when the world was young;
> He too it was, in Prophet's vesture stoled,
> Spake not but sang until life's roof-tree rung,
> And we who hear him still are crowned with gold.[72]

Alfred Austin similarly holds that the poet touches man's soul through song, not through rhetoric:

> O souls perplexed by hood and cowl,
> Fain would you find a teacher;
> Consult the lark and not the owl,
> The poet, not the preacher.

He may be recalling a delightful Keats fragment when he says in another poem that the throstle's song

> . . . was sent
> Nowise to deepen argument,
> Rather to teach me how, like thee,
> To merge doubt in melody.

But despite his preference for a life of melodies rather than of thoughts, Austin continues to regard the poet as an apostle of "The deep religion of the heart." In *Poets' Corner* he grants that some of England's greatest singers led stormy and often sinful lives. "Their temple was the earth, the air," not the church.

> Creeds were to them but chains to break;
> No formulas their thirst could slake,
> No faith their hunger feed.

"Yet it was wise as well as just" to inter their bones in the Abbey,

[72] *Poems*, p. 83.

For should there come that threatened day,
When creeds shall fade, when faith decay,
And worship shall have ceased,
Then, when all formal guides shall fail,
Mankind will in the Poet hail
A prophet and a priest.

. . .

Devotion at his touch shall wake,
The fountains of emotion quake
With tenderness divine;
His melody our cravings lift
Upward, and have the saving gift
Of sacramental wine.[73]

This desire for a noninstrumentally instrumental kind of poetry is characteristic of the group. Occasionally, however, they display traces of a purer aestheticism. Reluctant to accept the Heraclitean counsel of Pater's *Conclusion*, they usually try to associate the aesthetic experience with contemplation of permanence rather than with immersion in the relativistic flux. They would like to believe that a thing of beauty is a joy forever. If poetry reminds Austin of sacramental wine, *The Line of Beauty* reminds O'Shaughnessy of the Incarnation:

What is eternal? What escapes decay?
A certain faultless, matchless, deathless line,
Curving consummate. Death, Eternity,
Add nought to it, from it take nought away;
'Twas all God's gift and all man's mastery,
God become human and man grown divine.[74]

Symonds describes "the dreamland of art's beatitude" as a "fair region of perpetual good,"[75] and for Lee-Hamilton

Beauty's forms are ever young,
Sculptured, painted, writ, or sung;

. . .

While grows old the human clay,
Never can they feel decay;
But the while the world grows older
Grow no duller, grow no colder,
And from their eternal truth
Live in a perpetual youth.[76]

But it is difficult to believe that a thing of beauty is a joy forever unless

[73] *Lyrical Poems*, pp. 45, 101, 122.
[74] *Songs of a Worker*, p. 106.
[75] *New and Old*, p. 6.
[76] *Poems and Transcripts*, p. 99.

one also believes that Beauty is Truth, Truth Beauty. The latter belief is too Platonic for these poets (as indeed it was for Keats), and for them a sacramental view of sensuous delight is equally out of the question. Having neither philosophic nor religious foundation for the worship of beauty, they must after all make the best of Pater's flux, enjoying its intensest moments with a bliss made desperate and a little morbid by their knowledge that this is a world in which beauty cannot keep her lustrous eyes.[77] Despite the passage quoted in the preceding paragraph, Lee-Hamilton himself is fully aware of this fact. There are, he says, blessed moments

> When on the road of existence, we look not ahead, but around us,
> Holding the reins with loose hand, feeling secure for a while;
> When, as we look on the world through which we too fast have hurried,
> Nothing but beauty we see—beauty serene and divine.

But these good minutes are no less transitory than rare:

> Few are the moments of respite, when thus on the weary journey,
> Man can enjoy the scene; soon do they come to an end:
> Scarce have the coursers relaxed, when, lashed by invisible spirits,
> Wildly their race they resume, bearing us helpless away.[78]

The shape of beauty which most efficaciously moves away the pall from our dark spirits is a beautiful woman. Hers is also, however, the form which is hardest to view with complete aesthetic detachment: "secondary values" *will* intrude. It is therefore not surprising that in these poets a religion of beauty tends to become a religion of love. The transition may be observed in O'Shaughnessy's *Thoughts in Marble*, the series which contains his glorification of *The Line of Beauty*. This is the group of poems on which he was engaged when death stayed the hand of the sculptor. He said of it:

> I have kept strictly within the lines assigned to the sculptor's art, an art in which I have as yet failed to perceive either morality or immorality. They are therefore essentially thoughts in marble, or poems of form, and it would therefore be unjustifiable to look in them for a sense which is not inherent in the purest Parian. I have been represented as saying with Baudelaire, "Art for Art." . . . Truly, I think that a little "Art for Art" has already [i.e., by 1880] done much good in England, and that a little more is needed, and would be equally beneficial.

Here is as pure an aestheticism as we are likely to find in this period. Immediately, however, he winces away from Baudelaire to a less decadently

[77] I do not mean to imply that these poets were influenced by Pater's *Conclusion*. A good deal of my material antedates 1873, and even when it does not I have observed no unmistakable evidence of indebtedness to him.

[78] *Poems and Transcripts*, p. 80.

romantic Frenchman: "But with Victor Hugo I do not say, 'Art for Art,' but 'Art for humanity,' and my meaning is that Art is good—is an incalculable gain to man; but art, in itself equally perfect, which grows with humanity and can assist humanity in growing—is still better."[79] When we turn to the *Thoughts* themselves we find that several of them are far from being "poems of form", since they urgently advocate Hellenic paganism in connection with the thesis that nonmoralistic art is uplifting to the spirit. The others are personal love-poems. One of them is entitled *Living Marble.* His beloved is asleep; now he may gaze his fill upon

> The wayward Venus who for days hath hid
> Her peerless, priceless beauty, and forbid,
> With impious shames and child-like airs perverse,
> My great, fond soul from worshipping the sight
> That gives religion to my day and night—
> Her shape sublime that should be none of hers.

A Priest of Beauty laments that since he must go to work in the morning he cannot behold the fair one's loveliness every minute of the day:

> How is it that some bitter envious morn
> Compels me from her—intense haloes yet
> Above her breasts, and many a joy unborn
> In places that no kissing hath made wet.[80]

Not quite the purest Parian.

Being neither Platonists nor Christians, these poets have great difficulty in spiritualizing love despite their habit of talking about it in terms of worship, God, priests, sacraments, and so on. John Payne adds a Swinburnian spice of pain and damnation to his *Chant Royal to the God of Love*:

> Lord of liesse, sovran of sorrowing,
> That in thy hand hast heaven's golden key
> And hell beneath the shadow of thy wing,
> Thou art my Lord to whom I bend the knee![81]

But we learn from one of his sonnets that, again like Swinburne, he worships not one God but two. As the sunflower yearns toward the sun,

> Even so my heart, from out these darkling days,
> Whose little light is sad for winter's breath,
> Strains upward still—with song and prayer and praise
> Ensuing ever, through the gathering haze,

[79] *Songs of a Worker*, p. viii. (Quoted by A. W. Newport Deacon in his Preface.)
[80] *Ibid.*, pp. 95, 98.
[81] *Selections*, p. 94.

Those twin suns of our darkness—Love and Death—
That rule the backward and the forward ways.[82]

The case of Philip Bourke Marston claims our sympathy. He went totally blind at the age of three; a sightless worshipper of beauty is a pathetic contradiction in terms. His one chance of marriage was destroyed by the death of his fiancée, Mary Nesbit.[83] How many of his far too numerous love-poems have to do with her I do not know; my point is simply that he suffered much. He would like to believe that to love a woman is to love God—supposing that God exists, which He probably does not. One man, he says, worships God, another Art, another Liberty. As for him, he worships only

. . . her whose life these songs commemorate.
Yet, if indeed there should be God and heaven,
By loving solely what is good and great,
All that we deem in life is loveliest,—
Is not the worship His, though unconfessed?

Elsewhere he describes himself as an apostle of *The New Religion*—"I sing the Gospel of her life." She is "my land, my Christ, my God, my love!" (One thinks of Keats's letters to Fanny Brawne.) In heaven, where "My lady sits at Beatrice's feet," no voice is heard but hers:

There is no other sound in heaven, I trow;
God and his angels bow from their high place
To hear the smallest sound which that voice says:
And they do well, indeed, to listen so.

Although such poems do not remind us very strongly of the *Paradiso*, he insists that he is preaching Dante's love-doctrine in days when most men prefer lust. The following bit of wish-fulfillment hardly supports his contention:

She thrilled with passion, till her lips
Could nothing do but kiss and cleave;
Their souls were like sea-driven ships.
He felt her swelling bosom heave;
His lips her lips with kisses flaked,
Till both lips ached.

He wrung her long sweet fingers out;
He drained the passion of her mouth;

[82] *New Poems*, the prefatory sonnet.

[83] Another severe blow was the death of his sister Cecily, who had tended him in his blindness for many years.

Her hair was all his face about,—
'O life to life! O youth to youth!
O sea of joy, whose foam is fire!
O great desire![84]

The title of this poem, which one would like to see illustrated by James Thurber, is *Before Battle.*

We have already seen that the cult of beauty and love sometimes colors the work of the medievalists. But although an aesthete might conceive of the Middle Ages as richer in beauty and love than the nineteenth century, he could hardly pretend that the architecture, sculpture, and painting of those times exemplified the doctrine of *l'art pour l'art.* A good deal of medieval imaginative literature might seem to have no palpable design upon the reader, but almost all of it was produced by men who felt free to write without moral or spiritual thesis because they had no doubts as to life's purpose. They were playing within a walled garden, and the walls were built of stones which the Victorian aesthetes rejected. To be sure Coleridge and Keats, read in the incense-laden atmosphere of exaggerated Catholic Revival ceremonialism, did much to create the impression that the garden wall was merely a lath-and-paper stage setting. Thanks to this illusion, the Middle Ages provided the favorite pleasure dome for most pre-1880 escapists. Toward the close of our period, however, several poets of this group have found a more appropriate nostalgic vehicle for aesthetic doctrine in an equally unreal and wishful conception of ancient Greece.[85] *La Belle Dame sans Merci* was a perfect Pre-Raphaelite poem, but if one wanted to learn the *meaning* of art-for-art one must turn to the opening of *Endymion* and to the *Grecian Urn.* To object that a good aesthete should steer clear of all doctrine, including his own, would be excessively logical. The aesthetes quite often preach against preachment.

Lee-Hamilton, we know, greatly prefers Greece, "beauty's noblest world," to the Middle Ages despite his responsiveness to the flavor of superstitious piety:

The Middle Ages, like a sea of lead,
Extend immense and desolate; a sea
On which the sun appears for ever set,
And through the lasting twilight we perceive
Some few wrecks of Antiquity. Look back
With me upon those times of woe, when first

[84] *Collected Poems*, pp. 25, 30, 54–55, 131, 134, 139.

[85] The same remark applies in some measure to Hellenic ideals as revived in the Italian Renaissance. I shall have little to say about this subtendency, but the reader will think of Pater and Symonds.

The bell's dull tolling marked the close of day,
And rendered sadder nightfall's saddened hour.
The thousand woodland gods of Greece were gone;
The sunlit glades were empty, which had once
With joyous beauty teemed.

He concedes that the Middle Ages, "Barren and mean and cruel as they were," produced magnificent cathedrals,

But that was when the long-retarded dawn
Already struggled with the night. For lo,
A change was coming o'er the face of earth—

the Renaissance, of course. For Lorenzo,

The long-lost world of Hellas had been found;
The Sea of Ages, in whose silent depths
Antiquity lay buried, then cast up
Its richest treasures . . .

. . .

Italian painters did what once the Greeks
Had done in marble, and created forms
Of lasting beauty. Nay the very Gods
Of Greece revived, and on the canvas stood
Disguised as saints.

For this poet, revival of the Greek spirit by no means implies the imposition of classical curbs upon the romantic drive toward boundlessness. In *Venus Unburied*, he describes the effect of an excavated statue of the goddess on those who flocked to see it:

And each man owned, as on that form he gazed,
The force of love;
And felt his soul by heavenly power raised
To spheres above.

The statue speaks to them of a time

When Gods as men in every myrtle grove
Of Hellas trod;
And man, though proud of being man, yet strove
To be a God;

. . .

When life and art were one harmonious whole
To every Greek;
And men in all things found a hidden soul,
And made it speak.[86]

[86] *Poems and Transcripts*, pp. 5–6, 106.

Not only Lee-Hamilton but O'Shaughnessy bears witness to the fact that in the nineteenth century, as in the Renaissance, these Hellenic "forms of lasting beauty" are often used as holy images in the self-worship of man. *Dialogue Between Two Venuses* is one of the latter poet's *Thoughts in Marble*. The first Venus is the sacred Greek personification of all art, she whose "perfect birth / Fulfilled the life and made the dream of man." The second is the sterilely sexless "Venus of Gibson," the Victorian sculptor. She addresses her rival in the accents of Miss Barrett:

> *I* am the pure ideal of a day
> Purer than thine. Long since man put away
> The ancient sin thou symbolest, and broke
> Love's altars, and beat down his flowery yoke;
>
> . . .
>
> A new and holier faith gave man new strength
> And Athens lies a ruin, the ancient crowned
> Passion-gods writhe as bitter serpents, bound
> In the all-quenchless hell that gave them birth.

This, retorts the ancient goddess of love, is but "the language of some Gothic lie" which has robbed man of vitality and beauty:

> For whoso looks on me is filled with faith,
> And walks exalted in a transformed earth,
> Worshipping alway, serving no mere wraith
> Of dreaming, no frail vision's doubtful birth,
> Nor leaning on the word that any saith.

Man has been deluded by "covetous priests" who

> Have spoiled his good, and poisoned all his streams.
> He dare not sit at any of the feasts
> Of life, and wholly darkened, he blasphemes
>
> The goddess giver of true holiness
> To all his days.

Something of what O'Shaughnessy means by "true holiness" may be gathered from his *Eden*. Years after their expulsion, Adam and Eve return to the garden. It has grown delightfully wild; no angel guards it. The animals, "That broke man's laws the whole day long," are free and fearless. "There seemed no rule of right and wrong, / No fruit we might not taste." They eat again of the once-forbidden apples. No God now chides them. Eden, sheltered from "every cruel wind" of the world by the untended growth of flowers and trees, has become the ideal place to make love in:

And now we need not fear to kiss;
The serpent is our playfellow,
And tempts us on from bliss to bliss,
No man can see or know.

. . .

And while we joy in Eden's state,
Outside men serve a loveless lord;
They think the angel guards the gate
With burning fiery sword!
Ah, fools! he fled an age ago,
The roses pressed upon him so,
And all the perfume from within,
And he forgot or did not know;
Eden must surely win.[87]

This pretty piece of paganism is more attractive than the same poet's *Lines to a Young Murderess*, which end with

Will you not slay me? Stab me; yea, somehow,
Deep in the heart: say some foul word to last,
And let me hate you as I love you now.
Oh, would I might but see you turn and cast
That fair false beauty that you e'en shall lose,
And fall down there and writhe about my feet,
The crooked loathly viper I shall bruise
Through all eternity:—
Nay, kiss me, Sweet![88]

This poem provides a logical transition between *Eden* and Symonds's *Valley of Vain Desires*. The latter is a ghastly region where men are compelled by some inward obsession to gorge themselves with a loathsome fruit which they detest:

How can I teach you by what fearful fate
Foredoomed, dogged downward by what pangs, enticed
By what pale cravings, lured alike by hate

And love, these guilty things, of God despised,
Of man rejected, moaning crept beneath
The treacherous tree, and fed, and cursing Christ,

Dragged the slow torture of plague-stricken breath
Onward through days or weeks or months or years
To fade at last in horror-shrouded death?[89]

[87] *Poems*, pp. 59, 60; *Songs of a Worker*, pp. 112, 115, 116, 120. [88] *Poems*, p. 50.

[89] *New and Old*, p. 235. Symonds's rather nervously apologetic note, p. 248, reads: "This is an attempt to describe by way of allegory the attraction of vice that 'fascinates and is intolerable,' with its punishment by physical extinction or madness in this life." He is known to have had homosexual tendencies.

Even without anticipating what must later be said of Swinburne in this connection, we may infer that our aesthetes value Greek statues less as purposeless shapes of beauty than as weapons against Christian asceticism in general and Victorian prudery in particular. Doubtless they would not have yearned so wistfully toward "the ancient passion-gods" had they possessed more passion of their own. But they were at least genuinely sensuous, as artists should be, to an extent which set them at loggerheads with the puritanism of their times. They did indeed constitute the "Fleshly School," though Buchanan was wrong (especially since his motives were not disinterested) in permitting himself to be shocked by them. It is a pity that neither the Catholicism nor the Protestantism of the nineteenth century was qualified to show these poets the artistic and spiritual possibilities of *Christian* sensuousness. But anxious as I am that institutional Christianity should assume its fair share of the blame for modern unbelief, I doubt whether our aesthetes would have surrendered their self-will even to the most complete and sanely balanced orthodoxy. In their feebly tenacious way they wanted to be romantics, not Christians, and perhaps because of their distaste for hazy abstractions they felt the difference more keenly than most non-Catholics of that day. Beneath their hatred of Mrs. Grundy, and rendering the hatred more noxious than that lady herself, lay a deeper enmity toward the bondage of saying "Thy will be done."

Their unbelief goes beyond what might reasonably be expected of artists rebelling against prudish disapproval of "unpleasant" subjects. Although Scott gropes wistfully toward Christianity in some of his poems, he disavows all trust in supernatural guidance in *To the Sphinx* (*Considered as the Symbol of Religious Liberty*). Having seen many myths and deities come and go, the sphinx can view such changes with relativistic detachment. The poet reproaches her, however, for withholding from men the secret which might have liberated them from vain illusions,

> ... making them turn away,
> Earthward, not starward, searching for their home
> Inward and not down beyond the tomb,
> Nor over Styx for fairer days than ours;
> For night is certain on the further shore.[90]

Symonds holds, with Feuerbach, that all gods are man-made: Moloch, Astarte, Ashtaroth, Jehovah, Jesus—

> All these, and all besides whom all men fear,
> Are the phantasmal shadowy shows of man,

[90] *Poems*, pp. 164–165.

> Flesh of our flesh, soul of our soul, made clear
> And magnified for feeble eyes to scan;
> Our gods themselves are, glorious or base,
> As the dream varies with the varying race.[91]

The evolutionary-anthropological tone of the last line is symptomatic. Philip Marston compares "the fearful bitterness of hopeless love" to "the barrenness of prayer," asking, "My God, which thing is worse, to love or pray?" He justifies a dead man's (Parnell's?) adultery by blaming it on God:

> I swear, by these blank eyes and tortured breast,
> Though I should take upon me God's worst ban,
> 'Tis God that I abjure, and not this man.

This poet's address *To James Thomson, Author of "The City of Dreadful Night"* is warmly sympathetic, and he is doubtless imitating Thomson in *Counsel*:

> Oh, all my brothers, rest a space from strife,—
> Let each one with no murmur live his life.
> Will ye make glad our tyrant's eyes and ears,
> By sound of sighs and sight of bitter tears?
> Not so; but rather spite the God on high,
> By showing him how man can live and die.

"We are, and we are not," says Marston;

> We know not life's beginning, nor life's close,—
> 'Twixt dawn and twilight shine the sunny hours
> Wherein some hands pluck thorns and some hands flowers;
> 'Twixt light and shade are shed the sudden showers;
> Yet night shall cover earth as with a pall.[92]

Lee-Hamilton, in his bold unhackneyed way, calls life "a ladder that we all must climb." But very few of us reach the top,

> And, when once there, they heave a gentle sigh,
> And, scarcely conscious, softly smile—and die.[93]

For most of his fellows, however, death is no smiling matter. Morris's *Earthly Paradise* has been aptly described as "one interminable lyric on the memory of beauty and pain, the craving for rest, and the fear of death."[94] Payne strikes a defiant pose in *A Song Before the Gates of Death* ("Suggested

[91] *New and Old*, p. 131.
[92] *Collected Poems*, pp. 29, 61, 90, 91 332.
[93] *Poems and Transcripts*, pp. 10, 11.
[94] D. N. Bush, *Mythology and the Romantic Tradition in English Poetry*, p. 322.

by Mr. Burne Jones's Picture, 'A Lament' "). "The dead are gods" because they have found surcease from life's ills.

> The fierce gods chase us to the brink with scorn;
> Yet smite the strings! We are not so forlorn
> But we may die, seeing that death is best.
> Curse we the gods and die!

(Notice, incidentally, how often these poets speak of "the gods" rather than of God.) *The Last of the Gods*, says Payne in another poem, is Death:

> Lo! of all Gods that men have knelt unto,—
> Of all the dread Immortals fierce and fair,
> That men have painted on the vault of blue,—
> There is but one remains, of all that were.
> DEATH hath put on their crowns; and to him sue
> Mortals and Gods in parity of prayer.[95]

So far as our conduct in this life is concerned, the inference is that we should crowd into our trivial span of years the maximum amount of pleasurable sensation. As Marston puts it:

> A little time for laughter,
> A little time to sing,
> A little time to kiss and cling,
> And no more kissing after.[96]

Although the aesthetes were often reproached for their evasion of contemporary issues, we are not surprised to learn that in the seventies the aggressively secularistic *Fortnightly Review* "endorsed the excellence of the later romanticists . . . feeling that their 'paganism' was in harmony with the advanced spirit of the age."[97] Their hedonism, however, seems to have been singularly unfruitful of joy.

In *At Delphi,* Alfred Austin gives a peculiar arty twist to the eighteenth-century "progress piece" type. He cannot find Apollo amidst the ruins of his temple.[98] His search for the poet-god is hindered by a Greek Orthodox priest who stands for gloom and pain and fear, not for "light and poesy." Out in the sunshine, Austin begins to feel better:

> What if all the gods be dead?
> Nature reigneth in their stead.

[95] *Miles*, VII, 48 ; *New Poems*, p. 189.
[96] *Collected Poems*, p. 174.
[97] E. M. Everett, *The Party of Humanity: the Fortnightly Review and Its Contributors*, p. 249.
[98] Apparently Austin was on the very spot, for he dates the poem "Delphi, April 1881."

But the priest, who has followed him, manages to spoil even his enjoyment of nature. Just as he is about to conclude that poetry is indeed dead, he hears the voice of the god reassuring him:

> Though the Muses may have left
> Tempe's glen and Delphi's cleft,
> Wanderer! they have only gone
> Hence to murmuring Albion.
> Need was none to travel hither:
> Child of England, go back thither.
>
> . . .
>
> Back, and in thy native land
> Thou wilt find what thou dost seek.
> There the oracles still speak;
> There the mounting fumes inspire
> Glowing brain and living lyre.
> There the Muses prompt the strain,
> There they renovate my reign;
> There thou wilt not call in vain,
> "Apollo, Apollo, Apollo!"[99]

At least as far as the poets of this chapter are concerned, Austin's patriotic claims are ludicrous. Let us grant that the Aesthetic Movement conferred real benefit upon English literature by emphasizing aspects of the art of poetry which the Victorian age had too much neglected. Taking the group as a whole, it may at least be said that most of them know what poetry is and frequently try to write it. Compared with the groups discussed in previous omnibus chapters the desire to write versified lectures is somewhat weaker and the desire to make pleasing artifacts somewhat stronger. William Morris is a genuine poet though usually a tiresome one. O'Shaughnessy would be an accomplished lyricist if he had any idea of when to stop. But how utterly dead they are, even the best of them! Today who reads them for pleasure? What scholar studies them for purposes other than clinical?

It is not easy to say where the trouble lies. Despite their artiness, their work is seldom "pure" enough in George Moore's sense to illustrate the fact that when poetry tries to be *perfectly* pure it dies of its own dear loveliness. Their avoidance (by no means complete) of contemporary scenes and problems is not in itself culpable: the poet, as Matthew Arnold had been saying, claims the privilege of projecting his imagination into any period. Arnold might justly complain, however, that the aesthetes' cultivation of the past provided no fruitful criticism of the present. For the malady which

[99] *Lyrical Poems*, pp. 211, 213–214.

afflicts these poets is essentially a malady of the spirit. They do not steadily and firmly believe in *anything*—God, man, nature, beauty, love, or technique. They do not even believe in their own unbelief. They glorify pattern because their inner lives are formless. They have no center: the inconsistencies which pervade this chapter are theirs, not mine. Although they dislike overt didacticism more than most of their contemporaries, they cannot bear to abandon the romantic identification of poetry with prophecy. But they have nothing to prophesy *about*.

Their romanticism, when not merely decorative and nostalgic, voices the impossibility of being romantic in the modern world. It points toward the boundlessness of nihilism, not of creative self-assertion; the interfusion of man-made chaos, not of man-made cosmos.[100] They like to account for their disenchantment by complaining that there are no longer any "gods." Payne writes:

> No gods have we to turn to, new or older;
> The blue of heaven knows their thrones no more:
>
> . . .
>
> And lo! if any set his heart to singing,
> Thinking to witch the world with love and light,
> Strains of old memories set the stern chords ringing,
> The morning answers with the songs of night.
> For who shall sing of pleasance and delight,
> When all the sadness of the world is clinging
> About his heart-strings and each breeze is bringing
> Its burden of despairing and despite?[101]

Symonds, like Arnold, feels himself standing between two worlds, and so on:

> . . . Undone
> Is all the fabric of that former dream;
> Those songs we have unlearned, and, one by one,
> Have tossed illusions down the shoreless stream;
> Tearless and passionless we greet the sun,
> And with cold eyes gaze on a garish gleam.

Happy, he says in another poem, were the martyrs who died fighting wild beasts in the arena;

> But we who strike at shadows, we who fight
> With yielding darkness and with thin night-air,

[100] Schopenhauer did not count for much in England before 1880, but we are told that Payne was much impressed by him. (Lucy Robinson's Introduction to *Selections*, p. xv.) The spirit of Schopenhauer's pessimistically romantic aestheticism, if not its direct influence, is at work in other poets of this set.

[101] *Selections*, p. 43.

Who shed no blood, who see no hideous sight,
For whom no heaven is opened—our despair
And utter desolation infinite
Can not find calm nor comfort anywhere.[102]

But even their despair is flaccid and unreal, since they retain no tincture of belief in the "gods" whose passing they lament and whose return would greatly embarrass them. In the last analysis nothing remains for them but the trivial satisfaction of posing as the idle singers of an empty day, born out of their due time, too sensitive and peculiar to distill beauty from the ugly devaluated world in which they live. O'Shaughnessy feels utterly different from "the common folk I walk among." He inhabits a private spirit-realm, singing songs only to himself:

Do I not feel—ah, quite alone
With all the secret of my heart?

But his heart contains no secret other than that of its emptiness, and this he will not confront. He does not wish to scorn what stupid folk esteem,

Nor mock the things they hold divine;
But, when I kneel before the shrine
Of some base deity of theirs,
I pray all inwardly to mine,
And send my soul up with my prayers.[103]

Up to where? Up to what? As we know, he prays to nothing whatever. Payne admits his spiritual bankruptcy so much more frankly that the following stanzas may serve as the conclusion of this chapter:

Why are our songs like the moan of the main,
When the wild winds buffet it to and fro,
(Our brothers ask us again and again)
A weary burden of hopes laid low?
Have birds left singing and flowers to blow?
Is life cast down from its fair estate?
This I answer them—nothing mo'—
Songs and singers are out of date.

What shall we sing of? Our hearts are fain,
Our bosoms burn with a sterile glow,
Shall we sing of the sordid strife for gain,
For shameful honour, for wealth and woe,
Hunger and luxury,—weeds that throw
Up from one seeding their flowers of hate?

[102] *New and Old*, pp. 128, 129.

[103] *Poems*, p. 9.

Can we tune our lutes to these themes? Ah, no!
Songs and singers are out of date.

. . .

Winter holds us, body and brain:
Ice is over our being's flow;
Song is a flower that will droop and wane;
If it have no heaven toward which to grow.
Faith and beauty are dead, I trow;
Nothing is left but fear and fate:
Men are weary of hope; and so
Songs and singers are out of date.[104]

"Sterile glow" leaves nothing more to be said.

[104] *Selections*, pp. 190, 191.

Chapter Thirteen

DANTE GABRIEL ROSSETTI

ROSSETTI is almost certainly a better poet than Morris, and beyond doubt immensely superior to the eight other writers whom we have just been examining. Granting that poetry of completely noninstrumental form is inconceivable, he is also as nearly a pure aesthete as one can hope to find. This statement is supported, not denied, by the fact that he never tried to evolve a theory or form a school: he was too busy writing poems and painting pictures. He influenced his fellows as a vivid personality at work among words and pigments, not as a conscious leader. To a greater extent than they he sundered himself from the Ruskinian gospel of the morality of art; but unlike Whistler, he would not have troubled to fight Ruskin even if that prophetic bore had been a less profitable source of commissions. Nor did Rossetti deliberately use his poems for even the inferential preachment of a counter-gospel of aesthetic antinomianism. Today, except for those whose sensitiveness to the odor of decay is a little decadent, his fleshliness is cloying but not corrupt. His work, furthermore, seldom exhibits the stagy postures which irritate us in most other aesthetes—the nervous scorn of this ugly, mechanical, prudish age, the pretense of identifying impotence with distinction, the morbidly savored despair, the studio chatter *about* being an artist. These are perhaps symptoms of a craving to be more romantic than the doctrine of *l'art pour l'art* in itself can justify. Rossetti, on the contrary, successfully fabricated a good deal of legitimate romance because he was usually contented with the greatly restricted romantic satisfaction which could be obtained from concentrating on his two crafts.

What primarily concerned him was the application of technical skill to the production of various effects which interested him at various moments. In *The Raven*, Poe has done a splendid job with the feelings of the lover on earth; Rossetti will try his hand at the feelings of the beloved in heaven. *The Woodspurge*, that remarkable rendering of the blankness of exhausted sorrow, was suggested by a picture in a botany textbook. *My Sister's Sleep* is not related to any actual experience: it is a technical study in suspense, brittle silence, brittle cold, and different kinds of light. "Christ's blessing on the newly born!" is a touch of emotional color, not essentially more meaningful than the firelight picked up by the mirror in the corner. Submitting the exhumed volume of manuscript poems for Allingham's criticism, Rossetti says: "I never meant, I believe, to print the Hymn (which was written merely to see if I could do Wesley, and copied, I believe, to enrage my friends) nor the Duke of Wellington."[1] The experiment in doing Wesley was to remain unpublished, but we have *Wellington's Funeral*:

> Gabriel,
> Since the sound of thine "All hail!"
> Out of heaven no time hath brought
> Gift with fuller blessing fraught
> Than the peace which this man wrought
> Passing well.
>
> Be no word
> Raised of bloodshed Christ-abhorr'd.
> Say: "'Twas thus in His decrees
> Who Himself, the Prince of Peace,
> Sent a sword."

We also have *Vox Ecclesiæ, Vox Christi*, which satirizes the Christian habit of using the "not peace, but a sword" text to sanctify militarism. Probably the latter poem is more sincere than the former, but we cannot be sure.

It is not easy to get at the thought of a man who might have said, with the Keats whom he so warmly admired, "Not one word I ever utter can be taken as an opinion growing out of my identical nature. How can it, when I have no nature?"[2] But in dealing with an artist whose mind is "constantly informing and filling some other body," something may be learned about him from noticing what sort of body he customarily chooses to inform and fill. We must make what we can of that resource with such help as may be provided by the unsatisfying letters and the considerable mass of reminiscence and anecdote which has been assembled and interpreted by the biographers.

Allingham reports conversations with Rossetti which took place in 1867: "We talk of Home and other 'Spiritualists,' about whom D.G.R. has at the least a curiosity. . . . We talk of 'immortality,' but nothing new, and of 'suicide,' which R. thinks 'silly.' There are traces of superstition in him,

[1] *Letters to William Allingham*, pp. 244–245.

[2] Rossetti's surviving letters, furthermore, are meager and superficial compared to Keats's. He often destroyed correspondence and private papers, censored his brother's *Præraphaelite Diaries*, and left orders—too faithfully carried out—that the family should destroy various important documents and letters after his death. (Oswald Doughty, *Dante Gabriel Rossetti*, p. 8.)

none of religion."[3] This judgment is not contradicted by William Michael Rossetti's description of his brother as "superstitious in grain, and anti-scientific to the marrow . . . with the naturalism characteristic of Italian blood."[4] A superstitious fleshly unbeliever is not a contradiction in terms: Byron is a prime example of the compound. Rossetti's father, minus most of the fleshliness, is another. Although old Gabriele often called himself a Catholic he was, on mystico-political grounds, a violent opponent of the papacy. From the *Divine Comedy* he gathered that Dante was a member of a secret masonic sect whose only God was the free Man.[5] As one discovery led to another, the sect expanded to include St. Paul, St. John, the Cabbalistic writers, the Brahmins, Swedenborg, Petrarch (Laura was a masonic lodge), Boccaccio, Chaucer, Erasmus, Milton, Bunyan, Tom Moore (because of *The Epicurean*), and Victor Hugo. Such heroes he revered, probably under Comtian influence, as the saints of a religion of liberated humanity. At times, staggered by his own revelations, Gabriele retreated to what he conceived to be a more conventional position. In one such mood he composed a psaltery, *Iddio e l'Uomo*, only to see it placed on the Index: what he regarded as purest Catholic piety the Church condemned as rank man-worship.[6] He was a romantic who could believe, on what he supposed to be severely rational grounds, in practically anything but Christianity.

Such traits are not passed down through the chromosomes, but they may be potent factors in a child's early environment. In boyhood Dante Gabriel had before him an influential model of superstitious rationalism. As a poet, he would be able to exploit black magic in *Sister Helen* and *Rose Mary* with an enthusiastic, not merely a willing, suspension of disbelief, but without any sense of commitment to the Church which threatened practitioners of such magic with damnation. On the other hand he would always be both too superstitious and too genuinely sceptical to feel perfectly sure that damnation was nonsense. Meanwhile his mother, as a ritualist, may have encouraged in him an aesthetic conception of Christianity—a religion which, as his father was demonstrating, might mean whatever he chose.

[3] *Diary*, pp. 160, 162. As regards the first topic, William Michael Rossetti says that his brother derided Spiritualism in the 1850's but that "In later years (beginning, say, in 1864) he believed in it not a little." (*Letters to Allingham*, p. 204).

[4] Preface to *Collected Works of D.G.R.*, p. xxi. As a rationalist, William was perhaps not an impeccable judge of the difference between superstition and religion, but it is noteworthy that he never uses the former term in connection with Christina.

[5] One may conjecture that he had accepted quite seriously, and had interpreted in a favorable light, the nonsense about the "Illuminati" with which European Catholics were scaring themselves, more or less sincerely, during his boyhood.

[6] Oswald Doughty, *Dante Gabriel Rossetti*, pp. 34–46, *passim*, 141.

She was also a puritan, however, and under that aspect she may have planted in him an uneasy feeling that his sensuousness must be elevated and redeemed by some sort of supersensuous ideal.

From the ferment of his boyhood home young Rossetti moved into the aesthetic ferment which produced the P.R.B. The opposition between his view of Pre-Raphaelitism and Hunt's was at first not apparent even to the protagonists. Mr. Doughty is probably right as to Rossetti's initial motives: "For Gabriel, at least, the chief incentive was the excitement of an attack upon the Academicians . . . and the assertion of his own individuality."[7] But it was not immediately clear to him what direction the attack should take, what sort of individuality he should assert. He found himself among a group of young artists who by no means confined their discussions to painting. In an earnestly confused atmosphere which, despite its tinge of studio Bohemianism, suggests that of the Apostles Club, they talked also of literature, politics, and religion. "We had not yet," Hunt recalls, "balanced our belief in Voltaire, Gibbon, Byron, and Shelley. . . . Our determination to respect no authority which stood in the way of fresh research in art seemed to compel us to try what the result would be in questions metaphysical, denying all that could not be proved"—the familiar young-Shelley blend of romanticism and positivism. Sometimes, however, they felt that they could easily believe in God were it not for the Church: "In sober moments we had agreed that orthodox religionists made such claims to entrammel judgment, conscience, and will, that they drove thinking men to the extreme alternative of throwing away all faith in divine over-rule."[8]

Rossetti was not so inhuman as to be blankly indifferent to religious questions. Less than five years had elapsed since he had "enormously relished" Bailey's *Festus,* reading it "again and yet again;"[9] and even now Keats had not yet effaced his admiration for Shelley.[10] Hunt indicates the cleavage in Rossetti's religious feelings and the way in which it was to be reconciled: "The fact that so many modern poets had been defiant, captivated him with revolt, while the precedent of the older artists in song and

[7] *Ibid.*, p .67

[8] W. Holman Hunt, *Pre-Raphaelitism and the Pre-Raphaelite Brotherhood*, I, 110, 116.

[9] W. M. Rossetti, Preface to *Collected Works*, p. xxvi.

[10] Keats himself was not "blankly indifferent" to such questions, but Victorian aesthetes interpreted him wholly in the light of *l'art pour l'art.* We may add here that Rossetti always retained an unexpected capacity for admiring "meaningful" poetry which departed widely from the ideals of the Aesthetic Movement. Browning is the most striking example; others are Hake, Horne, C. J. Wells, James Thomson, Ebenezer Jones. He disliked, on the other hand, the extremer, more decadently Frenchified manifestations of *l'art pour l'art.* He was very English as well as very Italian.

design encouraged the ecclesiastical strain of work he favoured; supremacy of genius alone taxed his loyalty, and perfection in Art was synonymous in his mind with the amplest Wisdom."[11] This analysis, otherwise most helpful, telescopes two stages in Rossetti's early development. For a short time he seems to have defined "Wisdom" and "supremacy of genius" in a more broadly romantic sense than would make them quite synonymous with a strictly aesthetic view of "perfection in Art." In this brief phase he was willing, or almost willing, to worship creative genius as displayed by heroes in any field of accomplishment.

In this spirit he drew up a "manifesto" to which, says Hunt, "some of us" formally subscribed. The preamble reads: "We, the undersigned, declare that the following list of Immortals constitutes the whole of our Creed, and that there exists no other Immortality than what is contained in their names and in the names of their contemporaries in whom this list is reflected."[12] The Immortals are grouped in hierarchical levels by a system of stars. Pious readers will be glad to learn that four stars are the unique distinction of Jesus Christ.[13] Three stars: "The Author of Job" and Shakespeare. Two stars: Homer, Dante, Chaucer, Leonardo da Vinci, Goethe, Keats, Shelley, Alfred, Landor, Thackeray, Washington, Browning. One star: Fra Angelico, Boccaccio, Mrs. Browning, Patmore, Raphael, Longfellow, Tennyson. No stars in their crown: a miscellany of worthies, among them "Early Gothic Architects," "Early English Balladists," Byron, Wordsworth, Haydon, Milton, Cromwell, Hampden, Bacon, Newton, Poe, Hood, Emerson, Leigh Hunt, Columbus.[14]

The manifesto owes much to a Comtian conception of divinity and immortality, but no doubt the impact of Carlyle's hero-doctrine should also be recognized. Old Gabriele, too, would have been glad to include most of these great men in his crypto-masonic sect along with Dante and Boccaccio. The list itself is richly instructive. Although the arty bias is already dominant, we should observe the less aesthetically romantic element (Shelley, Wordsworth), the tinge of Ruskinism (Early Gothic Architects), the political liberalism (Washington, Hampden), and the positivisitic respect for science (Bacon, Newton). Noteworthy also is the lack of discrimination and of sense of humor in such clusters as "Fra Angelico, Boccaccio, Mrs. Browning," and "Bacon, Newton, Poe." We know what came of all this. "The older artists in song and design" triumphed over the moderns and the

[11] *Op. cit.*, I, 117. [12] These incoherent words mean that the list is illustrative, not exhaustive.

[13] But not because Rossetti believed Him to be God. This is obviously the religion-of-humanity Christ.

[14] Hunt, *op. cit.*, I, 111.

"ecclesiastical strain" over "secularistic revolt," while "supremacy of genius" narrowed to a more restricted and hence more attainably romantic ideal of "perfection in Art." These changes followed the grain of the man's nature; to ask precisely what caused them would be a waste of time.

As regards "the ecclesiastical strain," two facts must be juxtaposed and if possible reconciled. In the first place, despite a good deal of obvious fakery, Rossetti at his best is remarkably successful in creating an illusion not merely of Catholic surfaces but of Catholic feeling. Secondly, we know that he was never a Catholic or, for that matter, a Christian of any sort. To a large extent the anomaly has already been explained in the preceding chapter: a more accomplished artist than the other aesthetic medievalists, he often did more successfully what they were trying to do. Then too—a different though a related point—the sensuous and superstitious Rossetti was precisely the sort of man most liable to be captivated by the ceremonialism which had done so much to obscure the distinction between religious and merely aesthetic worship. In *Hand and Soul,* young Chiaro discovers "that much of the reverence which he had mistaken for faith, had been no more than the worship of beauty." Doughty applies these words to Rossetti himself and associates them with a recollection of the painter William Raymond, who, "when a boy, often saw Rossetti with Millais at the ornate musical services at St. Andrew's Church, Wells Street, then [about 1850–52] famous for its music and 'high' ritual."[15] But a letter which Rossetti wrote at Boulogne in 1849 suggests neither much reverence nor much ritualistic lore: "The evening before last I walked about the principal church of the town during Mass or Vespers or whatever they call it."[16] Perhaps, however, he is merely affecting ignorance as the easiest way of expressing contempt.

At all events, technical dexterity, half-superstitious romantic nostalgia, and the sensuous appeal of ceremonialism will suffice for that delightful fake, *The Blessed Damozel.* But we cannot so easily dismiss the apparently authentic religious quality of poems like *Ave,* or the sonnet on *St. Luke and the Painter,* "Who first taught Art to fold her hands and pray," or *World's Worth*:

> He stood within the mystery
> Girding God's blessed Eucharist;
> The organ and the chant had ceas'd.
> The last words paus'd against his ear
> Said from the altar: drawn round him
> The gathering rest was dumb and dim,

[15] *Op. cit.*, p. 135.

[16] Quoted by Graham Hough, *The Last Romantics*, p. 48*n*.

And now the sacring-bell rang clear
And ceased; and all was awe,—the breath
Of God in man that warranteth
The inmost, utmost things of faith.
He said: "O God, my world in Thee!"

Such lines suggest a warmer imaginative sympathy with the subject than is consistent with complete aesthetic detachment. I am half inclined, indeed, to say that Rossetti was sometimes visited by twinges of genuine Catholic belief. But this I cannot prove, and quite possibly the moments in which he nearly convinces us of his sincerity are those in which his art has most successfully deceived us. It is safest to stick to one's foreground impression of him as a craftsman trying for effects. Safest, but not wholly satisfactory, for one cannot feel sure either way. "Rossetti," I said in the preceding chapter, "thought of *Ecce Ancilla Domini* as 'the blessed white daub'—a teasing technical problem." Without rejecting this interpretation of his words, may we also make some allowance for the craftsman's reluctance to talk to fellow-artists about his work in other than technical language, although his feelings about the subject may be strong?

"The Bible," says William, "was deeply impressive to him, perhaps above all Job, Ecclesiastes, and the Apocalypse."[17] "The Author of Job," we recall, is triple-starred with Shakespeare in the hero-worshipping manifesto. In all stages of his career the poems show that he was deeply saturated in the language of the Scriptures. Not merely the title but some passages in the text of *The Burden of Nineveh* attest his familiarity with that very minor prophet, Nahum. Biblical allusions turn up even in the letters, as when he writes of hot weather at Hastings, "I wandered over the baked cliffs, seeking rest and finding none."[18] In 1852 he tells Hunt that he "had quite recently read the whole [New] Testament from the first word to the last"—but why?—"in the hope of finding some hitherto untreated circumstance for painting."[19] An artist's familiarity with the Scriptures implies nothing as to his religious beliefs: Swinburne knew his Bible even better than Rossetti.

A Last Confession does nothing to relieve our bewilderment. A dying Italian is making what appears to be a sacramental confession; but this is one of those self-expressive romantic confessions, in the tradition of *Lara*, where the priest is on hand to be shocked rather than to give absolution. The speaker has been a political liberal of the type which in Italy is always secularistic. His story is a grim "slice of life" with contrasting glints of

[17] Preface of *Collected Works*, p. xxv. William is speaking of his brother's early reading, but the statement is not inapplicable to Gabriel's maturity.

[18] *Letters to Allingham*, p. 22. See Matthew xii: 43.

[19] Hunt, *op. cit.*, I, 222.

idealism—rather like Mérimée's *Carmen* set to a Browning dramatic monologue. He adopted a little orphan girl and fell in love with her as she grew up. She was unworthy of his devotion. When he spoke his love she laughed at him precisely like the whore whom he had heard laughing at a street-fair; so he stabbed her with the knife he had planned to give her as a present. But, he tells the priest, he heard women's laughter of a different sort last night, when

> I dreamed I saw into the garden of God,
> Where women walked whose painted images
> I have seen with candles round them in the church.
> They bent this way and that, one to another,
> Playing: and over the long golden hair
> Of each there floated like a ring of fire
> Which when she stooped stooped with her, and when she rose
> Rose with her. Then a breeze flew in among them,
>
> . . .
>
> . . . and beneath that gust
> The rings of light quivered like forest leaves.

Although this decoration is excellent in its Italianate kind, any sufficiently gifted atheist might have fabricated it. But the penitent continues:

> Then all the blessed maidens who were there
> Stood up together, as it were a voice
> That called them; and they threw their tresses back,
> And smote their palms, and all laughed up at once,
> For the strong heavenly joy they had in them
> To hear God bless the world.

The lines are still very arty, but if they had not been written by Rossetti one would unhesitatingly describe them as *religious* art. Yet the supposed penitent ends his supposed confession by disclaiming all desire for absolution. He threatens his spiritual director:

> . . . If you mistake my words
> And so absolve me, Father, the great sin
> Is yours, not mine: mark this: your soul shall burn
> With mine for it.

He does not repent of his sin, and having told his story he whirls away to hell in a burst of melodramatic rant, "the strong heavenly joy" not only forgotten but spurned. This one poem combines the naturalism of late-nineteenth-century fiction, pseudo-ritualistic sensuous word-painting, apparently genuine religious feeling, and complete spiritual tone-deafness. Where, amidst these incompatibles, is the man himself?

Leaving this puzzle precisely where we found it, let us briefly consider Rossetti's dealings with a more esoteric sort of religion—the ostensibly Dantesque love-mysticism which appears in *The House of Life* and several other poems.[20] On this theme he speaks, if not unmistakably in his own person, at least without obvious dramatic disguise; he may tentatively be credited with a sincere attempt to mean what he says. The principal ideas are familiar enough. For him, the cult of beauty becomes a cult of love even more quickly and inevitably than for the poets of the preceding chapter. Fundamentally this love is a man's desire to possess the body of a beautiful woman, but Rossetti does his best to spiritualize it. He represents Love as the supreme value, including but also transcending "all kindred Powers the heart holds fair." It is a spirit, not a personality, but it may be addressed and worshipped as a god. (Whether Love is stronger than Death or Death stronger than Love is a question the answer to which depends on the mood of the moment: contrast sonnets XLI and XLVIII.) Love is made manifest in the physical beauty of woman, but our delight in that beauty is a means, not an end: the final purpose of love with a small letter is to draw our souls up toward Love with a capital letter. The upward pull is most strongly exerted after the beloved has died, but even while she is living we may anticipate it in some measure. To do him justice, Rossetti does not identify these ideas with Christianity. He thinks, however, that they represent the personal religion of Dante.

But in his own fashion he falsified Dante no less radically than his father had done. Of all the ways of trying to feel religious about human love, the most difficult for a man like Rossetti to understand and duplicate would be Dante's delicately balanced combination of personal sexuality, Platonized courtly love, and erotic mystical symbolism, all held within the framework of Christian theology. Despite his self-will[21] and his Bohemian eccentricities, Rossetti was not at all a bad fellow. Hake remembered him as "the noblest of men," with "a heart so good that I have never known a better, seldom its

[20] Critics have a way of speaking of *The House of Life* as if it were devoted wholly to the love-cult; but many of the sonnets, especially but not exclusively in Part II, have nothing to do with it. It is merely the principal theme of a work for which the most ingenious generalizer could hardly frame a topic sentence. In 1881 Rossetti brought together and published, under this title, a large number of sonnets which he had written sporadically all the way from 1848, "or even a year or so preceding," to a date shortly before publication. (William Michael Rossetti's note, *Collected Works*, I, 517.)

[21] "I never do anything I don't like," he said when reproached for being late to dinner. (Allingham, *Diary*, p. 161.)

equal. Illness changed him, but then he was no longer himself."[22] Nevertheless, when we think of his relations with women we are not strongly reminded of Dante and Beatrice. In *The House of Life* the beloved is sometimes Elizabeth Siddal and sometimes Jane Burden Morris. He married poor Guggums only when she had convinced him, at long last, that he could possess her Pre-Raphaelite body in no other way. Her death may have been suicidal; at all events he had some reason to think so, and to blame himself for the tragedy. Jane, a less "Early Christian" type of beauty, was the wife of his close friend. The woman with whom he was happiest was Fanny Cornforth—too frankly vulgar and sensual to be associated with the love that moves the sun and the other stars. I am not challenging Rossetti's right to use his imagination, but in the best poetry a man's imagination bears some relation to his life.

A remarkable passage in *Jenny* seems to be an outcropping of genuine emotional experience:

> Like a toad within a stone
> Seated while Time crumbles on;
> Which sits there since the earth was curs'd
> For Man's transgression at the first;
> . . .
> Which always—whitherso the stone
> Be flung—sits there, deaf, blind, alone;—
> Aye, and shall not be driven out
> Till that which shuts him round about
> Break at the very Master's stroke,
> And the dust thereof vanish as smoke:—
> And the seed of man vanish as dust:—
> Even so within the world is Lust.

This he actually knew, but in *The House of Life* he tries to forget the toad in order to say what a really high-minded love-poet and translator of *La Vita Nuova* should say about Love. No hypocrisy was involved: he uttered all these noble sentiments out of a guilty feeling of obligation to idealize his passions. It has been suggested that his sense of guilt was a symptom of the neurosis which at last became psychosis; that his mother gave him a streak of hysterical puritanism which conflicted with his sensuousness; that his grasp of reality was so deficient that he never outgrew an adolescent habit of erotic daydreaming. Without disputing any of these plausible explanations, one might also consider the possibility that he felt sinful because he knew that he *was* sinful; and that, having no notion of how to cope with his knowledge

[22] Thomas Gordon Hake, *Memoirs of Eighty Years*, p. 215.

religiously, he tried to sublimate it aesthetically by borrowing Dante's love-doctrine.

The attempt is a failure because he does not know what *intelletto d'amore* means. In *Dante at Verona* he says of the exiled poet:

> Each hour, as then the Vision pass'd,
> He heard the utter harmony
> Of the nine trembling spheres, till she
> Bowed her eyes towards him in the last,
> So that all ended with her eyes,
> Hell, Purgatory, Paradise.

In the *Paradiso* there is a great deal of talk about Beatrice's eyes, but they are in no sense the culmination of his journey: it is always perfectly clear that they are mirrors reflecting downward to him the light of the Divine Sun. But for Rossetti, as we see in Sonnet III of *The House of Life*, the relations between Dante and the dead Beatrice were like those between the lovers in *The Blessed Damozel*:

> O what from thee the grace, to me the prize,
> And what to Love the glory, when the whole
> Of the deep stair thou tread'st to the dim shoal
> And weary water of the place of sighs,
> And there dost work deliverance, as thine eyes
> Draw up my prisoned spirit to thy soul!

In short, Rossetti cannot see the difference between loving God and loving a woman. *Heart's Hope*, Sonnet V of *The House of Life*, substitutes a romantic muddle of flesh and spirit for Dante's Christian view of their symbolic and sacramental balance in harmonized tension:

> For lo! in some poor rhythmic period,
> Lady, I fain would tell how evermore
> Thy soul I knew not from thy body, nor
> Thee from myself, neither our love from God.

In Dante's thought, natural and supernatural are real, different, and related; Rossetti sunders them and then confuses an empirical conception of nature with a supernatural in which he has no belief at all.

The uneasy pose suggested by "lo," "lady," "fain," and "rhythmic period" warns us not to take Rossetti too seriously. So far as his artistic intentions are concerned, poems like *Sister Helen* are perhaps not very much more "impersonal" than the love-sonnets. In the former he is trying to sound like an old English ballad-maker; in the latter, he is trying to sound like a Florentine courtly poet. But in the love-poetry the mask does not sufficiently conceal the human face, and the two are incongruous. Thanks to his model, he achieves an elevation of manner which the poets of the preceding chapter usually miss when they write of love. But the rhythmic periods are hollow and unconvincing. The man's real sensuality is only enfeebled and falsified, not genuinely spiritualized, by the aesthetic figment of love-mysticism.

There is little or no evidence that Rossetti thought of writing poems and painting pictures as inherently religious activities. The early prose tale *Hand and Soul,* to be sure, embodies what Professor Hough has described as a creed of "fidelity to one's own inner experience, which is to be followed even if it contradicts formal morality. . . . This fidelity to experience is all that God demands of the artist, it is as acceptable to him as a formal religious faith, and an art carried on in this spirit is itself a worship and service of God."[23] Here is the aesthete's version of the religious subjectivism which has figured so largely in earlier chapters. This poet did not probe his mind very deeply or resolutely, but if his "own inner experience" be taken to mean his own conception of art, we may say that he was usually loyal to this sort of Inner Light throughout his career. The idea that the artist worships and serves God by creating works of art is, however, a youthful German-romantic, "Nazarene" notion which he seems not to have retained. Under pressure he might say, "My art is my religion," but he would have meant that he enjoyed being an artist so much that he felt no need of religion.

Yet there were moments when he acknowledged that words and colors were not enough. A fragment preserved by his brother reads:

> Would God I knew there was a God to thank
> When thanks rise in me!

Imbedded in the alien texture of *The House of Life* are several indications that he has thought of God not only in thankful but in remorseful moments. How, he wonders, would "the last days of my life" look if he could see their faces today?

> I do not see them here; but after death
>   God knows I know the faces I shall see,
> Each one a murdered self, with low last breath:
>   "I am thyself,—what hast thou done to me?"

[23] Graham Hough, *The Last Romantics*, p. 53.

Such passages raise a hypothetical question which might otherwise hardly seem worth asking. If Rossetti had more often chosen to use art as a way of grappling with life rather than as a way of insulating himself from it, what religious opinions would he probably have expressed?

The socio-political liberalism implicit in the early catalogue of heroes did not disappear from his thought so completely as is usually supposed. *A Last Confession* shows some sympathy with the *risorgimento,* and *On Refusal of Aid Between Nations* "refers," as his brother says, "to the apathy with which other countries witnessed the national struggles of Italy and Hungary against Austria."[24] As regards humanitarian sympathies, *Jenny* is more truly social-minded than the readers who were shocked by its "unpleasant" subject.

> And must I mock you to the last,
> Ashamed of my own shame,—aghast
> Because some thoughts not born amiss
> Rose at a poor fair face like this?
> Well, of such thoughts so much I know:
> In my life, as in hers, they show,
> By a far gleam which I may near,
> A dark path I can strive to clear.
>
> Only one kiss. Good-bye, my dear.

The Burden of Nineveh is serious criticism of a mechanized and soulless English society "That walked not in Christ's lowly ways." The story of *The White Ship*, narrated by a medieval butcher's son, includes an element of religious democracy:

> "O I am Godefrey de l'Aigle hight,
> And son I am to a belted knight."
>
> "And I am Berold the butcher's son
> Who slays the beasts in Rouen town."
>
> Then cried we upon God's name, as we
> Did drift on the bitter winter sea.
>
> And the hours passed; till the noble's son
> Sighed, "God be thy help! my strength's foredone!"
>
> "O farewell, friend, for I can no more!"
> "Christ take thee!" I moaned; and his life was o'er.

In the nineteenth century, democracy, secularism, and religious liberalism had been thrown into incongruous but potent alliance by the united forces

[24] *Collected Works*, I, 519.

of political oppression, social callousness, and ecclesiastical obscurantism. The son of an Italian radical would be especially disinclined to identify "Christ's lowly ways" with traditional Christianity. In the mid-sixties, the secularist Moncure D. Conway found the spiritual temper of the aesthetic set entirely congenial. At times Rossetti believed no more than his aggressively unbelieving brother, though his own unbelief was too sensuous and sentimental to be described as "rationalism":

> Let no priest tell you of any home
> Unseen above the sky's blue dome.
> To have played in childhood by the sea,
> Or to have been young in Italy,
> Or anywhere in the sun or rain,
> To have loved and been beloved again,
> Is nearer Heaven than he can come.

But this stanza was omitted when *Soothsay* was first published in 1881, and the following lines are more representative of the poem in its final state:

> Let lore of all Theology
> Be to thy soul what it *can* be:
> But know,—the Power that fashions man
> Measured not out thy little span
> For thee to take the meting-rod
> In turn, and so approve on God
> Thy science of Theonymy.

Here outright denial gives place to the subjectivist preference for believing in God without thinking about Him.

Rossetti was in fact too sensitive to beauty, too sceptical, too superstitious, and perhaps even a little too religious to be a thoroughly convinced unbeliever. Usually he felt more comfortable in an atmosphere of noncommittal theism, open at one end toward complete negation and at the other toward the very broadest Broad Churchmanship. His dislike of talking about such matters does not wholly conceal the familiar symptoms. In 1865 he told Smetham that he respected Christian beliefs but was unable to share them. Hall Caine, the friend of his last years, inferred that Rossetti rejected Christianity with scorn. "Yet he always professed 'faith in God,' . . . although beyond that, even towards the vaguest definition of his meaning, he could not go."[25]

[25] Doughty, *Dante Gabriel Rossetti*, pp. 575, 653. Such statements make it unwise to attach much importance to the fact that Rossetti, in his final breakdown, expressed "some inclination to consult a Roman Catholic priest." Nothing came of the fleeting hysterical notion. (Christina Rossetti, *Family Letters*, p. 102.)

But this undefined God could be addressed in apparently heartfelt prayer:

O Lord of work and peace! O Lord of life!
O Lord, the awful Lord of will! though late,
Even yet renew this soul with duteous breath;
That when the peace is garnered in from strife,
The work retrieved, the will regenerate,
This soul may see thy face, O Lord of death!

Heaven's peace, then, is to be attained through *work*—the application of a "regenerate" will to the performance of duty. Perhaps he is thinking merely of his work as an artist, but it seems to me that the lines imply a more "muscular," a more Carlylean or Kingsleyan, obligation to be up and doing. Sonnets LXXI, LXXII, and LXXIII of *The House of Life* constitute *The Choice*. How is one to live in view of the fact that "to-morrow thou shalt die"? Both the hedonism of "Eat thou and drink" and the asceticism of "Watch thou and fear" are rejected in favor of "Think thou and act." If we live in accordance with this spirit, which hardly seems to be that of the Aesthetic Movement, perhaps we shall not die tomorrow after all. Gaze out upon the expanse of ocean,

And though thy soul sail leagues and leagues beyond,—
Still, leagues beyond those leagues, there is more sea.

The symbol suggests the hope that self-expansion through thought and action may continue even beyond the grave.

Despite Rossetti's expressed desire to behold the face of the Lord of death, he always doubted and sometimes denied the doctrine of personal immortality. He was unwilling to go beyond the position expressed in *The Cloud Confines* —that after death the soul will be more or less Platonically reabsorbed into the cosmic reservoir of spirit from which it originally came. Of course it is all an inscrutable mystery, but

Still we say as we go,—
"Strange to think by the way,
Whatever there is to know,
That shall we know one day."

The hollow cheerfulness of this refrain reminds us of Clough, almost the last poet with whom we should usually dream of comparing Rossetti.

In short, if the aesthetic mask is removed we behold the face of a wavering but not altogether unhopeful humanitarian theist. By this stage of our investigation the type has become somewhat wearisome. Let us quickly replace the mask and pass on.

Chapter Fourteen

FRUSTRATED ROMANTICISM

THE TITLE of this chapter is by no means peculiarly applicable to the poets whom we are to consider in the remainder of this volume: the phrase and the predicament for which it stands have already appeared more than once. In their relatively specialized way, the aesthetes display awareness of the futility of the romantic aspiration. All romantics, indeed, are inevitably frustrated, since they demand more than life will grant. But up to the point where their position becomes intolerable they display great ingenuity in evading acknowledgment of defeat. We have often been impressed by the resourcefulness with which poets of this period draw sustenance for illusion even from trends which would seem to be essentially hostile to their desires. Even in the first eight chapters, however, we have also observed many signs of lassitude and despair. It is already clear to us that the age presented formidable obstacles to free, full, confident expression of the romantic impulse. Throughout the Victorian period romanticism exerts immense power, but it achieves that power only by entering into a compromise—on the one hand with Christianity and on the other hand with positivism—which forbids complete fulfillment of its aims.

But although the writers to be examined henceforward say much that we have heard before, they present on the one hand unusually severe cases of frustration, while on the other hand they resist definite assignment to any of the categories thus far established. It is more than a mere coincidence that they are all poets of considerable historical importance and literary merit: they have the insight to perceive that they are living in a sick world and the honesty to say so. They are indifferent or scornful toward old-fashioned Protestantism, they detest Catholicism, and they refuse to dupe themselves by romanticizing Christianity.[1] Several of them are related to the Aesthetic Movement, but none can be called an aesthete without so many reservations that the label would be misleading. They might be described as "Seekers," though hardly as "Seers," in a state of somewhat deeper and more chronic

[1] On the last point the Arnold of *New Poems* and Clough in his *New Sinai* vein are partial exceptions.

desperation than most poets of Chapter VII. But they vary so markedly in personal idiosyncrasy and in the cause and degree of their frustration that we had better deal with each of them as an individual problem. Five relatively minor poets will receive brief treatment in this chapter; the four special chapters which follow will discuss four major figures somewhat more intensively.

Emily Brontë (1818–1848) and her sisters were thwarted not by bewildering and painful experience of the nineteenth-century "march of mind" but by personal circumstances which withheld such experience from them. The expansive forces in their situation were intense imaginative vitality, avid curiosity about the whole of life, sexual longing, and desire for complete self-development as human beings. The restrictive forces were the Victorian conception of womanhood, lack of male society except that of stupid curates, poverty, schoolroom drudgery, the flinty drabness of Haworth, the nerve-racking restrictions of a remote country parsonage ruled over by an embittered man whose problematical beliefs had little or no effect upon his spirit. Solution of their predicament in actual living seemed to be impossible. For Charlotte the Brussels sojourn shook the wall a little, but the result was M. Emmanuel, not a husband. All they could do, in the last analysis, was to write, setting their imaginations to work upon their dammed-up feelings, upon the wild moors, and upon such scraps of enlarging experience as came their way. Never quite sure as to whether they would find more relief in a faithful report of their actual situation or in the luxury of wish-fulfillment, they usually attempted to combine both solutions in a single work. Branwell's way of escaping from Haworth is no business of ours.

So far as concerns their conscious motives, the sisters wrote not to provide data for amateur psychologists but to obtain a larger, freer life through fame and money. In this enterprise they relied much more upon recent and contemporary poetry and fiction than upon any religious tradition. It is interesting, however, to note the inverse ratio between the strength of their romantic impulse and their attitude toward Christianity. Anne, never much tempted to smash through the wall which surrounded her, was a mildly faithful Evangelical. Charlotte, in whose mind Jane Austen and Mrs. Radcliffe contended for mastery, was a Broad Churchwoman.[2] Emily, so pure a romantic that she reminded Matthew Arnold of Byron, cared nothing about Christianity, broad or narrow. No coward soul was hers. In those famous valedictory lines she spurns all creeds as "unutterably vain."

[2] A little broader in England, to be sure, than in popish Europe.

Emily was not merely a romantic person but a romantic poet. Although her best poem is *Wuthering Heights*, even her verse is often valuable for other than the diagnostic purposes to which we must confine ourselves. Those purposes are not seriously obstructed by doubts as to whether the poems represent her feelings or the feelings of the inhabitants of Gondal.[3] That realm was a part of her own being, and except when the situation is obviously dramatic or pseudo-historical we may safely ascribe to her the sentiments of the speaker.

"Liberty," Charlotte remembers, "was the breath of Emily's nostrils; without it, she perished."[4] Emily tells us so herself:

> And if I pray, the only prayer
> That moves my lips for me
> Is—"Leave the heart that now I bear
> And give me liberty."
>
> Yes, as my swift days near their goal
> 'Tis all that I implore—
> Through life and death, a chainless soul
> With courage to endure![5]

"Just leave my character alone," she says in substance, "but remove all hindrances to its expansion." She likes symbols which suggest a favorable answer to this prayer—the boundless moor, the boundless sky, the boundless ocean. Questioned by an adult, a child answers that to her the past is like an autumn leaf and the present like

> A green and flowery spray
> Where a young bird sits gathering its power
> To mount and fly away.

But better still, the future is like

> A sea beneath a cloudless sun;
> A mighty, glorious, dazzling sea
> Stretching into infinity.[6]

Emily refuses to rely on anything but a principle of goodness and strength which she finds within her own breast. Her feelings of power are corroborated and even heightened by the wild moors, but they are not created or controlled by any force external to herself:

[3] As regards the latter possibility see *Complete Poems*, pp. 4, 14.

[4] *Complete Works of Charlotte Brontë and Her Sisters*, IV, 338.

[5] *Complete Poems*, p. 163. Compare the prefatory sonnet of Byron's *Prisoner of Chillon*: "Eternal Spirit of the chainless mind, / Brightest in dungeons, Liberty! thou art."

[6] *Ibid.*, p. 30.

I'd walk where my own nature would be leading:
It vexes me to choose another guide.

. . .

What have these lonely mountains worth revealing?
More glory and more grief than I can tell:
The earth that wakes *one* human heart to feeling
Can centre both the worlds of Heaven and Hell.[7]

The function of the mountains is to provide a symbolic focus for the otherwise undefinable emotions of glory and grief which are the only Heaven and Hell she can believe in. Even if these lines were actually written by Charlotte,[8] their faithfulness to Emily's thought is attested by *No Coward Soul Is Mine.*

But Emily was too intelligent to be taken in by her own Byronism. She knew very well that her soul was not "chainless," and that the chains were not merely external:

'Twas grief indeed to think mankind
All hollow, servile, insincere;
But worse to trust to my own mind
And find the same corruption there.

Like the Byronic hero who impressed her imagination so deeply, she derives a certain morbid satisfaction, but no solution, from brooding over the chasm between aspiration and reality:

No promised Heaven, these wild Desires
Could all or half fulfil;
No threatened Hell, with quenchless fires,
Subdue this quenchless will!

O let me die, that power and will
Their cruel strife may close,
And vanquished Good, illustrious Ill
Be lost in one repose.[9]

These lines have reminded me of Byron, but in writing the last stanza she may have remembered Shelley's *Triumph of Life*:

[7] *Ibid.*, p. 256.

[8] The poem cited, the *Stanzas* beginning "Often rebuked, yet always back returning," was published by Charlotte among Emily's remains in 1850; but it is the only one of the eighteen poems thus published for which no manuscript source has been discovered. Mr. Hatfield suggests, *ibid.*, p. 255, that it was written by Charlotte under the guise of a self-portrait of Emily. I agree that parts of the poem are a little too slick for Emily, but the stanza about the mountains does not sound at all like Charlotte. It seems more probable that Charlotte has revised here and there the diction but not the thought of a lost manuscript by Emily.

[9] *Complete Poems*, pp. 36, 220.

And much I grieved to think how power and will
In opposition move our mortal day,
And why God made irreconcilable
Good and the means of good.[10]

But although Emily's poems talk *about* the glory and despair of being consumed by "quenchless fires," they provide nothing tangible for the flames to feed upon. Those who wish to see frustrated romanticism gnashing its teeth in a powerfully imagined world of people, actions, and places must turn to her prose masterpiece. The book was written in what she means by "Hell," but so well written that it must almost have given her the satisfactions of what she means by "Heaven."

Ebenezer Jones (1820–1860) also had quenchless fires.

He sat upon a stile apart,
The world's convulsion in his heart;
But in his fix'd space-searching eye,
Conquest—far off, eternally.

This is merely a scrap of unpublished boyhood verse preserved by his brother, but the same passion appears in his best poem, *The Waits*:

And I had heard the ungovernable sea
  Earth's quietness loud scorn;
I had mark'd afar his raging radiancy,
And proudly, in his pride, had felt that he
  And I were twain god-born.[11]

There are not many poets whose desire to be as ungovernable as the ocean has dashed itself against solider obstacles.

According to his brother Sumner, Jones's parents were prosperous but very rigid dissenting Calvinists. Except for Watts and Henry Kirke White, their children were permitted to read hardly anything but the Bible, tracts, and "books of over-wrought 'spiritual' experience and hysterical evangelicalism." Shakespeare and even Milton were forbidden. Byron was darkly mentioned as "a Satanic spirit. . . . Of Shelley we had never heard." Nothing is said in Sumner's Memoir of formal schooling, but Jones's poems are those of a man who has been educated much too little and a little too much. When the father went bankrupt because of illness, the ministers and other pious souls who had been dining very well at the Joneses' turned "to other quarters where high Calvinism would still be solidly supported by Consols."[12]

[10] Shelley's uncompleted poem was first published in 1824.
[11] *Studies of Sensation and Event*, pp. xxxviii, 11.
[12] Sumner Jones's Memoir, *ibid.*, pp. xxviii–xxxvi *passim*.

"Now was the veritable awakening of my brother's mind!" There was no spiritual conflict: he simply felt intuitively that everything he had been taught was wrong. (We may interject that Jones, even in his social-protest verse, almost never attacks Christianity but writes as if no such religion had ever existed.) He greatly admired Carlyle, but it was Shelley who taught him to think of poetry as

> Rapt adoration which no priestly scoffer
> Of thee and thy dear love may hope to know.

Under this influence "Poetry and religion became one with him." At seventeen he found clerical work in the City, loathed it, and took up political radicalism.[13] He was twenty-three when he published his one volume of verse, *Studies of Sensation and Event*, in 1843. It won him the private praise of several good judges[14] but had so bad a press that he left unfinished a sequel, which was to have been entitled *Studies of Resemblance and Consent*, and spent the rest of his short life as an unsuccessful radical journalist. He was very unhappily married. The Memoir explains that the numerous love-poems pertain not to his wife but to "one who was lost to him by change and estrangement, and who not long after was claimed by death." Sumner Jones says nothing about a physical disaster, but in the frontispiece of R. H. Shepherd's 1879 edition of *Studies of Sensation and Event* the poor fellow has no right hand. He died of tuberculosis at the age of forty. The gravestone was inscribed: "To live in hearts we leave behind is not to die."[15]

It is astonishing that a man so handicapped should have been described by Rossetti as "this remarkable poet, who affords nearly the most striking instance of neglected genius in our modern school of poetry," and whose poems "are full of vivid disorderly power."[16] Rossetti was fond of reporting such discoveries with warm-hearted extravagance. Jones is clumsy, immature, very uneven and lacking in self-criticism, sometimes flat and sometimes overambitious in a way that makes one think of the Spasmodics. But he has plenty of vivid disorderly power, and he has his own way of saying things. Although he writes few if any really good poems, one frequently feels that he should have been a poet.

[13] He agreed in general with the Chartist program but did not work directly for that cause. His "line" was republicanism and a sort of agrarian socialism. His fairly numerous poems of social indignation are shrill, vague, and trite. One doubts whether his radicalism was rooted in anything much deeper than personal misery.

[14] "Barry Cornwall," Horne, W. J. Fox, and Milnes. Rossetti, another admirer, did not meet Jones until several years later. Browning also thought well of Jones, but I find no record that he told him so.

[15] Memoir, *op. cit.*, pp. xix, xxi, xxv, xxxvi–lxi *passim.*

[16] D. G. Rossetti, *Collected Works*, I, 478.

He is trying to do something impossible: namely, to reconcile sensationalistic psychology with the romantic conception of creative genius. Wordsworth and Coleridge had made a similar attempt at an early stage in their careers; but Jones found a more congenial precedent in Shelley, to whose memory the *Studies* are dedicated "not so much in reverence for his perfection in art as in love of the infinite goodness of his nature, in which, partly for its celestial beauty and partly because it was human, it has often been given me to rejoice with joy unspeakable and full of glory." But probably Jones had other reasons for admiring the great romantic. He was in much the same state of mind as the Shelley of *Queen Mab*. Valuing above all else the untrammeled exercise of voluntary mental power, he has espoused a philosophy which denies the very existence of that power. On the one hand he believes that

> Man has no station; he must upward soar
> Towards bright-wing'd deities, or sink down towards fiends;
> Man cannot pause.—
> Go! bid the sun to rot within its heavens!
>
> . . .
>
> Deracinate the fruitful earth of growth!
> Though infinite space grow dark, the soul of man
> Shall soar triumphantly.[17]

On the other hand he has chosen to live in a world in which such beliefs are absurd. Doubtless the Christian Church herself is largely to blame for the fact that so many nineteenth-century lovers of freedom were willing to think of themselves as automata rather than submit to the yoke of "kingcraft and priestcraft." Following the established pattern, Jones has become an infidel, a republican, and a mechanical determinist. He finds, as usual, that the philosophy which he has seized upon as a weapon against Christianity turns in his hand and threatens his own romantic heart.

One fine day in the country he felt unaccountably indifferent to the beauty of the scene. It did not matter that the skies were blue and the birds were singing:

> The unity in the boundlessness of life
> Gave me no thrill.

Why did he shake off this mood after meeting a dog and petting it into rapture?

> Is it that man is all too great, to rest
> The passive slave of any heaven or earth,

[17] *Studies*, p. 167.

> Of Nature's shows and forces? Of a God,
> Hath man the causative destiny and essence?
> Must he fulfil such destiny, or find pain?
> And rose within my being this trembling gloom
> From passiveness continued? Did it pass
> While I was making glad the village cur,
> Because I commenced to influence?

Good men, he adds, use their power-craving for good ends, and bad men for bad ends, "But to influence both require."[18] Yet the wish to feel divinely causative is rebuked by the title *Studies of Sensation and Event*—in other words, studies in the necessitated mechanism of sensory stimulation and associative response. Precisely to the extent that his postulates have released him from slavery to heaven, they have forced him to acknowledge the absolute dominion of earth over every movement of his body and every thought of his mind.

In *Queen Mab* Shelley, like Wordsworth and Coleridge before him, is preparing to abandon the attempt to be a romantic mechanist; he has begun his retreat to the stronghold of transcendentalism. There are a few faint indications that Jones wanted to follow the same course, but he lacked the intellectual equipment which it demanded. Ordinarily he can only try to feel big by putting himself in the way of big sensations, forgetting that according to his own views our choice of stimuli is no less completely determined than the consequences of the choice. Despite his unfortunate marriage he thinks of love as a valuable way of awakening ourselves to "a wild sweet bliss." This mode of expansion he advocates not only in *A Plea for Love of the Individual* but in its companion-piece, *A Plea for Love of the Universe.* In the latter poem he urges:

> Love magnifies existence; love the world,—
> Thy soul shall grow world-great in its sensation;
> And 'neath the blaze of infinite life unfurl'd,
> Pant with the passion of a whole creation,
> Oh love then! love![19]

Love the universe to obtain the illusion of personal infinitude.

The recipient of this advice is a "minstrel." Jones would like to believe that although all sensations are produced mechanically the poet experiences them in a peculiar way. He tells how a little boy, rambling in the woods, is agitated by a feeling of awe exactly like that which moved him not long

[18] *Ibid.*, pp. 90, 91.

[19] *Studies*, pp. 147, 149.

before when he received "the high priest's blessing."[20] It is not that the blessing of the woods *reminds* him of the ecclesiastical blessing: the two experiences present themselves simultaneously to his imagination, equally present and equally vivid, "For both one essence possess'd." Jones explains:

> The essence of mind's being is the stream of thought;
> Difference of mind's being is difference of the stream;
> Within this single difference may be brought
> The countless differences that are or seem.
>
> Now thoughts associate in the common mind
> By outside semblance or from general wont;
> But in the mind of genius, swift as wind,
> All similarly influencing thoughts confront.

This exceptional boy, then, will be a poet,

> ... one of that band,
> Who, telling the sameness of far-parted things,
> Plants through the universe, with magician's hand,
> A clue which makes us following universe-kings.

It makes us not only gods but brothers. The normal associative process mingles similarities, which bring men together, and differences, which keep them apart. But the poet beholds only "fraternal essences," and beholds them all at once.

> Yea, at his glance, sin's palaces may fall,
> Men rise, and all their demon gods disown;
> For knowledge of hidden resemblances is all
> Needed to link mankind in happiness round Love's throne.[21]

Jones appropriately placed this untitled poem last among the *Studies of Sensation and Event*, for it set forth the theme which he had planned to illustrate in *Studies of Resemblance and Consent*. Of this uncompleted sequel we have only eight poems, published in 1879 by R. H. Shepherd in his edition of the 1843 volume. They do not, as a matter of fact, say anything very different from the less pessimistic of the poems issued in his lifetime, and they do not say it so well. If he had taken his scheme of classification seriously the second volume would imply that the first had not been poetry at all. But probably he merely wanted to publish more poems and made a new title from one of the ideas which he had already expressed.

[20] Presumably at Confirmation? Since Jones was bred a Dissenter the poem is not, as might otherwise be supposed, a personal reminiscence.

[21] *Studies*, pp. 179, 180–181.

In less sanguine moments—and they are many—he drops the notion of uniting mankind through metaphor and conceives of the poet (i.e. himself) as *The Naked Thinker*. Old Lord Aspwern dies, having discovered that the world is one mass of falsehood. In his will he specifies that for part of each day his heir shall sit stark naked in a perfectly bare room of the castle and write,

> Fiercely to rend life's meanings and
> Drag out the things that are.

The successor to the title obeys these instructions:

> Lord Aspwern's eyes are lightnings keen,
> So keen his world is not
> The world by other mortals seen,
> His thought is not their thought:
> Lord Aspwern glows with glorious pride,
> That lifts beyond earth's creeds,
> Its thoughts and laws beneath him tide,
> Hour storms he calmly reads;—
> But ever in courts, in marts, in farms,
> Whether we joy or moan,
> Yea, even in the lovingest lady's arms,
> Lord Aspwern is alone.

If one cannot achieve through poetry the delight of being a benevolent universe-king, this magnificently disenchanted poetic loneliness provides a way of satisfying romantic pride within the "fierce and mean" world described in *The Waits*,

> Where love loud rages, seeing throned the wrong
> That all his hope destroys;
> Where poetry pales, despairing, and for song
> Raves, till her utterance, erst so sweet and strong,
> Sinks to mere maniac noise.
>
> Where even science hath fall'n, with terrible dread
> Palsied his strenuous limbs,
> Dashing the diadem from his anguish'd head,
> And howling atheist howlings.[22]

To protest against scientific atheism seems inconsistent in so loyal a positivist; but by "atheist" Jones probably means denial of the potential divinity of man. In *Ways of Regard*, one of the 1843 poems, he tries to convince himself that sensationalistic determinism does not, after all, deprive

[22] *Ibid.*, pp. 8, 10, 15.

us of all spiritual reliance. The thought of this long and labored poem is at last summed up in an allegorical vision which owes much to *The Revolt of Islam.* Two young lovers, though members of the ruling caste, affirm that "Man has no station" and lead an uprising of slaves. The rebels, convening in a cave, seethe with high-minded indignation and love of the species. All their sensations are intense, noble, and shared. From their lips, consequently,

> ... stream'd high to the empyrean
> Radiance of powers unhuman. In a moment,
> Above all lower firmaments, and above
> All clouds and winds, it soar'd. Immortal calm
> Received its glory. To the immortal calm
> The unhuman powers rush'd ...
>
> . . .
>
> ... They circled round and round;
> Now sweeping vast and rapture-breathing curves,
> Now floating tremulously with happiness,
> Now solemnly moving in elated thought
> Of their own grandeur.

"Unhuman" is characteristically clumsy and misleading. Jones means that these powers, being products of the best collective feeling, transcend the sensations of any individual human being. Hence they become what men used to think of as gods. Having ascended into the empyrean, they enjoy the "high prerogative / Of blissful contemplation," which by no means excludes "elated thoughts / Of their own grandeur." But unlike the gods of Lucretius, they are not selfish or indifferent, for they derive their life from the life of man and what they contemplate is that life. "Rejoice, companions!" they sing to one another;

> ... Even now
> The race of man is culminating! Now,
> Big is the earth with the superior creatures
> Waiting to displace man. Their glorious slaughters,
> Their frenzied passions, their quick-ended lives,
> Await our gaze ...
>
> . . .
>
> All things beneath us change, and still we take
> From every change fresh joy. Beneath us roll
> Differently all things; everything us yields
> Joy differently. Sweep, sweep on, companions!
> And glory in our delight. Eternally
> All things intensify; and we must ever
> Intenselier contemplate, intenselier joy.[23]

[23] *Ibid.*, pp. 166, 170, 171.

Progress is infinite diversification and intensification of collective altruistic human feeling. This ferment of ascending change is a law of the universe. If we choose to call it "God" we need not think of ourselves as atheists.

Sixteen years later, to judge from *I Believe*,[24] both Jones's despair and his hope have taken on a Platonic tinge which seems inconsistent with his original sensationalism. Perhaps he is trying to move onward from the earlier to the later thought of Shelley. Man, he says, is doomed to endless discontent because the soul can "expand to / Fit delight" only in the presence of a perfection which does not exist in the world of appearances.

> And seems it then, while each fruit thou [the soul] pursuest
> Turns to dust,
> That, spite of all thy pride in thy pursuing,
> 'Twere more just
> That thou hadst never been into dead-sea apples
> Thus out-thrust.

Nevertheless "Endurance knows celestial consolations / Past belief," and one of the unbelievables which we must not relinquish is faith in necessitated progress:

> Dissatisfaction accident is of Earth,
> Not Earth's plan;
> Years come when even its name shall be a riddle
> None may scan;
> Perchance even now his plumes outspreads the hour that
> Ends the ban.

Then let the earth roll on, while maids continue to enchant us and painters to "exalt us Nature."

> Nor shake thou mockingly thy dart, oh Death;
> Know, oh king!
> We have made friends with Melancholy, and she
> Thee will bring
> Gently among us, yea to teach new music
> Them that sing.
>
> There is a heaven, though we to hope to pass there
> May not dare;
> Where adoration shall forever adore some
> Perfect fair;
> And we can wait thee, Death, our eyes enfixed
> Firmly there.[25]

[24] First published in *The Reasoner* for May 15, 1859, and reprinted by Shepherd in 1879

[25] *Studies*, pp. 195–199 *passim.*

Intellectual coherence is not the outstanding quality of this poem. Remembering, however, that Jones was to die a year later, we should at least admire the pluck of this confused and desperate man.

William Johnson (1823–1892), who later assumed the name of Cory, was shy, eccentric, sickly, bookish, weak-voiced, myopic almost to blindness, a latent homosexual, and a person of aspiring mind. He wanted to be a leader in patriotic action, a statesman, a sailor, an athlete, a rider to hounds. Some adjustment between his equipment and his dreams was obviously necessary. If he could not be a Wellington or a Nelson he could, as a master at Eton, form the characters of beautiful young English gentlemen. If he could not be an oarsman, he could write

> Swing, swing together,
> With your bodies between your knees.

Even in the less occasional poems of *Ionica* he could derive a modified sort of romantic satisfaction from interfusing the spirit of the Greek Anthology with the spirit of the playing-field. The results are often very pleasing, and not only to wearers of the old school tie.

This compromise, however, fell far short of satisfying the needs of Johnson's spirit. On seaside vacations the ocean breaks through the wall which he has built around his disquietude. Standing *On Livermore Sands*, he is distressed by nature's "wanton game." "The meteors into darkness haste," and so do we.

> Lo! myriad germs at random float,
> Fall on no fostering home, and die
> Back to mere fragments; every mote
> Was framed for life as thou, as I.

Scientists may rejoice in this spectacle, but not poets,

> Since that which yearns towards minds of men,
> Which flashes down from brain to lip,
> Finds but cold truth in mammoth den,
> With spores and stars, no fellowship.
>
> Say we, that our ungarnered thought
> Drifts on the stream of all men's fate,
> Our travail is a thing of nought,
> Only because mankind is great.[26]

[26] *Ionica*, pp. 123–124.

"Man's unhappiness comes of his greatness"—one would not have thought of associating this poet with Carlyle.

Pounding on *Clovelly Beach*, "the chainless sea" penetrates a deeper level of consciousness and brings to the surface a fragment of the past. He remembers how he felt when, long years ago, someone sang an old song in his grandfather's parlor:

> Then my cold childhood woke to strange desire.
>
> That was an unconfessed and idle spell,
> A drop of dew that on a blossom fell;
> And what it wrought I cannot surely tell.
>
> . . .
>
> Oh, had I dwelt with music since that night!
> What life but that is life, what other flight
> Escapes the plaguing doubts of wrong and right!
>
> Oh, music! once I felt the touch of thee,
> Once when this soul was as the chainless sea,
> Oh, couldst thou bid me even now be free![27]

These lines combine two sorts of chainlessness: that of Shelley's *West Wind*, "tameless, and swift, and proud," and that of mere escape from "plaguing doubts of wrong and right." Though he studied history and political economy with wistful enthusiasm he disliked argument on such subjects: when he pictured himself as a statesman he was thinking of leadership, not of debate. It was for a different reason that he shrank from the contemporary Babel of overconfident assertion and denial about matters of "wrong and right." As regards ethical and spiritual problems his mind was torn between deep scepticism and deep craving for certitude. Not unlike Matthew Arnold he needed, but could not find in the noisy eighteen-sixties, an area of peace and quiet within which to feel romantic. Hence as he stands on Clovelly Beach he does not know whether he wants the freedom of unhindered Titanism or the freedom of unhindered flight.

His conception of music as release from propositions suggests that he might have followed the way of the aesthetes, but he was too much of a thinker for that. In the more seriously Hellenic portions of *Ionica*, with their delicate blend of Epicureanism and Stoicism, he is groping toward a *modus vivendi* more appropriate to the life of a humanistic teacher and scholar. To

[27] *Ibid.*, p. 130. But apparently he associated music with spiritual expansion even in maturity, for he says in a letter, "Generally if I speak of music I should dwell on its being the Epthatha [Be opened] for all. The violin in particular is to me a symbol of infinity." (Quoted by Faith C. Mackenzie, *William Cory*, p. 60.)

a considerable extent it enables him to feel himself into a serene yet by no means impassive culture; to be impersonally personal and to pass critical judgment upon the present while seeming to ignore it; to cool his thwarted desire for self-expansion in an academically reputable tradition of regretful but unrebellious disenchantment, and thus to derive a bitter sort of sweetness from the inevitability of limitation. For most Greeks, however, humanistic pride was shadowed by dread of the total extinction of man's energies in death. This is a theme not infrequently treated in *Ionica*, and it is precisely here that Johnson's last alley of escape runs into a stone wall. Unlike the poets of the Anthology, he had to take account of the Christian hope of everlasting life: to write as if he had never heard of it would have been a psychological impossibility.

Although he feared death perhaps even more than most men—"Half my time I meditate the ceremony of dying"[28]—he was unable or unwilling to accept the faith which might have relieved this dread. He was not a man who could be deeply religious on a merely subrational basis, and he could not have fought his way to reasoned conviction without opening his ears to the controversial racket about *Origin of Species* and *Essays and Reviews*. Here I speak of the type of religious sensibility revealed in the poems. In daily life he seems to have maintained, as a sceptic and an English gentleman, a conventionally pragmatic loyalty to the external observances of the Establishment. From a liberal but not a destructively radical point of view he gave his Eton students the facts about theology and Church history which future leaders of the nation should know as a part of their heritage. Yet there is no evidence that he had a positive faith and a good deal of evidence to the contrary.

In what is probably his most effective poem he speaks not simply as the Greek Epicurean but as *Mimnermus in Church*, explicitly rejecting Christian consolation in favor of this knowable earthly life, which gains sweetness from its brevity.

> You promise heavens free from strife,
>   Pure truth, and perfect change of will;
> But sweet, sweet is this human life,
>   So sweet, I fain would breathe it still;
> Your chilly stars I can forgo—
> This warm kind world is all I know.
>
> . . .

[28] Quoted by Mackenzie, *William Cory*, p. 2. He said of a pet songbird: "He is happy. He does not know that he will die." (*Ibid.*, p. 136.)

Forsooth the present we must give
To that which cannot pass away;
All beauteous things for which we live
By laws of space and time decay.
But oh, the very reason why
I clasp them, is because they die.[29]

As a bewildered Victorian, however, Johnson was unwillingly drawn toward another Greek theme—the tragic conception of life as a vain struggle in the clutches of inscrutable doom. Mimnermus is refuted by *Phaedra's Nurse*—a free translation from the *Hippolytus* by a man who has read the Pauline epistles, *Hamlet*, and Wordsworth's *Immortality*:

The life men live is a weary coil,
There is no rest from woe or toil,
And if there's aught elsewhere more dear
Than drawing breath as we do here,
That darkness holds
In black inextricable folds.

Lovesick it seems are we
Of this, whate'er it be,
That gleams upon the earth;
Because that second birth,
That other life no man hath tried,
What lies below
No god will show,
And we to whom the truth's denied
Drift upon idle fables to and fro.[30]

From the modern strife of tongues Johnson withdrew to the serenely naturalistic Greeks only to find himself confronted by the very problems he had sought to evade.

In yet another respect Hellenism betrayed him. For many years it enabled him to feel quite harmlessly "Greek" toward a few favorite students. But at the close of the spring vacation of 1872 he did not return to Eton. He had written "an indiscreet letter" to a youth whose father had shown it to the headmaster, Dr. Hornby.[31] Whether Hornby, who had always disliked him, forced him to resign under threat of expulsion, or whether he resigned voluntarily in indignation at a "friendly" warning, is not known. There is no reason to suppose that even in this instance his homosexuality went beyond a very cloying pedagogic sentimentality. Everything was hushed up until

[29] *Ionica*, pp. 5–6. [30] *Ibid.*, p. 137. [31] H. S. Salt, *Memories of Bygone Eton*, p. 119.

long after his death, and his friends were able to persuade themselves that the eccentric William Johnson had simply decided overnight to retire from teaching because he was weary of it. The fact that he had recently inherited some money lent credibility to this explanation.

A few months later he changed his name to Cory without acquiring a new personality. For the remaining twenty years he lived with harmless and usually cheerful futility on his modest but sufficient income. At the age of fifty-five he was masterfully wooed and won by a woman in her twenties who had always wanted to marry a clever elderly man. They had a son, and apparently got along well enough. He taught Latin and Greek, *gratis,* to groups of young ladies; wrote some poems which were added to the 1877 and 1891 editions of *Ionica*;[32] published an unsuccessful two-volume *Guide to Modern English History*; died of consumption.

Of course it is not my fault, but I am sorry that several of the poets who flourish within the last two decades of our period are sexually peculiar. Remembering poor Dolben, I do not insist that they would have been normal if they had been Christians. The same example suggests, however, that control and sublimation of misdirected emotions are at least facilitated by belief in some suprapersonal reality. Like Johnson-Cory, Edward FitzGerald (1809–1883) was a latent homosexual. The fact would be no more than a tenable hypothesis had not the abnormality come rather close to the surface in his old age, when he too obviously fell in love with the coarse hard-drinking fisherman Joseph Fletcher. But even to readers who have no knowledge of this circumstance and who refuse to make unsavory guesses in the absence of tangible evidence, it must be obvious that this marvelously gifted man shrouded his personality and his art in a thick veil of repression. Almost certainly he himself did not know the reason: these matters are arranged by the inward censor.

On the rare and trivial occasions when he writes verse in his own person he says nothing useful for our purposes. Of the numerous translations which constitute almost the whole body of his work, only one is sufficiently a part of the history of English literature to deserve attention here. And of course the great version of the *Rubáiyát,* though extremely free, is not an original poem in the same sense as *In Memoriam.* Very frequently he alters, rearranges, or adds wholly new matter to Omar's quatrains, but even then we cannot be sure that he is speaking for himself. Much of the "freedom" may be unintentional mistranslation; many of the additions may be attempts to

[32] Most of the additional poems, however, had been written before he withdrew from Eton.

impart coherence to the fragmentary original without unfaithfulness to Omar's spirit and manner.

Some of the divergencies from Omar, however, are too striking to justify the supposition that the poem is a mixture of free translation and impersonal dramatic monologue from beginning to end. Consider the stanza:

> Oh Thou, who Man of baser Earth didst make,
> And ev'n with Paradise devise the Snake:
> For all the Sin wherewith the Face of Man
> Is blacken'd—Man's forgiveness give—and take!

W. A. Wright informs us that "There is no original for the line about the snake," and conjectures that the stanza "is FitzGerald's mistaken version of Quatr. 236 in Nicolas' ed. which runs thus:

> 'O thou who knowest the secrets of every one's mind,
> Who graspest every one's hand in the hour of weakness,
> O God, give me repentance and accept my excuses,
> O thou who givest repentance and acceptest the excuses of everyone.' "[33]

But one can hardly believe that "mistaken" is the right word for Fitz-Gerald's inversion of this humble prayer. He knew what he was doing.

Nor does it seem possible to doubt that the following lines express a personal repudiation of Christianity:

> I sent my Soul through the Invisible,
> Some Letter of that After-life to spell:
> And by and by my Soul return'd to me,
> And answer'd "I Myself am Heav'n and Hell."
>
> Heav'n but the Vision of fulfill'd Desire,
> And Hell the Shadow from a Soul on fire,
> Cast on the Darkness into which Ourselves,
> So late emerged from, shall so soon expire.[34]

A happy and confident romantic might use this solipsistic subjectivism in support of his prerogative of infinitude. He might even identify it with an extreme Feuerbachian sort of Broad Churchmanship. But FitzGerald is too honest and too intelligent to suppose that such an attitude is in the vaguest sense Christian. He also knows—without knowing the submerged *why*—that direct uninhibited outpouring of romantic desire is not for him. Sometimes he blames Christianity for his stultification and lashes out at it.

This is in the *Rubáiyát*. In real life, to judge from his letters and what

[33] *Letters and Literary Remains*, VII, 163, 186. [34] *Ibid.*, p. 160.

others have told us about him, he was by no means aggressively anti-Christian. Unable to convince himself that anything was objectively true or false, he disliked people who were positively or negatively cocksure about the deepest mysteries of life. Toward all sincere gropers in the dark he maintained that sceptical tolerance which can so easily be mistaken for Christian charity. He enjoyed a good sermon and occasionally went to church in the hope of hearing one. His attitude toward ideas was essentially aesthetic: when they were beautifully expressed by a flavorsome personality he appreciated them regardless of whether he agreed with them.[35] He protests against Niebuhr's attempt to apply scientific rigor to Roman history: "It is mean to attack old legends that can't defend themselves. And what does it signify in the least if they are true or not? Who ever *actively* believed that Romulus was suckled by a wolf?"[36] The same principle could be applied to the defenseless legends of Christianity. As Keats had said of the graceful postures of the human mind, "Though erroneous, they may be fine." What better thing can one hope for than a practicable myth? And there was just the chance that the myth might hit upon some fragment of the truth.

In this spirit he admired the religious lyrics of Vaughan and Herbert, even to the extent of making a "pilgrimage" to Bemerton. "I noticed the little window into which Herbert's friend looked, and saw him kneeling so long before the altar, when he was first ordained." Of a volume of selections from such seventeenth-century theologians as Taylor, Barrow, and South he writes: "It seems to me that our old Divines will hereafter be considered our Classics—(in Prose, I mean)." He also savors the style of *Religio Medici*, though here he feels compelled to add that the arguments are unconvincing. John Newton "was a man of great power," and his autobiography is "a fine book." On one of his sailing expeditions FitzGerald reads Virgil, Juvenal, and Wesley's *Journal*—"one of the most interesting books, I think, in the English language." He praises the Hare brothers' *Guesses at Truth*. Newman's Anglican sermons "are the best that ever were written in my judgment." Fifteen years later: "I think his Apology very noble; and himself quite honest, so far as he can see himself. The passage in No. 7 . . . where he describes the State of the World as wholly irreflective of its Creator unless you turn—to Popery—is very grand."[37] Grand, but of course no less incredible than Calderón, eight of whose dramas he translated.

[35] The anonymous first edition of the *Rubáiyát* (1859) was of course one of Rossetti's discoveries, and the immense popularity of the revised and enlarged edition of 1868 originated in the enthusiasm of the aesthetic group. The philosophy of the poem agreed with that of Pater's *Conclusion*.

[36] *Letters*, I, 97.

[37] *Ibid.*, I, 10–11, 12, 34, 41, 46, 53, 61, 73, 292; II, 57, 72.

Except for George Eliot, whose spirit is very different, it is hard to think of any other Victorian who enjoyed so many religious books of so many kinds without the faintest glow of personal conviction.[38]

If we assume that he admired Omar's irreligious quatrains with the same aesthetic neutrality and detachment, we are at a loss to explain why they inspired the only good poetry he ever wrote. Other Persian poets did not stir him to genuine creativity, nor did Aeschylus, Sophocles, or Calderón. Despite the already acknowledged ambiguity of the whole situation, it seems more reasonable to suppose that FitzGerald's *Rubáiyát* represents what he himself wanted to say. The conjecture may be valid not only for the passages in which he executes a free fantasia on Omar's theme but for those in which he translates the congenial text with relative faithfulness. We should not, of course, take what may be called the Persian Anacreontic element too seriously.[39] FitzGerald was a vegetarian and a teetotaler; he led a sexless life before, during, and after his unhappy marriage to Lucy Barton. The gazelle-eyed girl and the jug of wine are taken over merely as interestingly exotic symbols of escape from the pressure of unanswerable questions. We find more and more of FitzGerald himself, I believe, the further we move behind the factitious sensuality into the doubt and pain which constitute the real substance of the poem.

A Moment's Halt—a momentary taste
Of BEING from the Well amid the Waste—
   And Lo! the phantom Caravan has reach'd
The NOTHING it set out from—Oh, make haste![40]

Ignorant of the hidden reason why he can find no rosebuds to cull even in the few desperate moments which life allots to men, FitzGerald sometimes resorts to the crusty humor in which his letters are so rich:

Myself when young did eagerly frequent
Doctor and Saint, and heard great argument
   About it and about: but evermore
Came out by the same door wherein I went.

With sharper cynicism he can renounce the pleasure of regarding himself as unique:

[38] Matthew Arnold, an even more assiduous reader of devotional and theological works, developed religious convictions which prevent us from placing him in this category, although to be sure his convictions had very little to do with what he read.

[39] There is nothing to indicate that FitzGerald had any belief in the probably absurd theory that Omar was shrouding the truths of Sufi mysticism in sensual symbols.

[40] *Letters and Literary Remains*, VII, 156.

And fear not lest Existence closing your
Account, and mine, should know the like no more;
  The Eternal Sákí from that Bowl has pour'd
Millions of Bubbles like us, and will pour.

But neither in fictitious sensuality nor in wit was there surcease from the misery of being flung

Into this Universe, and *Why* not knowing
Nor *Whence*, like Water willy-nilly flowing;
  And out of it, as Wind along the Waste
I know not *Whither*, willy-nilly blowing.

. . .

There was the Door to which I found no Key;
There was the Veil through which I might not see:
  Some little talk awhile of ME and THEE
There was—and then no more of THEE and ME.[41]

That is the real message of the poem. "Come, fill the Cup" is traditional hedonistic swagger, not a solution.

But "message" is hardly the word, for FitzGerald was not engaging in antireligious propaganda. He hoped that contemporary doubters might derive some consolation from discovering, as he had discovered, that the "modern" predicament had been voiced by a Persian poet of long ago. There was a closely related aesthetic motive: despair, he felt, loses half its sting when beautifully expressed. On both counts one may agree with him. Young folk especially are often not merely consoled but edified by learning how very old their new negations are. It is also true that every sincere emotion, religious or antireligious, deserves the most adequate externalization that art can provide. The famous passages of the *Rubáiyát* are now almost as shopworn as those of Gray's *Elegy*; poets have found other ways of expressing spiritual bankruptcy. In its day, however, the work said very beautifully what many Victorians felt but were afraid to say for themselves. I have not studied the contemporary reviews; it is reported that some readers were shocked, unpleasantly or deliciously, by such lines as "Man's forgiveness give—and take!" But I doubt whether the poem was widely condemned as a corrupting influence. The first edition was almost wholly neglected, and by the time the second appeared few of those who could be expected to read it were likely to be staggered by it. After all, it was a "translation" from the Persian—a sort of exotic safety valve. It was also, I believe, a cry of despair.

[41] *Ibid.*, pp. 152, 153, 156.

The sense of inability to be either a Christian or a romantic in the teeth of the modern world grows stronger as our period nears its close; probably it will figure even more largely in the next volume than in this. John Byrne Leicester Warren, Baron De Tabley (1835–1895) wrote a good deal of poetry after 1880, but since he was steadily productive from 1859 to 1876 without any marked change of outlook he had better be discussed here. There is no substantial source of information about him, and the scale of this study does not justify original research into the circumstances of his life. The various short memoirs and essays give the impression that he had about the average human allotment of disappointments and sorrows but was inclined to make rather too much of them. Let us assume with a sigh of relief that he was sexually normal, abandon all pretense of explaining why he wrote as he did, and confine ourselves to the text of the poems.

They are the work of an intelligent, cultivated, aesthetically and spiritually sensitive, and somewhat thin-blooded aristocrat—certainly no genius, but graced with excellent poetic table-manners. "Vivid disorderly power," Rossetti's phrase for Jones, cannot be applied to his Lordship. His colors are faint; he lacks vigor; he has more order than is good for him. In style and choice of subject he leans heavily on greater poets. His dreamy-decorative-mellifluous vein makes us think, as he would wish us to think, of the Keatsian side of Tennyson. The Pre-Raphaelite influence on his aesthetic medievalism is obvious.[42] His dramatic monologues frequently recall Browning, and sometimes specific works of that poet. His Neo-Hellenism is Swinburnian but much chastened by his admiration for Landor and Tennyson and by his landed-gentry respectability.[43] Yet the comparisons which he suggests are seldom very odious. He is no mere plagiarist or slavish imitator, and although he fails to develop a voice of his own he has some interesting things to say.

He seems to detest the age in which he lives. At the close of his career we find him lamenting the disappearance of "the land of dreams":

> The hard world wakes in cold reality,
> Romance hath still'd her music, touch, and tone.
>
> . . .
>
> Gone? all shall go, the fable and the truth;
> Ambrosial glimpses of an antique day,

[42] But this is not a prominent tendency in his work, and since we have already seen a good deal of it in other poets we shall ignore it in this discussion.

[43] Of course Swinburne belonged to precisely the same class, but in his case other factors were stronger than the social determinants.

Lost, as the love dream of a withered youth
In wintry eyes where charmèd laughter lay.

This complaint may seem excessively Bunthornian, but it is rooted in a quite unaffected philosophic pessimism which he expresses less languishingly in *A Song of Despair*:

The earth is dust, dust,
Heaven is but empty air,
Faith falters in distrust.
The throne of God is bare.

The saint has worshipped wind,
The sun has seen a lie,
The round globe deaf and blind
Rolls on eternally.

The priests in golden domes
With blood and fire entreat
The hand that never comes,
The long-delaying feet.

. . .

Who sins, by Nature sins,
The pure by birth are so.
The game Death always wins,
Tho' we play high or low.

The heart is nerve and flesh,
The brain a mere machine,
Some slave in sensual mesh,
Some virtue saves serene.[44]

These lines are dated "July, 1894"—the year before his death. Although the prevailing tone of all his work is somber and disillusioned, he did not arrive at this utterly hopeless conclusion without a certain amount of spiritual wrestling. He does not impress us as a pessimist a priori or as a man who chose to be miserable for the morbid fun of it. It is with sorrow, not with glee, that he reports, "The throne of God is bare." A dramatic monologue entitled *The Prodigal* renders with no hint of unbelief the penitent but hopeful feelings of the errant son. But although the poet imaginatively sympathizes with those feelings he cannot make them his own. Elsewhere he asserts that his most heartfelt prayer has gone unanswered. He has begged for no miracle, he tells God, since he knows that "Nature is stronger than thou art divine,"

[44] *Collected Poems*, pp. 458–459, 485.

> But all my being withers in the want
> Of one ripe, excellent, and righteous thing,
> For which the sources of my nature pant
> And dwell in bitter thirst until thou grant.

The fact that De Tabley is borrowing from Part VI of *James Lee's Wife* does not imply that his emotion is spurious. Browning, similarly thwarted in his craving for "One fair, good, wise thing," tries to console himself by glorifying the imperfect. But his less robust admirer complains that he has prayed for this boon "seven times a day" and now demands value received for his devotions:

> Ah, deal not falsely, as a merchant may,
> Who takes thy merchandise and doth not bring
> Coin to reward its use for many a day—
> Nay, thou wilt hear, and, *if thou canst*, repay![45]

Since the fatted calf is not served up in response to this sneering demand, John Warren assumes that science has destroyed religion. "Nature is stronger than thou art divine."

Hence when he touches upon Christianity he tends to be either openly sceptical or ambiguously ironic. One attempt to reconcile supernaturalism and nature-worship may be worth noting. Refuting a bigoted "saint," the sun defends his worshippers:

> God's glory is my glory, and my praise
> Only his praising. They, who kneel to me,
> See thro' the waving of my orient wings
> A choir of stars with voices like the sea,
> Singing hosanna in the heavenly ways.

Of course they see nothing of the sort unless they are Christians—in which case they do not worship the sun. All but very rigorous bibliolaters will prefer *Jael*, a Browningesque dramatic monologue in which the slayer of Sisera, far from rejoicing in her deed, laments it as brutal, treacherous, and cowardly. She feels that God has condemned her for it. Her explanation is curiously up-to-date: a restless feminist housewife, she had wanted to show that she could do something really important. The poem has no essentially anti-Christian implications, but neither the author nor most of his readers would be aware of that fact. In *The Strange Parable* he advances a queer interpretation of Mark xii: 43–45, Christ's story of the man who returns home after his reformation only to consort with "seven other spirits more wicked than himself." According to De Tabley it means

[45] *Ibid.*, pp. 30, 67–68.

> That man with men must change [exchange] his words or die.
> And this I hold, man lonely is not man,
> Dowered with the curse and need of social bond,
> And leavened by his fellows into sin,
> Because he cannot take his path alone.[46]

One can be virtuous only in solitude, and hence only at the cost of ceasing to be a normal man; the social impulse, an essential law of human nature, inevitably breeds sin.

This poet shows some interest in the Vatican Council and its English repercussions. *Bishop Blougram's Apology* is the model for *The Cardinal's Lament.* In a note De Tabley rather anxiously insists that the poem is strictly dramatic: its ideas are not to be ascribed to him—a statement which, as usual, should be taken with several grains of salt. Professor Evans does not convey the precise flavor of the poem in calling it "an aroused, spirited presentation of the case for Catholic Christianity."[47] The Cardinal, who speaks with more obviously shifty casuistry than Browning's Bishop, insists that there can be no possible reconciliation between reason and faith:

> Their feud is old as ocean, keen as fire;
>
> . . .
>
> You cannot build a reasonable faith.

On this basis he satirizes the efforts of Broad Churchmen to

> Frame some mild creed with neither back nor bones,
> A mist of genial benevolences
> To please all round, Budd, Calvin, Moses, Comte.
> Fair bodes the scheme in its first fluid stage,—
> It makes a tidy pamphlet, well received,—
> But crystallize it can't, except around
> Some little tiny notion of a god,
> Some germ organic in the central haze
> To vivify and quicken the inert.

The trouble with liberals is that they try to be logical and scientific about these matters.

> Here your dilemma rises, man of mind,
> Either ignore your god-mote, leave your scheme
> A vapid thing to fester on grey shelves,
>
> . . .
>
> Or accept something which transcends your rules.[48]

[46] *Ibid.*, pp. 137, 283–290, 355.
[47] B. I. Evans, *English Poetry in the Later Nineteenth Century*, p. 356.
[48] *Collected Poems*, pp. 55, 56, 58*n*.

Such acceptance is faith, not reason. Then why not be a Catholic, since Holy Church embodies the only Christian tradition which frankly affirms that Christianity is irrational? De Tabley does not mean to champion Pio Nono against Dr. Jowett. The former is preferable to the latter only because his pretensions demonstrate so much more conclusively that Christianity is nonsense.

At the Council, another poem of not impenetrable irony, is dated "Rome, November, 1869." The cardinals glorify the infallible Pope,

> For God has made thy mouth his own, and error
> In thy voice is not heard.
>
> . . .
>
> Leave vain philosophies, old dreamer Teuton,
> Great drowsy fly in web of logic weak;
> We silenced Galileo, menaced Newton,
> And Darwin shall not speak.
>
> . . .
>
> Till Death and Doubt be thy tame sheep, O pastor,
> Pontiff of souls and vicar of God's choice,—
> Infallible, in whom the spirit master
> Hath breathed his spirit voice,—
>
> Explain our Faith! all faithful hear thy mandate,
> Emperors watch in dread our world debate;
> Thy fear is on all peoples! (but the bandit
> Who plunders at thy gate.)[49]

The closing lines, if not the preceding stanzas, prevent us from supposing that the author feels any enthusiasm for the papal claims.

Not that De Tabley is an ardent Protestant: he attacks the Church of Rome because he sees in it the most formidable organized expression of Christian belief.[50] To strike at Christianity through Roman Catholicism, a safe object of abuse in England, in the interests of deism or atheism is a good old eighteenth-century device which Swinburne also employs. Like the earlier Swinburne, however, Warren usually prefers to write as a pseudo-Euripidean pagan, rebelling not directly against God but against Zeus or "the gods." Sometimes he contrasts Christian and Hellenic standards to the disadvantage of the former. *Encrates*, an Athenian ex-athlete, refutes a headnote quoted from Bishop Wilson: "It seemeth to me that the young pagan, albeit in his pride of life he was as an animal oftentimes perfect, yet

[49] *Ibid.*, pp. 81–82.

[50] His political liberalism is also an important factor, but not important enough to provide a sufficient explanation of his attitude.

failed in that he had no hope beyond; old age being imminent when the flourish of those vanities must be abolished." In rebuttal Encrates instances the pleasures of civic pride, war, love, and so on.

Are not these worth the living? Canst thou make
Thy heart a lie, and say thou scornest all?

. . .

... Light and life
And energy are ours: and, crowning all,
Are silence and not undelicious peace.[51]

It is Browning's *Cleon* without the unconscious Christian longings.

As often happens, however, the glorification of human life on a purely naturalistic level collapses into a nihilistic pessimism which forbids all pleasure save that of defiance.

Mighty our masters and
Very revengeful,

. . .

Helming the seasons in
Pastime they sit;
Tossing the plague on some
Fortunate island,
Carelessly tossing it,
Watching it go
Strike and exterminate.

. . .

They cry to the nations,
"We strike, if ye pray not.
We bend down our eyes along
Temple and grove,
Searching the incense-curl
And the live smell of blood;
Hating the worshipper,
Craving his prayer."

The gods made man only that they themselves might feel strong and creative. They wanted something to bully:

... What avail
Omnipotence without some weaker thing
To be amazed? With only brother gods
To see, as strong as they, who would create?

But their puppets

Mutinous grew;
Requiring justice, beholding frailty

[51] *Collected Poems*, p. 45.

Among celestials,
They laughed and straightway
They made their reason god,
Which all gods hate.

Another poem acknowledges, however, that the only effectual way of rebelling against the gods is to die and thus elude their cruelty:

Strong are alone the dead,
They need not bow the head,
Or reach one hand in ineffectual prayer.
Safe in their iron sleep
What wrong shall make them weep,
What sting of human anguish reach them there?
They are gone safe beyond the strong one's reign,
Who shall decree against them any pain?[52]

Our last and surest refuge is the Garden of Proserpine.

In *Orestes*, a choric drama of 1867, the hero speaks:

O mother, there is no oracular voice
So fit to guide a man and keep him noble
As his own spirit.

This is what John Warren wanted to believe. One familiar result of trying to believe it may be seen in *A Ballad of Life*, written a few months before his death:

There is nothing new to say or do,
But to creep to a ditch and die.
There is no truth or faith or ruth
Beneath the barren sky.[53]

These causally related passages epitomize not only the case of Lord De Tabley but the entire historical tragedy to which this series of studies is devoted.

[52] *Ibid.*, pp. 166, 177, 310.

[53] *Ibid.*, pp. 207, 465. Hugh Walker, who knew the author, says of *Orestes*: "Into hardly any of his works has Warren put a larger share of his own deepest feeling." (*Lord De Tabley: A Biographical Sketch*, p. 17.) The later lines are obviously a personal outcry.

Chapter Fifteen

SWINBURNE

SWINBURNE was more than an emptily mellifluous lyricist, more than a sado-masochistic pornographer. Beneath the alliterative spate of words, the blur of imprecise images, the hypnotic gallop of anapaests, may be discerned historically significant ideas on art, sex, politics, science, and religion. Although he liked to flaunt his psychopathic peculiarities in the face of Mrs. Grundy, he was fundamentally sincere. His best poetry is not of the ivory tower. His aestheticism was sometimes a sword with which to thrust at Victorian respectability and sometimes a shield with which to protect himself against criticism; but until all the fight was drained out of him it was not a mere evasion of life. He deserves to be taken seriously.

At Oxford two Swinburnes existed side by side. One was the arty young friend of Rossetti, Morris, and Burne-Jones who shared their medievalistic enthusiasms and their admiration for *The Heir of Redclyffe*. He was, or had recently been, an Anglo-Catholic. His parents were devoutly "high," and "as child and boy . . . I went in for that as passionately as for other things (e.g., well-nigh to unaffected and unashamed ecstasies of adoration when receiving the Sacrament.)"[1] By this time the ecstasies had dwindled to ritualistic medievalism, but they had not wholly given way before that "turbid Nihilism" which the letter to Stedman mentions as the next phase of his spiritual history. His Anglo-Catholic boyhood, indeed, exerted some influence throughout his career. Not only was he essentially a ceremonialist to the end of his days, but he retained strong religious feelings and an active interest in theological controversy. His deep saturation in the language of the Bible and of the Liturgy was always a prominent feature of his style even—or rather, particularly—in his most rampantly irreligious poems. He never actually disbelieved in the God of Christianity: he merely disliked Him very much. Writing to W. M. Rossetti in 1904, he speaks not without tenderness of "that particular uppermost 'high' branch of the Anglican Church to which our mothers and sisters belonged. In them that creed

[1] *Complete Works*, XVIII, 182. This letter of 1875 to E. C. Stedman is Swinburne's fullest account of the development of his religious thought.

certainly was compatible with an adorably 'beautiful type of character' which yet, I cannot but think, might have been better in some ways and happier on the whole with a saner and wider outlook on life and death."[2] He would never accept any middle ground between the Catholic tradition and denial of all supernaturalism, "for," he tells Stedman, "a Theist I never was; I always felt by instinct and perceived by reason that no man could conceive of a *personal* God except by crude superstition or else by true supernatural revelation; that a natural God was the absurdest of all human figments."[3]

The other Swinburne at Oxford was the young libertine, republican, and freethinker who consorted with John Nichol and to a less extent with other members of the convivial "Old Mortality" set. The pattern for this Swinburne had been established not by his parents but by his paternal grandfather —that worldly, cultivated, eighteenth-century infidel who had brought to England from France an exotic flavor of cosmopolitanism and a strong sense of the interdependence of organized religion and political tyranny. A virtuoso of curious learning and exquisite forms, a morally irresponsible *grand seigneur*, a foe of *l'infâme*,—the combination was irresistible. The Hellenic republican Landor and the Hugo of *Les Châtiments*, both read with wild enthusiasm at Eton, linked his grandfather's influence with the art of poetry. At Oxford the work was completed by Nichol, who had met Mazzini and Kossuth and whose political and religious rebellions were tinged with the European type of secularism. In his very different way, Jowett may also have done something to weaken Swinburne's orthodoxy, but he seems to have had little sympathy with his pupil until the strange youth had become a famous poet. What sapped Swinburne's High Churchmanship was not Balliol Hegelianism but indignation against institutional Christianity in general and the Catholic Church in particular as the agent of obscurantism and oppression. His refusal to distinguish between the Christian faith and the historical record of Christian institutions was not wholly unjustified: there is dismayingly high authority for supposing that there should be some relation between the two. One could, however, sympathize more fully with Swinburne's passion for liberty had it not been sullied by his passion for libertinism. Unfortunately, he detested Christianity too largely because it forbade the satisfaction of impulses which had already begun to assume a perversely sinister form.

[2] *Ibid.*, p. 481.

[3] *Ibid.*, p. 182. Such poems as *Hymn of Man* and *Hertha* are certainly dedicated to a sort of "natural God," but as used in this letter the phrase means a supernatural God revealed *in* nature. This concept he always repudiates.

Nevertheless the revolt had its impersonal and ideal side. Such poems of the Oxford days as *A Song in Time of Order* and *The Cup of God's Wrath* indicate that the feelings of *Songs before Sunrise* had crystallized even earlier than those of *Poems and Ballads*. The *Ode to Mazzini* is reminiscent of Shelley's *Ode to Naples*; the great romantic would always exert a strong influence on both the negative and positive aspects of Swinburne's religion.[4] He addresses Italy in characteristically Scriptural language:

> Thine eyes beyond this Calvary look, altho'
> Brute-handed Austria smite thee on the cheek,
> And her thorns pierce thy forehead, white and meek;
>
> . . .
>
> Yet is thy spirit nobler than of yore,
> Knowing the keys thy reverence used to kiss
> Were forged by emperors to bow down before,
> Not for free men to worship: So that Faith,
> Blind portress of the gate which opens death,
> Shall never prate of Freedom any more.

Turning from kingcraft and priestcraft, he makes his final Shelleyan appeal to

> Thou! whose best name on earth
> Is Love—whose fairest birth
> The freedom of the fair world thou hast made.
>
> . . .
>
> We keep our trust tho' all things fail us—
> Tho' time nor baffled Hope avail us,
> We keep our faith—God liveth and is love.

In Swinburne's early poems this antimonarchical, anticlerical love-cult is mingled with, and for a time submerged by, the subject matter and style of Pre-Raphaelitism. Admiration for Morris's *Guenevere* poems and the personal magnetism of Rossetti were important factors. Then too, the noble and the ignoble were so incongruously mingled in Swinburne's desire for freedom that art for art's sake, especially of the medievalistic variety, offered a relief from increasingly painful tensions. On the one hand, it was a kind of revolt against the Victorian suspicion of beauty; on the other hand, its remoteness had the soothing quality of an anodyne. And it enabled him to breathe the incense of ritualistic Anglo-Catholicism without subjecting himself to *l'infâme*.

He employs a more or less Pre-Raphaelite manner from time to time

[4] Dining at Monckton Milnes's in 1863, Matthew Arnold meets "a sort of pseudo-Shelley called Swinburne." (Arnold, *Letters*, I, 227.) The phrase is perceptive.

throughout his career; it is not a favorite club in his golf bag, but he uses it for certain strokes. He is, however, classifiable as a Pre-Raphaelite poet only during this early period of experimental groping. When writing in this vein he shows an uncanny ability to reconstruct not only the trappings but what seem to be the essential emotions of medieval Catholicism, and at the same time to render those emotions ambiguous. *St. Dorothy*, a tale of the martyrdom of a Christian virgin, is a remarkable feat of historical imagination and stylistic mimicry; but the Emperor Gabalus is a little too obviously a precursor of the Marquis de Sade, and the account of Dorothy's sufferings goes somewhat beyond the necessities of edification. Theophilus, the young pagan who had asked Gabalus to force her to marry him, is converted by the spectacle of her heroic death and himself undergoes martyrdom. He is now united in heaven with his Blessed Damozel, who had loved him even when she rejected him:

> But truly for his love God hath him brought
> There where his heavy body grieves him nought,
> Nor all the people plucking at his feet;
> But in his face his lady's face is sweet,
> And through his lips her kissing lips are gone:
> God send him peace, and joy of such an one.

A queen whose "mouth was most fair" sings *A Christmas Carol*, "Suggested by a drawing of Mr. D. G. Rossetti's." A very innocent or hasty reader might credit Swinburne with having made at least one charmingly reverent contribution to the poetry of the Catholic Revival. But the half-submerged implication is that the Mother of Jesus was an adulteress, and that the queen who sings the carol feels special kinship with her because she herself has sinned in the same way. *The Queen's Tragedy* contains lines which look forward to *Atalanta*:

> And prayer is vain. Moreover I have prayed
> And seen no face of God nor any saint,
> And have not peace.

These doubtless intentional ambiguities suggest that Swinburne's Pre-Raphaelitism is associated with a desire to use Christian materials for discrediting Christianity. A wistful recognition of the beauty of medieval faith is mingled with the pleasure of desecrating it. He has already begun to chant the Black Mass. Soon, however, the pain of unrequited love, the influence of *Justine* and *Les Fleurs du Mal*, the nervous excitation of his increasingly corrupted mind, and the maturing of his artistic aims under the guidance of

Monckton Milnes impelled him to cast off the Pre-Raphaelite disguise and attack Christianity with bolder, more uncompromising weapons. Let us pass on, then, to the "turbid Nihilism" of *Atalanta in Calydon* and *Poems and Ballads*.

Concerning *Poems and Ballads* Swinburne declared:

> The book is dramatic, many-faced, multifarious; and no utterance of enjoyment or despair, belief or unbelief, can properly be assumed as the assertion of its author's personal feeling or faith. . . . Byron and Shelley, speaking in their own persons, and with what sublime effect we know, openly and insultingly mocked and reviled what the English of their day held most sacred. I have not done this. I do not say that, if I chose, I would not do so to the best of my power; I do say that hitherto I have seen fit to do nothing of the kind.[5]

If this statement is not deliberately untruthful it betrays the most astonishing facility in self-deception. By 1866, to be sure, he had moved onward from moderate Pre-Raphaelite aestheticism to become the leading English protagonist of the French theory of *l'art pour l'art* which Baudelaire had derived from Gautier and Poe. Swinburne wished to demonstrate the irrelevance of subject matter for criticism by showing that a poet could write beautifully on themes of horror and evil. Cultivation of such themes would also affirm the complete moral irresponsibility of the artist. It is impossible, however, to believe that the philosophy of *Poems and Ballads* is purely aesthetic. Swinburne is hardly less aware of his readers than Tennyson. And he does not merely wish to shock them: that desire, though strong, is rooted in genuinely perverse convictions which he insists on projecting into the stream of contemporary thought. More than Shelley, more even than Byron, he "openly and insultingly mocked and reviled what the English of [his] day held most sacred." In his own strange fashion, Swinburne is one of the Victorian prophets.

Glancing back to *Atalanta* from *Poems and Ballads*, we see how little dramatic objectivity inheres in its hopeless but undaunted defiance of the gods. "All we are against thee, against thee, O God most high!" is a personal utterance, as is the appeal from divine tyranny to "the holy spirit of man." Here, as in *Poems and Ballads* and sometimes in later poems, he attempted to integrate the aesthetically "pure" and the subversively instrumental aspects of his thought by giving a peculiar twist to nineteenth-century Hellenism.[6] According to Professor Bush, "Swinburne's intoxicating neopaganism gave a fresh and powerful stimulus to the old conflict between

[5] *Complete Works*, XVI, 354–355.

[6] Swinburne's Hellenism was peculiar so far as the English tradition is concerned; but, as Professor Graham Hough reminds us, it was considerably influenced by Gautier's "general conception of pagan antiquity as something nude, splendid, rapacious, and cruel." (*The Last Romantics*, p. 188.)

Christ and Pan which the names of Schiller and Mrs. Browning will recall. . . . He had no small share, though a devout Hellenist, in creating that deplorable conception of Greece as a Bohemian paradise of beauty, art, love, and no morals."[7] Swinburne tells Lord Houghton that he prefers the pure classicism of Landor to Tennyson's "magnificent hashes of old and new with such a sharp sauce of personality as *Œnone* and *Ulysses*." Tennyson is a great poet, "But he is not a Greek or a heathen, and I imagine does not want to be. I greatly fear he believes it possible to be something better; an absurdity which should be left to the Brownings and other blatant creatures begotten on the slime of the modern chaos."[8] Swinburne's Hellenism, however, is not much purer than Tennyson's: the difference is between two refracting personalities, not between authenticity and falsification. Nor is *Atalanta* less thickly bedaubed with the slime of the modern chaos than *Balaustion's Adventure*. The implications of Dionysus and of Sade are perhaps not mutually exclusive, but they diverge more widely than Swinburne was able to perceive.

In a letter of 1865 to Lady Trevelyan, Swinburne prefers Carlyle's *Frederick* to his *Cromwell*: "I must say Frederick's clear, cold pluck, looking neither upward nor around for any help or comfort, seems to me a much more wholesome and more admirable state of mind than Cromwell's splendid pietism. . . . It is the old question between Jews and Greeks, and I, who can understand Leonidas better than Joshua, must prefer Marathon to Gilgal." Widely as Swinburne's Greece differs from Arnold's, this preference helps to explain why Swinburne will admire Arnold's efforts to "Hellenize" Christianity. The following words, addressed to Stedman in 1875 during the composition of *Erectheus*, might almost have been written by Arnold himself: "I always feel the Greek history and mythology (in its deeper sense and wider bearing) much nearer to us even yet than those of the Jews, alien from us in blood and character. Even the poet of Job is a Semitic alien, while the poet of Prometheus is an Aryan kinsman of our own: his national history of far more real importance to us, his poetry far closer to our own thoughts, passion, speculation, conscience, than the Hebrew."[9]

Swinburne would like to draw from Greek paganism more romantic values than "Frederick's clear, cold pluck." From the gray world of the pale Galilean he turns to

> . . . the fair days when God
> By man as godlike trod,
> And each alike was Greek, alike was free.

[7] D. N. Bush, *Mythology and the Romantic Tradition in English Poetry*, pp. 352–353.
[8] *Complete Works*, XVIII, 20.
[9] *Ibid.*, pp. 29, 183–184, 209.

His psychological condition at this time impelled him to express the contrast between Christian slavery and Greek freedom chiefly in sexual terms. The sorrowful maiden of Christianity, "slave among slaves," is spurned in favor of the joyous and joy-giving Aphrodite,

> Her deep hair heavily laden with odor and color of flowers,
> White rose of the rose-white water, a silver splendor, a flame.

As everyone knows, however, the force of this contrast is marred by Swinburne's perverse transformation of Venus into Our Lady of Pain. A decadent romanticism supplants the fresh and vital amorality of paganism. Only "the insatiable Satiety" results from

> . . . the strange loves that suck the breasts of Hate
> Till lips and teeth bite in their sharp indenture.

How seriously to regard his desire to bite and be bitten? He seems to have been physically undersexed and mentally oversexed.[10] To what extent he cultivated perverse practices in the hopeless endeavor to close the gap between mind and body is a question for the biographers, but there can be no doubt that his imagination hugely outstripped his capacity and even his desire actually to inflict or suffer the horrors of which he dreamed. We may also be sure that a strong factor in his literary exploitation of sadism and masochism was a desire to *épater les bourgeois* by showing that authentic flowers of evil could be grown on English soil. In later years he denied his assertion of the pure aestheticism of *Poems and Ballads* by confessing that he had felt "a touch of Byronic ambition to be thought an eminent and terrible enemy to the decorous life and respectable fashion of the world; and, as in Byron's case, there was mingled with a sincere scorn and horror of hypocrisy a boyish and voluble affectation of audacity and excess."[11] Here, however, he seems to be remembering, with more gratitude than he had felt in 1865, Lord Houghton's review of *Atalanta* in the *Edinburgh*. The critic, who of all men should have known better, had associated the defiant fatalism of the piece with Byron. Swinburne responded: "I should have bowed to the judicial sentence if instead of 'Byron with a difference' you had said 'De Sade with a difference.' The poet, thinker, and man of the world from whom the theology of my poem is derived was a greater than Byron. *He* indeed, fatalist or not, saw to the bottom of Gods and men."[12]

[10] See Edward Shanks's Introduction to his edition of *Selected Poems* for what seems to me a very satisfying statement of the situation.

[11] *Complete Works*, XIX, 281.

[12] *Ibid.*, XVIII, 32–33.

Unquestionably the merely pornographic side of De Sade's writings appealed strongly to Swinburne:

> But there is nothing, nor shall be,
> So sweet, so wicked, but my verse
> Can dream of worse.

Since by no means all of these dreams were shared with the public, we must assume that his perversion was a private pleasure as well as a means of shocking his readers. Mr. Welby rather tantalizingly reports that *Anactoria* and *The Leper* are nursery rhymes compared with "such unpublished and unprintable verses of his as I have had pass through my hands."[13] Not all of these were casual impromptus tossed off to amuse himself and friends like Simeon Solomon. At intervals from 1861 to 1881—for Mazzini by no means dispelled the obsession—he worked with loving care at *The Flogging Block*, an elaborate epic of flagellation.[14]

But the author of *Justine* was also an exciting philosopher of nihilism, an apostle of romantic self-expansion in its most extravagant and desperate form—"Thy prophet, thy preacher, thy poet," as Swinburne describes him to Dolores. His devotion to the "gratuitous act," like that of a modern existentialist, was based on principle. The philosophic sadist rises superior to everything—decency, human-kindness, love, chivalry, man-made law, ethical precept, God. No knowledge, no experience, is closed to him. *Homo sum, nihil ergo inhumani a me alienum puto.* For Swinburne, the inversion and desecration of religious values was especially attractive. Sappho desires to torture her beloved as a means of emulating and outstripping God's cruelty to man and ultimately of being cruel even to Him:

> Me hath God made more bitter toward thee
> Than death toward man; but were I made as he
> Who hath made all things to break them one by one,
> If my feet trod upon the stars and sun
> And souls of men as his have always trod,
> God knows I might be crueller than God.
>
> . . .
>
> Him would I reach, him smite, him desecrate,
> Pierce the cold lips of God with human breath,
> And mix his immortality with death.

These are the reveries of a nineteenth-century, not of a genuinely Hellenic, psychopath. Swinburne finds the celebration of the Black Mass more titillating than mere pagan unawareness of sin. One must deliberately

[13] T. E. Welby, *A Study of Swinburne*, p. 41.

[14] Mario Praz, *The Romantic Agony*, p. 215.

choose the raptures and roses of vice in preference to the lilies and languors of virtue, knowing full well that the vice is vice and that the virtue is virtue. That is the theme of *Laus Veneris*:

> Alas, Lord, surely thou art great and fair.
> But lo her wonderfully woven hair!
>   And thou didst heal us with thy piteous kiss;
> But see, now, Lord; her mouth is lovelier.
>
> . . .
>
> I dare not always touch her, lest the kiss
> Leave my lips charred. Yea, Lord, a little bliss,
>   Brief bitter bliss, one hath for a great sin;
> Natheless thou knowest how sweet a thing it is.
>
> . . .
>
> Ah love, there is no better life than this;
> To have known love, how bitter a thing it is,
>   And afterward be cast out of God's sight.[15]

Laus Veneris is useful for critics who wish to institute damaging comparisons between Swinburne and Baudelaire. That the French poet is a much greater artist than his English admirer there can be no doubt. Perhaps, however, the difference in their *thought*, especially as regards religion, has been somewhat exaggerated. *Les Fleurs du Mal*, more impressively than *Poems and Ballads*, mingles a genuinely horrified awareness of sin with the pose of diabolistic desecration. Baudelaire knows nothing of salvation, but he experiences the reality of damnation more intensely than Swinburne. It should, however, be possible to observe this fact without insisting that Baudelaire was a great religious poet and Swinburne a decadent guttersnipe who merely pretended to be a condemned blasphemer. *Ave Atque Vale* at least suggests that Swinburne *wanted* to be as serious about these matters as the Frenchman. Once he emerges from the *Poems and Ballads* phase, furthermore, Swinburne is for several years (witness *Hertha*) a more constructive religious thinker than Baudelaire.

But we have not yet done with *Poems and Ballads*. They illustrate the fact that sadism and masochism are opposite faces of the same coin. Swinburne's craving for unbounded liberty is inseparable from the delight of enslavement. The worship of Dolores at "the shrine where a sin is a prayer" implies the suffering of pain even more than the infliction of pain. And the quest for increasingly perverse sensation, like nobler romantic aspirations, is endless. One can never quite abandon the hope of novelty:

[15] Observe how the style and tone of the Pre-Raphaelites, the verse pattern of FitzGerald's *Rubáiyát*, and the characteristic themes of *Poems and Ballads* are united in this poem.

What new work wilt thou find for thy lover,
What new passions for daytime or night?
What spells that they know not a word of—
Whose lives are as leaves overblown?
What tortures undreamt of, unheard of,
Unwritten, unknown?

But the permutations and combinations of lust are arithmetically finite, and Swinburne must ask the unbearable question:

Ah, where shall we go then for pastime,
If the worst that can be has been done?

Yet the satiety is "insatiable":

We are fain of thee still, we are fain,
O sanguine and subtle Dolores,
Our Lady of Pain.

Bitten or biting, however, she refuses to "come down and redeem us from virtue."

The high defiance becomes a mechanical compulsion from which the only escape is "the sleep eternal / In an eternal night." Hence the pagan goddess to whom Swinburne finally pays his vows is not Venus in either her joyous or her rapacious aspect, but the daughter of Ceres:

Thou art more than the gods who number the days of our temporal breath;
For these give labor and slumber; but thou, Proserpina, death.

The death-wish, of course, is psychiatrically orthodox in Swinburne's situation. At Oxford, W. H. Mallock was one of a group of admiring undergraduates who were told by Swinburne that *The Triumph of Time*, *Dolores*, and *The Garden of Proserpine* represented three successive stages in a spiritual autobiography.[16] The sequence, then, runs from frustrated would-be-normal love to frustrated perversity and thence to longing for oblivion.

That is the story through 1866 or so.

Then he stood up, and trod to dust
Fear and desire, mistrust and trust,
And dreams of bitter sleep and sweet,

. . .

. . . and his spirit's meat
Was freedom, and his staff was wrought
Of strength, and his cloak woven of thought.

[16] *Memoirs of Life and Literature*, p. 57.

The Prelude to *Songs before Sunrise* exaggerates a little. No radical transformation has occurred. The political poetry of the late sixties and early seventies revives feelings and themes which he had cultivated at Oxford during his friendship with Nichol. While singing of Italian liberty he lived no more edifyingly than while singing of Faustine. One can see a thread of psychological coherence running from *Poems and Ballads* to *Songs before Sunrise*. The old sadism is reflected in the angry destructive violence and the uneasily overasserted virility of the later volume; the old masochism, in the swooning hero-worship and the emphasis on the sufferings of the persecuted. Nevertheless a marked change, and one highly creditable to Swinburne, has taken place. To an astonishing degree he achieved imaginative sublimation of his imaginative perversities. His poems of freedom may be inadequate aesthetically, intellectually, and spiritually; but few minds which have sunk so low have managed to rise so high. One is glad that he said of *Songs before Sunrise*: "My other books are books; that one is myself."[17] The statement is not completely true, but the feeling that it *should* be true expresses what is best in his nature.

As propaganda for anticlerical liberalism, almost all of Swinburne's political poems have some bearing upon our subject. The analogy between Mazzini and Christ sometimes broadens to embrace the conception of a crucified and resurrected Italy. *Super Flumina Babylonis* shifts from Psalm 137 to images of Easter morning:

> Lo, the graveclothes of Italy that are folded up
> In the grave's gloom!
> And the guards as men wrought upon with a charmèd cup,
> By the open tomb.
>
> And her body most beautiful, and her shining head,
> They are not here;
> For your mother, for Italy, is not surely dead;
> Have ye no fear.

Italy, "Who is risen indeed," tells her sons that he who lays down his own life for human freedom wins true immortality, since he has given himself to that which is inherently deathless. He has become a member of George Eliot's "Choir Invisible."

"I have written," Swinburne told Powell in 1870, "a modern companion in arms and metre to my *Hymn to Proserpine* called *Hymn of Man* . . . by the side of which *Queen Mab* is as it were an archdeacon's charge and my own

[17] *Complete Works*, XVIII, 200.

previous blasphemies are models of Catholic devotion."[18] The new poem was written in protest against the Oecumenical Council of 1869–70, and the author dreamed of its being read as a "Te Hominem Laudamus" before Ricciardi's Anti-Catholic Council in Naples. Swinburne and W. M. Rossetti sent Ricciardi a collaborative letter, translated into Italian by Rossetti, but the opposition assembly was dissolved by the authorities before the manifesto could be made public. Lafourcade quotes from the manuscript a paragraph which he ascribes wholly to Swinburne: "The Liberty we believe in is one and indivisible: without free thought there can be no free life. That democracy of the spirit without which the body, personal or social, can enjoy but a false freedom, must, by the very law of its being, confront a man-made theocracy to destroy it. Ideal or actual, the Church or priests, and the Republic, are internecine enemies."[19]

But to insist overmuch upon the topical aspect of the religion of *Songs before Sunrise* is to ignore its larger significance. "Love, the beloved Republic, that feeds upon freedom and lives" transcends Mazzini's ideal of a liberated secularistic Italy. *Hymn of Man* is much more than a protest against Papal Infallibility and the *Syllabus Errorum*. Negatively, it is an outcry of hatred against the man-made God who denies the infinitude of man; positively, it is an assertion of belief in the independent goodness and power of human love. If there is any validity in the interpretation of romanticism which unites this series of studies, we can find no more uncompromising expression of the romantic faith than "Glory to Man in the highest! for Man is the master of things." The poem, however, simply repeats, in more violent language though not with more fundamental extravagance of thought, the victory of Shelley's Prometheus over Jupiter.

> Thou art judged, O judge, and the sentence is gone forth against thee, O God.
> Thy slave that slept is awake; thy slave but slept for a span;
> Yea, man thy slave shall unmake thee, who made thee lord over man.
> For his face is set to the east, his feet on the past and its dead;
> The sun rearisen is his priest, the heat thereof hallows his head.
> His eyes take part in the morning; his spirit outsounding the sea
> Asks no more witness or warning from temple or tripod or tree.

Hybris has attained its climax. But there is a note of anxiety as well as of impatience in the question, "Till his corpse be cast out of the sun will ye know not the truth of his death?"

Swinburne does not assert that each individual man is God:

[18] Quoted by Georges Lafourcade, *Swinburne*, p. 174.

[19] *Ibid.*, pp. 172–174.

. . . God, if a God there be, is the substance of men which is man.

. . .

Not men's but man's is the glory of godhead.

Divinity, then, is Humanity—not you or I or Swinburne. Yet to the extent that we are all outward and visible signs of the human substance, "each man of all men is God." My inability to think of Collective Man except as a huge aggregation of individuals—Jones plus Cohen plus Perez plus Tojo and so on to the inclusion of every weak, faulty human being in the world—is perhaps a spiritual limitation. Thus limited, I am compelled to doubt whether for Swinburne, a passionate individualist, the concept of divine Collective Humanity is much more than a subconscious means of giving his lust for personal boundlessness a quasi-religious sanction. He recognizes, at all events, that in practice each separate man must be his own God. The statement in the Prelude of *Songs before Sunrise* that "man's soul is man's God still" can refer only to the individual:

Save his own soul's light overhead,
None leads him, and none ever led,

. . .

Save his own soul he hath no star,
And sinks, unless his own soul guide,
Helmless in middle turn of tide.

Reliance on the Divine Humanity is self-reliance. In *On the Downs*, Swinburne is uplifted by "the wise word of the secret earth":

There is no God, O son,
If thou be none.

He would agree, then, with Blake's

Thou art a man; God is no more;
Thine own humanity learn to adore.

He deifies man in order to deify himself.

He is equally romantic in calling upon nature to authenticate the divinity of man. As we have just seen, in *On the Downs* it is the voice of the earth that assures him of his godhead; and "Glory to Man in the highest" is "the love-song of earth." The oppressed peoples of Europe address to Mother Earth a reverent but rather disillusioned *Litany of Nations*:

We thy children, that arraign not nor impeach thee
Though no star steer us,
By the waves that wash the morning we beseech thee,
O mother, hear us.

(We may note in passing that the cult of Proserpina has not wholly been abandoned, for the bride of Pluto is the daughter of Ceres.) "The Republic" appears as *Mater Dolorosa*, a sort of Kathleen-ni-Houlihan who wistfully longs for the hour when "the soul of man and her soul and the world's be one."[20] *Walt Whitman in America* is hailed as one who has identified "the earth-God Freedom" with "The great god Man, which is God."

We must turn to *Hertha*, however, for a complete setting-forth of the "God = Freedom = Man = Earth" equation. "Of all I have done," said the author, "I rate *Hertha* highest as a single piece, finding in it the most of lyric force and music combined with the most of condensed and clarified thought."[21] In this remarkable poem Hertha is not merely external matter—"I am the soul." But although she is the World Soul she is also the physical universe. In fact she is literally everything: "Beside or above me / Naught is there to go." Man is not to invoke her as a transcendent spiritual force: fully developed human power is the very power of Hertha. "I am thou, whom thou seekest to find him; find thou but thyself, thou art I." Hence "she stirs not for all who have prayed." But she is not quite accurate when she declares that her growth has "no guerdon / But only to grow." This all-encompassing impersonal force has a beneficent desire. From the very first "dim changes of water" she has labored to give birth to man—free, strong, happy, loving, self-sufficient man, "pulse of my center, and fruit of my body, and seed of my soul." She says to her children:

I bid you but be;
I have need not of prayer;
I have need of you free
As your mouths of mine air;
That my heart may be greater within me, beholding the fruits of me fair.

Thus the mother-and-child metaphor, though poetically indispensable, falls short of the full truth. Hertha desires not merely to produce men but to become fully human.

Why then have the children in which her being is consummated gone whoring after strange gods who only terrorize and oppress them? Since every physical atom and every action and thought of man is a part of Hertha, she herself would seem to be responsible for his religious aberrations. Nevertheless she blames man for his disloyalty to her:

O my sons, O too dutiful
Toward gods not of me,

[20] *Mater Triumphalis*, the companion-piece, voices the more confident mood of *Hertha*.
[21] *Complete Works*, XVIII, 184.

Was I not enough beautiful?
Was it hard to be free?

How, we vainly wonder, can there be gods external to that which includes everything? Hertha herself seems to recognize a God "not of me" who is her deadly enemy. But since these are *Songs before Sunrise* she assures her incomprehensibly erring sons that the celestial tyrant will soon be destroyed:

Thought made him and breaks him,
Truth slays and forgives;
But to you, as time takes him,
This new thing it gives,
Even love, the beloved Republic, that feeds upon freedom and lives.

And the creed of the Republic of love is that the only God is Hertha-Man—"Man, equal and one with me, man that is made of me, man that is I."

By Swinburne's day the river of human sufficiency had been fed by so many tributary streams that the sources of *Hertha* cannot be determined with much precision. Mazzini had declared in his *Credo* of 1867: "Humanity is not an aggregation of individuals but a Collective Being. . . . Humanity is a man who lives and works for men. . . . The best Interpreter between Individual man and God is Humanity."[22] But Swinburne goes further than this: his Collective Being is not an interpreter of the Unknowable, but very God of very God. The influence of Comte seems obvious at this point. In the official cult of the Positivistic state, furthermore, Man as the Great Being was to be worshipped in and through individual great men and women. This might have encouraged Swinburne's combination of Man-worship and personal hero-worship. Also if the First Person of the Comtian Trinity is the Great Being, the Second Person is the Grand Fetich, Earth. The fact may have been suggestive to the poet, though in the religion of Positivism, Man and Earth are not identified as in *Hertha*. But even at his most visionary Comte would be too systematic and too authoritarian for Swinburne. If Hegel's Absolute were completely identified with human mind (no very difficult feat) the essential theme of *Hertha*—the universe as the self-creation of mind through nature—would be thoroughly Hegelian. After the publication of *Poems and Ballads* Swinburne became more intimate with Jowett than in the Oxford days, and the Master of Balliol may have told his former pupil something about his favorite philosopher. *Hertha* also smacks a little of Hindu pantheism:

[22] Quoted by Lafourcade, *Swinburne*, p. 175.

I the mark that is missed
And the arrows that miss,
I the mouth that is kissed
And the breath in the kiss,
The search, and the sought, and the seeker, the soul and the body that is.

Might Emerson's *Brahma* have been an intermediary between Swinburne and the monistic Orient?

Swinburne would be inclined to associate Comte's Great Being with such earlier conceptions of Cosmic Man as Blake's Albion, Swedenborg's Grand Man, and perhaps the Adam Kadmon of the Cabala. Since he was himself a romantic poet, we may safely emphasize the influence of Blake, to whom he devoted one of his most substantial critical studies, of Shelley (*Cor Cordium*), of Whitman (*To Walt Whitman in America*), and of Victor Hugo, in whose *Religions et Religion* he was to detect "an unconscious echo and indeed the very voice of William Blake."[23] Professor Beach associates the poem with Goethe's views as to the relations between man and nature.[24] As other possible sources Lafourcade mentions Cleanthes' *Hymn to God*, Tennyson's *The Higher Pantheism*, Schopenhauer, and Darwin.[25]

The last name deserves particular attention. "With Swinburne," says Joseph Warren Beach, "we come at length to an English poet in whom evolutionary ideas have borne fruit in a nature-poetry militantly 'naturalistic.'" In *Songs before Sunrise*, "he apparently takes for granted the derivation of man by process of evolution from the substance of the material earth." In *Hertha*, "It is from earth, from nature, that man derives his being, his mind, his aspirations, his morality."[26] It seems to me, however, that Professor Beach somewhat exaggerates the materialistic element which the poem undoubtedly includes. The evolution described by Swinburne is not only a physical but also, and more essentially, a spiritual process. The business of Hertha is not mechanically to *produce* man, but to *become* the humanity that she possessed in potentiality from the beginning of time. Man to her is "fruit of my body" only because he is "pulse of my center" and "seed of my soul." Through her, the human spirit *produces itself.* To say that this kind of evolution is more Hegelian than Darwinian is not to deny that Swinburne associated modern science with intellectual liberty and the downfall of supernaturalism. As late as 1887 *The Commonweal* hails scientific enlightenment in precisely the spirit of an eighteenth-century Whig:

[23] *Complete Works*, XIII, 202, 205, 342.
[24] J. W. Beach, *The Concept of Nature in Nineteenth-Century English Poetry*, pp. 461, 474
[25] *Swinburne*, pp. 175–176.
[26] *Op. cit.*, pp. 455, 605.

What Newton's might could not make clear
Hath Darwin's might not made?

The forces of the dark dissolve,
The doorways of the dark are broken:
The word that casts out night is spoken,
And whence the springs of things evolve,
Light born of night bears token.

In more pessimistic moods, evolution can give a modern tinge to the Greek sense of all-controlling doom. But when Swinburne sings as a champion of freedom he has no intention of subjecting "the holy spirit of man" to the physical mechanism of the universe. He will agree than man belongs to nature if you will agree that nature belongs to man. Matter is strong, but human pride is stronger.

In *Hymn of Man* and frequently elsewhere, Swinburne combines assertion of his own faith with attacks upon the Christianity which denies it. His enmity toward Roman Catholicism is especially bitter, largely because of his espousal of Mazzini's anticlericalism but also because in Swinburne's day the Catholic Church, of all expressions of Christian belief, insisted most firmly on the transcendence of God and the insufficiency of man. His own Anglo-Catholic rearing may further help to explain his marked tendency to identify Christianity with Catholicism. He had more sympathy with Protestantism to the extent that it implied revolt against ecclesiastical authority. Writing of *Bothwell*, he tells Lord Houghton that John Knox "is in effect, beneath the outer shell of Protestant bigotry, the prophet or at least the precursor of democracy and the popular spirit of the future."[27] Evidently Swinburne—with Carlyle, Kingsley, Ruskin, and Mr. Middleton Murry—feels a psychological kinship between the Protestant temper and his own faith in human energy. Concerning "Protestant bigotry" as represented by contemporary Evangelicals and Nonconformists he has practically nothing to say; it had no bearing on the *risorgimento*, and in any case he was after bigger game. That he scorned it may be inferred from his warm approval of *Literature and Dogma*:

> I am personally delighted that a critic hitherto regarded as so safe and considerate a thinker, when compared with "such as this republican," should, while dwelling so warmly on the value and significance of the Bible, have so distinctly repudiated that most objectionable "Person," the *moral and intelligent* governor of the universe. I do not despair of seeing the day when any reference to the Bible as an

[27] *Complete Works*, XVIII, 140.

> authority will be equivalent, in the eyes of all respectable persons, to an open avowal of atheism.[28]

He liked Bibliolatry no better than Ecclesiolatry; he merely regarded the latter as the more formidable enemy.

With a ribaldry sometimes witty and sometimes blatant, Swinburne derides Christian beliefs and practices in his letters and in many unprintable bits of verse.[29] Even in his serious published poems his violence is often too extravagant to be effective. Something of the old tradition of "flyting" seems to have descended from his Border ancestors to his poetry as to his controversial prose. Such a poem as *Christmas Antiphones* shows that he is more persuasive when less violent. The first section, "In Church," is a mournful but reverent prayer to Jesus:

> Bid our peace increase,
> Thou that madest morn;
> Bid oppressions cease;
> Bid the night be peace,
> Bid the day be born.

These petitions are unanswered, and in the second section, "Outside Church," we hear the furious, despairing outcry of the people against oppressors both human and divine:

> Man on us as God,
> God as man hath trod,
> Trod us down with might.
>
> We that one by one
> Bleed from either's rod,
> What for us hath done
> Man beneath the sun,
> What for us hath God?

In the third section, "Beyond Church," the Religion of Humanity is proclaimed to mankind:

> Man shall do for you,
> Men the sons of man,
> What no God would do
> That they sought unto
> While the blind years ran.

It is not a very good poem, but the device of a "historical" ascent from false religion to no religion to true religion makes more effective propaganda than war-whoops of "Thou art smitten, O God, thou art smitten!"

[28] *Ibid.*, p. 108.

[29] See T. E. Welby, *A Study of Swinburne*, pp. 268–269.

From the early Deists to the religious liberals of our own times, the human Jesus has been used as a weapon against traditional Christianity. Swinburne, like Shelley, is glad to praise the Jesus whose message of love has been so grossly perverted by His worshippers. And like Blake, though much more rarely, he is willing to regard Him with reverence as a beautiful personification of "the great god Man, which is God." The autobiographical letter of 1875 to Stedman asserts that "we who worship no material incarnation of any qualities, no person, may worship the Divine humanity, the ideal of human perfection and aspiration, without worshipping any god, any person, any fetish at all. Therefore I might call myself, if I wished, a kind of Christian (of the Church of Blake and Shelley), but assuredly in no sense a Theist." To the phrase, "a kind of Christian," he appends an explanatory note: "That is, taking the semi-legendary Christ as type of human aspiration and perfection, and supposing (if you like) that Jesus may have been the highest and purest sample of man on record."[30] All of Swinburne's favorable references to Christ may be interpreted in the light of this statement.

But although he feels entitled to worship Jesus as the Divine Humanity in the Church of Blake and Shelley, he is unable to do so because whatever may be real in the legendary Christ has been completely obscured and corrupted by the false religion which bears His name. Oliver Elton seems to ignore this fact when he describes *Before a Crucifix* as "not only an explosion against the Christ of theology, but a true, a heartfelt, and sometimes a splendid offering to the Christ of Galilee."[31] As a symbol of "Christian creeds that spit on Christ" the crucifix is to be loathed and derided; but it deserves worship as a symbol of suffering Humanity, of "the common face of man." Yet this true Humanity-Christ we *cannot* worship, for

When we would see thee man, and know
  What heart thou hadst toward men indeed,
Lo, thy blood-blackened altars; lo,
  The lips of priests that pray and feed
While their own hell's worm curls and licks
The poison of the crucifix.

Nay, if their God and thou be one,
  If thou and this thing be the same,
Thou shouldst not look upon the sun;
  The sun grows haggard at thy name.
Come down, be done with, cease, give o'er;
Hide thyself, strive not, be no more.

[30] *Complete Works*, XVIII, 183.

[31] *A Survey of English Literature, 1830–1880*, II, 61.

The "real" Jesus is too valuable a means of rebuking the Church to be abandoned entirely; but priestcraft has made it impossible for us to use Him as the image of human self-redemption. Rather than grope back into the ambiguous past, it is better to move forward with Hertha.

Sincere devotion to Christianity is entirely consistent with lack of enthusiasm for Pio Nono. Much of what Swinburne branded as evil was evil indeed. But the common idea that the sole requisite for being a good Christian is hostility to organized Christianity is probably fallacious. Let us wildly dream that in the eighteen-seventies there existed one universal Christian Church, perfectly loyal in every belief and practice to the teachings of Jesus; loving, tolerant, joyous; friendly to all truth; free from superstition and trickery; unspotted from the world, but alive to social responsibilities, the champion of the humble and the foe of the tyrant. Against such a Church Swinburne would assuredly not have hurled the *Hymn of Man* as it now stands. But if this imaginary Church represented anything that could be called a religion, it would proclaim a God external to man and ineffably superior to him; and it would insist that the price of communion with this God is human self-surrender. Furthermore, if this were a Christian Church, it would insist that Jesus Christ, in however shadowy and undefined a sense, was a revelation to man of the nature and the will of God. Swinburne would not have accepted either article of this minimal creed, for Man was the only God in whom he was willing to believe. To avoid any imputation of personal prejudice on this point I shall quote Mr. Welby, who seems not to be offensively bigoted. He holds that "Liberty is the vital principle of Swinburne," and that this liberty is to be defined as

> complete self-realization for man in obedience to the common human will, in satisfaction of the general aspiration of humanity. . . . It is because he is, in his own mode, religious that it becomes so urgently necessary for him . . . to assail not only conventional Christianity, but every theology which postulates a divinity exterior to man. . . . The religion of Swinburne . . . acknowledges no creative or moral energy external to the universe. Theism of any kind is impossible for him because he denies not only the possibility of any revelation, but the possibility of the human mind [*sic*] conceiving of any God who shall not be made in man's likeness.[32]

Although there is much in Swinburne's tirades against organized religion which deserves the respect of believers, one cannot imagine a Christianity, or any supernaturalistic religion, so uncorrupted—or so corrupted—that he would have accepted it. He loathed Christianity not because he was a Christian but because he was a romantic.

[32] *A Study of Swinburne*, pp. 22–23, 114.

He never abjured the gospel of *Hertha*, but his confidence in it as a means of transforming the world rapidly subsided with the subsidence of the political excitement which had provided it with fuel. After about 1873, physical and mental exhaustion turns him toward a dreamily melancholy aestheticism much more "escapist" than that of *Poems and Ballads*. It may be worth noting that his aestheticism includes a remnant of his faith in human energy. This power, however, is now the prerogative of the Poet rather than of Man. All readers of romantic poetry will be aware how flexibly, in accordance with the degree of the writer's confidence, it expands to confer the creative force upon all mankind or restricts it to the individual genius. As early as *Anactoria*, Swinburne had made Sappho declare that God cannot utterly destroy her, for she will live eternally as a song in nature (compare *Adonais*), in human passion, and in "all high things."

Essentially the same theme is revived in *The Last Oracle* (1876) as a sort of transition from *Hymn of Man* to the less purposeful poetry which he has now begun to cultivate. "Destroyer and healer, hear!" cries Swinburne to Apollo the poet-god, borrowing a little too obviously from Shelley. Poetry, he continues, is the creative element in the universe. It has made all the deities whom man has ever worshipped,

> For no thought of man made Gods to love or honour
> Ere the song within the silent soul began.

We have deserted Apollo for the pale Galilean, but at last "the Gods that ruled by grace of sin and death" have been conquered and destroyed. Unfortunately, however, we are now left with no gods at all. We must seek redemption through Apollo,

> For thy kingdom is not passed away,
> Nor thy power from the place thereof hurled;
> Out of heaven they shall not cast the day,
> They shall not cast out song from the world.

But since Apollo himself, like all other gods, is the product of man's poetry, there is little use in asking him to restore our god-making poetic faculty. "Song should bring thee back to heal us with thy song" is as circular as *Ode to the West Wind*, where Shelley prays to be uplifted by a power whose existence depends upon "the incantation of this verse." According to *The Interpreters* all human thought is essentially creative, but only in poetry does it achieve full beauty and potency. Natural objects are dead and meaningless until

Man gives them sense and soul by song, and dwelling
In thought.

. . .

In human thought have all things habitation;
Our days
Laugh, lower, and lighten past, and find no station
That stays.

But thought and faith are mightier things than time
Can wrong,
Made splendid once with speech, and made sublime
By song.

The fact that Swinburne is imitating the guitar music of Shelley's lines to Jane Williams beginning "The keen stars were twinkling" should warn us against regarding this aesthetic transcendentalism too solemnly.

During his long residence with Watts-Dunton he became, of course, milder, more conventionally "wholesome" and patriotically British, and toward the end more completely immersed in his beloved Elizabethan and Jacobean plays. But the Putney period extends far beyond the limits of this study, and in any case it would be a waste of time to attempt to distinguish between what he actually thought and what his late-found Victorianism permitted him to say. He avoids violent utterances on matters of religion, toys with the notion of a transmigration-of-souls kind of immortality, and speaks admiringly of Jesus as a good and gentle man who, like himself and Victor Hugo, was fond of little children.[33]

There is nothing, however, to indicate that he relaxed his opposition to all supernaturalistic religion and to Christianity in particular. His guardian, indeed, provides clear evidence to the contrary. When Swinburne died, his Anglo-Catholic sister Isabel was extremely anxious that his body should receive Christian burial, but Watts-Dunton—and it does him credit—stuck to his promise to Swinburne "that the burial service should never be read over his grave. . . . If he had made a slight matter of his antagonism to Christianity as so many freethinkers do it would have been different, but with him it increased with his years and at the last (if I must say what I am sorry to say) it was bitterer than ever."[34] Finally, however, a fumbling sort of compromise was arranged. At what must have been unusually high speed even for an Anglican clergyman, the Rector of Bonchurch read the committal office not over the grave, but as the coffin was removed from

[33] *Complete Works*, XVIII, 330.

[34] Letter from Watts-Dunton to Isabel Swinburne, quoted by Lafourcade, *Swinburne*, p. 301.

the hearse at the cemetery gates. He might more appropriately have read the lines:

> For thee no fruits to pluck, no palms for winning,
> No triumph and no labor and no lust,
> Only dead yew-leaves and a little dust.
> O quiet eyes wherein the light saith naught,
> Whereto the day is dumb, nor any night
> With obscure finger silences your sight,
> Nor in your speech the sudden soul speaks thought,
> Sleep, and have sleep for light.

Chapter Sixteen

THOMSON

JAMES THOMSON's unfortunate childhood became firmly linked in his memory with the least attractive manifestations of Christianity. At the Royal Caledonian Asylum, however, the orphan boy supplemented his meager schooling with books which admitted him to a world much pleasanter than his actual environment. At fifteen, Byron was for him the ideal romantic poet, but during the following year Shelley became the polestar. De Quincey, himself a wanderer in the City of Dreadful Night, was another favorite. Fielding, Smollett, and Defoe helped to shape the realistic side of his divided character. In later years romance and renunciation of romance would combine in his admiration for Heine.

But the immediate necessity was to find some means of making a living. In 1852, after a year of training school and a year of apprenticeship, he became a civilian schoolmaster in the army, and served in that repugnant capacity until 1862, when he was cashiered for a minor breach of discipline.[1] During this period the chief formative influences of his career were exerted upon him.

In 1851, while serving as an assistant teacher in a village near Cork, he had become engaged to the fourteen-year-old Matilda Weller. Her death in 1853 provided a favorite theme for Thomson's poetry during the next ten years. It gave him his first conclusive evidence of the impotence of man's desires. It also, however, gave him a flattering analogy: by thinking of her as Sophie von Kühn he was able to think of himself as Novalis.[2] He claimed spiritual kinship with both Shelley and Novalis in adopting the pen-name "Bysshe Vanolis" (almost always abbreviated as "B. V."). Whether the loss of Matilda was a major cause of his melancholy or mainly a medium for the release of hitherto unfocused neurotic feelings is a disputed question. I incline strongly to the latter view without being able to substantiate it. That a seventeen-year-old should enter into a "some day we'll marry" sort

[1] He went swimming with a group of soldiers in an "off bounds" area and refused along with the others to give his name to the officer who caught them.

[2] Imogene Walker doubts whether he had any firsthand acquaintance with Novalis's work at the time of Matilda's death. (*James Thomson*, p. 61.) But soon he read the German romantic with care and began translating the "hymns" inspired by the loss of Sophie.

of engagement with a girl of fourteen is not a disquieting circumstance. But a well-adjusted boy does not find his ideal lover in Friedrich von Hardenberg or rest long content with the knowledge that he has a little heavenly soul-bride—especially if he does not believe in heaven. What Thomson writes about the dead Matilda does not sound quite healthy. There is too much talk of her purity, too much uneasiness about his own carnality. He seems to have shrunk from the physical side of love as if it were shameful. He never married and apparently had no sex-life at all. The horse-boat-pipe-girl manliness of *Sunday Up the River* is factitious. In his attitude toward Matilda, in his alcoholism, and in the general manic-depressive pattern of his nature, he reminds one of Poe. No, there was already something wrong with Thomson when he met Matilda-Sophie-Ulalume. He used her as a loveless way of being "in love."

In 1851 he also made friends with an army private who was destined to achieve fame in fields other than military. There is no reason to suppose that Charles Bradlaugh was wholly responsible for Thomson's conversion to secularistic rationalism. By the time they met, the disturbed young school-master had doubtless reacted sharply against what he took to be Christianity. But Bradlaugh introduced him to a well-defined tradition of aggressive unbelief; gave him a cause and comrades, arguments and ammunition, and eventually a sort of trade. At least up to the time of his discharge, however, the dead Matilda claimed Thomson's heart about as strongly as Bradlaugh claimed his brains. She had been more pious than he and had sometimes voiced gentle Gretchen-like distress at her Faust's bold opinions. After her death, her purity and her piety combined to preserve early influences which would otherwise have been cast off without much hesitation. Always in need of something to feel guilty about, he felt guilty about his irreligion. It was a sin. Yet, would not acceptance of her beliefs constitute a sin against reason? Either way he could be sure of sinning. That was something, but not enough.

Hence the poems written between 1853 and 1862 point in several incongruous directions. The somber tone of *The Doom of a City* predicts that of his masterpiece, but the poem shows him still trying to reconcile the reality of evil with the reality of a benevolent God. In *A Recusant* he longs to go to church but feels a moral obligation to remain outside:

How sweet to enter in, to kneel and pray
With all the others whom we love so well!
All disbelief and doubt might pass away,
All peace float to us with its Sabbath bell.

Conscience replies, There is but one good rest,
Whose head is pillowed upon Truth's pure breast.

But the breast of truth, as Thomson conceives of truth, is no less flinty than pure. In 1860 he can derive no ray of hope for human betterment from *The Dead Year* which has just passed. He tries to rejoice in the "heathen manhood" of *Robert Burns*:

He felt scant need
Of church or creed,
He took small share
In saintly prayer,
His eyes found food for his love;
He could pity poor souls condemned to hell,
But sadly neglected endeavours to dwell
With the angels in luck above.

But healthy animalistic paganism was impossible for Thomson.[3] He was never able to suppress his awareness that a godless life is a devaluated life. When he tries to be sheerly naturalistic he shows us nothing but the bestial horrors of *A Real Vision of Sin*. According to a note penciled by the author on his manuscript, this poem was "Written in disgust of Tennyson's, which is very pretty and clever, and silly, and truthless."[4] The characters in this Zolaesque slice of life are a vile old thieving beggar, his vile old doxy, and their vile old dog, each consumed with hatred of the other two. Urged on by his mate, who possesses a nihilistic philosophy too sophisticated for her station, the old man agrees to commit suicide with her in the nearby stream; but he craftily pulls back at the last moment and leaves her to drown alone. His glee is short-lived, for the dog, whom he has recently beaten, leaps at his throat; they fall into the stream and drown each other.

From such labored loathesomeness Thomson's imagination recoils in quest of some faith which will replace the one he has rejected. A poem of 1855 was *Suggested by Matthew Arnold's "Stanzas from the Grande Chartreuse,"* which Thomson regards as a fitting "dirge for a mighty Creed outworn." Part I assumes that Christ is dead; but Part II, in a way which reminds us more strongly of Clough than of Arnold, avers that although "the great Form" is dead "the Divine" is an undying spirit which requires some new mode of expression. In Part III, however, Thomson fears that no man of this age can be looked to for a modernized revelation. We had

[3] The reader of Volume III of this series will have been reminded that it was also impossible for Burns.

[4] *Poetical Works*, II, 391.

better maintain provisional loyalty to the dead Christ "Till the diviner One appear."

> Nay,—our adoring love should have
> More faith than to believe that He,
> Before Another comes to save,
> Can leave us in blind misery
> Without a Guide: God never can
> So utterly depart from man.
>
> We will move onward!—let us trust
> That there is life and saving power
> In this dear Form which seems but dust.

If dead *men* can inspire us, he asks, why not a dead *God*? From such pathetic nonsense he rather often turns, during this period, to a pantheism which he vainly attempts to reconcile with both the struggle-for-existence conception of nature and with the religion of humanity. *Shelley* (1861) hails that poet as an angelic spirit sent down from heaven to teach a corrupted world that the Soul of the Universe is "infinite love for all things that exist." How these poor souls gravitate toward Shelley!

Such ideas continued to exert some emotional appeal even after his intellect had rejected them. His admiration for Shelley, Novalis, and—inevitably—for Blake and Whitman was maintained to the end of his life. His tastes, as his critical essays bear witness, were always more affirmatively romantic than his official philosophy. After 1862, however, his gropings toward a romantic substitute-religion are largely though not quite completely abandoned in favor of more thoroughgoing unbelief. Upon his dismissal from the service he lived for several years in the home of Bradlaugh, who had left the army and was rising rapidly to leadership in secularistic and radical circles. Through his good offices Thomson became something like a professional propagandist against Christianity, contributing frequently to The *National Reformer*. Before long, however, it proved hazardous to rely on him for regular and systematic service: as early as 1863 he was drinking hard.

The *National Reformer*, edited by Bradlaugh, was the organ of the Secularist Society. That organization had been founded after the collapse of Chartism by George Jacob Holyoake, the veteran politico-religious radical, to preserve and foster the ideals of intellectual freedom and human brotherhood which the Chartist platform had vainly endeavored to implement.

For some twenty years the Society led a seedy, precarious existence; but in the eighteen-sixties, encouraged by the changing climate of opinion, it grew much more prosperous and aggressive. In one of the 1868 issues of the journal Christopher Charles summed up the Secularist program: "It takes reason for its guide, morality for its principle, and utility as the test of all the actions and institutions of men. . . . Secularism adopts reason instead of faith, science instead of revelation, nature instead of providence, work instead of worship and prayer, and holds that humanity, instead of divinity, should occupy the thought of men and command their service."[5] A familiar cluster of ideas. But since the leaders of the movement were rough-and-tumble propagandists rather than scientists or philosophers they were rather old-fashioned in their up-to-dateness. Their faith was tinged with the eighteenth-century perfectibilitarianism of Godwin and Condorcet; their conception of great poetry was fully satisfied by *Queen Mab*. The Protestantism which they attacked was already obsolescent, and the satirical devices which they employed against it were borrowed from Voltaire and Paine.

In the eighteen-seventies, "Secularism" in this special restricted sense and the more philosophic secularism of the major Victorian intellectuals partly coalesced, the former becoming more deeply versed in contemporary ideas and the latter employing more aggressive controversial tactics. Yet there remained an essential difference between the two wings of the movement. Huxley's primary aim was not to destroy religion: he attacked it only when bishops got in his way. Bradlaugh, on the other hand, cared little about science except as a weapon with which to slay a deadly foe.[6] The socio-political motive was naturally stronger among the middlebrows than among the highbrows. There cannot have been many agnostics who subscribed to both the *Fortnightly Review* and the *National Reformer*. The journal of the Secularist Society was read chiefly by radical workingmen—intelligent, ambitious, and thwarted products of the popular education movement who, not without reason, associated religion with opposition to their advancement. They had little or no impersonal philosophic interest in the ideas which were rendering it difficult for more learned and well-to-do Victorians to retain the traditional faith, but they were delighted to learn that those ideas were making trouble for their old enemies, kingcraft and priestcraft. It sufficed them to be told, again and again, that thanks to Strauss and Darwin it was now an open secret that Christianity was nonsense.

[5] Quoted by Imogene Walker, *James Thomson*, p. 44.

[6] The difference is relative, not absolute: H. K. Clifford combined Huxley's enthusiasm for science with Bradlaugh's detestation of Christianity.

In many ways Thomson found the opinions and aims of the Secularist Society congenial enough. He himself was an unusually gifted member of the class which he addressed in the *Reformer*. His self-made culture, almost wholly linguistic and literary, too thinly covered the native vulgarity which he had no chance to outgrow. He lacked a philosophical center from which to judge his second-hand notions of "scientific law," and he identified theology with the crudest fundamentalism. The negative side of Bradlaugh's program appealed to him strongly: whatever else might or might not be true, Christianity was false and must be destroyed. That conviction provided a small rock of sureness in the bleak ocean of his incertitude. For many of his associates, the political aspect of the cause was paramount, since in a nation of free men religion would die a natural death. This, Thomson thought, was putting the cart before the horse: if England was ever to be a republic, her people must *first* be cured of their addiction to spiritual opiates. His prose attacks on Christianity use all the tricks of the trade.[7] Some of the essays are quite serious rationalistic tracts. For example, he argues that "unlike most myths, which have a certain justification in their beauty, in their symbolism of high truth," the myth of Jesus as God "distorts the beauty, degrades the sublimity, stultifies the meaning of the facts wherein it has been founded." But of course "Jesus, as a man, commands my heart's best homage."

He writes more zestfully when he engages in satire. On *Christmas Eve in the Upper Circles,* "Poor dear God sat alone in his private chamber, moody, miserable, sulky, weary, dejected, supernally hipped." He was old and rheumatic, "his back bent, his chin peaked, his poll bald, his teeth decayed, his body all shivering, his brain all muddled, his heart all black care; no wonder the old gentleman looked poorly as he cowered there, dolefully sipping his Lachryma Christi. 'I wish the other party would lend me some of his fire,' he muttered, 'for it is horribly frigid up here'." He dislikes the priggish Jesus but talks to him for want of better company. He tells the unattractive youth that in earlier days he envied the loves of Zeus.

> So I, like an old fool, must have my amour; and a pretty intrigue I got into with the prim damsel Mary! Then a great thought arose in me: men cannot be loyal to utter aliens; their gods must be human on one side, divine on the other; my own people were always deserting me to pay homage to bastard deities. I would adopt you as my own son (between ourselves, I have never been sure of the paternity) and admit you to a share in the government.

And so on. It is difficult for a Christian to evaluate such vivacities with

[7] The best examples, both serious and satirical, have been edited by G. W. Foote in *James Thomson. Satires and Profanities*, the source of my quotations from Thomson's prose.

complete detachment. Considering the purpose and the audience, the satire has a swashbuckling effectiveness. More cultivated secularists than the readers of the *National Reformer* would, however, probably agree that it is so crudely extravagant as to defeat its own purpose, that it reveals more of the vulgarity of Thomson than of the absurdity of the Christian faith.

Toward the more constructive aspect of the Society's program Thomson could not feel wholeheartedly enthusiastic. A great deal of Victorian romanticism, as we know, expressed itself through the religion of humanity; but the Secularists enveloped this faith in an atmosphere so drably utilitarian that they denied rather than encouraged the manic side of Thomson's divided nature, while on the other hand their shallow optimism was unsatisfying to his depressive side. Some remnants of boyhood Calvinism prevented him from associating evolution with perfectibility. If man is the helpless puppet of mechanistic predestination, how can he prate of self-improvement through voluntary effort? Science was no less the enemy of romantic aspiration than of Christian superstition and obscurantism. Even after 1870, when he found a kindred spirit in the hopeless Leopardi, Thomson sometimes tried to follow the complete party line, but not with full conviction. As late as the year before his death the laureate of pessimism was persuaded to compose the *Address on the Opening Night of the New Hall of the Leicester Secular Society*. Let us picture to ourselves that hall and that audience as we read:

> Who loveth not the brother at his side,
> How can he love a dim dream deified?
>
> We know our lives at best are full of care,
> But we may learn to bear and to forbear,
> By sympathy and human fellowship.
>
> . . .
>
> This is the spirit in which we have wrought
> To build our little Temple of Free Thought
> And mere Humanity—to us Divine
> Above the deity of any shrine:
> This modest Hall for Club and Institute
> Which we now open; may it bear good fruit!
> No rigid barriers of sex or sect
> Or party in these halls do we erect:
> *In*clusion not *ex*clusion is our aim.
>
> . . .
>
> Our creed is simple, All men are one man!
> Our sole commandment, Do what good you can.

The only really Thomsonian line is the one least appropriate to the occasion—"We know our lives at best are full of care." Otherwise he says all the proper things, but plainly the eviscerated cheerfulness of these godless conventicles is repugnant to him. He is a freethinker who does not believe that thought is free.

Therefore most of the poems written between 1864 and 1870 depart rather widely from orthodox secularism in the direction of a philosophy, or anti-philosophy, of unreflecting vitality fabricated as a remedy for his deepening melancholy. In *Vane's Story*, to be sure, there is much that would please Bradlaugh. The poem is obviously autobiographical. Returning to him in vision from the spirit world, Matilda is distressed to find him still an unbeliever, but he rallies her tenderly:

> You good Child! I beseech no more
> That one and one may make up four,
> When one and one are my assets,
> And four the total of my debts:
> Nor do I now with fervour pray
> To cast no shadow on broad day:
> Nor ever ask (as I asked once)
> That laws sustaining worlds and suns
> In their eternal path should be
> Suspended, that to pleasure me
> Some flower I love,—now drooping dead,
> May be empowered to lift its head.

He adds that he is not an atheist but an agnostic who doubts whether God wishes us to pry too urgently into His inscrutability. Yes, it is true that he consorts more with sinners than with saints. The latter

> . . . want no earthly friend,
> Having their Jesus: but perpend;
> What of the wild goats? what of us,
> A hundred times more numerous,
> . . .
> And in the next life (as they tell)
> Roasted eternally in Hell!

Furthermore he has seen too many saints who thought only of getting *themselves* into heaven:

> Their alms were loans to poor God lent,
> Interest infinity-per-cent;
> Their earnest prayers were coward cries,
> Their holy doctrines blasphemies;

Their faith, hope, love, no more, no less,
Than sublimated selfishness.

Now my gross, earthly, human heart
With man and not with God takes part;
With man, however vile, and not
With seraphim I cast my lot.

"If any human soul at all" is to be condemned to eternal torture,

Then I give God my scorn and hate,
And turning back from Heaven's gate
(Suppose me got there!) bow, *Adieu!*
Almighty Devil, damn me too!

Answering the beloved revenant's question as to whether he feels remorse for his unbelief, he says that he faintly remembers how "years ago" he tortured himself in this way:

What passionate secret prayers I prayed!
What futile firm resolves I made!
As well a thorn might pray to be
Transformed into an olive-tree;
As well a weevil might determine
To grow a farmer hating vermin;
The *I am that I am* of God
Defines no less a worm or clod.
My penitence was honest guile;
My inmost being all the while
Was laughing in a patient mood
At this extreme solicitude,
Was waiting laughing till once more
I should be sane as heretofore.

Having spurned all such delusions, he now stands in the broad daylight—a free, sane, iconoclastic, laughing, loving, human sinner. He has not forgotten his wish to be like Robert Burns. In *The Naked Goddess* he rejects both ascetic piety and the utilitarian cult of progress through reason. Artemis reappears in modern England to her own bewilderment and to the horror of all Britons except children and young lovers, who understand her perfectly. The message of *Philosophy* is that we should abandon philosophizing:

If you will analyze the bread you eat,
The water and the wine most pure and sweet,
Your stomach soon must loathe all drink and meat.

Life liveth but in Life, and doth not roam
To other realms if all be well at home:
"Solid as ocean-foam," quoth ocean-foam.

In an untitled fragment the earth good-humoredly derides the importunity of her over-inquisitive children:

"Dear Mother Earth, tell us, tell us, tell us!
What is the meaning of all the things we see?"—
Oh! what a family of puny little fellows,
Calling me always, *Tellus, Tellus, Tellus!*
Eat your bread, drink your wine, snatch at all you see;
But I am very busy, do not bother me.

The not very realistic cockneys of *Sunday Up the River* make love in accordance with a sentimentalized version of this gospel of vitality:

Let my voice ring out and over the earth,
Through all the grief and strife,
With a golden joy in a silver mirth:
Thank God for Life!

Let my voice swell out through the great abyss
To the azure dome above,
With a chord of faith in the harp of bliss:
Thank God for Love!

Let my voice thrill out beneath and above,
The whole world through:
O my Love and Life, O my Life and Love,
Thank God for you!

But since Thomson has no God, no love, and no life worth mentioning, and since he cannot stop thinking, these attempts to be earthy, vital, and breezily grateful to Something can give him little or no real satisfaction.

Singing is sweet; but be sure of this,
Lips only sing when they cannot kiss.

Statues and pictures and verse may be grand,
But they are not the Life for which they stand.

They can, however, bear much closer organic relationship to a man's personal apprehension of life than any work which Thomson had thus far produced. If he was to externalize his deepest self in authentic poetry he must affirm despair, not seek to suppress it. He had reached the point where he could satisfy the romantic desire for power only through a powerful expression of the impossibility of being romantic:

> Because it gives some sense of power and passion
> In helpless impotence to try to fashion
>   Our woe in living words, howe'er uncouth.

By 1870 he was working at his essay on Leopardi, and he had begun to compose *The City of Dreadful Night*.[8] We shall return to it at the close of the chapter.

After the publication of the *City* in 1874 he still functioned from time to time as a propagandist in prose. *Great Christ Is Dead* inverts Miss Barrett's Evangelical theme: it is Jesus, not the eternal Pan, who has died:

> More then eighteen hundred years have passed since the death of the great god Pan was proclaimed; and now it is full time to proclaim the death of the great god Christ. . . . Fate, in the form of Science, has decreed the extinction of the gods. Mary and her babe must join Venus and Love, Isis and Horus; living with them only in the world of art. Jesus on his cross must dwindle to a point, even in the realms of legend under Prometheus and Caucasus.

Here Thomson may owe something to Winwood Reade, who three years before had written in *The Martyrdom of Man*: "Where now is Isis the mother, with the child Horus on her lap? They are dead; they are gone to the shades. Tomorrow, Jehovah, you and your son shall be with them."[9] Reade, however had sweetened his unbelief with a rather mystical form of the religion of humanity; Thomson, in this essay, would like to transform "Fate, in the form of Science" into romantic pantheism: "Christ the Great is dead, but Pan the Great lives again . . . not as a God, but as the All, Nature, now that the oppression of the Supernatural is removed." Perhaps his acquaintance with Roden Noel has renewed his loyalty to Shelley.[10]

Thus freed from the oppression of the Supernatural, Thomson is beginning to go to pieces.[11] In 1875, the year in which *Great Christ Is Dead* was published, he quarreled with Bradlaugh. He occasionally supports the cause of rationalism in *The Secularist*, a rival of the *Reformer*, and he contributes

[8] Completion of the poem was delayed by his trip to Colorado as agent for a mining company and by his service in Spain as a war correspondent during the following year. It was first published in the *National Reformer* March 22–May 17, 1874.

[9] *The Martyrdom of Man*, p. 443.

[10] See above, pp. 222–223.

[11] I do not mean to imply any necessary causal relationship between his principles and his miserable end. There have been plenty of cheerful sober atheists and plenty of melancholy drunken Christians. If the believer insists that the drunken Christians were not *real* Christians, the unbeliever may retort that the drunken atheists were not *real* atheists.

some of his best non-propagandist work to *Cope's Tobacco Plant*; but he is drifting steadily into the hopeless misery of dipsomania.

He goes down fighting; not all of the poems which he continues to write in soberer moments are utterly devoid of light. To be sure *Insomnia*, devoted to a major theme of his masterpiece, voices the hysterical dread that he alone will be denied the boon of sleep even in the grave. In the *Proem* to an unwritten work which might well have been a slightly softer sequel of the *City*,

> We stagger under the enormous weight
> Of all the heavy ages piled on us.

And we have lost the illusions which made life endurable for our forebears: "Our world is all stript naked of their dreams." For us there can be "No God . . . / No Heaven . . . / No life beyond death." Our only remaining hope is that of a better life for future generations. If *that* prove a mirage, then there remains

> In all our world, beneath, around, above,
> One only refuge, solace, triumph,—Love,
> Sole star of light in infinite black despair.

At least there is a star. Thomson views the shattered dreams of the past not with the arid glee of a triumphant rationalist but with the sentimental regret of a thwarted romantic, for the *Proem* ends:

> O antique fables! beautiful and bright,
> And joyous with the joyous youth of yore;
> O antique fables! for a little light
> Of that which shineth in you evermore,
> To cleanse the dimness from our weary eyes,
> And bathe our old world with a new surprise
> Of golden dawn entrancing sea and shore.

Again we see that Leopardi has not wholly supplanted Shelley. In *A Voice from the Nile* the personified river feels no scorn, but rather a puzzled pity and admiration, for men's vain efforts to find spiritual goods within the visible world:

> Poor men, most admirable, most pitiable,
> With all their changes all their great Creeds change:
> For Man, this alien in my family,
> Is alien most in this, to cherish dreams
> And brood on visions of eternity.

. . .

My other children live their little lives,
Are born to reach their prime and slowly fail,
And all their little lives are self-fulfilled;
They die and are no more, content with age
And weary with infirmity. But Man
Has fear and hope and phantasy and awe,
And wistful yearnings toward unsated loves,
That strain beyond the limits of his life,
And therefore Gods and Demons, Heaven and Hell:
This Man, the admirable, the pitiable.

She advises men to abandon these illusions and bend in reverence before the phenomenal world, saying, "Blessèd for ever be our Mother Earth"; but she knows, and seems half glad to know, that her counsel will never be accepted.

It is not surprising that Thomson, largely released from doctrinaire commitments and moving further and further into the fragments of his disintegrating nature, should slightly have relaxed the utter pessimism of *The City of Dreadful Night* in favor of "wistful yearnings toward unsated loves." Moreover the last seven years of his life do not constitute one unbroken downward plunge. They derive peculiar pathos from gleams of hope like those which sometimes delude the hero of a Greek tragedy just before the catastrophe. Prior to 1874, Thomson lived and wrote in a specialized circle which had little connection with the literary world. Rossetti, with his flair for such discoveries, had read and admired some of his earlier poems, but otherwise Thomson was practically unknown among his peers. *The City of Dreadful Night*, however, possessed a power which swept beyond the bounds of the Secularist Society. Men like George Meredith, Philip Marston, Roden Noel, and Bertram Dobell praised the poem and sought his acquaintance. Here was an excellent poet, a sensitive literary critic, an interesting though difficult human being, a wreck well worth salvaging. Just as Thomson approached his nadir, he saw that he had a chance of becoming a reputable man of letters if only he could pull himself together. Through Dobell he published two volumes of verse in 1880 and a volume of prose *Essays and Phantasies* in the following year.

Hence the mixture of real midnight and false dawn in *The Poet and His Muse*. Oppressed by deepest melancholy, he calls upon the muse to help him sing more joyously. She appears in answer to his summons, but she is no less pale and worn and sad than he. Bitterly she reproaches him:

Lo, you have ravaged me with dolorous thought
Until my brain was wholly overwrought,

Barren of flowers and fruit;
Until my heart was bloodless for all passion,
Until my trembling lips could no more fashion
Sweet words to fit sweet airs of trembling lyre and lute.

Now she is dead, and ghosts can sing no songs. But the poet refuses to accept her message of despair,

For lo, this beating heart, this burning brow,
This spirit gasping in keen spasms of dread,
This agony of the sting:
What soulless clod could have these tears and sobbings,
These terrors that are hopes, these passionate throbbings?
Dear Muse, revive! we yet may dream and love and sing!

If he could still feel agony, he had not lost all capability of feeling joy. So long as his heart leaps in passionate throbbings, Bysshe Vanolis need not admit complete frustration.

Too late. By this time the depressive troughs of the curve were much deeper than the manic peaks were high. *The Poet and His Muse* was written in 1882. Before the year was out he had died of intestinal hemorrhage after a six-day bout of drinking. We are told that his last words were so extravagantly blasphemous that no one has ever ventured to print them.[12] I should be quite willing to break the silence if I knew what they were, for in my opinion all facts and ideas about important matters deserve to be in print, no matter how shocking they may be to this person or that. At all events, it is clear that he did not permit himself to be scared into affirming beliefs which he did not possess, and for this he deserves our respect. What God thought (and eternally thinks) about James Thomson is no business of ours, but we are entitled to hope that the Recording Angel may have been directed to file the case under "Invincible Ignorance": the poor soul had so little chance, on this side of the grave, to learn the real meaning of the faith which he denied.

The City of Dreadful Night may be lengthy, repetitive, and awkwardly constructed, but it is one of the most powerful poems produced within the nineteenth century. Both before and after 1874, as we have seen, Thomson could write more hopefully in more hopeful moods, but it is right that he should be remembered for his greatest and blackest poem. Its importance for our subject is obvious. Its ideas and feelings are far from unique in this period, but nowhere else are they set forth with such uncompromising

[12] Imogene Walker, *James Thomson*, p. 172*n*.

intensity of despair. After observing so many attempts to extract from unbelief the satisfactions of belief, we are delighted to meet a good honest atheist who has the courage to write:

All substance lives and struggles evermore
Through countless shapes eternally at war,
  By countless interactions interknit;
If one is born a certain day on earth,
All times and forces tended to that birth,
  Not all the world could change or hinder it.

I find no hint throughout the Universe
Of good or ill, of blessing or of curse;
  I find alone Necessity Supreme,
With infinite Mystery, abysmal, dark,
Unlighted ever by the faintest spark
  For us the flitting shadows of a dream.

Now at last we know where we are. This is rock bottom. Such negation is radical enough to raise the possibility of affirmation.

But this is a strange poem to have been published in a journal devoted to making the godless life attractive. Perhaps Bradlaugh felt that its impressiveness as a statement of thoroughgoing unbelief outweighed the misery which it depicted, or perhaps he could not resist the temptation to show that really "high class" poetry could bloom from the dry soil of the Secularist Society. For whatever reason, he printed in the *National Reformer* a crushingly pessimistic interpretation of the principles which official rationalism advocated as a source of enlightenment, freedom, and happiness:

The world rolls round forever like a mill;
It grinds out death and life and good and ill;
It has no purpose, heart or mind or will.

. . .

Man might know one thing were his sight less dim;
That it whirls not to suit his petty whim,
That it is quite indifferent to him.

Nay, does it treat him harshly as he saith?
It grinds him some slow years of bitter breath,
Then grinds him back into eternal death.

Though probably not many readers of the *National Reformer* were orthodox Comtian Positivists, practically all of them would accept Comte's view of human history as ascending from the religious through the metaphysical to the positive or scientific stage of development. In Section XX of his poem Thomson allegorizes this theory with grimmest irony. The angel (man believing in God), the warrior (man believing in his own powers), and the unarmed man (man believing in nothing) successively collapse in impotence before the steady gaze of the sphinx. The symbolism of the sphinx herself is complex. She is "Necessity Supreme," but she is also "infinite Mystery"—Demogorgon, and the black void which enshrouds Demogorgon. She means knowing too much, and she means knowing nothing at all. In the next section she melts into the figure of Melancholia, "That City's somber Patroness and Queen." Then she reveals herself as

> The sense that every struggle brings defeat
> Because Fate holds no prize to crown success;
> That all the oracles are dumb or cheat
> Because they have no secret to express;
> That none can pierce the vast black veil uncertain
> Because there is no light beyond the curtain;
> That all is vanity and nothingness.

Not much consolation can be drawn from the discovery that "There is no God . . . / Whom we must curse for cursing us with life." The loss of any such object of vital hatred is perhaps the bitterest deprivation which an unbeliever can suffer. Equally unconvincing—to Thomson no less than to us—is the mock-stoicism of "No hope could have no fear."[13] The City is not the abode of ataraxy: it reeks with

> Infections of unutterable sadness,
> Infections of incalculable madness,
> Infections of incurable despair.

This poem is not the tragedy of a convinced positivist: positivism in itself knows no tragedy. It is the tragedy of Bysshe Vanolis, a romantic who has cast off the chains of Christianity in order to enjoy "All the sublime prerogatives of Man" and who finds that the aspirations of Shelley are no less completely thwarted by "Necessity Supreme."[14]

We cannot say, however, that *The City of Dreadful Night* simply shows us what "science" has done to romantic aspiration. When Thomson asserts that the universe has "no secret to express . . . no light beyond the curtain," he has no firm belief that he is stating the objective truth about the real

[13] The line translates a statement in one of Leopardi's letters: "Where is no hope is no place for inquietude." (Walker, *James Thomson*, p. 100*n*.)

[14] For no ascertainable reason, the mechanistic universe seems a trifle less hostile to Novalis than to Shelley. See the curious appearances of Matilda in Sections IV and IX, which seem wholly inconsistent with the philosophy of the poem. Thomson has no God, but he clings at times to a German-romantic sort of goddess.

nature of things. The poem represents the nemesis of subjectivism rather than the power of ineluctable fact to crush the heart's illusion. Thomson knows very well that the emptiness of the universe is the product of his imagination. Both *In Memoriam* and *The City of Dreadful Night* say "I have felt"; the difference is that Tennyson and Thomson feel differently. Thomson declares that he is not describing the world of "the hopeful young, / Or those who think their happiness of worth," or the superficially contented Philistines,

> Or pious spirits with a God above them
> To sanctify and glorify and love them,
> Or sages who foresee a heaven on earth.

No, he is addressing, and representing, a very special "sad Fraternity" of doomed souls,

> . . . desolate, Fate-smitten,
> Whose faith and hope are dead, and who would die—

men who have come "through the desert," who suffer from Leopardian *noia,* who have lost their Matildas, who cannot sleep, who drink too much. These are the sole inhabitants of the City of Dreadful Night, and they are not very numerous in proportion to the population of the globe. Every one of them, in fact, is James Thomson.

But of course, although he has no criterion of the reality of anything except its existence as a vivid impression in the mind, Thomson wants his misery to be *both* unique and universal. The poem certainly implies that those who have been initiated into the "sad Fraternity" are peculiarly qualified

> To show the bitter old and wrinkled truth
> Stripped naked of all vesture that beguiles,
> False dreams, false hopes, false masks and modes of youth.

On the other hand, since "life is but a dream," how is one to distinguish between "false dreams" and the real truth? The City itself is an illusion,

> For it dissolveth in the daylight fair;
> Dissolveth like a dream of night away.

The dream, however, is real for those who habitually dream it, since

> . . . when a dream night after night is brought
> Throughout a week, and such weeks few or many
> Recur each year for several years, can any
> Discern that dream from real life in aught?

> For life is but a dream, whose shapes return,
> Some frequently, some seldom, some by night,
> And some by day, some night and day; we learn,
> The while all change and many vanish quite,
> In their recurrence with recurrent changes
> A certain seeming order; where this ranges
> We count things real; such is memory's might.

Thus Thomson's pessimism arises not from acceptance of "the findings of science," but from a morbid subjective state of mind. Reality is the consistency of your dream. The subjectivism which enables happier romantics to assert the divinity of man has deprived Thomson of everything but "infinite void space." Perhaps the saddest feature of the poem is the absence of conviction that anything is really true or really false. The Inner Light has willed to extinguish itself.

To place Swinburne and Thomson last among our Victorian poets would greatly enhance the rhetorical effectiveness of my thesis. The device would show us romantic pride soaring to its climax in "Glory to man in the highest!" and descending to the inevitable catastrophe in *The City of Dreadful Night*, the final outcome of the tradition of Blake and Shelley. But the history of nineteenth-century religious ideas is too disorderly, inconclusive, and undramatic to justify so shipshape a conclusion. Both Swinburne and Thomson are sick men. Their cases, though clinically precious, are too exceptional to reflect the normal situation. Not unreluctantly, therefore, I have chosen to reach further back into the period and conclude our survey with Arnold and Clough—two poets who are more representative of the Victorian temper in being more hesitant, more willing to compromise, more resourceful in avoiding spiritual shipwreck by throwing out anchors in various directions, some romantic and some unromantic.

Chapter Seventeen

ARNOLD

IN STUDYING the religious bearings of Arnold's poetry, we should concern ourselves especially with the decade preceding his appointment to the Oxford professorship in 1857. Few of the poems which he wrote after this period have contributed much to his reputation as an analyst of the Victorian predicament. For intelligently bewildered young moderns, *Rugby Chapel* is as dead as *Merlin and the Gleam* or *Rabbi Ben Ezra*, but *Dover Beach* speaks to them in the language of their own hearts. Nor is it surprising that they should derive a kind of relief from the probity of his despair. There is something sanative in any honest description of a spiritual malady even though the diagnostician, himself deeply smitten by the disease, is unable to propose a remedy.

Time has not refuted Arnold's well-known words to his mother: "My poems represent, on the whole, the main movement of mind of the last quarter of a century, and thus they will probably have their day as people become conscious to themselves of what that movement is, and interested in the literary productions which reflect it."[1] He was referring, of course, not to the official progress-cult but to the doubt and confusion fermenting beneath it. What then are the symptoms of "this strange disease of modern life"? How to describe "the something that infects the world"? For Arnold, the root of the disease is lack of integration and clarity of purpose in the individual and in society. The tide of faith is receding, and no normative ethical, political, or aesthetic principles exist which might provide the meaningfulness no longer to be expected from religion. A whirl of aimless irrational activity gyrates about an emptiness through which we vainly grope in search of our buried selves. Uncertain of our ends, we glorify means—all kinds of "machinery," but especially the ugly, vulgar, antisocial machinery of getting and spending. Even those who refuse to admire the works of Philistinism can find little else to admire. In an age so lacking in moral grandeur, what is there to sustain one's faith in human greatness? Each man lives alone, walled up within a selfhood which he does

[1] *Letters*, II. 10.

not understand, deprived of vitality and joy but deprived equally of calm. The wheels go round faster and faster; all is noise and confusion; the changes are too rapid for interpretation; the torrent of unintelligible experience leaves us no time to breathe. Having no center to steady us, we oscillate from one extreme to another without urbanity or graciousness. When we try to be wise we grow hard and cold; when we try to be gay we are merely frivolous. If we revolt from meaningless drudgery it is only to make futile gestures of irrational defiance against laws which are incomprehensible to us. Such is "the hopeless tangle of our age." Possibly Arnold's picture is overdrawn; if it were a photograph, it would not be a drawing. We who also live in an "iron time / Of doubts, disputes, distractions, fears" will concede its essential faithfulness.

Carlyle, whose attack upon machine-civilization was launched much earlier than Arnold's, stubbornly clung to his romanticism throughout the successive phases of its debasement. In Arnold, on the other hand, the romantic impulse was frustrated not merely by the age but by his own nature. He shrank from the expansiveness for which he longed. He wanted free creative personality, but with plenty of poise and calm. Perhaps in revolting against machinery one cast off servitude only to put on madness. Expansiveness and manifoldness without reasoned aim merely aggravated spiritual bewilderment and resulted at last in melancholy exhaustion. Inchoate and disorderly aspiration he distrusted. Aspiration proceeding from what source of self-knowledge? Directed toward what clearly conceived goal? Those were the essential questions, and they could not be answered. Rationalism was suspect because it denied aspiration; aspiration was suspect because there seemed to be no rational basis for it. How to be passionate without eccentricity? How to be intelligent without desiccation of vital feeling?

But if his mind was thus racked by inner conflicts, one may well ask whether the malady which he describes is actually the strange disease of modern life or the strange disease of Matthew Arnold. To suppose that he confronted his environment with Sophoclean detachment, seeing it steadily and whole, is to misunderstand him. This unsparing critic of the *Zeitgeist* was one of its most helpless though most intelligent victims. I disagree, however, with what seems to be a growing tendency to repudiate Arnold's description of the predicament of modern man on the ground that it is merely a description of his own deficiencies. If he had not been a rather extreme example of the weaknesses which he deplores he would not have felt the contemporary malaise so keenly or expressed it so movingly.

Arnold was torn between the wish to be exactly like his father and the wish to be as different from him as possible. An uneasy and inhibited lover, he desired Marguerite but felt that her vitality would be bad for his *Bildung*.[2] He was introspective and melancholy but wanted so much to be a eupeptic extrovert that he often succeeded in behaving like one. When he mingled with the world of action he lost his sense of personal integrity; when he retreated into himself he felt lonely and selfish. He was overly sensitive to noise and muddle and tended to confuse reality with vulgarity. A genuine lover of mankind, he was also an intellectual and social snob of the first water. He was a complete subjectivist who strove to devise objective value-standards not only for himself but for all Englishmen; an ardent liberal who wished (up to the last decade of his career) to preserve the ideals of the French Revolution by means of a paternalistic State, an Established Church, and a National Academy. To credit such a man with a solidly integrated character would be rash. It can hardly be said, however, that his inconsistencies were so unique as to disqualify him from understanding the conflicts which plagued other members of the intellectual class of the nineteenth century—or for that matter of the twentieth.

According to M. Bonnerot, Arnold was primarily a sufferer from the *mal du siècle*, a belated romantic who looked upon the strenuous, confident world of the eighteen-fifties with the lackluster eyes of Obermann, René, Manfred, and Ortis.[3] He clung to the mood expressed in Tennyson's *Second-Rate Sensitive Mind* and Browning's *Pauline*. But the *mal du siècle*, beneath the affected posturings in which it often found expression, was a deeply real thing—the bewilderment of men who had found that the human mind had shaped a world unfit for the habitation of the human spirit. This melancholy uneasiness, with the struggle to surmount it, constituted precisely what Arnold meant by "the main movement of mind of the last quarter of a century." His own too abundant share of the *mal du siècle* enabled him to detect its presence in the hearty eighteen-fifties and to realize that it was of greater historical importance than the cult of energy which tried to shout it down. Before long the official optimism began to crack; and by 1880, when Arnold's poetry came into its own, there were many who acknowledged that he had been right. Today we do not express our despair in the manner of *Werther*, but we are not so free from the essential spirit of *Weltschmerz* that we can dismiss Arnold's melancholy as anachronistic either for his age or for our own.

[2] Personally I have no doubt that Marguerite was a real person, but this is the way he felt about her even if she was imaginary.

[3] Louis Bonnerot, *Matthew Arnold, Poète*. See especially pp. 123–124, 127, 160–161, 221.

To this important extent Arnold was a wise man. But the same deep personal involvement which made him exceptionally sensitive to the real rather than to the apparent spirit of his times also rendered him incapable of healing that spirit in himself or in others. He was too completely immersed in the age to have any notion of how to get out. To say this is to imply that Arnold never attained his ideal of the poet as consoler and fortifier of man's spirit. Nevertheless his pre-1857 poetry, precisely because it does no more than grope toward answers to the painful questions that it asks, is perhaps truer to his nature and therefore more valuable than his prose, which fabricates interesting but inadequate solutions.

In the pre-1857 poems Arnold's melancholy is occasionally, though very rarely, relieved by hopes that might loosely be described as religious. Man still has his soul, "And while it lasts, we cannot wholly die." Conceivably the river of time

> May acquire, if not the calm
> Of its early mountainous shore,
> Yet a solemn peace of its own

as it draws nearer to the "Murmurs and scents of the infinite sea." Yet the world which he confronts is one from which positive religious belief has almost wholly vanished. It has vanished from his own mind no less than from his environment. He frequently speaks of "God" as an eighteenth-century poet might speak of "great Jove" or "the gods." Sometimes the term carries a little more significance, but it never implies the real existence of a Divine Being with whom he seeks communion in remorse and love and fear and joy. He tells Clough that

> with me a clear almost palpable intuition is necessary before I get into prayer: unlike many people who set to work at their daily self-denial etc. like furies in the dark hoping to be gradually illuminated as they persist in this course. Who also may be sheep but not of my fold, whose one natural craving is not for profound thoughts, mighty spiritual workings etc. etc. but a distinct seeing of my own way so far as my own nature is concerned.[4]

Indirectly, however, the subsidence of faith was a disaster because it rendered the distinct seeing of one's own way more difficult.

> What bard,
> At the height of his vision, can deem
> Of God, of the world, of the soul
> With a plainness as near,
> As flashing as Moses felt?

[4] *Letters to A. H. Clough*, p. 110.

Things had been much clearer when people believed in God, and Arnold longed for clarity.

Even more importantly, however, the decay of religion was a main cause of that desiccation of vital feeling which he shared with his disillusioned contemporaries. "God keep us both from aridity!" he writes Clough in 1852. "*Arid*—that is what the times are."[5] Hence although he never pretends to believe in Christianity during this period he almost never attacks it. The rather aggressive scepticism of *Mycerinus* is exceptional. In *Progress* he warns those rationalists who regard their spiritual emptiness as a sign of intellectual advancement:

> Say ye: the spirit of man has found new roads,
> And we must leave the old faiths, and walk therein?—
> Leave then the Cross as ye have left carved gods,
>   But guard the fire within!

Weaker spirits who could not guard the inner fire without cleaving to the Cross should conform to Christianity as a means of preserving the necessary warmth:

> If one loved what was beautiful and interesting in itself *passionately* enough, one would produce what was excellent without worrying about religious dogmas at all. As it is, we are *warm* only when dealing with these last and what is frigid is always bad. I would have others—most others—stick to the old religious dogmas because I sincerely feel that this *warmth* is the great blessing, and this frigidity the great curse—and on the old religious road they would have still the chance of getting the one and avoiding the other.[6]

Like Tennyson and Browning, Arnold felt that cold-blooded morality is a contradiction in terms, and that religion, be it true or false, raises ethics to a suitable temperature. "The noblest souls of whatever creed," he was to say in his essay on *Marcus Aurelius*, "have insisted on the necessity of an inspiration, a joyful emotion, to make moral action perfect. . . . The paramount idea of religion is, that it has *lighted up* morality; that it has supplied the emotion and inspiration needful for carrying the sage along the narrow way perfectly, for carrying the ordinary man along it at all."[7]

On apparently religious grounds, Arnold can be suspicious of romantics who have a fire which burns without being stoked by any sort of suprapersonal spiritual fuel. As early as 1844 he had written in *Stagirius*:

> When the soul, growing clearer,
> Sees God no nearer;

[5] *Ibid.*, p. 131. [6] *Ibid.*, p. 43. [7] *Essays, First Series*, p. 348

When the soul, mounting higher,
Sees God no nigher;
But the arch-fiend Pride
Mounts at her side,
Foiling her high emprise,
Sealing her eagle eyes,
And, when she fain would soar,
Makes idols to adore,
Changing the pure emotion
Of a high devotion
To a skin-deep sense
Of her own eloquence;
Strong to deceive, strong to enslave—
Save, oh! save.

Speaking partly of the "disagreeable" nature of *Villette* and partly of the personality of its author, he describes Charlotte Brontë to Clough as "a fire without aliment—one of the most distressing barren sights one can witness. Religion or devotion or whatever it is to be called may be impossible for such people now; but they have at any rate not found a substitute for it and it was better for the world when they comforted themselves with it."[8]

Arnold's own inner fire burned low, and his efforts to supply it with some alimentary substitute for religion or whatever it is to be called were not very convincing even to him. Nevertheless he thinks that excessive indulgence in religious feeling is vulgarly disproportionate though perhaps pragmatically desirable for less cultivated persons. He finds that Francis Newman, in *Phases of Faith*, "bepaws the religious sentiment so much that he quite effaces it to me. This sentiment now, I think, is best not regarded alone, but considered in conjunction with the grandeur of the world, love of kindred, love, gratitude etc. etc."[9] The religious sentiment points toward no absolute external truth, and it is not the normative basis of other goods. It is merely one of many feelings, and with those feelings it withers away in the drought of the *Zeitgeist*.

In his poetry Arnold usually assumes as axiomatic that religion is dead or dying and proceeds to explore some aspect of the resultant confusion. There is probably not a single poem, indeed, in which his own inability to believe is a direct rather than an indirect cause of his melancholy. Even in *Dover Beach*, loss of faith is not so much a personal as a historical disaster. The loss of God is a tragedy not in itself, but in its consequences for intellectual, emotional, and ethical clarity and vitality.

[8] *Letters to Clough*, p. 132.

[9] *Ibid.*, p. 115.

Stanzas from the Grande Chartreuse is less exceptional than it appears at first glance. The fascination which the monastery exerts upon him is complex. The Tinker-Lowry commentary emphasizes its ritualistic aspect: "The organ music, the appeal of 'the high altar's depth divine,' the flickering tapers, and the 'cloistral round' have doubtless some reference to the followers of Pusey, Keble, and the leaders of the Anglo-Catholic Movement. The whole poem, in fact, should be read with the background of the Oxford Movement in mind."[10] Similarly Bonnerot regards the piece as one of several examples of Arnold's lively interest in the aesthetic side of Catholicism. He quotes from the essay *Irish Catholicism and British Liberalism* (1878): "The need for beauty is a real and now rapidly growing need in man; Puritanism cannot satisfy it, Catholicism and the English Church can."[11] Arnold preferred the *style* of Catholicism to that of Protestantism.[12] He might almost be termed a High Church agnostic, for in reciting the Creed in the chapel at Harrow he punctiliously turned to the east even when the clergy neglected to do so.[13] The "Church of the future," he believed, would be a Catholicism divested of Catholic belief but maintaining its beautiful forms as the unifying element of the State cult.[14] Newman was for him a charming example of "the sentiment of Oxford for beauty and sweetness." In his warfare against Philistinism, Arnold was grateful to the Oxford Movement for "the deep aversion it manifested to the hardness and vulgarity of middle-class liberalism, the strong light it turned on the hideous and grotesque illusions of middle-class Protestantism."[15] Keble had been his sponsor in baptism.

Arnold, in short, liked almost everything about Catholicism except its Christianity. That fact, however, is perhaps not of cardinal importance for interpretation of *Stanzas from the Grande Chartreuse.* He envies the monks chiefly for their exemption from the sick hurry of the modern world. On his romantic side, to be sure, he is impressed by the traditional stage properties of monasticism—dim corridors, flickering candles, "cowled forms"; but except in the penultimate stanza singled out by Tinker and Lowry he does not seem particularly interested in the very simple ceremonial of the Trappists. The mention of organ music in this passage is strangely contradicted by the seventh stanza—

[10] C. B. Tinker and H. F. Lowry, *The Poetry of Matthew Arnold*, p. 252.

[11] Quoted by Bonnerot, *Matthew Arnold, Poète*, p. 173.

[12] *Essays, First Series*, p. 141.

[13] E. M. Chapman, *English Literature in Account with Religion*, 1800–1900, p. 442.

[14] *St. Paul and Protestantism . . . and Last Essays on Church and Religion*, p. 337.

[15] *Culture and Anarchy*, p. 60.

> The chapel, where no organ peal
> Invests the stern and naked prayer.

In the same stanza Arnold astonishingly speaks of the monks' "Passing the Host from hand to hand." As Tinker and Lowry suggest, he may have been thinking of "the plaque bearing the image of the Crucified which the Carthusians pass about at the Pax (Kiss of Peace);"[16] but the error is hardly that of a liturgiological enthusiast or even of an attentive ill-informed observer. As regards the specifically religious ideas and emotions which ceremonial symbolizes, Arnold is tone deaf; he does not know what a monastery is for. These monks are merely "shy recluses" who live in "secluded dells" and who think of the altar as a stand for "yellow tapers." To the blandishments of the world they have nothing to say but "Leave our desert to its peace!" Their days, to be sure, are a "cloistral round / Of reverie, of shade, of prayer," but the three nouns are on the same level of importance.

Nevertheless the Chartreuse possesses qualities which Arnold wistfully admires. The monks are somewhat like the stars in *Self-Dependence.* They are withdrawn from the strife and din; their lives are calm, disciplined, obedient, peaceful. They know the secret of *Quiet Work*—"toil unsevered from tranquillity." Somehow they appear to have found the center of their being. Arnold does not understand what that center is; but he knows that these happy silent men are Catholic Christians, and for one moment he feels that he would almost be willing to share their beliefs and their discipline for the sake of their peace. The "rigorous teachers" of his youth have conditioned him against any such relapse into superstition. And yet the new world which those teachers had promised him, the world of enlightened happiness won through rational inquiry, seems powerless to be born. His faint Catholic hankerings can therefore be expressed only in terms of *Weltschmerz*:

> Oh, hide me in your gloom profound,
> Ye solemn seats of holy pain!
> Take me, cowled forms, and fence me round
> Till I possess my soul again.

The plea is no more religious, and no more conducive to self-integration, than the psychologically equivalent lines in *Parting*:

> Fold closely, O Nature!
> Thine arms round thy child.

What the monastery offers him is an anodyne, not a faith or even a liturgical show.

[16] *The Poetry of Matthew Arnold*, p. 250.

But although Arnold's most characteristic poems are not those of a man who believes in any sort of supernaturalistic religion, they are deeply saturated in a desire to attain what are now called "spiritual values." "Like as the hart desireth the waterbrooks, so longeth my soul after thee, O values. My soul is athirst for values, yea, even for living values: when shall I come to appear before the presence of values? My tears have been my meat day and night, while they daily say unto me, where are now thy values?" What then *were* his values, and on what foundation did they rest?

There can be little doubt that almost from the first he subscribed more or less consciously to the doctrine which he was later to formulate in the words: "More and more mankind will discover that we have to turn to poetry to interpret life for us, to console us, to sustain us."[17] But if the poet is to provide a consoling and sustaining interpretation of life his ideas must be derived from observation of the world in which men live—observation so acute and sympathetic that it constitutes quite as real a participation in life as if he bustled about in the marketplace. On the other hand, he must not become so involved in the superficies of everyday experience that he dissipates his creative individuality. Callicles names the essentials: "The rest of immortals, the action of men." Arnold failed to harmonize the two factors. Greatly preferring the former, he claimed for the poet the right to withdraw from the world and contemplate it with the serene all-seeing detachment of a Lucretian god. But he knew that poets are not gods, but men: they are doomed to feel the misery they see.

> These things, Ulysses,
> The wise Bards also
> Behold and sing.
> But oh, what labour!
> O Prince, what pain!

He was not quite willing to pay the price.

It was of course the poet's prerogative to draw his material from all times and places no less than from the here and now. But although Arnold could write *about* any period of culture, he could not escape the necessity of writing *in* the noisy, centrifugal, ignoble society of which he was a part. How could an artist hope to preserve his integrity in such an environment? How could he maintain true disinterestedness when he must evaluate everything that he read or thought or wrote as a more or less efficacious prescription for this strange disease of modern life? "My dearest Clough these are damned

[17] "The Study of Poetry," *Essays in Criticism, Second Series*, pp. 1–2.

times—everything is against one."[18] In less bewildering ages, poets could more easily achieve a synthesis of passion and reason;

> But we, brought forth and reared in hours
> Of change, alarm, surprise—
> What shelter to grow ripe is ours?
> What leisure to grow wise?

The petty vulgarities of the age were almost harder to bear than its profounder evils. In his longing for some sort of wholeness there were times when Arnold leaned toward art for art's sake: "People do not understand what a temptation there is, if you cannot bear anything not *very good*, to transfer your operations to a region where form is everything. Perfection of a certain kind may there be attained, or at least approached, without knocking yourself to pieces."[19] To yield to this temptation would be to transgress the principle that "For poetry, the idea is everything." It was hard, however, to convey fortifying ideas without preaching and arguing in the manner of poor Clough. The poet, Arnold insisted, must be an artist—an artist who understands life without losing his identity in its flux.

On the whole, then, it seemed best to withdraw from the action of men into his private inwardness. But when he attempted to do so he frustrated his strong impulse toward vitality, joy, love, communion with humanity and with nature. He could not bear society, and he dreaded loneliness. Bewailing the poet's lot, Empedocles addresses Apollo:

> The jars of men reach him not in thy valley—
> But can life reach him?
> Thou fencest him from the multitude—
> Who will fence him from himself?
>
> . . .
>
> Where shall thy votary fly then? back to men?—
> But they will gladly welcome him once more,
> And help him to unbend his too tense thought,
> And rid him of the presence of himself,
> And keep their friendly chatter at his ear,
> And haunt him, till the absence from himself,
> That other torment, grow unbearable;
> And he will fly to solitude again,
> And he will find its air too keen for him,
> And so change back, and many thousand times
> Be miserably bandied to and fro
> Like a sea-wave, betwixt the world and thee,
> Thou young, implacable God!

[18] *Letters to Clough*, p. 111.

[19] *Letters*, I, 72.

It is an unhappy poet, not an unhappy scientist, who leaps into the crater of Etna. The Victorian Empedocles, however, continued to oscillate between the poles of a complete poetic vocation, disconsolately murmuring:

> Ah! Two desires toss about
> The poet's feverish blood.
> One drives him to the world without,
> And one to solitude.

Temperamentally he was not well qualified to create that bracing sort of poetry which is to replace "what now passes with us for religion and philosophy."

Except for its greater intensity, the dilemma of the modern poet was the dilemma of modern man in general. We have been told that Arnold is "the formulator of modern Humanism,"[20] and a humanist should believe in the greatness of man. Arnold tries to do so. Goethe represented one of his most ardently cherished though least attainable ideals. Human personality, "God's harmonious whole," transcends the analytical peeping and botanizing of the psychologists, for it is

> Centred in a majestic unity;
> And rays her powers, like sister islands, seen
> Linking their coral arms under the sea:
> . . .
> Whereo'er the chariot wheels of Life are rolled
> In cloudy circles to eternity.

This is the sonnet *Written in Butler's Sermons*. The sonnet *Written in Emerson's Essays*, also published in 1849, is more sceptical. The poet—ironically, as it transpires—reproaches the "monstrous, dead, unprofitable world" for refusing to hear the "voice oracular" of the American seer:

> . . . Yet the will is free:
> Strong is the Soul, and wise, and beautiful:
> The seeds of godlike power are in us still:
> Gods are we, Bards, Saints, Heroes if we will.—
> O barren boast, O joyless Mockery!

The last line was later changed to "Dumb judges, answer, truth or mockery?" But the revised version, though less overtly pessimistic than the original, is no more encouraging: dumb judges can render no intelligible decision.

Man's enduring rock of reliance, the *Palladium* of his life, is the soul—

[20] J. E. Baker, "Our New Hellenic Renaissance," *The Reinterpretation of Victorian Literature*, p. 27.

the central core of individual personality. A man discovers his soul and understands its nature by obeying the great maxim, "Know thyself." The conflict between action and contemplation would be reconciled if we could discover

> . . . our own only true, deep-buried selves,
> Being one with which we are one with the whole world.

The alternative is subjection to "some bondage of the flesh or mind." But the self-knowledge which is necessary is also impossible. What we like to call self-knowledge is merely *Self-Deception*, since

> . . . he, who placed our master-feeling,
> Failed to make our master-feeling clear.

The Buried Life is buried too deep for our powers of introspection. We must try to believe that the palladium exists, but we must acknowledge our inability to find it.

Withdrawal into the self is fruitless if the self, so far as we are able to know it, merely reflects that ebb and flow of human misery which we are trying to escape. Hence the Stoicism which Arnold frequently recommends has more of the weakly agitated *ennui* of Sénancour than the calm of Marcus Aurelius. Genuine ataraxy is impossible for the

> . . . unquiet heart
> That neither deadens into rest
> Nor ever feels the fiery glow
> That whirls the spirit from itself away,
> But fluctuates to and fro,
> Never by passion quite possessed
> And never quite benumbed by the world's sway.

Stoicism clashes not merely with his *Weltschmerz* but with his social-mindedness. In *Kensington Gardens* he prays to the "Calm soul of all things":

> The will to neither strive nor cry,
> The power to feel with others give.

The two gifts would seem to be mutually exclusive.

If contraction of desire is a vain reliance, perhaps he can achieve self-realization through the most intense form of feeling with others—that is, through love. In that good minute (for we think of Browning) "When a belovèd hand is laid in ours," one seems to catch a glimpse of *The Buried Life*;

And then he thinks he knows
The Hills where his life rose,
And the Sea where it goes.

But Arnold was too fearful of the vitality for which he longed to make much of these moments. On further reflection it seemed improbable that self-knowledge could be achieved through so undisciplined a young person as Marguerite. In the nick of time he reminds himself, with a sigh of mingled sadness and relief, that "We mortal millions live *alone*." She must remember "Our different past":

Far, far from each other
Our spirits have grown.
And what heart knows another?
Ah! who knows his own?

The renunciation of Marguerite (granting that it was an actual occurrence) was a cause of Arnold's melancholy mainly in the sense that it revealed to him with painful clarity the cleavage in his nature. Both fortunately and unfortunately, he was no D. H. Lawrence. In 1865 he wrote from Turin to his wife at home: "Since I have been in Italy I have rather wished you wore ear-rings—the great gold ear-rings of this country, in such a variety of styles, please me so much—however, it is perhaps as well you do not."[21] Even if the reader refuses to join me in feeling a certain pathos beneath these words, he will probably agree that love would not, after all, be for Arnold the best means of transcending the conflict between contraction and expansion. The lovers at the close of *Dover Beach* must be true to one another merely because no other truth is visible on the darkling plain; their embrace is desperate, not triumphant.[22]

In *Parting*, therefore, he turns from Marguerite to nature. At first glance the lines are simple enough, but under closer scrutiny they reveal the ambiguity which renders his thought on this subject so perplexing to us and to him.

Blow, ye winds! lift me with you!
I come to the wild.
Fold closely, O Nature!
Thine arms round thy child.

[21] *Letters*, I, 327–328.
[22] In any case the last stanza is probably a fragment of a separate poem. It is not organically related to *Dover Beach*. See Tinker and Lowry, *The Poetry of Matthew Arnold*, p. 173.

Here a rather Shelleyan desire to be lifted up and made one with a great wild energy immediately becomes a desire to be rocked and lulled by a soothing earth-mother. He addresses her:

To thee only God granted
A heart ever new:
To all always open;
To all always true.

Mother Nature, then, has the personal qualities which Arnold, as he confesses to Clough, feels to be lacking in himself.

Ah, calm me! Restore me!
And dry up my tears
On thy high mountain platforms
Where Morn first appears,

Where the white mists, for ever,
Are spread and unfurled;
In the stir of the forces
Whence issued the world.

Here again, as in the first stanza quoted, he wants both calm and the stir of mighty forces.

When Arnold's approach to natural objects is most direct and sensuous, he values them chiefly for their power to relax overstrained nerves. Essentially an anodyne, they give peace and quiet, surcease from torturing perplexities. This healing power operates both directly and through poetry which expresses it, notably that of Wordsworth. But if nature often soothes Arnold when he desires refuge from agitation, she no less often confers vitality, excitement, and feelings of self-expansion when he desires to escape from the cold sluggishness of acedia:

Murmur of living
Stir of existence!
Soul of the world!

. . .

Yearn to the greatness of Nature!
Rally the good in the depths of thyself!

Here, in *The Youth of Man,* his use of the World-Soul concept suggests that when he wants vitality his concept of nature becomes more cosmological and less "scenic" than when he wants calm. Much as he admires Spinoza, however, the feeling-tone of this pantheism is more romantic than Spinozistic. He is too good a Wordsworthian completely to abstract *natura naturans* from *natura naturata*. Empedocles unites his spirit with cosmic force, but he does so by leaping into phenomenal smoke and flame and uproar.

There are two quite different motives for the suicide of Empedocles. On the one hand, he seeks oblivion to still the painful ferment of thought and feeling. On the other hand, he seeks to be swept out of his *ennui* through union, as in *Parting*, with "The stir of the forces / Whence issued the world." The latter motive is by far the stronger just before the leap, where the almost Spasmodic lines recall the ancient legend that Empedocles jumped into the crater to prove himself a god.

> No,no, ye stars! there is no death with you,
> No languor, no decay! Languor and death,
> They are with me, not you! ye are alive!
>
> . . .
>
> ... And thou, fiery world,
> That sapp'st the vitals of this terrible mount,
> Thou, too, brimmest with life ...
>
> . . .
>
> Oh that I could glow like this mountain!
> Oh that my heart bounded with the swell of the sea!
> Oh that my soul were full of light as the stars!
> Oh that it brooded over the world like the air!

This is suicide for the sake of romantic self-expansion. Even the profusion of "Oh's" and exclamation-points, so characteristic of this poet, reveals the craving to find in nature stronger emotions than he possesses. Arnold's inability to decide whether he felt too much or too little is clearly reflected in his dealings with nature.

An effort to reconcile the conflicting claims of involvement and detachment is seen in his frequent insistence that we should try to learn from nature the lesson of *Quiet Work*—"Toil unsevered from Tranquillity."

> Weary of myself, and sick of asking
> What I am and what I ought to be,

he finds in the stars his favorite symbol of this harmony of quietude and dutiful action. In *Self-Dependence* and *A Summer Night* they go about their business "Ohne Hast, ohne Rast." They teach that true vastness has nothing to do with morbid introspection or Byronic rant. Though perfectly serene they are not impassive, for "with joy the stars perform their shining." The source of that joy is perfect self-knowledge: "Who finds himself, loses his misery." Discovery of his personal center, however, is precisely what Arnold feels himself unable to achieve. He must realize, also, that the fallacy of ascribing calm, joy, wisdom, and *Entsagen* to lumps of incandescent matter is a little *too* pathetic to make this view of nature anything more than a wistful flight of fancy. One might as well admire a table for the probity with which it resists external pressure, its uncompromising squareness, the courage with which it stands on its own four legs.

Nevertheless Arnold insists that the moral values which we seem to apprehend in nature are objective, not imposed upon it by our shaping spirit of imagination. "They are here—they are set in the world." Wordsworth is dead, but *The Youth of Nature* is eternally lovely and good. Arnold clings to this belief because he needs an extrapersonal ethical reliance. Herein, however, he runs counter to a formidable intellectual trend of his day. Although an enthusiastic amateur botanist, he seems to have known little and cared less about contemporary scientific theories. His grudging attitude toward the function of science in education will be remembered. Most of his poems are pre-Darwinian both chronologically and psychologically, and in any case he generally avoided topical controversies in his poetry. There is plenty of evidence, however, that he was uneasily aware of the discrepancy between the scientific view of nature and his own. Indeed one may conjecture, though one cannot quite prove, that this awareness was the chief reason for his final abandonment of nature as a source of moral inspiration. We have seen that Empedocles dies as a weary poet who seeks to revitalize himself in union with cosmic energy—the desperate old romantic device of self-expansion through self-annihilation. In the preceding scene, however, he had addressed Pausanias not only as a disillusioned Stoic but as a sadly Epicurean precursor of evolutionary science. Professor Stevenson rightly finds it "significant" that Arnold "took the first evolutionist as a mouthpiece to express the fatalism of the nineteenth-century rationalists. . . . He declares that man is conditioned by environment and heredity; his life is but a trivial repetition of an endless recurrent process; he deceives himself with illusions about life, while the world moves on indifferently. Nature has no special regard for humankind."[23]

For man to merge himself with a universe of unfeeling, soulless mechanism would be to lose his humanity, not to enlarge it. Hence the poet who longs to be enfolded in the arms of Mother Nature is forced to cultivate that man-*versus*-nature dualism for which he has been lauded by the New Humanists. He cannot, however, completely stifle the longing to think of nature as his "brother-world." Platonic withdrawal from phenomena

[23] Lionel Stevenson, *Darwin Among the Poets*, p. 46.

aggravates his feeling of loneliness—"Who hath a monarch's hath no brother's part." On the other hand, reconciliation with Earth means abnegation of human dignity. Such is the dilemma of one who tries to live *In Utrumque Paratus*.[24]

The sonnet *Religious Isolation* is uncompromisingly antinaturalistic. The desire to find in nature the same spiritual qualities as those of the human soul, he warns Clough, is

> . . . unworthy of a man full-grown.
> What though the holy secret which moulds thee
> Moulds not the solid Earth? . . .
>
> . . .
>
> Live by thy light, and Earth will live by hers

We are reminded of the Emersonian distinction between "law for man and law for thing" which the New Humanists adopted as their cardinal text. *The Independent Preacher Who Preached That We Should Be "In Harmony with Nature"* is scorned for his inability—which the poet certainly shares—"To be like Nature strong, like Nature cool." But in the lines more usually cited Arnold goes on to contrast an evil Tennysonian nature with the humanity which must either improve upon her or "rest her slave." Since these sonnets seem to pave the way for the humanistic culture-doctrine of Arnold's prose, it is strange that both appeared in the 1849 volume, while many pieces expressing more favorable views of nature were written considerably later.[25] Apparently he became convinced with the passing years that these early attempts to elevate man above nature had pointed in the right direction after all.

No very definite conclusion arises from this brief sketch of Arnold's dealings with nature. When he did not try to think about his feelings, grass and flowers and running water relaxed his nerves, and he had genuine personal comradeship with ponies and dachshunds. But his efforts to extract from these soothing simplicities something like a philosophy or religion of nature were too confused and inconsistent to be satisfying to him or to the reader. After all his admiration for the *Tüchtigkeit* of the stars, he knew only what he had known in 1849—"Nature and man can never be fast friends."

A man who arrives at this conclusion is offered a choice between religion and humanism. Arnold went down the latter fork in the road. Modern man

[24] The striking 1869 revision of the last stanza of this poem must be considered later.

[25] It is also noteworthy that *To an Independent Preacher* was not reprinted by Arnold until 1877. Perhaps he regretted the note of personal animus in the opening lines.

must seek integration not by uniting himself with nature but by cultivating those moral insights and creative powers which bear witness to the higher worth of his independent humanity. Needless to say, it is in classical literature that we may find the most fortifying examples of wholesome poise, high seriousness, calm without frigidity, sweetness and light. This theme, like that of man's moral superiority to nature, appears as early as 1849 in *To a Friend*, and it is voiced more delicately and imaginatively in the final song of Callicles in *Empedocles on Etna*. The 1853 Preface states in explicit prose that to moderns who are trying to write poetry "amid the bewildering confusion of our times" the ancients offer "the only solid guidance, the only sure footing." But their benign influence is not confined to creative writing: "I know not how it is, but their commerce with the ancients appears to me to produce, in those who continually practise it, a steadying and composing effect upon their judgment, not of literary works only, but of men and events in general." Here of course is the germ of the doctrine which he developed as Professor of Poetry at Oxford between 1857 and 1867.

Since the criticism-and-culture gospel which characterizes this second stage of Arnold's career is a kind of substitute-religion it is germane to our subject; but its tenets are so familiar and so scantily set forth in his poetry that we need not examine them closely. Naturally they will be unsatisfactory both to materialists and to those who believe that it takes the superhuman to keep the human from becoming subhuman. The high ethical value of humanistic culture for the few exceptional persons who are willing and able to acquire it is undeniable. Even for them, however, its value as a nostrum for this strange disease of modern life is limited, since the serene wisdom of the ancients (Arnold's, not Swinburne's) depended too largely on the greater simplicity of the circumstances which they confronted. In the nineteenth century one could read Greek tragedy with wistful admiration, but one could not think and feel like Sophocles.

Arnold's gospel of culture was not a private aristocratic luxury but a social ideal. The entire British public must be regimented into "a disinterested endeavour to learn and propagate the best that has been known and thought in the world." Hence sweetness and light became involved in potentially totalitarian political theories which descended to Matthew from his father. This personal heritage, being implicit in "reason and the will of God," must be made to "prevail." But as Trilling has already observed, the program is circular: there can be no culture without a good state, and the only good state is one whose members possess culture.[26] The authoritarian

[26] Lionel Trilling, *Matthew Arnold*, p. 252.

element in Arnold's humanism is discordant with those democratic impulses which never deserted him and which find unexpectedly vigorous expression at the very close of his career.

There were times, too, when he felt that the best antidote for the sluggish vulgarity of the Philistine was not Hellenic poise but Celtic magic and passion. The Americans, of course, needed this stir of excitement even more than the English. In a way, the assassination of Lincoln did the Yankees unexpected credit:

> If Lincoln had been killed two years ago it would have been an immense loss to the North, but now he has done his work. All the recent matters have raised America in one's estimation, I think, and even this assassination brings their history something of that dash of the tragic, romantic, and imaginative, which it has had so little of. *Sic semper tyrannis* is so unlike anything Yankee or English middle class, both for bad and good.[27]

The apostle of sweet reasonableness realized that he himself would benefit from a dash of the tragic, romantic, and imaginative. If he envied the steady wholeness of Sophocles, he envied also the colorfulness of Booth. As we have seen, he *almost* wanted his wife to wear large gold ear-rings—but perhaps she had better not.

It is hard to say, indeed, whether Arnold was a classicist with romantic longings or a romanticist with an uneasy sense of obligation to be classical. One can only be sure that he was a frustrated nineteenth-century man engaged in a hopeless search for his buried life. Pitying both himself and his fellow-wanderers, he often writes as a victim of the *mal du siècle*. Less frequently he tries to combat his lassitude and bloodlessness by cultivating romantic emotions of the more energetic and masterful sort. These efforts, however, are inhibited by his inability to aspire without knowing what he is aspiring toward and by his distrust of everything violent and excessive. Had not the romantic poets, with all their greatness, bequeathed to the Victorians a ferment of disordered insatiable passions which aggravated rather than assuaged their misery?

> For what availed it, all the noise
> And outcry of the former men?—
> Say, have their sons achieved more joys?
> Say, is life lighter now than then?
> The sufferers died, they left their pain—
> The pangs which tortured them remain.

[27] *Letters*, I, 300.

The ancients, with a few later poets who retained something of their gift for producing touchstones of high seriousness, offered a safer means of reconciling his desire to feel and his dread of feeling. Safer, but not wholly satisfactory to a man who was so deeply moved by Byron.

If Arnold's classical humanism is not completely classical, still less is it completely humanistic. It is mingled with abortive religious hankerings which deprive him of the satisfactions of a resolute secularism without fulfilling the demands of a positive religion. Although the basic ideas of the gospel of culture are implicit and often explicit in Arnold's literary criticism,[28] they are not systematically formulated and brought to bear upon "men and events in general" in a program for the transformation of society until the publication of *Culture and Anarchy* in 1869. But in that volume his Hellenism, which had been relatively pure in *On Translating Homer*, lost its disinterestedness and became submerged in the politico-theological concerns which had been looming larger and larger in his mind during the past six or seven years. By the time the theory of culture achieves its fullest, broadest expression, it is primarily a weapon in Arnold's campaign "to deliver the Middle Class out of the hands of their Dissenting ministers."[29]

The remarks on *Empedocles* in the 1853 Preface show that Arnold had already begun to feel that his poetry, if it was to fulfill the highest functions of the art, should be more wholesome, encouraging, and constructive. His appointment to the Oxford professorship four years later was an irresistible invitation to become a Victorian prophet—albeit an exceptionally urbane and witty one. But since the poetic level of his nature was confused and melancholy, it was necessary for him to prophesy almost wholly in prose. For several years he preached classical humanism; but the letters of the 1860's, together with the articles on *The Bishop and the Philosopher* and *Dr. Stanley's Lectures on the Jewish Church* (both of 1863), indicate a growing desire to come to terms with Christianity by reinterpreting it in the light of a Hellenized latitudinarianism. The *Note-Books* show that during the same period he became an avid reader of theological and devotional literature. The evidence which they provide makes it impossible to doubt that Arnold was intensely curious about religious ideas and feelings and warmly responsive to them when they were expressed in wise and beautiful words. The sightless chasm between what he admiringly read about religion and what he wrote

[28] Most notably in *The Function of Criticism at the Present Time*.

[29] *Letters*, I, 263. To his mother, February, 186

about it is a mystery partly explained by Walter de la Mare's juvenile poem in which the child marvels at the fact that

> Whatever Miss T. eats
> Turns into Miss T.

In Arnold's mind the great religious classics turn into "morality touched by emotion."

Arnold's later poetry is by no means transformed by his desire to be more bracing, but it shows that some change has occurred. He is still a groper and a doubter, and not infrequently a melancholy one. But *Dover Beach*, though not published until 1867, was composed in the period of *Weltschmerz*; and the melancholy *Growing Old* may, as De Vane suggests, be a recoil from the unbearable optimism of *Rabbi Ben Ezra*. Most of the poems actually composed during the 1860's are relatively sanguine. Rather surprisingly, however, they rely much less upon classical humanism than does the prose of the same period. Perhaps the culture-philosophy is meant to be implicit in them, but if so the relationship is far from obvious. Disregarding a good many slight occasional pieces, what one finds is a little undefined hopefulness, a little of the Carlylean hero-cult, and a good deal of Broad Churchism which looks forward to the prose of the seventies.

Of several cases in which he revises earlier poems into closer agreement with his present temper, *In Utrumque Paratus* is the most interesting. The original version of 1849, we remember, offered no decisive choice between lonely philosophic detachment and dehumanizing submergence in nature.[30] The poem was not reprinted until 1869, when it appeared with a new concluding stanza which advocated a more or less Meredithian union between man and the world of evolutionary science:

> Thy native world stirs at thy feet unknown,
> Yet there thy secret lies!
> Out of this stuff, these forces, thou art grown,
> And proud self-severance from them were disease.
> O scan thy native world with pious eyes!
> High as thy life be risen, 'tis from these;
> And these, too, rise.

On this subject, however, Arnold remains a hard man to pin down. In 1877, when he next reprinted the poem, he dropped this stanza and returned to the melancholy inconclusive ending of 1849.

Thyrsis is a beautiful idyll of the Cumner region, but as an elegy on Clough

[30] See above, p. 490.

it is evasive. Of course their friendship has been dead for some years, and even while it lasted it was strained by radical differences in their responses to the bewilderment which they shared. Nevertheless it seems clear that Arnold wishes to avoid grappling with the real problem of Clough because it is too like his own real problem to be treated firmly in these days of hard-won *Tüchtigkeit*. Two gingerly stanzas, far enough part, glance at the submerged distress. The main body of the poem delightfully combines the pastoralism of Theocritus with the pastoralism of Oxford, but it buries the tortured author of *Dipsychus* in a heap of white and purple fritillaries. The hopeful conclusion—the voice, the light, the tree, the scholar-gipsy—is almost Tennysonian in its follow-the-gleamishness.

Obermann Once More is much richer in the old authentic misery. Arnold recalls so vividly the feelings with which he formerly read Sénancour that one doubts whether those feelings have vanished even now. Obermann's own melancholy review of Western history—the downfall of loveless Rome, the rise and collapse of the Christian ideal, the shattering of the revolutionary vision—is surely more than dramatic. Finally the dramatic figment wholly evaporates when Sénancour, speaking completely out of character and out of relation to the rest of the poem, reads Arnold a heartening Victorian lecture:

> Though late, though dimmed, though weak, yet tell
> Hope to a world new-made!
>
> Help it to fill that deep desire,
> The want which racked our brain,
> Consumed our hearts with thirst like fire,
> Immedicable pain;
>
> . . .
>
> What still of strength is left, employ
> That end to help attain:
> *One common wave of thought and joy*
> *Lifting mankind again!*

"The vision ended," but as Arnold looked out over the Valais he "saw the morning break." Yet he feels a little too old and weak, and not sufficiently free from his earlier sadness, to shoulder the redemptive task which the shade of Obermann has imposed upon him. He must try to build up the temper of heroism within himself by recommending it to others. In *The Last Word*, he pictures the struggle to lift mankind as a desperate battle in which the individual must accept defeat although his cause will eventually conquer:

Charge once more, then, and be dumb!
Let the victors, when they come,
When the forts of folly fall,
Find thy body by the wall.

He remembers an authentic example of the hero as prophet: for some time the thought has been dawning on him that he should try to be more like the father whom he had once found too overwhelmingly "zealous, beneficent, firm." Hence, of course, *Rugby Chapel.* Although they grant that Arnold's agnosticism had relaxed considerably by the time he completed the poem, Tinker and Lowry believe that the traditional Christian language which it employs was mainly a consequence of the subject. "How much of this attempt to lend a religious ardour to 'Rugby Chapel' represents a genuine conviction on the poet's part must be left to the judgment of the individual reader." They seem to have their doubts. Much depends, of course, upon the date of composition. If the poem was finished soon after "November 1857," the date given by Arnold himself when he published it a decade later, the Christian element is almost wholly factitious; but if, as these commentators think probable, the poem "could hardly have been completed for [i.e., until] many years" later than 1857,[31] its religiosity is by no means inconsistent with the general tone of the *New Poems* of 1867.

For this volume includes several indications of the fact that Arnold has been working his way toward the views which, beginning in 1869, he will express more systematically in his theological prose. He has begun to regard with reverent enthusiasm Christian formulas which he has deprived of most of their Christian content. He now firmly believes in God, if you will allow him to assume that "God" is an emotional way of saying "morality":

God's wisdom and God's goodness!—Ay, but fools
Mis-define these till God knows them no more.
Wisdom and goodness, they are God!—what schools
Have yet so much as heard this simpler lore?
This no Saint preaches, and that no Church rules;
'Tis in the desert, now and heretofore.

This situation was soon to be remedied by *St. Paul and Protestantism.*

The message of *Anti-Desperation*[32] is that since Christianity is a matter of conduct, nothing absolutely essential to it is lost even if Jesus was a mere man and there is no divine judge of our actions and no immortality:

[31] *The Poetry of Matthew Arnold*, pp. 239, 241–242.
[32] So in 1867, but finally entitled *The Better Part.*

Hath man no second life?—Pitch this one high!
Sits there no judge in heaven, our sin to see?—

More strictly, then, the inward judge obey!
Was Christ a man like us—Ah! let us try
If we, then, too, can be such men as he!

Pis-Aller views rather superciliously those who are unable to practice the Christianity of the inner judge without accepting the traditional *Aberglaube*:

Nay, look closer into man!
Tell me, can you find indeed
Nothing sure, no moral plan
Clear prescribed, without your creed?

"No, I nothing can perceive;
Without that, all's dark for men.
That, or nothing, I believe."—
For God's sake, believe it then!

The last line seems to be merely a fling of contemptuous impatience. But perhaps it is not too Empsonian to conjecture that it may also mean: "If you cannot achieve goodness without your creed, then, even for the sake of that purer God in whom I believe, stick to your creed and be good." Arnold, as we know, had never wished to perplex the faith of weaker spirits who needed the support of popular superstition.

The sonnet *Immortality* can be paraphrased in words which Arnold will soon use of St. Paul: "Death, for him, is living after the flesh, obedience to sin; life is mortifying by the spirit the deeds of the flesh, obedience to righteousness. Resurrection, in its essential sense is therefore for Paul, the rising, within the sphere of our visible earthly existence, from death to life in this sense."[33] William Taylor, the Congregational minister whom Arnold meets in *East London*, has attained this sort of immortality—"Thou mak'st the heaven thou hop'st indeed thy home." The good man, who had told Arnold that in confronting the horrors of the slums he had been "Much cheered with thoughts of Christ, *the living bread*," must have been puzzled by the poet's interpretation of his words. He sheds a similar mist of amiable vagueness over *Monica's Last Prayer*. She says, as Arnold had found in her son's *Confessions*,[34] that she does not care where her body is buried, "*But at God's altar, oh! remember me!*" Her request, of course, is that Augustine

[33] *St. Paul and Protestantism*, p. 70. It is true that Paul conceives of death and life in this way. The misinterpretation lies in supposing that he therefore could not really have believed in actual resurrection and the afterlife of the blessed in heaven.

[34] Book IX, Chapter xi.

shall pray for her soul in celebrating the Mass. This *Aberglaube* must be supplanted by the truer interpretation:

> Creeds pass, rites change, no altar standeth whole;
> Yet we her memory, as she prayed, will keep,
> Keep by this: *Life in God, and union there.*

This might be a fair paraphrase of Monica's desire if "God" and "union" meant to the poet what they meant to her. Arnold's treatment of such subjects closely resembles his friend Dean Stanley's.[35]

There is not the slightest reason to suppose that the Broad Churchism of *New Poems* is insincere, but one doubts whether it lay very close to the core of his being. His eldest son died in the following year. "I was with the bereaved father," writes G. W. E. Russell, "on the morning after the boy's death, and the author with whom he was consoling himself was Marcus Aurelius."[36] Not Sénancour, at least. When Arnold looks forward to his own death in *A Wish* (1867), he turns to another non-Christian reliance. He will have in the sickroom no throng of whispering friends, no pompous physician, and above all no clergyman

> To canvass with official breath
>
> The future and its viewless things—
> That undiscovered mystery
> Which one who feels death's winnowing wings
> Must needs read clearer, sure, than he!

Let the dying man be moved to the window, whence he can "once more" behold

> The world which was ere I was born,
> The world which lasts when I am dead;
>
> . . .
>
> There let me gaze till I become
> In soul, with what I gaze on, wed!
> To feel the universe my home;
>
> . . .
>
> Thus feeling, gazing, might I grow
> Composed, refreshed, ennobled, clear;
> Then willing let my spirit go
> To work or wait elsewhere or here!

He did not change very fundamentally from the man who wrote *A Summer Night*.

But by this time, of course, Arnold would insist that Marcus Aurelius

[35] See above, pp. 69–70.

[36] *Letters*, I, x.

and Wordsworth were prime exemplars of what he meant by Christianity. "Matt is a good Christian at bottom," declared his wife, but she could never be persuaded to read his theological studies. The scholar is less fortunate than Mrs. Arnold. If, however, his subject is religious thought in Victorian *poetry,* the extent of his obligation not merely to read but to discuss these works is debatable, especially since Arnold had abandoned poetry by the time he wrote them. I should nevertheless feel moved to undertake the task had not Lionel Trilling already performed it so admirably. As a high-minded agnostic he was free to expose the defects of Arnold's views with a trenchancy which, if employed by a believer, might well elicit protests against his bigotry —such protests as Mr. Trilling himself has elsewhere leveled against my own treatment of the major romantic poets. It is fortunate for me as well as for the reader that the work has been done.

Mr. Trilling recognizes that Arnold helped to break down an unimaginatively literalistic conception of the Bible. He acknowledges the real value of his literary, psychological, and developmental approach to the study of Christian doctrine. Nevertheless he conclusively demonstrates that Arnold's religion, far from being a liberalized form of Christianity, is not a religion at all. The famous definition of religion as "morality touched by emotion" is spurious; for, as Trilling says in words which perfectly express my own objection to the faith of the romantics, "It is not *any* emotion that touches morality and translates it into religion but specifically an emotion about an outside and transcendent force, or help, or criterion."[37] He proceeds to show that such a transcendent power could not be established by Arnold's purely subjective ethical pragmatism. The attempt to interpret the Hebrew passion for righteousness, the person and teachings of Christ, and the theology of St. Paul in the light of this conception of religion was doomed to failure.

Trilling rightly stresses the very strong political motivation behind Arnold's theological writings. It seems to me, however, that he underestimates the importance of aesthetic fastidiousness and social snobbery as factors in Arnold's ten-year campaign against the Nonconformists. His aversion was of long standing. As early as 1848 he is writing his mother: "I see a wave of more than American *vulgarity,* moral, intellectual, and social, preparing to break over us."[38] That vulgarity was the vulgarity of Dissent.

[37] Mr. Trilling makes it clear that on this as on some other points about Arnold's theology he is anticipated by F. H. Bradley, whose devastating attack on Arnold insists that religion implies "the belief, however vague and indistinct, in an object, a not-myself; an object, further, which is real." (*Ethical Studies*, p. 316.)

[38] *Letters*, I, 4. See the 1869 Preface of *Culture and Anarchy*, where America provides an example of how culture deteriorates in the absence of a state religion.

In 1853 he tells Clough: "The woman [Harriet Beecher] Stowe by her picture must be a Gorgon—I can quite believe all you tell me about her—a strong Dissenter-religious middle-class person—she will never go far, I think."[39]

Such feelings were kept in a constant state of irritation by his inspectorship of Nonconformist schools, which threw him into contact with impossible persons who bore names unknown on the banks of the Ilyssus—Wragg, Higginbottom, Stiggins, Bugg, Bottle, Jupp. That their beliefs were narrow was distressing; that they expressed their beliefs with such hideous crudity was unforgivable. The hymns they sang! "Sing glory, glory, glory to the great God Triune!" or even worse,

> My Jesus to know, and feel His blood flow,
> 'Tis life everlasting, 'tis heaven below.[40]

"Of all dull, stagnant, unedifying *entourages*, that of middle-class Dissent . . . seems to me the stupidest," he confides to his mother in 1855.[41] The voyage of the Pilgrim Fathers was fruitful of much good, but "think what intolerable company Shakespeare and Virgil would have found them" had they been on the *Mayflower*![42]

Arnold was not concerned with the fact that these dreadful people, however crude in their tastes and unbalanced in their theology, possessed more of the Christian religion than he would ever be able to understand. Nor did he recognize that he himself was an end-product of the Puritan tradition. Despite all his whimsical urbanity and all his talk about the sweet reasonableness of true Christianity, the emphasis on righteousness and conduct in his theology was far too Hebraic, in terms of his own criticism of the Victorian temper, to be brought into harmony with the Hellenism of his culture-doctrine. His antidote for Puritanism was merely Puritanism *in extremis*.

Arnold's aesthetico-social snobbery adds a special animus to the cultural, political, and theological aspects of his ten-year struggle "to deliver the Middle Class out of the hands of their Dissenting ministers." The bitterest enemies of sweetness and light, the Philistines par excellence, were the bourgeois Nonconformists. And how do Englishmen "come to have such light belief in right reason, and such an exaggerated value for their own independent thinking, however crude?" It is because they are so deeply

[39] *Letters to Clough*, p. 133.

[40] *Literature and Dogma*, p. 349. For the latter hymn, which Arnold regarded with particular horror, see also *ibid.*, p. 39, and *Essays, First Series*, p. 142.

[41] *Letters*, I, 49.

[42] *Culture and Anarchy*, p. 54.

immersed in Hebraism, which cares nothing about quality of intelligence.[43] The Dissenters are not only arch-Hebraists but political liberals who will be highly resistant to Arnold's idea of making reason and the will of God prevail through the authority of the State. To promote culture, the State must be animated by a concern for righteousness. The national morality must be embodied in "a national society for the promotion of goodness"[44]—his father's ideal of a State Church. If this Church is to include all Englishmen, as it should, it cannot stand for anything in particular so far as creeds and dogmas are concerned. If the Dissenters would only worship like cultivated gentlefolk, what they believed would matter very little. But they are hostile to the conception of an Established Church, and they hold very precise beliefs. So also do the Anglican Evangelicals, but Arnold takes care to leave them alone. They remain within the Establishment, they are less outrageously vulgar than the chapel-goers, and in any case they seem to be growing more and more latitudinarian.[45] It is the Dissenters, then, who constitute the chief obstacle to the propagation of culture by a National Church which, calling itself Christian, will interpret Christianity as morality in a state of earnest but urbane and cultivated excitement. Arnold must take the wind out of their sails by showing that St. Paul, the cornerstone of their theology, was not a Puritan at all, but an apostle of sweet reasonableness whose vestigial Hebraism was not essential to his real teachings.

The resultant theological crusade came to an end in 1877, when Arnold declared in his essay on *The Church of England*:

> And I, for my part, now leave this question, I hope, for ever. I became engaged in it against my will, from being led by particular circumstances to remark the deteriorating effect of the temper and strifes of Dissent upon good men, the lamentable waste of power and usefulness which was thereby caused; and from being convinced that the right settlement was to be reached in one way only: not by disestablishment, but by comprehension and union. However, as one grows old, one feels that it is not one's business to go on forever expostulating with other people upon their waste of life, but to make progress in grace and peace oneself.[46]

He believes, as he admits to Grant Duff two years later, that his effort "has produced very little result." But one must give up the notion that such changes can be effected in a single lifetime. "Perhaps we shall end our days in the tail of a return current of popular religion, both ritual and dogmatic. Still, the change, for being slower than we expected, is not the less sure."[47]

[43] *Culture and Anarchy*, p. 144.

[44] *St. Paul and Protestantism . . . and Last Essays on Church and State*, p. 213. ("A Psychological Parallel.")

[45] *Ibid.*, pp. vii–x.

[46] *Ibid.*, pp. 342–343.

[47] *Letters*, II, 187.

The only change which he actually expects, however, is the continued growth of secularism. In 1881 he writes Fontanès:

> Man feels himself to be a more various and richly endowed animal than the old religious theory of life allowed, and he is endeavouring to give satisfaction to the long repressed and still imperfectly understood instincts of this varied nature. I think this revolution is happening everywhere; it is certainly happening in England, where the sombreness and narrowness of the religious world, and the rigid hold it long had upon us, have done so much to provoke it. I think it is, like all inevitable revolutions, a salutary one, but it greatly requires watching and guiding. . . . The moral is that whoever treats religion, religious discussions, questions of churches and sects, as absorbing, is not in solid sympathy with the movement of men's minds at present.[48]

Many years earlier he had expressed exactly the same thought to Clough when he said that nowadays the religious sentiment "is best not regarded alone, but considered in conjunction with the grandeur of the world, love of kindred, love, gratitude etc. etc."[49] There are few men who seem to change more but actually change less than Matthew Arnold. But when he writes in a similar vein to Grant Duff in 1882, he regards the secular revolution less complacently, concluding his letter with a "very profund sentence" of Ewald's: "Eigentlich von der Verkehrtheit des Verhaltens gegen das Gottliche alles Unglück ausgeht."[50] One doubts, however, whether Arnold would have thought this sentence so profound if Ewald had written "Gott" instead of "das Gottliche."

During the last decade of his life Arnold revives the gospel of culture in a more flexible and realistic form, advocating it from a point of view considerably more democratic than that of *Culture and Anarchy*. Not regimented order but the equality of educated individuals becomes the sharpest weapon against Philistinism. This final phase is interesting and praiseworthy, but it produces no poetry and it has little to tell a student of his religious thought.

We may observe, however, that although Arnold now steers clear of specific theological and ecclesiastical questions he combines with his ideas on education and literary criticism much of the essential spirit which animated the religious writings of the preceding decade. If religion is emotionalized morality, its values are preeminently to be sought in poetry:

> The future of poetry is immense, because in poetry, where it is worthy of its high destinies, our race, as time goes on, will find an ever surer and surer stay. There is not a creed which is not shaken, not an accredited dogma which is not shown to be

[48] *Ibid.*, pp. 220–221. [49] See above, p. 479. [50] *Letters*, II, 234.

questionable, not a received tradition which does not threaten to dissolve. Our religion has materialized itself in the fact, in the supposed fact; it has attached its emotion to the fact, and now the fact is failing it. But for poetry the idea is everything; the rest is a world of illusion, of divine illusion. Poetry attaches its emotion to the idea; the idea *is* the fact. The strongest part of our religion to-day is its unconscious poetry. . . . More and more mankind will discover that we have to turn to poetry to interpret life for us, to console us, to sustain us. Without poetry, our science will appear incomplete, and most of what now passes with us for religion and philosophy will be replaced by poetry.[51]

Poetry, then, expresses those ideas (normative moral concepts and attitudes) which constitute all that is really true in religion. It is therefore a superior substitute for "what now passes with us for religion," which has stultified itself by its attachment to supposed facts. Reading great poetry is even more purely religious than worshipping virtue in the State Church, which after all would probably entail some degree of commitment to the objective truth of the traditional formulas. But here we may object that in poetry the idea is *not* everything, is indeed nothing at all unless the poet attaches the idea to supposed facts—the facts of image and symbol. It might be more accurate to say of poetry not that "the idea is the fact" but that the fact is the idea. Religion works with ideas in much the same way: it resembles poetry less in its concern with truth and goodness than in its imaginative concreteness. This had repeatedly been recognized by Arnold himself in his theological essays: "We have to renounce impossible attempts to receive the legendary and miraculous matter of Scripture as grave historical and scientific fact. We have to accustom ourselves to regard henceforth all this part as poetry and legend."[52] When we are trying to think about religion, Arnold bids us renounce all the poetry; when we are reading poetry, he bids us observe how truly religious it is.

His thought wavers back and forth between two different conceptions of religion which respectively correspond to two different conceptions of poetry. We may think of historic Christianity as a great poem in the sense of being a body of truth-telling symbols—some instituted and revealed to man by God, whose metaphors are absolute truth; some devised by man under God's direct or indirect guidance; some wholly the product of human imagination at work within the spiritual experience of the believing community. Arnold repudiates all this symbolism as "mere" poetry which must be renounced if we are to arrive at the high ethical concern for wisdom, righteousness, and love which is all that Christianity really *means*. When

[51] "The Study of Poetry," *Essays in Criticism, Second Series*, pp. 1–2.
[52] *God and the Bible*, p. 338.

these values are released from their stultifying attachment to "supposed facts" they become the subject matter of *true* poetry as distinguished from the poetry of *Aberglaube*. But a poetry consisting of conceptual statements about ethical abstractions would be no poetry at all. If the poet's feelings about moral truths are warm and strong, they will necessarily be concretized in images. There is no one source from which the symbols of true religious emotion *must* be derived, but there are obvious aesthetic and psychological advantages in drawing them from that "world of divine illusion," the traditional reservoir of "popular" Christian symbolism. In doing so, however, we must remember, just when our feeling becomes most intense, that the illusion *is* illusion: otherwise the poetry of high seriousness would relapse into the poetry of superstition. "The future of poetry is immense" because it will soon become the only way of talking elevated nonsense without involving oneself in genuine belief.

These ideas concerning the relations between poetry and religion are of doubtful value for literary criticism. As regards their validity for religion I am so deeply committed a witness that I prefer to fall back upon Mr. Trilling, whose agnosticism, as so often happens, embraces a clear perception of what religion means.

> That Christianity is true: that is, after all, the one thing that Arnold cannot really say. That Christianity contains the highest moral law, that Christianity is natural, that Christianity provides a poetry serving the highest good, that Christianity *contains* the truth—anything but that *Christianity is true*. . . . Feeling is all, says Faust. But Gretchen knows what neither Faust nor Arnold knew, that feeling is *not* all in poetry and religion. . . . The emotions which a sensitive non-believer experiences from a well-sung requiem mass or any other elaborate ritual may have much in common with the religious emotion; they are clearly not religious. Here is poetic experience merely, and however much the poetic experience may order our lives, however much pseudo-statement may organize our emotions, its effect is not so great as that of "statement" or what we firmly believe to be statement. To keep in mind, as Arnold recommends, that all the language of prayer is the result of a great but charming mistake about the nature of a fundamental reality is, for the religious person, scarcely fortifying; for the non-religious person, it is scarcely persuasive to faith.[53]

With these illiberal remarks I find myself in complete agreement. For such reasons both the religious and the nonreligious person may prefer to remember Arnold for those early poems in which he expresses, with unrivaled elegiac pathos, the bewilderment of his generation and of ours.

[53] *Matthew Arnold*, pp. 364, 365.

Chapter Eighteen

CLOUGH

It is perhaps unfortunate that Arthur Hugh Clough chose verse as the vehicle for his perplexities: although he desired to write "poetry" he was not sufficiently an artist to be much interested in making *poems*. At times he can be very refreshing when he seems to be working toward a poetry of seriously witty conversation not unlike that of W. H. Auden's lighter vein. Usually, however, he accepted the dominant Victorian fallacy that poetry is the prophetic utterance of bards who have made up their minds about the great mysteries; and since he could *not* make up his mind about them his efforts to write what the age called "true" poetry were largely stultified. For that very reason, however, his poems are rewarding for anyone who wishes to understand the spiritual difficulties of the period.

Rather too much has been said of how Dr. Arnold, completing the work begun by Arthur's formidable mother, made him a morally overstrained young prig. The fact provides a partial explanation of one element in his character, but it should not be made the starting point for a Stracheyan exposure of the absurdities of Victorian seriousness. Clough deserves to be treated with much sympathy and respect. The problems which disturbed him were well worth worrying about. He was a highly intelligent man with a natural bent toward cheerfulness, clarity, intellectual honesty, and wholesome realism; but the age pulled him in too many different directions to enable him to fulfill his best potentialities. Only a very great mind could have synthesized all the disparate thoughts and feelings which beset him.

At Balliol the ideal sixth-former took his place among a liberal bookish set, several of whose members were products of Dr. Arnold's teachings. There is much truth, however, in Walter Bagehot's seemingly paradoxical statement that the Rugby headmaster played into the hands of his prime aversion, John Henry Newman. The most solid bulwark against Newmanism was the intellectual and spiritual apathy of the English schoolboy. "But," says Bagehot, "it was exactly this happy apathy, this commonplace indifference, that Arnold prided himself on removing. He objected strenuously to Mr. Newman's creed, but he prepared anxiously the very soil on which that creed was sure to grow. A multitude of such minds as Mr. Clough's, from being Arnoldites, became Newmanites,"[1] "Multitude" is an exaggeration, but the shift from Arnold to Newman was by no means uncommon. It was often followed, however, by a counterturn to a more than Rugbeian liberalism as the Oxford Movement developed tendencies which were repugnant to the Protestant sensibilities of many of the young men who had been saying, "Credo in Newmannum." This for example was the course followed by J. A. Froude. Clough had attached himself to W. G. Ward when that brilliant youth was still a disciple of Thomas Arnold. As Ward veered toward Newman, Clough rather hesitantly followed; but even before the conversion of Ward and Newman he had found that Catholicism, Anglican or Roman, was completely alien to his nature. In the turmoil of reaction he could find no alternative reliance. His earnest seeking spirit was whirled off into a bewildering medley of Coleridge, Carlyle, Emerson, Mill, Strauss, Hegel, Broad Churchism, the gospel of service, scientific materialism, intellectual pessimism, sentimental optimism.

In 1844 he describes himself to Gell as a Christian who has lost his enthusiasm for Christianity:

> Without in the least denying Christianity I feel little that I can call its power. Believing myself to be in my unconscious creed in some shape or other an adherent to its doctrines, I keep within its pale; still, whether the spirit of the age, whose lacquey and flunkey I submit to be, will prove to be this kind or that kind I can't the least say. Sometimes I have doubts whether it won't be no Christianity at all.

He adds that he often wonders if Christ may not be doing His work quite outside of what now passes for the Christian Church. By 1847, as a letter to his sister shows, he doubts whether *true* Christianity necessitates belief in the historicity of Christ: "I cannot feel sure that a man may not have all that is important in Christianity even if he does not so much as know that Jesus of Nazareth existed." Why then should we be troubled by doubts as to the factual accuracy of the Gospels?

> Trust in God's justice and love, and belief in His commands as written in our conscience, stand unshaken, though Matthew, Mark, Luke, and John, or even St. Paul were to fall. The things which men must work at will not be critical questions about the Scriptures, but philosophical problems of Grace, and Free Will, and Redemption as an idea, not as a historical event.[2]

The flunkey of the age was to resign his fellowship and tutorship in the following year.

[1] *Literary Studies*, II, 276–277.

[2] *Letters and Remains*, pp. 67–68, 85–86.

Here, one feels inclined to say, is one more victory for the Inner Light. But although romantic motivation is strong in Clough's thinking, he is not a typical "frustrated romantic." It would be more accurate to say that in his character romanticism was one of several elements strong enough to frustrate one another and weak enough to succumb to such frustration. Yet only in a few exceptionally desperate moments does he deny the existence of some sort of absolute spiritual reality that is more than a mere projection of his feelings.

> It satisfies my soul to know
> That, though I perish, Truth is so.

What tortures him is the difficulty of knowing what the Truth is, of discovering some rational basis for believing in its existence, and of achieving union with it. Though he never found a religion, he was more religious than his friend Matthew Arnold. He desired God as God, not as a poetic symbol of morality.

Most of us, says Bagehot in his review of the posthumous 1862 volume, are content to live by hand-to-mouth guesswork about the ultimate questions which we cannot hope to answer. But Clough was one of those uncomfortable people who "will not *make their image*. They struggle after an 'actual abstract,' " refusing to accept a pattern for their ignorance. Yet they cannot be called unbelievers in the ordinary sense.

> No one knows more certainly and feels more surely that there is an invisible world, than those very persons who decline to make an image or representation of it, who shrink with a nervous horror from every such attempt when it is made by others. ... If you offer them any known religion, they "won't have that"; if you offer them no religion, they will not have that either; if you ask them to accept a new ... religion, they altogether refuse to do so. They seem not only to believe in an "unknown God," but in a God whom no man can ever know.[3]

That Clough himself would smilingly admit the accuracy of this diagnosis is suggested by a canceled passage in an early draft of *Amours de Voyage*, where Claude explains to Eustace:

> No, I am not, you may trust me, in any true sense a Sceptic,
> Not in the highest things a Sceptic, however I seem so.
> Look you, most people accepting, as Time or Locality, Birth or
> Education suggests, some *particular* things, are therefore
> Credited largely for faith, heaven help us, in *things in general*.
> I, who sincerely believe, as I fancy, in *things in general*,
> That is, in God, you know, am a sceptic, forsooth, as I do not
> Make-up instanter my mind to believe in your *things in particular*.

[3] *Literary Studies*, II, 268–272. The phrase "actual abstract" is drawn from *Amours de Voyage*, Canto III, line 132.

I am, believe me, at bottom nor sceptic nor unbeliever,
Misbeliever perhaps, as I go the wrong way about it;
So it would seem; yet rather account me an over-believer
Young and romantic; perhaps as you say a little bit cracky.

Reading these lines in conjunction with the Bagehot passage, a present-day neologist would approvingly infer that Clough wanted a very "high" religion with a God who soars above all attempts to say anything definite about him. That is indeed what he desired, and he paid the penalty for desiring it. Christians affirm an ineffably high, purely spiritual God who made Himself low and specific and human in order to force Himself into the thick skulls and hard hearts of men. It has never been easy to achieve perfect spiritual equilibrium in responding to this stupendous miracle. No doubt many professed Christians believe in concrete particulars of creed and cult without genuinely believing in Almighty God. On the other hand, to love and worship and serve a completely unrevealed and imageless *deus absconditus* is an extremely difficult if not an impossible psychological feat. "High" religion needs a considerable tincture of "low" religion if it is not to die of its own abstractness or slough down into a welter of subjective sentiments and impotent moral platitudes.

Clough tried hard to evade this disaster by insisting that although the Divine Being could not be formulated or imaged there must be rational grounds for believing in His existence if only one could discover them. The abstractly rational, however, could not be sundered from the concretely and personally pragmatic. The intellectual validity of belief in God could be tested only by the impact of that belief upon human lives. The truth for which Clough thirsted must be metaphysically absolute, but it must also be empirically verifiable in experience.[4] In another discarded passage of *Amours de Voyage*, Claude writes to his friend:

I am a thing to be known, and a knower will somewhere know me.
Still you perceive that knowledge on this hypothesis claims a
Far, far higher place; while Love, God love us, and Action
Prove but subordinate branches of Experimental Science.

More even than a God of pure reason Clough wanted a God of love and beneficence, but for such a God he needed more images than he was able to accept.

With a few uninteresting exceptions, Clough's poetry is the record of his hopeless struggle to be simultaneously religious, romantic, rational, and

[4] On this point see Édouard Guyot, *Essai sur la formation philosophique du poète Clough: Pragmatisme et intellectualisme.*

realistic. In *Dipsychus*, the conflicting elements are juxtaposed but not harmonized. Here Clough divides his own personality into a Quixotic sort of Faust and a Sancho Panza-ish sort of Mephistopheles, each canceling out the other.[5] But the self-division is really quadruple rather than dual. For Clough sees in himself two Dipsychuses, a noble idealist and a muddle-headed Spasmodic prig; and two Spirits, a corrupting mocker and a keen-witted champion of common sense.

Dipsychus delights in the variegated welter of Venetian life,

> The faces, and the voices, and the whole mass
> O'the motley facts of existence flowing by![6]

This rich phenomenal world would be

> . . . perfect, if 'twere all! But it is not;
> Hints ever haunt me of a More beyond:
> I am rebuked by a sense of the incomplete,
> Of a completion over-soon assumed,
> Of adding up too soon.

But if it would be presumptuous to infer that the sum total of sense-appearances constitutes reality, would not belief in a supersensuous "More" also be "a completion over-soon assumed"? Shall he trust his eyes, or his desires?

> . . . Oh, oh these qualms,
> And oh these calls! And, oh! this woman's heart
> Fain to be forced, incredulous of choice,
> And waiting a necessity for God.

On the dreary treadmill of everyday life the moments when he feels sure of "a More beyond" are brief and rare, but they provide the sole evidence that life is worth living. He *must* believe in them, for

> If this pure solace should desert my mind,
> What were all else? I dare not risk this loss.
> To the old paths, my soul!

The Spirit retorts by reminding him of what his "old paths" actually amount to:

> O yes.
> To moon about religion . . .

. . .

[5] In the early drafts the speakers are Faustulus (the ironic diminutive is characteristic) and Mephistopheles. In the latest draft they are Dipsychus and Spirit (a very misleading name for him). But the Spirit is once called "Mephistopheles" by Dipsychus, and he accepts the appellation as one of many possibilities.

[6] We think of Browning in Italy, and observe the Browningesque "O'the."

. . . to debate in letters
Vext points with earnest friends; past other men
To cherish natural instincts, yet to fear them
And less than any use them. Oh, no doubt,
In a corner sit and mope, and be consoled
With thinking one is clever, while the room
Rings round with animation and the dance.
Then talk of old examples, and pervert
Ancient real facts to modern unreal dreams,
And build up baseless fabrics of romance
And heroism upon historic sand;
To burn, forsooth, for Action, yet despise
Its merest accidence and alphabet;
Cry out for service, and at once rebel
At the application of its plainest rules:
This you call life, my friend, reality;
Doing your duty unto God and man—
I know not what.

Here the Spirit speaks not as an external corrupter, but as Arthur Hugh Clough reporting what he fears may be the truth about himself.

He refuses to abandon the hope that beneath the ferment of these qualms and calls there abides a deeper undivided self which is somehow a part of the suprapersonal reality. But for him, as for Arnold, this integrating self-knowledge is both necessary and impossible. The Wordsworthian title of an early poem, "*Blank Misgivings of a Creature moving about in Worlds not realised*," is interpreted in a way which reminds us less of the *Immortality Ode* than of Tennyson's *Confessions of a Second-Rate Sensitive Mind*:

How often sit I, poring o'er
   My strange distorted youth,
Seeking in vain, in all my store,
   One feeling based on truth;
Amid the maze of petty life
   A clue whereby to move,
A spot whereon in toil and strife
   To dare to rest and love.

. . .

Excitements come, and act and speech
   Flow freely forth;—but no,
Nor they, nor aught beside can reach
   The buried world below.

This mood cannot be dismissed as adolescent mawkishness, for it remains essentially the mood of Dipsychus, who cries:

To thine own self be true, the wise man says.
Are then my fears myself? O double self!
And I untrue to both.

St. John, Clough elsewhere remembers, says that it "doth not yet appear" what we shall be when we see God face to face. "Ah," mourns the poet, "did he tell what we are here!" We have no notion of who we are or what we are for.

Clough's most fundamental conflict is much like that expressed in Arnold's *In Utrumque Paratus*. If in our quest of "a More beyond" we soar with Plato to the empyreal sphere we lose the color and concreteness of everyday existence and the ethical values of vital relationship with man and nature; if on the other hand we immerse ourselves in mere phenomena we lose our apprehension of the "More." The only solution is a compromise. As we behold the visible world we must say to ourselves:

This that I see is not all, and this that I do is but little;
Nevertheless it is good, though there is better than it.

But this sensible (and potentially Christian) balance is seldom fully satisfying to Clough. He usually oscillates between one extreme and the other. We hear him praying:

. . . O Good and Great,
In whom in this bedarkened state
I fain am struggling to believe,
Let me not ever cease to grieve,
Nor lose the consciousness of ill
Within me;—and refusing still
To recognize in things around
What truly cannot there be found,
Let me not feel, nor be it true,
That while each daily task I do
I still am giving day by day
My precious things within away
(Those thou didst give to keep as thine)
And casting, do whate'er I may,
My heavenly pearls to earthly swine.

The "precious things within," obscured by everyday experience, come alive only when he raises his mind to the noumenon. Once when he gazed in bewilderment at the starry heavens,

Then Plato to me said,
"'Tis but the figured ceiling overhead,

With cunning diagrams bestarred, that shine
In all the three dimensions, are endowed
With motion too by skill mechanical,
That thou in height, and depth, and breadth, and power,
Schooled unto pure Mathesis, might proceed
To higher entities . . .
In the sole Kingdom of the Mind and God.
Mind not the stars, mind thou thy Mind and God."

Thus instructed, when he heard savants bemusing themselves with cosmological puzzles,

Talk they as talk they list,
I, in that ampler voice,
Unheeding, did rejoice.

But perhaps those higher entities are mere figments of wishful imagination. What, in any case, has their abstract perfection to do with the actual life of men? In *Amours de Voyage* Claude concedes:

Yet we must eat and drink, as you say. And as limited beings
Scarcely can hope to attain upon earth to an Actual Abstract,
Leaving to God contemplation, to His hands knowledge confiding,
Sure that in us if it perish, in Him it abideth and dies not,
Let us in His sight accomplish our petty particular doings,—
Yes, and contented sit down to the victual that He has provided.

Clough is whistling to keep his spirits up: he would like much more than this if only he could get it. A passage in the *Bothie* attempts to bridge the gap between eating-and-drinking man and contemplative God by means of a personally pragmatic rather than a Platonic sort of ideal aspiration:

Yes, we must seek what is good, it always and it only;
Not indeed absolute good, good for us, as is said in the Ethics,
That which is good for ourselves, our proper selves, our best selves.

But in order to seek this individual good we must know what our best and proper selves *are*; and this, we have seen, is precisely what Clough is unable to discover.

The Spirit in *Dipsychus*, of course, is all for realism and common sense. His detestation of *Schwärmerei* is sometimes rather ignobly cynical, but in the following lines Clough uses him as the vehicle for searching and serious self-criticism:

. . . Come, my pretty boy,
You have been making mows to the blank sky

Quite long enough for good. We'll put you up
Into the higher form. 'Tis time you learn
The Second Reverence, for things around.

. . .

Why will you walk about thus with your eyes shut,
Treating for facts the self-made hues that float
On tight-pressed pupils, which you know are not facts?
To use the undistorted light of the sun
Is not a crime; to look straight out upon
The big plain things that stare you in the face
Does not contaminate; to see pollutes not
What one must feel if one won't see; what *is*,
And will be, too, howe'er we blink, and must
One way or the other make itself observed.

Clough often tries to practice this Second Reverence—extending the term, however, to include not merely the honest confrontation of facts but the use of them in beneficent action. The relation between this doctrine and belief in God is indicated by lines which he uses in two letters and which finally appear in *Dipsychus*:

. . . It seems His newer will,
We should not think at all of Him, but trudge it,
And of the world he has assigned us make
What best we can.

"Best" of course not merely for ourselves, but for mankind. Dipsychus's social conscience is so tender that it even reproaches him for enjoying the gondola ride while the gondolier sweats for his pittance:

My very heart recoils
While here to give my mirth a chance
A hungry brother toils.

The joy that does not spring from joy
Which I in others see,
How can I venture to employ,
Or find it joy for me?

But the Spirit, speaking no less surely for Clough, calls Dipsychus a prig.

Several of the poems preach a gospel of duty—Carlyle softened and socialized by Kingsley. *Last Words* contrasts the dying Napoleon's "Tête d'armée" with what Clough imagines the dying Wellington *might* have said:

"That humble, simple duty of the day
Perform," he bids; "ask not if small or great:

Serve in thy post; be faithful, and obey;
Who serves her [duty] truly, sometimes saves the state."

"*Blank Misgivings*" suggests that the bliss of contemplation may be the ultimate reward of such faithful service:

The Summum Pulchrum rests in heaven above;
Do thou, as best thou may'st, thy duty do:
Amid the things allowed thee live and love;
Some day thou shalt it view.

But there are higher and lower conceptions of duty, and it is difficult to prevent the former from collapsing into the latter. What the term means to Victorian society is described in one of the *Ambarvalia* pieces:

Duty—'tis to take on trust
What things are good, and right, and just;
And whether indeed they be or be not,
Try not, test not, feel not, see not:
. . .
'Tis the stern and prompt suppressing,
As an obvious deadly sin,
All the questing and the guessing
Of the soul's own soul within:
'Tis the cowardly acquiescence
In a destiny's behest,
To a shade by terror made,
Sacrificing, aye, the essence
Of all that's truest, noblest, best.

This early poem expresses, with youthful crudity and extravagance, a difficulty that Clough continued to feel throughout his career. Did not the active life, however practically beneficent, entail so many compromises with vulgarity and evil that one's higher nature was inevitably smothered in the lower? On the other hand, could one attain the Summum Pulchrum without immersing oneself in the baseness of actuality and struggling through it to the "More beyond"? Compelled to answer the first question affirmatively and the second negatively, Dipsychus despairingly submits himself to the control of his Mephistopheles,

Not to please thee, O base and fallen Spirit!
But One Most High, Most True, whom without thee
It seems I cannot [please]. O the misery,
That one must truck and practise with the world
To gain the vantage-ground to assail it from;
To set upon the giant one must first,
O perfidy! have eat the giant's bread.

God wants him to act for the good of mankind; he cannot so act on any effective scale without money and power; he cannot obtain money and power without adopting the Machiavellian tactics of the Spirit; he cannot use those tactics without being corrupted. That Dipsychus is indeed corrupted in the process of becoming Lord Chancellor may be inferred from Part II, but this rough unfinished draft is too feeble and fragmentary to enable us to tell whether he was to find some means of escape from the vicious circle.

Although we can attain union with God neither from the active nor from the theoretic life, the mere thought of a godless world is intolerable. Dipsychus tells the Spirit of a dream in which a Venetian bell, now merrily tinkling and now ominously tolling, seems to say:

> Ting, ting a ding! Come dance and sing!
> Staid Englishman, who toil and slave
> From your first breaching to your grave,
> And seldom spend and always save,
> And do your duty all your life
> By your young family and wife;
> Come, be't not said you ne'er had known
> What earth can furnish you alone.
> The Italian, Frenchman, German even,
> Has given up all thoughts of heaven;
> And you still linger—oh, you fool!
> Because of what you learnt at school.
>
> . . .
>
> Ah, well, and yet—dong, dong, dong:
> Do, if you like, as now you do;
> If work's a cheat, so's pleasure too;
> And nothing's new, and nothing's true;
> Dong, there is no God; dong!

The nonexistence of God confers exemption from Grundyism, but for the atheist the life of pleasure and the life of duty end in the same blank emptiness.

The Spirit answers that there are indeed those who disbelieve in God or are indifferent to the problem; but that country folk, clerical families, most married couples,

> Youths green and happy in first love,
> So thankful for illusion;
> And men caught out in what the world
> Calls guilt, in first confusion;

And almost every one when age,
  Disease, or sorrows strike him,
Inclines to think there is a God,
  Or something very like Him.

For a moment we are perplexed: should not these lines have been assigned to Dipsychus, and the outright denial of God to the Spirit? But the Mephistopheles of this poem is not the *Geist der stets verneint*. He is the Spirit who will say "Yes" to any idea that makes him comfortable, regardless of whether it is true or not. Dipsychus, on the other hand, hungers for the truth, be it positive or negative.

Both the speakers in this poem, we must keep reminding ourselves, are aspects of the poet's own character. But although Clough is doubtless tempted to believe on grounds of merely conventional expediency, he is too honest and at bottom too religious to succumb to this snare. His envy of the stupidly orthodox is partly genuine and partly ironic:

O happy they whose hearts receive
The implanted word with faith; believe
Because their fathers did before,
Because they learnt, and ask no more.

. . .

O happy they, nor need they fear
The wordy strife that rages near:
All reason wastes by day, and more,
Will instinct in a night restore.
O happy, so their state but give
A clue by which a man can live;
O blest, unless 'tis proved by fact
A dream impossible to act.

But although Clough is pretty thoroughly convinced that their creed is indeed a dream, he is by no means convinced that he has found anything more reasonable:

"Old things need not be therefore true,"
O brother men, nor yet the new;
Ah! still awhile the old thought retain,
And yet consider it again!

In *Amours de Voyage* he permits his spokesman to acknowledge the power which Catholic Rome exerts upon him:

Is it religion? I ask me; or is it a vain superstition?
  Slavery abject and gross? service, too feeble, of truth?

> Is it an idol I bow to, or is it a god that I worship?
> Do I sink back on the old, or do I soar from the mean?
> So through the city I wander and question, unsatisfied ever,
> Reverent so I accept, doubtful because I revere.

Claude also pays tribute to

> ... the calm and composure and gentle abstraction that reign o'er
> Mild monastic faces in quiet collegiate cloisters.

But Catholics even more than other Christians are willing to "make their image"; and this, as Bagehot says, is precisely what Clough refuses to do. Far from accepting the dogmas of Rome, he can no longer accept even those of Rugby. Although the new is not *necessarily* truer than the old, he has some hope of the former and none of the latter. The Voice of *The New Sinai* seems to declare that the old Revelation is utterly dead:

> And as of old from Sinai's top
> God said that God is One,
> By Science strict so speaks He now
> To tell us, There is None!

After all, however, this is not "the Voice" but "the cloud" from which the Voice spoke in ages past and within which He remains hidden

> Till idol forms and idol thoughts
> Have passed and ceased to be.

We need a new prophet-soul, someone like Carlyle or Emerson, who will penetrate the cloud and reveal to us a God untainted by the infantile superstitions which now obscure Him. This poem, as Clough himself doubtless realized, illustrates what the Spirit means when he speaks of Dipsychus's proneness "to pervert / Ancient real facts to modern unreal dreams." Neither here nor elsewhere is Clough at all explicit as to the content of the modern revelation. The only clue is the statement already quoted from *Dipsychus*:

> ... It seems His newer will,
> We should not think at all of Him, but trudge it,
> And of the world He has assigned us make
> What best we can.

Mount Sinai is certainly not what it used to be.[7]

Although, as we have seen, Clough accuses traditional believers of relying on instinct rather than on reason, he himself sometimes wearies of brain-

[7] See above, pp. 268–269, for Digby Dolben's answer to *The New Sinai.*

work and seeks a more romantic solution. "*Hang* this thinking!" cries Claude:

> . . . what good is it? oh, and what evil!
> Oh, what mischief and pain! like a clock in a sick man's chamber,
> Ticking and ticking, and still through each covert of slumber pursuing.
>
> . . .
>
> Let me, contented and mute, with the beasts of the field, my brothers,
> Tranquilly, happily lie,—and eat grass, like Nebuchadnezzar!

The next step, of course, is to transform disillusion into illusion by mysticizing this naturalism:

> All that is Nature's is I, and I all things that are Nature's.
> Yes, as I walk, I behold, in a luminous, large intuition,
> That I can be and become anything that I meet with or look at;
>
> . . .
>
> Yea, and detect as I go, by a faint but a faithful assurance,
> E'en from the stones of the street, as from rocks or trees of the forest,
> Something of kindred, a common, though latent vitality, greet me;
> And, to escape from our strivings, mistakings, misgrowths, and perversions,
> Fain would demand to return to that perfect and primitive silence,
> Fain be enfolded and fixed, as of old, in their rigid embraces.

One's own instinctive urges, thus united with the vitality of nature, are easily promoted from the subrational to the superrational level. Why, asks Clough, should we puzzle our heads over "vain Philosophy,"

> While from the secret treasure-depths below,
>
> . . .
>
> Wisdom at once, and Power,
> Are welling, bubbling forth, unseen incessantly?
> Why labour at the dull mechanic oar,
> When the fresh breeze is blowing,
> And the strong current flowing,
> Right onward to the Eternal Shore?

Breezes without, breezes within. Such intuitions are stifled not only by analytical reason but by conventional worship. In church on a fine Sunday morning, the poet longs to escape:

> Why stay and form my features to a "foolish face" of prayer,
> Play postures with my body, while the Spirit is not there?
> Not there, but wandering off to woods, or pining to adore
> Where mountains rise or where the waves are breaking on the shore?

Few moderns think very long about the nexus between cosmic and human vitality without thinking about sex. In *The Bothie of Tober-na-Vuolich*,

Philip Hewson, the worried, overintellectualized young radical and humanitarian, is soothed by Highland scenery and refreshed by bathing in Highland streams, but he does not discover the secret treasure-depths until he discovers the beautiful, simple, intuitive Elspie. The nonintellectual beauty insists that she must read hard to become worthier of him. Philip protests:

> This is the way with you all, I perceive, high and low together.
> Women must read, as if they didn't know all beforehand.
>
> . . .
>
> Weary and sick of our books, we come to repose in your eye-light,
> As to the woodland and water, the freshness and beauty of Nature,
> Lo, you will talk, forsooth, of the things we are sick to the death of.

In her noblest moments, however, Elspie is not troubled by her intellectual and social inferiority to her lover:

> No, I feel more as if I, as well as you, were,
> Somewhere, a leaf in the one great tree that, up from old time
> Growing, contains in itself the whole of the virtue and life of
> Bygone days, drawing now to itself all kindreds and nations,
> And must have for itself the whole world for its root and branches.
>
> . . .
>
> Yes, and I feel the life-juices of all the world and the ages
> Coming to me as to you.

Romantic evolutionary pantheism, sexual vitalism, the cult of progress, the cult of humanity—a familiar cluster.

To judge from *Dipsychus*, however, Clough's efforts to draw religious satisfaction from romantic nature-experience were not very satisfying. Toward such illusions the Spirit is extremely sceptical. Dipsychus tries to find union with "the life-juices of all the world" in a swim at the Lido:

> Aha! come, come—great waters, roll!
> Accept me, take me, body and soul!
> That's done me good.

Straightway his mocking *alter ego* deflates the illusion:

> Pleasant, perhaps. However, no offence,
> Animal spirits are not common sense.
>
> . . .
>
> They're good enough as an assistance,
> But in themselves a poor existence.
> But you, with this one bathe, no doubt,
> Have solved all questions out and out.
> 'Tis Easter Day, and on the Lido
> Lo, Christ the Lord is risen indeed O!

The irony of that last couplet cuts deep. Clough is reminding himself of Part II of his own *Easter Day*, in which, after repudiating the Resurrection as a historical event, he asserts that "Christ is yet risen" as a feeling in the heart. At this point in *Dipsychus* the poet seems to admit that redemption through swimming and redemption through subjectivized Christianity are about equally futile. Similarly the Spirit, weary of his companion's barcarole endlessly rhyming "Ah" and "gondola," refers to a more philosophically romantic mood only to poke fun at it:

> Quote us a little Wordsworth, do!
> Those lines that are so just, they say:
> "A something far more deeply" eh?
> "Interfused"—what is it they tell us?
> Which and the sunset are bedfellows.

Knowing also that Dipsychus-Clough is doomed

> To cherish natural instincts, yet to fear them,
> And less than any use them,

the Spirit does not encourage him to cultivate the mystico-primitivistic sexuality of Philip and Elspie. He has been urging Dipsychus to pick up some Venetian *cocotte* not in order to corrupt him but in order to free him from illusion:

> I know it's mainly your temptation
> To think the thing [sex] a revelation,
> A mystic mouthful that will give
> Knowledge and death—none know and live!
> I tell you plainly that it brings
> Some ease; but the emptiness of things
>
> . . .
>
> Is the sole lesson you'll learn by it—
> Still you undoubtedly should try it.
> Once known the little lies behind it,
> You'll go your way and never mind it.

Clough is extremely idealistic about women, and deeply suspicious of his own idealism.

Although he died only two years after the publication of *Origin of Species*, he was too sensitive to the doubts raised by contemporary science to embrace the romantic religion of nature or the Christian view of natural revelation.[8] In *The New Sinai*, "Science strict" is the cloud of negation which has

[8] See F. W. Palmer, "The Bearing of Science on the Thought of Arthur Hugh Clough," *PMLA*, LIX, 212–225.

obscured our awareness of God. *Natura Naturans,* to be sure, interprets evolution as the ascent, from the geologic to the human level, of a cosmic spirit of love which at last attains full self-consciousness in man. Here, despite the Spinozan title, the influence of Hegel is probably at work. Clough also has deep respect for the willingness of the true scientist to face the facts whatever they may be. But his efforts to emulate this probity are undermined by his dread of mechanism. He cannot bear to think that

> Earth goes by chemic forces; Heaven's
> A Mécanique Céleste,
> And heart and mind of human kind
> A watch-work like the rest.

One means of evading this disastrous conclusion is hinted at in the Goethean title of *Wen Gott betrügt, ist wohl betrogen.* The threat aimed by science at the cult of creative imagination is expressed in lines which ask the cheating gods:

> Is it true that poetical power,
> The gift of heaven, the dower
> Of Apollo and the Nine,
> The inborn sense, "the vision and the faculty divine,"
> All we glorify and bless
> In our rapturous exaltation,
> All invention, and creation,
> Exuberance of fancy, and sublime imagination,
> All a poet's fame is built on,
> The fame of Shakespeare, Milton,
> Of Wordsworth, Byron, Shelley,
> Is, in reason's grave precision,
> Nothing more, nothing less,
> Than a peculiar conformation,
> Constitution and condition
> Of the brain and of the belly?

Precisely because he abhors this idea he desires to confront it disinterestedly:

> Oh say it, all who think it,
> Look straight, and never blink it!
> If it is so, let it be so,
> And we will all agree so.

But just at this crucial point his courage wavers, and he adds the cryptic lines:

> But the plot has counter-plot,
> It may be, and yet be not.

Whom God deceives is well deceived. Belief in "all a poet's fame is built on," if an illusion, may be a beneficent and necessary illusion which God wishes us to embrace in order to preserve us from rhyming "Shelley" with "belly." The poem veers from "Face the facts" to "Let's pretend."

In other words, as so often happens, the objective empirical pragmatism which we have observed as an important element in Clough's thinking melts into a subjective, romantic, *als ob* pragmatism. It both attracts him and arouses his self-distrust. Shall we, he wonders, adopt "some arbitrary judgment" as to life's purpose, "and wilfully pronounce it clear" although we know full well that it is not? Or shall we "pace the sad confusion here," frankly confessing our inability to fathom its meaning? The latter course may be more honest and courageous, but it cuts across the grain of human nature:

> The heart still overrules the head;
> Still what we hope we must believe.

Rather than lapse into a merely animal existence it is

> . . . better far to mark off this much air
> And call it heaven, place bliss and glory there;
> Fix perfect homes in the unsubstantial sky,
> And say, what is not, will be by-and-by.

These lines assert the will to believe with an irony which comes close to denying it. We are not surprised that the Spectrum-Deity of *Shadow and Light* pricks the bubble in words which Hardy might have written:

> And yet withal, 'tis shadow all
> Whate'er your fancies dream,
> And I (misdeemed) that was, that seemed,
> Am not, whate'er I seem.

But although the philosophy of *als ob* is not really convincing to him, it derives some reinforcement from his considerable knowledge of German Bible-criticism. The Straussian conception of Jesus added to his doubts concerning traditional Christianity, but it could be used to illustrate the fact that *Wen Gott betrügt, ist wohl betrogen*. The thought of *Epi-Strauss-Ium* is set forth more fully and explicitly in *Easter Day*. In Part I the voice relentlessly asserts

> . . . the one sad Gospel that is true,
> Christ is not risen.

But the voice in Part II proclaims the inspiring paradox:

> Though dead, not dead;
> Not gone, though fled,
> Not lost, though vanished.
> In the great gospel and true creèd,
> He is yet risen indeed;
> Christ is yet risen.

On Straussian premises, this is not the irresponsible juggling which it must otherwise appear to be. In historical fact, no divine-human Saviour burst from the tomb on Easter morning. But the *Jesus-feeling* within our hearts is an eternal truth, and we are entitled to externalize that feeling in a beneficent myth. In "the great gospel and true creed" of human love, what the Resurrection *means* is unshaken. We recall Clough's words to his sister: "I cannot feel sure that a man may not have all that is important in Christianity even if he does not so much as know that Jesus of Nazareth existed." The position is more romantic than Christian, since it implies that we are redeemed only by what is best within ourselves.

It is not my fault that this chapter moves like a seesaw: Clough never advances an important idea which he does not elsewhere deny. We already know that there are times when the Gospel according to Strauss has no more spiritual potency than a dip in the ocean. Speaking as the Spirit in another passage of *Dipsychus*, Clough derides *Easter Day* because "There is a strong Strauss-smell about it." Bishop Butler was wiser than the Germans: he proved that " 'Twas useless to explain things."

> At any rate this rationalistic
> Half-puritanico-semitheistic
> Cross of Neologist and Mystic
> Is, of all doctrines, the least reasonable—
> And of all topics most unseasonable.
> Why should you fancy you know more of it
> Than all the old folks that thought before of it?
> Like a good subject and wise man,
> Believe whatever things you can.
> Take your religion as 'twas found you,
> And say no more of it—confound you!

One of Clough's many unfinished poems implicitly rejects the consolations of German neologism. The poet dreams that Jesus returns to earth as a mere ghost briefly emerging from the shades. He declares, "I am that Jesus whom they slew"; but He knows nothing of His divinity or miraculous birth or resurrection. Christ's refusal to confirm any of the Christian myths creates a most embarrassing situation. The man of the world is outraged:

> His wife and daughter must have where to pray,
> And whom to pray to, at the least one day
> In seven, and something definite to say.
>
> . . .
>
> And the poor Pope was sure it must be so,
> Else wherefore did the people kiss his toe?

A Jesuit cardinal sees no great difficulty:

> Whatever may befall,
> We Catholics need no evidence at all,
> The holy father is infallible, surely!

An Anglican canon says that on the contrary there *should* be evidence; but the testimony of a ghost is notoriously untrustworthy, and there is no reason to abandon the Christian faith on such dubious grounds. Other dignitaries of the Establishment have more practical reasons for clinging to their orthodoxy:

> It had been worth to some of them, they said,
> Some £100,000 a year a head.

Pious women demand of the bewildered honest ghost

> What should they teach their children and the poor?
> The Shade replied, he could not know,
> But it was truth, the fact was so.

In short Christ is *not* risen, and here there is no attempt to transform the harsh fact into a soothing myth.

This poem, together with *The Latest Decalogue*, *In the Great Metropolis*, and several other satirical poems or passages already cited in this chapter, reminds us once more how much the shortcomings of the Church and the un-Christian conduct of its adherents have done to prevent men of high spiritual gifts from embracing the Christian religion. Clough's criticisms of a society only nominally Christian have considerable merit; but Mr. Humbert Wolfe's thesis that he was a great satirist and wit forced into seriousness by influences alien to his true character seems overstrained.[9] The satires lack any high distinction of form and phrase; their sarcasm is extravagant and loose; they reveal more discomfort than they inflict. Clough has no firm center from which to judge what he condemns.

[9] See "Arthur Henry Clough," *The Eighteen-Sixties*, pp. 20ff.

His real desire was to write wholesomely constructive serious (not necessarily solemn) poetry for his own benefit and for that of his fellows. Since, however, God's "newer will" decrees that we should live as nobly as possible in this world without thinking of Him, Clough's most sanguine poems are usually ethical with a quasi-religious flavor rather than specifically religious. Much in the manner of Browning, he often preaches the gospel of robust activity, courageous struggle, and inspiring failure. *Qui Laborat, Orat, Life is Struggle, Say Not the Struggle Nought Availeth*—the titles are usually quite sufficient.[10] No one can say where the ship of life has sailed from or whither it is going, but for that very reason the voyage is a joyous adventure. How delightful to stroll the deck on calm sunny days! Better still,

> On stormy nights when wild north-westers rave,
> How proud a thing to fight with wind and wave!
> The dripping sailor on the reeling mast
> Exults to bear, and scorns to wish it past.

Yet we remember that the Spirit has described Dipsychus as one of those who

> . . . burn, forsooth, for Action, yet despise
> Its merest accidence and alphabet.

Hope Evermore and Believe! has more philosophical content than most of these robustious pieces. The idea that nature depends for its meaning upon the mind of man is stock romantic doctrine, but here Clough's way of expressing it suggests the influence of Hegel:

> Hope evermore and believe, O man, for e'en as thy thought
> So are the things that thou see'st, e'en as thy hope and belief.

What though life be full of obstacles?

> All, with one varying voice, call to him, Come and subdue;
> Still for their Conqueror call, and, but for the joy of being conquered
> (Rapture they will not forego) dare to resist and rebel.

In short this is a good world because it is a good world to strangle.[11] The same transcendentalism supports the belief that *Even the Winds and the Sea Obey* the shaping spirit of imagination. Clough will not quite maintain, with "the mystical German," that America did not exist until Columbus beheld its shores,

[10] But the reader should be warned that many of the titles which have become familiar to him were posthumously devised by Mrs. Clough, and that the definitive 1951 Oxford Edition admits these only to the notes.

[11] Here I paraphrase or misquote a sentence of Santayana's which I cannot place.

And yet I would deem it was so,
As o'er the new waters he sailed,
That his soul made the breezes to blow,

. . .

The resolve of his conquering will
The lingering vessel impelled.

Imbedded in the visible world there are mysterious powers that can overrule nature's mechanical laws, but even these powers are subject to our creative will. They

Can cause, so to say, every cause,
And our best mathematics befool;
Can defeat calculation and plan,
Baffle schemes ne'er so wisely designed,
But will bow to the genius of man
And acknowledge a sovereign mind.

He "would deem it were so," for if it *were* so he would be relieved of the fear that "all a poet's fame is built on" is merely

. . . a peculiar conformation,
Constitution and condition
Of the brain and of the belly.

His selfhood, however, is too divided and confused to permit such feats of self-assertion. At best, romantic transcendentalism will do no more for him than justify the softer, more subjective aspect of his pragmatism, encouraging him to say:

O let me live unto myself alone,
And know my knowledge to the world unknown;

. . .

And worship thee, with thee withdrawn apart,
Whoe'er, whate'er thou art,
Within the closest veil of mine own inmost heart.

But again the seesaw tips, and we hear Claude saying:

What with trusting myself and seeking support from within me,
Almost I could believe I had gained a religious assurance,
Found in my own poor soul a great moral basis to rest on.
Ah, but indeed I see, I feel it factitious entirely;
I refuse, reject, and put it utterly from me;
I will look straight out, see things, not try to evade them;
Fact shall be fact for me, and the Truth the Truth as ever,
Flexible, changeable, vague, and multiform, and doubtful —
Off, and depart to the void, thou subtle, fanatical tempter.

In these lines Clough resolutely abjures romantic inwardness, at the same time describing Truth in such a way that he can never conceive of it as other than subjective.

Certainly this wavering tortured doubter wrote many poems suitable for use on inspirational calendars, but his optimism is so utterly devoid of foundation in reason or in faith that to me it is more depressing than the blackest pessimism.

> 'Twill all be well: no need of care;
> Though how it will, and when, and where,
> We cannot see, and can't declare.
> In spite of dreams, in spite of thought,
> 'Tis not in vain, and not for nought;
> The wind it blows, the ship it goes,
> But whence and whither, no one knows.

Compared with that, *The City of Dreadful Night* is positively bracing.

Chapter Nineteen

CONCLUSION FOR HISTORIANS

As I BRING this book to a close I find myself wondering, perhaps rather tardily, whether it contributes anything really useful to the history of ideas. The religious thought of this period has already been competently treated by other scholars. Anyone who hopes to improve on their work must re-examine the primary sources—the solid blocks of expository-argumentative prose which embody the normative thinking of the nineteenth century.

A quite different but equally legitimate enterprise might, however, concern itself not with Victorian religious ideas as a phase in the history of theology and philosophy but with the impact of those ideas upon the spiritual sensibilities of the educated Victorian public as a whole. To study the impact of an idea is to study the way in which human beings respond to it with their intellects, their emotions, and their imaginations; and to study past responses is to scrutinize and interpret the written record of those responses. Evidence could be drawn not only from belles-lettres but from popular sermons and tracts, artless autobiographies, diaries and letters, newspapers, sectarian and secular journals of opinion, book reviews, textbooks, advertisements, reports of university debates and lectures to workingmen, vestry minutes, choir programs, jokes in *Punch,* lending-library records, epitaphs, children's names, legal and legislative documents—Lord knows what else. Paintings and drawings would provide an important body of supplementary evidence. But who combines enough learning, breadth of interest, patience, and assurance of longevity to digest materials so limitless and so diverse and to synthesize them in a complete history of the religious temper of the Victorians? While "general education" labors to produce the all-integrating scholar of the future, there will be plenty of time, and a moderate amount of justification, for old-fashioned pedants to study particular areas of the whole field. I have nibbled at the segment which I personally find most toothsome.

In writing the successive volumes of this series I have, to be sure, sometimes wished that I had undertaken to discuss religious trends not only in poetry but in drama, fiction, and perhaps the less technical kinds of expository prose. This widened scope would, however, have compelled me either to treat the subject with unrewarding superficiality or to write six books of such length that, supposing I lived to complete them, even the Columbia University Press could not be expected to publish the monstrous lumps.[1] Granting the propriety of choosing a single branch of literature, the choice of poetry demands no apology. I like it best and know most about it. It is the literary type in which intellectual, emotional, and imaginative responses to religious stimuli are most closely interfused and find most intense and meaningful expression. On these bushes, too, the berries of our quest grow thickest. As for the present volume, there are few Victorian poets who are not obsessed by the problem of the status of religion in the modern world. The critics and the reading public felt that there was something religious about poetry and something poetical about religion. As time went on they depended more upon poetry than upon the pulpit for the most truly elevating sentiments and attitudes concerning "the things of the spirit."

For the larger uses of intellectual historiography the evidence provided by poetry is quantitatively small and qualitatively peculiar. It needs to be supplemented by evidence drawn from nonliterary sources. Although there were all too many Victorian poets, they constituted only an infinitesimal fraction of the population—and not a wholly representative fraction, for even the most ordinary poet is not, statistically speaking, quite an ordinary man. Ignorance and torpor, however, are colorless invariables which resist analysis and characterization. Historiography defeats its own purpose when it struggles too hard to restore to life that which has never lived. We learn most of what is worth knowing about a culture from the utterances of its most perceptive and articulate members. Poets are unusual not in seeing less of their world than other men but in seeing more of it and in being more sensitive to the deeper implications of appearances. They represent what moves below the surface of an age if not the superficial phenomena. They shuttle back and forth between the technically formulated theories and the subconscious emotional drives of which the theories are a rationalization. Thanks to the steam printing press and to the pathetic reverence of the public for the authority of words, the Victorian poets, though numerically negligible, constituted one of the most powerful social groups of the age. They expressed what the reading public really thought and felt but could not say. If we cancel out the cases in which the poet is too idiosyncratic to represent anyone's views but his own (these are not always the best poems)

[1] Treatment of the discursive prose would also entail invasion of the field cultivated so fruitfully by Basil Willey, whose *Nineteenth Century Studies* is to be supplemented by another volume of the same type.

and the cases in which he obviously does not mean what he says,[2] we are left with a large body of writing which tells the historian a great deal, though by no means all he needs to know, about the religion of nineteenth-century Englishmen.

In the preceding chapters the material has been described and its meaning discussed with, I hope, due heed to the differences between fact and opinion. It is a *fact* that Thomson in his poem on Arnold's *Stanzas from the Grande Chartreuse* hopes to be inspired and guided by a dead God. When I call this idea "pathetic nonsense" I express an *opinion* with which the reader may agree or disagree without altering the status of the fact.[3] Even the strongest disagreement will not justify him in asserting that I expect my statements of opinion to be accepted as statements of fact; to entertain any such hope would be excessively naïve. My obvious desire to *influence* the reader's view of the subject will be less corrupting than if I had tried to conceal it. His own predispositions and commitments will provide a sufficient antidote. The danger that his ideas about religion will be modified by these opinionated pages is infinitesimal.

Although no point-by-point summary of the book seems necessary, I should like to expatiate a little on its principal theme. In approaching the religious trends of the Victorian period through the poets we have, I believe, come to recognize the importance of a factor which has been ignored or at best greatly underestimated by scholars who have studied the history of religious thought more directly and technically. If a visitor to the chapel of Trinity College, Cambridge, walks up to the altar steps, turns his back on the Cross, and looks straight down the center aisle into the antechapel, the first object in his line of vision will be the famous statue of Newton. Were one a poet, or even a historian wistfully trying to be lively, one might be tempted to use Cross and Statue as polar symbols of the Victorian tension between belief and unbelief. But after our long immersion in the poets we see that this dichotomy would be misleading even if it were handled with full recognition of the fact that it is less simple than it looks. For the twofold symbolic scheme fails to take account of the *tertium quid*—man's undying desire for self-sufficiency and personal infinitude. The Cross will not sym-

[2] But these may be historically significant as indicating his awareness of what the age wants him to say.

[3] See above, p. 459. I may add that the unusually large amount of quotation in this series of studies is intended to give the reader full opportunity to see what the poet actually says and to form his own judgment of it. When this safeguard is neglected, the gap between a scholar's ostensibly objective description of the thought of a poem and the poem itself often proves to be astonishingly great.

bolize romanticism: it denies man's independent boundlessness and proclaims his need of divine aid. Nor will the Statue function as a romantic symbol, for it implies the subjection of the human spirit to the dominance of matter in motion. The Victorian tension pulls in three, not two, directions: toward faith in God, toward faith in man, and toward faith in matter. Should we not perhaps add a fourth faith? I have in mind what Ruskin calls "Traffic"—reliance on material progress through money-making, quantitative production, *laissez-faire* competition, mechanized industry. But although genuine science and Traffic are extremely different, the latter depends for its existence upon the former. It is science applied—and misapplied—to commercial life. Traffic is what selfish empiricism makes of the disinterested scientific endeavor to understand the mechanisms of nature. When the average Victorian said "science," he meant the invention of machines to facilitate the getting and spending of money. Mammon-worship is not a separate religion, but simply the basest form of faith in matter.[4]

The threefold scheme has been quite sufficient to render our historical enterprise bewilderingly complex. When I said a moment ago that "no point-by-point summary of the book seems necessary," I should have been honest enough to say that no such summary is possible. For although the three faiths are essentially different they perplexingly intertwine as they move outward from their central principles. Statue and Cross are not completely antithetical: at Trinity, they appropriately confront each other within an edifice which symbolizes the totality of Christian culture. Newton himself was religious, as were not a few Victorian scientists. Both Cross and Statue, furthermore, stand for that recognition of the suprapersonal objectivity of truth which is hostile to the romantic spirit, and both symbolize great unromantic rational systems. On the other hand, romanticism and science seem to be allied in opposition to the Christian belief in a transcendent deity. Up to a certain point, the accomplishments of science are richly satisfying to romantic pride. For Wordsworth, Newton's statue represented the high adventure of "Voyaging through strange seas of thought, alone." We have observed the ability of some of our poets to transform science into the stuff of romantic illusion by means of pantheism or transcendentalism. Nor should it be forgotten that those who profess faith in man or faith in matter remain about equally loyal to the ethical standards of the religion in which they no longer believe. Christianity and romanticism in turn are united against science by their refusal to concede the dominance of matter over

[4] Under the head of "science" we may also include, for the purposes of this brief schematic discussion, the sensationalistic philosophies of utilitarianism and positivism.

mind. Thanks to the dread of disturbing the *status quo* and to the association of secularism with radicalism, all but the most uncompromising romantics wish to think of themselves as Christians. They manage to do so by subjectivizing Protestant Christianity into more or less close agreement with the romantic faith in man. In this interfusion Protestantism meets romanticism halfway by falling back upon an immanentist and "inward witness" type of apologetics in order to evade the threats of science. Catholic Christianity, on the other hand, makes only superficial concessions to the romantic spirit, while romanticism rejects all that is essential in Catholicism but uses its flavor and trappings as something to feel romantic about. Traffic, the bastard child of science, would seem to be a deadlier enemy of both Christianity and romanticism than its parent. Innumerable avowed Christians, however, achieved a comfortable working compromise between the service of God and of Mammon; and many romantics derived a feeling of boundlessness from regarding the upward sweep of "progress" with humanitarian or patriotic enthusiasm. In short each of the three faiths influences, and is influenced by, the other two. Some of these developments reach their peak earlier than others, and some later. Speaking very broadly and generally, we may say that the thirties and forties represent the gradual integration of the Victorian complex, the fifties its time of relative stability, and the sixties and seventies its gradual disintegration. But the poetry shows very clearly that the ferment of attraction and repulsion agitates our three faiths throughout the entire period; it does not, so far as I can see, subject itself to precise chronological plotting from year to year or even from decade to decade.

Trinity College Chapel contains no object which conveniently symbolizes the romantic tradition—nothing like Novalis's Blue Flower. But in the antechapel, among the effigies of Newton and other illustrious alumni, stands (or sits) a statue of Tennyson. Except perhaps in his earliest and latest working years, he was able to satisfy a chastened sort of romantic impulse not by defying the age but by coming to terms with it. Despite occasional outcroppings of the more passionate affirmations and denials which brooded in the deeper levels of his nature, he established uneasily friendly relations between science and Christianity by suffusing them with a romanticism which they in turn considerably modified. Thus in religious as in other matters his voice was that of the Victorian Compromise. It would not, however, be quite accurate to describe him as the representative Victorian *poet*. Let us rather say that he was the most nearly representative *Victorian* who also managed to write poetry. Disregarding the petty scribblers who will say anything that publishers will pay for, I can think of no other serious poet who was both able and willing to combine faith in God, faith in man, and faith in matter approximately as those faiths were synthesized in the general culture of Mid-Victorian England. Combinations of two of the three faiths in other poets are very common, especially the blend of half-romanticized Christianity and half-Christianized romanticism. Swinburne's *Hertha*, on the other hand, illustrates the anti-Christian union of romanticism and science. Even these two-sided compromises are often rejected in favor of a single faith. We have seen no poet so suicidally devoted to science as to spurn all dealings with either Christianity or romanticism, though R. H. Horne almost provides the unique exception. But the orthodox Christian poets cleave to faith in God without any tincture of faith in man or in matter; while a small but qualitatively important group of romantics are willing to condemn themselves to complete frustration rather than conciliate the Cross, or the Statue, or Britannia of the Marketplace.

In short the material which we have been studying points in every conceivable direction. But as I reviewed the preceding chapters in preparation for writing this conclusion I felt very strongly that Victorian poetry, taken as a whole, was much more uneasy, doubtful, and confused than the apparently prosperous, confident, integrated society in which it was written. The fact enhances rather than diminishes the usefulness of the poetry for the historian who wishes to delve below the surface phenomena in order to establish psychological coherence between the nineteenth century and the twentieth.[5] More clearly than any other sort of historical evidence the literature of the period shows that the Victorian Compromise was a temporary façade of expediency hastily improvised from materials so incongruous that it was doomed to disintegration. One may well ask why, in that case, poetry enjoyed such high prestige in a society so anxious to shut its eyes to its own uneasiness. But in the first place the bracingly "idealistic" poets were of course more highly esteemed than the questioning ones. Many Victorians, too, derived a certain relief from having their own wordless qualms expressed for them in poetry. It was too remote from their everyday concerns to be deeply disturbing unless it threatened the code of respectability. And they were so stubbornly determined to be edified by high-minded, mellifluous, hypnotically rhythmic language that they could obtain an astonishing amount of encouragement from essentially discouraging ideas, as in the case of *Idylls of the King*. If a poet expressed bewilderment with eloquent solemnity he was readily accepted as an idealist and a prophet.

[5] Victorian prose is of course indispensable for the same purpose; perhaps only the partiality of a specialist leads me to believe that the poetry takes us even deeper into the heart of the *Zeitgeist*.

The pseudo-synthesis of three incongruous faiths was already beginning to break down in the eighteen-sixties, and in the seventies the disintegration accelerated so rapidly that by 1880 the cultural complex which we have in mind when we say "Victorian" had almost disappeared.[6] How and why did it come to an end? To what sort of intellectual and spiritual environment would a young poet beginning his career in the seventies have to adjust himself? What was the religious temper of England at the point where the present volume closes and the next may some day begin?

The appropriate symbol of the Victorian Compromise in its most triumphant phase was a house of glass—the Crystal Palace at the time of the Great Exhibition of 1851. It proclaimed not three faiths but one. It showed what human intelligence and energy could do to nature, and what nature would do for man if he worked in accordance with her laws. Those laws were also God's laws. In a sense it was really He who had invented all these profitable machines and designed all these astounding works of art. He believed in progress. What God willed, what man wanted, and what nature provided were identical, or could be made so in the not very distant future. With His usual discrimination, God had been especially good to the English; but the international character of the exhibits denied any conflict between industrial competition and the Christian ethic. Among nations as among individuals, getting ahead of one's neighbor was the best way of loving him. Unrestricted commerce would make the world one seamless garment of brotherhood and peace.[7]

In 1870 Prince Albert's vision of the Table Round was shattered by Bismarck—a more practical sort of German.[8] After the end of the American Civil War, England had been forced to recognize a formidable economic rival in the United States. Now Prussified Germany—busy and prosperous, armed to the teeth and quick on the trigger—must be watched very carefully. France would never be satisfied until she had her revenge. Italy, now welding her states into national unity, would soon have claims of her own. And what about Russia? John Morley and a few others of his type believed that the only hope for peace and the democratic way of life lay in something like Tennyson's "Parliament of man, the federation of the world;" but this ideal

[6] All such statements are relative. There is a sense in which the Victorian period lasts until 1914, and even today some individuals are still living in it.

[7] The poets have shown us that there were dissident voices even in 1851, but this is a fair statement of the official view which was accepted by most Englishmen.

[8] Until quite recently, thanks to the Atlantic Ocean, such dreams have died more slowly in the United States than in England. I myself, born in 1894, was brought up to believe in the American equivalent of this one. But of course I do not mean that the Franco-Prussian War made it *immediately* apparent to Englishmen that the Crystal Palace had been smashed.

smacked too much of Prince Albert. No, Britannia must rule the waves or drown. Under Disraeli's leadership the romance of liberalism gave place to the romance—at once more picturesque and more realistic—of imperialism. To be thoroughly successful, however, this exciting and perilous form of romantic expansion requires a more confident unity of feeling than England at this time possessed. After thirty years of prosperity her luck changed in the mid-seventies, when a series of bad harvests made it impossible to meet American competition in cheap grain and brought about a collapse of agriculture which caused in turn a general economic depression. The long-dwindling power of the landed aristocracy now vanished almost completely before the power of the bourgeois plutocrat. Yet the triumph of urban civilization was hollow, for at the moment it had very little to feel triumphant about. During hard times it becomes difficult to derive spiritual satisfaction from the worship of Mammon. Even as Empress of India, Queen Victoria was not an adequate substitute for the fallen idol; he must somehow be set back on his pedestal. The masses were grumbling as in the days of Chartism; trade unions gathered strength. Although the increasingly active Socialists were dangerous, as the Paris Commune seemed to prove, on the other hand the whole fabric of *laissez-faire* liberalism, free trade included, must be overhauled and revised—just enough but not too much. And how much was that?

In the sphere of philosophy and religion, the first effect of the breakdown of the Compromise was that each of the three faiths became somewhat more distinct from the other two and spoke its own mind with considerable vigor. Precisely because the old certainties were crumbling, for a time one could *assert* the certainty of almost anything with less dread of being crushed by some irrefutable mass of hostile evidence. Science had provided the main integrating factor in the Mid-Victorian social synthesis. Here was a body of objective fact in which not only scientific materialism but utilitarianism and positivism were firmly rooted. Much more importantly, however, the whole system of Traffic as an object of quasi-religious devotion depended on acceptance of the claims of science to tell the whole truth about the universe and man's place in it. In the seventies, as the triumphant onrush of material progress wavered, faith in matter lost some of its authority. The new imperialistic program, furthermore, demanded more color and passion than the laboratory and the factory could provide. There were signs of an anti-scientific reaction, a reaching out in search of some rational foundation for believing that subjective emotion possessed objective validity. Empiricism was challenged by a revival of intuitionalism: by 1880 a sentimentalized version of Hegel had become the official academic philosophy and the authority for a great deal of looser, less technical thinking along mind-over-matter lines.[9]

Emboldened by all this confused freedom and less hindered by earlier scruples against disturbing the balance on which "progress" depended, every variety of belief and unbelief set forth its claims. The weakness of the Vatican as a secular power assuaged the anxieties which had been aroused in 1870; hence Roman Catholicism was able to assume something like its present place in English life as a definite body of dogma which must be accepted or rejected in its entirety. Despite strong opposition, Anglo-Catholicism of the ritualistic type was extremely active, but there were also signs that the heirs of the Oxford Movement were once more beginning to use their brains. They were also, along with most other Christian groups, developing a more genuine social-mindedness in response to the reproaches of the secularists. Under the same pressure there was a panicky but beneficent trend toward greater clerical conscientiousness and efficiency in all branches of the Church. Meanwhile the revivalistic movement of the seventies, with Moody and Sankey as its chief figures, showed that the power of Evangelicalism, both Anglican and Nonconformist, was by no means spent—a fact to which the rise of the Salvation Army also bore witness. The Reform Act of 1867 had increased the power of Dissent by extending the franchise downward into the lower-middle and upper-lower classes. Now left-wing Dissenters, especially Unitarians, were stimulated to renewed activity, chiefly political to be sure, by the efforts of John Morley to preserve liberalism through an alliance between his group of intellectuals and the forces of Joseph Chamberlain.

Both within and without the Establishment, Broad Churchmen emphasized the social gospel and maintained an approving attitude toward the evolving universe. Their position was slightly weakened, however, by the fact that it was becoming less important to associate the term "Christian" with every manifestation of religiosity. Substitute-religions no longer hesitated to assert that they *were* substitutes, and superior ones, for the traditional faith. The seventies teemed with them: several kinds of non-Christian theism, Comtian Positivism and various less formalized versions of the religion of humanity, socialism, anarchism, Utopian communities, emergent evolution and "cosmic emotion," Pater's gospel of the hard gem-

[9]Throughout the entire nineteenth century, of course, German transcendentalism had lent aid and comfort to English romanticism and had proved useful in the subjectivizing of Christianity; but it was much less generally influential than utilitarianism up to the Hegelian revival which began to challenge Mill in the eighteen-sixties and rose to dominance during the next two decades.

like flame, the cults of Schopenhauer and of Hegel, Spiritualism, Swedenborgianism, Rosicrucianism, mental healing, Hindu occultism, theosophy, astrology, mesmerism, "self-help" through diet or exercise or will-power, unclassifiable parlor-mysticisms invented by prophets who were willing to sell their secrets to restless women for a fee. The combined forces of romanticized Christianity and openly non-Christian "spirituality" were much stronger than those of Roman and Anglican Catholicism and fundamentalist Protestantism—which were further weakened by the fact that they did *not* combine.[10]

Angered and alarmed by what seemed to them a widespread revolt against reason, the secularist intellectuals cast aside their philosophic detachment, adopted the aggressiveness though not the coarseness of the Bradlaugh school, and leveled frontal attacks against Christianity, theism, and intuitional philosophy. Veteran popularizers of science like Huxley and Tyndall became more actively antireligious but were outstripped in violence by Clifford. Walter Cassel, Winwood Reade, Romanes, Butler, Morley, and Leslie Stephen rushed into the breach. Besides contributing directly to the hostile criticism of supernaturalism, Morley and Stephen in their biographical and literary studies invited admiration for the eighteenth century as the fountainhead of sanity and intellectual freedom. The *Fortnightly Review* and *Fraser's Magazine* opened their pages to secularistic propaganda. Even the sober old *Cornhill* ran Arnold's *St. Paul and Protestantism* and *Literature and Dogma*. Under James Knowles *The Nineteenth Century* featured symposia on such questions as immortality and the dependence of morality on religion, with participants representing every shade of opinion from complete orthodoxy to complete atheism. It is probably safe to say that by 1880 very few members of the intellectual laity felt any positive moral obligation toward any kind of supernaturalistic religion.

In this closing decade of our period the romantic impulse is a factor in imperialism, in liberalized Christianity and most of the non-Christian substitute-religions, in neo-Hegelianism, in art for art's sake, and perhaps even in the rationalistic defiance of spiritual authority.[11] On the other hand, it is from the poetry of the seventies that we have heard the most desperate outcries of frustrated romanticism. We may resolve this apparent anomaly by remembering that the romantic faith varies in depth and intensity

[10] This does not imply that, on the other hand, James Martineau and Annie Besant were conscious allies. I mean that a psychological kinship unites all religious subjectivists against all religious objectivists and *vice versa*, but that among the latter this kinship is obscured by differences of doctrine and cult which are less important to the former.

[11] Romantic motivation is strong, for example, in Clifford and Reade, easily discernible in Tyndall.

according to the temperament of the individual.[12] If it was relatively mild and subject to dilution by other tendencies it could find sufficient scope in the rich centrifugal confusion of the decade. But a really passionate and uncompromising drive toward infinitude would not be satisfied so easily.[13] The true romanticist does not deny the existence of an objective world. He needs such a world as the plastic stuff of his exploits: dominance would be no fun if there were nothing real for his spirit to dominate. His only grudge against reality is its refusal to bend to his will. He therefore withdraws into the depths of his own being, but not with any notion of remaining in that last and surest place of refuge if he can help it. The motive for his subjectivism is the desire to lay hold upon an inward principle of independent goodness, wisdom, and creative energy, and then, in the omnipotence of that selfhood, to rush out again into the objective and mold it into a reflection of the higher reality of his vision. To a genuine romantic Titan, boundlessness does not mean a pleasantly unhindered oozing out of idiosyncrasy: it means the conscious imposition of godlike mastery upon the external world. If he is not only a romantic man but a romantic poet, he will think of this outrush of energy chiefly in terms of creativity—what Coleridge called "the esemplastic power." Why do romantic poets take such delight in the diversity of things and yet describe the function of imagination as unifying and synthetic? Because the greater the manifoldness of the material the more glorious the triumph of subduing it to a pantheistic interfusion which will present no obstacle to man's self-enlargement.

Anything more than momentary recreative enjoyment of the illusion is possible only when the irreconcilable difference between the reality of the universe and the pseudo-reality fabricated by the imagination is not too crushingly obvious. Even a dream, to be healthy, must derive enough nourishment from actuality to support the belief that one is "dreaming true." The stronger the romantic impulse, the less this condition was satisfied by the eighteen-seventies. There was plenty of diversity, but it was the manifoldness of decay—the whirling fragments of a disintegrating culture. What imagination could subject it to synthesis and express its meaning for the future? The Mid-Victorian prophets in prose and verse were fading out. Those who still survived in 1880 were disenchanted and disenchanting old men who surveyed with more or less plucky dismay the ruins of the world they had known. Fresh voices could be heard, but none of them

[12] Needless to say, it also varies with the changing moods of the individual himself, but these modulations are too swift and subtle for analysis.

[13] Least of all when, as in several cases which we have noted, the individual is thwarted not only by his environment but by inward suppressions.

spoke with the old confidence. The prospects for a "New Sinai" seemed remote. Though it had become harder to feel sure that anything was false it had become correspondingly harder to feel sure that anything was really true. From this scepticism even the power of the transcendental will was not exempt. Since the days of Bain and Herbert Spencer, evolutionary science had invaded that romantic holy of holies, the autonomous creative mind, with an apparent authoritativeness more formidable than that of the old sensationalism. Thought itself was the passive product of the mechanical processes which had shaped man's body. Even in the subjective, then, there was no refuge from reality, no chance to make a higher truth by the exercise of free will. More recently a revival of transcendental philosophy had come to the aid of the romantic faith, but the resultant hopes were clouded and in some cases destroyed by the violence of the scientific counterattack. With much tactical acuteness Huxley, Tyndall, Romanes, and Clifford disclaimed a dogmatically materialistic theory of mind. They merely presented, against a richer background of specific facts than had been available to Bain and Spencer, the parallelism between brain and mind, and challenged the intuitionalists to propose any nonmechanistic theory which could account for it. Roden Noel and some other spiritual ancestors of Middleton Murry were almost able to persuade themselves that Hegel had validated Shelley, but many romantics were frustrated by the fear which had oppressed Clough even in less bewildering days—the fear that

> All invention, and creation,
> Exuberance of fancy, and sublime imagination,
> All a poet's fame is built on,
>
> . . .
>
> Is, in reason's grave precision,
> Nothing more, nothing less,
> Than a peculiar conformation,
> Constitution and condition
> Of the brain and of the belly.

While the biological scientists were busily confirming this dread as an antidote to the revival of "superstition," a younger generation of physicists, the heirs of Michael Faraday, were preparing to develop ideas which would eventually expose the incompleteness and crudity of nineteenth-century materialism. But even if the Haldanes and Clerk Maxwell had realized the final implications of their researches the age would not have been receptive to them: scientific and economic materialism were too firmly associated and too deeply entrenched in the history of popular education. An even more formidable obstacle to general acceptance of novel scientific concepts was the growth of specialization in intellectual life. The professional scholar of today cannot regard this late-Victorian development with unqualified disapproval: the greater the abundance and complexity of knowable facts, the greater the need of experts in particular fields. To a considerable extent, however, modern specialization represents a failure of intellectual nerve. The scholar's field, like the ivory tower of the aesthete, too easily becomes a refuge. In the seventies the creative thinker in every sort of intellectual endeavor begins to lose contact with the intelligent and fairly well-educated person who is not deeply versed in any particular subject.

Mid-Victorian society had been held together not only by community of intellectual interests but by loyalty to the Christian ethic—an obligation recognized no less strongly by unbelievers than by believers. Toward the close of our period, however, it becomes more difficult to coast on the ever-slackening moral impetus of the religion which is denied or only nominally professed. Conduct, Arnold's "three-fourths of life," is catching up with principles. Psychologically speaking, the "naughty nineties" begin in the seventies. There is a new and ugly growth of merely frivolous unbelief motivated by a desire to dissolve moral standards in a relativistic flux rather than to know the truth and make it prevail. Not only among the increasingly decadent aesthetes was the weakening of moral fiber apparent. In his very different way, the Prince of Wales was no less a hedonist than Walter Pater. With the widowed Queen in retirement at Balmoral, he restored something of the old Regency tone to the court and to "society" in general, but he found *nouveaux riches* who were eager to spend their money more congenial company at the baccarat table than genuine seedy aristocrats. The bourgeois, in their upward-looking snobbery, no longer felt certain whether they should emulate the life of duty or the life of pleasure. The old code of respectability was breaking up. That in itself was a blessing, but no higher standard seemed likely to take its place.

By 1880 or soon thereafter the confused polemic ardors of the past decade had relaxed into a Pyrrhonistic agreement to ignore insoluble problems. None of the three faiths was decisively victorious and none was crushingly defeated. What finally emerged was the assumption that if nobody insisted on the absolute objective truth of any proposition we could all live together peaceably, each man in his private universe of home-made values. Although this pragmatic subjectivity would seem to be the natural outcome of the liberal tradition, the most thoughtful representatives of that tradition do not like it. The Mid-Victorian liberal, after all, had believed very strongly in the reality of certain truths and goods: it was his opponents' dogmas, not his own, which illustrated the vices of absolutism. From now on the old champions of *laissez-faire* will be the new champions of the welfare state, while the Tories will defend individual enterprise.

The triumph of *fin-de-siècle* subjectivism had been predicted and deplored in the seventies by two great Victorian liberals. Leslie Stephen's *Essays on Free-Thinking and Plain-Speaking* (1873) and John Morley's *On Compromise* (1874) are both, in a way, contributions to the antireligious counterattack. For these secularists, however, the survival of Christianity was even less distressing than the intellectual flabbiness and irresponsibility of most Christians. One might as well argue with a cloud. Except for Roman Catholics, Puseyites, and Evangelicals, whose obviously moribund superstitions were beneath contempt, nobody who called himself a Christian seemed willing to affirm anything in particular other than the undesirability of calling himself anything else. According to Stephen, "It may be said, with little exaggeration, not only that there is no article in the creeds which may not be contradicted with impunity, but there is none which may not be contradicted in a sermon calculated to win the reputation of orthodoxy, and be regarded as a judicious bid for a bishopric." From the success of the Oberammergau Passion Play he infers that we no longer believe in the actual truth of religion, but regard it aesthetically as a more or less effective expression of feeling.

> Worship is merely an agreeable mode of stimulating certain emotions without implying any particular theory as to the objects of worship; and one method of treatment may be as effective as another.... A dogma is only offensive when you are asked to believe it; but we may be all members of a Church in which a dogma is no more essential than a vestment, and is simply an arbitrary sign of certain emotions.... The one objectionable thing is to believe anything very strongly; that is bigoted, and makes a man painfully narrow-minded. Look at religions from the serene heights of philosophy, and you must admit that all are beautiful in their way, and may be turned to account by the genuine liberal. Dr. Newman expounds a very beautiful and touching creed; so does Comte, and possibly even Mr. Bradlaugh. Let us agree to differ.[14]

On these points Morley is at one with Stephen, but he is more deeply concerned about the intellectual spinelessness of Christians as the most striking but by no means the sole example of a general indifference to truth which has gradually sapped the vitality of the English liberal movement. Germans, Spaniards, Americans, and Frenchmen, he says, regard their

[14] *Essays on Free-Thinking and Plain-Speaking*, pp. 47, 54, 64, 69, 132.

homelands in a spirit of high idealism, but "What stirs the hope and moves the aspiration of our Englishman? Surely nothing either in the heavens above or on the earth beneath. . . . Within the last forty years England has lost one by one each of those enthusiasms which may have been illusions . . . but which at least testified to the existence among us, in a very considerable degree, of a vivid belief in the possibility of certain broad general theories being true and right, as well as in the obligation of making them lights to practical conduct and desire." Where now are that belief and that sense of obligation to implement it in deeds? "Indolence and timidity have united to popularise among us a flaccid latitudinarianism, which thinks itself a benign tolerance for the opinions of others. It is in truth only a pretentious form of being without settled opinions of our own, and without any desire to settle them." Innumerable ideas are toyed with, but who believes that any of them is really true? "There are too many giggling epigrams; people are too willing to look on mutually hostile opinions with the kind of curiosity which they bestow on a collection of mutually hostile beasts in a menagerie." The cause of our fatal readiness to compromise is "the slow transformation now at work of the whole spiritual basis of thought. . . . Religion, whatever destinies may be in store for it, is at least for the present hardly any longer an organic power. It is not that supreme, penetrating, controlling, decisive part of a man's life, which it has been, and will be again."[15] The consequent timorous hesitation of Christians to assert what they believe has gradually infected our whole intellectual life. "Conscience has lost its strong and on-pressing energy, and the sense of personal responsibility is sicklied o'er with the pale cast of distracted, wavering, confused thought. The souls of men have become void. Into the void have entered in triumph the seven devils of Secularity."[16]

The spectacle represented by Morley is both ironic and saddening. In 1874 an eminent representative of all that is finest in nineteenth-century liberalism is found hungering for absolutes, decrying latitudinarianism, confessing the emptiness of mind and soul which eventually results from lack of positive commitment. The age of the Victorian prophets has ended; that of the Hollow Men is close at hand.

Within the sphere of empirical observation, science had been able to resist

[15] The unexpectedly religious tone of the final clause requires explanation. Though a less orthodox Comtian than Frederic Harrison, Morley pinned his hopes for the future on an alliance between scientific knowledge and the religion of humanity. Liberalism was to be cured by the hair of the dog that bit it.

[16] *On Compromise*, pp. 6–7, 12, 36–37, 127, 130.

the nemesis of inwardness as Morley has described it. Spurning this limitation, however, the theory of evolution had undertaken to provide a philosophy which told the whole truth about man's individual and social existence. It had gone so far beyond its factual base of supplies that it had laid itself open to subjectivist interpretations. Spencer's view of evolution was at least more vulnerable to romantic infiltration than Darwin's; Hegel, still more encouragingly, taught that the growth of the universe is the development of free creative mind. Even deeper confusion arose from the fact that while science was imposing a philosophy and a method on every aspect of history, history was imposing a relativistic outlook upon science. If history could be regarded as a branch of evolutionary science, evolutionary science could also be regarded as a branch of history. When history denies or ignores the existence of objective moral and spiritual norms it becomes a purely relativistic study of social change. Nineteenth-century science owed its original authority to a kind of absolutism: it could appeal to "the unchanging laws of nature." But the only unchanging law involved in the doctrine of evolution was a law of ceaseless change. Natural selection was a hypothesis suggested by the history of organisms, a history whose only standard of value was adaptability to environment. So far as anyone could discover, the organic variations which provided the evidential starting point for the whole theory were mysterious accidents. Even when it confined itself to its proper business, Darwinism was steeped in an atmosphere of chance and change. Hence outside the sphere of experimental demonstration late-Victorian intellectuals could interpret man and society in terms of relativism, pragmatism, and subjectivism without feeling that they were false to the spirit of true science.

Writing in 1926, the good pragmatist John Herman Randall admits that

> The biological and psychological attitude of evolution has with curious irony reinforced the very irrationalism it has sought to combat. If beliefs are primarily means of adaptation to an environment, what becomes of truth, nay, of science itself? . . . Cannot then any belief that works be true? To many the gate is opened to a new justification of their cherished faiths. . . . Are not all our beliefs but more or less concealed rationalizations? . . . Here is a disquieting question indeed! It has already destroyed the naïve faith of the Enlightenment in the unclouded reason of the average man, the very basis of liberalism and toleration; to many it seems the very suicide of science. It is indeed a difficult problem. But however we solve it theoretically, it is evident that we must have faith in our ability to find truth; and if our early confidence has gone, a knowledge of the difficulties in the way must serve to make it easier to overcome them.[17]

[17] *The Making of the Modern Mind*, p. 480.

Having delivered himself of this heartening *non sequitur*, Professor Randall closes his chapter on "The World Conceived as a Process of Growth and Evolution" with an even more hopeful quotation from John Dewey.

Shortly before his death in 1873 the same problem is worrying John Stuart Mill. Since the beginning of the century, he says in *Theism*, the conflict between belief and unbelief has assumed a changed aspect. "Experience has abated the ardent hopes once entertained for the regeneration of the human race by merely negative doctrine—by the destruction of superstition." Nowadays we think more in terms of history. Unbelievers regard Christianity and Theism as "things once of great value but which now can be done without; rather than, as formerly, as things misleading and obnoxious *ab initio*." The historical outlook has been strengthened by analogies between the development of religion and the course of biological evolution. Hence secularists have come to think of religion "less as intrinsically true or false than as products thrown up by certain states of civilization." Mill approves of this view with one important reservation: it must not be allowed to obscure the fact that "the most important quality of an opinion is its truth or falsity."[18]

But what scientific basis is there for asserting that any idea, favorable or unfavorable to religion, "now can be done without by the human race as a whole"? If a single individual declared that he found it necessary for his personal survival in the struggle for existence, his right to retain it would be unassailable from the historico-evolutionary point of view. The question of the "truth or falsity" of the idea would, however, be meaningless. In *On Compromise*, Morley asserts that improper use of the historical method has helped create the present "tendency . . . to make men shrink from importing anything like absolute quality into their propositions." All truth is now relative to time, place, personal circumstance. Hence

> a distinct and unmistakable lowering of the level of national life; a slack and, lethargic quality about public opinion; a growing predominance of material, temporary, and selfish aims, over those which are generous, far-reaching, and spiritual; a deadly weakening of intellectual conclusiveness, of clear-shining moral illumination, and, last, of a certain stoutness of self-respect for which England was once especially famous. A plain categorical proposition is becoming less and less credible to average minds. Or at least the slovenly willingness to hold two distinctly contrary propositions at one and the same time is becoming more and more common. In religion, morals, and politics, the suppression of your true opinion, if not the positive profession of what you hold to be a false opinion, is hardly ever counted a vice, and not seldom even goes for virtue and wisdom. One is conjured to respect the beliefs of others, but forbidden to claim respect for one's own.[19]

[18] *Three Essays on Religion*, pp. 125–128 *passim*.

[19] *On Compromise*, pp. 17–18, 31–32.

Thus although many romantics felt that their aspirations had been crushed by science, in other than purely experimental fields the romantic spirit had been hardly less successful in subjectivizing the fruits of evolutionary science than in subjectivizing Protestant Christianity. This victory, to be sure, had been achieved at an apparently disastrous cost—abandonment of the feeling of certitude and mastery. But there remained the chance that some would-be Titan might see in the great emptiness a precious opportunity for a reinterpretation of the romantic faith which would offer something more substantial and potent than the notion that nothing is really true or really false. If there is no suprapersonal absolute, what is to hinder a man from shaping an absolute out of his own inwardness? If there is no objective truth, what stands in the way of the great lie?

Moncure D. Conway once spent a congenial weekend in the home of Charles Bray, the amiable and high-minded Unitarian whose *Philosophy of Necessity* had helped to wean young Mary Ann Evans from Evangelicalism.

> On Sunday after breakfast I was present at the usual religious service of the family. . . . This service consisted of the rendering on the piano of Handel's "Messiah" (the whole) without words or singing. It was a beautiful day, the low windows opened on the flower garden and the landscape dressed in living green and blossoming trees. There we sat, souls who had passed through an era of storm and stress and left all prophetic and Messianic beliefs, but found in the oratorio hymns of an earth in travail.[20]

There they sat, trying very hard not to think of the words, in a spiritual vacuum which rebellious human nature might some day fill with almost anything.

The incident calls to mind the climactic portion of a recent magazine article describing a tour of the United Nations headquarters in New York:

> The tour moves next to the Meditation Room, which has a tremendous impact upon the emotions of many tourists. Of all the stops this one, according to the girl guides, is where eyes are most frequently observed moistening. The room is designed to have a religious atmosphere without containing any symbol or furnishing peculiar to any particular religion—for instance, no cross, no stars, no prayer rugs. It's simply a small, windowless room entered through a doorless doorway, walled in with white draperies, adorned with a few chairs, which can be turned in any direction [a fine touch], and a waist-high mahogany log set upright and topped with a bowl of fresh white flowers.[21]

[20] *Autobiography*, II, 156.

[21] Don Wharton, "Manhattan's Biggest Side Show," *Saturday Evening Post*, May 9, 1953, p. 41.

Here are focused the spiritual resources of the as-yet-free world. The article does not tell us how often the tourists find those latitudinarian chairs occupied by contemplative delegates.

What, in this affectingly aseptic chamber, would one meditate about? A fruitful subject might be provided by a report in the New York *Times* of a birthday interview with Carl Sandburg, a man deservedly admired as poet, biographer, and human being. He volunteers this to the reporter: "My grand-daughter once said to me, 'Is God real?' I said to her, 'If God is real to you, then He is real.' " Almost bowled over, the reporter adds his final comment: "A basic answer to a basic question, given by a pretty basic sort of person."[22]

Mr. Sandburg's answer is very basic indeed, and it probably represents the type of religiosity which moistens the eyes of tourists in the Meditation Room. Here, we may feel, is a thoroughly harmless kind of Inner Light, a subjectivism too wistful, tentative, and undogmatic to kindle the anarch's torch. But can we, on second thought, be perfectly sure of that? The American romantic, heir of Emerson and Whitman, has assured his grand-child that the existence of God depends upon her feelings—a thought more encouraging to pride than to humility. In maturer years she might move onward to the idea that God is the achievement of her creative will. She might even decide that since the only divinity is the divinity of her own mind, she herself is God. What is to prevent her? Anything is real if it is real to her.

Of course it is very unlikely that this particular little girl will grow up to be a new scourge of the world. Knowing the difference between reality and make-believe, she probably received her grandfather's basic answer with the clear-eyed scorn of childhood. Nevertheless the anecdote suggests the ex-pansive potentialities of romantic inwardness even in its vaguest and mildest form. The pride of man exhibits phenomena of chain-reaction not altogether unlike those of the atom. And if the former should lay hold upon the latter . . .

[22] Book Review Section of the New York *Times*, January 4, 1953.

Chapter Twenty

CONCLUSION FOR CRITICS

THIS SUPPLEMENTARY CHAPTER would have been presented as an appendix had I not hesitated to diminish its chances of being read. But although the historical study which I have actually written ended on the preceding page I should like to think that it is not altogether irrelevant for critical evaluation of Victorian poetry in the twentieth century. If such relevance exists it deserves to be emphasized in the interests of academic peace and good will. The present relations between historical scholars and "new critics" in our American departments of English fall a trifle short of perfect harmony. Let us hope that scholars will always claim for themselves, and freely grant to their colleagues, the right to study literature in different ways. But although imposed uniformity is a curse, sympathetic understanding and cooperation are blessings. We might enjoy them more abundantly if on the one hand the literary historian more frequently reminded himself that he was tracing the development of one of the fine arts, while on the other hand the critic were more willing to concede the value of historical knowledge for reasoned appreciation of particular poems. There would still be two markedly different points of view, but each would enrich the other.

I am poorly qualified to illustrate the possibilities of such a *rapprochement*, not only because my own studies are too benightedly historical for the purpose but because my ideas about literature are too invertebrate. Indeed, the reader may wonder how a religious absolutist can so suddenly transform himself at the last into an extreme critical relativist. Some explanation of this apparent inconsistency may be in order. Although we have nothing to reason with except the impressions which stream through consciousness, our existence becomes much sweeter and saner when we use what Santayana calls our "animal faith" to the extent of assuming that we live within a real world of absolute objective truths. On the other hand we are lost unless we remain sensitive to the perils of pretending to be completely sure of what those truths are and of trying to force our sureness upon our fellows. This is not the place to attempt a refutation of the objection that there is no practical difference between living in a world of unknown absolute truths and living in a world where all values are held to be inherently relative and man-made. I can only say that I have tried both worlds and have found the difference unspeakably great.

But although it is almost always safer not to talk or, if possible, even to feel as if our ignorance were certitude, there are a few fundamental questions about which a man must make up his mind. In these rare instances, unfortunately, the dangers of intolerance and coercion are particularly great; but they must be risked if one is to live, and they are not insuperable. In accordance with this principle, I posit, on grounds no less satisfying to my reason than to my feelings, the objective reality of God and of His creation. Unable to believe in God without asking myself what I believe *about* Him, I further posit the doctrines of historic Christianity. My commitment to this faith is very strong: I *feel* not the slightest doubt that it is true not only inwardly and personally but outwardly and universally. At the same time, since my religion includes much more than I can prove to other men or even to myself, I cannot deny the possibility that I may be partly or wholly mistaken; and I recognize an obligation to manifest this awareness, not of personal incertitude but of human limitation, in my relations with my fellows.

One advantage of accepting the religious solution of the ultimate mystery is that we are thereby enabled to confront the innumerable lesser mysteries without agonizing over them. Otherwise, we must strain so terribly hard to be right about *everything*. I enjoy expressing my literary preferences and aversions, but I neither pretend to know nor very solemnly care what makes a good poem. As regards suprapersonal objective criteria for aesthetic judgments I have no faith at all and see no necessity for having one. Here there is no forced option, nothing which irresistibly claims the allegiance of my entire being, no overmastering sense of having been granted a means of satisfying my deepest need. To suppose that the unknown real world contains unknown absolute truths concerning literary values and to refrain from all dogmatism on questions so lacking in urgency is wholly consistent with my philosophy. If on the other hand we derive what we call our religion chiefly from aesthetic experience, then the questions "What shall I do to be saved?" and "Why do I dislike this poem?" are equally crucial, and to feel perfectly sure in our literary judgments assumes a quality of numinous obligation. Hence criticism bids fair to become the theology of the twentieth century—a development anticipated in their several ways by Carlyle, Arnold, and Pater. In this as in many other fields the most dogmatic thinkers are often those whose relativism sets them free—or perhaps forces them—to devise dogmas of their own. Deficient in this sort of inventiveness, I hesitate to condemn Tennyson for his failure to write like Donne, or Swinburne for his failure to write like Mr. Auden, or Arnold for his failure to write as I should write if I happened to be a poet.

What the critic says about the Victorians will largely depend, as I have been trying to suggest, on whether his conception of poetry is tight and precise or large, loose, and easy. Rather than saddle myself with some theory which would forbid me to enjoy a great deal of writing which seems to me obviously enjoyable, I probably lean too far in the latter direction. Yet I have some notions about books, and though I claim no importance for them I am aware of a quite definite irritation when they are not agreed with. So perhaps I am a critic after all. In the present discussion, however, we had better concern ourselves with the way in which our judgments of Victorian poetry are conditioned by our attitude toward critical problems more specifically related to the subject of this book. The material which we have been studying raises the general question of the relations between religion and poetry; our ideas on that question will influence in turn our critical estimate of that material.

"Gladstone and Tyndall," Tennyson told Allingham in 1884, "were sitting at my table. . . . Tyndall began talking in his loose way about 'This Poem—or Poetic Idea—God.' Gladstone looked at him and said with severity, 'Professor Tyndall, leave God to the Poets and Philosophers, and attend to your own business.' Tyndall fell quite silent for several minutes."[1] Now every human being is entitled to talk about God, and scientists of all men should be encouraged to do so. If God is to be left to poets and poetical-minded philosophers, Gladstone's rebuke merely repeats Tyndall's own statement that God is a piece of poetry. But if Gladstone means that science *as such* has nothing to do with religion, and that poetry and philosophy (in the sense of metaphysics) have a great deal to do with it, he is to that extent probably correct. Poetry and philosophy dissociate themselves from science, and associate themselves with each other and with religion, in their attempt to apprehend and express more of the truth than can be accounted for by observation and measurement.

This implies that poets and philosophers may, and ultimately must, be concerned with the religious *problem,* not that they are obligated or peculiarly empowered to arrive at an encouraging solution or indeed at any solution whatever. The result of their quest may be completely negative; they may report that result cynically, or despairingly, or triumphantly. But when

[1] William Allingham, *A Diary*, p. 340.

Victorians appealed to the authority of poets and philosophers from that of scientists they were thinking not of atheistic poets and of positivistic philosophers, but of men who had the sort of wisdom which soars above mere knowledge and arrives at ennobling conclusions about "the things of the spirit." Philosophers were included among these seers as a tribute to the Platonic tradition and perhaps to the intuitive Germans; but it was preeminently the poets—the *true* poets, of course—who could be relied on for the right sort of insight. The dominant view is Carlyle's: "Prophet and Poet, well understood, have much kindred meaning . . . in this most important respect especially, that they have penetrated both of them into the sacred mystery of the Universe."[2] The prophetic conception of poetry is no mere historical curiosity. Many old-fashioned literary scholars continue to cherish it as the spiritual basis for the "save the humanities" campaign. It is responsible for the notion, still entertained by all but our most intelligent students, that poetry is noble nonsense and that this noble nonsense is what one means by "religion." Professors who like to function as trumpets for the lips of prophet-poets usually prefer to give courses in Wordsworth and Shelley rather than in Tennyson and Browning. And quite understandably, for as the nineteenth century goes on the struggle to maintain the romantic cult of genius becomes too obviously desperate. But although the Victorian poets know very well that they have *not* "penetrated into the sacred mystery of the Universe," they usually cannot bear to relinquish the privilege of writing as if they thought they had done so. This chasm between pretension and actuality constitutes one of the major shortcomings of the poetry of this period.

In lumping together "true" poets and intuitional philosophers as men of supra-scientific spiritual insight, the Victorians were also tempted to forget that poetry is a language, and a language of a very different sort from that of philosophy. The philosopher uses words to explain and discuss his meaning; the poet uses words to shape an object which is intended to *be* his meaning. But the dividing line should not be drawn too rigidly. Symbols unsupported by statements are like jewels without a setting. Our present-day horror of rhetoric in poetry, our insistence that everything must be done through the image, ignores the fact that almost all great poetry has freely mingled imaginative and conceptual language, each enhancing the effect of the other.[3]

[2] *Heroes and Hero-Worship*, p. 313.

[3] The twentieth century moves so rapidly in so many different directions that it is hard to keep strictly up-to-date. At present one discerns the return of a more friendly attitude toward the rhetorical element in poetry. If this reaction continues it will necessarily entail a more charitable view of the Victorians.

Although communication is seldom the primary motive for *writing* a poem, there seems to be no reason for inviting anyone to *read* it unless it renders an experience which is worth sharing and which is sharable by readers who are able and willing to meet the poet half way. Poets do not even now enjoy being told by intelligent persons that their work is unintelligible. A symbol (other than a desperately trite one) which says something to the poet often says nothing at all or something quite different to the reader unless there is enough rhetoric to steer his understanding of the symbol into the poet's associative channel. Frequently also the connotations of the symbol are not clear even to the poet himself: it is not so much his meaning as a trial shot in the direction of a meaning as yet unknown to him. He may attempt to discover what in the world it *might* mean by associating it with conceptual statements. Even granting that the symbol *ought* to be ambiguous, its sevenfold Empsonian possibilities may not be fully apparent either to the poet or to the reader without some admixture of the language of analysis and discussion.

Despite these reservations the fact remains that what is distinctive and indispensable in the language of poetry is the expressed or suggested image which, ideally speaking, synthesizes sense, emotion, and intellect as in an act of sacramental (*not* mystical) worship; whereas what is distinctive and indispensable in the language of philosophy is the rhetorically developed proposition as in a theological treatise. Now of course it would be absurdly unjust to assert that more than a few poems of the Victorian period are versified theological treatises or even versified sermons. Just as the "true" poet was more deeply spiritual and prophetic than almost any philosopher, so poetry was supposed to reveal the sacred mystery of the Universe in language more elevated, rhythmic, impassioned, melodious, and decoratively metaphorical than that of edifying prose. But the more earnestly the Victorians strain to fulfill this requirement the more uneasily we feel that what they give us is not precisely poetry but rather a sort of bedizened inspirational public address. The images are on the surface, but not at the center. The desire to shape a lovely meaningful object is often nonexistent, sometimes secondary, very seldom primary.[4] Hence, perhaps, the excessive wordiness of Victorian poetry. When a poem is conceived of as a thing, there is a fair chance that the poet will leave off once the thing has been made; but when a poem is conceived of as a succession of *ideas about* some great inexhaustible subject, there is no reason why it should ever stop so long as the

[4] To some extent it becomes primary for the anti-prophetic aesthetes; but they are so sick of preachment that they try, with equally disastrous results, to sunder formal beauty from significant content.

poet's thoughts continue to flow. "More and more," Arnold writes his sister in 1849, "I feel bent against the modern English habit (too much encouraged by Wordsworth) of using poetry as a channel for thinking aloud, instead of making anything."[5] Although Arnold is often more truly a maker than most of his fellows, his practice falls short of his critical penetration: he is too fond of "thinking aloud" in his own poems. This characteristic Victorian fault may be attributed partly to inadequate ideas concerning poetry, religion, and the relations between them.

Let us turn back for a moment to Tyndall's phrase, "This Poem—or Poetic Idea—God." It probably irritated Gladstone because this particular scientist's religious position was notoriously ambiguous. A great admirer of Carlyle, Emerson, and Fichte, he was nevertheless too loyal a materialist to assert the romantic or any other faith. He assigned religion to poetry as a means of enjoying its flavor without committing himself to believing in it. In his famous 1874 address at Belfast he granted that religion and art can never be destroyed by science. "It will be wise to recognize them as the forms of a force, mischievous if permitted to intrude on the region of objective *knowledge*, over which it holds no command, but capable of adding, in the region of *poetry* and *emotion*, inward completeness and dignity to man."[6]

From this rather Arnoldian idea one could move in either of two directions. One could emphasize "mischievous if permitted to intrude," dismissing religion and poetry as kindred aspects of dangerous unreason; or one could emphasize "capable of adding . . . inward completeness and dignity to man," and arrive at a pragmatic justification of myth-making. Negatively, Strauss taught that Christianity was nonsense; positively, he taught that it was a beautiful poem. If poets were prophets it followed that prophets were poets. You could still be spiritual if you approached all such impossible but lovely and elevating tales with a willing suspension of disbelief. Thus, well before the close of the period which we have been studying the prophetic conception of poetry is sophisticating itself into that quest for a "usable myth" which figures so largely in present-day criticism. It is now frequently asserted that the poet would write more effectively if he could give himself the illusion of believing in something or other. Unless he wants to feel like a fool he cannot affirm any familiar myth in its original form or invent a new one. He can, however, summon up the ghost of creative faith by tinkering with one of the old myths, say that of Christianity, in such a way as to make its traditional form the vehicle for some new meaning that derives its impressiveness from

[5] *Unpublished Letters*, p. 17. [6] *Fragments of Science*, II, 209.

symbols which originally meant something quite different. This practice is clearly an extension of a Victorian trend. It usually convinces the reader of nothing but the poet's lack of conviction. Genuine myth-makers were not wistfully trying to revive a state of mind favorable to the composition of poetry; they really believed that they were telling the truth.

This line of thought cannot further be pursued without consideration of a related problem. Most poems which have any claim upon our serious attention pertain to matters important not only for the poet but for us. Frequently it is obvious that the poet is expressing—symbolically or conceptually, positively or tentatively—an idea, opinion, or belief with which we feel impelled to agree or disagree. Even in the least explicitly communicative poem, we can usually detect a point of view, a state of mind, a type of sensibility which seems to us desirable or undesirable for the confrontation of experience. To what extent is our attitude toward the poet's thought relevant for literary criticism? This difficult question has often been discussed, perhaps most interestingly by I. A. Richards and T. S. Eliot; but if I attempted to give my opinion on Eliot's opinion on Richards's opinion on the critical legitimacy of having an opinion on the poet's opinion I should never be able to finish this chapter. It will be less confusing to make a fresh start.[7]

As I have already confessed, I am allergic to abstract conceptions of pure poetry, pure criticism, pure aesthetic experience. Abandoning all attempt to dogmatize as to how poetry *should* be read, I shall examine four passages in the company of an imaginary fellow-critic who, as a romantic sort of humanist, denies what I affirm concerning religion and affirms what I deny. Let it be supposed that we are equally knowledgeable, equally sensitive to aesthetic values, equally disinclined to identify poetry with versified preachment. We fully realize that readers who concern themselves only with what a poem "says" do not understand the nature of poetry. Our reaction against such stupidity does not, on the other hand, impel us to the opposite extreme of insisting that the poet's view of life is of no importance for his poem as a work of art.

First we take a stanza from Ernest Jones's *Corayda:*

> While the mind still reigns in its kingly dome,
> While the heart in the breast beats still,
> There is nothing so stubborn, wherever we roam,
> But must yield to the conquering will.

[7] But of course the reader should see, or see again, the chapter on "Doctrine in Poetry" in Richards's *Practical Criticism* and the essays on "Shakespeare" and "Dante" in Eliot's *Selected Essays*.

My colleague and I are at one in dismissing these lines as doggerel. My distaste for them is aggravated only a little, if at all, by the fact that they embody a statement which I regard as wildly untrue. His distaste for them is mitigated only a little, if at all, by the fact that he regards the same statement as the expression of a lofty ideal. Respectable critics never praise rubbish no matter what they may think of the writer's beliefs.

Now a passage about Jesus Christ by the elder De Vere:

> . . . He took
> Our Being, and assumed Humanity,
> With Power; and therefore, was He God and Man.
> Not by commixture; so, being different
> From each, He could be neither: nor conversion,
> For how could God be changed? nor in division,
> Distinguishable; for there is but one Christ:
> But joined forever, and inseparably;
> Persistent God and Man; even when the bond
> Of soul and flesh were, humanly, dissolved!

This for me is absolute saving truth, but I refrain from calling it bad poetry only because it is not poetry at all. My colleague will surely agree with me, and on grounds which make it quite unnecessary for him to enter into theological controversy. He may suspect me of liking the passage a little better than he does, but I beg him to discard so slanderous a notion.

The situation grows more complicated when we move on to these lines from the "Prelude" to *Songs before Sunrise*:

> Passions and pleasures can defeat,
> Action and agonies control,
> And life and death, but not the soul.
>
> Because man's soul is man's God still,
> What wind soever waft his will
> Across the waves of day and night
> To port or shipwreck, left or right,
> By shores and shoals of good and ill;
> And still its flame at mainmast height
> Through the rent air that foam-flakes fill
> Sustains the indomitable light
> Whence only man hath strength to steer
> Or helm to handle without fear.
>
> Save his own soul overhead,
> None leads him, and none ever led,

> Across birth's hidden harbor-bar,
> Past youth where shoreward shallows are,
> Through age that drives on toward the red
> Vast void of sunset hailed from far,
> To the equal waters of the dead;
> Save his own soul he hath no star,
> And sinks, unless his own soul guide,
> Helmless in middle turn of tide.

My friend and I recognize that we are now reading poetry. The passage suffers from the fact that the poem in which it occurs is cluttered and disunified. Also the proportion of imagery to real imagination in the quoted lines is rather large, and the thought circles around instead of getting up and speeding straight ahead. In other words the lines were written by Swinburne. Nevertheless here is a man's passionate apprehension of life projected with considerable power through rhythm and symbol. We take his experience into ourselves and are moved by it.

But it is psychologically impossible that we should be moved in the same way and to the same extent. My fellow-critic shares Swinburne's faith in man; I repudiate it. I do not for this reason condemn the lines as bad poetry; indeed I like them partly because they are so vitally and outspokenly untrue that they clarify my conception of the truth. But I should like the passage even better if it did not tell a lie. Neither here nor in his more extravagantly blasphemous assertions of man's divinity and God's nonexistence does Swinburne shock or anger me. I firmly believe that poets should be encouraged to say precisely what they think on any subject, and that when they do so with imaginative power the result is a good poem. All enhancement of our ability to understand the thought and feeling of other men is valuable not only aesthetically but morally and spiritually. Nevertheless it seems fantastic to deny that there is a difference between reading what you think is true and reading what you think is false. Possibly my dislike of Swinburne's ideas incapacitates me for criticizing his poem. On the other hand, my imaginary colleague's approval of them may incline him toward an excessively enthusiastic estimate. Who is to judge between us? A third critic with his own set of presuppositions? Ideally speaking, the prerequisite for sound criticism is the ability to feel the poem precisely as the author felt it, but this theoretical goal cannot be achieved in practice. The poem that men read is never the poem that the author wrote; the poem that A reads is never the poem that B reads. Instead of laying claim to an impartiality which he does not possess, the critic had better give his readers fair warning of the respects in which his mind is liable to refract whatever the truth about the work may be.

What my hypothetical colleague and I think about Swinburne's religion is relevant for literary criticism. Poetry may be less important than some people suppose, but it is not so trivial that one bit of nonsense will serve as well as another for effective writing. It would be bad criticism to detach the proposition "Man's soul is man's God," assert that it *is* the poem, and call the poem great or worthless according to our attitude toward the proposition. But it would be equally bad criticism to detach the so-called "aesthetic" values of metaphor, rhythm, tone color and so on, call *them* the poem, and insist that the proposition has nothing to do with criticism because it has nothing to do with poetry. The aesthetic values would be on the same level as those of *Jabberwocky* unless Swinburne had something to say. For him, as we know, the idea expressed in this passage is important for human life. Therefore it must be important for me as a critic, and I shall say that I think it interestingly and eloquently and characteristically false. My fellow-critic will, I hope and believe, exercise the same liberty from his own contrary point of view.

Finally, the opening of Christina Rossetti's familiar Christmas poem:

> In the bleak mid-winter
> Frosty wind made moan,
> Earth stood hard as iron,
> Water like a stone;
> Snow had fallen, snow on snow,
> Snow on snow,
> In the bleak mid-winter
> Long ago.
>
> Our God, Heaven cannot hold Him,
> Nor earth sustain;
> Heaven and earth shall flee away
> When He comes to reign:
> In the bleak mid-winter
> A stable place sufficed
> The Lord God Almighty
> Jesus Christ.

This passage is related to De Vere's lines on Christ in somewhat the same way as the Swinburne passage is related to Jones's effusion. My colleague and I agree that we are reading an authentically poetic expression of the belief which De Vere versifies without one glimmer of imagination. Our opinions as to the value of this belief diverge as in our judgments of Swinburne, except that here I share the poet's thought and my colleague does not.

Probably, however, we shall disagree about this passage less markedly than we did about the Swinburne lines. The affirmation is here less oratorical and obviously purposive. As we begin the poem, we even feel that the artfully contrived effect of snowiness and long-agoness possesses an aesthetic value quite independent of any belief or disbelief. "Here at last," we may say, "is *pure* poetry." But almost immediately we discover that this poem concerns the birth of Almighty God, and that the snowiness and long-agoness are therefore very different from the remote bitter chill in which *The Eve of St. Agnes* is enveloped. Let us suppose that my fellow-critic is an open-minded, easy-going, relativistic sort of secularist. He grants that Christina has found a myth which has helped her to write an effective poem. He can imagine how the poem *would* impress him if he could believe what she believes. He can work up a kind of "Hoping it might be so" feeling about it. But this poem cannot be read as one reads Hardy's *The Oxen* without transforming it into something quite foreign to what it was meant to be. Even the more affirmative subjectivism of "God is real if he is real to you" comes nowhere near Christina's intention. In this case it is I who have the better chance of experiencing the poem as it was written, and I who incur the greater danger of overestimating its literary value. The question of whether I do in fact succumb to this peril must be held in abeyance until we are all perfectly sure of what constitutes a good poem.

These remarks, I believe, illustrate the relations which actually exist between the beliefs of the poet and the beliefs of the critic. Whether different conditions *should* exist seems to me an idle question. Poetry is the most humanly interesting of the arts because it is, aesthetically speaking, so hopelessly impure. It is impure because it is made of words, not of tones or pigments, and words express or imply statements about man's thought and action. Meanwhile poetry is also a fine art in the sense that music and painting are fine arts; and the critic has a special obligation to give full weight to this aspect of poetry because the ordinary reader is inclined to ignore it. The critic may even choose to confine himself wholly to matters of form and expression, but he will not then be discussing all that human beings, himself included, mean by "poetry." He will not even be discussing rhythms and images in any fruitful way, for in poetry the aesthetic and the nonaesthetic are so closely intertwined that each draws its life-blood from the other. In the last analysis, the content of poetry is no less important for literary criticism than for historical scholarship. These facts were universally recognized until men fell back upon the desperate expedient of supposing that there is no such thing as truth. Prior to 1900 at the latest there has never been a poet (outside of a small handful of extreme aesthetes) who would not have been astonished and angered to be told that the value of what he said had nothing to do with the value of his poems.

It is, I think, *historically* demonstrable that some religious beliefs are more resistant than others to the spiritual disintegration which has landed us in our present predicament. Is it then *critically* demonstrable that some beliefs are more favorable than others to the health of the art of poetry? I think not. One might argue that, other things being equal, a valid religion is conducive to the writing of good poetry, and the lack of such a religion a handicap. But other things never *are* equal: too many factors are involved which have nothing to do with religion. Creedal differences resist correlation with differences in vitality, sincerity, imaginative apprehension of what is believed or disbelieved, emotional power, sense of rhythm, sense of form, desire and ability to shape thoughts and feelings into aesthetic objects. I feel no inclination whatever to rank Victorian poems, as poems, according to the extent to which they approximate my own beliefs. To my mind Adelaide Procter has a religion and Matthew Arnold has not, but *Dover Beach* is an immeasurably better poem than *The Lost Chord.* I prefer *The Dream of Gerontius* to *Merlin and the Gleam,* but I prefer *The City of Dreadful Night* to *The Dream of Gerontius.* Swinburne almost never wrote anything as bad as the best portions of *The Christian Year.* In general I like strongly felt, interestingly imaginative expressions of real belief or real disbelief, and dislike vague, mealy-mouthed "idealistic" smudges of unfocused thought and feeling. The nonliterary motivation of my tastes is probably strong, but many critics who do not share my beliefs seem to agree that these soft wordy smudges are the curse of Victorian poetry.

The use which any poet makes of his religion depends to some extent upon the general religious conditions of the age in which he lives. Here again the history of ideas may serve the ends of literary criticism. If the contemporary culture possesses a universal or strongly dominant spiritual consensus which the poet shares, he can voice his faith with confidence and vigor, free to experience it as beautiful since he does not need to argue that it is true. Thus Dante could write great Catholic poetry in the Middle Ages; and Milton, despite a less homogeneous religious environment, could write great Protestant poetry in seventeenth-century England. But no Dante or Milton could have arisen within the period of our study. For the large majority of Victorians, Roman Catholicism was a sinister un-English superstition and Anglican Catholicism an irritating contradiction in terms.

Protestantism, meanwhile, was disintegrating too rapidly to provide a normative spiritual tradition. Hence Catholic or Protestant poets who continued to believe that Christianity meant anything in particular were alienated from their environment and were forced to struggle, scold, argue, preach, and dream nostalgic dreams with results detrimental to their art.

These outmoded believers were deprived of another great blessing. When the culture possesses a homogeneous spiritual tradition, poets *can* write specifically religious poetry but are under no obligation to do so. They need only take the world which God has made and write about the joy and horror, glory and baseness, of human life within that world. But in the absence of any spiritual consensus religious-minded poets must everlastingly be talking *about* God, and wondering whether He really does exist, and scolding themselves for wondering.[8] This uneasiness is felt even more strongly, however, when the poet's own spiritual experience reflects rather than denies the centrifugal disharmony of the age. Then there is division and strife both within and without—a situation which makes it impossible either to arrive at a personally satisfying solution of the religious problem or to abandon the effort to do so. Such poets, to be sure, are more in tune with the actual trend of Victorian culture than those who hold more precisely formulated beliefs in opposition to that trend. Does one make better poetry by being in tune, or out of tune, with a predominantly tuneless religious ambience? The question is probably unanswerable. The most one can say is that belief in some sort of external spiritual reality is favorable to the firmness, centripetality, and concreteness which characterize good poetry, but that too much uneasily self-conscious fuss *about* religion is aesthetically detrimental. There was an immense amount of such fuss during the Victorian period.

Pure Evangelicalism is poetically sterile in the nineteenth century: it is too suspicious of any writing which is not motivated by the wish to convert or edify. This barrenness is in large measure the natural consequence of an intense but narrow and excessively "Hebraic" religious sensibility in which distrust of "outward forms" is deeply rooted. But Milton's example is sufficient to remind us that there can be great Puritan poetry in which very gorgeous and elaborate imagery appears as an almost necessary compensation

[8] I see no necessity for burdening the reader with a discussion of the famous passage in Johnson's *Life of Waller* on the difficulty of writing good "sacred" poetry. Fundamentally, it seems to me, he is saying that it would be impossible to turn his own private meditations into a poem like *The Vanity of Human Wishes*. That is probably true, but there are other kinds of religious experience and other kinds of poetry in which to express them. But I do believe that the ability to write expressly devotional poetry is a very special gift, and that on the whole religion influences the poet most beneficently not in giving him traditionally sacred subjects but in giving him a sacred way of regarding *any* subject.

for the imageless character of Protestant worship; and there seems to be no reason why Evangelical belief per se should have prevented the appearance of such poetry in the Victorian era. The influence of doctrine and cult is important, but additional nonreligious factors must be recognized. Most of the strict Evangelicals, as practical men of business, were deeply affected by the antiaesthetic spirit of bourgeois utilitarianism. And although they had lost contact with healthy folk poetry, they had risen only to a level which was undercultivated and subliterary in relation to conscious art. For reasons congruous with their religious position but not necessarily inherent in it, they were not the sort of people from whom much poetry is to be expected.

Theoretically at least, Victorian Catholics, Roman or Anglican, were in a more favorable position. Catholicism harbors no grudge against "outward forms" either of dogma or of worship. It is friendly to art in being sensuous, symbolic, and sacramental. Its focus is the poetic altar, not the rhetorical pulpit. "The Word was made Flesh" defines poetry as it defines the Incarnation, and the Mass is the great "objective correlative" of Christian thought and emotion. For these very reasons the Catholic may sometimes feel that the poetry of the Church has rendered the poetry of man superfluous; but a strong creative spirit should be able to find inexhaustible possibilities in rendering fine shades of personal response to various aspects of the faith and in applying the sacramental principle to everyday secular life. On the whole the advantages would seem to outweigh the disadvantages. We have seen, however, that Catholic poets of this period usually fail to exploit their opportunities.[9] They veer away from genuine poetry either toward religious and politico-ecclesiastical propaganda or, later in the period, toward emptily ritualistic aestheticism. One can only conclude that the antipoetic pressure of the Victorian environment conditioned their writing more strongly than did their inherently poetic religion. This is a striking example of the difficulty of establishing any fixed correlation between religious belief and poetic merit.

But the main body of Victorian poetry, as we know, cannot be given a label which implies commitment to any classifiable variety of supernaturalistic religion. The major tendencies involved are the subjectivizing of the Protestant tradition by romanticism and the frustration of the romantic faith by science and Traffic. Most critics will grant, I suppose, that the creative

[9] Since Hopkins has been held over for the next volume, Christina Rossetti has been the principal though not quite the sole exception. From the Catholic point of view Patmore's esotericism is highly ambiguous.

process which produces poetry is a drive toward a center, toward concretion, toward the making of an organized thing, toward the performance of an integrated act. Both of the two dominant religious trends, on the other hand, are inherently centrifugal, disintegrative, and resistant to firm symbolic organization. Furthermore the two religious trends point in contrary directions, the former implying a victory for the romantic faith in man and the latter a defeat. By about 1880 the conflict has resulted, for the time being, in a stalemate of slack Pyrrhonistic indifference, a condition unfavorable to the intensity and vitality which art demands. Under these circumstances it is remarkable not that the Victorians produced so much bad poetry, but that they often wrote so well. Nevertheless, I agree with the majority of contemporary critics that on the whole the poetry of the age of Tennyson is disappointing as compared with the poetry of the age of Shakespeare, of Milton, of Wordsworth, or of T. S. Eliot.[10] It would be wildly absurd to say that the history of nineteenth-century religious thought provides a sufficient explanation of this fact. That it provides a partial explanation seems probable enough: there may well be some causal relationship between spiritual and aesthetic disintegration.

Let me tentatively suggest, in a last-minute effort to be very pure and aesthetic, that Victorian poetry failed to achieve a *style* appropriate to the underlying bewilderment of the period. It seems to me that the "new critics" are excessively bigoted in their insistence that poetry must be hard, dry, fragmentary, ironic, ambiguous, and cryptic. If they are right, a great deal of obviously delightful poetry is not fit to read. Personally, I like the full-voiced, single-minded, confidently believing, explicitly communicative manner when it expresses the poet's apprehension of a relatively harmonious and integrated world of sharable human experience. But when we look back at the nineteenth century from the twentieth, we doubt whether the most representative Victorian poets truly felt that they were living in such a world. Their immediate obligation as artists in an age of bewilderment was the scrutiny of little fragments of personal confusion, not the fabrication of synthetic universes. Too often, however, they attempt to maintain the prophetic style in the almost complete absence of prophetic feeling. They want to sound like bards but have nothing to sound bardic about. Even when frustration forces them to admit this fact they seldom find the appropriately broken, tentative, exploratory language in which to express their actual situation. They are living in a deeply ironic, ambiguous, and difficult era;

[10] I do not think that Victorian poetry is inferior to eighteenth-century poetry, but there is no need to argue the question here.

yet they continue to voice their confusion and despair as smoothly, eloquently, and decoratively as if they really believed something. They say "Lo!" and pretend to hear "voices" long after the pose has become meaningless.

Matthew Arnold writes to Mrs. Forster concerning his poems: "The true reason why parts suit you while others do not is that my poems are fragments—i.e. that I am fragments . . . and a person who has any inward completeness can at best only like parts of them; in fact such a person stands firmly and knows what he is about while the poems stagger weakly and are at their wit's end."[11] This is admirably perceptive, but one does not feel that Arnold's intellectual and emotional fragmentation is faithfully reflected in the form and language of his poetry. He tries too hard *not* to write like a man who is at his wit's end. Although his understanding of the modern predicament is unusually keen, many of his contemporaries similarly insist on expressing disorganized ideas in carefully organized language. Their style, in short, has not caught up with their state of mind. The objection applies even to poets who possess an integrating religious faith. Their writing does not reflect the confusion and pain of the intelligent believer confronted by an unbelieving world; it does not sufficiently immerse itself in the agony which it seeks to heal; it does not sound as if it had been written in the nineteenth century.

But even if this objection is valid it should not be expressed with impatience or contempt. The Victorian age is sadder to us than it was to the Victorians. We know what happened in the sequel; the poets of 1830–1880 were not prophetic enough for that. It is unreasonable to scold them for not moving more rapidly toward a disaster of which most of them felt only faint uneasy premonitions. We can hardly blame them for clinging to formal and stylistic order as firmly as possible while they drifted toward incoherence of mind and spirit. If our historical study of their religious ideas contributes something to a critical understanding of why their poetry seems to us inadequate, it should also help to make that understanding more flexible and sympathetic.

[11] *Unpublished Letters*, p. 18.

Appendix I

PRIMARY SOURCES

A LIST of the poetic material on which this study is based, with letters and other prose writings of poets when these have been used. Readers will observe, with varying degrees of disapproval and sympathy, that in a few cases I have neglected more up-to-date and scholarly editions in favor of the heavily penciled books in my small, old-fashioned personal library. It does not seem to me that perfect bibliographical finesse is of prime importance in a work of this kind. All the texts are quite sound enough to show us what the poet thinks about religion.

Place of publication is London unless otherwise specified. The abbreviation "Miles" signifies: The Poets and the Poetry of the Nineteenth Century. Eds. A. H. Miles, *et al.* London, 1905–07.

Adams, Sarah Flower. Selections. Miles, VIII, 141–154.

Alford, Henry. Selections. Miles, XI, 237–246.

Allingham, William. A Diary. Eds. H. Allingham and D. Radford. 1907.

—— Songs, Ballads, and Stories. 1877.

Arnold, Edwin. The Light of Asia. Boston, 1891.

Arnold, Matthew. Culture and Anarchy. Ed. W. S. Knickerbocker. ("Modern Readers Series.") New York, 1925.

—— Essays in Criticism. First Series. 1895.

—— Essays in Criticism. Second Series. 1898.

—— Friendship's Garland. *In* Culture and Anarchy . . . and Friendship's Garland. New York, 1883.

—— God and the Bible. New York, 1883.

—— Letters, Ed. G. W. E. Russell. 1895.

—— Letters to A. H. Clough. Ed. H. F. Lowry. Oxford, 1932.

—— Literature and Dogma. New York, 1906.

—— Note-Books. Eds. H. F. Lowry, Karl Young, W. H. Dunn. 1952.

—— Poems. Ed. H. S. Milford. 1913.

—— St. Paul and Protestantism. With an Essay on Puritanism and the Church of England, and Last Essays on Church and Religion. New York, 1902.

—— Unpublished Letters. Ed. Arnold Whitridge. New Haven, 1923.

Ashe, Thomas. Poems. 1886.

Austin, Alfred. Lyrical Poems. 1891.

Bailey, Philip James. Festus. 1860.

Bamford, Samuel. Passages in the Life of a Radical, and Early Days. Ed. Henry Dunckley. 1893.

Bamford, Samuel. (*Continued*)
—— Poems. Manchester, 1843.
Barham, Richard H. The Ingoldsby Legends. 1860.
Barnes, William. Poems of Rural Life in the Dorset Dialect. 1887.
Bennett, William C. Poems. 1862.
Bickersteth, Edward Henry. Yesterday, To-day, and For Ever. New York, 1869.
Bigg, John Stanyan. Night and the Soul. 1854.
—— Shifting Scenes, and Other Poems. 1862.
Blackie, John Stuart. Selections. Miles, IV, 267–280.
Bonar, Horatius. Hymns of Faith and Hope. New York, 1867.
Bowden, John William. Lyra Apostolica, p. 155.
Bowring, John. Selections. Miles, XI, 147–156.
Brontë, Anne. Poems. The Complete Works of Charlotte Brontë and Her Sisters, IV, 309–334, 357–371. [1905.]
Brontë, Charlotte. Poems. The Complete Works of Charlotte Brontë and Her Sisters, IV, 219–276. [1905.]
Brontë, Emily Jane. Complete Poems. Ed. C. W. Hatfield. New York, 1941.
Browning, Elizabeth Barrett. Letters. Ed. F. G. Kenyon. New York, 1897.
—— Letters to Her Sister, 1846–1859. Ed. Leonard Huxley. New York, 1930.
—— Poetical Works. 1905.
Browning, Robert. Complete Poetical Works. Ed. Augustine Birrell. New York, 1919.
—— An Essay on Shelley. The Complete Poetic and Dramatic Works of Robert Browning. Cambridge Edition. Boston and New York, 1895, pp. 1008–1014.
—— Letters. Collected by T. J. Wise. Ed. T. L. Hood. New Haven, 1933.
—— New Letters. Eds. W. C. De Vane and K. L. Knickerbocker. New Haven, 1950.
Browning, Robert, and Elizabeth Barrett Barrett. Letters. New York and London, 1899.
Browning, Robert, and Julia Wedgwood: A Broken Friendship as Revealed by Their Letters. Ed. Richard Curle. New York, 1937.
Buchanan, Robert Williams. Complete Poetical Works. 1901.
—— The Drama of Kings. 1871.
Bulwer-Lytton, Robert, Lord Lytton. *See* "Meredith, Owen."
Burns, James Drummond. Selections. Miles, XII, 23–36.

Call, Wathen Mark Wilks. Golden Histories. 1871.
Calverley, Charles Stuart. Complete Works. 1901.
Caswall, Edward. The Masque of Mary, and Other Poems. 1858.
Clough, Arthur Hugh. Letters and Remains. 1865.
—— Poems. Eds. H. F. Lowry, A. L. P. Norrington, and F. L. Mulhauser. Oxford, 1951.
—— Poems and Prose Remains. With a Selection from His Letters and a Memoir Edited by His Wife. 1869.
Cook, Eliza. Selections. Miles, VIII, 269–282.
Cooper, Thomas. Poetical Works. 1877.

Cory, William Johnson. Ionica. 1891.
Courthope, William John. Selections. Miles, X, 559–574.
Craik, Dinah Maria. Selections. Miles, VIII, 377–384.

De Tabley, John Byrne Leicester Warren, Lord. Collected Poems. 1903.
De Vere, Aubrey (1788–1846). A Song of Faith, Devout Exercises, and Sonnets. 1842.
De Vere, Aubrey Thomas (1814–1902). Irish Odes and Other Poems. New York, 1869.
—— Poetical Works. 1884–98.
—— Recollections. New York and London, 1897.
—— Selections. Ed. G. E. Woodberry. New York, 1894.
Dixon, Richard Watson. Christ's Company and Other Poems. 1861.
—— Lyrical Poems. Oxford, 1887. (Privately printed.)
—— Mano: A Poetical History of the Time of the Close of the Tenth Century. 1883.
—— Poems. A Selection with a Memoir by Robert Bridges. 1909.
—— The Story of Eudocia and Her Brothers. Oxford, 1888. (Privately printed.)
[Dobell, Sydney.] Balder, Part the First. By the Author of "The Roman." 1854.
Dobell, Sydney. Poetical Works. Ed. John Nichol. 1875.
—— Thoughts on Art, Philosophy, and Religion. 1876.
Dolben, Digby Mackworth. Poems. Ed. Robert Bridges. 1911.
Dowden, Edward. Selections. Miles, VII, 81–98.
Dublin Book of Irish Verse, The. Ed. John Cooke. Dublin and London, 1909.

Elliott, Ebenezer. Poetical Works. Ed. Edwin Elliott. 1876.
Ellison, Henry. Selections. Miles, XI, 261–298.
Evans, Sebastian. Brother Fabian's Manuscript; and Other Poems. 1865.

Faber, Frederick William. Poems. 1867.
Fane, Julian. Poems. 1852.
Ferguson, Samuel. Selections. The Dublin Book of Irish Verse, pp. 203–235.
FitzGerald, Edward. Letters. Ed. W. A. Wright. 1894.
—— Letters and Literary Remains. Ed. W. A. Wright. 1902–03.
Flower, Sarah. *See* Adams, Sarah Flower.
Fox, William Johnson. Selections. Miles, XII, 298–301.
Froude, Hurrell. Lyra Apostolica, p. 170.

Gilbert, William Schwenck. H.M.S. Pinafore and Other Plays. Modern Library. New York, n.d.
Gill, Thomas Hornblower. Selections. Miles, XI, 361–370.
Gray, David. Selections. Miles, VI, 355–370.
Greenwell, Dora. Selections. Miles, VIII, 341–358.

Hake, Thomas Gordon. Legends of the Morrow. 1879.
—— Memoirs of Eighty Years. 1892.
—— Poems. Selected with a Prefatory Note by Alice Meynell. 1894.
Hallam, Arthur Henry. Writings. Ed. T. V. Motter. New York, 1943.

Havergal, Frances Ridley. Selections in E. Davies, Frances Ridley Havergal: A Full Sketch of Her Life, with Choice Selections from Her Prose and Poetical Writings. Reading (Mass.), 1884.

Hawker, Robert Stephen. Poetical Works. Ed. Alfred Wallis. 1899.

Horne, Richard Henry [or Hengist]. Orion: An Epic Poem. Boston, 1872.

—— Prometheus the Fire-Bringer. Melbourne, 1866.

Houghton, Lord. *See* Milnes, Richard Monckton, Lord Houghton.

How, William Walsham. Poems. 1886.

Ingelow, Jean. Poetical Works. New York, 1868.

Ingoldsby, Thomas. *See* Barham, Richard H.

Johnson, William. *See* Cory, William Johnson.

Jones, Ebenezer. Studies of Sensation and Event. Ed. R. H. Shepherd, with Memorial Notices . . . by Sumner Jones and William James Linton. 1879.

Jones, Ernest. The Battle-Day: And Other Poems. 1855.

—— Corayda: A Tale of Faith and Chivalry, and Other Poems. 1860.

Keble, John. The Christian Year, Lyra Innocentium, and Other Poems. 1914.

Keegan, John. Selections. The Dublin Book of Irish Verse, pp. 182–190.

Kemble, Frances Anne. Selections. Miles, VIII, 253–268.

Kingsley, Charles. Alton Locke, Tailor and Poet. 1911.

—— Poems. New York, n.d.

—— Yeast. 1908.

Lee-Hamilton, Eugene. Gods, Saints, and Men. 1880.

—— Poems and Transcripts. Edinburgh and London, 1878.

Leighton, Robert. Selections. Miles, V, 73–84.

Lynch, Thomas Toke. Selections. Miles, XI, 313–336.

Lyra Apostolica. Ed. H. C. Beeching. Introduction by H. S. Holland. 1899

Lytton, Robert Bulwer-Lytton, Lord. *See* "Meredith, Owen."

MacDonald, George. Poems. Selected by V. D. S. and C. F. New York, 1893.

Mackay, Charles. Selections. Miles, IV, 505–516.

Mangan, James Clarence. Selections. The Dublin Book of Irish Verse, pp. 124–156.

—— Selections. Miles, III, 453–485.

Manners, Lord John. England's Trust, and Other Poems. 1841.

[Mansel, Henry Longueville.] Scenes from an Unfinished Drama Entitled Phrontisterion, or, Oxford in the Nineteenth Century. Oxford, 1852.

Marston, John Westland. Dramatic and Poetical Works. London, 1876.

Marston, Philip Bourke. Collected Poems. Boston, 1892.

Massey, Gerald. My Lyrical Life: Poems Old and New. 1889.

"Meredith, Owen" [Robert Bulwer-Lytton, Lord Lytton]. Poems. Boston, 1881.

Miles, A. H., *et al.* (eds.). The Poets and the Poetry of the Nineteenth Century. 1905–07.

Milnes, Richard Monckton, Lord Houghton. Selections. Miles, IV, 241–266.

Montgomery, Robert. Satan: A Poem. 1830.

Morris, William. Chants for Socialists. 1885.
—— The Defence of Guenevere, The Life and Death of Jason, and Other Poems. The World's Classics. Oxford and London, 1933.
—— Letters to His Family and Friends. Ed. Philip Henderson. 1950.
—— The Pilgrims of Hope. 1886.
Mulock, Dinah Maria. *See* Craik, Dinah Maria.
Myers, Frederick W. H. Collected Poems. Ed. Evelyn Myers. 1921.

Naden, Constance Caroline Woodhill. Selections. Miles, IX, 387–394.
[Neaves, Charles, Lord Neaves.] Songs and Verses Social and Scientific, by an Old Contributor to Maga. Edinburgh and London, 1879.
Newman, John Henry. Apologia pro Vita Sua. Ed. Charles Sarolea. Everyman's Library. 1912.
—— Loss and Gain. 1874.
—— Verses on Various Occasions. 1890.
Noel, Roden Berkeley Wriothesley. Essays on Poetry and Poets. 1886.
—— A Modern Faust, and Other Poems. 1888.
—— Poems. A Selection. Ed. Robert Buchanan. Canterbury Poets. n.d. [1892.]

O'Shaughnessy, Arthur William Edgar. Lays of France. 1874.
—— Poems. Ed. W. A. Percy. New Haven, 1923.
—— Songs of a Worker. 1881.

Palgrave, Francis Turner. Selections. Miles, V, 275–294.
Patmore, Coventry Kersey Dighton. Poems. Ed. Basil Champneys. 1921.
—— The Rod, the Root, and the Flower. Ed. Derek Patmore. 1950.
Payne, John. New Poems. 1880.
—— Selections. Miles, VII, 37–60.
—— Selections. Eds. Tracy and Lucy Robinson. New York, 1906.
Pfeiffer, Emily Davis. Under the Aspens. 1882.
Pollok, Robert. The Course of Time. Ed. J. R. Boyd. New York, 1854.
Procter, Adelaide Anne. Poems. With an Introduction by Charles Dickens. Boston, 1881.
—— Selections. Miles, VIII, 359–376.

Rands, William Brighty. Selections. Miles, V, 147–162.
Rossetti, Christina Georgina. Family Letters. Ed. William Michael Rossetti. 1908.
—— Poetical Works. Ed. William Michael Rossetti. 1928.
Rossetti, Dante Gabriel. Collected Works. Ed. William Michael Rossetti. 1906.
—— Letters to William Allingham. Ed. G. B. Hill. 1897.
Rossetti, William Michael (ed.). Præraphaelite Diaries and Letters. 1900.
Ruskin, John. Poems. Ed. J. O. Wright. New York, 1884.
—— Selections. Miles, IV, 1819–1900.

Scott, William Bell. Poems. 1875.
Skipsey, Joseph. Carols from the Coal-Fields, and Other Songs and Ballads. 1886.

Smedley, Menella Bute. Poems. 1868.
—— Selections. Miles, VIII, 327–340.
Smetham, James. Literary Works. Ed. William Davies. 1893.
Smith, Alexander. Poetical Works. Ed. William Sinclair. Edinburgh, 1909.
Smith, Walter Chalmers. Selections. Miles, XII, 109–128.
Smythe, George Sydney. Historic Fancies. 1844.
Stanley, Arthur Penrhyn. Letters and Verses. Ed. R. E. Prothero. 1895.
Sterling, John. Selections. Miles, IV, 179–190.
Sutton, Henry Septimus. Poems. Glasgow, 1886.
Swain, Charles. Poems. Boston, 1871.
Swinburne, Algernon Charles. Complete Works. Bonchurch Edition. Eds. Edmund Gosse and T. J. Wise. 1925–27.
—— Selected Poems. Ed. Edward Shanks. 1950.
Symonds, John Addington. New and Old: A Volume of Verse. Boston, 1880.

Talfourd, Thomas Noon. Dramatic Works . . . To which are added, A Few Sonnets and Verses. 1852.
Tatham, Emma. The Dream of Pythagoras, and Other Poems. London, n.d. [1863?].
Tennyson, Alfred Tennyson, Lord. Poetic and Dramatic Works. Ed. W. J. Rolfe. Cambridge Edition. Boston and New York, 1898.
—— Works. Eversley Edition. Ed. Hallam Tennyson. London, 1907–08.
Tennyson, Charles. *See* Turner, Charles Tennyson.
Tennyson, Frederick. Daphne and Other Poems. 1891.
—— Shorter Poems. Ed. Charles Tennyson. 1913.
Thomson, James. Poetical Works. Ed. Bertram Dobell. 1895.
—— Satires and Profanities. Ed. G. W. Foote. 1884.
Trench, Richard Chenevix. Selections. Miles, IV, 191–206; XI, 225–228.
Tupper, Martin Farquhar. Proverbial Philosophy: A Book of Thoughts and Arguments, Originally Treated. New York, 1849.
Turner, Charles Tennyson. Collected Sonnets. 1884.

Wade, Thomas. Selections. Miles, III, 597–620.
Waring, Anne Lætitia. Selections. Miles, XI, 387–396.
Warren, John Byrne Leicester. *See* De Tabley, John Byrne Leicester Warren, Lord.
Webster, Augusta. Selections. 1893.
Wells, Charles Jeremiah. Joseph and His Brethren: A Dramatic Poem. With an Introduction by Algernon Charles Swinburne and a Note on Rossetti and Charles Wells by Theodore Watts-Dunton. The World's Classics. 1908.
Williams, Isaac. The Cathedral, or the Catholic and Apostolic Church. Oxford, 1853
—— Lyra Apostolica. pp. 143–144.
Williams, Sarah. Selections. Miles, IX, 179–182.
Woods, George Benjamin (ed.). Poetry of the Victorian Period. Chicago, 1930.
Woolner, Thomas. My Beautiful Lady. 1866.
—— Poems. 1887.
Wordsworth, Christopher. Selections. Miles, XI, 229–236.

Appendix II

SECONDARY SOURCES

A LIST of books and articles, other than the writings of the poets, which have been cited in the notes of this study. To these are added some other works which, though not expressly cited, have provided information or ideas concerning Victorian poetry and its background.

Altick, R. D. The Private Life of Robert Browning. Yale Review, XLI (1952), 247–262.

Angeli, Helen Rossetti. Dante Gabriel Rossetti. London, 1949.

Annan, N. G. Leslie Stephen. London, 1951.

Atkins, G. G. Reinspecting Victorian Religion. New York, 1928.

Atkinson, Henry George, and Harriet Martineau. Letters on the Laws of Man's Nature and Development. London, 1851.

Badger, Kingsbury. Arthur Hugh Clough as Dipsychus. Modern Language Quarterly, XII (1951), 39–56.

Bagehot, Walter. Literary Studies. Everyman's Library. London, n.d.

Baker, J. E. The Novel and the Oxford Movement. Princeton, 1932.

—— Our New Hellenic Renaissance. The Reinterpretation of Victorian Literature, pp. 207–236.

Barham, R. H. Dalton. Life and Letters of the Reverend Richard Harris Barham. London, 1880.

Barlow, George. On the Spiritual Side of Swinburne's Genius. Contemporary Review, LXXXVIII (1905), 231–250.

Barzun, Jacques. Darwin, Marx, Wagner. Boston, 1941.

—— Romanticism and the Modern Ego. Boston, 1943.

Battenhouse, H. M. Poets of Christian Thought. New York, 1947.

Baum, P. F. Tennyson Sixty Years After. Chapel Hill (N.C.), 1948.

Beach, J. W. The Concept of Nature in Nineteenth-Century English Poetry. New York, 1936.

Beale, Dorothea. The Religious Teaching of Browning. Browning Studies, pp. 76–91.

Benn, A. W. History of English Rationalism in the Nineteenth Century. London, 1906.

Berdoe, Edward. Browning and the Christian Faith. London, 1899.

—— Browning's Message to His Time. London, 1897.

Berger, Pierre. Quelques aspects de la foi moderne dans les poèmes de Robert Browning. Paris, 1907.

Blackburn, William. The Background of Arnold's Literature and Dogma. Modern Philology, XLIII (1945), 130–139.

Bonnerot, Louis. Matthew Arnold: Empédocle sur l'Etna. Étude critique et traduction. Paris, 1848.

—— Matthew Arnold, Poète. Paris, 1947.

Bradley, A. C. A Commentary on Tennyson's In Memoriam. London, 1929.

Bradley, F. H. Ethical Studies. Oxford, 1927.

Bray, Charles. Phases of Opinion During a Long Life. London, 1884.

Brilioth, Yngve. The Anglican Revival. London, New York, Toronto, 1933.

Brinton, Crane. Ideas and Men. New York, 1950.

Brookfield, Frances M. The Cambridge "Apostles." New York, 1907.

Brown, A. W. The Metaphysical Society. New York, 1947.

Brown, E. K. Matthew Arnold: A Study in Conflict. Chicago, 1948.

Browning Studies. Being Select Papers by Members of the Browning Society. Ed. Edward Berdoe. London, 1895.

Buchman, Rolf. Martin F. Tupper and the Victorian Middle Class Mind. Berne, 1942.

Buckley, J. H. The Victorian Temper: A Study in Literary Culture. Cambridge (Mass.), 1951.

Burrows, Margaret F. Robert Stephen Hawker. Oxford, 1926.

Bury, J. B. Browning's Philosophy. Browning Studies, pp. 28–46.

—— The Idea of Progress. London, 1924.

Bush, D. N. Mythology and the Romantic Tradition in English Poetry. Cambridge (Mass.), 1937.

—— Science and English Poetry. New York, 1950.

Carlyle, Thomas. Critical and Miscellaneous Essays. Complete Works, Vols. I and II. New York, n.d.

—— Sartor Resartus. On Heroes, Hero-Worship, and the Heroic in History. London, Toronto, New York, 1926.

Champneys, Basil. Memoirs and Correspondence of Coventry Patmore. London, 1900, 1901.

Chapman, E. M. English Literature in Account with Religion, 1800–1900. Boston and New York, 1910.

Chesterton, G. K. Robert Browning. London, 1903.

—— The Victorian Age in English Literature. New York and London, 1913.

Church, R. W. The Oxford Movement. London, 1909.

Clark, Kenneth. The Gothic Revival. London, 1928.

Clifford, W. K. Lectures and Essays. Eds. Leslie Stephen and Frederick Pollock. London, 1901.

Conway, M. D. Autobiography. Boston and New York, 1904.

Cornish, F. Warre. The English Church in the Nineteenth Century, Part I. London, 1933.

Corson, Hiram. The Idea of Personality, as Embodied in Browning's Poetry, Browning Studies, pp. 47–75.

Crum, R. B. Scientific Thought in Poetry. New York, 1931.

Cruse, Amy. The Victorians and Their Reading. Boston and New York, 1935.
Curtin, F. D. Aesthetics in English Social Reform: Ruskin and His Followers. Nineteenth-Century Studies, pp. 199–245.

Davies, E. Frances Ridley Havergal: A Full Sketch of Her Life, with Choice Selections from Her Prose and Poetical Writings. Reading (Mass.), 1884.
De Vane, W. C. Browning and the Spirit of Greece. Nineteenth-Century Studies, pp. 179–198.
—— A Browning Handbook. New York, 1935.
—— Browning's Parleyings: The Autobiography of a Mind. New Haven, 1927.
Digby, Kenelm Henry. The Broad Stone of Honour: or, The True Sense and Practice of Chivalry. London, 1877.
Disraeli, Benjamin. Coningsby, or The New Generation. London, 1927.
Doughty, Oswald. Dante Gabriel Rossetti: A Victorian Romantic. New Haven, 1949.
Drachman, J. M. Studies in the Literature of Natural Science. New York, 1930.
Drinkwater, John. The Poetry of the 'Seventies. The Eighteen-Seventies, pp. 96–110.
Dugdale, Giles. William Barnes of Dorset. London, 1953.

Eighteen-Seventies, The. Essays by Fellows of the Royal Society of Literature. Ed. Harley Granville-Barker. Cambridge, 1929.
Eighteen-Sixties, The. Essays by Fellows of the Royal Society of Literature. Ed. John Drinkwater. New York and Cambridge, 1932.
Eliot, T. S. Selected Essays. New York, 1932.
Elliott-Binns, L. E. Religion in the Victorian Era. London, 1936.
Elton, Oliver. A Survey of English Literature, 1830–1880. London, 1920.
Emerson, R. W. Selected Prose and Poetry. New York, 1950.
[Essays and Reviews.] Recent Inquiries in Theology, by Eminent English Churchmen; being "Essays and Reviews." Ed. F. H. Hedge. Boston, 1861.
Evans, B. I. English Poetry in the Later Nineteenth Century. London, 1933.
Everett, E. M. The Party of Humanity: the Fortnightly Review and Its Contributors, 1865–1874. Chapel Hill (N.C.), 1939.

Faber, Geoffrey. Oxford Apostles. London, 1936.
Fairbairn, A. M. Catholicism, Roman and Anglican. London, 1899.
Fairchild, H. N. Browning the Simple-Hearted Casuist. University of Toronto Quarterly, XVIII (1949), 234–240.
—— Browning's Heaven. Review of Religion, XIV (1949), 30–37.
—— Browning's Pomegranate Heart. Modern Language Notes, LXVI (1951), 265–266.
—— Browning's "Whatever Is, Is Right." College English, XII (1951), 377–382.
—— The Immediate Source of *The Dynasts*. PMLA, LXVII (1952), 43–64.
—— *La Saisiaz* and *The Nineteenth Century*. Modern Philology, XLVIII (1950), 104–111.
—— Religious Trends in English Poetry. New York, 1939, 1942, 1949.

Fairchild, H. N. (*Continued*)
—— Rima's Mother. PMLA, LXVIII (1953), 357–370.
—— Romanticism and the Religious Revival in England. Journal of the History of Ideas, II (1941), 330–338.
—— "Wild Bells" in Bailey's *Festus?* Modern Language Notes, LXIV (1949), 256–258.
Feuerbach, Ludwig Andreas. The Essence of Christianity. Translated from the Second German Edition by Marian Evans. New York, 1855.
Froude, J. A. Essays in Literature and History. Everyman's Library. London and New York, 1906.
—— The Nemesis of Faith. London, 1849.

Gaselee, S. The Aesthetic Side of the Oxford Movement. Northern Catholicism, pp. 423–445.
Gaskell, Elizabeth Cleghorn. Mary Barton and Other Tales. London, 1891.
Gingerich, S. F. Wordsworth, Tennyson, and Browning: a Study in Human Freedom. Ann Arbor (Mich.), 1911.
Gohdes, Clarence. American Literature in Nineteenth-Century England. New York, 1944.
Gosse, Edmund. Father and Son. New York, 1923.
—— Life of Algernon Charles Swinburne. Complete Works of A. C. S., Bonchurch Edition, Vol. XIX. London, 1907.
Green, Joyce. Tennyson's Development During the "Ten Years' Silence" (1832–1842). PMLA, LXVI (1951), 662–697.
Grennan, Margaret R. William Morris, Medievalist and Revolutionary. New York, 1945.
Griffin, W. H., and H. C. Minchin. Life of Robert Browning. London, 1938.
Guyot, Édouard. Essai sur la formation philosophique du poète Clough: Pragmatisme et intellectualisme. Paris, 1913.
Gwynn, Dennis. Lord Shrewsbury, Pugin, and the Catholic Revival. London, 1946.

Haldane, Elizabeth S. George Eliot and Her Times. New York, 1927.
Halévy, Élie. The Growth of Philosophic Radicalism. Tr. Mary Morris. New York, 1928.
Hammond, J. L. and Barbara. The Bleak Age. Pelican Books. London, 1947.
Harrison, Frederic. Tennyson, Ruskin, Mill, and Other Literary Estimates. New York, 1900.
Harrold, C. F. Carlyle and German Thought. New Haven, 1934.
—— John Henry Newman. London and New York, 1945.
—— The Oxford Movement: A Reconsideration. The Reinterpretation of Victorian Literature, pp. 33–56.
Heitland, W. E. Cambridge in the 'Seventies. The Eighteen-Seventies, pp. 249–272.
Hewlett, Dorothy. Elizabeth Barrett Browning: A Life. New York, 1952.
Hinton, James. Life in Nature. Ed. Havelock Ellis. New York and Toronto, 1931.
Holland, Bernard. Memoir of Kenelm Digby. London, 1919.
Holloway, John. The Victorian Sage. London, 1953.

Hough, Graham. The Last Romantics. London, 1949.
Hudson, Derek. Martin Tupper: His Rise and Fall. London, 1949.
Hunt, John. Religious Thought in England in the Nineteenth Century. London, 1896.
Hunt, Leigh. The Religion of the Heart. A Manual of Faith and Duty. London, 1853.
Hunt, W. Holman. Pre-Raphaelitism and the Pre-Raphaelite Brotherhood. New York, 1914.
Hutton, R. H. Literary Essays. London, 1888.
Huxley, T. H. Man's Place in Nature and Other Essays. Everyman's Library. London and New York, 1908.

James, D. G. The Romantic Comedy. London, 1948.
Jay, Harriet. Robert Buchanan. London, 1903.
Johari, G. P. Arthur Hugh Clough at Oriel and at University Hall. PMLA, LXVI (1951), 405–425.
Johnson, E. D. H. The Alien Vision of Victorian Poetry: Sources of Poetic Imagination in Tennyson, Browning, Arnold. Princeton, 1952.
Johnson, Samuel. Life of Waller. Lives of the English Poets. Ed. G. B. Hill. Vol. III, pp. 249–300. Oxford, 1905.
[Jolly, Emily.] Life and Letters of Sydney Dobell. Edited by E. J. [So says title-page, but her preface says that the narrative connecting the letters is her own.] London, 1876.
Jones, Henry. Browning as a Philosophical and Religious Teacher. New York, 1891.

Kenyon, Ruth. The Social Aspect of the Catholic Revival. Northern Catholicism, pp. 367–400.
Kingsmill, Hugh. After Puritanism. London, 1929.
Kirkman, J. Introductory Address to the Browning Society. Browning Studies, pp. 1–20.
Knickerbocker, Frances W. Free Minds; John Morley and His Friends. Cambridge (Mass.), 1943.
Knickerbocker, W. S. Creative Oxford. Syracuse (N.Y.), 1925.
Knox, R. A. Enthusiasm: A Chapter in the History of Religion. New York and Oxford, 1950.

Ladd, Henry. The Victorian Morality of Art: An Analysis of Ruskin's Aesthetic. New York, 1932.
Lafourcade, Georges. Swinburne: A Literary Biography. London, 1932.
Lecky, W. E. H. History of Rationalism in Europe. London, 1865.
Lewes, G. H. A Biographical History of Philosophy. London, 1893.
Lewis, C. S. The Great Divorce. New York, 1946.
Lounsbury, T. R. The Life and Times of Tennyson. New Haven, 1915.
Lubac, Henri de, S.J. The Drama of Atheist Humanism. Tr. Edith M. Riley. New York, 1950.

Lucas, F. L. The Decline and Fall of the Romantic Ideal. New York, 1936.
—— Ten Victorian Poets. Cambridge, 1948.
Lyttelton, A. T. Modern Poets of Faith, Doubt, and Paganism, and Other Essays. London, 1904.

Macan, R. W. Oxford in the 'Seventies. The Eighteen-Seventies, pp. 210–248.
McCrie, George. The Religion of Our Literature. London, 1875.
Mack, E. C. Public Schools and British Opinion, 1780 to 1860. London, 1938.
Mackail, J. W. Life of William Morris. London, 1922.
Mackenzie, Faith Compton. William Cory: A Biography. London, 1950.
Mallock, W. H. Memoirs of Life and Literature. London, 1920.
—— The New Republic. London, n.d.
Marchand, L. A. The Athenaeum: A Mirror of Victorian Culture. Chapel Hill (N.C.), 1941.
Marks, Jeannette. The Family of the Barrett. New York, 1938.
Martineau, Harriet. Autobiography. Ed. Maria Weston Chapman. Boston, 1877.
Masterman, C. F. G. Tennyson as a Religious Teacher. London, 1910.
Mattes, Eleanor B. In Memoriam, the Way of a Soul. New York, 1951.
Mead, George H. Movements of Thought in the Nineteenth Century. Ed. M. H. Moore. Chicago, 1936.
Merz, J. T. History of European Thought in the Nineteenth Century. London, 1896–1914.
Mill, John Stuart. Autobiography. New York, 1924.
—— Three Essays on Religion. London, 1874.
Miller, Betty. Robert Browning: A Portrait. New York, 1953.
Mineka, F. E. The Dissidence of Dissent: The Monthly Repository, 1806–1838. Chapel Hill (N.C.), 1944.
Morley, John. On Compromise. London, 1903.
Muirhead, J. H. How Hegel Came to England. Mind, XXXVI (1927), 423–447.
Murry, J. M. Looking Before and After. London, 1943.
—— Things to Come. London, 1928.
Myers, Frederic. Catholic Thoughts on the Bible and Theology. London, 1874.

Naish, Ethel M. Browning and Dogma. London, 1908.
Nash, Henry S. History of the Higher Criticism of the New Testament. New York, 1906.
Neff, Emery. Carlyle. New York, 1932.
—— Carlyle and Mill. New York, 1926.
Newman, Francis William. Phases of Faith: or, Passages from the History of My Creed. London, 1865.
Nicolson, Harold. Swinburne. London, 1926.
—— Tennyson. London, 1925.
Nietzsche, Friedrich. The Philosophy of Nietzsche. Modern Library. New York, 1927.
Nineteenth-Century Studies, Eds. Herbert Davis, W. C. De Vane, R. C. Bald. Ithaca (N.Y.), 1940.

Northcott, Herbert. The Development and Deepening of the Spiritual Life. Northern Catholicism, pp. 309–335.
Northern Catholicism. Eds. N. P. Williams and Charles Harris. New York, 1933.

Orr, Alexandra. Life and Letters of Robert Browning. Revised by F. G. Kenyon. London, 1908.
—— The Religious Opinions of Robert Browning. Contemporary Review, LX (1891), 876–891.
Overton, J. H. The English Church in the Nineteenth Century, 1800–1833. London, 1894.

Page, Frederick. Patmore: A Study in Poetry. London, 1933.
Palmer, F. W. The Bearing of Science on the Thought of Arthur Hugh Clough. PMLA, LIX (1944), 212–225.
Pater, Walter. Marius the Epicurean: His Sensations and Ideas. Ed. J. C. Squire, London, 1929.
—— Studies in the History of the Renaissance. London, 1888.
Patmore, Derek. The Life and Times of Coventry Patmore. London, 1949.
Pattison, Mark. Memoirs. London, 1885.
Phare, Elsie Elizabeth. The Poetry of Gerard Manley Hopkins. Cambridge, 1933.
Pigou, A. C. Robert Browning as a Religious Teacher. London, 1901.
Pope-Hennesy, Una. Canon Charles Kingsley. New York, 1949.
Praz, Mario. The Romantic Agony. Tr. Angus Davidson. London, 1933.

Quinlan, M. J. Victorian Prelude. New York, 1941.

Randall, J. H. The Making of the Modern Mind. Boston and New York, 1926.
Raymond, W. O. The Infinite Moment and Other Essays in Robert Browning. Toronto, 1950.
Reade, Winwood. The Martyrdom of Man. New York, 1926.
Reilly, Sister M. Paracleta. Aubrey de Vere: Victorian Observer. Lincoln (Neb.), 1953.
Reinterpretation of Victorian Literature, The. Ed. J. E. Baker. Princeton, 1950.
Renan, Ernest. La Vie de Jésus. Paris, 1928.
Richards, I. A. Practical Criticism. New York, 1929.
Robertson, J. M. Modern Humanists Reconsidered. London, 1927.
[Romanes, George John.] A Candid Examination of Theism. By Physicus. London, 1892.
Rosenblatt, Louise. L'Idée de l'art pour l'art dans la littérature Anglaise pendant la période Victorienne. Paris, 1931.
Routh, H. V. Towards the Twentieth Century. New York, 1937.
Ruskin, John. The Stones of Venice, Vol. II. Unto This Last. The Crown of Wild Olive. *In* Works. Library Edition. Eds. E. T. Cook and A. D. O. Wedderburn. London, 1902–12.
Russell, Bertrand. History of Western Philosophy. London, 1948.
Russell, Frances T. One Word More on Browning. Stanford University, 1927.
"Rutherford, Mark" [William Hale White]. Autobiography. London, 1936.

Salt, Henry S. Memories of Bygone Eton. London, n.d.
Sanders, C. R. Coleridge and the Broad Church Movement. Durham (N.C.), 1942
Santayana, George. Interpretations of Poetry and Religion. New York, 1918.
Schilling, Bernard. Human Dignity and the Great Victorians. New York, 1946.
Seeley, John Robert. Ecce Homo. London, 1910.
Shuster, G. N. The Catholic Spirit in Modern Literature. New York, 1922.
Simpson, W. J. Sparrow. The Revival from 1845 to 1933. Northern Catholicism, pp. 36–74.
—— The Spiritual Independence of the Church. Northern Catholicism, pp. 401–422.
Spencer, Herbert. The Data of Ethics. London, 1879.
—— First Principles. New York, 1890.
Stange, G. R. Tennyson's Garden of Art: A Study of *The Hesperides*. PMLA, LXVII (1952), 732–743.
Stephen, Leslie. The English Utilitarians. London, 1900.
—— Essays on Free-Thinking and Plain-Speaking. New York and London, 1905.
Stevenson, Lionel. Darwin Among the Poets. Chicago, 1932.
Storr, V. F. The Development of English Theology in the Nineteenth Century, 1800–1860. London, 1913.
Strauss, David Friedrich. The Life of Jesus. Tr. Marian Evans. New York, 1855.

Tennyson, Charles. Alfred Tennyson. New York, 1949.
—— Six Tennyson Essays. London, 1954.
Tennyson, Hallam. Alfred Lord Tennyson: A Memoir. New York, 1898.
Thackeray, W. M. Vanity Fair. Boston, n.d.
Thirlwall, J. C. Connop Thirlwall. London, 1936.
Thorp, Margaret F. Charles Kingsley. Princeton, 1937.
Thureau-Dangin, Paul. La Renaissance catholique en Angleterre au dix-neuvième siècle. Paris, 1899–1906.
Tillotson, Geoffrey. Criticism and the Nineteenth Century. London, 1951.
Tinker, C. B., and H. F. Lowry. The Poetry of Matthew Arnold. New York, 1940.
Tracy, C. R. Browning's Heresies. Studies in Philology, XXXIII (1936), 610–625.
Trevelyan, G. M. English Social History. New York, 1947.
Trilling, Lionel. Matthew Arnold. New York, 1939.
Tulloch, John. Movements of Religious Thought in Britain During the Nineteenth Century. New York, 1885.
Tyndall, John. Fragments of Science. New York, 1902.

Waddington, M. M. The Development of British Thought from 1820 to 1890, with Special Reference to German Influences. Toronto, 1919.
Walker, Hugh. John B. Leicester Warren, Lord De Tabley: A Biographical Sketch. London, 1903.
—— The Literature of the Victorian Era. Cambridge, 1913.
Walker, Imogene B. James Thomson, B.V. Ithaca (N.Y.), 1950.
Welby, T. E. A Study of Swinburne. New York, 1926.
—— The Victorian Romantics, 1850–1870. London, 1929.

Wellek, René. Immanuel Kant in England, 1793–1838. Princeton, 1931.
Whibley, Charles. Lord John Manners and His Friends. Edinburgh, 1905.
White, William Hale. *See* "Rutherford, Mark."
Willey, Basil. Nineteenth Century Studies. New York, 1949.
Williams, N. P. The Theology of the Catholic Revival. Northern Catholicism, pp. 130–234.
Wilson, S. L. The Theology of Modern Literature. Edinburgh, 1899.
Wingfield-Stratford, Esmé. The Victorian Cycle. New York, 1935.
Wolfe, Humbert. Arthur Hugh Clough. The Eighteen-Sixties, pp. 20–50.

Yonge, Charlotte M. The Heir of Redclyffe. London, 1868.
Young, G. M. Victorian England. London, 1937.
Young, Helen H. The Writings of Walter Pater. A Reflection of British Philosophical Opinion from 1860 to 1890. Bryn Mawr (Pa.), 1933.

Zaturenska, Marya. Christina Rossetti. New York, 1949.

INDEX OF NAMES

INDEX OF TOPICS